HOW TO FORECAST GOLD AND SILVER USING THE WAVE PRINCIPLE

All Prechter's Real-Time Elliott Wave Precious Metals Commentary from 1978 to 2001

New Classics Library

How to Forecast Gold and Silver Using the Wave Principle

Third Edition 2021

Printed in the United States of America

ISBN: 978-1-61604-126-7
Library of Congress Control Number: 2021919005

Publisher: New Classics Library
Gainesville, Georgia USA

Elliott Wave International
www.elliottwave.com
Address for comments: customercare@elliottwave.com

ACKNOWLEDGMENTS

Special thanks go to Angela Hall, who formatted this book. Over the years, Dave Allman, Leigh Tipton, Angie Barringer, Rachel Webb and Sally Webb all had a hand in creating the charts when they were published. The jacket design is by Marc Benejan and Brett Heckman.

ROBERT R. PRECHTER

Robert R. Prechter, CMT, is founder and president of Elliott Wave International. He has been publishing financial market commentary since 1976. In 1984, Bob set a record in the options division of the U.S. Trading Championship with a real-money trading account.

Bob's *Elliott Wave Theorist* twice won Hard Money Digest's Newsletter Excellence Award. In December 1989, Financial News Network (now CNBC) named him "Guru of the Decade." Bob served for nine years on the Board of the Market Technicians Association and in 1990 – 1991 served as its president. Bob has written 14 books on finance, including his two-volume set, Socionomics – The Science of History and Social Prediction. His recent title, *Conquer the Crash – You Can Survive and Prosper in a Deflationary Crash and Depression*, was a New York Times® Best Seller. In 1999, Bob received the CSTA's first annual A.J. Frost Memorial Award for Outstanding

Contribution to the Development of Technical Analysis. In 2003, Traders Library granted him its Hall of Fame award.

Table of Contents

PUBLISHER'S NOTE

This volume presents every word Prechter wrote about the precious metals complex, first in the 1978 book, *Elliott Wave Principle*, then in *The Elliott Wave Theorist* beginning with the Special Report of November 1979 – as gold and silver were roaring into a major top – and carrying through the year of 2001, when gold reached a low after 21 years of bear market. Prechter's commentary shows how wave analysis can serve to negotiate the most difficult maze of all: a long, deceptive period of bear market action, an environment that stymies most analysts. Rare is the approach that can give you a proper vision of the big picture while also keeping you on the right side of intermediate swings most of the time, particularly when markets fluctuate as wildly as gold and silver did during this two-decade span. Another challenging aspect of the period was that the two metals parted company halfway through the period. Silver bottomed in 1993, years before gold. It was a tricky event but one that *The Elliott Wave Theorist* nevertheless anticipated.

Over this period, Prechter made one major forecasting error in gold and one other error regarding the shape of the larger wave, but each time meticulous analysis quickly forced him to reinstate the proper vision. A careful reader will note that the forecasting error stemmed from distortion in the data caused by government price-fixing, which obscured the two opening waves in 1967-1970. Prechter was aware of the quandary and discussed it in advance. Developing waves soon provided the solution because of their unequivocal implications about the position of the larger pattern. Such are the values of knowing what waves can and cannot do.

This exciting metals saga begins at a time when Prechter and his staff had to search for data in obscure places and then draw the charts and apply their titles by hand, letter by letter. It carries into the computer age, when data became readily accessible and software could help them draw the graphs. Despite this and other sweeping changes in technology, the waves, as you will see, stayed true to form.

In late 1995, others at Elliott Wave International began writing the firm's monthly metals commentary. Prechter's comments for this historic period ended then except for two Special Reports, included here. For a later view, as well as a detailed guide to buying precious metals, see *Conquer the Crash* (2002), Chapters 13 (final page) and 22.

The commentary herein is unedited except that we have removed or added some commas, omitted references to EWT's page numbers, corrected "which" to "that" when required, de-italicized phrases, and a few similar small things. To keep the focus on metals, we have also omitted occasional, brief references to opinions on other markets, monetary conditions and the economy that were included in some of these discussions.

All dates listed in the headers are *publication* dates. The writing was typically completed one day before that date. Parenthetical references to "text" refer to *Elliott Wave Principle* by Frost and Prechter, but be aware that page numbers differ in later editions.

After reading this book, we hope you will see the value of Elliott wave and supporting technical analysis for forecasting financial price trends. If you want to become an Elliottician, this book can start you on your way.

Elliott Wave Principle, 1978

COMPOSED JULY 1978; PUBLISHED NOVEMBER 1978

Gold in the recent past has often moved "contra-cyclically" to the stock market. A reversal in the price of gold to the upside after a downtrend often occurs concurrently with a turn for the worse in stocks, and vice versa. Therefore, an Elliott reading of the gold price has upon occasion provided confirming evidence for an expected turn in the Dow.

In April 1972, the U.S. government raised its long-standing fixed price for gold from $35 an ounce to $38 an ounce, and in February 1973 increased it again to $42.22. This "official" price used by central banks for currency convertibility purposes and the rising trend in the unofficial price in the early seventies led to what was called the "two-tier" system. In November 1973, the official price and the two-tier system were abolished by the inevitable workings of supply and demand in the free market.

The free-market price of gold rose from $35 per ounce in January 1970, reaching a closing "London fix" peak of $197 an ounce on December 30, 1974. The price then started to slide, and on August 31, 1976 reached a low of $103.50. The fundamental "reasons" given for this decline were U.S.S.R. gold sales, U.S. Treasury gold sales and I.M.F. auctions. Since then, the price of gold has recovered substantially and is trending upward again.

Despite the efforts of the U.S. Treasury to diminish gold's monetary role and the highly charged emotional factors affecting gold as a store of value and a medium of exchange, its price has traced out an inescapably clear Elliott pattern. Figure 6-11 is a graph of London gold, and on it we have indicated the correct wave labels. Note that the rise from the free-market liftoff to the peak at $179.50 an ounce on April 3rd, 1974 is a complete five-wave sequence. The officially maintained price of $35 an ounce before 1970 prevented wave

Figure 6-11

formation prior to that time and thus helped create the necessary long-term base. The dynamic breakout from that base fits well the criterion for the clearest Elliott count for a commodity, and clear it is.

The rocketing five-wave advance forms a nearly perfect wave, with the fifth terminating well against the upper boundary of the trend channel (not shown). The Fibonacci target projection method typical of commodities is fulfilled in that the $90 rise to the peak of wave ③ provides the basis for measuring the distance to the orthodox top. $90 x .618 = $55.62, which added to the peak of wave III at $125 gives $180.62. The actual price at wave V's peak was $179.50, quite close indeed. Also noteworthy is that at $179.50, the price of gold had multiplied by just over five (a Fibonacci number) times its price at $35.

Then in December 1974, after the initial wave Ⓐ decline, the price of gold rose to an all-time high of nearly $200 an ounce. This wave was wave Ⓑ of an expanded flat correction, which crawled upward along the lower channel line, as corrective wave advances often do. As befits the personality of a "B" wave, the phoniness of the advance was unmistakable. First, the news background, as *everyone knew*, appeared to be bullish for gold, because legalization of American ownership was due on January 1, 1975. Wave Ⓑ, in a seemingly perverse but market-logical manner, peaked precisely on the last day of 1974. Second, gold mining stocks, both North American and South African, were noticeably under performing on the advance, forewarning of trouble by refusing to confirm the assumed bullish picture.

Wave Ⓒ, a devastating collapse, accompanied a severe decline in the valuation of gold stocks, carrying some back to where they had begun their advances in 1970. In terms of the bullion price, the authors computed in early 1976 by the usual relationship that the low should occur at about $98, since the length of wave Ⓐ at $51, times 1.618, equals $82, which when subtracted from the orthodox high at $180, gives a target at $98. The low for the correction was well within the zone of the previous fourth wave of lesser degree and quite near the target, hitting a closing London price of $103.50 on August 25, 1976, the month just between the Dow Theory stock market peak in July and the slightly higher DJIA peak in September.

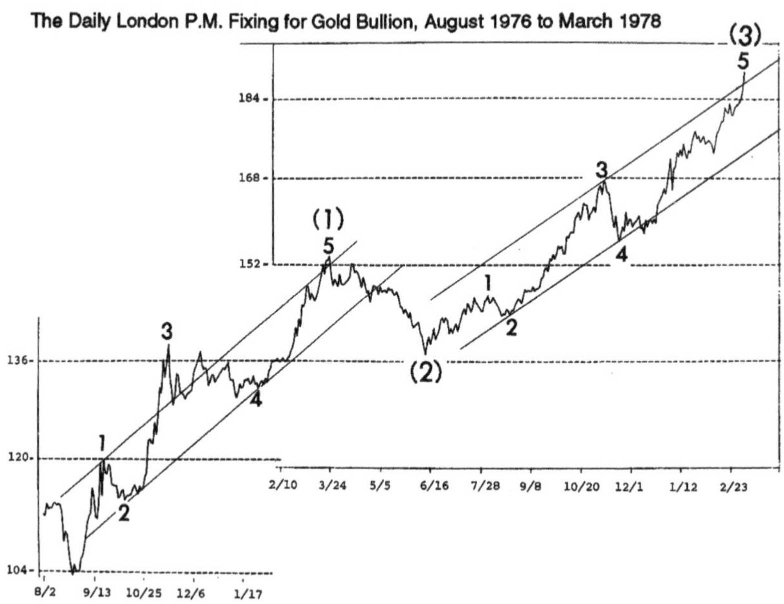

Figure 6-12

The ensuing advance so far has traced out four complete Elliott waves and entered a fifth, which should push the gold price to new all-time highs. Figure 6-12 gives a near term picture of the first three waves up from the August 1976 bottom, where each advancing wave divides clearly into a five-wave impulse. Each upward wave also conforms to an Elliott trend channel on semilog chart paper. The slope of the rise is not as steep as the initial bull market advance, which was a one-time explosion following years of price control. The current rise seems mostly to be reflecting the decline in the value of the dollar since in terms of other currencies, gold is not nearly as close to its all-time high.

Since the price of gold has held the previous fourth wave level on a normal pullback, the count could be a nearly completed five-wave sequence or a developing third wave extension, suggesting coming hyperinflationary conditions under which both the stock market and commodities climb together, although we offer no definite opinions on the subject. However, the Ⓐ-Ⓑ-Ⓒ expanded flat correction implies great thrust in the next wave into new high ground. It should be remembered, though, that commodities can form contained bull markets, ones that need not develop into waves of higher and higher degree. Therefore, one cannot necessarily assume that gold has entered a giant third wave from the low at $35. If the advance forms a distinct five-wave sequence from the low at $103.50 adhering to all Elliott rules, it should be regarded as at least an interim sell signal. Under all cases, the $98 level still should be the maximum extent of any important decline.

Gold, historically speaking, is one of the anchors of economic life, with a sound record of achievement. It has nothing more to offer the world than discipline. Perhaps that is the reason politicians work tirelessly to ignore it, denounce it, and attempt to demonetize it. Somehow, though, governments always seem to manage to have a supply on hand "just in case." Today, gold stands in the wings of international finance as a relic of the old days, but nevertheless also as a harbinger of the future. The disciplined life is the productive life, and that concept applies to all levels of endeavor, from dirt farming to international finance.

Gold is the time-honored store of value, and although the price of gold may flatten for a long period, it is always good insurance to own some until the world's monetary system is intelligently restructured, a development that seems inevitable, whether it happens by design or through natural economic forces. That paper is no substitute for gold as a store of value is probably another of nature's laws.

The Elliott Wave Theorist, 1979

NOVEMBER 18, 1979 – SPECIAL REPORT

Elliott counts suggest important tops in silver, gold, the major commodity market indexes, and short term interest rates.

Silver

It is difficult to find commodities charted on semilog paper, but in dynamic bull markets they are absolutely necessary for correct Elliott channeling. I transferred the monthly price ranges for silver from an arithmetic chart to semilog paper and found that both the wave count and the channel conform to the classic Elliott pattern.

There are some characteristics of this structure that may be of interest to Elliott students:

1) The advance contains two examples of a descending triangle, a fairly uncommon structure.

2) The low at 2 falls below the beginning of wave 1 only because the price of silver was controlled prior to 1967, when the true "market" price would have been below $1.29 per ounce.

3) The correct method of constructing an Elliott trend channel begins with connecting the terminal points of waves 2 and 4. This leaves a good deal of the early part of wave 5 in silver outside the trend channel, but results in a perfect fifth wave target meeting the upper parallel almost exactly.

4) Although Elliott did not recognize 9-wave triangles as valid structures, a case can be made for a triangle ending in December 1977 [See Figure 1-44 in *Elliott Wave Principle* – Ed.] It's as if the triangle's fifth wave "extends" into a five-wave triangle itself. Theoretically, since triangles are five waves each of an a-b-c structure and since triangles are corrective substitutes for a-b-c's, why cannot one of the triangle legs be a triangle?

5) Given the concept of a fourth wave ending in December 1977, all the price action would be held within the lower

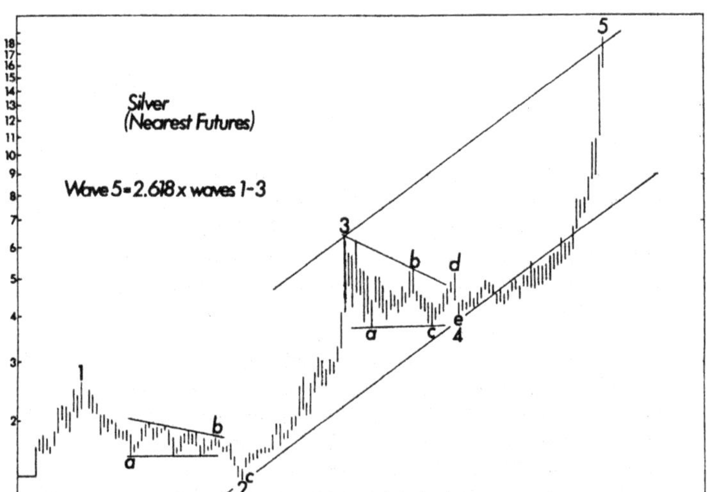

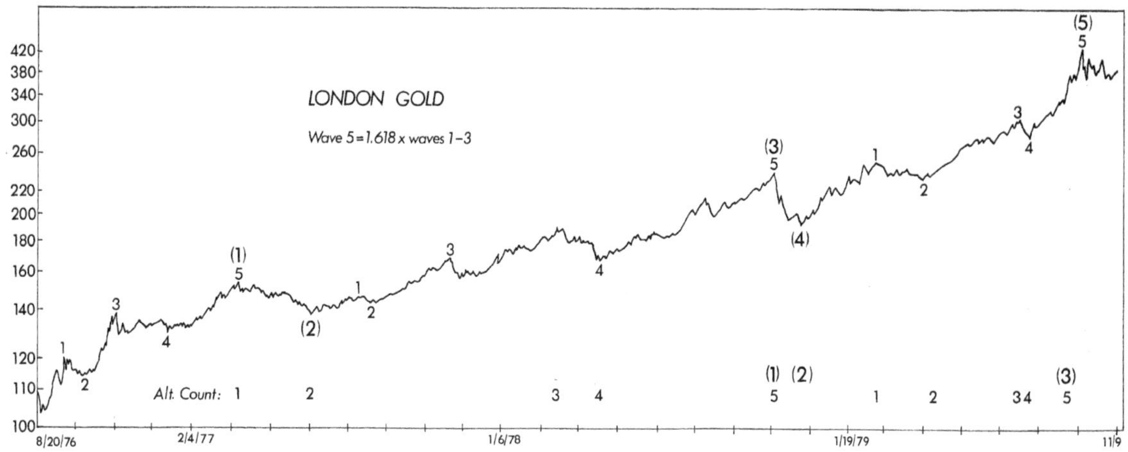

trendline (not shown), while the fifth wave would show a climactic break through the upper trendline.

6) Wave 5 is just over 2.618 times as long as waves 1 through 3, a typical Elliott relationship.

The dramatic series of increases in margin requirements on silver futures contracts has coincided with what appears to be an Elliott wave peak. If my wave count is valid, silver can be expected to drop back to between $4 and $6 some time in the next decade. The Elliott outlook for depression in the latter 80s may go hand in hand with such a price collapse. If the upper trendline is pierced by too great a margin in coming months, however, silver will have to be recounted.

Gold

At least on an intermediate basis, gold appears either to have peaked already or to be on the verge of a final thrust to the upper 400's. The chart at the top of this page shows two alternative counts. The count marked below the chart pattern shows an extended first wave ending in late 1978 and a simple third wave (both longer and stronger than wave 1) ending at the recent high. A fifth would then be on the verge of developing and a short term blowoff would be expected to begin quite soon. The count marked on the chart pattern itself indicates a completed advance.

If gold has peaked after a five-wave advance from its August 1976 low, wave 5 is then 1.618 times as long as waves 1 through 3, a normal Elliott relationship. Furthermore, the entire rise from the low at $103.50 to the morning fix on October 10 at $437 was an exact 4.236 multiple ($103.50 x 4.236 + $438), where 4.236 is the ratio between second alternate Fibonacci numbers. The closing high the day of the top was $424, a representation of the Fibonacci ratio itself (423.6).

These target ratios, plus an acceptable Elliott count, suggest that the three-year bull market rise in gold is over or nearly so. The downside target for gold is at least $282.50, the low of wave 4.

One all-important question, in Elliott terms, is whether the 1967-68 rise in gold stocks (see silver chart) was actually wave 1 of the long term gold bull market. If the true first wave was masked by the artificial price controls on gold at $35 per ounce, then we are witnessing the peak of the final fifth wave advance in gold from a true low in 1967! Specifically supporting this conclusion is the obvious inability of gold stock indexes to register new highs to anywhere near the extent that gold bullion has risen above its 1974 peak. This lagging action is characteristic of fifth waves, and its occurrence is telling. I might add that the irregular correction from 1974 to 1976 is a formation more characteristic of fourth waves than second waves, strengthening the argument.

Furthermore, the gold bullion rise from 1971 to 1974 was so dynamic that it disrupted normal Fibonacci targets and is unchannelable on semi-log paper. Could this be because the rise was packing in three waves' worth of upside price action, delayed because of government price-fixing, into one? It makes sense to me, especially when we take into account the other charts in this report (notably silver). A normal upside target under this count would be $482, where ($179.50 - $35) 2.618 + $103.50 = $482. The downside risk thereafter would be $103.50, a figure which sounds highly unlikely unless we factor in the Elliott forecast of late '80s depression, which could be deflationary.

The six-year gold cycle, postulated by market analyst and friend Charles Curtopelle, is due to peak out in early 1980, ushering in a three-year period of decline. I have found that, without exception, when the waves and cycles are both in gear, it pays to beware.

By the way, I notice that both silver and gold have advanced approximately 13 times (a Fibonacci multiple) their government-controlled price levels of a decade ago. Spot silver has peaked at $17.60 (London price), just over 13 times $1.29 and gold has so far peaked just under 13 times $35. I should note that one more rally in gold to $480 would equalize their bull market advances.

DECEMBER 9, 1979

Most Elliott evidence points to the conclusion that this decade's historic rise in gold prices is coming to an end along with the decade itself. In the November 18 Special Report on commodities and inflation, I offered two counts for gold, where "gold appears either to have peaked already or to be on the verge of a final thrust to the upper 400's." As I pointed out, the "normal upside target would be $482, where ($179.50 - $35)2.618 + $103.50 = $482." Now there is further evidence that this target has validity.

In the last regular issue I outlined my thoughts on the triangular formation gold had formed near term, suggesting that the triangle was wave b of and a-b-c correction. This interpre-

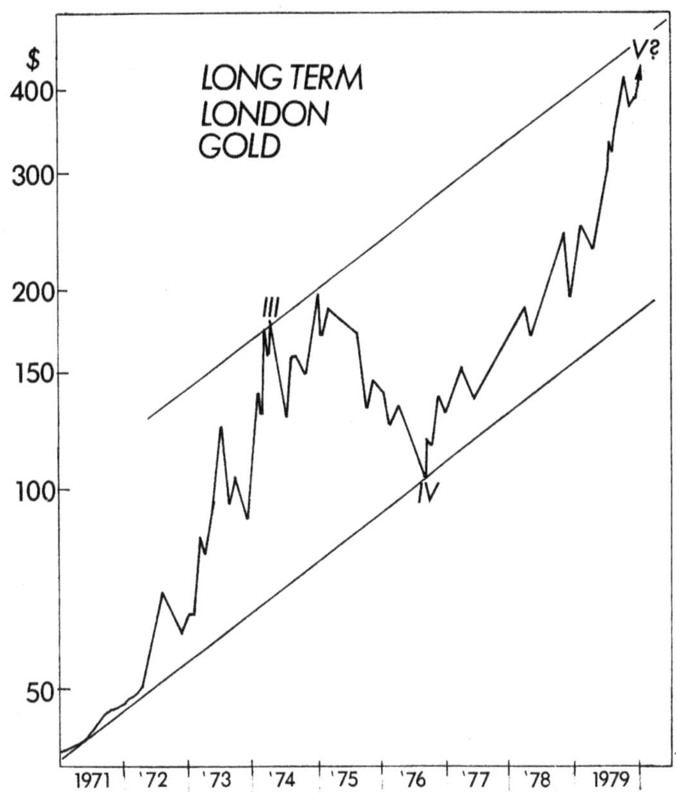

tation is still admissible if we count wave c as a failure since it fell only to $372.80, and did not drop below the low of wave a at $367.50 as I expected it to. Since failures in a-b-c corrections are fairly rare, however, I think the "alternate count" shown in the Special Report is the correct one. In this case, our triangle is wave (4) of the advance, a normal position for corrective wave triangles (see text, p. 41). This count also satisfies the rule of alternation (see text, p. 50) in that wave (2) is a simple zigzag while wave (4) is a complex triangle.

The Elliott rule in roughly estimating triangle breakouts is that they tend to travel about the same distance as the widest part of the triangle (see text, p. 44). Thus an approximate target for the fifth wave up would be ($437 - $367.50) + $390 - to - $396, or around the $460 to $466 area, quite near the $482 target computed above from the long-term wave structure and the $455 target computed from the 13x Fibonacci multiple of the $35 price (see August and September letters). Finally, the upper trendline of the 10-year trendchannel (see long term chart) will be met by any move to the $475-$500 level, another argument for a peak coming quite soon in the upper $400 area. The downside support target at $282.50 would again become operative if and when we get our fifth wave completed on the upside.

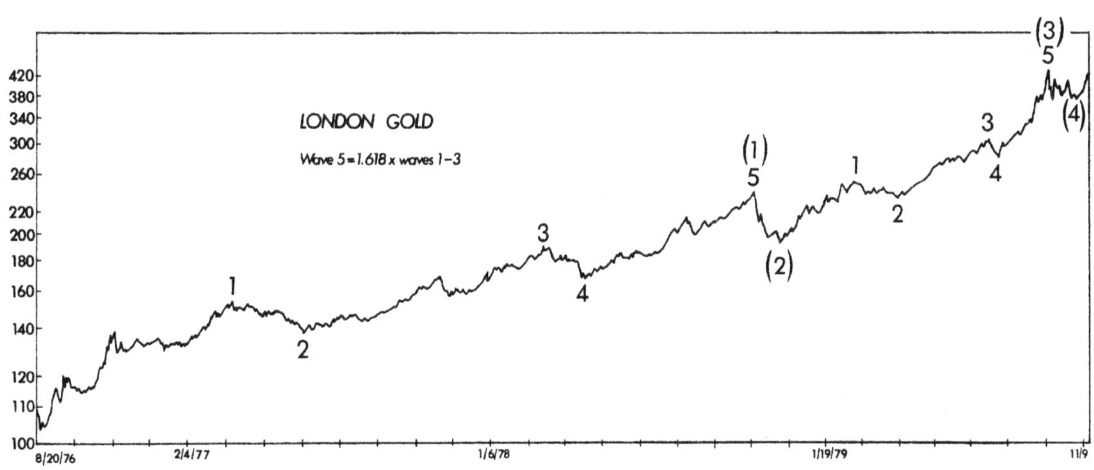

Gold stocks as a group appear to be rallying in a wave "b" of an a-b-c correction. Individual chart patterns show new highs in the South African golds with upside but lagging action in the North American golds. The inability of gold stocks to perform as well overall as they did in the 1972-74 upswing is further evidence that on a major trend basis gold is probably in the process of completing its fifth and final wave. A near term blowoff in gold here could coincide with the expected "test" pullback in the stock market, the expected pullback in the bond market, and a continuation of the current rebound in short term interest rates.

Commodities magazine—January 1980

Elliott counts suggest bear moves

"Elliott counts suggest important tops in silver, gold, the major commodity market indexes and short-term interest rates," says well-known Elliott wave analyst Robert Prechter in a recent special report of his newsletter, *The Elliott Wave Theorist.*

Prechter's Elliott conclusion coincide with the thinking of several other authors in this issue of *Commodities* and suggest some bear markets ahead.

"If my wave count is valid, silver can be expected to drop back to between $4 and $6 per oz. sometime in the next decade," Prechter says. "The Elliott outlook for depression in the late '80s may go hand in hand with such a price collapse."

Prechter does caution that if the upper trendline on his semilog silver chart is pierced by too great a margin in coming months, he may have to do some recounting.

Prechter's gold charts indicate an upside target of $482 per oz. and a downside target of $282.50, the low of Wave 4.

On interest rates, Prechter points out the charts of both the prime rate and 90-day T-bill yields show channelable five-wave advances with an exhaustion break of the upper trendline on the surge in rates after the Federal Reserve's Oct. 6 actions. The fifth wave in T-bill yields is even subdivided into five clear waves, he says of his charts.

"This count should mark the end of the three-year rise in short-term interest rates," he concludes. "Even if this is only an intermediate top, a normal Elliott pullback based on the five-wave count would bring the prime rate back to 11½% and T-bill yields back to 9%."

The conjunction of five waves on various interest rate charts, according to Prechter, "all seems to point to the same conclusion: The world is about to begin a phase of general deflation."

The Elliott Wave Theorist, 1980

JANUARY 6, 1980

Gold

Seven years after President Richard Nixon claimed "We're all Keynesians now," the gold market is still screaming "OH YEAH?" For those who recognize the damage to the currency that fifteen years of intense and accelerating inflation in this country must wreak, dollars are nothing but tulip bulbs. The gold rise is really a crash in tulip bulb dollars plotted upside-down. When the dollar falls to the level it is really worth (assuming we avoid hyperinflation), the "crash" will be over and the gold rise will be over. As Frost and I said in our book (p.144), "Gold, historically speaking, is one of the disciplines of economic life; it is the time-honored store of value. That paper is no substitute for gold is probably another of nature's laws."

As for the intermediate term, the action in the precious metals on January 3 was not atypical of the blowoff top I was expecting. While my target of $482 now looks overly conservative, I did caution that "blowoffs tend to be unruly and an overshoot is possible." So far, the "overshoot" has amounted to $150!

Several factors appear to indicate that a blowoff has occurred. First, the bullion price rise was nearly vertical. Secondly, many gold stocks did not open for two hours that morning, and volume in the shares was tremendous. Thirdly, by the end of the day, all but the South Africans closed down on the day and quite near their intraday lows. And in the background, a headline from the November 30 issue of Western Mining News reads, HECLA'S FUTURE "COULDN'T LOOK BETTER." Agreed, but that's what they said about General Motors in 1928.

On the other hand, the possibilities that this is not "the" final top but just "a" top have increased, since the upper trendline of what I had assumed was a valid long term channel was penetrated decisively, as it was with silver. This event supports the count that labels all of the price action in gold from the August 1976 low at $103.50 as the *third* major wave (III) up from the $35 price in 1970.

You may recall that I suggested in November that the first wave up in gold, masked by price controls, may have occurred in the late 1960s, when silver bullion and precious metals stocks both registered a first wave up. Since the upper channel line has been penetrated much beyond normal for a fifth wave, however, that assumption is highly questionable. The altered wave count implies another astronomical rise in gold several years hence. The target for such a fifth Cycle wave would depend upon the turning points of the third and fourth waves. Whether such a rise would be spurred by more inflation or by severe social unrest is anyone's guess.

Frost's View

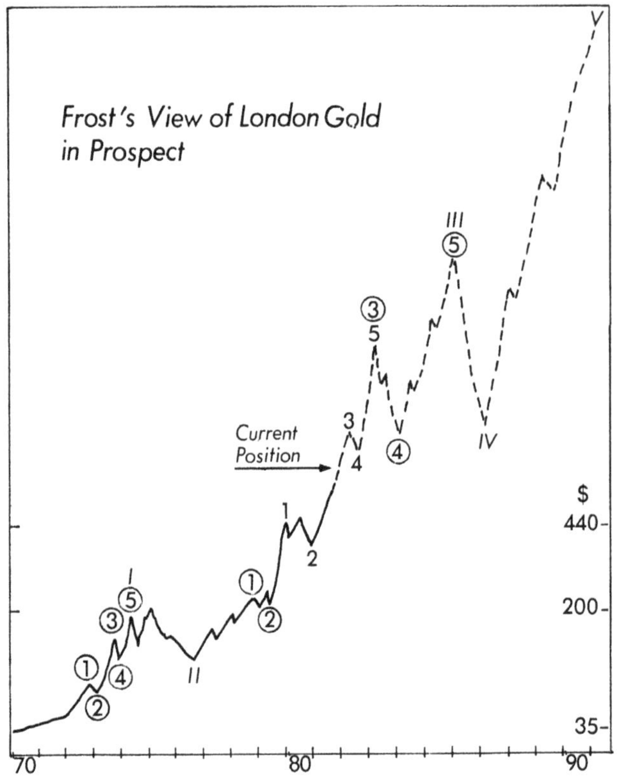

Ending points for third waves are more difficult to forecast than those for fifth waves. We may have seen the peak with last week's blowoff or we may be in the center area of a third wave extension. The volatility of the rise last week can support either interpretation, and the break of the upper trendline, unless it fails to hold, gives the extension idea great credibility.

A.J. Frost sent me his thoughts on gold last month on a chart he originally drew on October 2, 1979. So you'll have the benefit of an expert interpretation from the reigning dean himself, I've reproduced his amazing forecast for you. As he explains, "Three up waves, each shorter in length and subdividing into smaller corrections carries tremendous potential, as a rule. It is seldom a completed 5."

Frost's projection supports an outlook for continued inflation. His Elliott reasoning is flawless, as long as gold follows the same Elliott rules as stock averages do. Most commodities do not follow all the rules. For instance, the greatest thrust in the stock market comes at the center point, the third of the third. But in most commodities, the greatest thrust occurs at the culmination, the fifth of the fifth. Gold is not "most commodities," however, as Frost and I explained in our book (see p. 140). My experience so far with charts of gold bullion supports Frost's assumption that it adheres to typical wave action. If this outlook for gold is correct, it may explain why there will be no "crunch" in 1980 for the stock market to discount. As Frost concludes, "The buoyancy we see in gold will soon get transposed to the DJIA."

FEBRUARY 9, 1980

Gold

According to the gold and bond markets, the outlook for continued inflation has worsened. Not only did gold break through the upper end of what might have been a valid long-term trend channel (see January letter), thus suggesting another major rise a year or so hence, but the bond market (see next section) has collapsed after taking a glance at the Carter "guns and butter and steak and eggs and two Cadillacs" budget.

For the time being, however, gold has registered a fairly classic blowoff, which I now believe has finished off the major leg III from the 1970 fixed-price low. While the bond market is only now catching up to the ravages of inflation, gold is well ahead of the inflation rate now, and a substantial correction lasting a year or more should be getting underway. If Frost's interpretation is correct (see January letter), gold should experience one or two more run-ups to new highs before the wave IV correction begins.

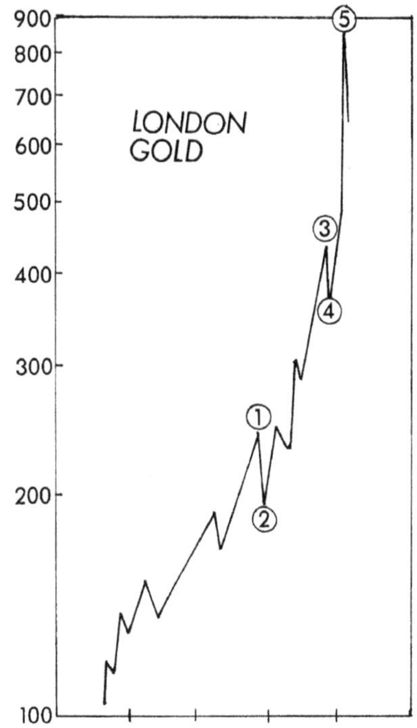

I think the most eloquent way that one can express the truth of the utterly dismal mismanagement of this nation's currency by the terminal idiots in Washington is not by words, but by charts. Toward that purpose, I have reproduced three-year charts of both gold and bonds for your masochistic delight.

MARCH 9, 1980

Gold, bonds and short term rates are all continuing as expected. Major support for gold over the next two years is the $388 level, with interim support at $477.

Gold

Last month I commented, "For the time being, gold has registered a fairly classic blowoff, which I now believe has finished off major leg III from the 1970 fixed-price low. A substantial correction lasting a year or more should be getting underway." The recent action of gold and gold stocks, which took their worst drubbing in quite a while late last week, continues to confirm this interpretation. Silver has already experienced a drop from $50 per ounce at the November peak to $30 per ounce. The accompanying chart shows the long term picture of London gold from 1972, and sums up my viewpoint.

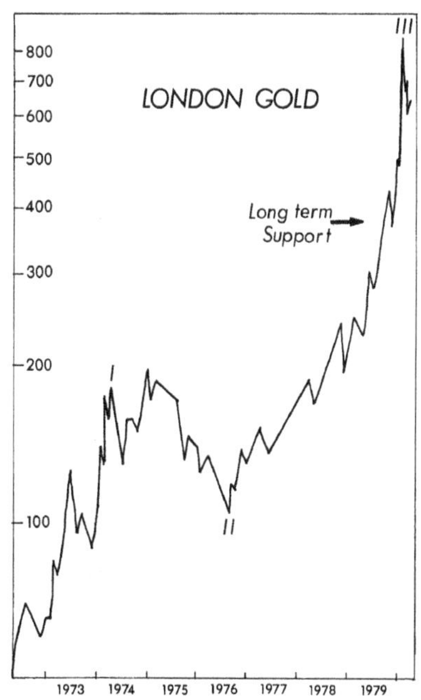

Fibonacci support levels for gold are $565, $477 and $388. The $388 level would correspond with a .618 retracement of wave III *and* with the area of the previous fourth wave of lesser degree, a normal Elliott support level. The $388 level is the most reasonable target for the eventual end to the large wave IV correction. An ideal Elliott scenario for gold over the next year or two would be an Ⓐ wave down to $477, forming the first retracement of the extended fifth wave within wave III. Then a strong rally would ensue forming wave Ⓑ, followed by a declining wave Ⓒ down to the final target of $388.

APRIL 6, 1980

Gold appears to be days away from an intermediate low.

Gold

On the front page of last month's issue I commented, "Major support for gold over the next two years is the $388 level, with interim support at $477." Gold has since declined to a low of $474 on March 18. A minor low was registered ten days later at $485, and Thursday's close was $485.75. Obviously Elliott support at $477 is having an effect. Last month I outlined the "ideal" Elliott scenario as one in which gold would form "an Ⓐ wave down to $477...then a strong rally forming wave B, followed by a declining wave Ⓒ down to the final target of $388." My current reading of gold suggests that the first important phase of reaction (an a-b-c forming a larger Ⓐ) is almost over. The current fifth wave down should penetrate the $474 low slightly and lead to the best rally since the highs. By the way, the exact reading at the second wave low in December 1979 was $471.50. If the current downleg is indeed finishing an "Ⓐ" wave, it should stop just about exactly at that level. If I am wrong on the near term, look to $388 as the next stop.

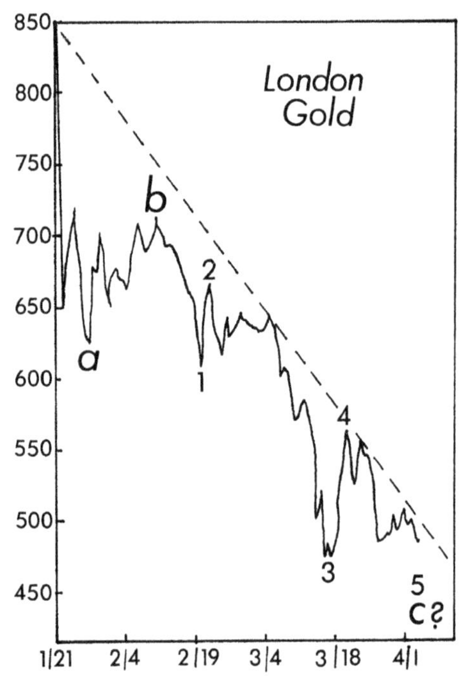

MAY 12, 1980

Gold remains in a major bear wave decline.

Gold

There is nothing to add to my expectations for gold. For this year at least, gold is a dead issue. The $850 peak began a "bear" phase which should last at least a year. The first support level at $477, which I computed two weeks after the peak, has held all declines during the past six weeks. The ultimate target is still $388. Intervening rallies are nearly impossible to gauge by Elliott methods, so I will refrain from too much pontification on the near-term swings. Suffice it to say that the peak of wave c's fourth wave down at $560 (see April letter) should continue to provide upside resistance, while a .618 retracement of the decline to just over $700 should be the maximum potential of any intermediate rally.

JUNE 10, 1980

Gold is in a one- to two-year Elliott bear market but could trade at new all-time high levels within the corrective pattern.

Silver

The gold and silver markets have been acting as if following a pre-written Elliott script ever since their highs. First let's look at silver. The accompanying chart is a model of Elliott clarity. It has a striking beauty to its simplicity. Wave ① was a clear five, and wave ② was a clear a-b-c. Wave ③ was a clear five and constituted the longest and strongest part of the entire wave, in textbook fashion. Wave ④ was a clear a-b-c, and wave ⑤ was a clear five, with a loss in momentum, a failure to meet the support trendline and a path that "hugged" the downtrend line, all typical characteristics of the final wave in a sequence.

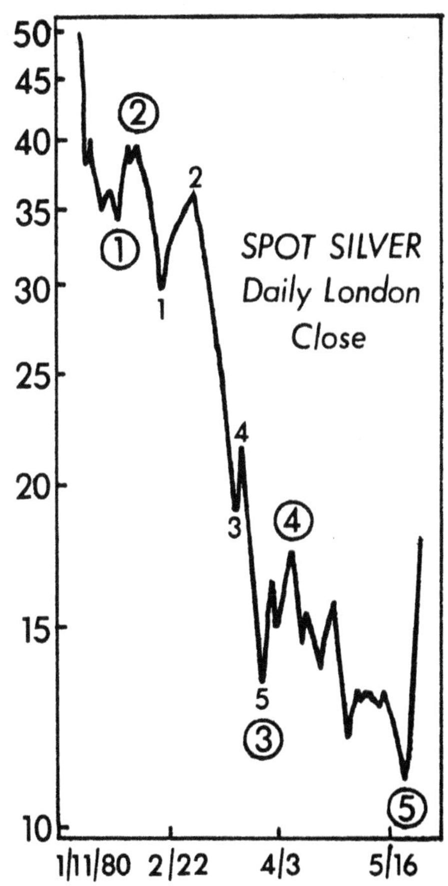

As for the Fibonacci relationships, wave ⑤ traveled 6.5 points (roughly .618 x 10), wave ① traveled 16 points (1.618 x 10), and wave ③ traveled 26.3 points (2.618 x 10). All these lengths are 10x multiples of the three main Fibonacci ratios, making the three impulse waves related to each other by Fibonacci multiples. In addition, wave ② at 6 points was just over .618 times as long as wave ④ at 4 points, thus roughly relating the corrective waves by Fibonacci as well. And finally, note that wave ① bottomed at the exact level that marks a Golden Section of the entire decline. At that point 38.2% of the decline had occurred, leaving 61.8% left to go. This makes wave ① equal to .618 of the travel from its low to the final low.

As for the present situation, the Ⓐ wave down in silver was completed on May 22, and the B wave rally is underway. Since the Ⓐ-wave decline was a clear five-wave structure, we can assume with conviction that the ultimate low for silver has NOT been seen, and that after the B wave has run its course, another decline should get underway, taking silver to lower lows. Based on the rule that bear markets generally end in the span of travel of the fourth wave of lesser degree, I expect silver's ultimate low to be in the vicinity of $4-$6 per ounce, the area of the 1974-1976 "trading range."

As for the B wave currently underway, the minimum target would be the peak of the fourth wave of lesser degree, or $17.50. That level was reached on Friday's close for silver. A 50% retracement would be $30.50. A maximum target after the first wave of a zigzag is the .618 retracement point, which is the $35 level, where wave ① bottomed.

Gold

As you know, I lean toward the idea that we have completed only three major waves up in gold from the 1970 fixed-price low. If this is true, then the action since $850 is the beginning of major wave IV. The outlook for silver also precludes any thoughts that gold might be in for another huge-multiple runup directly from here.

In the March 9 letter, I outlined a "perfect" Elliott scenario as one in which gold would form "an Ⓐ wave down to $477...then a strong rally forming wave B, followed by a declining wave Ⓒ down to the final target of $388." The recorded low for gold was $474 on March 18, $3 off the projected target for wave Ⓐ, and about as close as I'll ever get to projecting a turn in advance. The orthodox low occurred either April 7 (a day when the London spot market was closed) or April 21 (concurrently with the orthodox low in stocks). Whichever low is used, it was slightly higher than $474, leaving a small fifth wave failure (see text, p.33).

As far as the Fibonacci ratio is concerned, I have taken the chart of gold and placed a Golden Section (see text, p.83) alongside. As you can see, the top in early February marks the exact point of division, making the final decline equal to .618 of the length of the entire decline.

Now that the B wave rally is underway, I have done some thinking about the potential for this gold rally. The action since the April 7 low is not crystal-clear, and several options are

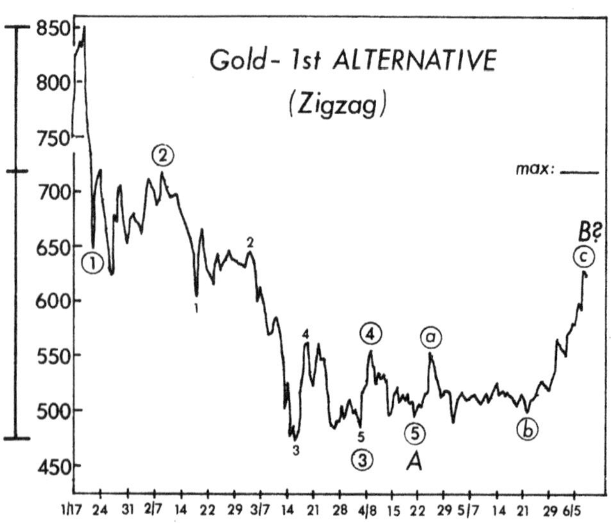

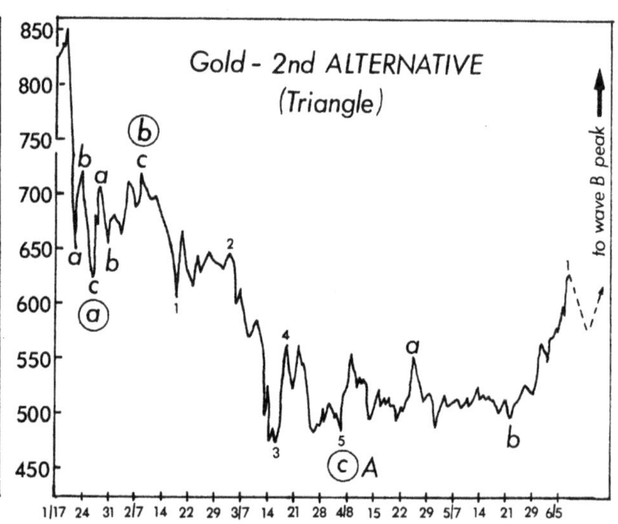

left open. One important point is that since the 1974-1976 correction in gold was an irregular correction, the current correction should be a *zigzag* or a *triangle* by rule of alternation.

Zigzag

I can count wave A as a "five" by accepting a fifth wave failure on April 21 and by labeling the bottom of wave ① at $650. This count portends an ⓐ-ⓑ-ⓒ rally to follow with resistance at $630 (a.382 retracement) and $710 (a.618 retracement). Yesterday's high was $627.50 and may have completed an ⓐ-ⓑ-ⓒ rally, with wave ⓒ subdividing into a clear five. The $710 level should be kept in mind, though, since the double failure [at the bottom of wave A] (both the fifth wave of wave ③ and wave ⑤ itself) suggests strength in the current rally.

Triangle

Unfortunately, the gold decline is one of those rare occurrences that can be counted just as easily as a "three." This makes the action since April 7 classifiable as waves a and b of a larger three-wave rally, with wave c upward currently underway. If this count is valid, the triangle alternative would be the most attractive, both from the standpoint of the rule of alternation and because the triangle is a typical *fourth* wave formation.

What type of triangle might we expect? Well, I arrived at my original target of $477 by expecting the extension in the huge fifth wave blowoff to be doubly retraced (see text, p.29). The first wave from 1976 was technically the extended wave, but the fifth wave made such a phenomenal upside rush that it seemed a candidate for double retracement, and following the guidelines, the *first* retracement can be expected to stop at the bottom of wave ② of the extension, which was $477. Now if indeed a double retracement is underway, this rally should carry at least back to the highs at $850. The only types of triangles that allow for this possibility are ascending triangles and reverse symmetrical triangles. While either is possible, a reverse symmetrical triangle would be the only one that could *also* give me my ultimate potential downside target of $388. Therefore that formation seems the most logical based on current information.

Let's take this analysis one step further. Often the final wave of a reverse symmetrical triangle is related to the first wave by 1.618. The triangle in the DJIA in 1976, for instance, proceeded exactly in this manner. (For a full discussion of that period, ask New Classics for reprints of my 1976 reports – $13 will cover reprinting and mailing). Now since the first wave traveled $376 ($850-$474), then the final wave would be expected to travel $608 ($376 x 1.618). We have already established that our final target is $388, which marks *both* a .618 retracement of major wave III and the bottom of the previous fourth wave

EXPANDING or REVERSE SYMMETRICAL

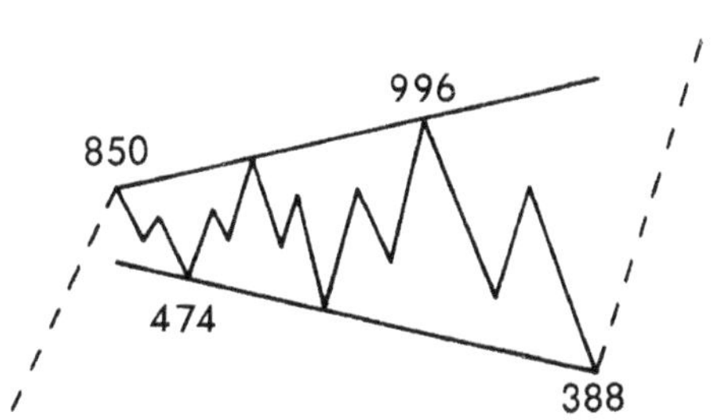

A Possible Outlook for Gold

of lesser degree (each a normal target point in its own right). Therefore the final high in the triangle would be $388 + $608 or $996. This illustration, from page 43 of *Elliott Wave Principle*, should give you the idea.

JULY 6, 1980

Gold continues on its way to at least $710, and has potential for a new high in the current corrective wave. The recession may be ending.

Gold & Silver

Nothing special has happened to gold in the past few weeks. I still feel that the $710 level is a very likely target for this rally. Don't forget that the failures at the April lows (see June 10 letter) suggest strength in the current rally, and the triangle alternative still allows for new all-time highs for gold even in the current *corrective* wave. Thus if $710 is exceeded, I would expect highs slightly above $850 to follow soon afterwards. Gold stocks, as a group, have registered new highs as expected. This occurrence seems to give additional support to the reverse symmetrical triangle alternative.

Silver met its minimal target of $17.50 in early June (see June 10 letter) and has yet to manage to climb above it. This action reveals continuing relative weakness, from an Elliott standpoint, in silver as compared to gold. Silver remains in an a-b-c zigzag bear market and has a lower low ahead of it, likely in the $4-$6 range some time in the next two years. The Elliott position of silver strongly supports my interpretation that gold is in a corrective wave.

AUGUST 10, 1980

Gold continues in a primary Elliott wave bear market, although new highs may occur within the corrective pattern.

Gold

The Primary degree bear market continues in gold. The orthodox top at $850 should stand for about two years before the next major impulse wave gets underway. Two main possibilities remain for the shape of the current corrective wave, a *zigzag* and a *reverse symmetrical triangle*, both of which have ultimate downside targets of $388. These two patterns were spelled out completely in my June letter.

Jim Arnold, who edits one of my favorite letters, *The Primary Trend* (700 N. Water St., Milwaukee, WI 53202), has beaten me to the punch in taking the next logical step in Elliott channeling (see text, p.59). Jim's letter always has a sexy centerfold feature, and the July 9 issue is no exception. If you'd like to feast your eyes on weekly gold for twelve years, you'll have to ask Jim for his chart since it's too big for me to reproduce in this letter. However, I do have my own compact model featured at right.

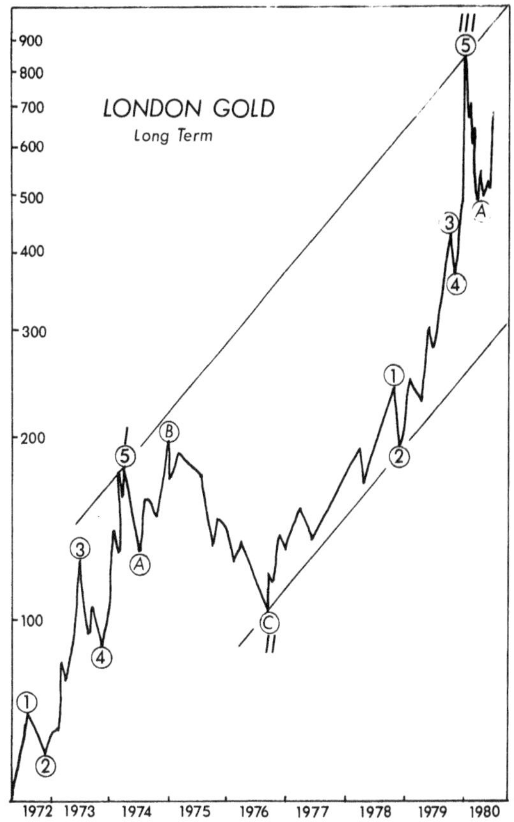

Now that wave III has peaked, the long term Elliott trendchannel must be redrawn by connecting the peaks of wave I and III, and then constructing a parallel line from the bottom of wave II. One fascinating result of this exercise is that the progress of gold from the August 1976 low through early 1979 is now shown to have been hugging the true major uptrend support line. Furthermore, the chart indicates that if my $388 downside target for the current Primary wave correction is to be met, it will probably occur as a zigzag and end by mid-1981, when the uptrend line will be crossing the $388 level. A full two-year-plus correction may have to take the shape of a *symmetrical triangle* to stay within the trendchannel boundaries.

As for the near term, the recent action has been quite lethargic and inconclusive, but I would still lean toward further potential in the current bear market rally since we saw either an a-b-c into the $474 low or a fifth wave failure, each of which implies strength in the upward correction to follow. Remember that the triangle alternative allows for new all-time highs in bullion *within the corrective* wave. However, don't let new highs in gold, if they occur, convince you that a new giant upwave has begun. The action of gold over the *next* two years could resemble the action in the Dow Industrials over the *past* two years, with the final shakeout providing the best buying opportunity.

Take a close look at the action in gold since 1974. Who says the principle of countercyclicality hasn't been working? Within one month's error, the Dow *bottomed* at 570 when gold *topped* at $195, topped at 1020 when gold bottomed at $103.50, *bottomed* at 740 when gold topped at $850, and is now streaking to new highs as gold begins its bear market. By the way, each wave interpretation currently supports the other.

AUGUST 21, 1980

Gold continues in its bear market rally to at least $710. Remember that I am fully prepared for new highs in gold within the corrective wave before the next serious decline.

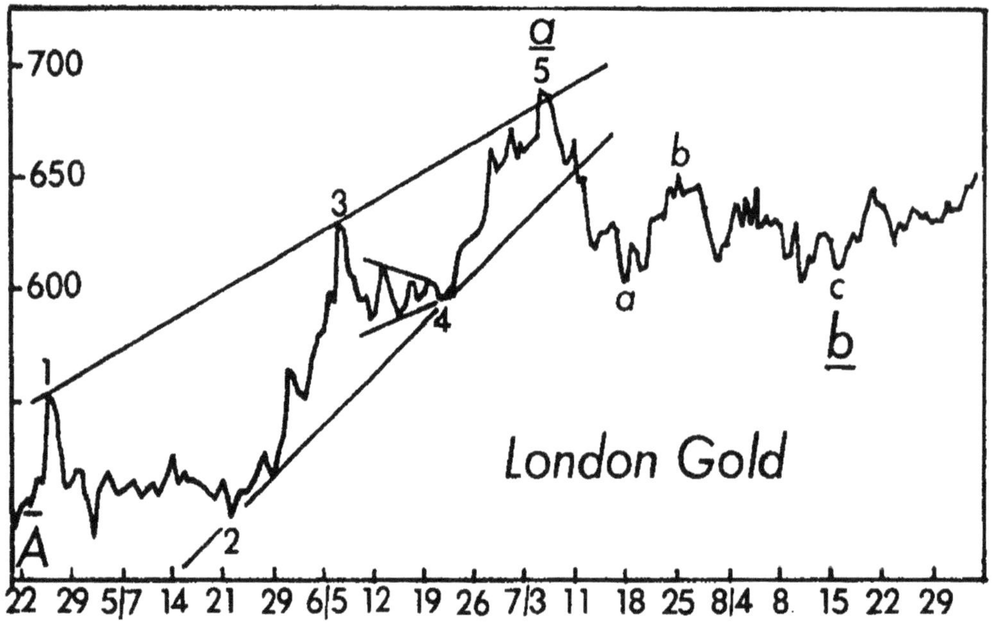

SEPTEMBER 9, 1980

Gold has entered wave C and is finally approaching its *minimum* rally target at $710, although higher targets remain a distinct possibility. Gold *stocks* should continue to out-perform gold bullion.

Gold has entered wave c of its a-b-c bear market rally and should meet the minimum Elliott target of $710 within days. Remember that the possibility still exists for a new high above $850 before the next important down wave. One of my subscribers, Sam Robbins of Robbins Planning Co., wrote recently that when compared to the prices of "everything else, gold is now more expensive than it has ever been in the last 400 years." Clearly gold did more than "catch up" to inflation in Primary wave III from $103.50 to $850. This fact in itself adds support to the idea that gold is going to be marking time for at least another year.

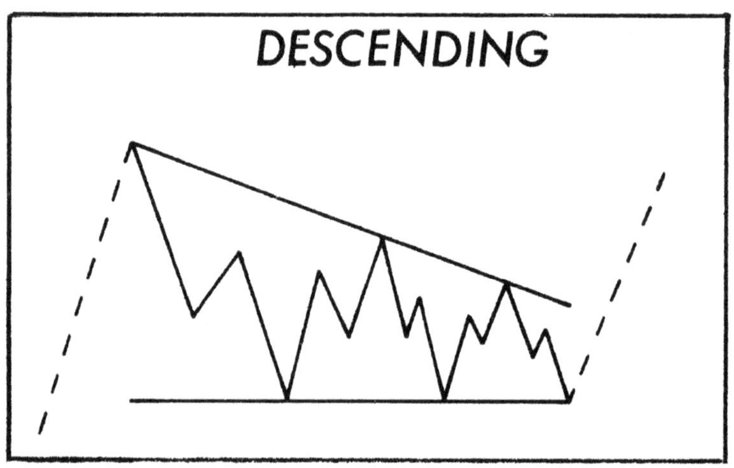

What about the gold *stocks*? Don't they have to go dull along with gold? On the contrary, in the June 10 letter I commented as follows:

> Gold stocks are acting extremely well. It looks to me as if most will register new highs during 1980. Certainly if gold bullion can be expected to hold up at lofty levels during most of the corrective period, the income potential of gold mines is phenomenal. Thus while gold itself "corrects" by going sideways, gold mining companies may enjoy particularly good earnings, earnings which may not have been discounted as yet.

In fact, gold stocks are registering those new highs now, and the status of the waves in my gold stock average does not appear to be any kind of blowoff, but a continuation move. Therefore I do expect further gains, with intermittent pullbacks, in precious metals stocks over the next few months.

Silver

Silver held underneath its minimum retracement level at $17.50 (see June letter) for three solid months, and has just broken out to new highs. The peak of wave A came after a clear 5-wave move, and wave B is a textbook descending triangle. The illustration is from page 43 of *Elliott Wave Principle.*

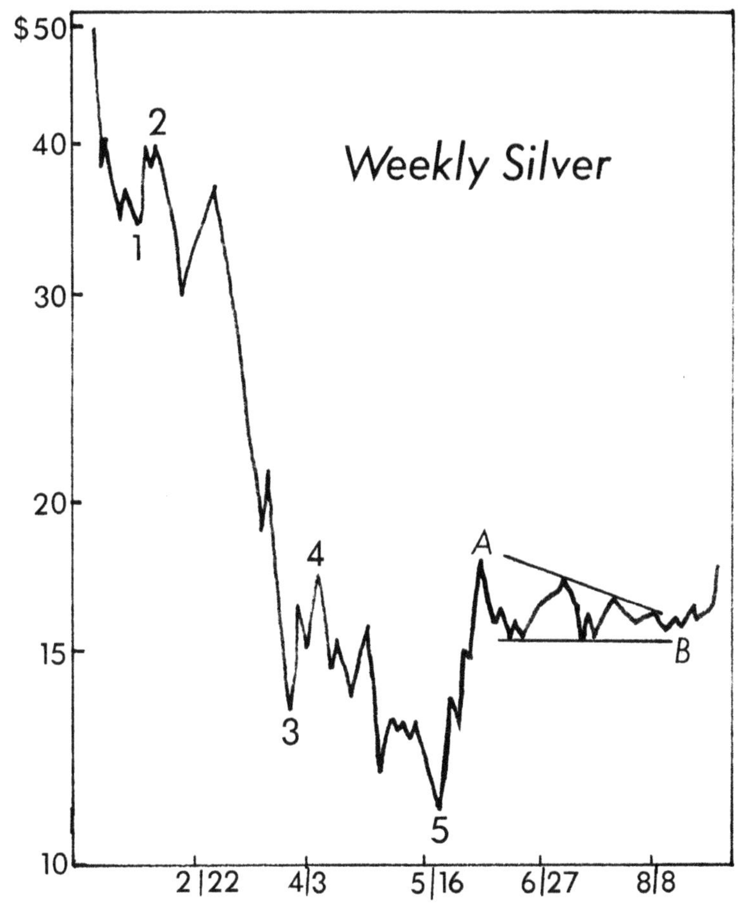

Wave C upward is now underway, and several levels present themselves as possible targets. The recent breakout ushers in the potential for a complete .618 retracement at $35, which coincidentally is exactly a double of the $17.50 price. A 50% retracement would be $30.50. In another computation, wave equality between waves A and C would give $22-$23 as a target.

SEPTEMBER 23, 1980 – INTERIM REPORT

Gold has now hit its minimum target of $710 per ounce London fixing. The failure at the $477 low did imply strength and thus an overrun of the $710 level, but from here on out, I'd rather let the other guy have the profits. The "guaranteed" part of the rise is behind us. Yesterday's action in gold stocks smacked of a near-term blowoff, and the wave count on gold shows a completed "five" for wave C. If gold goes higher, it will probably be as part of a triangular structure as discussed in the June letter.

OCTOBER 3, 1980

Gold appears to have topped out its B-wave just above my long-standing target of $710 per ounce, and silver its B-wave at $24.

Gold

Last month's wave analysis indicated, "Gold has entered wave c of its a-b-c bear market rally and should meet the minimum Elliott target of $710 within days." In the September 23 Interim Report, the day gold registered its peak London fixing to date, I suggested getting out of the long side:

> Gold has now hit its minimum target of $710 per ounce London fixing. The failure at the [April] low did imply strength and thus an overrun of the $710 level, but from here on out, I'd rather let the other guy have the profits. The "guaranteed" part of the rise is behind us.

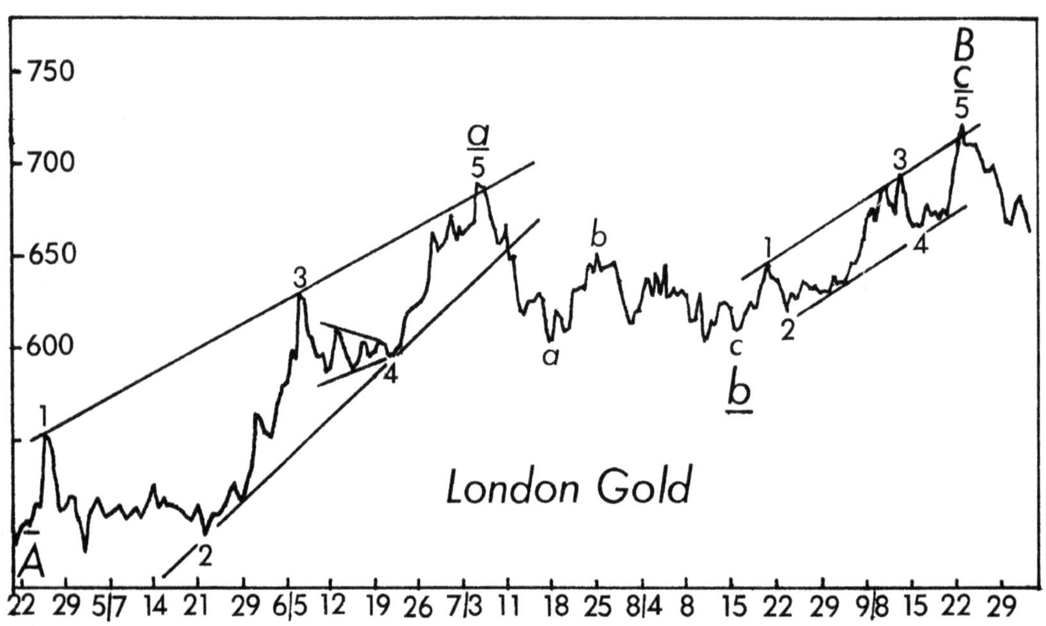

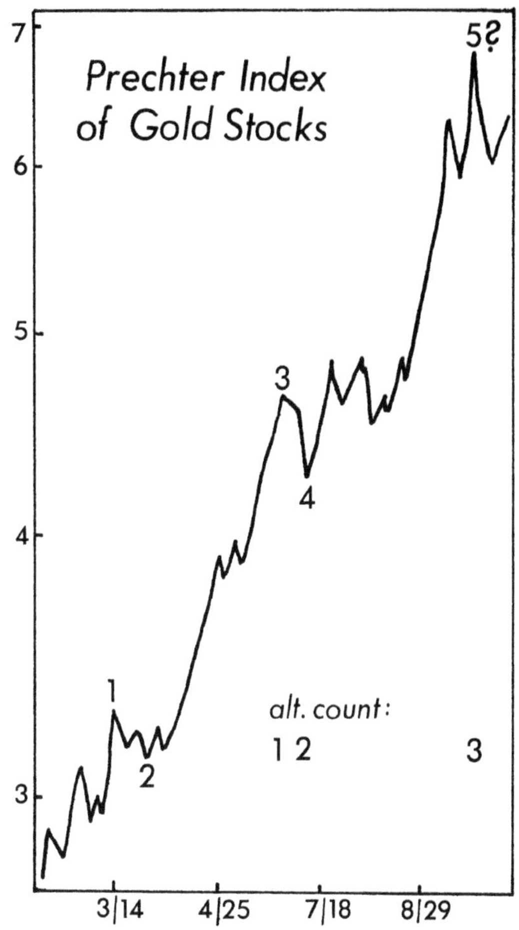

If indeed the high has been seen, the overshoot at the high was about the same as the undershoot at the orthodox low, typical wave behavior. Using another possible orthodox low at $495 on April 21 (the same day as the orthodox stock market low), I find that wave c is .618 times as long was wave a, helping confirm the top at $720. For a look at the two possible orthodox lows, see the June 10 letter.

Here are some things to keep in mind while watching the gold market over the next few months. The reverse symmetrical triangle alternative as outlined in the June 10 letter could still be operable, and highs above $850 within the corrective wave are still possible, although less probable now that a reversal has taken place at $720. I think $720 should be used as a stop point if you are now short gold. A drop below $605 will virtually confirm the recent high, since that level marks the low of wave b. If a symmetrical (contracting) triangle is underway, the current decline would have a target equal to .618 times the rise just completed, or between *$568 and $584* per ounce. While a descending triangle should not be ruled out, a decline below $568 would increase the chances that a zigzag decline is in force with its maximum downside target of *$388*. A zigzag implies that the bear phase will take its toll in terms of *price*; a triangle implies that the bear phase will take its toll in terms of *time*.

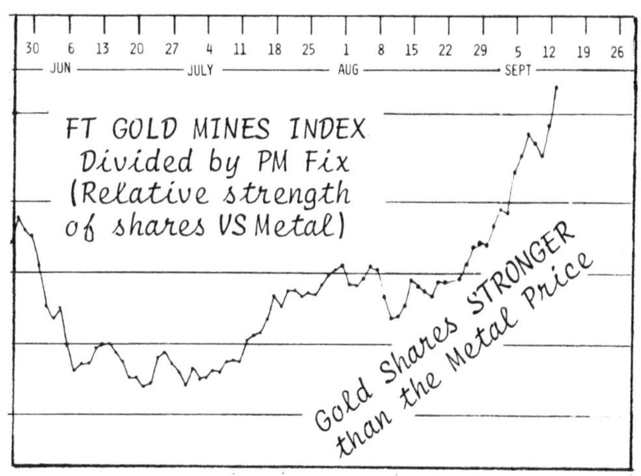

Gold Shares

This is a tough area, but I currently feel that gold shares have made or are about to register their fifth wave tops from the 1976-1977 lows. They were one cycle off from bullion and continued in their *impulse* wave sequence while gold has been only in a B wave. The fact that gold bullion has failed by a wide margin to confirm the breakout to significant new highs in gold shares is in itself an important sell signal of intermediate significance pertaining to the whole gold picture.

As I said on September 23, "Yesterday's action in gold stocks smacked of a near-term blowoff." The accompanying chart of PIGS shows either a completed five or three waves in the advance from the late March low, suggesting that *a top either has been seen or will be registered upon one final new high.*

The continuation of gold shares in their Primary *impulse* wave was part of the reason I indicated in the June 10 letter that gold stocks would outperform gold bullion during the Primary wave correction in bullion. The latest copy of Ian McAvity's *Deliberations* (P.O. Box 182, Adelaide St. Station, Toronto, Canada M5C 2J1) contains a chart of the relative performance of the two areas and shows that my timing wasn't too far off on that score. The first phase of outperformance was January-February 1980, and the second phase (shown) began in June.

Silver

Silver hit a brick wall at its first Elliott upside resistance zone of $22-23. The high reading on September 23 was $24.15, an exact ⅓ retracement prior to the subsequent fallback. My guess is that silver has peaked along with gold and that its zigzag B-wave rally has ended. There is no reason to expect exceptional strength from silver, since its overall bear market pattern is clearly a zigzag. Therefore, prepare for a final C wave down to lows significantly under the last low at $11 per ounce, probably closer to $4-$6 per ounce. If a new high above $24.15 occurs contrary to my expectations, see the September 9 letter for the next two resistance levels.

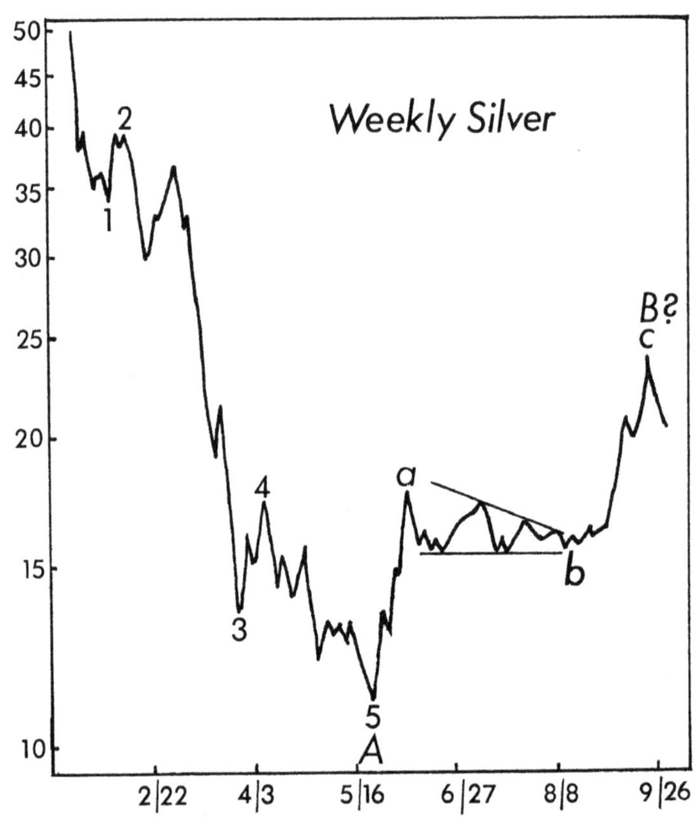

Gertrude Shirk, writer for *Cycles*magazine (124 S. Highland Ave., Pittsburgh, PA 15206), predicted the January top in silver over a year in advance based on the 5.58-year silver cycle. The next ideal low is scheduled for *1982.8*, a perfect time zone for a symmetrical triangle in *gold* (see August 10 letter) to meet the rising lower trendline for its Supercycle bull market.

OCTOBER 31, 1980 – SPECIAL REPORT

Gold should go *sideways* in a triangle formation to meet its lower trendchannel boundary by mid to late 1982; the dotted line shows the alternate possibility of a zigzag decline to $388 by mid-1981. The ultimate high in gold is forecast at $5040 as a minimum and most likely target level by 1986-87. The 5x multiple of wave I ($35 x 5) and the 8x multiple of wave III ($103.50 x 8) suggest to me a 13x multiple for wave V. Using the current downside limit of $388, which marks a .618 retracement of wave III, I project a target of $5040 per ounce as the minimum and most likely target for the orthodox fifth wave high in gold. Not only does this level mark a 13x multiple, but it touches the upper trend-channel line perfectly in the 1986-1987 time period and also happens to mark almost the exact level of a 144x multiple of the original $35 per ounce price! It is worth noting that Elliott considered 144 (the first Fibonacci number which is also a square) as the "largest number of practical value" when applying the Fibonacci sequence to markets.

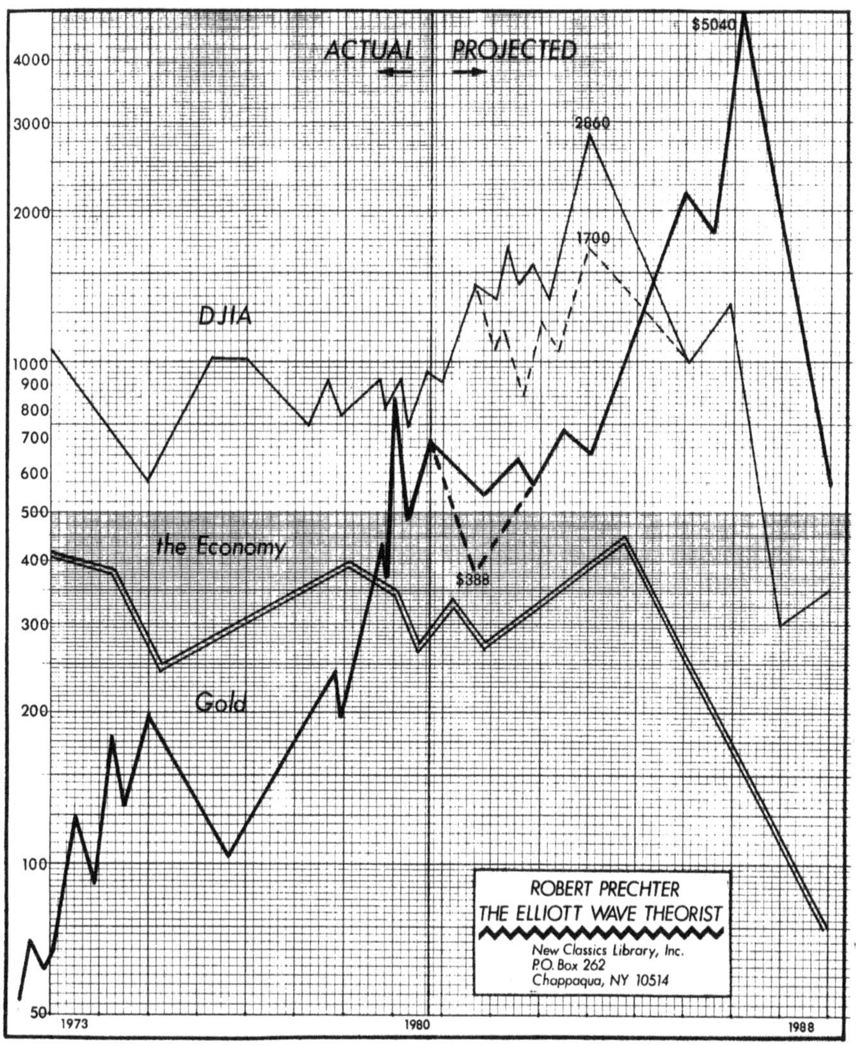

NOVEMBER 20, 1980

Gold remains in a bear market but should undergo a near term a-b-c rally before collapsing below the $600 level.

Gold & Silver

As you know, Elliott analysis caught the gold top at $720 to the day after forecasting a $710 peak for several months. The recent action in the gold price appears to have confirmed that assessment, not just because the price declined 17% from the high, but because it did so in a five-wave pattern. An Elliotter must conclude that further downside action lies ahead. If you take a look at the daily chart of gold, you can see the beautiful five-wave decline from the top, complete with extended third wave and parallel channel. Right now it looks as if gold should immediately begin a minor a-b-c rally back to about $655, the peak of the previous fourth wave of lesser degree. Since this a-b-c rally would be wave 2 in the declining sequence, there is no guarantee that $655 will be met precisely, but it is a guideline. The next decline in gold should be a real killer, as wave 3 of Ⓒ cracks the "support level" at $600. Hold all shorts from $720, and use any rally from here as an opportunity to add to the short side. Use $720 as a stop.

Last month's comments remain relevant:

> If a symmetrical (contracting) triangle is underway, the current decline would have a target equal to .618 times the rise just completed, or between $568 and $584 per ounce. While a descending triangle should not be ruled out (providing a floor at $474), a decline below $568 would increase the chance that a zigzag decline is in force with its maximum downside target of $388.

Gold shares have also followed the script. The chart of gold stocks in the October 3 letter indicated, "A top either has been seen or will be registered upon one final new high." Several days later, the final rally in gold stocks peaked out, with about ⅔ of the gold issues managing new highs and the other ⅓ failing by small margins. After a near-term rally coinciding with

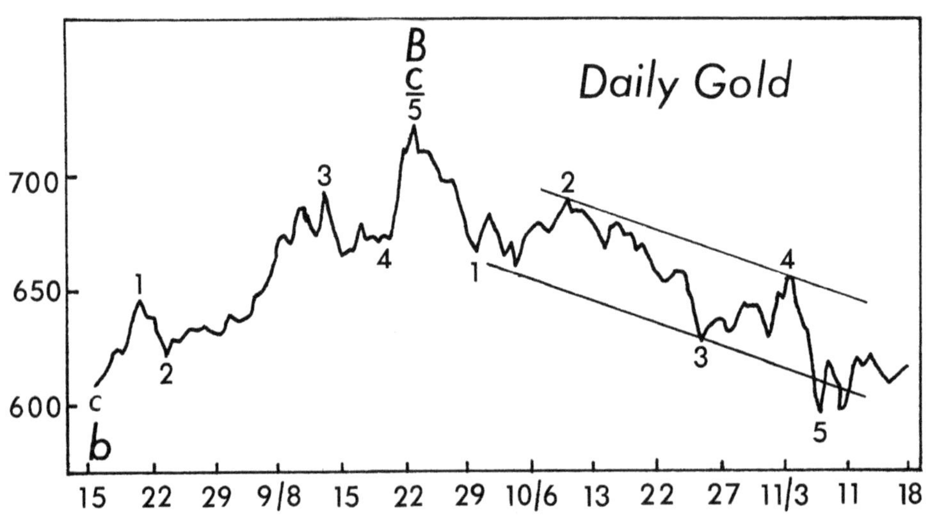

the a-b-c upward correction in bullion, gold stocks should join bullion on the downside.

Silver peaked out exactly as expected and has traced out the same pattern as gold, a beautiful five-wave decline. Eventual target is below $11 ounce.

DECEMBER 14, 1980

Gold & Silver

Like that famed 13th-century Italian ballerina Fibonacci, the price of gold has been tripping from one side of the Elliott stage to the other, dancing to the sounds of a Golden Symphony: 5th of a 5th at $850; 50% retracement at $477; .618 retracement at $720. And now a perfect five-wave decline, an a-b-c, and a vicious 3rd-wave crack below "support" at $600.

Encore, encore! Here is a comment from the November 20 issue:

> The next decline in gold should be a real killer, as wave 3 of C cracks the "support lever" at $600. Hold all shorts from $720, and use any rally from here as an opportunity to add to the short side.

The nature of the decline in gold last week was such that I think the zigzag scenario is becoming by far the most likely. Not only did gold fall below .618 triangle support at $568, but it declined in a typical third wave manner – hard and fast. These observations increase the chances that gold will hit my downside target of $388 before Primary wave V begins.

By the way, the B wave peak in December 1974 coincided with a huge divergence between the new highs in the gold price and the distinctly laggard behavior of gold *shares*. This time, at the B wave peak at $720, it is gold shares which have run to new highs and gold *bullion* whose performance has lagged. In terms of interpretation, a non-confirmation is a non-confirmation. It's bearish. In terms of Elliott, it's the Rule of Alternation manifest in yet another way.

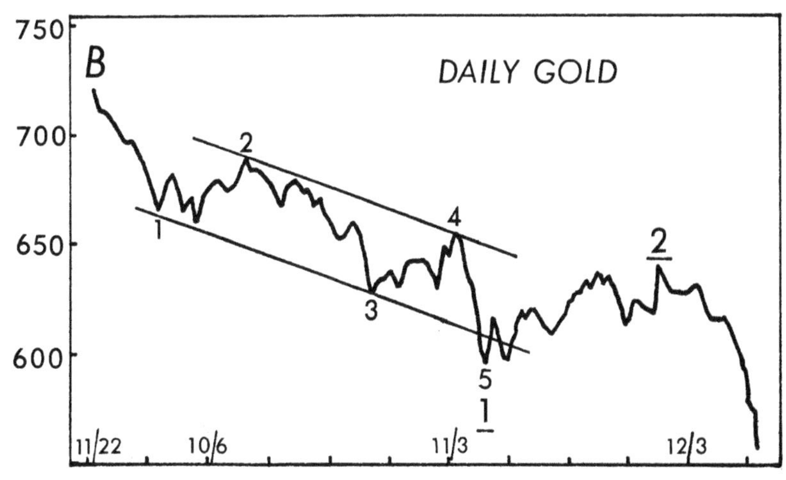

Silver is on its way to below $11 an ounce, possibly into the $4-6 range, the area of the previous fourth wave of lesser degree.

The Elliott Wave Theorist, 1981

JANUARY 9, 1981

Gold continues to head south and still appears to have much further to go.

Gold

In June 1980 I made a presentation at Jim Blanchard's NCMR Conference in Montreal, in all a thoroughly enjoyable experience. I gave my outlook for a $710 maximum upside in gold for the rest of 1980 to a roomful of 1200 slowly shaking heads to be sure, but most listened politely. I do remember one particularly cynical speaker however, who, after projecting a continued runup to $1000, $2000 and $3000 gold, remarked to the audience and the tape recorder that "Unfortunately, when Elliott Waves were developed, there was no OPEC around and the Russians don't seem to have studied the cycles." They don't, eh? Well they'd better start soon!.

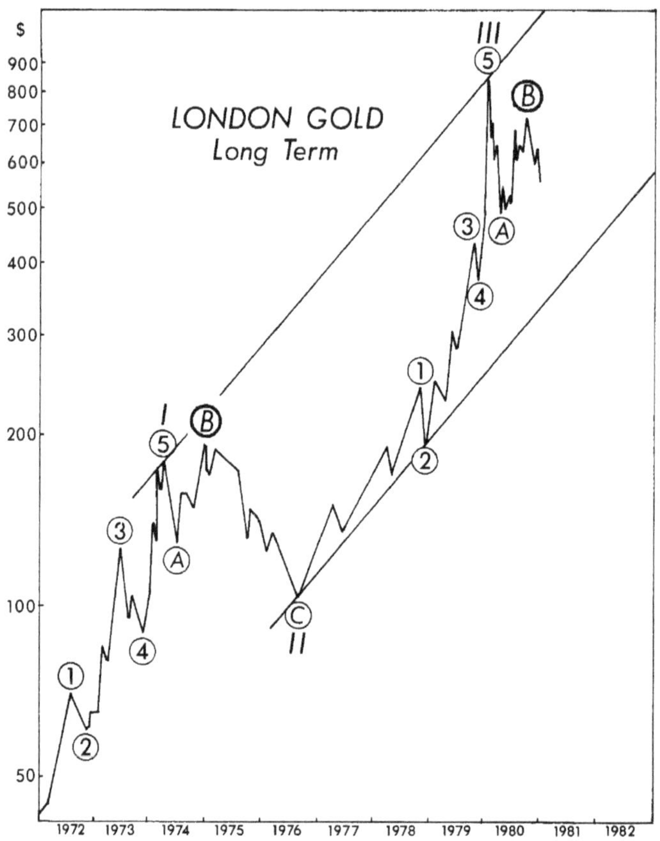

The long term picture is the handsomest, so I'll show that one this month. Based on normal Elliott expectations, we should await either wave C of a zigzag or waves C-D-E of a triangle. Maximum and most likely downside target is still $388, a .618 retracement of wave III and the area of the previous fourth wave of lesser degree, wave ④ (see chart).

FEBRUARY 6, 1981

The maximum downside momentum for gold has now passed, although prices should continue to work their way lower in the months ahead.

Gold

After staying with the short side since the September 23 top in gold at $720, it is finally time to think about switching tactics in some areas. The "third of the third," or period of maximum downside thrust, has just ended. Thus while bullion should continue lower over the next several months down to its ultimate target of $388, gold stocks may sense the slowing of downside momentum and begin to resist further weakness.

In the March-October rally, ASA climbed from just over 35 to just under 92, a perfect 161.8% rise. ASA has now declined from 92 to near 50, one heck of a healthy retracement. Even if it manages to fall a full 61.8% back to 35, it may take a long time to fulfill the remaining portion of that objective. These considerations coupled with the extremely high yields now offered by gold stocks seem to make it prudent to use the current low levels to *take profits on gold stock shorts and get out of all gold stock puts.* With high-premium options such as those in ASA, low downside momentum could make the puts nearly worthless, even if you've got the direction right.

On the other hand, investors on the short side in gold futures should hold positions until the final bottom. *Traders* in this area, for the first time, can start trading around their short positions, that is, shorting on near term rallies and covering on near term declines, as the next two "fourth" waves create a downwardly biased trading range situation in bullion. I am *not* ready at this time to recommend any long positions in gold or silver.

To understand where I think we are in the gold picture, take a look at the chart below of the twice-a-day London gold fix. Taking into account the tenets of the Wave Principle regarding overlapping and length of waves (see text, p. 53), I think gold is developing the most typical of all impulse waves, one containing an extended third. To examine this formation, see text, p. 28 and reverse & invert Figure 6.

Within larger wave 3 of the current C wave, gold has completed waves 1 and 2 and has nearly completed 3. If this pattern is to remain true, gold should drop to a slight new low to finish off wave 3, then enter a sideways period for several weeks for wave 4, then undergo another short drop for wave 5. At that point larger wave 3 will have ended, and wave 4, a

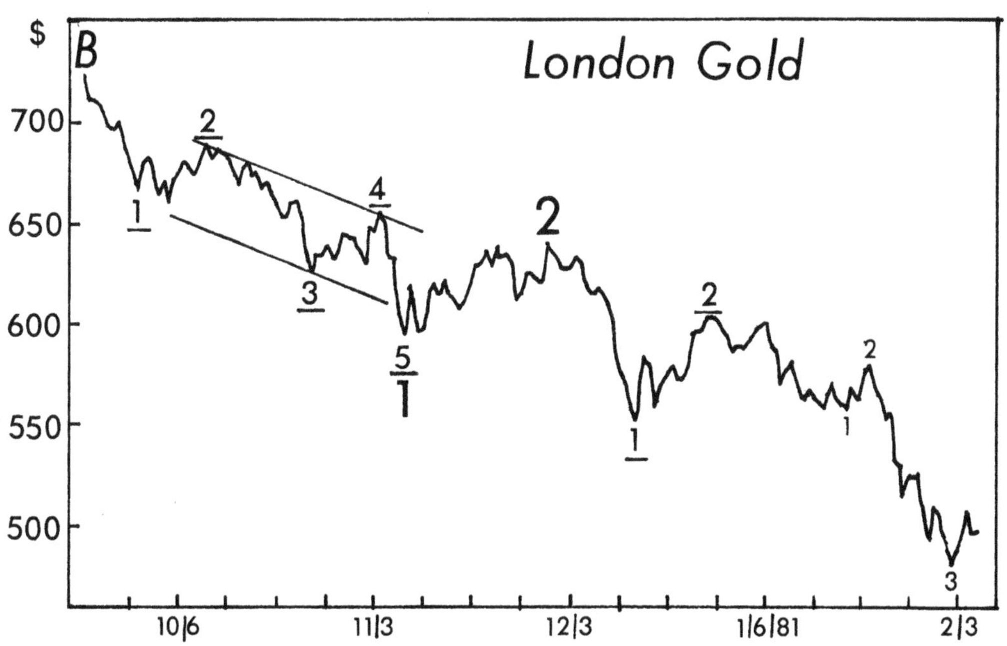

sideways-to-up period lasting a month or more, should precede the final drop into the low of wave 5. This low would finish off the entire C-wave decline from $720. Since both upward second waves so far have been zigzags, I expect the fourth waves to be flats or triangles, that is, *sideways* structures rather than significant rallies.

An *alternate count* is still possible in gold, one that would allow for a better rally after one more minor wave down to the area of the previous low at $474. At this point, gold could complete a zigzag down from $720, constituting wave c in an a-b-c-d-e triangle formation (see below, from *Elliott Wave Principle*). As I outlined in the June 1980 letter, a larger triangle pattern from the $850 top is a distinct possibility. At this point in the corrective wave, the only possible triangular pattern remaining is the *descending triangle*. Until $474 is broken decisively, this count remains a viable alternative to the more likely zigzag, and provides another good argument for lightening up on the short side here. If wave d of a triangle is about to begin, the rally could carry back into the low 600s before the final wave e drop.

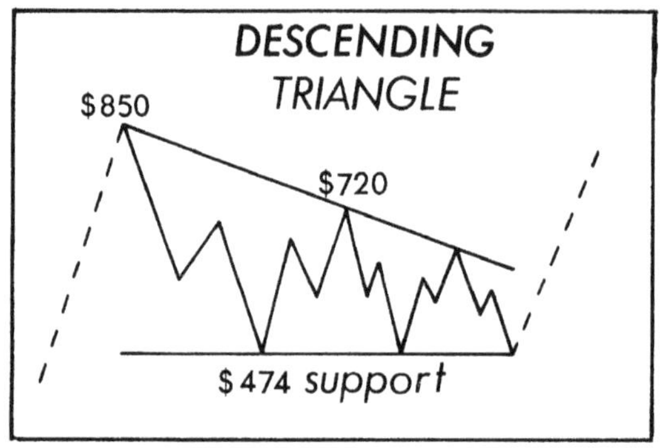

MARCH 6, 1981

Gold is completing wave 3 on the downside and should undergo a flat fourth wave "holding pattern" between approximately $450 and $520 before breaking down again a month or two from now.

Gold

It is a great pleasure to be "on track" for so long in any particular market, especially with a degree of confidence that continues high because of the perfect clarity of the wave structure during this entire correction in gold from $850. Last month was no exception, as the extended wave 3 continued to unfold, falling to a point at the current juncture that should mark the end of wave 5 of 3. As it was outlined last month, "Gold should drop to a slight now low to finish off wave 3, then enter

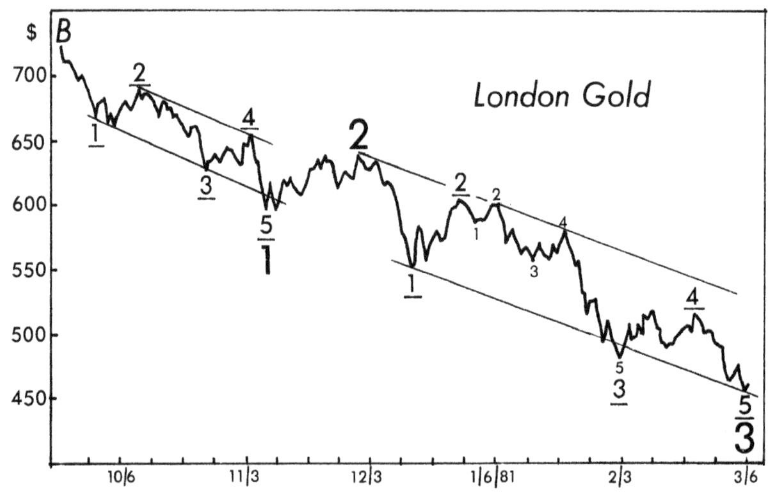

a sideways period for several weeks for wave 4, then undergo another short drop for wave 5." The chart on this page shows how my expectations worked out.

Besides the near perfection of the wave form, one reason I expect a trading low here is the Wave Equality guideline (see text, p. 57). Note that on the accompanying chart of the twice-a-day London gold fix, wave 1 of 3 from $640 to $555 covered $75. If waves 1 and 5 are to be approximately equal in length, then the distance of wave 5 should be close to $75. Measuring from the peak of wave 4 ($515-$520), we obtain a downside target area for wave 5 of $440-445, which has quite nearly been met.

If wave 3 down from $640 is indeed ending, then we should expect wave 4 to commence. It should be a *flat* upward correction since wave 2 was a zigzag. Although we should remain flexible as to the exact shape of wave 4, a typical flat a-b-c correction would result in a "wave a" rally to the peak of the previous fourth wave of lesser degree ($515-520), a "wave b" drop back to the low of wave 3, and a "wave c" return to the $515-520 area before the final wave 5 drop gets underway. This process should take a month or more. The target for wave 5 of C remains $388.

I noticed more than one advisor who, basing his conclusion on the Wave Principle, declared the gold decline over at $490 in early February. The flaw in that count involved "overlapping" and/or a third wave which was the shortest in the sequence, breaking fundamental rules of Elliott. Don't ever fall into that trap when you're counting waves. The third wave rule is particularly helpful, and keeps you on the right track when extensions are developing.

Silver is on a perfect track with gold, and has exactly the same count. I still expect to see silver below $11 per ounce before its wave C is over.

APRIL 12, 1981

Gold and silver are each in the fifth wave down within wave C of their bear markets and should reach bottom within four to six weeks. The target for gold remains $388.

Gold

A lot of people have called "the" final bottom in gold recently, but as I read the picture, *the bear market in gold is still intact and not yet over.* Elliott analysis was able to recognize *one day off the bottom* the end of wave 3 of C last month (see March 6 letter). A countertrend rally was indicated, and I expressed my expectations as follows:

> Although we should remain flexible as to the exact shape of wave 4, a typical flat a-b-c correction would result in a "wave a" rally to $515-520, a "wave b" drop back to the low of wave 3, and a "wave c" return to the $515-520 area before the final wave 5 drop gets underway.

As it happened, the crisis in Poland helped get wave 4 over very quickly, and it appears to have done its upward "correcting" in terms of *price* rather than time. Therefore rather than waiting for a flat wave's "b" and "c", I conclude that the rally was not a flat but a zigzag, which ended at $547.25 a.m. London fix (the closing fix was $538.75). Traders who participated in the excellent rally from $457 to $515-520 should now be short again. "Investor" shorts are still in effect from $710. Traders should place a stop at $535 London fix because as yet the alternate count of a descending triangle from the $850 high, while very unlikely, has yet to be proven impossible (see text, p. 43 and p. 99 of the February issue).

Wave 5 should now carry down to the final fifth wave target at *$388*, and with the speed at which this wave is progressing, the month of May appears a likely time period for that target to be met. My only concern is that the "380" level recently began popping up in an amazing number of gold prognosticators' writings. Why pick 380? As far as I know, only an Elliotter would be focusing on such an otherwise unlikely level. I hope the camp expecting that level is not becoming overcrowded. On the other hand, if gold does get there, I expect that many of these "targets" will be lowered to $250 just as the buy point is at hand.

Silver

Silver remains on track with gold and is clearly into its fifth wave down within wave C. While a majority of hard-money forecasters predicted that silver would "outperform" gold in 1980-81, *for almost a full year now I have been predicting silver back under $11 per ounce*, and this down wave is now culminating right on target. In the June 10, 1980 issue, I explained it this way:

> The A wave down in silver was completed on May 22, and the B wave rally is underway. Since the A-wave decline was a *clear* five-wave structure, we can assume with conviction that the ultimate low for silver has NOT been seen, and that after the B wave has run its course, another decline should get underway, taking silver to lower lows.

While I'm less confident about forecasting an *exact* level for the final low, at that time I projected a low of silver between $4 and $6 per ounce, based on the rule that bear markets

generally end in the span of travel of the fourth wave of lesser degree (see text, p. 55), in this case the 1974-1976 trading range. Since then, two new developments have strengthened that ultimate downside target. First, it is often the case that in an a-b-c zigzag, waves a and c tend toward equality in length. Since wave A down in silver covered 39 points, a 78% drop, it seems quite reasonable to expect that wave C will also fall 78%. A 78% drop from the B wave peak at $24.15 yields *$5.31* as a potential target. The second target support comes from the tenet that when the third wave in a sequence is extended, the first and fifth tend toward equality (see text, p. 57). Now, within the C wave in silver, the third wave was clearly extended (see chart), so the fifth wave may well be the same length as the first wave, which covered $6.65. A $6.65 point drop from the recent fourth wave peak at $13.03 would give a target of *$6.38.* These price levels are merely guidelines; when silver finishes counting out a "fifth of a fifth," it will be a great buy and we'll be buying silver by the truckloads.

How could such a tremendous drop in the price of silver occur? Well, it was the Hunt *buying* that pushed the fifth wave up to tremendous heights in the first place, and it may well be Hunt *selling* that forces the fifth wave of C down to a price well below what anyone would consider reasonable, even at this juncture. After all, there are rumors that armored trucks are delivering Hunt silver to Delaware, where there is no sales tax....

MAY 11, 1981

Gold

The most important piece of information that I can glean from Elliott analysis is that *gold's bear market is not yet over.* One can certainly *argue* that wave 5 of C is ending now on a failure (the inability to make a low below that of wave 3 – see text, p. 32), but other Elliott evidence to date does not support that argument. First, the uptrend line of the long term trendchannel has not been met; secondly, gold has yet to fall within the span of travel of the previous fourth wave of lesser degree, the $366-$437 range of October 1979's triangle formation; and finally, the Fibonacci retracement target of *$388* is still the most compelling target using typical Fibonacci relationships.

As for the near term picture, it is my tentative conclusion, as I said in the April letter, that wave 4 ended at the $547.25 a.m. London fix on March 27. This count indicates that wave 5 is already underway. It is highly likely that the final wave down of this bear market will not cause a panic type low that will be easily recognized by gold followers. I expect a slow, lethargic, even boring decline, as the bulls slowly abandon gold one at a time. This development would allow plenty of time for gold to get down to $388 by the time its uptrend line passes through that price level, my best estimate for which is the month of August.

This type of action would also fit what I expect to be the psychology near the final low in gold, a feeling not of "I'll lose my shirt," but of "who needs the stuff?" After all, with Reagan's budget and tax packages passed, it may appear as if the U.S. is on the road to solving its economic problems. In other words, it should be a low of *neglect*, not of panic.

I also notice that the bullish/bearish opinion polls on gold still show what I consider to be too many bulls. At the final bottom of a bear market already over a year old, the consensus opinion on gold should be *negative*, not neutral as it is currently. Finally, the bottom-fishers among gold prognosticators are numerous. Generally, there doesn't seem to be any particular reasoning involved by those calling the $470 area a "probable low;" it just appears to be named a "support level." When nobody wants to miss the bottom, you're probably not there yet.

While I continue to feel that the "descending triangle" alternative (see February 6 letter) is highly unlikely and getting more so with each passing day, an important alternate count does exist for gold on the *near term*. It's important, that is, if you're a futures trader, since an $80 countertrend move could bankrupt your account.

In last month's issue, I labeled wave 4's peak at $547.25. But Elliott's rule of alternation (see text, p. 50) reminds us that when wave 2 is a *simple* construction, wave 4 is likely to be *complex*. Therefore, it may be that the $547.25 price is only wave "a" of 4, the current decline wave "b", and a "c" wave rally back up to $550 is needed to complete a *large, complex, flat wave 4*. The March low was easy to recognize and led to a profitable "long" trade; if gold rallies to $550, it will again be an easily recognizable point to go short. The current position of the wave is ambiguous enough that I prefer *new* traders to be *out* of the gold market entirely, awaiting either a super shorting opportunity at $550 or a super buying opportunity at $388.

Long term shorts from $720 should *stay short*. I absolutely do *not* recommend going long now. There is no change in my outlook for silver (see April issue), which is tracking gold perfectly.

JUNE 9, 1981

Gold is in wave 5, finishing off wave C of its A-B-C bear market from the January 1980 peak; target is still $388.

Gold

Remember in January 1980 when gold was at $850 and ounce and a typical forecast was for about $2000 an ounce by the end of the year? Now, with gold having lost almost 50% of its value from the peak, I suggest you get prepared for the exact same phenomenon to occur again, this time on the downside. *One of the best tipoffs to the end of a trend long in motion is the sudden general raising or lowering of sights to a great percentage beyond current price.* This sudden "snap" in mass psychology has accompanied almost every important trend change in history.

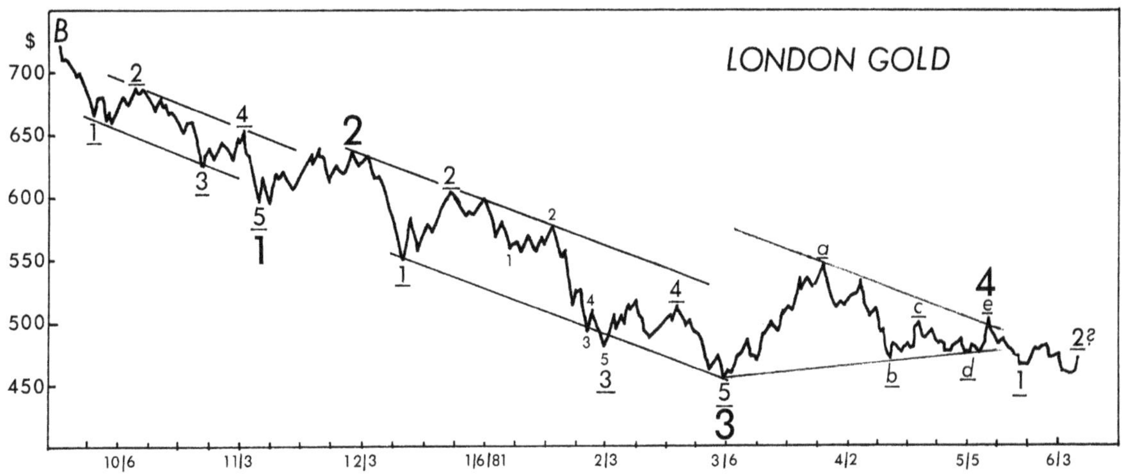

In my opinion, the catalyst for the dramatic change in psychology necessary to indicate the end of the bear market in gold will be a break of the "magic" but totally irrelevant $450 level. From my experience, a knowledge of the Wave Principle can be invaluable in helping determine which *apparent* support levels are of *actual* importance. As far as I'm concerned, action at the $450 level now has no meaning whatsoever in terms of making one "more bearish" or "more bullish" on the outlook for gold. The Elliott target of $388, which I have held for well over a year, is still the level of greatest importance — more important, even, than the $710 level on the B-wave rally which peaked in September of last year.

In the April 12 issue, I voiced this worry:

> My only concern is that the "380" level recently began popping up in an amazing number of gold prognosticators' writings. Why pick 380? As far as I know, only an Elliotter would be focusing on such an otherwise unlikely level. I hope the camp expecting that level is not becoming overcrowded. *On the other hand, if gold does get there, I expect that many of these "targets" will be lowered to $250 just as the buy point is at hand."*

Now comes an article in Friday's *WSJ*, with comments as follows: "Gold Again Nears Critical $450 Support Level With Analyst Calling Any Break 'Devastating'. A drop of the gold price below $450, he says, would open the way, technically, for the decline to the $250-290 area." Oho! *We're finally setting up for fifth wave psychology.*

The point to be made is not whether someone's analysis is good or bad, but whether the consensus opinion becomes influenced by publicity for a particular outcome in the market. According to the writer of the column, "The $450 level looms so large because it has stopped several major declines since gold prices peaked near $850 an ounce in early 1978" (sic; he meant 1980). True, but it only stopped those declines that it was meant to stop. The A wave down in gold had an Elliott-based target of $477, which was met within $3. The recent minor wave lows all had normal targets in the $460-$475 range and were all part of a textbook pattern. From here on out, however, $450 has no meaning. And if a majority of investors becomes convinced that it *does* have meaning, we'll have the right conditions for disinterest in gold at $388.

In summary, it appears that a break of $450 could be the catalyst for the psychology we need to create a bottom. After all, how does a "long" justify selling a position that is already down 50%? He tries to make it look as if he is not embarrassingly late in his decision by "forecasting" prices *much* lower. This phenomenon explains how investors rationalize selling right into the bottom.

The Outlook

Last month's comments still hold: *Stay short or stay out*. I still expect $388 on London gold by August of this year. The "alternate possibility" of a near-term rally back to $550 before the completion of the bear market has increasingly less likelihood, and the preferred wave count appears right on target. At this point, wave 2 of 5 probably ended on yesterday's news of Israel's bombing in Iraq, and I expect wave 3 to break the supposed "support level" at $450 rather dramatically quite soon, probably leaving a downside gap in the price structure.

As for the next near term stopping level, wave 3 of 5 could bottom around $405-$420, causing the round number $400 to appear to have significance as well, but when $400 is broken, I expect the few remaining bulls finally to give up on gold. I would begin mental preparation now for some aggressive buying this summer.

A Change in Count

An alternate count with the same implications as the one I have been presenting (with wave 4 ending at $547 on March 27 – see April letter) has been suggested to me by several subscribers. The most thorough argument for this count came from a conscientious student, Robert H. McCormac of Chicago. His argument that wave 4 formed a *contracting triangle* (see text, p. 43) rather than a zigzag is entirely sound and most likely correct. Despite the fact that the triangle is quite "damped down," with an uncharacteristically short c wave, various other considerations make a triangle the most likely count:

–It is a wave 4, a typical place for a triangle to form.

–It is composed of five waves of three legs each.

–Wave e, in typical fashion, breaks through the triangle outline.

–A triangle is a complex pattern, satisfying the Rule of Alternation (see text, p. 50) with regard to the simple structure of wave 2.

–The thrust (see text, p.44) following a triangle should travel "approximately the distance of the widest part of the triangle." Now since the widest part of a triangle in this case is about $120 (the vertical distance between the end of wave 3 and the upper triangle boundary), and $120 from the wave e peak at $501 is *$381*, we have one confirmation on a micro scale of the target first computed on a macro scale.

–Since the triangle ended on May 11 at $501, the expected distance for wave 5 will satisfy the guideline that when wave three is extended, waves one and five tend toward equality in time and magnitude (see text, p.57). If wave 5 bottoms at $388, it will be 114 points long. Wave 1 fell from $720 to $595, or 125 points, quite close indeed. However, we should remember that the $720 peak was $10 above the *calculated* peak of $710. Wave 1, then, was $10 longer than it "should" have been, suggesting that a 115-point length for wave 5 (to $386) would be quite a satisfactory target. In terms of time length, wave 1 took 32.5 trading days. 32.5 trading days from May 11 would project June 25 as s reasonable time for our ultimate target of $388. Based on the long term trendchannel, this time period seems about two months too early, but if gold hits the target near that date, I suggest you cover shorts and go long immediately.

–If wave 4 was a triangle that ended on May 11, that upward correction coincided exactly with the end of a downward correction in the stock market, which ended with a closing low of 963.44 on May 11. *Orthodox* turning points in the various markets of stocks, gold and interest rates tend to coincide.

–Triangles portend thrusts, or swift, sharp movements that serve to complete an entire sequence of waves. Certainly the importance placed upon $450 could cause some dramatic selling when that level is broken.

–By labeling wave 4 as a triangle, we can now see that its orthodox peak was indeed *perfectly within the span of the previous fourth wave of lesser degree*, wave 4 of 3 (see text, p. 55), meeting my original expectations for the extent of the countertrend rally!

For me, that's plenty of evidence that wave 4 is best labeled a triangle. For those Elliott students who still want to keep track of the previous count labeling wave 4 at $547, you can label wave 1 of 5 on April 29, at a slight fifth subwave failure, and wave 2 of 5 on May 11. We won't know for certain which count is correct until we count either five waves or three waves down from the $501 peak on May 11. Whichever is the correct count, our strategy is not affected.

By the way, the only other newsletter I know that uses the Fibonacci ratio to obtain price targets is Dennis Sanders' and Thomas Gaughan's *Commodity International Advisor* (141 W. Jackson Blvd., Suite 1765, Chicago, IL 60604). They have been correctly bearish on gold all the way down and currently project a low for August 1981 at $400, with an outside chance of $325. While they do not take the time to explain their work, if you like concise advice and unhedged suggestions for strategy, theirs is one of the best.

A FALLACY

About three times a week I hear the comment, "Rising interest rates are bearish for gold." This assumption is based upon the argument that high interest rates make it "expensive" to hold gold, thus putting downside pressure on the price. This "reasoning" kept legions of investors out of the most lucrative rise in gold in history. The truth is that under Nixon, when interest rates soared, gold went up more than *fivefold.* Under Ford, when interest rates fell from 12% to 4%, gold's price was *cut in half.* Under Carter, when interest rates quadrupled, gold went up *eightfold.* Tell me, were rising interest rates bearish for gold? NO? Then what is the real answer to the relationship?

The way I see it, it is the perception of the *reason* for high interest rates that determines their bullishness or bearishness in relation to the price of gold. If interest rates are rising in response to inflationary pressures while still trailing the rate of inflation, gold will go up. If, however, interest rates are rising *ahead* of the inflation rate in an attempt to rein in inflation, gold will go down. And the reason it will go down is that the gold market will be anticipating a *lower* rate of inflation in the future, and consequently, lower interest rates as well. While we have yet to experience this occurrence, if interest rates were deliberately pushed down below market rates *artificially* by government fiat in order to provide "cheap money," then gold would most certainly go up. Again, I think the reason behind the change in interest rates is the most important factor, not the change itself.

Silver

Month after month for over a year, the Elliott wave message on silver has been the same:

1) Expect a final low below $11 an ounce.

2) Don't buy silver until gold has completed its bear market.

3) Silver will underperform gold.

4) The possibility exists for silver's low to be as low as $4-$6 per ounce.

None of these comments was accepted as rational when they were first made, but the incredible foresight that Elliott analysis can provide is being demonstrated once again, even to my own amazement. Last week, prices for silver dropped briefly to *three digits* for the first time in this ongoing bear market. I don't see the bottom yet.

JUNE 29, 1981

Gold is in wave 3 of 5, declining to the culmination of its bear market from $850; target still $388.

Gold

The June 1981 issue of Hard Money Digest, a publication which tracks the various market letters' opinions on gold and silver trends, crossed my desk just a day or so after my June issue was mailed. Their comments certainly reduced the "worry level" on my outlook for gold. Here's what they said:

> It's been a long time since we've seen *so few newsletters* recommend selling gold short term and so many recommend buying it. We're almost up to the strongest consensus we've ever had on gold — 50 per cent in favor of buying it.

Clearly the $450-480 level is considered a buy point by most chart followers. As you know, *The Elliott Wave Theorist* was not one of the consensus last month, voicing radical comments such as these:

> *Stay short or stay out.* I still expect $388 on London gold by August of this year. Wave 2 of 5 probably ended on yesterday's news of Israel's bombing in Iraq, and I expect wave 3 to break the supposed "Support level" at $450 rather dramatically quite soon, probably leaving a downside gap in the price structure.

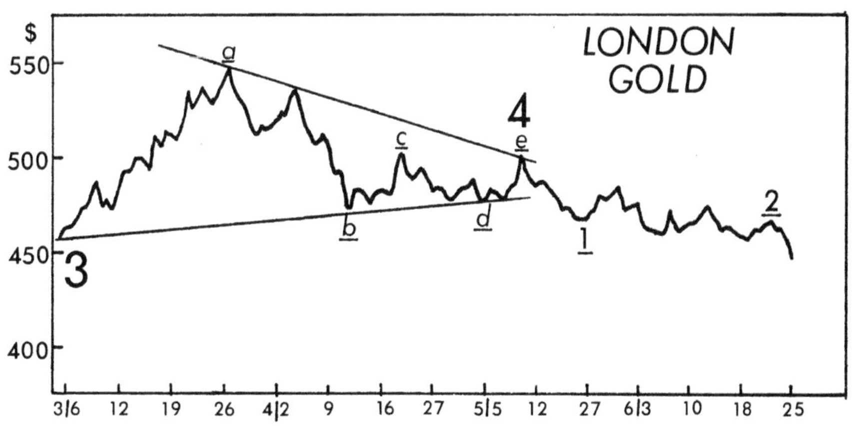

The $473.50 closing price the day before that comment was the highest level gold has seen since. The wave count appears to have been correct, particularly since the latest decline took on some of the characteristics of acceleration typical of third wave action (see text, p. 67). Wave 2 did form a slightly longer holding pattern than I expected and evolved into a "triple three" correction. If you look closely at the gold chart, you'll see that each mini-wave in the sideways period labeled wave 2 subdivided into an a-b-c, typical of corrective wave patterns. The breakdown from that pattern appears to be a typical impulse wave.

I still expect wave 3 to carry down to the $405-420 area before a wave 4 countertrend rally takes place. Since I've counted wave 2 as a complex pattern, wave 4 should be a simple zigzag by rule of alternation, producing a sharp upside bounce lasting about a week. That should set the stage for the final move down, wave 5 of 5 of C, which I hope will terminate close to my ultimate target at $388. Traders should stay short or stay out; "investor" shorts are still in effect from $710. But starting now, you should begin preparing yourself for stepping in and *buying* gold when every one else begins talking about $250. If London gold hits $390 this month, cover all shorts and go long, with a mental stop at $375.

AUGUST 2, 1981

Gold's 19-month bear market is ending, and the $388 target computed a year and a half ago should be met *this week. Cover all shorts in gold bullion and gold futures and begin aggressive accumulation of both gold and gold stocks.*

Gold

Last month served its purpose of answering the comment (reprinted in Australian Investor's Digest, GPO Box 1811, Adelaide 5001) from one writer who said, "PROOF that $457 is the low; yes, it's true. Believe me, $457 will be the bottom on gold. *Publishers who are looking for a $400 or $350 gold should be ignored.*" What's the excuse for that kind of dogmatic comment? I hope at least some of you didn't ignore us dumb publishers who suggested postponing your buying.

In June I commented that "I expect wave 3 to break the supposed 'support level' at $450 rather dramatically quite soon, leaving a downside gap in the price structure." We got the break, a typical third wave "kill," and we got the gap. I expected mini-wave 3 to carry to the $405-420 level before bouncing in wave 4; however, the actual low was $397, out of the range by $8. Elliott analysis suggested that wave 4 would be a "simple

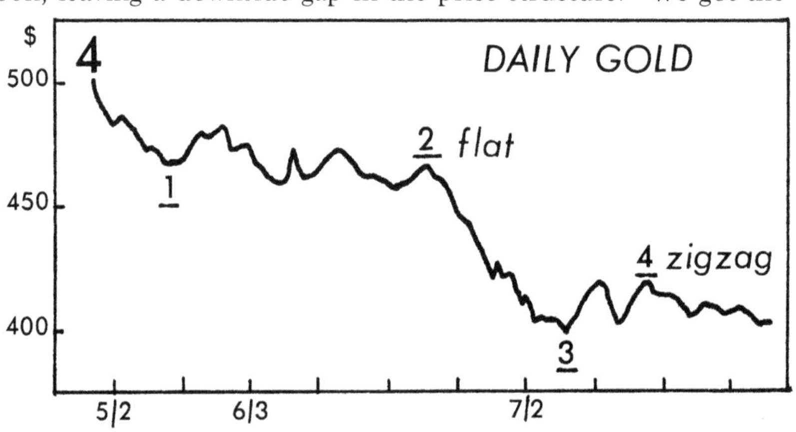

zigzag by Rule of Alternation, producing a sharp upside bounce lasting about a week." That expectation worked out quite well, as you can see on the accompanying chart.

The target of $388 computed a year and a half ago is fast approaching, and the time zone of "mid-1981," first estimated a year ago and refined last May to "August 1981," is now upon us. The a-b-c zigzag in gold has traced out a textbook pattern from January 1980 to the present. As I read it, the fifth of the fifth of wave C is in progress, and the bear market low in gold should be met within days. The target area of $388 London or slightly below should be hit *this week* as the $400 level is cracked in mini-wave 3 of 5, probably leaving a small gap at $400 on the nearby futures chart on Monday.

Whether you have been short since September at $710 in an investment position or more recently from $500+ in a trading position, *cover all shorts in gold bullion and gold futures and buy aggressively right now.* Older subscribers will remember that short sales in gold stocks were covered and puts sold in *February* (see Feb. 6 letter) at the bottom of wave 3 of 3 in anticipation of the relative strength, which then developed in the stocks vs. the metal. The bullish "double bottom" in my gold stock average against a bullion price fully $70 lower than it was in February make South African gold stocks, which now yield 20% on average, one of the most attractive investments I can find. I'd buy them now.

Silver

Silver is also entering its final leg down. We've avoided silver throughout one of the most devastating bear markets in history for any commodity. It's now time to *buy* silver while everyone else is throwing it overboard. Those who loved it at $50 an ounce now hate it at $8. Does that make sense to you?

I would ease into silver a bit more defensively because silver has been known to bottom shortly *after* gold. Also, the *percentage* risk on this final leg in silver is greater, with prices under $6.50 still possible. Spread your buying through this week during selling waves and your average price should be excellent.

AUGUST 5, 1981 — SPECIAL REPORT

Major Buying Opportunity in Gold

Yesterday the Fibonacci ratio target of $388 per ounce computed a year and a half ago was satisfied quite closely, and the time zone of "mid-1981," refined last May to "August 1981," is upon us. The "fifth of the fifth" of wave C broke down perfectly with what appeared to have been an exhaustion gap on Monday August 3. Keep in mind that August isn't over yet and the fifth wave could subdivide further to somewhat lower lows, but as I read it, yesterday's low reading marked the precise bottom, and I am concluding that a major bear market in gold has ended. If not, it's close.

August 4's low on the London p.m. fixing was $391.25, just $3.25 from the ideal target level of $388. While that reading is certainly close enough for comfort, nothing was quite as amazing as yesterday's exact intraday low tick for the nearest futures contract (the "spot month") on the COMEX. Take a look at this table, from this morning's Wall Street Journal. No, I didn't have to bribe anyone to get that price put in! Now, if gold will just turn up from here, the Elliott picture could look extremely good.

In this *the* bear market bottom for gold? No one can know beyond doubt. But it is indeed a major buying opportunity for anyone following the principles of R.N. Elliott. A major buying opportunity is one that carries low risk, and the $388 level certainly qualifies, for a long list of reasons. If the price of gold turns up from here, we can move "stops" up to $388, limiting our risk to zero. If we're stopped out, so be it. But a major opportunity has presented itself, and since we've been well prepared by Elliott's rules and guidelines, I suggest taking advantage of it.

Despite the common usage of arithmetic charts for commodities, it is absolutely essential that wave patterns of this large a degree be viewed on *semilog* scale so that the relative proportions of

Futures Prices

Tuesday, August 4, 1981

Open Interest Reflects Previous Trading Day

	Open	High	Low	Settle	Change	Lifetime High	Lifetime Low	Open Interest
GOLD (CMX) – 100 troy oz.; $ per troy oz.								
Aug	390.50	392.00	388.00	391.20	+ 2.70	963.10	388.00	6,844
Sept	392.00	396.00	392.00	394.70	+ 2.30	432.50	392.00	230
Oct	398.50	399.50	395.50	398.80	+ 2.10	1026.4	395.50	20,249
Dec	408.00	409.30	405.00	408.50	+ 2.00	981.00	405.00	33,318
Fb82	417.50	419.50	415.00	418.70	+ 2.00	887.30	415.00	19,584
Apr	427.60	428.00	425.50	429.10	+ 2.00	898.00	425.50	18,930
June	437.00	440.00	437.00	439.60	+ 2.00	925.00	437.00	24,428
Aug	446.90	447.50	446.90	450.10	+ 2.00	887.00	446.90	25,570
Oct	....	....	....	460.80	+ 2.00	842.00	463.00	23,633
Dec	469.00	472.00	469.00	471.70	+ 2.00	666.50	469.00	18,630
Fb83	482.00	482.50	482.00	482.70	+ 2.00	642.00	480.50	18,923
Apr	492.50	492.50	492.50	493.70	+ 2.00	604.00	492.50	7,576

Est vol 24,000; vol Mon 44,578; open int 217,915, + 2,054

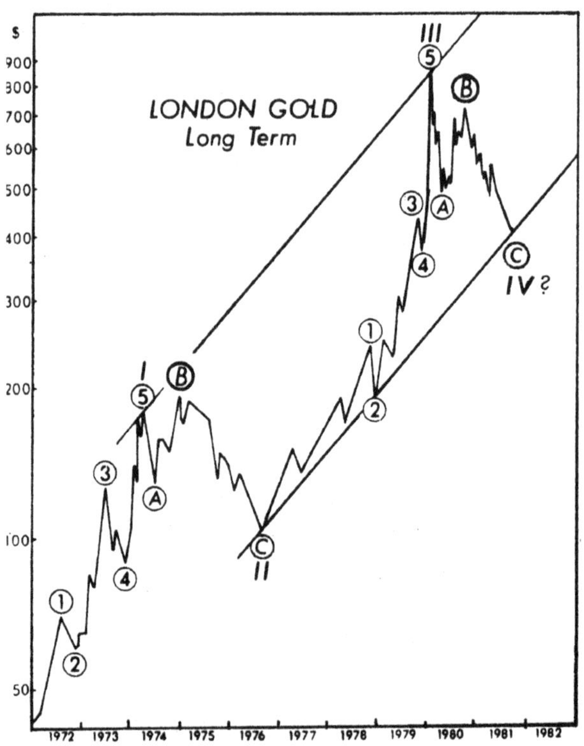

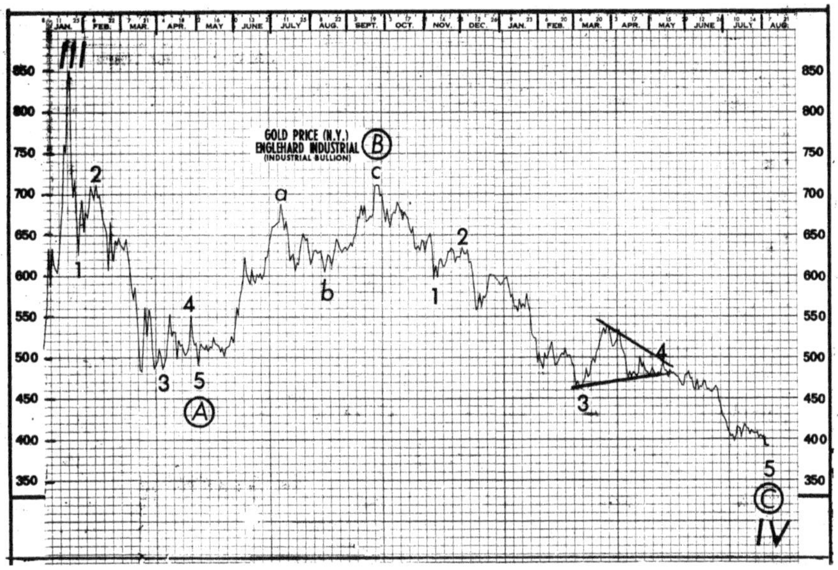

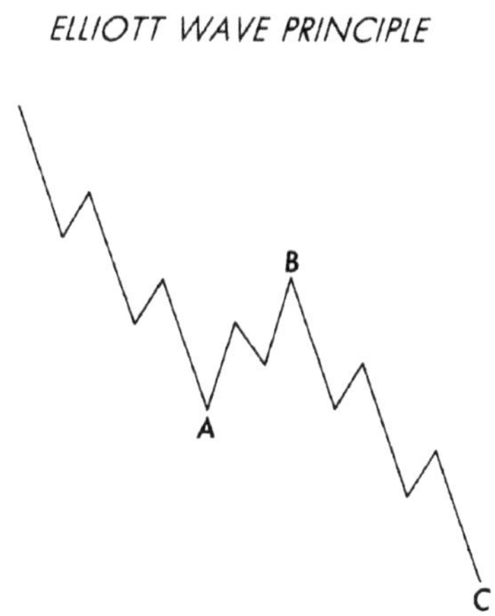

waves can be judged correctly and so that Elliott's channeling techniques can be successfully applied. As you can see from the 10-year chart of gold bullion, the price of gold has been following Elliott's principles to the letter from its $35 starting point back in 1971.

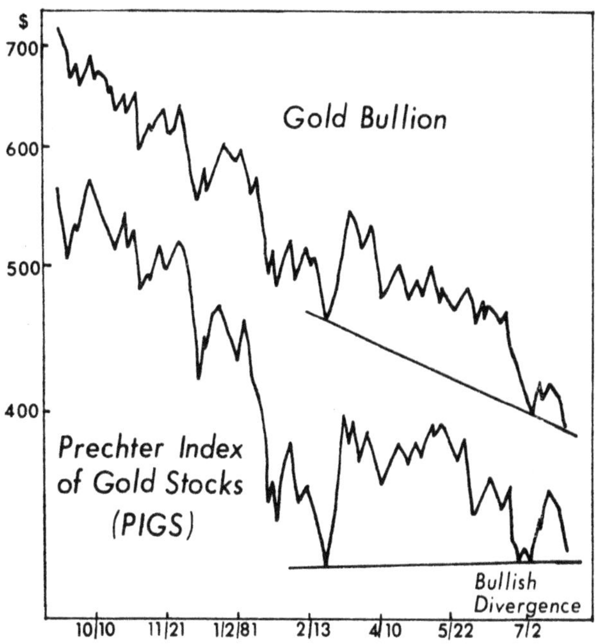

Shown also is the weekly chart of gold bullion from January 1980 to the present. Next to it is an illustration of a typical a-b-c zigzag bear market reprinted from Frost's and my book, *Elliott Wave Principle.* As you can see, the recent bear market has traced out a *textbook Elliott pattern.* The decline subdivides into a clear 5-3-5 wave structure, it retraces 61.8% of the previous advancing wave, and, as shown in the long term chart, it falls exactly to the level of the rising support trendline of the Elliott-style parallel trendchannel. If you look closely, you'll see that each wave in the direction of the next larger trend subdivides into a clear five waves as well.

Except for two profitable "long" trades on the way down, Elliott analysis has dictated being *out or short* for the entire bear market to date. At this juncture, whether you have been short since September at $710 in an investment position or more recently from $500+ in a trading position, I suggest that you cover all shorts in gold bullion and gold futures and buy aggressively right now. According to calculations that I have previously explained [See October 31, 1980 issue. — Ed.], if gold holds near the $388 level (and *only* if it holds in that area) the next bull market target for bullion is $5040 an ounce by 1986 (see Appendix).

Subscribers will remember that short sales in gold *stocks* were covered, and puts sold, in *February* at the bottom of wave 3 of 3, in anticipation of the relative strength that then developed in the stocks vs. the metal. The bullish "double bottom" in the Prechter Index of Gold Stocks (PIGS) against a bullion price fully $70 lower than it was in February makes *South African gold stocks*, which now yield 20% on average, *one of the most attractive investments I can find*. I'd buy them now. If the political situation warrants, it may be prudent to trade out of gold stocks in favor of bullion at some point in the next two or three years, but for now I think they will make excellent investments.

Here's a brief summary of why I am changing from a bear to a bull on gold:

1) The lower support line of the long term Elliott trendchannel has been met.

2) Wave IV from January 1980 is a perfect 5-3-5 zigzag decline, alternating with wave II, an irregular flat, thus satisfying Elliott's "Rule of Alternation."

3) The Fibonacci target at $388, a 61.8% retracement of wave III, has been met.

4) Gold is within the zone for the bottom of a normal bear market, the previous fourth wave of lesser degree (see EWP, p. 55), which in this case is the area of wave 4 of III, or $366 - $437.

5) The price damage in gold bullion in wave II occurred from January 1975 to August 1976. The price damage in wave IV is occurring from January 1980 to August 1981, a bear phase of the *same time length*.

6) Wave II's price damage was a drop from $197.50 to $103.50, falling just shy of a 61.8% Fibonacci ratio retracement of the rise from the $35 low. Wave IV's price damage is almost exactly a 61.8% retracement of the rise from $103.50 to $850, a bear phase of nearly the *same percentage retracement*.

7) The Prechter Index of Gold Stocks (PIGS) has failed to confirm the new low in gold bullion, giving a "buy signal"

8) The Wave Principle is a *law of nature*, and selective foreknowledge won't change things. No matter how much publicity my $388 target has gotten, such publicity will not affect the outcome of the wave structure one bit.

Negative Psychology

Many analysts will tell you that "everybody else" believes one thing, so they're going "contrary." Have you ever noticed that the other camp usually says the same thing? What is needed is at least some *documentation* of the majority opinion, supported by objective numerical measures, so that a basis for contrary opinion can be established.

Here's the current sentiment situation in gold:

1) A recent poll of commodity brokers revealed only *13% bulls* on the price of gold, to my knowledge the *lowest figure ever recorded.* Silver was down to a 15% reading.

2) The July 20 issue of The Wall Street Journal featured an article entitled "Commodity Experts Were Wrong on Inflation, Offer New Picks in Latest Investment Survey." According to the article, these experts picked four commodities for price appreciation last January, and "all four choices turned out to be wrong." What are their current comments on gold? *All bearish,* with one of the analysts comfortable enough to say "*I wouldn't buy gold with counterfeit money.*" Little does he realize that that's the only kind of money you can buy it with....

3) Remember when the commodity futures exchanges were *raising* the margins on precious metals in the frenzied climb to the peak? Typical "top" phenomenon. Well, on July 28, the Comex *decreased* the margins on gold and silver futures. That action is typical of market bottoms.

4) The Comex August gold futures contract has been trading quite consistently *below the spot price for bullion.* This is not a market that expects prices to go up.

5) The July 17 issue of The Wall Street Journal carried a front-page article on the commodity bust, starting the piece with exclamation, "Commodities are out." Other comments from the article and those interviewed in it were, "The reason for the slide is simple. For the first time in forty years, people believe that Washington is going to control inflation." "I just don't see a lot of incentive to be in commodities." "You'd have to be crazy to buy commodities" As I said in the May 11 letter:

> It should be a low of neglect, not of panic. The psychology near the final low in gold should be a feeling not of "I'll lose my shirt," but of "who needs the stuff?" As I see it, we're there.

6) There is wide publicity on the idea of remonetizing gold. Certainly that event would be negative for gold holders, at least for awhile, *but that's exactly the point.* The *bearish* news is making the headlines. There are *no* good reasons to buy gold. Therefore, the sellers must surely be finished with their selling.

7) Joe Bradley's Investor's Hotline tape for July had, among the four analysts interviewed, zero bulls on gold. That occurrence may be a "first."

8) Besides the fact that its history is too brief for high reliability, the 5½-year gold cycle, which projects a low late in 1982, has been very widely publicized (much more so than my $388 target). Many gold commentators have decided to "relax" until that time. As an interviewee in the July 6 issue of Forbes put it, "The investment climate

> for...gold shares will be grisly over the next 12 months." To me, it just seems too easy to happen. In fact, based on the evidence, gold shares should virtually explode in price quite soon.

In summary, the record shows that psychology toward gold has completely changed. At $850, gold bugs were deliriously shouting for $1000, $2000 and $3000 gold. Now they're focusing on the *downside* and accepting targets as low as $250. According to the Forbes article, "As a hot speculation, gold has probably had it." They weren't saying that at $850.

Cheap Money, Cheaper Ideas

In the June 9 issue of *The Elliott Wave Theorist*, I commented, "While we have yet to experience this occurrence, if interest rates were deliberately pushed down below market rates *artificially* by government fiat in order to provide 'cheap money,' then gold would most certainly go up." Well, you'd better brace yourself for increasing cries from the camp arguing for a forced lowering of interest rates The first salvo was fired in an article in The New York Times on June 21, 1981 by a Mr. John Winthrop Wright. He argues, and I quote, that:

> Although inflation can be caused by excessive monetary growth, there has been no such excessive growth in the United States during the last decade[!].... High interest rates, instead of curing inflation, have stimulated it[!].... Interest rates *can* be reduced safely and promptly. Adequate money and credit can be supplied, provided that there is *selective control* in the application of credit. [Aha!] A system of variable reserve requirements related to the mix of bank loan portfolios can produce a communion of profit-making interest between our banks and our national economic objectives.

His "solution" to high interest rates is twofold. First, *force* rates lower by fiat. Secondly, *force* banks to comply with loan policies dictated by federal government bureaucrats by easing reserve requirements when the "correct" loans are made. Do you like that idea? Do you think it will work? Do you believe in fascist fairy tales?

Until this kind of talk is tossed into the ashcan of discredited theory, *gold* will be a fine store of value and hedge against inflation. Mismanaged government money merely increases the demand for more stringent mismanagement. Money, of course, is a good that should be supplied in the free marketplace, not regulated by government. As is true with any other good the free market has to offer, "good" money would always drive out "bad.' Some day an enlightened citizenry will get rid of that "barbarous relic," government-monopolized paper money.

What If I'm Wrong?

I don't claim infallibility, and I don't offer dogmatic "proof" of anything; I do offer analysis. What you're getting is strictly my *opinion*, and I know it and you should know it.

Since each investor's hard-earned money is at stake, I always try to let my readers know what to do if my conclusions turn out to be incorrect. In this instance, suppose that, despite my current conclusions, there is an *alternative wave count* that is actually the correct one? Suppose gold *is* destined to go to $250 per ounce?

The beauty of choosing an entry point well in advance is that it prepares you psychologically for buying when everyone else is selling out at a loss. Both your pocketbook and your resolve are strengthened by the fact that you haven't been wiped out earlier by riding a market all the way down or in this case by acting on every so-called "support level" in the entire $460 slide in the price of gold.

In addition to the psychological advantage, a calculated target offers you a *low-risk entry point*. Since the low end of the allowable Elliott target area is $366, simply place a stop in the market equivalent to $360 basis London. If you're *not* stopped out, and gold moves up sharply from the target zone, you've caught the *exact bottom* after 19 months of decline. You can then move your stop up to the level of the exact bottom and limit your total risk to commissions only. On the other hand, if you *are* stopped out at $360, you can calmly take your $30 loss, sigh, and park your money in your favorite money market fund while yours truly dashes back to the drawing board. Since you've got a few hundred dollars' worth of profits on the short side behind you, a $30 loss shouldn't be too difficult to handle given the worst case outcome.

Important

I would conclude, on a significant break below $388, that the deflationists' argument is correct and that gold at $850 registered a bull market high that will stand for at least several decades That conclusion would not rule out excellent rallies in gold, but would indicate that the Supercycle rise from 1970 had ended in January 1980.

Silver

The bear market in silver has been right on track with gold's, as you can see from the accompanying long term chart. The only difference is that silver's decline is of *one greater degree* than that for gold. [This dichotomy will resolve; see chart, April 1982 issue. – Ed.] Silver had completed a full five waves up from 1967 at the January 1980 peak, thus projecting a devastating decline in that metal relative to gold despite early 1980's popular notion that silver would "outperform" gold on any decline.

As with gold, silver appears to be ending its final leg down. Elliott analysis has kept investors out of silver throughout one of the most devastating bear markets in history for any commodity. As I see it, now is the time to *buy* silver while everyone else is throwing it overboard. Those who loved it at $50 an ounce now hate it at $8.30. Does that make sense to you?

I would ease into silver a bit more defensively because silver has been known to bottom shortly after gold. Also, the *percentage* risk on this final leg in silver is greater, with prices under $6.50 still possible. I would invest fifty per cent of targeted funds immediately, then do additional buying during selling waves over the next few months, and your average price should be excellent.

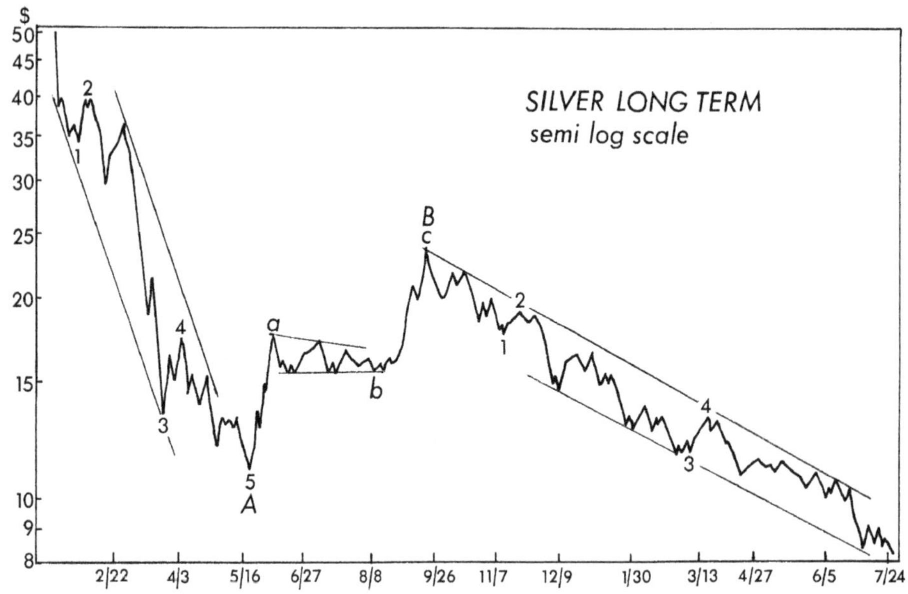

The main problem with silver here is that I have no way of calculating the likely extent of any rise. Since silver has completed an entire bull and bear market cycle, it will be beginning a new bull phase unrelated to its previous upswing. We can deal with this obstacle by closely watching the wave structure unfold in silver, trading out on fifth waves and repurchasing during a-b-c corrections. We can also trade in and out of silver on the signals from gold.

Only time will tell if my current conclusions for the precious metals markets are correct. However, no matter what the outcome, I'm certain that I've derived more pleasure tracking the intricacies of this bear market in gold than any analyst alive. Without a doubt, the Elliott Wave Principle is not only the most fascinating phenomenon ever discovered in the field of mass human behavior, it is by far the most enjoyable method of market analysis ever constructed.

Addendum: Excerpts from THE ELLIOTT WAVE THEORIST

FEBRUARY 9, 1980

For the time being, however, gold has registered a fairly classic blowoff, which I now believe has finished off the major leg III from the 1970 fixed-price low. While the bond market is only now catching up to the ravages of inflation, gold is well ahead of the inflation rate now, and a substantial correction lasting a year or more should be getting underway.

MARCH 9, 1980

The $388 level would correspond with a .618 retracement of wave III *and* with the area of the previous fourth wave of lesser degree, a normal Elliott support level. The $388 level is the most reasonable target for the eventual end to the large wave IV correction. An ideal Elliott scenario for gold over the next year or two would be an Ⓐ wave down to $477, forming the first retracement of the extended fifth wave within wave III. Then a strong rally would ensue forming wave Ⓑ, followed by a declining wave Ⓒ down to the final target of $388.

MAY 12, 1980

There is nothing to add to my expectations for gold. For this year at least, gold is a dead issue. The $850 peak began a "bear" phase, which should last at least a year. The first support level at $477, which I computed two weeks after the peak, has held all declines during the past six weeks. The ultimate target is still $388. ...while a .618 retracement of the decline to just over $700 should be the maximum potential of any intermediate rally.

SEPTEMBER 23, 1980 – INTERIM REPORT

Gold has now hit its minimum target of $710 per ounce London fixing. The failure at the $477 low did imply strength and thus an overrun of the $710 level, but from here on out, I'd rather let the other guy have the profits. The "guaranteed" part of the rise is behind us. Yesterday's action in gold stocks smacked of a near-term blowoff and the wave count on gold shows a completed "five" for wave C.

MAY 11, 1981

As for the near term picture, it is my tentative conclusion, as I said in the April letter, that wave 4 ended at the $547.25 a.m. London fix on March 27. This count indicates that wave 5 is already underway. It is highly likely that the final wave down of this bear market will not cause a panic type low that will be easily recognized by gold followers. I expect a slow, lethargic, even boring decline, as the bulls slowly abandon gold one at a time. This development would allow plenty of time for gold to get down to $388 by the time its uptrend line passes through that price level, my best estimate for which is the month of August.

SEPTEMBER 8, 1981

Gold bottomed right on target at $388 in Primary wave IV and has now entered Primary wave V in an ongoing Cycle wave bull market from 1971; first target area $501-547.

Gold

On August 4, the day of the low, gold completed an Elliott pattern that was like a laser print photograph in its striking clarity. As you undoubtedly know, the lowest London fixing was *$391.25* on August 4, just $3.25 from a target computed in March 1980. The exact low on the COMEX nearby futures contract was *$388.00*, and the lowest price for a cash gold bullion sale was *$388.00* by the Bank of Nova Scotia, both on the same date. Since gold has now risen comfortably above the $400 level, we can move our stops up to $390, limiting risk to zero.

It was a rare pleasure to have been negative on gold from the $710 level on September 23, 1980 and to have finally covered short sales at the exact bottom August 3 and 4. I had several calls from subscribers who had placed with their skeptical brokers good-til-canceled "cover short" orders at $390 several months ago, completing their transactions at that level within hours of the low.

Most encouraging is that the wave counts of very small degree now show repeated *five*-wave structures during advances and *a-b-c* formations for reactions. This tendency of pattern indicates a positive underlying force in the gold market. Furthermore, the advance from $388 has been all the more bullish since it has been inexplicable to most analysts. Remember all the way down when each rally in gold had a reason? — Russian sabre-rattling, OPEC meetings, etc. Now, particularly with the high interest-rate background, the question most often heard is "Why?" As long as you don't know the answer to that question, you can feel comfortable staying long. When the answer becomes obvious, we will look to sell to those who had waited until they'd figured out the reason.

As for now, a Minor wave rally is underway in gold. Within that structure, Minute waves i and ii have been completed and wave iii is underway. Note the following Elliott phenomena already displayed in the small bit of advance to date:

1) Wave i was a clear "five" and channeled perfectly by Elliott rules.

2) Wave 1 of i subdivided into five waves.

3) Wave 3 of i displayed typically strong characteristics (see text, p. 67).

4) Wave 5 of i formed a clear extension (see text, p. 25).

5) The extended wave 5 was precisely .618 times as long as the entire wave i.

6) The extension has been doubly retraced, and the first retracement stopped at $409.75, just .25 from the $409.50 price at the "beginning of the extension," the low of wave two of 5 of i, exactly as it should (see text, p. 29).

Gold's Glitter May Be Gone

These are tough times for gold bugs. In spite of continued political tension around the world — which traditionally leads to rising activity in bullion markets — gold prices have been dropping since last October. After falling below $400 an ounce last month for the first time since 1979, prices have bounced back slightly. However, the downward spiral seems likely to continue.

High interest rates seem to have defused the inflationary pyschology which allowed investors to bid gold up as high as $875 an ounce on the COMEX last year. And major purchasers from OPEC oil producers have lost interest in recent months. Gregory Kipnis, chief economist at ACLI International, a commodity service firm, says the reason is simple: shrinking trade surpluses leave fewer dollars to invest in gold.

Most analysts said they believe gold will be pressured for some time, and some analysts don't see substantial buying resuming until gold drops to $350 an ounce. For now, most speculators are staying out of the market. Robert Miller, a trader for coin dealers at Mantra Tordella and Brookes Inc., said business was light yesterday, perhaps in reaction to pessimistic gold price projections. "When you hear $350 from every newsletter, it scares people off," he said.

COIN WORLD, Wednesday, September 2, 1981

Mysterious jump in price puzzles bullion experts

Volatility returned to the precious metals markets during the week ended Aug. 19. In London, the price was fixed at $407.50 per troy ounce on Aug. 13, a sharp $10 drop from the previous afternoon. It held relatively steady in the afternoon, at $407.25; then advanced to $411.50 and $413 on Friday afternoon.

The primary action occurred during the new week, however, as the price climbed from a modest morning fix of $409.50 on Monday morning, Aug. 17, to $422.50 the following morning; and $433.50 on Wednesday, Aug. 19, settling back to $431.50 in the afternoon.

The experts were at a loss to explain the takeoff in the price of gold, and some experts, such as Vincent Martinelli, an investment advisor with the Deak Perera Group in New York, said they did not believe the bear trend had ended. "There weren't any fundamental reasons for this move," he said.

7) Wave ii formed a clear a-b-c zigzag.

8) Wave ii in most futures contracts retraced 61.8% of wave i.

At the point when wave v appears to be ending, traders may wish to sell and await an a-b-c correction to repurchase. Although no Fibonacci target calculations are possible at this early stage in the advance, it does appear that a normal wave "look" would cause wave v to peak no lower than $501 per ounce (the 4th wave triangle apex) and as high as $547 per ounce (the highest point in wave 4 down). Since four to six weeks would be a normal time span for the remainder of this Minor upwave, gold may be approaching its initial objective around the time of the next issue of *The Elliott Wave Theorist* in October.

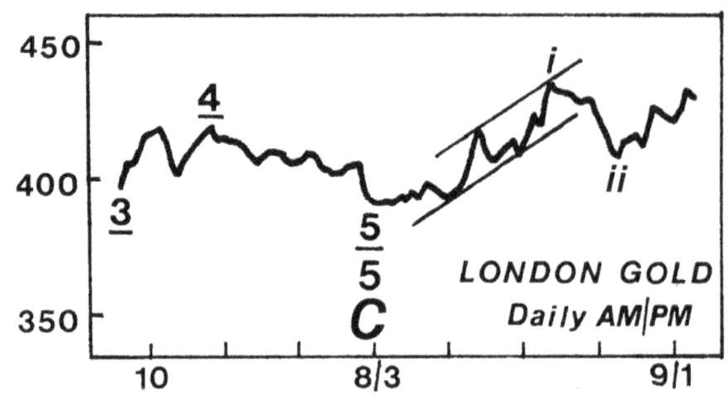

Gold Price in Swiss Francs

The Wave Principle works in wondrous ways. Consider the Rule of Alternation. Subscribers may remember that one of the many reasons a .618 retracement of wave III in gold was likely at this particular juncture was that wave II was an irregular flat, so by alternation IV should be a zigzag or a triangle, and zigzags often retrace 61.8% of a previous wave. You may remember that wave II in gold in terms of Swiss francs was a *zigzag* decline since it did *not* register a new high in December 1974 as did the price in dollars. Thus we should expect a *flat* for wave IV in terms of Swiss francs, and that's just what we have, even while the price in dollars traced out a zigzag! (See the accompanying chart, courtesy of Ian McAvity's *Deliberations*, P.O. Box 182, Adelaide St. Station, Toronto, Canada M5C 2J1.) In each instance, the Rule of Alternation is satisfied.

By the way, while I'm very happy to have kept subscribers *out* or *short* during the down waves of one of the most vicious bear markets in precious metals on record, we still *don't know yet* whether or not my conclusion that $388 was a once-in-a-lifetime buying opportunity is correct, and I'm not about to make any claims to fame yet. Before treating it as a certainty, I prefer to await further evidence which substantiates my calculation that $5040 is the next stop. And of course, if $388 is broken, my entire analysis will change.

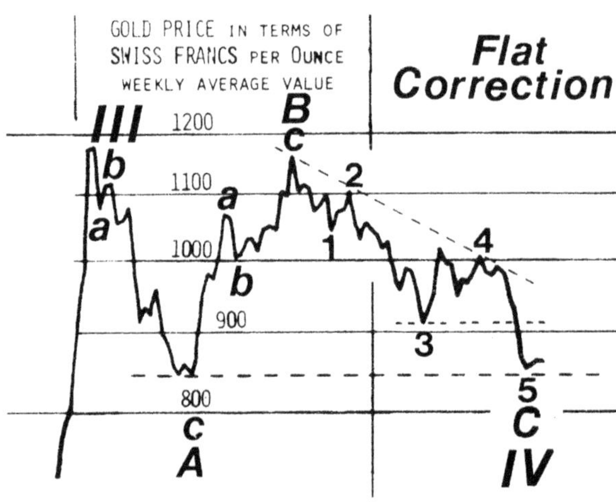

Silver

I've concluded that, as long as the $8.30 low holds, a new bull market in silver has begun. In the August 2 issue, I emphatically insisted, "It's now time to *buy* silver while everyone else is throwing it overboard." While I will still do my best to calculate targets on the way up, I cannot even attempt to estimate where the ultimate high in silver will be in this new bull market. Remember, commodities prices, as with individual stock prices, do not follow the Wave Principle in the purest sense of the theory. They can form what Frost and I call "contained waves," waves which *overlap* in the Primary and higher degrees (see text, p. 136). When a Primary bear market ends in a commodity, I look for a Primary bull market, but I don't try to forecast the next price peak because the new bull market is not necessarily related to the old. All we can count on at this time is that silver has entered a new Cycle degree advance which will consist of five Primary waves following the rules of the Wave Principle.

The most bullish occurrence for silver recently was the *break of the C-wave downtrend line on semilog scale* and the subsequent successful "test" (see chart). The message is clear: the 11-month downtrend in silver is over; the new trend is to the upside. Now that 50% of targeted funds were placed into the silver market at the $8.30 low, additional buying should be done during selling waves over the next few months. The first target for silver is the peak of the previous fourth wave of lesser degree, or the *$13.03* of March 27. From $8.30 to *$13.43* would be a 61.8% rise and may support the idea that the *$13* range will be the first stop for silver.

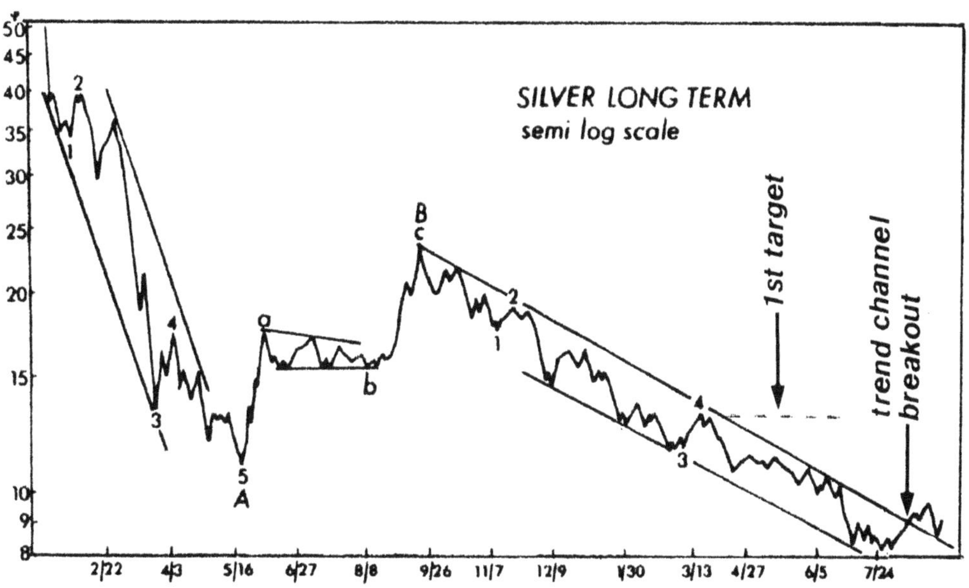

SEPTEMBER 25, 1981 – INTERIM REPORT

Gold has done nothing abnormal. The New York close brought bullion back to a .618 retracement of the last wave up and stopped on the uptrend line from the $388 low, a normal place for this minor pullback to stop. Hold long. If further selling pushes the London fix for gold under $430, it will be a warning sign. A break under $410, the low of wave ii, will be an indication that $388 is vulnerable. On any break of $388, reverse long positions bought at that level and go short once again, holding short as long as gold stays below that level. Silver, although still profitable from the buy point, has broken hard enough to show only an a-b-c rally from the August 4 low. Traders should sell out at breakeven on a fall to $8.30, while long term investors should keep the current 50% investment and wait a five-wave decline before putting in the second 50%. Re-read my comments about the possibilities of lower lows in silver in the August Special Report. Long term, the government sales of silver should prove to be the last super buy for that metal.

OCTOBER 5, 1981

Gold is in an area which is providing a long term buying opportunity.

Gold

According to the Wave Principle, the price of gold is at a very critical juncture on a long term basis.

As for psychology toward gold today, the bears continue to outnumber the bulls by a wide margin. Jim Blanchard, whose Gold Newsletter (4425 W. Napoleon, Metairie, LA 70001) tracks virtually all publications and opinions on gold, concludes as follows:

> Several investment advisors have mistakenly assumed, from seeing 5 or 6 bears turn bullish in the last several weeks, that most of the hard money newsletter writers have turned bullish when, in fact, they have not. Since 65.4% [as reported by Silver & Gold Report] of hard money newsletter writers and the more traditional stock market analysts are still bearish on gold, contrary opinion reinforces that $390 in early August was indeed the low.

Newspaper articles have continued to reflect the current environment of opinion. From The Wall Street Journal: "Business Turns Down for Gold Bugs." From Coin World: "Experts Ask: Why is Gold Price Rising?"

If August 4 marked the low, then gold is entering wave 3 of iii, the explosive center of the first Minor wave rally. The upside potential of this first Minor must be raised to around $600 now that the third wave has begun subdividing into such a massive extension. *Confirmation* of the low, however, has not been given since as yet the market has *not* shown explosive tendencies. While it certainly may do exactly that starting immediately, *until it does*, we must be aware of alternate interpretations.

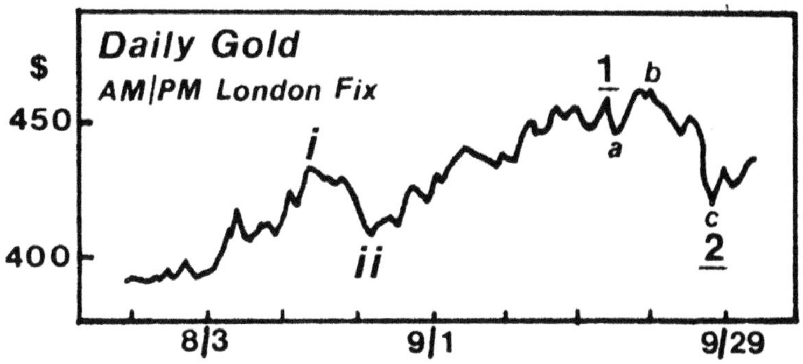

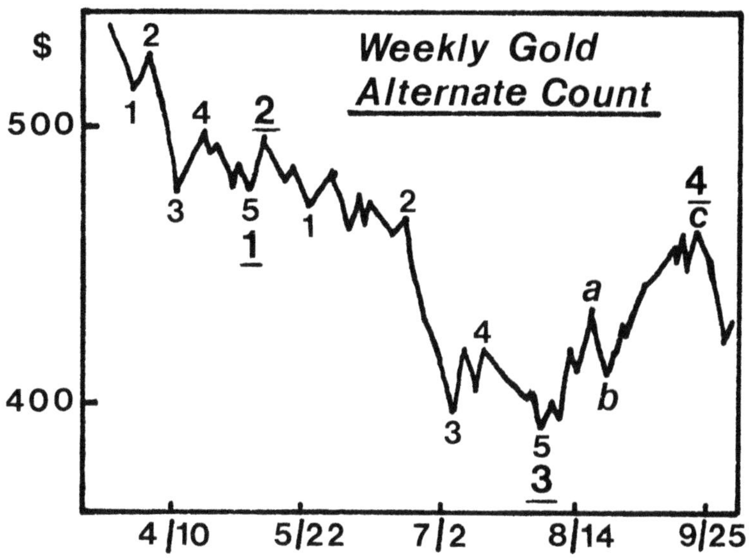

If I place the wave 4 peak at the nominal high on March 27 where I had labeled it prior to adopting the triangle interpretation, it is possible to show only three waves down into the August 4 low, followed by an a-b-c rally into the recent high at $463. If the true fifth wave down has just begun, gold should again break $400 and bottom after five Subminuette waves have completed, probably within two weeks. Even with this count, the picture is one of underlying health, since the fourth wave is extremely strong. Furthermore, the guideline of "wave equality" (see text, p.57), indicates that when a third wave is extended, the first and fifth tend toward equality in length. If the fifth in this case were *exactly* the same length as the first, it would bottom at $394, resulting in a bullish fifth wave failure (see text, P.32), giving the profile of a "double bottom." A move *above* the $463 high from here would confirm for me that the August 4 low at $388 was the final bottom.

One increasingly utilized argument for abandoning gold now is the fear that gold may be monetized soon by the authorities. Personally I doubt it, but what if it is? Would that place a tombstone on the price of gold? Did it work the last time? Absolutely not. In my opinion, *the waves come first*. They'll tell you when gold is likely to change direction or stop going up. It is my firm conclusion that if gold is remonetized too early in the wave count, the official value of gold will have to be repegged over and over again as inflationary pressures return. As an excellent article by Lindley Clark of the 9/1 WSJ pointed out, a return to the gold standard is not the *first* step to fiscal responsibility, it's the *last*. Citing the French experience in the 1920s he states, "The very first thing [Poincare did] was to get the government's budget back into balance. The order of events is important here. Once he had made sure the franc was as good as gold, he went through the formality of returning to convertibility." If gold convertibility is done correctly, gold will be dead as a profit vehicle long before it occurs. If it's done prematurely, it will be no guarantee of stability.

Hold long positions bought at $388 for an eventual target of $5044. If gold dips below $388, I'd prefer to exit long positions at no loss. If it then comes back up through that level, I'd be a willing holder. Sometimes this strategy can result in some frenetic trading. But if a real break does occur, it could save you a ton of money.

Gold Stocks

South African gold stocks rose an average of 20% from the 8/4 low and have since settled back. Further support for my conclusion that gold stocks have bottomed comes from subscriber A. P. Haft of New York City, who sent in this tabulation of the swings in a Gold Stock Index (reproduced in the Jorsey & Co. chart book), which started at 47 in 1962:

Years of Decline	Drop in Index	% Loss
1966-1967	132 → 89	32.6
1968-1969	231 → 89	62.0
1974-1976	622 → 196	68.5
1980-1981	1290 → 500	61.2

Note that the percentages of decline tend toward 61.8%, except for the first one, which is closer to the 38.2% Fibonacci ratio. The value of the index itself at each turning point is remarkably close to numbers in the Fibonacci sequence: 55, 89, 144, 233 and 610. The last three turning points are essentially *200, 1300* and *500*, representing 100x multiples of simple Fibonacci numbers. Whatever the numbers, though, the ratios certainly appear significant. Note also that the *rises* in the index approximate Fibonacci *ratios*, the first two near *262%*, the ratio between alternate Fibonacci numbers, and the second two neat *580%*, [close to] the ratio between third alternate Fibonacci numbers.

For that part of a portfolio reserved for gold-related assets, I recommend a split of 60% bullion-type coins and 40% gold stocks. At some point, when the political and social situation becomes less calm, I expect to be selling gold stocks in favor of gold coins only.

Alternate Counts?

My friend Donald Hoppe (Business and Investment Analysis, P.O. Box 513, Crystal Lake, IL 60014), an avid follower of the Wave Principle, recently raised again the valid question of whether gold, on an Elliott basis, should be considered to have peaked in its fifth Primary wave in January 1980 with the first wave having been limited by governmental interference in 1968-69.

As subscribers know, I've been dealing with this question for several years. I described the problem in the November 18, 1979 issue, which also included a long term chart illustrating the five-wave count in *silver* from 1967. My comments then were as follows:

> One all-important question, in Elliott terms, is whether the 1968-69 rise in gold stocks (see silver chart) was actually *wave 1* of the long term gold bull market. If the true first wave was masked by the artificial price controls on gold at $35 per ounce, then we are witnessing the peak of the final fifth wave advance in gold from a true low in 1968.

However, by the publication of the January 6, 1980 letter, that idea became highly suspect:

> You may recall that I suggested in November that the first wave up in gold, masked by price controls, may have occurred in the late 1960s, when silver bullion and precious metals stocks both registered a first wave up. [However,] the possibilities that this is not "the" final top but just "a" top have increased, since the upper trendline of what I had assumed was a valid long term channel was penetrated decisively.... This event supports the count which labels all of the price action in gold from the August 1976 low at $103.50 as the *third* major wave (III) up from the $35 price in 1970, [implying] another astronomical rise in gold several years hence. The target for a fifth Cycle wave would depend upon the turning points of the third and fourth waves.

Besides that occurrence, the most compelling argument at that time for beginning the count at the 1971 low was that the price was not lower in 1968 than it was in 1970. Second waves can retrace as much of first waves as they wish. There is most emphatically not a 50% limit or a 61.8% limit; a look at almost any chart in any market will show that second wave retracements are not limited to 61.8%. But for correct counting in first and second waves, there *is* a 100% limit. If one were to allow retracements of 100% or more within impulse waves (the waves of progress), the Wave Principle clearly wouldn't be worth two cents. Discipline would be gone, and any interpretation would be valid. Thus, in my opinion, a second wave with a 100% retracement is an uncomfortable interpretation.

Since that January 1980 issue, more evidence has accumulated supporting the wave IV interpretation. Since the January 1980 peak, I have continually pointed out the likelihood that silver would underperform gold, based strictly upon the *difference* between their long term wave counts from 1968. The fact that gold fell only 54.0% while silver fell a full 83.4% doesn't just serve to "prove I was right" but has supportive implications for the overall counts. In other words, the fact that gold has held up as expected relative to silver supports the case that its correction is of one lesser degree. In fact, if *silver* were only down 54% at this time, I would be a bit worried. But with a smash almost equal to the 1929-1932 collapse in stock prices, I'm quite satisfied that silver has fulfilled at least its minimum Supercycle downside potential. Another point: the percentage decline in gold is *64.7%* of the percentage decline in silver. Since that relationship is quite close to the Fibonacci ratio of *61.8%*, I think that my ongoing argument that silver was experiencing a decline of *one greater degree* than gold is exactly correct.

Despite what I consider overwhelming evidence, however, I cannot flatly discard the alternate interpretation at this time, nor can I dismiss Don Hoppe's and others' legitimate concerns. *The problem with that early period for gold is that government meddling may have masked its true wave structure.* The count from 1967 is not flat-out invalid, it is just unlikely *given current evidence.*

Theory aside, an entry point on gold at $388 was an inarguably good bet. With stops now moved up to $388, our risk is absolute zero. When the Wave Principle supplies you with a high-reliability, low-risk entry point, it always pays to take advantage of it. If it works out, you've caught the exact low. If not, your risk is minimal and by staying on top of the waves, you may still get out at a higher lever than you got in, even if a breakdown *is* the eventual outcome.

OCTOBER 30, 1981

Gold is at a very critical point as well but the pattern should resolve to the upside. Paul M. Montgomery of Legg Mason Wood Walker, Inc. (2600 Washington Ave., Newport News, VA 23607) agreed with me earlier in the year that gold would hit its low in early August. You might want to check out his work.

Gold

This point is a critical juncture in gold. Here's what we have. The long term trendline from 1971, which cut through the chart at $388 in August, has now climbed to about the $420 level. A 61.8% retracement of the rise from $391.25 to $463.50 targets $419 as a pullback low. A satisfactory a-b-c decline from the rally peak on September 21 can be counted into October 29 when London gold hit $422. And momentum oscillators are set to give a divergence buy signal on any dip below the September 28 low at $421.50. All these factors combine to suggest that gold's wave 2 "test" is ending now and that another buying opportunity is at hand. They also indicate that a *break* of this level would spell trouble. I expect that the gold question will be resolved in the month of November.

The accompanying chart shows five waves into the September 21 high, a count offered by subscriber Steve Barrett of Melbourne, Australia, and the most likely count under the bull market scenario. It is not a "pretty" count, but it is acceptable under the rules of the Wave Principle and allows an a-b-c to be counted from the high to present. If a third wave does begin soon, it should be explosive and carry into the 600s.

The bottom line is that while I still prefer bullish wave counts, bearish counts are still valid (see October letter). In other words, there has been no *confirmation* that the bottom at $388 was the beginning of a new bull market. Only a clear five-wave intermediate term advance will prove that conclusion. Until then, I prefer to use the overwhelming evidence at the $388 low that a bear market had ended to mold my strategy. Hold long or use this pullback to buy if you're not invested. Keep in mind that, as I've said before, a break of $410 would indicate that $388 is vulnerable, and if $388 is broken, I would no longer want to hold positions.

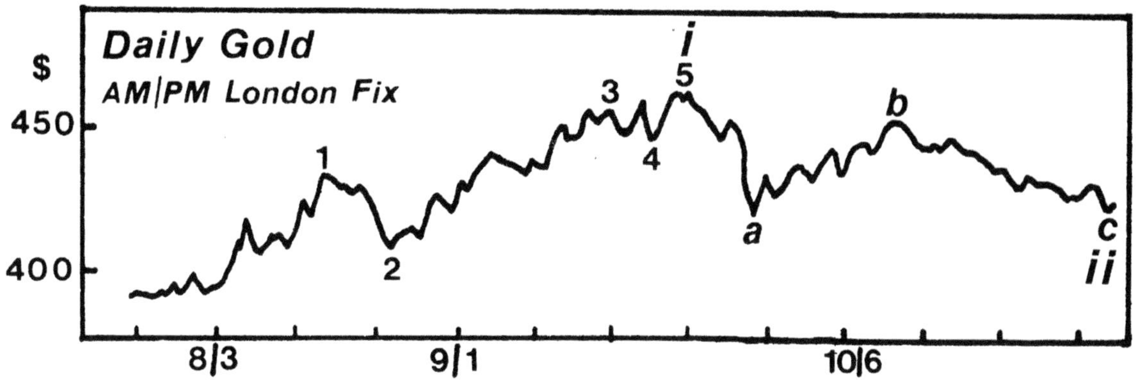

Gold Stocks

Last month I included a table of percentages of decline for the S&P Gold Stock group as submitted by a subscriber, but found an error in the figures shortly thereafter. The last decline in the index was from 1290 to 678 (not 500), or a loss of approximately 50% in value. 50% declines are common, and the correction did stop within the span of the previous fourth wave of one lesser degree.

My gold stock index (PIGS) is now only 8% above its bear market low, being dragged down by North American golds. South Africans currently average about 17% above their lows. While it has remained acceptably healthy to date, if the stock average *breaks below* its 1981 low, such action will undoubtedly signal a new and substantial decline. Since a 61.8% drop would bring the S&P Gold Stock index down to 491 and since the bottom of the previous fourth wave of one lesser degree is at 525, this range would be the next target zone.

Silver

I'm quite convinced that silver saw its bear market low on August 4. That low has held despite the world financial panic on September 25/28 and the government's silver sales. That's quite a performance. I still have an upside resistance area at $13, the previous fourth wave of one lesser degree, and as long as the $8.30 London spot closing low holds, that is where I want to take profits.

Commodities have a way of tracing out long base patterns after the end of bear markets, usually a series of a-b-c's back to back until the commodity makes up its mind to begin a new bull sequence. Until the market adjusts to the silver auctions, this type of "trading range" with a floor at $8 may be what's in store. A break of $8.30 would reinstate my previous long term target area of $4-$6.50, the area of previous bull market's fourth wave.

NOVEMBER 13, 1981 – INTERIM REPORT

Gold has broken $419, the short term support level, and caution is warranted for traders. I have said before that breaking $409 would put the $388 level in jeopardy and that break has not occurred. If gold can move back above $419, the short term picture would be back in bullish gear.

DECEMBER 7, 1981

Gold has begun wave iii upward, which should provide dramatic upside run.

Gold

The decline in gold from $463.50 on September 21 to $395.75 on November 17 traced out what can only be counted as an a-b-c decline. This count is bullish for the immediate future and supports the five-wave count for wave i up as presented in the November letter. What looked like the entire wave c on October 29 was only an extended first wave within wave c. As it turns out, the "double bottom" profile suggested in the October letter, with gold bottoming on a second bottom at $394, appears to have been a near-perfect description of what actually occurred.

However, since the second decline was an a-b-c, it could not have been a fifth wave down within the pervious bear market structure. Either it's a second wave within the new bull market structure, as I expect, or it's a "B" wave within a large A-B-C inverted flat correction. Even this "bear market" count offers a consolation since it still needs wave C upward to slightly above wave A at $463.50, a nice move if you're trading futures. If my overall thesis is correct, of course, gold will not stop there but will carry well into the 600s.

Strategy remains the same: Investors hold all long positions in gold for an eventual target of $5044. If $388 is broken, I would reverse to the short side and stay short as long as the price stays below $388.

For traders, as I said last month, "If gold can move back above $419, the short term picture would be back in bullish gear." Traders who stopped themselves out of gold just below

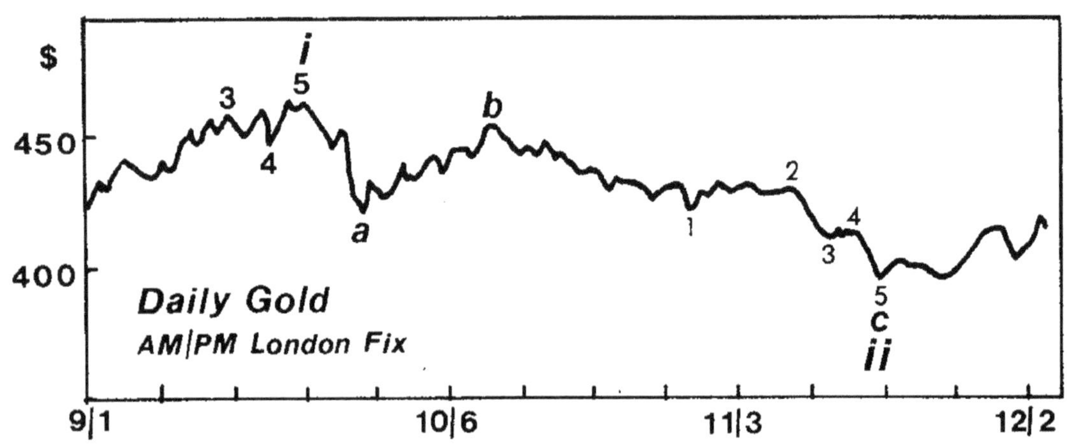

$419 should be long again now that gold has fixed at $423. For most futures traders, being out of the market for that last $25 plunge was worth the trouble of stopping out the position.

Technical and Psychological Background

Being a gold bull at the giant NCMR Conference in New Orleans in November was like walking through Lion Country Safari in a meat loaf suit. It is difficult to recall more than one or two people with whom I spoke who did not ask, "Well, now that gold's going to break $388, what's your next support level?" Well, nothing is for certain; maybe it will break. But it's curious to note that most people have already assumed that it will.

NCMR's president Jim Blanchard, a staunch gold bull, found himself hosting a bevy of bears. One media sensation, a sophisticated study which forecast a further drop to $320, reportedly sold 2000 copies to an audience of 3000. (And a good percentage of the attendees were spouses.) Not to say the study isn't valid: it's good technical work; in fact, just the kind I appreciate most. But it was embraced too enthusiastically to make a contrarian comfortable being bearish. By the end of the weekend, the intense gold pessimism had me panting to buy gold as the conference attendees rushed to the phones to sell out. Although it's too early to tell if a low has been seen, the London a.m. fixing on the Monday following the conference was $396, and it hasn't been lower since.

Keep in mind that the conference was a hard money crowd, and out of eighty speakers, a mere handful took the "daring stand that gold should be bought right now. What's going on? As I see it, "what's going on" is that gold-price pessimism. Which came out of the woodwork on the wave (5) of C down to $388, is now positively rampant as gold slips into what I believe is a "wave 2" low. And, as I have stated in many speaking presentations, "It is usually the case that pessimism is more pronounced at second wave lows than at actual bottoms." Read this description of second waves from page 66 of Frost's and my book, *Elliott Wave Principle*:

> Second waves often retrace so much of wave one that most of the profits gained up to that point are eroded away by the time it ends. This is especially true of call option [or futures] purchases, as premiums sink drastically in the stepped-up selling during second waves. Investors have finally gotten "one more rally to sell on," and they take advantage of it. Second waves often produce downside non-confirmations and Dow Theory "buy spots," when low volume and volatility indicate a dry-up of selling pressure.

Sound familiar? Now what about "downside non-confirmations"? How about the following:

1) Gold futures contracts made new lows in November, but gold bullion did not.

2) Gold stock averages made new lows in November, but gold bullion did not.

3) Silver made a new low in November, but gold bullion did not.

Are there any fundamental arguments for a higher gold price? As you know, I prefer to use interpretation of markets to predict fundamentals rather than vice versa. Since the wave counts are forecasting renewed inflation, I was intrigued to read Norman Fosback's comments in recent issues of his fine letter Market Logic (Institute for Econometric Research, 3471 N. Federal Way, Fort Lauderdale, FL 33306):

> True Money Supply: If you add money market mutual fund deposits to Ml-B, monetary growth has been anything but restrained. Measured by this true money supply criterion, liquidity growth is far outstripping the growth capacity of the economy, a situation that virtually assures more inflation ahead.

And on the government's budget:

> The bottom line, by our calculations, is that unless the economy turns around quickly, the 1982 deficit, including off-budget expenditures, will be closer to $125 billion. The degree of monetary restraint necessary to win the battle of inflation cannot possible be maintained in the face of the need to fund such a prolific deficit.

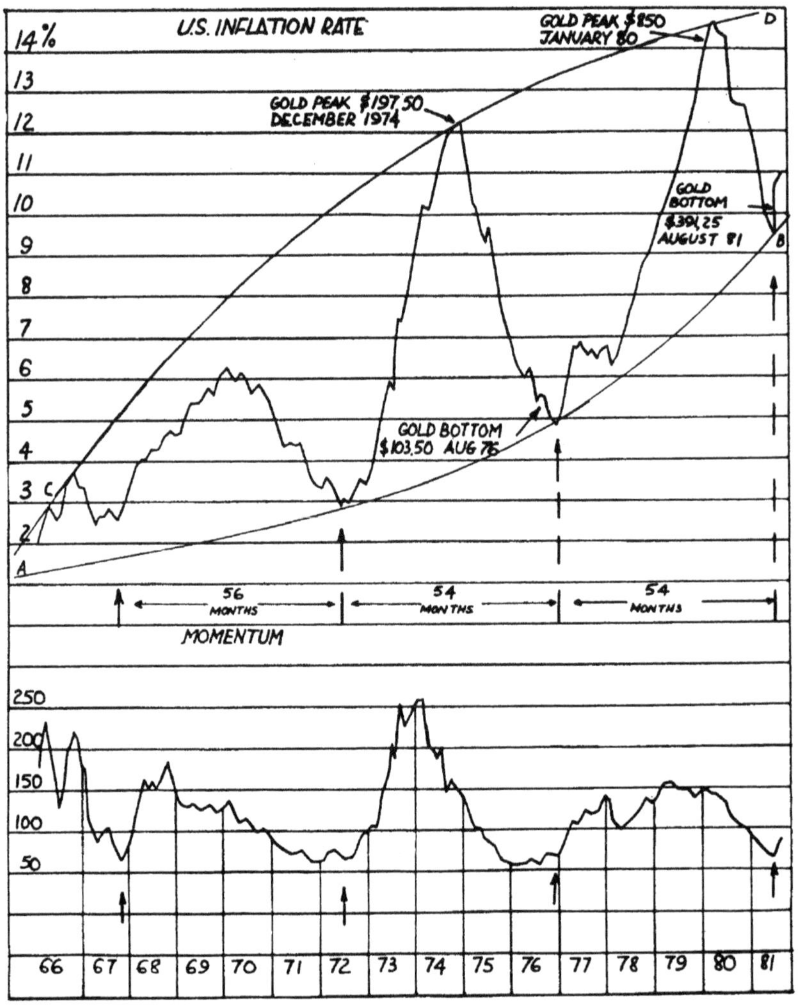

And in the face of this potential, the Professional Chart Service (61 South Lake Ave., Pasadena, CA 91101) tabulated only 18% bulls in a survey of opinions on gold, the lowest percentage since the week of the low in August.

One of the few speakers at NCMR who went against the crowd was Tony Henfrey, editor of Tony Henfrey's Gold Letter (P.O. Box 5577, Durban 4000, South Africa). Tony and I escaped with some friends to spend some time zipping around the French Quarter. I wouldn't trusted anyone's analysis after that foray was over, but luckily Tony and I had done our work before we got to New Orleans. Tony has correlated the gold price with the direction of the U.S. inflation rate, and the accompanying chart show his excellent analysis.

Note the length of the three inflation-rate cycles since 1967. At 56 months, 54 months and 54 months, it's clear that the average is quite close to a Fibonacci number of 55 months. Coincidence perhaps, but the combination of a Fibonacci time period, a regular periodicity and new evidence that inflation is again beginning to accelerate, thus verifying an inflation cycle low, makes a powerful case that the low in gold has been seen.

Silver

Yes, silver has made a new low, which means to me that my original long term target of $4-6.50 can no longer be ruled out. However, I have rarely gone wrong trading silver by following the waves in gold. Since the August low, it appears that silver has traced out an a-b-c "A-wave" advance followed by an a-b-c "B-wave" decline. If a large A-B-C inverted flat (see text, p.38) is developing, the next move in silver would be a C-wave advance to between $11 and $13. Keep in mind that in commodities, a series of a-b-c's can develop, following an orthodox bear market low, which can create long sideways patterns going nowhere until a new bull market takes hold.

THE ELLIOTT WAVE THEORIST, 1982

JANUARY 11, 1982

Gold

The short term wave count in gold is indicating that a break of the $388 level is now extremely likely. As much as I would *hope* that the level holds, the evidence for a break is beginning to mount. Remember, "hope" is a four-letter word in the world of investment, and only a cold reading of the technical factors can keep you on track for more time than you're off.

The art of Elliott wave analysis is in choosing the highest probability outcome from the evidence at hand. Unfortunately for us gold bugs, the short term wave structure now indicates a much higher probability that the bearish majority will be correct. The count I have as the "most likely" is one that involves a sequence of 1's and 2's of decreasing degree. This count indicates that *the "third of the third," or point of maximum downthrust, is due any day*. Of course, as old-time subscribers know, the break of an important Fibonacci support level is usually accomplished at exactly that point in the wave count (see text, p. 67).

From an Elliott wave perspective, I find it impossible to count the current downward structure from the peak at $463.50 as a standard ending fifth wave because the peak on December 4 at $426 overlaps the bottom on September 28 at $421.50. No true five-wave structure may contain a fourth wave which overlaps the first (see text, p.53). Overlapping may occur in fifth wave diagonal triangles (see text, p.30), but diagonal triangles contain five waves of *three legs each*, and the decline from $463.50 to $421.50, which would be the first down wave, appears to be clear "five." However, if I label that wave's bottom as a failure on September 30 at $426.50, I can push the count into this pattern.

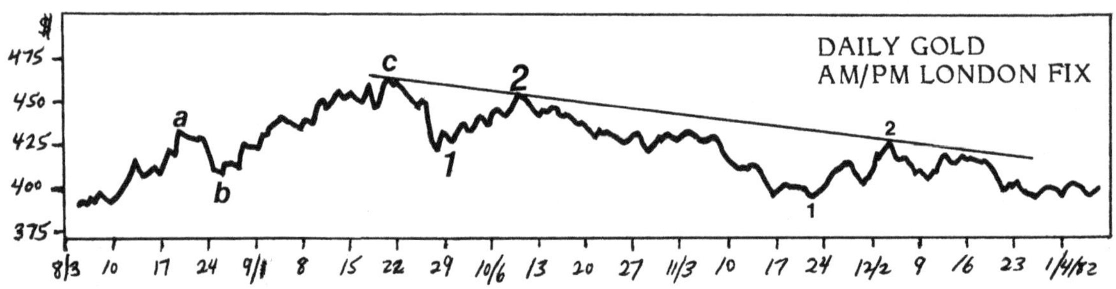

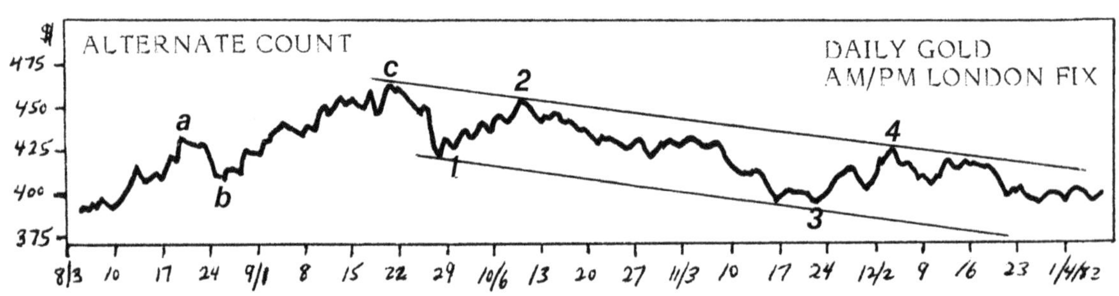

From experience, I know that jammed counts rarely work, but there are two reasons why I am entertaining this possibility. The first is psychology. Professional Chart Service's (61 S. Lake Ave., Pasadena, CA 91101) percentage for bulls on gold is still in low territory, at 30% having risen to only 43% after a November low at 18%. Hard Money Digest commented in the December issue, "The strongest consensus from the newsletters we review indicated to sell gold or to go short." A decline in gold here would satisfy the majority, and the majority is rarely satisfied. Secondly, this count would be on the right side of Jim Sibbett's Demand Index, which is currently showing a bullish divergence. (For a regular look at Jim's work, contact him at Let's Talk Silver and Gold, 61 S. Lake Ave., Pasadena, CA 91101 – $77/yr.)

As for strategy, Elliott analysis kept us on the "bear" side of the gold market from the September 1980 peak at $720 to the August 4 low at $391.25. If gold fixes *below* $380, I suggest reinstating your short position. *The net result will be as if we had never exited the short side at all.* We'll merely be picking up just about where we left off. Shorts should be held unless gold can fix above $410 basis London fix, the current level of the declining resistance trendline. That would be a trigger point to reinstate longs. Gold stocks also have acted extremely weak and are falling into a wave pattern that indicates lower lows ahead. Both traders and investors who would rather play conservatively may prefer to place money in T-bills and collect near-record yields for the time being. By the way, *never* sell that small part of your gold assets which is held as disaster insurance.

JANUARY 11, 1982 – SPECIAL REPORT

For the non-speculator, the one and only place to put your money to insure that it will hold *some* purchasing power relative to the total of goods and services available is into money itself: *physical gold.* I did not include gold in the above list of "investments" because gold is not an investment; it is money. Have you ever traveled abroad and taken a look at the local currency and wondered how the citizens of that country could take seriously what looks like "Monopoly money"? I've got news for you. You're using the same stuff. Monopoly money is the money over which some government has a monopoly. It is the currency of the realm only because the governments makes it illegal to use any other type. If a completely free market in money were available, I am quite certain that the market's choice would be gold, as it has been throughout the centuries wherever a free market for money has existed. This preference will undoubtedly remain until something better comes along. Sad to say, keeping money in the form of money does not add to productive capacity or prosperity. But in times of profligate government counterfeiting, there is no other choice but to hold something which will at least retain its value. However, since gold may drop in price in an initial deflationary stage, the best "parking place" for now is short-maturity T-bills. Later, when the financial crisis is at its nadir, a swift shift to gold will be essential.

JANUARY 28, 1982 – INTERIM REPORT

Since gold did not break my long-standing "breakdown confirmation" level at $366, and it has held that level with one of the lowest percentage of bulls in quite a while, the potential exists for this minor rebound in gold to turn into something better. The ideal posture toward gold for both traders and investors is still to be *short as long as it is below $388 and long when it is above.* This tactic may force several reversals of position (and then again it may not), but I know of no better approach at this critical level when the wave count is ambiguous. And when the direction of the big move is revealed, we'll be with it. A previous fourth wave of minor degree sits at $402, and will provide resistance if a bear market is still in progress. Getting above that level would be a bullish sign.

FEBRUARY 8, 1982

Gold's important support levels, calculated by Elliott methods, are $388, $366, $344, and $105-110.

Gold

As indicated in the last letter, I'm still leaving open the possibility that gold is making a major low here. There are several reasons why.

1) I can't easily forget how *low* $388 looked when gold was back in the 700s. It's come a long way and much lower than almost anyone expected. Why is the consensus now so convinced that it's way too high?

2) The break of $388 has yet to result in any desperate selling, which would be typical of a third wave breakdown. It still may, but it hasn't yet.

3) On January 26, The Wall Street Journal carried a detailed article that explained why South African Gold Shares were terrible investments because their dividends were in jeopardy. With ASA down from over $90 a share to $38 a share, might this be the news that the market has been discounting for the past year and a half?

4) Western Mining News, which has a vested interest in rising gold prices, had four articles on the front page of the January 22 issue. Here are the titles: "Arab Selling Likely to Depress Gold Prices," "Bullion Dealers Say Gold to Remain Bearish," "Hong Kong Dealers Say $350 Gold" and "Swiss Banks Forecast Depressed Gold in 1982." In these articles, every reason imaginable is given for further gold price weakness. Is this overkill? (By the way, that paper is a must for anyone interested in speculative gold mining stocks. Their address is North 3019 Argonne Rd., Spokane, WA 99206.)

5) With the recent low at $369.75, gold has yet to break my "confirmation" level at $366. I've mentioned that level before as a maximum (but, I felt, unlikely) retracement

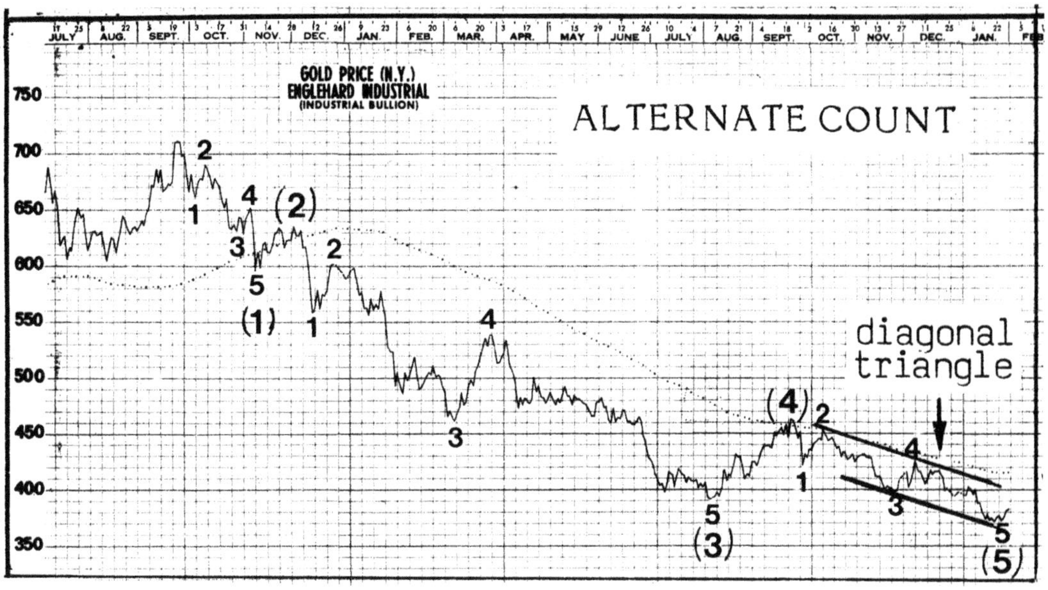

level for gold if the bull market which began in 1970 was still intact. The reason it's important is that it marks the low of the range of the previous fourth wave of lesser degree, wave ④ of III, which occurred in 1979.

6) It is possible, without breaking any Elliott rules, to recount the Ⓒ wave down from September 1980 as a five-wave sequence ending at the recent low. That count is shown on the accompanying chart. To get it, I changed the labeling on the extended third wave. The count does not provide for alternation between waves (2) and (4), however, and is therefore suspect. If $366 is broken, this alternative can be scrapped, and we'll know for sure that the wave sequence which began in 1967 completed its fifth wave in 1980.

7) The Trend & Cycles department of Dominion Securities in Toronto runs computerized trend smoothings on all commodities, currencies, and stock markets. Currently their gold model is poised to give its first simultaneous intermediate *and* long term "buy" signals since August 1976. I've highlighted their work in the past, and it has remained at the highest level of consistency and integrity. (Outside the Dominion Securities network, their analysis is available to institutional clients only. Highly recommended if you can afford it.)

8) Tony Henfrey, a sharp gold analyst and editor of Tony Henfrey's Gold Letter (P.O. Box 5577, Durban 4000, South Africa), recently showed a chart of 13-week momentum in the dollar price of gold and pointed out a clear divergence. Gold fell below $388, but the momentum indicator failed to exceed its level at the $388 low. This could be a traditional momentum-based "buy" signal.

9) The U.S. government is using tax funds to cover $71 million that Poland owes U.S. banks (including Citibank, Chase Manhattan, Morgan Guaranty, Chemical, Marine Midland, and Bank of America). An "extraordinary procedure" was devised so that Poland would not even have to declare the loans in default (admit bankruptcy). The "loans" total $1.6 billion and were made or, in this case, guaranteed by the Department of Agriculture to "finance" purchase of American grain. In actuality, the grain was purchased by U.S. taxpayers and given away by the USDA. The U.S. economy received nothing in return. This is what government calls "trade." This state of affairs could eventually result in the creation of a lot of inflationary funny money to cover the costs.

Supercycle Bear?

Whatever my personal preferences, I must take the break of $388 and the Elliott trend-channel support line from August 1976 as significant occurrences. Furthermore, strictly from the standpoint of wave form, it is more likely that my original count of a five-wave decline from $720 to $391.25 is correct (see August 1981 Special Report), and that wave C of this bear market is subdividing into a *much larger five-wave sequence,* indicating that the bear market is of one degree larger than I originally anticipated in 1980. If so, then gold finished wave (1) of C in August 1981 and has since finished wave (2), or at least wave a of (2), at $463.50 in September. Any *dramatic* selling in upcoming weeks, indicating typical behavior for a third wave (see text, p.67), would confirm this count and bring the support levels calculated below into effect.

Fibonacci Calculations

How low could wave C carry if a bear market of Supercycle dimension is indeed in force? Here are the Elliott support points that are available at this stage in the wave structure:

1) *$344.* This level marks the point at which wave C from $720 will exactly equal the length of wave A from $850 to $474. This relationship is typical in zigzags. Amazingly enough, as Stan Marzsalk (CMI, 1133 N. Camano Dr., Camano Is., WA 98292) pointed out to me recently, this level marks the exact point which is a 61.8% retracement of the entire gold bull market from $35 to $850. I consider this point very important for these two reasons.

2) *$242.* Here is where wave C would terminate at a point that lies below A by 61.8% of the length of A (see text, p.107). I consider this point the least important. No other Elliott evidence supports a low in this area, as far as I can see.

3) *$103.50-$111.63.* $103.50 is the level of the bottom of the previous fourth wave of lesser degree if a five-wave sequence occurred from 1967 to 1980. $111.63 is the point at which wave C from $720 will be 1.618 times as long as wave A from $850 to $474. These two points are generated by two of the most powerful calculations under Elliott

(see text, pp. 55 and 107), and the fact that they are very close together reinforces their validity. In sum, if $344 cannot hold the decline in gold, then a major deflation will probably send the price of the yellow metal to somewhere in the vicinity of $105-110 an ounce. I don't see any serious support in between those levels, although the area near $242 could act as a temporary stopping point. I find it interesting that the new consensus for a bottom in gold seems to be around the $300-320 area. If they're right, more power to 'em. But as of now, that's where the Wave Principle sees a serious vacuum. We'll take a graphic look at the bigger picture if $344 is taken out. Until then, I prefer to watch and wait. Tactics remain unchanged. Stay out or short as long as gold is under $388, and long as long as it is above that level. Until we've got a clear move underway, I don't know a better way to deal with this problem. If you do, use your own tactics, with my blessing.

Silver

I expected a series of a-b-c patterns between $8 and $13 to begin from the August low. So far, price action has occurred much closer to the $8 level than the $13 level. Despite last month's dip beneath $8, silver still shows strong evidence of support at that level. However, if gold breaks down, I expect silver will fulfill my previous long-standing target of $4-$6.50 per ounce and more likely the lower end. That area marks the zone of the previous fourth wave of lesser degree, the long consolidation pattern that occurred from 1974 to 1978.

MARCH 15, 1982

Gold's bear market remains in full force; near term support is *$285-305*; next important Fibonacci support *$242*. Silver's target is *$5.28*.

Gold

The trading tactics for gold have been very profitable recently. Despite all other technical and fundamental input, the implications based on the *Wave Principle* dictated being "out or short" again upon the break of the $388 level in January. Despite all the apparent evidence that "everybody" was bearish on gold, it was right to bet on the downside. When the Wave Principle gives a clear signal, it's still good to keep other data in mind, but it pays off to let the E.W.P. guide your actions. That's what I've done in gold, and it's worked.

Clearly the current deflation is more severe than originally anticipated in March 1980 when the forecast for a drop to $388 was made. At the time, however, even that expectation exceeded the worst fears of any other hard-money advocate in print, and it was invaluable information for 1980 and 1981. After several months of uncertainty, the gold picture has now cleared up again substantially.

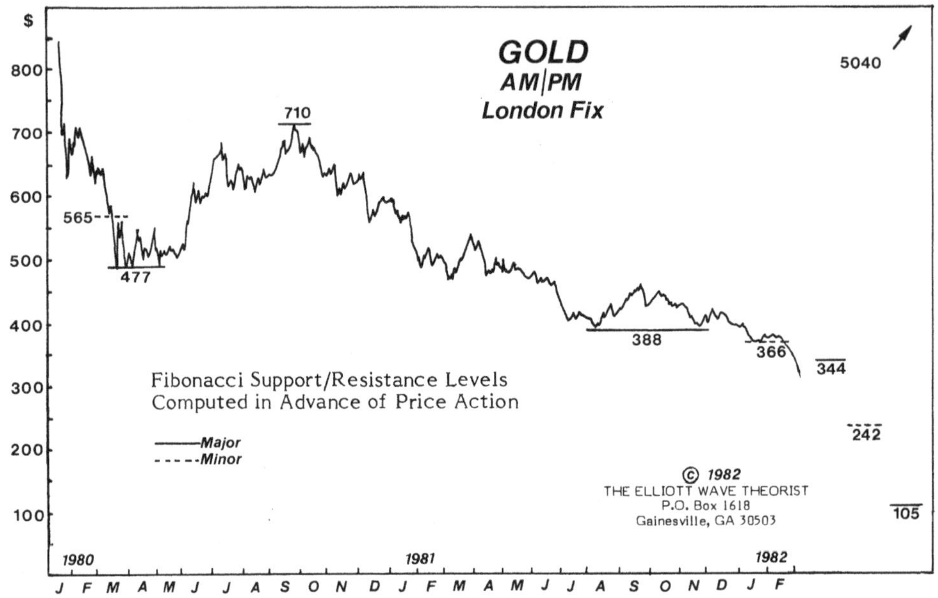

Gold has given several bearish signals since it first touched $388 in August 1981. The first was the a-b-c (three-wave) rally into September of last year. At the time, the other Elliott evidence was so bullish that I gave that countertrend pattern every benefit of the doubt, particularly since our purchases at $390 were safe from loss at that point. But in the end, it certainly revealed how important it was.

The second bearish signal was the break of $388. The January letter finally concluded that a break was likely, and suggested "reinstating short positions" if it occurred. $388 was indeed penetrated, and two important conclusions could then be drawn. One was that the calculated target of $5040 for the next advance in gold was "out the window." That calculation was made in October 1980 and was based upon a low being *met and held* at $388 in August 1981. As explained in the August 1981 Special Report on gold, "if gold holds near the $388 level (and *only* in it holds in that area) the next bull market target for bullion is $5040 an ounce by 1986." It didn't, so the lofty upside target, as well as expectations for renewed inflation, had to be scrapped, at least until the current bear is over.

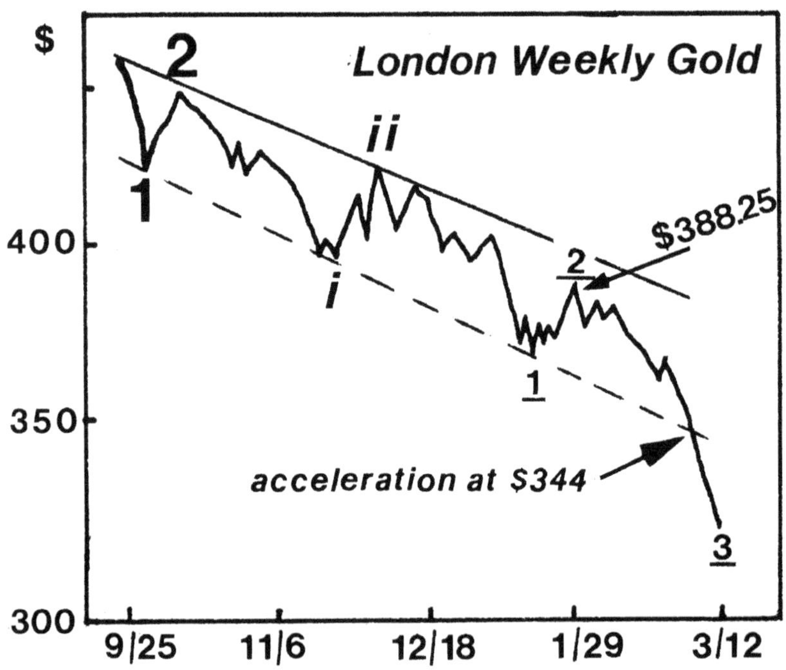

The second conclusion to be drawn was that the decline was *one larger degree* than I originally thought, which necessitated calculating likely mathematical support points for that large a "bear." Those points were *$344*, *$242* and *$105-110* (see February issue).

The third bearish occurrence was the typical "test" rally immediately after $388 was broken. The subsequent rally peaked at exactly *$388.25* on January 29, giving the $388 level a deadly "kiss goodbye" in classic Godfather fashion. Fibonacci supports that are *broken* are usually given this courtesy by the market. As another example on the gold chart, look at the rebound back toward the $565 level in early April 1980 after that minor Fibonacci level was penetrated in March.

The most recent bearish signal that gold has made is its penetration of $344. It always fascinates me how chart patterns will form to *reinforce* the importance of crucial Fibonacci levels. For instance, on the accompanying chart, notice that the $344 level, which satisfies two important Fibonacci calculations, is also the *exact point* at which the phony (i.e., not Elliott based, see text, p. 59) "channel" from the September peak was cracked on the downside. It also appears to be at the accelerating center of the "third of the third," wave 3 of iii of 3 in the wave count, where such breaks often occur (see text, p.67).

The implications of this break are that gold's bear market probably has *at least another $100 to go* and may have over $200 to go. I took a closer look at the *$242* level, by the way, and found that it just happens to be the first point of real chart support below $366. The peak of wave 1 in 1978 was exactly $242.75 on October 30. And from February through April of 1979, wave (2) of 3 stayed in a narrow trading range between $232 and $254, further establishing the only decent technical support level which still remains above $200 an ounce.

The Short Term

The only evidence of any tradable chart support before $242 is in the *$285-305* zone. There are no important Fibonacci calculations at that level, but I mention it for two reasons. First, there was some price hesitation there on the way up in 1979; secondly, the long term trendline which connects the 1970-71 and 1976 lows on semilog scale comes through that area in March 1982. The highly-acclaimed Aden Gold Study (Adam Smith Publishing, 4425 W. Napoleon Ave., Metairie, LA 70001; $25) forecast that this line would stop the great gold bear market in the $300-325 area. Additionally, Market Vane's (61 S. Lake Ave., Pasadena, CA 91101) tally of opinion last week showed only *16% bulls* on the price of gold, an extremely low reading that suggests a rally soon. Finally, gold is very oversold short term.

Although I do not think gold is hitting "the" bottom, the wave structure does show that the point of sharpest downthrust is passing, and that the trend should change from "straight down" to "choppy down" as a series of fourth and fifth waves of increasing degree drive gold into a tradable bottom. And staying short with the bearish sentiment this extreme is dangerous. Therefore I would suggest that traders cover short sales in the $285-305 zone and be ready to put them out again on a rally. Investors stay out of the long side. I expect that $344 will now be a *resistance* level to rallies.

Rules and Guidelines

Forecasting markets using Elliott is not an exact science, but it is an objective discipline. Each minor low in gold in the past two months was hailed as definitely "the" bottom by some well-meaning analysts who claimed to be using Elliott, even though such interpretations were either impossible or clearly less likely than the bearish ones. Most of them justified incorrect counts by referring to futures charts (which tell lies, as I've explained before) or worse, by saying that it's OK to break rules and ignore guidelines when analyzing in current time. The rules and guidelines have had their revenge, as they always do. When you put your own wishes ahead of the message of the market, the market will kill you.

"Insurance" Gold

Quite a few people have asked whether they should sell their "insurance" gold since the risk of further price decline increased when $388 was broken. My answer to that question is "definitely not." This portion of your portfolio (5-10%) is for just what it's labeled, "insurance" against the worse possibilities. Suppose you sell your core holding at $388 and put the money in a bank CD or standard money market fund. Then gold collapses all the way to $105 in a deflationary crash and you go to the bank or fund to withdraw your money to buy back the gold and, guess what, it isn't there. There's a moratorium on withdrawals. Then you've lost not only your money, but your gold as well. Don't cash in your catastrophe-insurance policy!

Silver

Gold did break down, and silver did break the $8 level significantly. As I said last month:

> If *gold* breaks down, I expect *silver* will fulfil my previous long-standing target of $4-6.50 per ounce, and more likely the lower end. That area marks the zone of the long consolidation pattern that occurred from 1974 to 1978.

Now that it's time to try to compute an exact target for the silver decline, I've come up with some observations that lead to a conclusion. Waves A and C in a zigzag are often equal in length. Since we are dealing with a semilog equivalency, the lengths must be expressed in percentages. Wave A of silver's bear market fell from $50 to $11, or 78%. If wave C also falls 78%, it will bottom at $5.28. Just as a wave C low at $5.28 would be 48% of wave A's low at $11, so the B wave peak at $24 was 48% of the high at $50. Here's where the Fibonacci ratio enters, since 48 is 61.5% of 78! In other words, the percentage distance between the two highs will be equal to the percentage distance between the two lows *and* equal to 61.8% of the percentage distance between both the first high to low and the second high to low, only at the $5.28 figure! (That's a mouthful, so you might want to take a look at the chart to visualize what I'm talking about.)

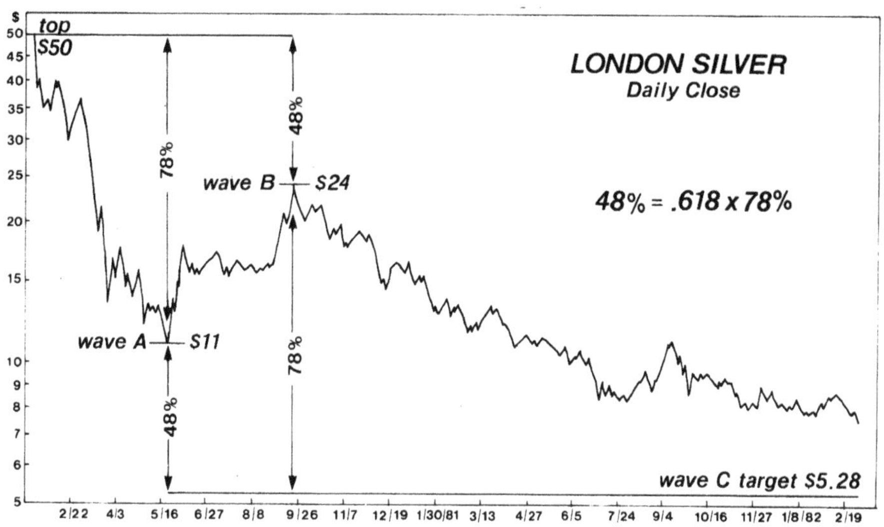

Furthermore, I would bet that the percentages of these daily closing figures are actually 80% and 50% when dealing with *hourly* figures (which I don't keep), representing the Fibonacci numbers *8* and *5*(x10). Anyway, I'll use *$5.28* as a target for the final bear market low until something better comes along.

APRIL 12, 1982

The decline in gold needs one more downward wave to finish off a five-wave sequence, although gold stocks appear to have bottomed intermediate term and should be bought on the "wave 2" pullback.

Gold

Gold has yet to reach the $285-305 zone to provide what I think will be an excellent point to cover short sales from $388. The extent of the current rally has forced a slight change in count as well. However, this rally is still best counted as a fourth wave in the sequence that began at the $463 high, so it appears that gold

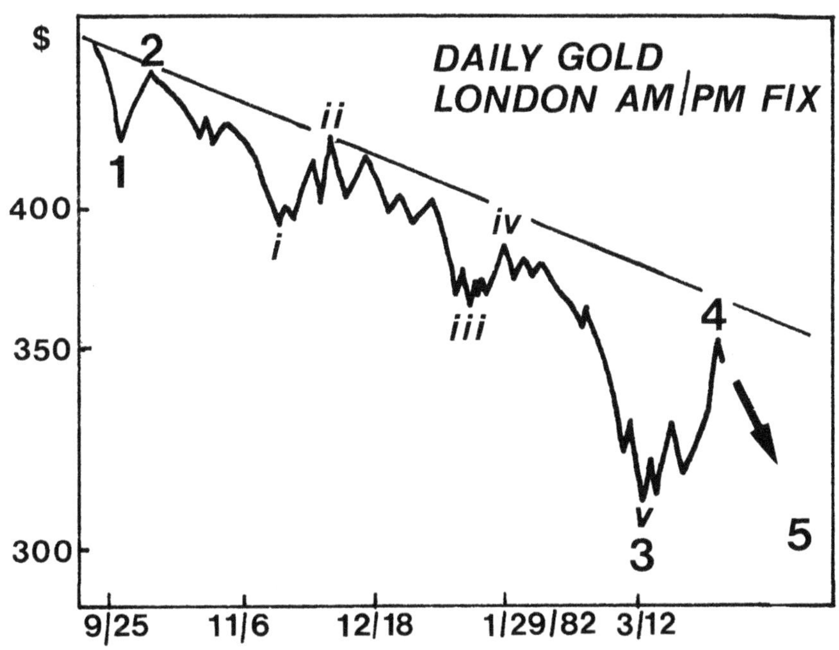

still needs another decline in order to complete a five-wave pattern from last September. Whether that decline will bring gold below the $312 bottom on March 15 remains to be seen, although fifth waves usually do make new lows. Therefore my inclination is to stay short for now and cover shorts during the next declining wave, which should begin immediately. After a fifth wave down, the next rally could carry as high as $388-405.

It's nearly impossible to count the current situation in bullion as a major bottom. At most, it's an intermediate bottom, using an alternate count as follows: I can interpret the decline from last September's peak as having ended on a fifth wave failure (see text, p.32) on March 29. Frankly, I doubt that this count is the correct one. Gold and silver are already back to a 50% reading on the Market Vane sentiment poll, probably due to the various forecasts that the $300-320 area would be the final low in gold. A fifth wave down here appears necessary from a psychological viewpoint as well.

The Long Term Picture

I revised my long term count when bullion broke $388 to indicate that wave V ended at the $850 peak in January 1980. The chart here shows the count that is now the most likely for the long term. You'll notice that gold has currently bottomed on top of the support line that stretches back to 1970. This is *not* the parallel to the line connecting the tops of III and V that appeared on my charts last year, but it is a valid support line. If it's taken out (and I expect that it will be later), no more arguments will exist to say that gold's bull market from 1970 is still intact.

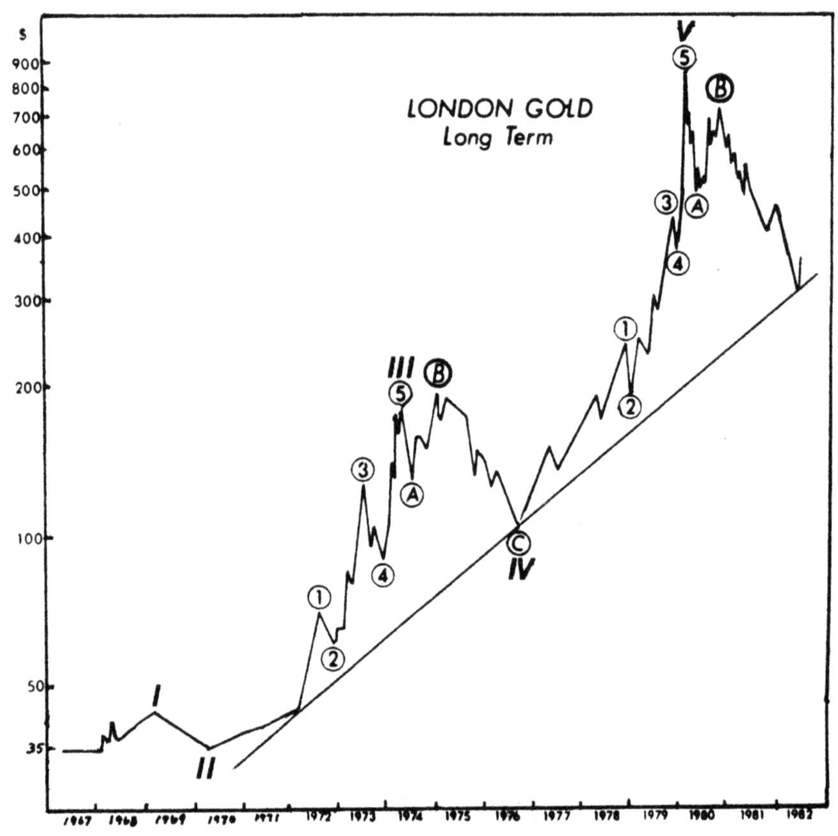

Gold Stocks

Unlike bullion, my index of gold stocks (PIGS) has traced five waves down from September 1981, further completing a full A-B-C zigzag pattern from its orthodox peak in September 1980. (You may remember that gold *stocks* made their fifth wave peaks at the $720 high in bullion (see October 3, 1980 letter), since they were out of phase with bullion and got going late in bullion's wave V advance.) What's more, the daily chart patterns for Anglo, Homestake, and ASA all show clear five wave patterns to the upside off their March 8 lows, complete with extended third waves. It appears, therefore, that gold *bullion* may drop to a new low soon while gold *stocks* will fail to confirm that new low, since they will merely be undergoing a second-wave pullback. This kind of non-confirmation often occurs at intermediate turning points in the gold market. I've often noticed them in the past, but I've yet to try to forecast one; let's see how it turns out. Tactically, I would start buying gold stocks for a trade on a 50% retracement of their March-April rallies, and particularly if bullion completes a fifth wave down as expected.

Aden Gold Study

One of the most common questions I get asked is "do you agree with the Aden Gold Study?" Answer: It's a good piece of technical analysis with a solid argument for a major gold bottom here and now and an ultimate target near $4000 per ounce by 1986. It is an exercise in forecasting, and I enjoy any well-done forecasting attempt. Right now, I don't agree with the conclusions, although I think this level will serve up a good-sized intermediate rally. But listen, folks, I've been wrong before, and I suggest you make up your own mind if you're interested. To make it easier for you, you can get a copy by sending $25 to us at New Classics Library, P.O. Box 1618, Gainesville, GA 30503. We'll have the publisher send you a copy.

MAY 10, 1982

Gold appears to be in its fifth wave down from last September's peak. When that wave has been completed, gold should undergo an intermediate rally to upside resistance at $388, and then resume its bear market.

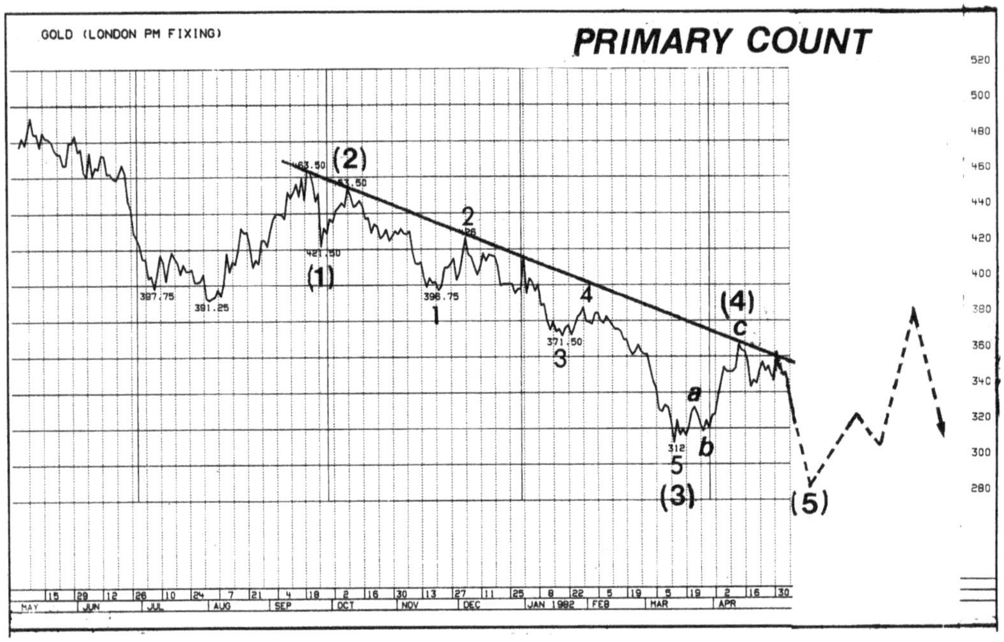

Gold

"It seems to defy all rational expectation." That was the comment from one of the anchorpersons on the Financial News Network on May 3rd when gold refused to rally on the escalation of the Falklands crisis. The Wave Principle is a rational explanation of what otherwise seem to be irrational price movements. Only if you are utterly convinced that prices are tied to current events will the markets seem irrational to you. (This isn't to say that an Elliotter

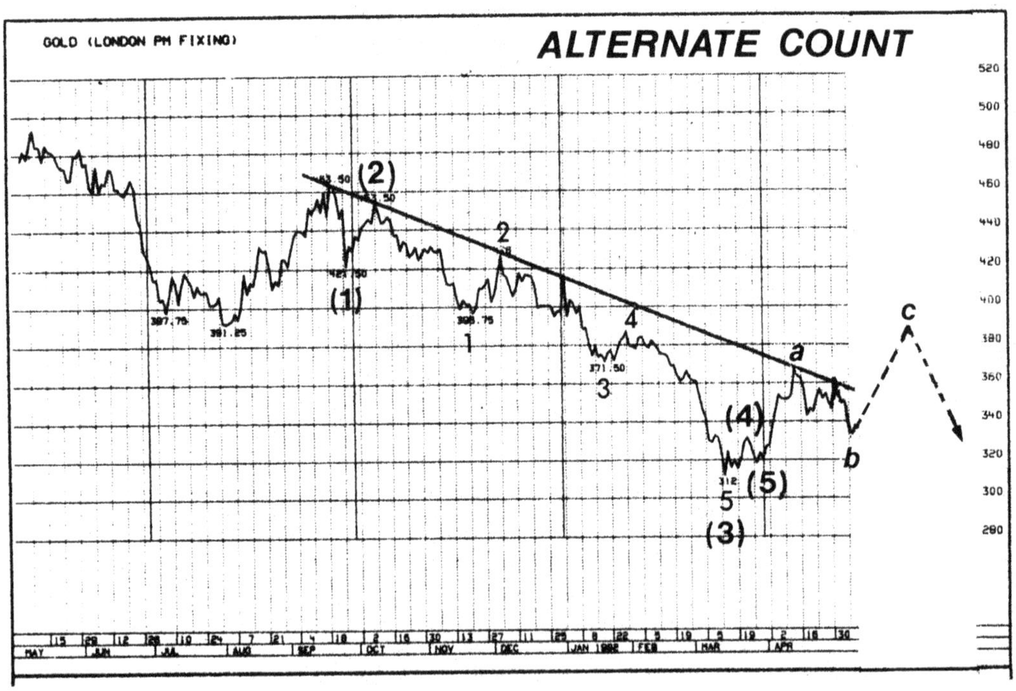

always knows what's going to happen next, merely that the wave patterns always fit rationally into the theory of the Wave Principle, while they do not fit rationally into the fluctuations of current events.)

Last month's issue (April 12) concluded that gold was at a fourth-wave peak and that a decline back toward the $312 low of March 15 was imminent. The peak occurred two days later at $366.75, concluding a $55 rally from the low at $312, and a decline is underway. At no time was the downtrend line from last September broken on the upside. Silver, of course, hardly reacted to the Falklands crisis at all and has since fallen to a new low. Gold stocks have pulled back as expected but should hold their March lows and perform well on the next advance in bullion.

The most likely intermediate downside target zone is still $285-305, although in order to protect against a fifth wave failure, I would suggest beginning to cover short sales below $320, which will yield about $70 profit from $388. After the upcoming short term low, five waves will have been completed from the $463 peak last September, and an intermediate a-b-c rally back to the $367-388 level will be highly likely. At that point, gold will be set up to crash again.

Deja Vu

The current news background and gold price action are exactly what they were during the March 1981 rally (remember that one?). At that time, the Polish crisis was intense (now it's the Falklands crisis), gold was rallying in a fourth wave (as it did here), the advance overshot its normal upside target (as it did here) and climbed 20% in value (the recent rally climbed 18% in value). It was even the same time of year!

Alternate Count: If gold stops here and begins to rally immediately, then the orthodox low for the last decline was on March 29 at $318.50, on a fifth wave failure (see April letter). This count would imply that waves "a" (Fibonacci $55) and "b" (Fibonacci $34) of the intermediate rally have already been completed and that wave "c" upward would carry gold to the $388-389 level, which would mark the point at which "a" and "c" of the inverted zigzag would be equal in length (both $55). Either way, the $388 level will be an excellent point to short gold once again.

Long Term Target Still $105-110

New major advances rarely begin with such an accommodating news background. As for those who tell you gold is "ridiculously cheap," you might want to show them the chart below, courtesy of the American Institute for Economic Research (Great Barrington, MA 01230). It shows the purchasing power of gold in terms of all other commodities, and is quite a shocker. The low end of the range is below $100 in 1981 dollars, again showing that while an ultimate target of $105 may be difficult to imagine, it isn't "off the wall."

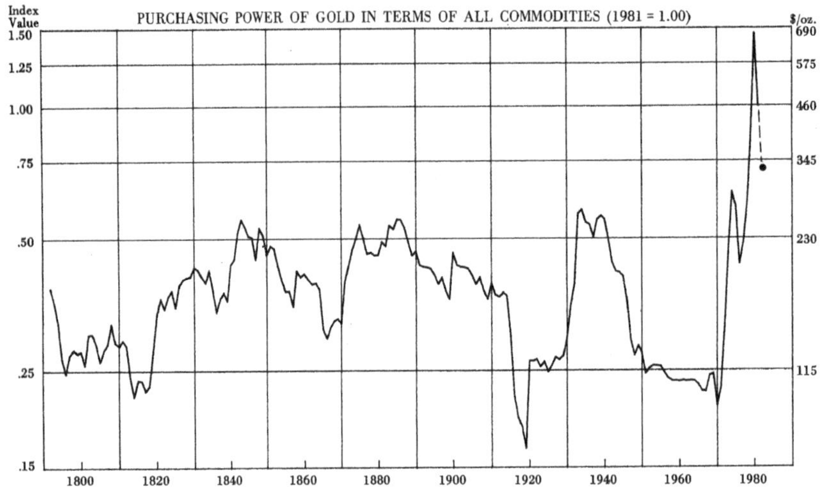

I mentioned in the February issue that $103.50 marks the low of the previous fourth wave of lesser degree and that $111.63 is the point at which wave C from $720 will be 1.618 times as long as wave A from $850 to $474. These are two strong Elliott magnets, which make that area a highly probable level for a low given a severe bear market. While not part of Elliott wave guidelines, it is worth noting that the $105 price is also a kind of "center" for two Fibonacci multiples. $105 divided by the Fibonacci number 3 gives the fixed-price low of $35, while $105 multiplied by the Fibonacci number 8 gives $840, just $10 off the all-time high.

Donald J. Hoppe, in the March 12 issue of his Analysis (Box 513, Crystal Lake, IL 60014), argues that precious metals may be undergoing a bear market of the same magnitude as the bear market for stocks in 1929-1932. He notes that at that time the Dow's initial drop was 48%, while gold's was 44%; the ensuing recovery in the Dow was 52%, and in gold was 65%. If the final drop in gold is equivalent to the 89% loss in the Dow, gold's ultimate low would be $94 per ounce. On this basis, Hoppe projects a low for silver of $5.50, which isn't far from my Fibonacci ratio calculation (see March issue) of $5.28 silver.

JUNE 7, 1982

Gold bullion should continue lower, breaking below the $300 level this month.

Gold

Downside momentum seems to have slowed in gold, but the wave count suggests that it's just the calm before the storm. As in the stock market, gold bullion sits at a critical support level, and indications are that it will break. Take a look at the long term chart. The support trendline that originated in the early '70s was hit again at the $312 low in March, and prices have once more come back to touch that trendline. It might be considered a successful "test," except that the minor wave count does *not* appear to be complete.

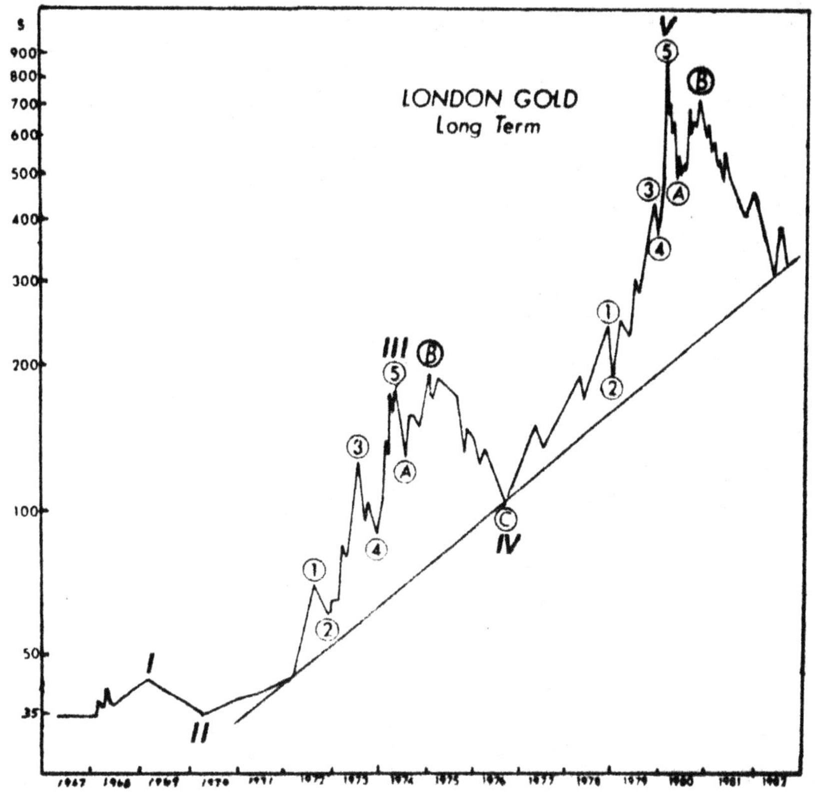

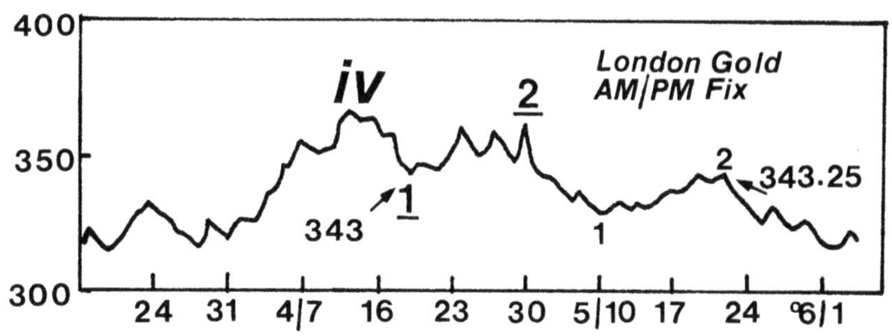

As you can see from the daily chart, the overlapping of waves makes it impossible to count this decline as a nearly completed "five," so wave 3 of v is likely breaking down into an extension. If my primary count is correct, gold will break down immediately. Hold short positions from $388. My "cover short" area of $285-305 now actually looks conservative because of the intricate subdivision in the declining wave from the $366.75 peak on April 14. But just to protect some profits, and in deference to the low number of bulls in Market Vane's bull/bear tally, I would cover half the short positions on a break of $300. Also, a stop at $350 basis London would be prudent.

My gold stock index (PIGS) has retraced 90% of its March-April rally, exceeding the 50% I thought would mark a trading buy point. With continued risk in both gold bullion and the stock market, gold stocks are no longer worth holding for a trade on the long side. Avoid.

If the Hunts have a silver hoard to sell, what could drive down the price of gold? How about continued massive sales by the Soviet Union, which, after all, is in a similar position to the Hunts? They've got tons of gold, but their empire is in danger of collapse. It's losing value in the deepening political depression, and they *have* to sell assets madly just to keep the empire intact.... Fundamentals are fun sometimes, aren't they? But I'd rather hang my hat on this WMN headline: "Dealers Surprised by Weak Gold Prices."

JULY 12, 1982

Gold finally entered the $285-305 downside target area for traders' short covering. The current rally should carry to approximately the $388 level before gold resumes its bear market decline.

Gold

Expectations in June that "Gold bullion should continue lower, breaking below the $300 level this month" worked out well. The low London fix was $296.75 on June 21, and the *long-awaited traders' target zone of $285-305 was finally met.* After that long time on the short side from $388, I'm annoyed that last month I recommended covering only half the position upon a break of $300. But the $90 trade on the short side is one of the best I've seen in this gold market lately, with most buy-siders getting taken out at stop after stop on the long and torturous way down. Cover the other half now, at a $50 gain.

Major Bottom?

Sentiment toward gold is at a very low ebb, supporting the argument for an intermediate rally. Two of the staunchest and most prominent gold "bulls," who have been holding out all year, finally threw in the towel in June, and Market Vane's bull/bear poll shows a large preponderance of bearish sentiment.

As with the stock market, however, I still do *not* count that as a major bottom. Sliver, gold, and precious metals stocks all made joint new lows on June 21, despite the jawboning that gold "might not confirm" the new low in silver. Thus, there were no non-confirmations at the low. Furthermore, silver has soared a full 25%, while gold has climbed only 10% from the low. Gold appeared to be showing "relative strength" going into the low, but it isn't displaying it on the rally as one might expect it to do if it had hit a major bottom.

I consider the major bear trend still intact for these reasons: The .618 Fibonacci retracement at $388 was penetrated and should now be a point of heavy resistance, the long term Elliott support line was broken in January and the major support trendline from 1970 was broken briefly in May. These observations make a strong argument that a major bottom is still far ahead of us, with the $105-110 area still a likely target.

Two Wave Counts

I still hold that gold bottomed on wave A of a Supercycle decline in April 1980 and peaked wave B in September 1980. At that point, wave C began. The intermediate-term wave count, which I haven't addressed in a while, allows for two main interpretations from there. One thing that appears certain is that the decline from April is probably *not* the fifth wave of the decline that began in September 1981, as I had been counting it. It is better to count one full five-wave decline into a fifth-wave failure in late March. (This alternate was mentioned in the April 12 issue.)

From there, my main interpretation is that the second wave within wave ③ of C is still underway from last March (see first chart). This count was presented in chart form as an *al-*

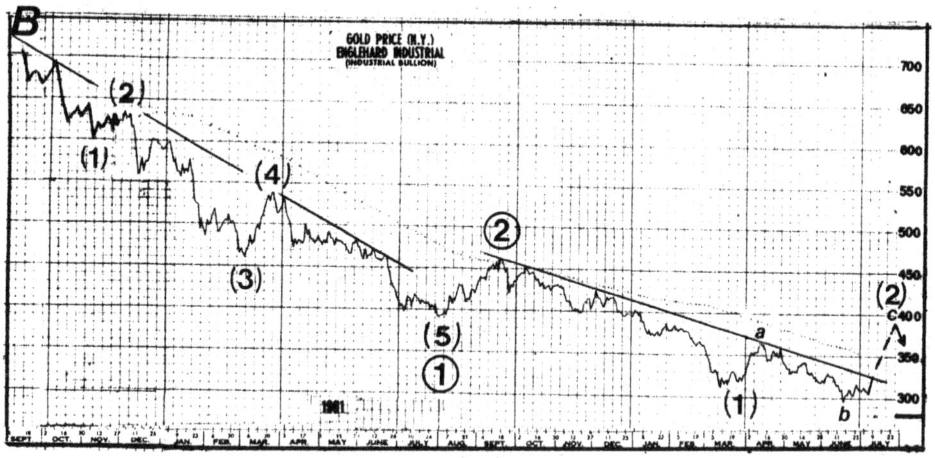

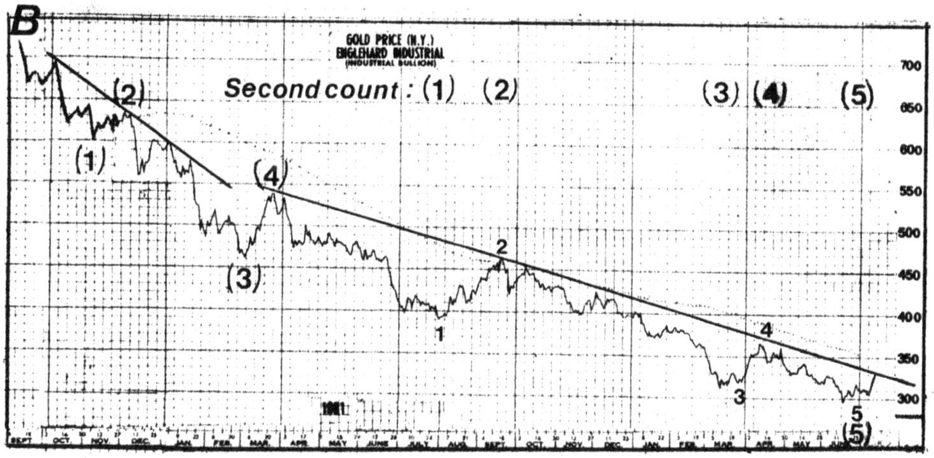

ternate in the May issue, with a dashed-line projection of a rally back to $388. Some analysts, including accomplished Elliotter Alf Field of Sydney, Australia, have held this view throughout the recent decline (although most thought that $312 would not be broken). The main reason that the decline from April should be counted as a "b" wave is that it is clearly best described as an overlapping seven-wave sequence. Such a formation is a *corrective* wave and fits the interpretation of a "b". An illustration of this formation is shown (inverted) in Figure 25 on page 174 of *The Major Works of R.N. Elliott.*

For the first time since gold was approaching $388, an alternate count allows for gold to be in the process of completing a fifth wave down. There are two acceptable ways to count a five-wave decline from September 1981 (see second chart), and one indicates that the recent low in gold was a bottom preceding the best intermediate rally since April-September 1980. However, the minor wave structure is nearly impossible to count as a "five" from last April to the present, making this clearly an *alternate* count. I'll go into more detail on what the *major* trend interpretation would be if $388 is exceeded. Even with this count, I doubt that gold has finished the *entire* wave C from $720, more likely just wave a of C.

Upside Targets

Wave c in an irregular correction is usually 1.618 times as long as wave a. Wave a in gold (during the Falklands crisis) climbed from $312 to $366.75, a total of *54.75* (Fibonacci 55) points. A 1.618 multiple of that length is 88.59 (Fibonacci 89) points. Since wave c started at the June 21 low of 296.75, it should peak at $385.34, confirming the importance of the old "388" resistance level.

If the *alternate* count is in force, targets are either $366.75, the previous wave (4) under one count, or $547.25, the previous wave (4) under the other count (see the second gold chart). As you can see, there is a tremendous difference in the two possibilities, underscoring how important a penetration of $388 resistance would be. The second resistance level is strengthened by the fact that on the long term gold chart, the broken Elliott support trendline from 1970 crosses through current price action at $500 per ounce and crosses $547.25 around October. An upside "test" of a broken trendline is a common technical occurrence, so as wild as this projection seems at the moment, it's a valid calculation.

In sum, the resistance levels are *$367*, *$385-388*, which is my current target, and *$547*. Because of the implications of the alternate count, both traders and investors should enter the long side with a stop at $305. Raise the stop to $340 if $360 is exceeded. Gold stocks are a buy as well.

AUGUST 9, 1982

Gold peaked exactly at $366.50, a Fibonacci resistance point calculated last month. As long as $388 is not exceeded, gold should now undergo a substantial decline. Bonds completed their 6-week rally on August 2.

Gold

The points of resistance for gold, calculated in the last letter, were $366.75, $385-388 and $547.25. The exact peak to date, reached on the London p.m. fix July 21, was $366.50, just .25 from the first Elliott wave resistance point. Anyone still skeptical about Elliott and Fibonacci targeting will find it difficult to ignore the precalculated peak in gold bullion last month. For most people, getting the direction right is tough enough, but being able to pinpoint probable turning points in advance even occasionally is something very few disciplines will achieve.

This juncture in the intermediate-term picture is a tough one, but I am concluding that for all practical purposes, gold's bear market rally has peaked out. There is some minor uncertainty in the daily wave structure in late June, making a final run to $385-388 still possible. But the structure can be counted as a full five waves up, and it reached the peak of the previous a-wave, thus fulfilling the requirements for wave c upward in last month's preferred count. My feeling here is that even if gold can make it to $388, let the other guy have the last $20. In the meantime, I'd rather stay out or play the short side. The risk is that gold is now entering wave (3) of ③, a crash phase.

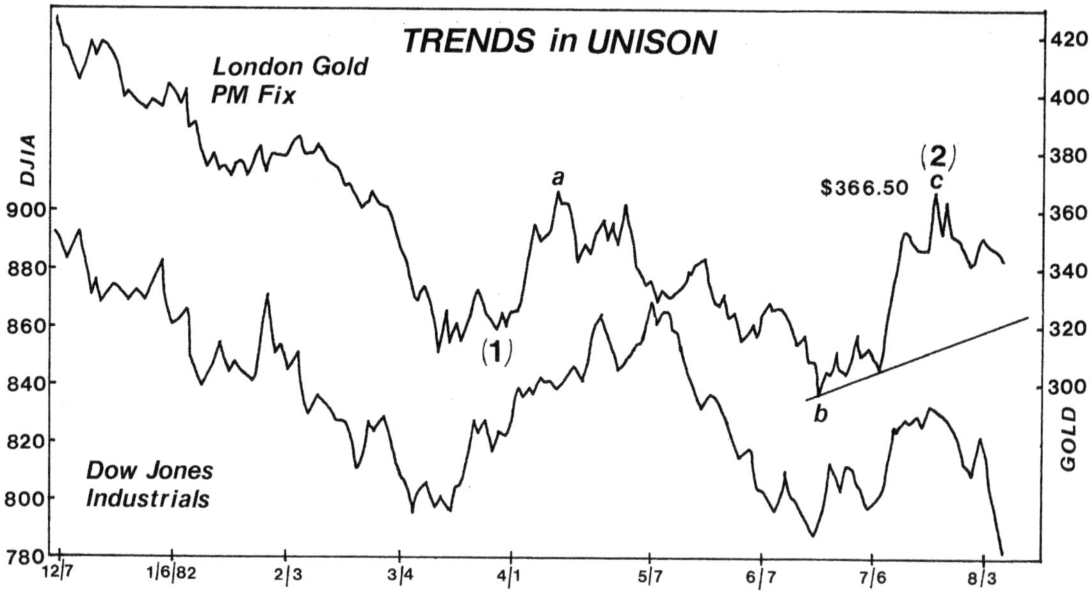

Alternate Counts

I won't re-hash the alternate wave counts, since I went over them in detail in last month's issue (new subscribers just write us for a copy). I urge you to refer to those charts, since they are still entirely valid. Suffice it to say that a dramatic push upward through $388 would have a profound effect upon my intermediate expectations with regard to the gold price, since the next resistance level would be $460 (the peak of the second wave of the extension), with a potential target point at $547 before a resumption of the bear.

If gold has actually started a substantial intermediate advance, then the maximum extent of its current a-b-c correction should be .618 of the length of the rally, or $323, which also happens to be the current position of the uptrend line connecting the mid June and early July lows. While this is a guideline, not a firm rule, any break of that level would be an important step in confirming the resumption of the bear market. If an a-b-c pattern develops, traders may wish to try a purchase near that point with a stop at $320 for a low-risk trading attempt. As a fail-safe, if gold does get above $388, buy and hold as long as gold stays above that level.

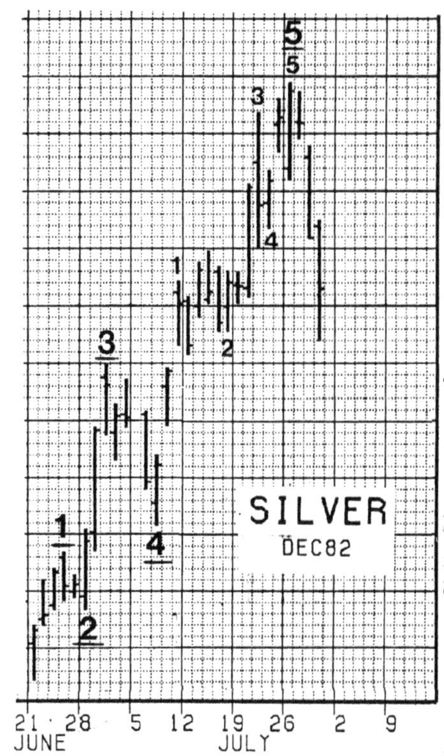

Silver

From the $4.90 low (basis London close), expectations were for a rally to "just under $8." The peak at $7.15 didn't quite make it, but it was close. The advance was a clear five waves (as the December futures chart shows), which helps substantiate a five-wave count in gold. Silver did penetrate its intermediate downtrend line dating back to last September. That line now sits just above $6 and should act as support. Under normal wave action, the fourth wave low at $5.50 would be the maximum allowable pullback level if $7.15 is to be exceeded. I'm still counting it as part of a rally in a bear market.

SEPTEMBER 13, 1982

Gold

Sell the next rally! If gold is in a bear market rally as I suspect, then the next new high could mark the exact peak. The Fibonacci target based on the *internal* wave construction is $515.50, the point at which wave (c) will be 2.618 times as long as wave (a). For this reason, the $547 "maximum" target may not be reached, and I would take $110+ profit on this rally on a fix above $500. For those so inclined, sell short between $547 and $500, with a stop at $560 basis London fix. If (1) of C ended at $296.75, then wave (2) of C is in its final stages now. See the July 12 issue.

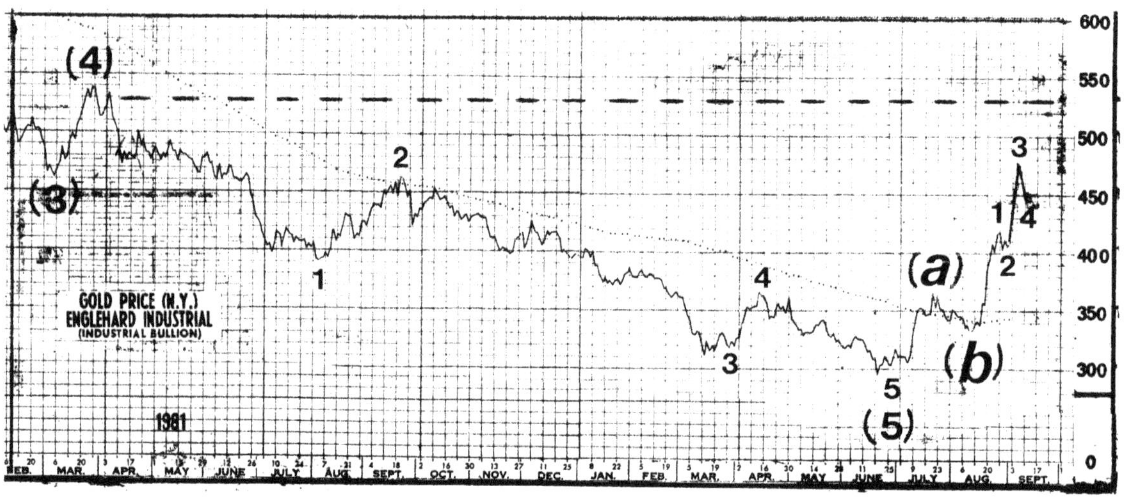

I didn't expect gold to get through $388, but it did trip the "buy" stop. The push through $388 was powerful, as it should have been, and once through, it never fell below to provide even one whipsaw. These Fibonacci levels make excellent points around which to base strategy, whether the "most probable" forecast works out or not. Let's see if the low 500s area acts as I expect it to. For the moment, I am concluding that gold is most likely to stumble.

OCTOBER 4, 1982

Gold is a muddle of if/then, but I would not want to hold aggressive long positions again until the right events occur.

Gold

Bullion has fallen over $50 since I wrote, "Gold may have already peaked." It's now a crucial juncture for the whole bull market/bear market question. The odds favor counting the recent rally as an a-b-c bear market rally, but confirmation of that opinion has not yet occurred. Since gold stocks have been holding up well during the latest slide in bullion, another rally of some type is likely from Thursday's low, if only to set up a non-confirmation.

Here's why the bull market argument remains alive: The drop from the high has taken a 5-3-5 form so far, bottoming Thursday just below the previous fourth wave of lesser degree (see EWP, p.55) and just $6 from the $389 level, at which waves a and c would be of equal length, a normal relationship in zigzags. If the next rally *clears $415* and traces out *five* waves, gold will likely have entered another intermediate wave up to over $500/oz. That rally will be countable as either wave "C" from the June low or as wave 3 up in a new bull market. The final answer must await more evidence.

You might ask, if sugar and some other commodities may be starting large B waves upward, why wouldn't I conclude the same about gold? The answer is that gold is miles ahead of the rest of the list and currently way overpriced relative to its historic relationship to a broad list of commodities.

By the way, the recent peak ($488 London fix; $515 Hong Kong peak) is interesting in two ways. First, $480 would mark the point at which bullion would have advanced exactly 61.8% from its low at $296.75, and $508 would mark the point at which bullion would have retraced 50% of the drop from $720 to $296.75.

A note on sentiment. The roar that a new bull market in gold has begun is deafening, and affirmations that it's going to $3000 are widespread. The public appears a lot more ready to believe it now than when my forecast low at $388 was hit in August of last year. The accompanying graph shows the results of a survey tabulated in February by Jim Sinclair (Sinclair Securities, 90 Broad St., New York, NY 10004). He added the totals of 36 out of 57 market letter writers polled by Jim Blanchard (Gold Newsletter) who were *specific* about their forecast for an ultimate bottom in gold. 39% said $300. Either the majority called it right, or gold will see $100 before the bear breathes its last.

South Africa's Tony Henfrey (Gold Letter, P.O. Box 5577, Durban 4000), one of the rare breed of capable and honest analysts, included an Elliott wave count in his last issue. He used a count different from mine but concluded last month, as I did, that one more minor new high in gold was forthcoming. Well, Tony, you did spell "Elliott" correctly, and you even counted according to the rules. Now if we can just get the market to follow our forecasts! Tony sees gold up until 1984 but not highs above $850.

Silver

Silver appears to have climbed in five waves off its low, so once this correction ends, silver should rally to a new high. Since the gold/silver ratio still favors silver, it should continue to outperform gold on a percentage basis. Given the extended first wave up, the pullback could fall as low as $6.25 before bottoming. First support is at $7.70.

NOVEMBER 8, 1982

September's "sell" recommendation for gold, three days after the peak, has been confirmed by recent technical developments. Gold should continue to trend lower, perhaps accelerating on the downside.

Gold

Amidst a sea of "buy" advice from every conceivable source, the September 13 issue of *The Elliott Wave Theorist* introduced the gold section with, "Sell the next rally!" Not only do I see no reason to turn bullish at this point, but in fact numerous technical occurrences have strengthened my overall feeling that gold is not embarking on a super move to $3000/oz.

For months now, I have been arguing that all three markets (stocks, bonds and gold) could not go up together on a long term basis. Stocks and bonds are OK together, and stocks and gold are OK together, but not all three at once. The September issue [said], "For the moment, I am concluding that gold is most likely to stumble."

That was written three trading days after the blowoff peak in gold. What's happened since? First, the wave count for the October rally was an a-b-c, not a "five," giving another point to the bears. Secondly, the wave count on the gold stock indexes and on ASA shows a completed "five" from the June low. That five-wave count implies at least a good correction, and since that rise probably completes wave C from last March, it could be the highest valuation for gold stocks for several years.

Thirdly, the "Dow Theory Gold" method gave a powerful intermediate "sell" signal on October 14, the day we went short on the hotline. (I thought I had invented this method in 1976 and found out later that several other people had invented it before I did. So much for innovative research.) In any case, it is an excellent method of discovering divergences in the gold market. I know that untold numbers of advisors have been saying that "gold stocks lead gold bullion," but they're flat-out wrong. The fact is that a new high in either stocks or bullion unconfirmed by the other will mark a "sell" point 8 times out of 10. What is more mysterious is that most analysts judge markets based on the last cycle, so why aren't more gold forecasters bearish? After all, at the $720 peak, gold stocks were streaking to new all-time highs while bullion lagged. That divergence led to a collapse in both, as it should have. I can only conclude that gold watchers are bullish anyway and are coloring their interpretations of the technical evidence.

Finally, did you notice that the frenzied gold rally occurred when the fear of widespread bank failures had reached panic proportions? It appears to me that the gold runup was the fear spike that coincided with the maximum fear registered at the stock-market bottom. The stock market, by doubling the value of bank stocks, says flatly that those worries are over. Gold apparently began to recognize this fact in early September, but the distribution phase is taking awhile, probably because of the widespread conviction that gold has embarked on a huge new bull market.

As for the near term, the dominant trading cycle in gold is due to bottom in late November, and could lead to a bounce. I suggest staying out or short for now, with a stop at $448 basis London fix.

Gold Loans

The main advantage of gold is not that you can get rich trading it but that it functions as a stable store of value. Those who say that gold's price is unstable do not realize that its wild fluctuations in recent times are a function of two things: The wild fluctuations in the value of the paper currencies in which gold's price is measured, and the ebb and flow in the level of fear regarding the rapidity of the further debasement of those currencies.

Conrad Braun, President of Gold Standard Corp., has considered a plan for getting together lenders and borrowers who would like to write their contracts in gold. I.e., "Mr. X will lend Mr. Y 100 ounces of gold. At the end of one year, Mr. Y will pay Mr. X the original 100 ounces plus 3 ounces interest." This type of contract should be of particular interest if you have concluded, as I have, that gold will not be soaring to $3000 per ounce any time soon. Gold contracts are the basis for a sound private money system. If you're interested, write him at 1600 Genesee, Kansas City, MO 64102 and ask for his booklet entitled, "Successful Precious Metals Investing."

Silver

All the way down in the silver collapse, Elliott analysis was one of the few proponents of the argument that silver would underperform gold all the way down. Ever since silver bottomed within 38¢ of my $5.28 downside target, I've been arguing the opposite. Silver has several things going for it relative to gold:

1) Silver lost over 95% of its value from the peak, making it extremely undervalued.

2) Gold is still very expensive relative to all other commodities.

3) Based on historical relationships, the gold-silver price ratio favors silver.

4) The price of silver reflects an industrial component as well as a monetary component. The stock market says that the economy will soon begin to improve, so silver should continue to benefit.

> 5) The next several years should be an environment of economic stability, the one primary enemy of gold.

My upside target for silver is $17, plus or minus $1. Interim resistance is at $11. In my opinion, establishment of a long silver/short gold spread would be very profitable in the long run.

NOVEMBER 30, 1982

Gold is still in a bear market, although as long as it holds above $405, it retains the potential for a final lunge to $550.

Gold

So far, gold's wave structure this year is typical of a bear market, not a bull market. The only uncertainty is whether or not it has one more advancing wave ahead of it before another decline begins in earnest. As I see it, the current position in gold is setting up for the last chance to get another leg going in its bear market rally. Let's look at the two possible wave counts.

First let's examine the case for another wave to the upside. From the low in June, I still count the rally as an a-b-c. The only rally pattern that would allow for another advance to develop is a "flat" correction, where the a-b-c rally is only wave A of a larger A-B-C. Question: Is wave B subdividing correctly for such an interpretation? Answer: Yes, it's forming a symmetrical triangle (see text, p. 43), which is nearly completed. When it's over, an explosive wave C would carry gold to the maximum target of approximately $547 and finish off the entire bear market rally sequence from June 1981. This argument is supported by the fact that silver looks bullish, and gold stocks, despite a 10% correction, have not yet cracked.

The negative case is that each decline from the $488 high can be counted as a first wave down. The current rally would peak around $430-435 and lead to a severe "third of a third" downside break. This argument is supported by the position of the intermediate term cycles, which aren't due to bottom until late January.

Last month's issue gave this strategy:

> As for the near term, the dominant trading cycle in gold is due to bottom in late November, and could lead to a bounce. I suggest staying out or short for now, with a stop at $448.

OK, the bounce is occurring on schedule, and a trader has covered shorts at a profit and is watching a minor rally. What to do now? This month is a little more iffy, but I think an intelligent strategy is still possible. Given that the *primary* trend is down, I would have to stick with a defensive strategy for investors; the stock market is a better investment. If you're a trader, trade long *only as long as the London fix stays above* $404.50. A break below that level would confirm the likelihood of a sharp break.

Silver

Last month's analysis showed the resistance level for silver at *$11*, a number no other method had recognized, as far as I've seen. As it happened, top tick for the December silver futures contract was *$11.01*. From there the contract dropped over $2 to hit $8.98 last week. London spot close hit $10.58 before reacting to $9.01. The resistance level did its job, and now silver may be ready for another upside assault.

Silver continues to look more bullish than gold. The recent formation can be counted as an a-b-c irregular correction. If this count is correct, silver's next move is *up strongly*. However, it must get through $10.20 to prove it's off and running. Anything less still allows for another wave to the downside. Next support is $8, plus or minus 30¢. Ultimate target still $17, plus or minus $1.

The Elliott Wave Theorist, 1983

JANUARY 10, 1983

Gold still has potential to $547, but it is the most precarious of the major markets and could begin a decline at any time. Silver has more reliable upside potential.

Silver

One trading day after silver bottomed at $9.01, the December issue recognized the end of an "a-b-c irregular correction," indicating that silver's next move was to the upside. Six weeks later, it's up 29%. Gold, in the meantime, is up 12%. The long silver/short gold spread is working well. My ongoing preference for silver over gold, based upon their different Elliott wave structures, has paid off for both of us.

Is there a fundamental reason for silver to outperform gold? Yes. The stock market says there's an economic recovery on the way, and the "industrial use" component is a much greater part of silver's value than gold's. That, coupled with the extreme compression and undervaluation at the mid-1982 lows, continues to make silver more attractive and supports the case for continuing the spread position.

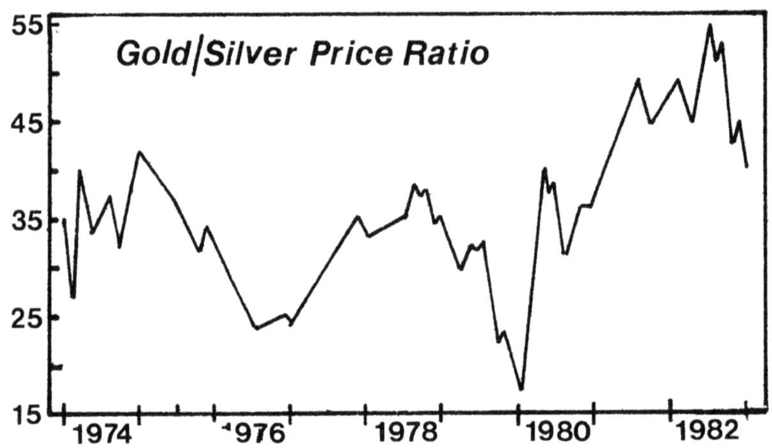

I still expect $17, plus or minus $1, for an ultimate target. For those interested, this target was generated by taking the length of wave A, at $5, and computing a likely length for wave C as 1.618xA, or $8. Adding that to the low at $9 gives $17. While zigzags often show waves A and C the same length, the strong irregular correction in the "B" position (see chart, December issue) indicates the potential for a long "C." Interim resistance is at $12, the peak of the previous fourth wave, and $14, the point at which the length of wave C would equal the length of wave A.

Short term, I can make a case that silver is topping in wave "B" of an irregular correction dating from early November. The risk is a drop back under $9 in a five-wave "C." Traders should keep this possibility in mind, but I'm not recommending selling here because a "third of a third" blastoff is more likely, and I wouldn't want to miss that move.

Gold

Last month, I was again willing to trade gold from the long side, "as long as the London fix stays above $404.50." Gold closed that Friday at $417.75, and has now traded up to the $460+ area.

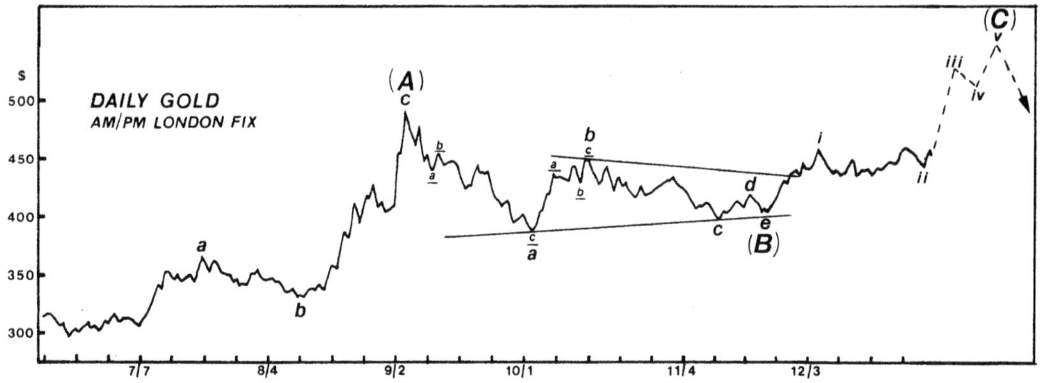

At this point, the technical background for gold is becoming increasingly dangerous. The divergence between gold shares and the bullion price is still signaling a major non-confirmation, which is getting larger with each passing week. A new high for gold could wipe that non-confirmation out, of course, but the difference in their performances will still be dramatic. Moreover, gold stocks have tripled from their lows, and the trend-chasers are beginning to notice. And quietly behind the scenes, despite all the return-of-inflation rhetoric, the utility stocks have scored a major breakout, providing a strong foundation for the "continuing dis-inflation" argument. In other words, inflation may be rekindled for a few months at a time, but each occurrence should appear as a temporary lift in an overall drop in the rate. As I see it, these factors make gold riskier than the stock market at this time.

The wave structure from the June low still appears to be characteristic of an upward correction rather than a new impulse wave. However, it does appear that the first count from last month's issue is the one that is unfolding. That is, gold is likely in the midst of a five-wave advance to between \$500 and its maximum target of \$547, as shown in the chart above. The guideline that post-triangle thrusts usually travel about the distance of the widest part of the triangle indicates that this rally could miss its maximum potential and peak at just over \$500.

If you're trading the metal long, place a stop at \$450 basis London fix and plan to sell out above \$500. Go short either at the maximum target of \$547 with a stop at \$560 or upon a break of \$450, using \$475 as a stop.

The B-wave triangle that formed during September, October and November adds even more weight to the "bear market rally" argument, since triangles generally precede the final wave in a movement (see text, p.44). Keep in mind, though, that if gold roars through \$550, I may be forced to concede that it really is a "new bull market."

Gold Stocks

The last "buy" suggestion I had for gold stocks occurred in early July, 1982. HM had just closed at 20, ASA at 26½ and Amgold at 44⅝. In the November issue, after these stocks had racked up a 100% gain, I reported what looked like a top developing. Since then, these stocks are up another 50%!

Why have the gold shares so powerfully outperformed bullion? The main reason, in my opinion, is that U.S. interest rates have been cut in half, and gold stocks, which have notoriously high yields, had record yields in June of last year after the average blue chip gold stock had lost 72% of its value. Meanwhile, the price of gold, merely by holding up, will provide the mines with an excellent average price for their sales, which in turn will keep the dividends secure. The market, however, figured this out well before I did but may have discounted the best by now. Gold stocks appear very overpriced. Still, there is not yet enough technical evidence to suggest shorting them.

FEBRUARY 7, 1983

Gold and gold stocks are starting to form a major top, while *silver has at least one more upleg to go* after a 4th wave correction.

Gold: Major Top Approaching

The headline pretty well sums up my feelings about gold for the first quarter of 1983. Although the top is not yet complete, there is so much rhetoric to combat that it seems prudent to make a case now rather than be dramatic and wait for "top tick." That way, you'll have time to digest my argument. Of course, if the final peaks in gold and silver are clear, I'll send out a bulletin, but it's more important now to have time to prepare for reducing exposure on climbs into new highs. Here are the factors that go into my conclusion:

1) The *wave count* in gold shows that the short term price action is following the forecast chart from the January letter. As a result, a large A-B-C pattern from the $296 low is completed or nearly so. This formation will fulfil the scenario for wave ② of C in an ongoing bear market from the high at $850.

2) When gold was emerging from its low at $296, the maximum retracement that gold was expected to manage, assuming that the bear market from $850 was still intact, was $547 *per ounce*. Last week's high was 7% from that price, making the potential further *reward* very low and the potential *risk* very high.

3) *Gold stocks* are counting out full five-wave advances. Meanwhile, the put/call ratios on the gold stocks (as reported by Paul Montgomery of Legg Mason, Newport News, VA) are at very low levels, suggesting that the express-train runup in gold stocks is now over and that a top-building phase (which may include one more new high) has begun.

4) *Sentiment*, as measured by Market Vane (61 S. Lake Ave., Pasadena, CA 91101), has recorded between 80% and 90% bulls on gold for the past *four weeks in a row*, suggesting that the current top is not "minor," but *at least* of intermediate significance. These figures reflect that most participants in the gold market have become convinced that

the forecasts for "$3000 gold" and a "massive new inflation cycle" will be fulfilled. Books and monographs on gold are coming out at the rate of one every two months, all selling the idea that gold is going up 1000% and rare coins up 2000%. And on January 31, the WSJ headlined, "Gold Fever Strikes on Canadian Exchanges As Talk About Finds Spurs Wild Trading." This is the beginning of a long bull market? Aren't gold rushes spurred by prices which are perceived to be very *high?* (And besides, won't a "gold rush" eventually result in increased gold production, depressing the price?)

5) Rate-of-change *momentum* was greater on the September peak than on the current new high, yielding a powerful divergence "sell signal." Momentum signals are particularly reliable when the other technical data supports the argument for a turn in the market.

The Wave Count

As you can see from the next chart, I'm counting the gold rally as wave ② of C, which suggests that wave C has a long way to go on the downside. If this count is correct, the ultimate target of $105 per ounce should be reached within the next several years as the deflationary forces of the Kondratieff cycle become more and more evident. The old parallel Elliott channel has been left on the chart to show the current rally as a typical "pull-up" back to the old support line.

The peak of the previous fourth wave, wave (4) of ① of C, occurred at $547 per ounce, and a .618 retracement of wave ① would project $558 per ounce. Therefore, the $550 area is a good place to look for "top tick" in the current rally. As I have said repeatedly, a good case *can* be made that an entire A-B-C correction from $850 ended at $296, but for the time being, "you pays your money and you takes your choice." The two main reasons I feel gold's prior bull market ended at $850 are that the last correction was greater than 61.8% (*highly* unusual for a fourth wave) and that the perfectly parallel trendchannel, which was met at the $338 low in August 1981, was subsequently broken. If $560 is substantially surpassed, I may be forced to

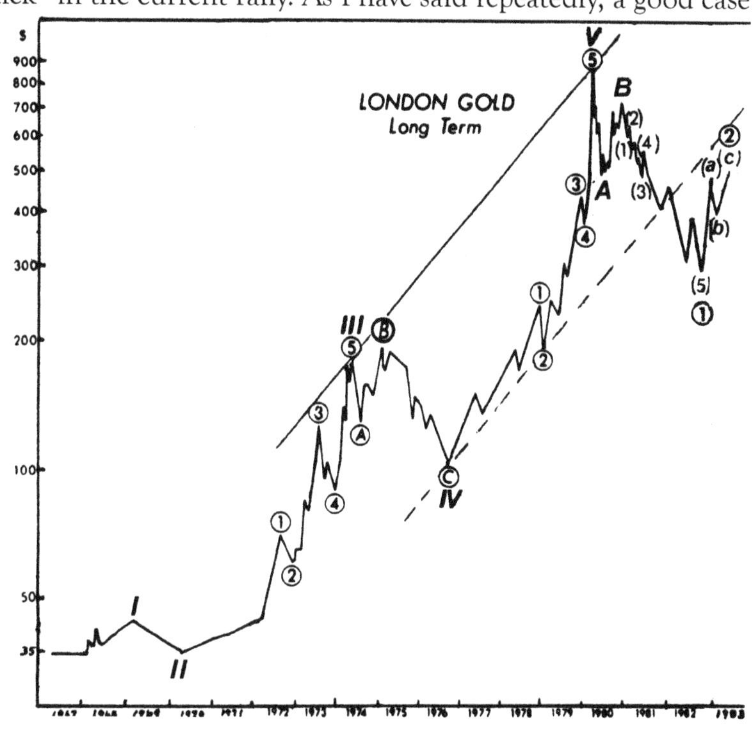

conclude that a grand new bull market is indeed underway, and that the Elliott trendchannel must be re-drawn connecting the lows at $103.50 and $296.75 (see text, p.59).

Tactically, I think it's prudent to *sell out* on strength in this area over the next several weeks. If I'm wrong and gold *does* continue to rise substantially, your repurchase price will be only $20 or $30 higher than your sale price; if I'm right, you'll be selling out at the top.

Silver

Silver's position is different from gold's. While gold may or may not climb to new highs on its next rally, *silver's pattern virtually demands another wave (or even two) to new highs.* By the most conservative count, silver has just finished only wave 3 of (C), and has now begun wave 4. Wave 4 should be either a "flat" or a triangle, fulfilling the Rule of Alternation, since wave 2 was a zigzag. Wave 4 should take place between $12.30 and $14.70 per ounce, and last three to five weeks. I still expect the final fifth wave to carry silver to my long-standing target of $17 per ounce.

The spread between silver and gold continues to move in our favor, and speculators who have followed Elliott analysis are continuing to profit from the narrowing spread. Once again, from the December low, silver soared 59% while gold struggled to only a 26% gain, less than half that for silver. I strongly recommend that traders hold their spread position until the final advancing wave in silver has ended.

By the way, a *single* $5000 futures contract purchased the day the December issue was written ("Silver's next move is *up strongly*") would now be worth $30,000 (this was an actual completed trade on the Telephone Hotline). If we can catch a low near $12.50, we should be able to multiply a silver futures position six times in value for the second time in a row. A close under $11.50 should be used as a stop.

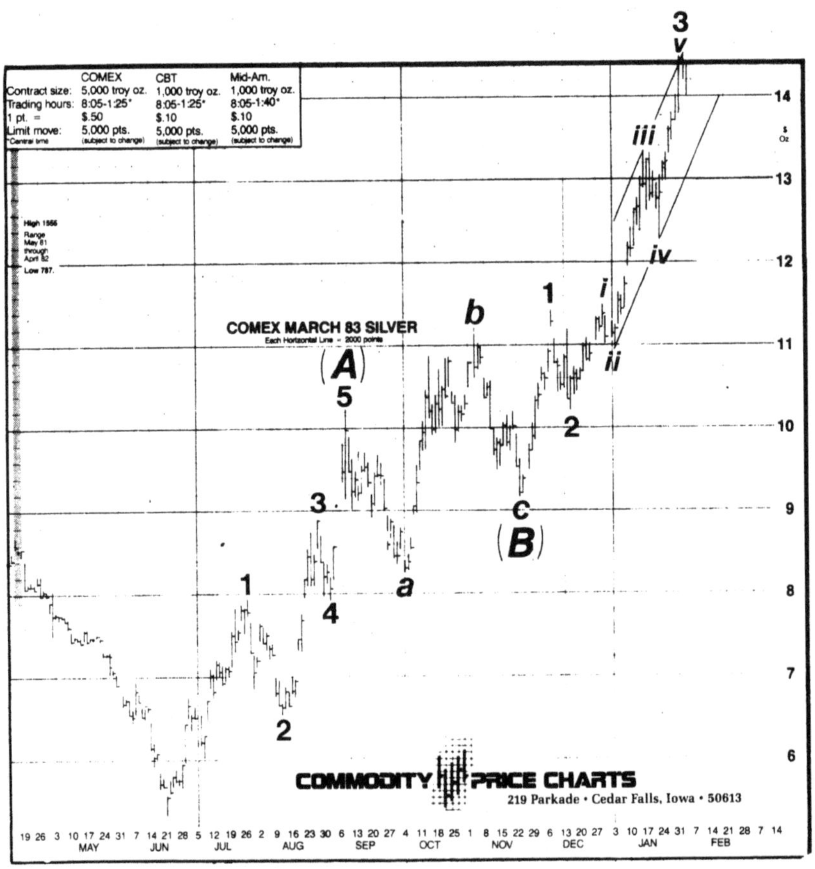

MARCH 7, 1983

Gold

Tactically, there's not much more to say about this market. The January and February issues of *The Elliott Wave Theorist* explained in detail the tremendous technical danger in the gold market and argued forcefully for a major top and a collapse in the price of gold. Since then, it's undergone the biggest two-week percentage drop (20%) since March 1980. If you followed the trading tactics given in January, you sold out all longs above $500 and, if so inclined, went short at $450 on the way down.

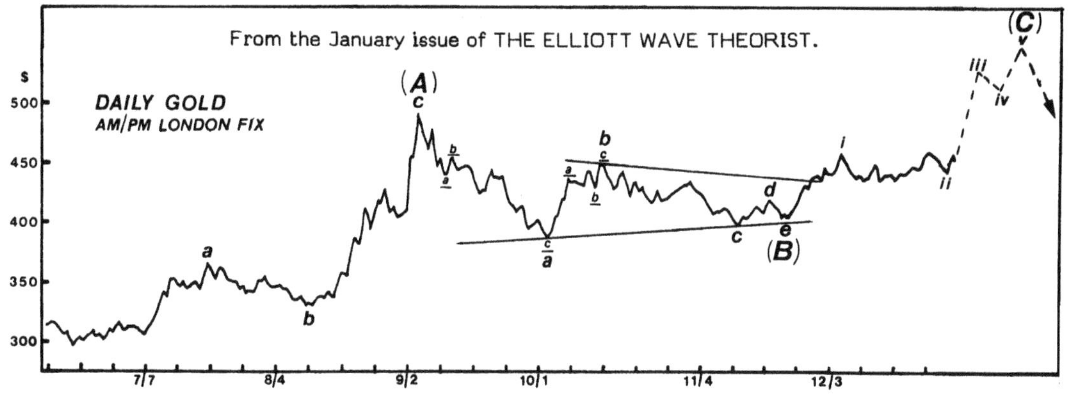

Wave analysis did a good job in recognizing the top, but it did an even more useful job in anticipating it. The first chart is taken from the January issue and illustrates the value of using expectations based on a knowledge of wave patterns. The actual path of gold followed along these lines almost exactly. I don't think it's coincidence that wave (C) was very close to .618 times as long as wave (A), or that wave b of the triangle retraced .618 of wave a.

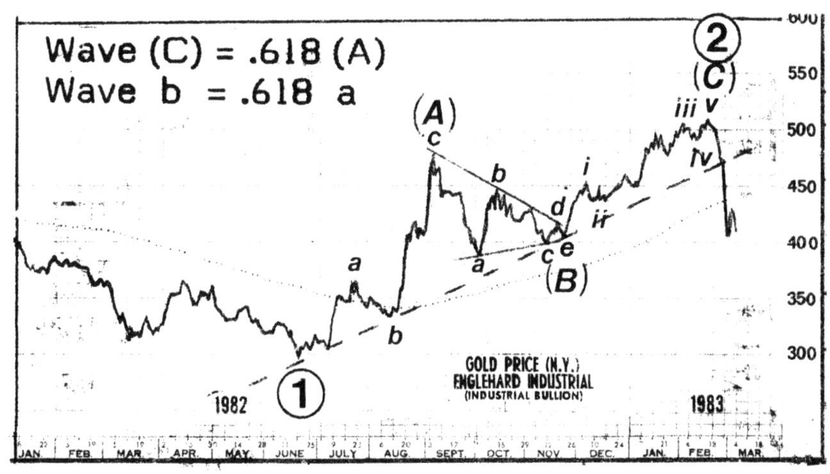

Despite the violence of the panic, most gold-related services are calling the decline a "correction" and urging further purchases for the inevitable march to $4000 an ounce. (Two notable exceptions are Walt Bressert, Box 223958, Dallas TX 75222, and Tony Henfrey, Box 5577, Durban 4000 S. Africa, who have been conservative in their projections, warning of the intermediate top in advance.) Certainly it's not impossible that this decline was a "correction," but usually vertical price drops after prolonged struggling advances are the first step in serious bear markets. This is particularly true when real technical deterioration occurs as the peak is being formed.

Do you remember in the second week of 1977, when the number of bearish advisors in the stock market fell to a record low of 4.5%? The Dow then fell steadily for 14 months without so much as a 5% upward correction. When the bearish contingent increased on the way down, many forgot that the market was still responding to the extremely negative figure recorded at the top, and those too quick on the draw bought prematurely several times. The recent top in gold was accompanied by six straight weeks of 80%-90% bullish sentiment, according to Market Vane (61 S. Lake Av., Pasadena, CA 91101), and I doubt that the long term implications of those figures will be resolved by the recent "correction."

What's even more amazing is that there were many more bullish advisors at last month's peak than at any time since the entire gold rush began 16 years ago (and, by implication, more than at any time in at least 50 years)! This incredible statistic, illustrated below, was reported by James Dines (Box 22, Belvedere, CA 94920) and is probably the single most important technical statistic of the recent top. I find it fascinating that the last time sentiment was exceedingly bullish was in the fall of 1980, at the secondary peak months *after* the major top in gold. In fact, I remember having to answer all sorts of erroneous "Elliott" counts on gold at that time. Evidence of this type supports the argument that the psychology at the February top was typical B-wave (corrective wave) psychology, a conclusion which fits my wave count to a "T".

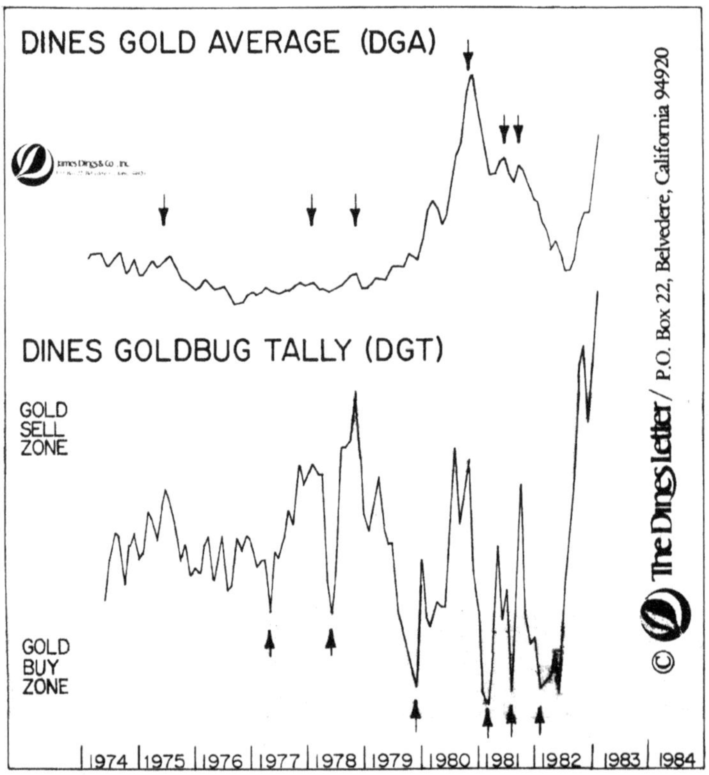

Tactics: Stay out or stay short. If you're short, move your stop to $490 basis London fix. The next short term low should occur in the $387-$405 zone, which marks the low area of the B-wave triangle. Bounces should terminate in the $430-$455 zone. If the 5½-year cycle is still operative in the precious metals, and if it has just peaked, as I expect, then the declining phase to its ultimate target of $105 per ounce should take at least 4½ years.

February 24, 1983

Krugerrand Sales Hit High

- February 14, 1983 -

High on Silver

THE WALL STREET JOURNAL, Thursday, February 10, 1983

Fear of Inflation: Many Economists Predict Price Rises May Accelerate

FEBRUARY 28, 1983

The Bear Market in Silver is Over!

FREE REPORT:
SILVER
Is It headed for $50?

The Gold Bonanza: Just The Beginning

New York--CNS--The price of gold is expected to rise significantly over the next few years, with overall supply falling below growing fabrication demand, an industry official said recently.

18 February 1983

there is still an incredible boo ...ing on in low-priced "penny" gold & silver shares,

February 21, 1983

Mutual Funds' Success:

Most of the Best Performers Hold Yellow Metal

Best Over 15 Years/ Best Over 10 Years

They Worry About Deficits, Recovery

Wednesday, they will mail hundreds of envelopes to a clientele clamoring to invest in International Investors Inc.'s gold fund, spurred by the glittering rise in the price of the precious metal, from $295 an ounce in June to about $500 today. And as

everybody should absolutely have a minimum of 20% of their portfolio in Republic of South Africa gold mines if they want to survive financially." Apparently, a lot of other people feel the same way. Every business day, $1 million pours into Strategic Investments' gold fund from investors whose number now totals 14,000.

February 18, 1983

J. ARON PREDICTS HIGHER GOLD PRICES

"B" waves -- Upward B waves are phonies. They are sucker plays, bull traps, speculators' paradise, orgies of odd-lotter mentality. They are often emotional, rarely technically strong, and virtually always doomed to complete retracement by wave C. If the analyst can easily say to himself, "There is something wrong with this market," chances are it's a B wave.

-- The upward correction of 1930 was a B wave within the 1929-1932 A-B-C zigzag decline. Robert Rhea describes the emotional climate well in his opus The Story of the Averages (1934):

> ...many observers took it to be a bull market signal. I can remember having shorted stocks early in December, 1929 after having completed a satisfactory short position in October. When the slow but steady advance of January and February carried above the previous high , I became panicky and covered at considerable loss. ...I forgot that the rally might normally be expected to retrace possibly 66 per cent or more of the 1929 downswing. Nearly everyone was proclaiming a new bull market. Services were extremely bullish, and the upside volume was running higher than at the peak in 1929.

Excerpted from ELLIOTT WAVE PRINCIPLE by Frost & Prechter

The outlook for gold says that the gold bugs are wrong on two counts: (1) that inflation will heat up again immediately to new high levels, and (2) that the big banks are on the verge of collapse due to the difficulties of the oil-producing nations. The Kondratieff cycle is bigger than either of these arguments and still calls for mild deflation [actually disinflation] with no economic disaster during the plateau period. It appears that the supply-siders will be vindicated, at least for awhile, as a surge in economic production and lower interest rates takes care of inflation and deficit worries. As for the banks, what could be better for them than to have the world's capitalist countries, helped by lower oil prices, producing *real wealth*, some of which has to be deposited in banks? I seriously doubt that the OPEC nations will default on loans to money-center banks. No country wants to lose its financial credibility entirely. And if you were an Arab sitting on a huge stockpile of GOLD and knowing you had to *sell something* to make up for the shortfall in your oil income.... After 1987, we'll worry about the banks, and after 1990, we'll worry about hyperinflation.

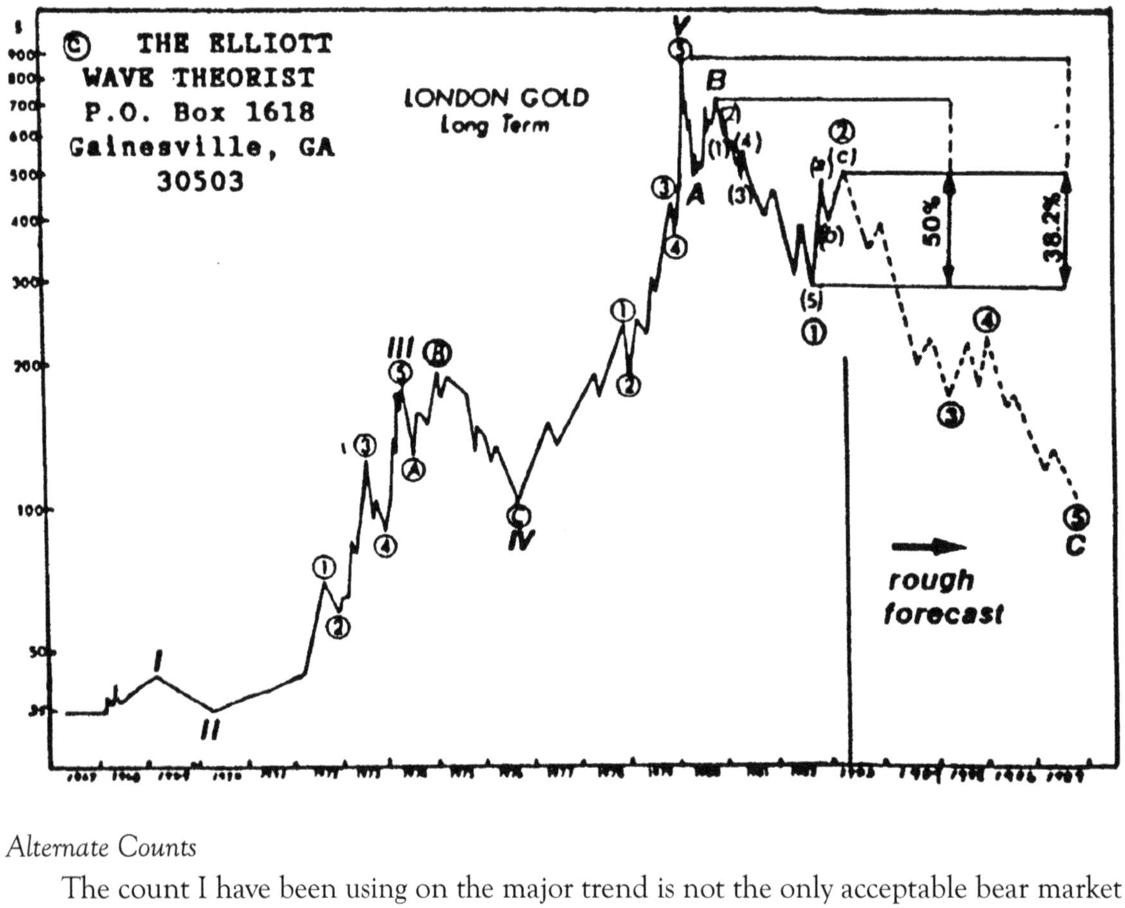

Alternate Counts

The count I have been using on the major trend is not the only acceptable bear market count, but it is supported by the fact that the recent rally, which peaked at $511.50, retraced almost exactly 50% of the decline from $720 to $296.75. This typical relationship among related waves argues that they are waves ① and ② of the same C-wave structure.

Just as compelling is the possibility that a "double zigzag" is forming. The idealized double zigzag shown here is taken from page 37 of *Elliott Wave Principle*. Interestingly, by this count, the X wave in gold has retraced 38.8% of the first A-B-C, a nearly perfect occurrence of the Fibonacci 38.2% retracement that usually occurs in this wave position. Which count is correct is almost irrelevant, since by either count we should expect two more downward thrusts of five waves each, separated by a three-wave rally. Several quick calculations suggest that the double zigzag pattern may bottom higher, in the $167-$179 area. What interests me about these numbers is that all the Fibonacci calculations fall within the span of the previous fourth wave of lesser degree, which had an orthodox peak at $179.50 and a low at $103.50 (see III and IV on the previous chart).

Strictly speaking, one could still make a case that a bull market started at $296.75 last June by counting the rise since then as a "five," completing wave (1) of the new bull market. The current drop would be wave (2). I do not favor this count, but only a drop below $296.75 can confirm its invalidity. Since wave (2) under this count would be expected normally to stop around $387-$405, a drop below that level would make it all the more unlikely.

Silver

Silver wasn't as cooperative as gold in hitting the expected target, but it did complete the necessary wave pattern, as you can see on the accompanying chart. The fifth wave within wave (C) came quickly and topped at just under $15 per ounce.

Tactically, traders had sold out between $14 and $14.50 after a $5 gain and were standing by to repurchase for $17 if silver's fourth wave fell as low as $12.50. It didn't, and even if you mistook the beginning of the recent drop as part of wave four, most

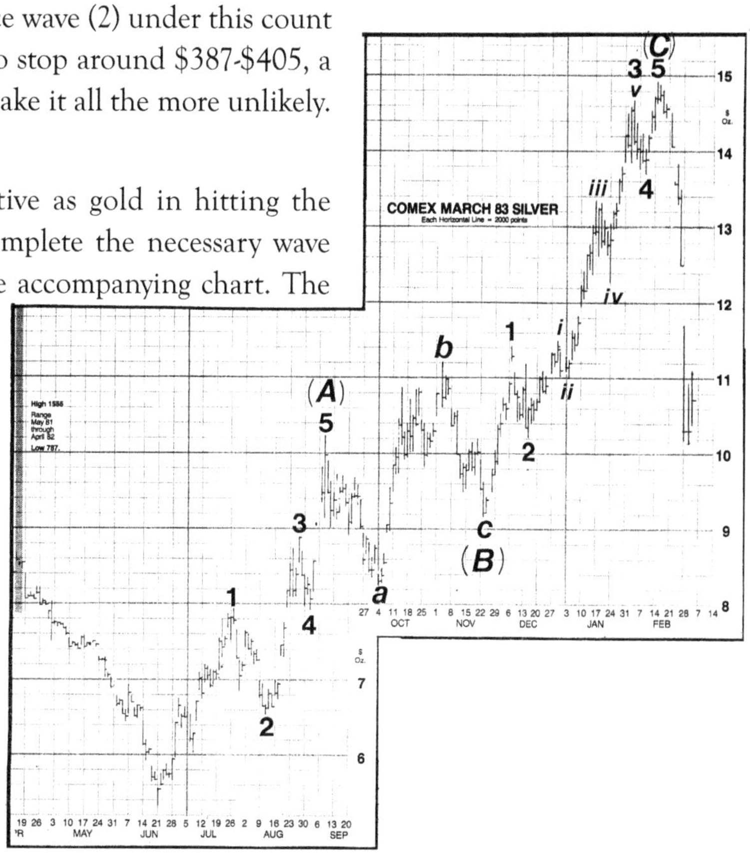

contracts opened through $12.50 and the protective stop at $11.50 simultaneously. Officially, though, I'll count it as the quickest $1 loss in silver trading history.

Silver, then, has completed its full A-B-C bear market rally and is due to follow gold down to below last year's low at $4.90 per ounce. It would take a move above $14 to force me to have second thoughts.

APRIL 11, 1983

I expect gold's current rally to peak well short of this year's highs and lead to a severe selling wave to below $300 by summer.

Gold

As I count it, gold is rallying in wave (2) of a declining 5-wave sequence from the top at $512. Although there are no firm rules for second wave retracements, wave (1)'s drop was so severe that I don't expect more than a .382 retracement, which would be the $448 level basis London fix. The maximum retracement should be $475, which is both a .618 retracement and, by one count, the peak of the previous fourth wave of lesser degree.

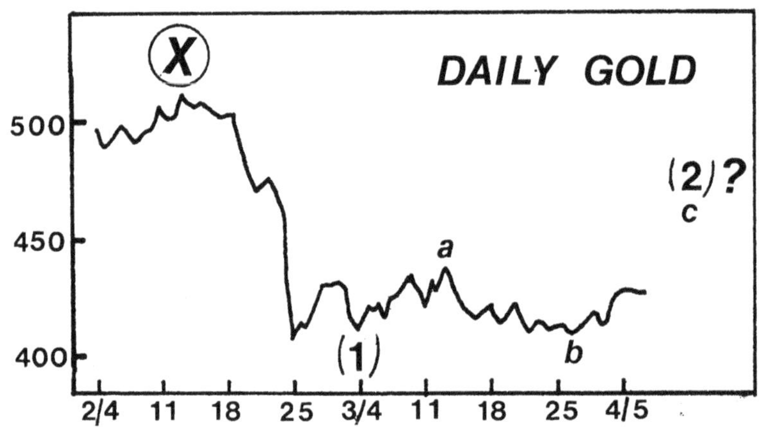

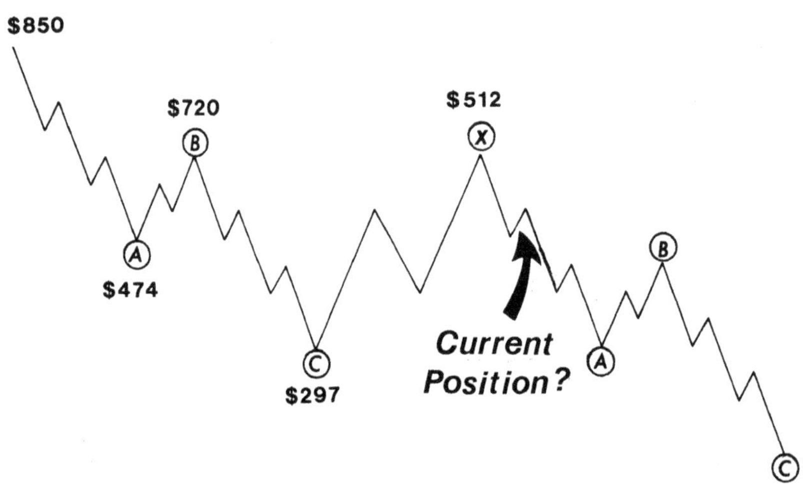

The next move of consequence should be wave (3), and since third waves are never the shortest, it will likely be a serious price decline.

The pattern for ASA from the top is a clear 5-wave decline, lending strong support to the bearish interpretation. ASA puts would be an excellent speculation on the current rally in the stock, which is now re-entering the 65-70 zone.

Long time subscribers might be interested to know that at the final second of panic in the February crash, gold touched exactly $388 in Hong Kong before reversing. The $388 level, you may recall, was the point at which the decline from $850 would have retraced .618 of the rise from $103.50. It was the exact low in August 1981 and could have preceded another super rise in gold had that low held. Since then, $388 also proved important as the support level for the B-wave triangle last October and November. It is often the case that important Fibonacci support or resistance levels have an effect on subsequent price action.

Despite a change in opinion by two top newsletters after the $100 drop, sentiment toward gold has changed very little as a result of the decline. Even so, what is most important, as I have stressed, is not the current state of opinion, which may be characterized as neutral, but the wild extreme of bullish sentiment at the $512 peak. That extreme has long term implications. Besides all the evidence already presented, consider that in the last eight months, at least six special books and reports on the precious metals have been published: *On Gold*, *The Case for*

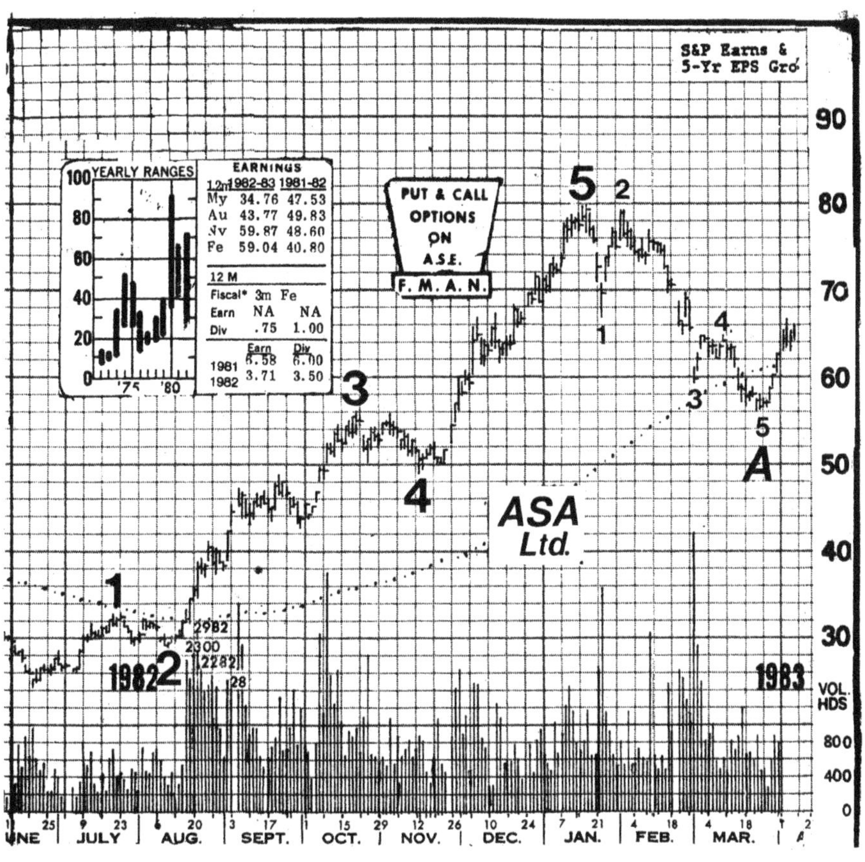

Gold, Silver Profits in the '80's, *Aden Gold Study Part II*, David Hall's *Rare Coin Study* and Horst Balzer's *Forecasting the Price of Gold*. One of the publishers has released a letter saying, "sales during the first three months have exceeded our expectations!" You can make millions selling gold books only if the public has an appetite for them. (Undoubtedly, *Elliott Wave Principle*, which forecasts a 3000 [revised in September 1982 to as high as 4000] Dow, will peak in sales a year after the Supercycle top in stocks!) And here's one for the files: a paper placemat in a Virginia restaurant was sent to me by a reader last February. Gilt-edged and filled with advice on purchasing coins, jewelry, futures and options, its headline boldly reads, "GOLD FEVER!"

Every reader of *The Elliott Wave Theorist* is smart enough to realize that in the end, he must make his own decisions. You should take into account, then, that a large contingent of analysts is violently bullish on gold and disagrees with my opinion strongly. The majority of hard money followers is referring to the drop as a "correction," calling the current price the "last chance to get aboard." The most widely circulated financial newsletter said last week that ASA calls were the best bet on the board, and another highly regarded letter called the idea that gold could fall below $200 an "absurd rumor."

Disagreement is what makes markets, of course, and a move back above $512 would force me to reconsider my opinion. However, regarding the purported "bargain price" that gold is now selling for, I suggest you take a good look at the next chart, courtesy Deliberations (Box 182, Adelaide St. Sta., Toronto, Ont. M5C 2J1). This comparison of weekly prices reveals that relative to the long list of food commodities (wheat, cattle, corn, coffee, soybeans, sugar, cocoa, etc.), gold at $512 was as expensive as it was at $850! Next month, space permitting, I'll show a chart of gold vs. commodities for the last 200 years.

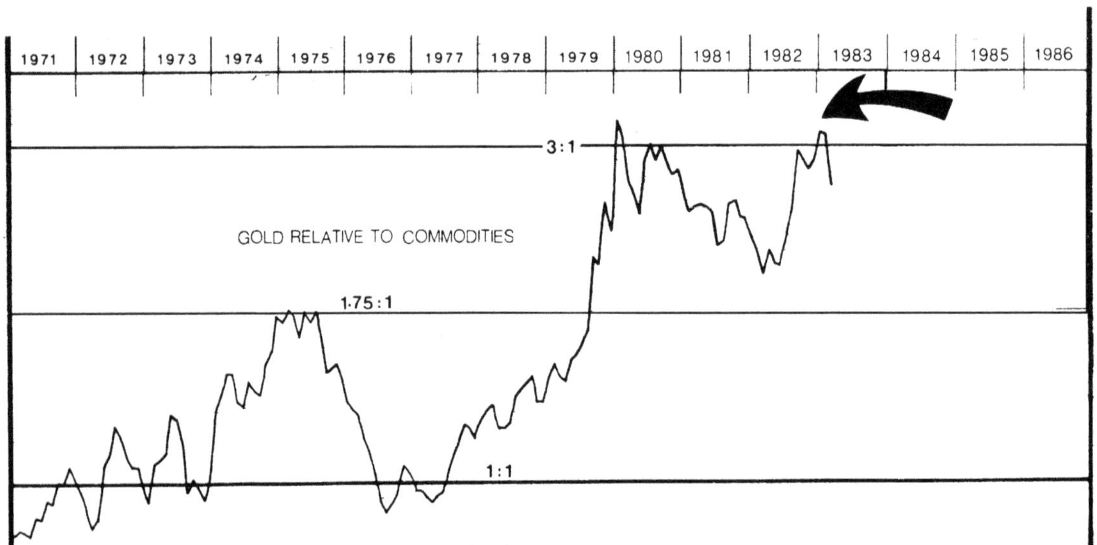

Gold relative to food commodities (in U.S. Dollars)

As I see it, the only thing that can keep gold at such a high premium over commodities is an immediate acceleration in the destruction of the value of the dollar and a resulting panic into real money. While I fully expect these conditions in the late '80s and early '90s, the technical condition of the gold chart says *it won't happen now*. Either way, our strategy was the correct one. Having sold out above $500, we can wait, at no risk, for the market to prove us wrong.

Silver

Silver's count is the same as gold's, rallying in wave (2), with wave (3) down just ahead. Silver's outlook will remain bearish unless it fills the gap at $13, a feat which is now highly unlikely.

MAY 2, 1983

Gold and silver appear to have peaked their wave (2) rallies in April.

Gold

The best wave interpretation still labels the $512 peak as wave Ⓧ in a double zigzag. This count implies that $512 will not be surpassed and that the final low will occur *below* $200 in late 1987-early 1988. That's when the 5½-year cycle in gold is due to bottom. It may also be significant that after a Fibonacci *13* years of advance from 1967, a final bottom in gold in 1987-88 would complete a Fibonacci *8* years of decline, so that the declining phase would last *.618* times as long as the advancing phase. For now, I expect things to unfold in exactly this manner.

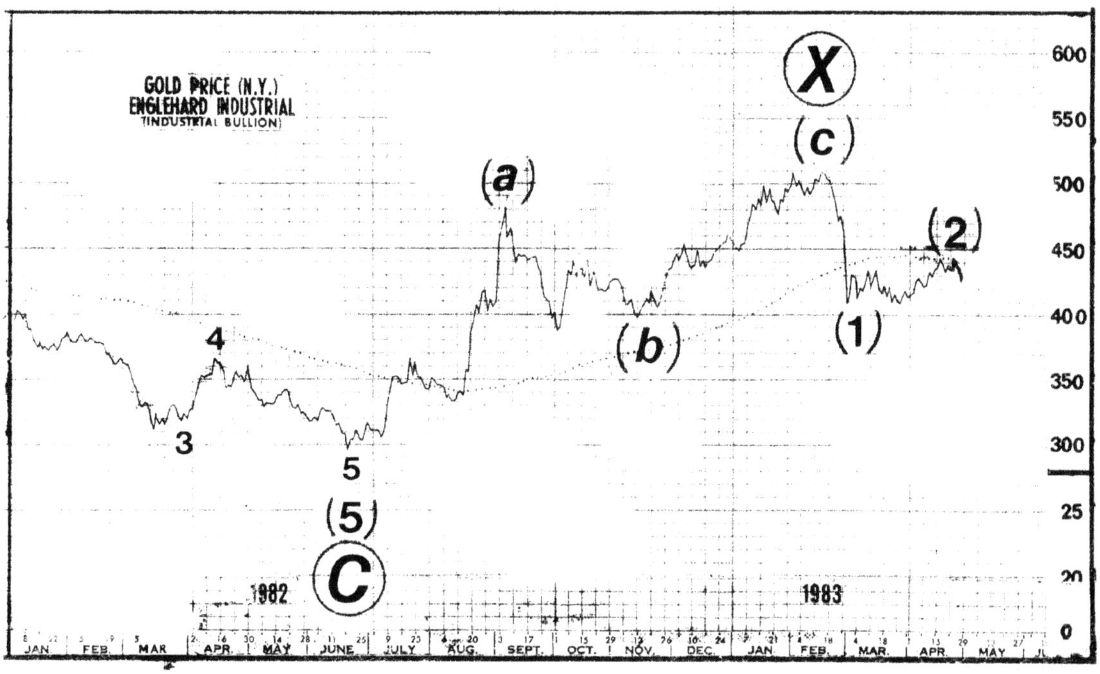

As for the short term, my forecast for a wave (2) peak near $448 basis London fix was hit almost exactly with a peak reading of $443 on April 18. Therefore I'm tentatively labeling that wave as complete and assuming that wave (3) is underway on the downside.

The chart of ASA, featured last month, also appears to have peaked on the upside at 73¾. The daily close chart shows an a-b-c subdivision in the rally, helping confirm that wave B in an A-B-C bear market has been completed. Wave C should carry ASA at least down to the level of the bottom of the previous fourth wave at 49½, if not substantially lower. If you're short, place a stop at 78, then lower the stop to 70 if ASA falls below 60.

Sentiment toward gold hasn't changed, and that is a big weakness in the bulls' argument. On April 11, two of Barron's' regular columns were devoted almost exclusively to gold. First was the options column, headed "November Gold Calls in Demand." Read this vivid description of what exists in place of the *disinterest* that *should* be evident at a bottom:

> Drexel Burnham's Marc Chaikin pointed out the extraordinary action in ASA calls, with out-of-the money Novembers often climbing more than the stock. That's not the way the game is played. In-the-moneys move point for point with the stock, not out-of-the-moneys. However, by Thursday's close, the November 70 (which was four points out-of-the-money) was up 4¼ on a 3⅜ upturn in the stock. On Thursday alone, the November 75, even further out-of-the-money, rose almost as much as the stock (⅜ on a ½ point rise) in heavy volume (772 contracts)—triple the prior *week's* pace. Normally, trading in November options is low at this time of year.
>
> At Friday's close, the stock was off ¼ on the day, but the November 70 was up ¼ and the November 75 gained ⅜ as 734 calls changed hands. The Amex reported it was investigating, but knew of no reason for the surge in prices and volume.

Next was the commodities column, which devoted a page and a half to explaining every conceivable argument for being bullish on gold. Here's an excerpt:

Gold: "Long-Term, We Are All Bullish"

Has Gold Found a Bottom?

> The bullion analysts we chatted with last week to a man were bullish. They tended to stress as reasons a resurgence of inflation and the possibility of a world banking crunch. Technicians pointed to a support level just above $400 and thought gold shortly would break out of its accumulation phase.

Alternate Count

The reason I try to present alternative counts is to protect against shock and confusion if the market goes against expectations. Usually, alternates are outlines of specific courses of action that are less likely but still possible under the rules of the Wave Principle. You should always have such possibilities in the back of your mind when holding a speculative position of any kind. It helps you decide where to place stops and when to change course.

I still see no better count than the "double zigzag," which was illustrated in the last two issues of *The Elliott Wave Theorist*. However, it is certainly possible that wave Ⓧ, the rally that serves to separate the two phases of bear market, has not yet ended, and that only wave (a) of Ⓧ was completed at $512. Wave (b) would be underway now, and wave (c) would carry back to the level of the September 1981 high at $720 before the second long bear phase begins.

The only Elliott guideline supporting this conclusion is that "X" waves often reach the same level as the preceding "B" wave. An additional argument is that the 5½ year cycle should exert a longer upside influence than a mere 8 months.

The reasons why I'm currently betting *against* this interpretation are as follows:

1) A move back to $720 would be a huge 77% retracement of the first A-B-C zigzag pattern, an unlikely event.

2) As illustrated in the March letter, the rally from $296.75 to $512 completed a beautiful conjunction of percentage retracements: *38.2%* of the decline from $850 and *50%* of the decline from $720.

3) An orgy of bullishness existed at the $512 peak, as documented in the February and March letters. That extreme sentiment would be more characteristic of the *end* of wave X than of the halfway point.

Strategy

Tactically, there is little to worry about. We sold out above $500 and can easily get back in at that price if forced to do so. As for the short term, gold should fall *at least to $370*, so buying is still not warranted at these levels. Since wave (3) portends a strong decline, traders who sold short at $450 on the way down or at the recent wave (2) peak should hold short with a stop at $450 basis London fix. A break substantially below $370 would wipe out the alternate count as a possibility.

Is Gold Cheap?

Last month I showed gold's value in relationship to food commodities in a chart going back to 1970. One might have responded that the current value is only *apparently* high because decades of price controls made gold artificially cheap in 1970. In answer to that is this chart (courtesy of AIER, Great Barrington, MA 01230) showing that *gold in the 1980s*, using annual average prices, *is more expensive than it has been for the last 200 years!*

This high valuation doesn't *necessitate* a decline, since a continued headlong rush toward destruction of the world's paper currencies would be a sound reason for the high value placed on gold by the marketplace. The technical picture, however, argues that we will be enjoying a five-year respite from paper money inflation. If anything, I expect that the gold bulls have gotten caught by a news "hook" in their reliance on increasing money supply figures as a guarantee of higher gold prices. As a well-reasoned article in the 4/27 issue of the WSJ argued, "This Money Bulge Isn't Inflationary," citing similar situations in other countries whose currency was increasing in value, as the US$ is.

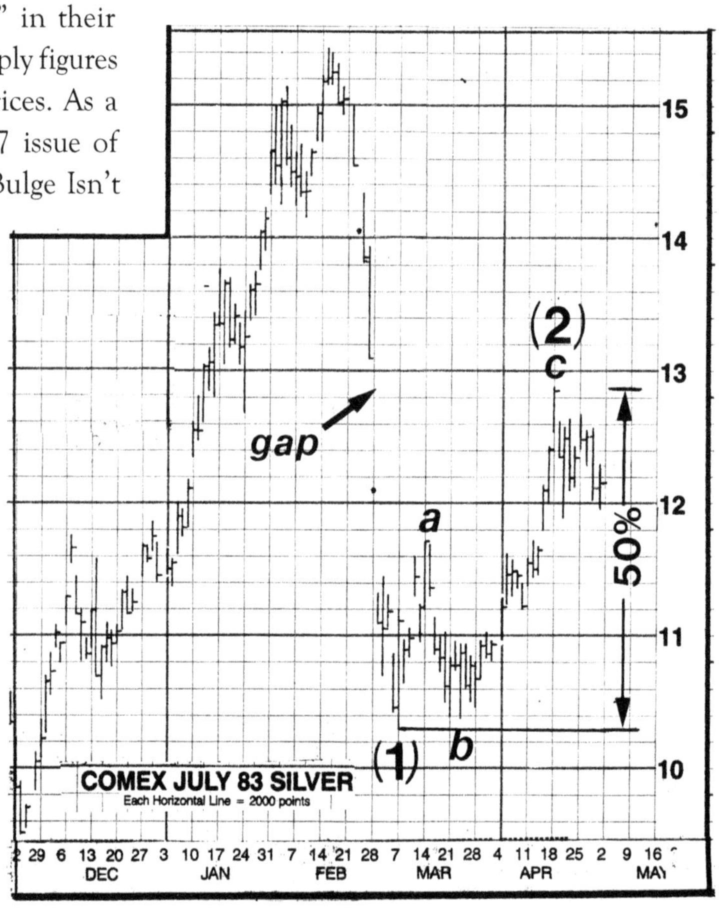

Silver

Silver shows the same count as gold, and appears to have completed its wave (2) countertrend rally in a perfect 50% retracement of wave (1). As I said last month, I would be quite surprised if the gap at $13 were closed, so that level would be a good place for a stop if you're playing the short side.

MAY 31, 1983

Fibonacci resistance in gold has held firm at $448. Gold is the least attractive investment vehicle and has the greatest downside risk. It should be trading below $200 per ounce in 1987.

Gold

All year, gold has been right on track with expectations, from the top in February at just over $500/oz. to the wave (1) low near $400 to the wave (2) peak, which was expected near $448. For the past six weeks, gold has paid a lot of respect to that 38.2% Fibonacci retracement target. Ever since bullion climbed above $440 in mid-April, it's hit a brick wall, with the highest London fix so far at $443.75 on May 10. Fibonacci targets usually show up as important support or resistance even if they are subsequently penetrated, however, so it's too early to say that the peak on the rebound has been confirmed. Remember that if $450 is exceeded, the next resistance level is $475, which is a .618 retracement of the February/March decline. If gold breaks down from here, I'll update the very long term picture in next month's issue.

I see no reason to change tactics. Stay out of the gold market; it's the least attractive of the major markets from a technical standpoint, and has the most downside potential, with prices under $200 likely before the next major bull market begins in 1987. If I'm wrong and bullion climbs back above $500, we'll get back in at no net loss and start speculating, along with everybody else, about the emerging inflationary spiral. Traders who are short should keep the stop at $450 basis London fix. If you're stopped out, sell short again at $472 with a stop at $480. We're still short ASA and long the puts, with no profit as yet to show for our efforts. Our stop at 78 remains intact.

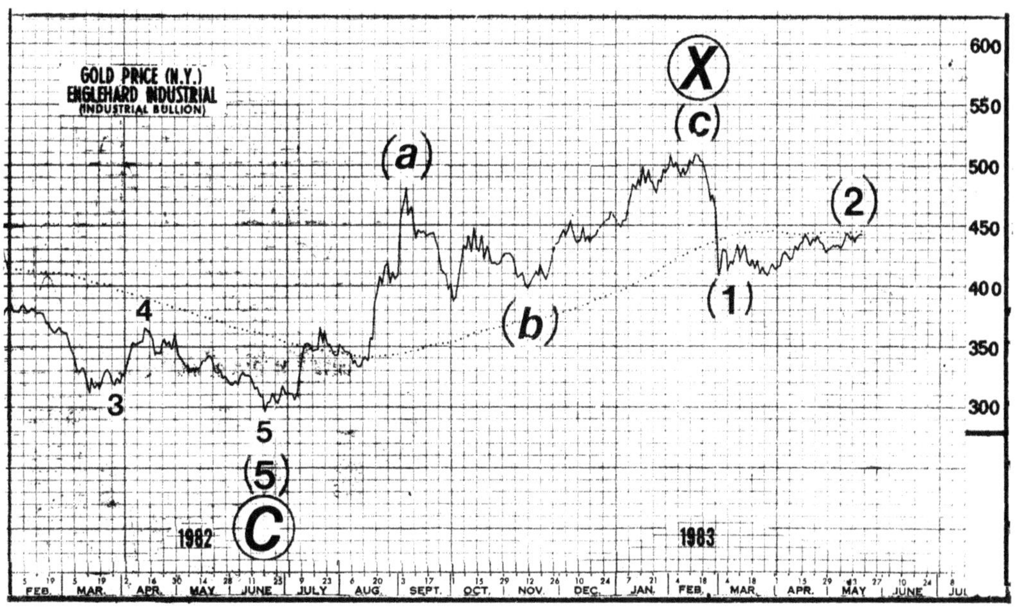

As I've documented ever since January, sentiment toward gold remains extremely bullish, and such conviction is not to be expected at bottoms. When gold first climbed above $440 in April, the bullish consensus as reported by Market Vane (61 S. Lake Av., Pasadena, CA 91101) had climbed to a moderate 60%. Now, with *no net progress* in the price of gold, the bullish consensus has hovered over 70% for six straight weeks, helped along by continual bullish articles on gold in the financial media.

Value: Gold vs. the Stock Market

The consensus is rarely bullish on *anything* that truly offers value. The charts on the next page show that the *stock market* offers value. But *the gold market is another story entirely.* The chart below, created by Richard Russell (Dow Theory Letters, Box 1759, La Jolla, CA 92038) presents the value picture better than anything I've seen to date. This is the kind of historical perspective that can help you make sound investment decisions. Anyone involved with the Wave Principle finds himself geared to looking at the present with a long historical perspective, since the big picture is often the real message. That's why charts like this interest me.

As Russell points out, the Dow/Gold ratio is currently near the low levels attained in the Great Depression! In other words, gold is *expensive* relative to stocks. While the Dow "bought"

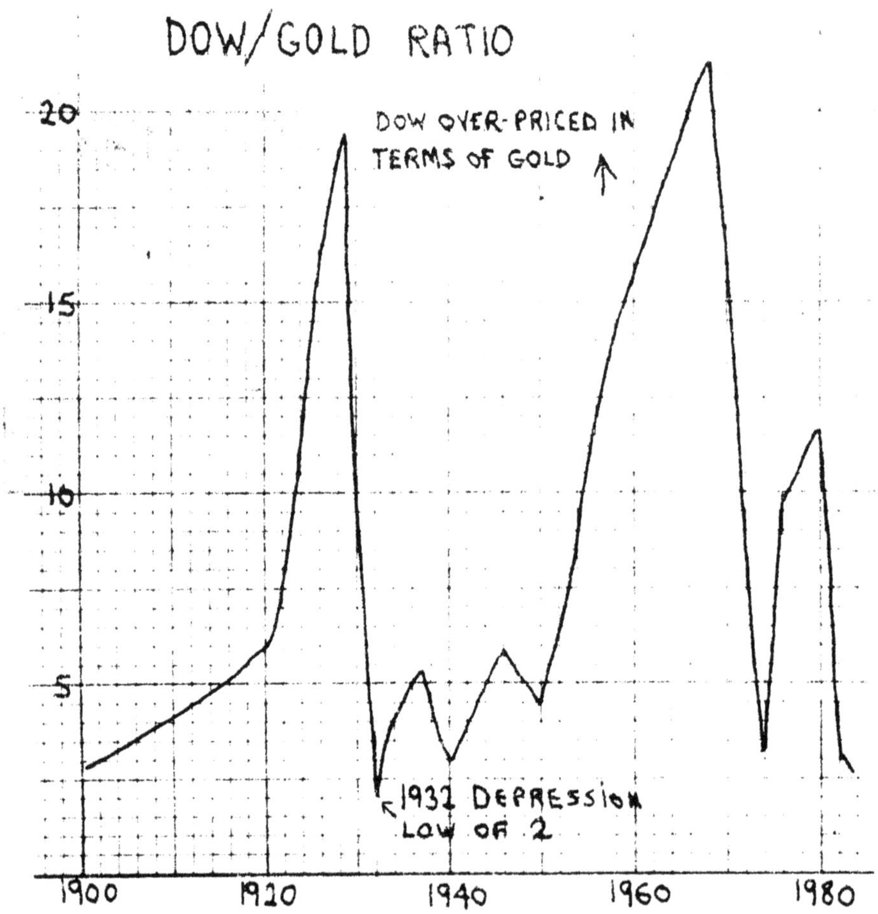

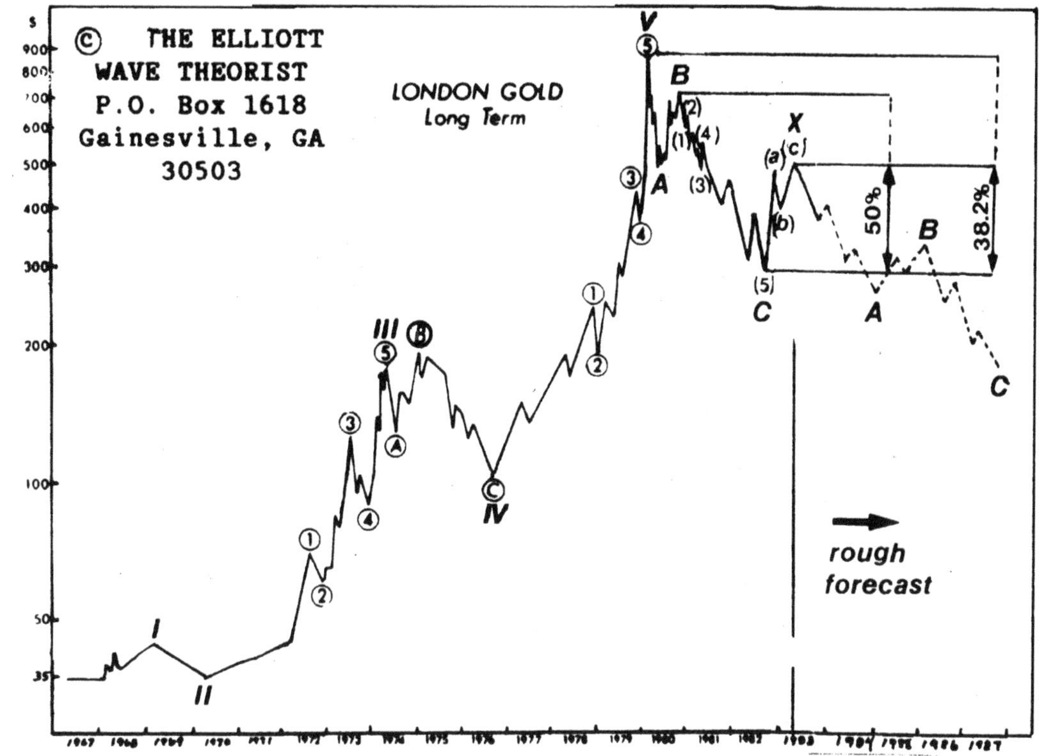
© THE ELLIOTT
WAVE THEORIST
P.O. Box 1618
Gainesville, GA
30503
LONDON GOLD
Long Term
rough
forecast
50%
38.2%

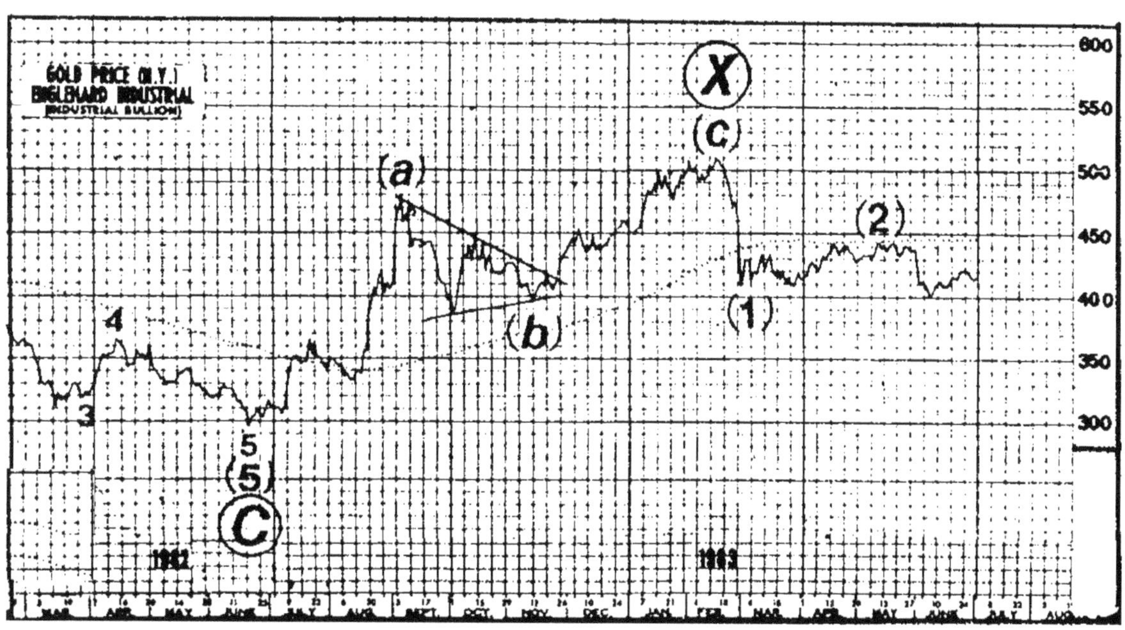
(a)
(b)
(c)
X
(1)
(2)
(5)
C

as many as 23 ounces of gold in 1968, today it buys less than 3! The reason is that the public has put a *high* premium on an asset that reflects *fear* of the future and a *low* valuation on one that reflects *confidence* in the future. The Elliott wave outlook for the stock market argues unequivocally that confidence will return, and in fact, that an exuberant over-confidence will characterize the mass psychological environment four years from now. As long as that forecast appears to be on target, there is no reason to put your money into gold.

Silver

I didn't expect silver to exceed $13, but the May rally brought the July contract to an intraday peak of $13.88 and the London closing price to $13.36. Near term, it appears that silver has traced out a full five waves from late March, making a drop back to the $12-12.50 level basis the July contract very likely. That is the area of the previous second wave of lesser degree, a normal Elliott target when the first wave is extended. It still counts acceptably as an a-b-c bear market rally, but the orderly shape and impressive extent of the rally could mean that its bull market remains intact.

At this point, I can't make a high-probability forecast for silver. I *can* say that if $12 is broken on the downside by a substantial margin, the bear market case will improve tremendously. On the other hand, as I said in March, "it would take a move above $14 to force me to have second thoughts" about the resumption of the major bear market in silver. A rise above $14 will argue that the bull market is still alive and on its way to my original upside target of $17.

Tactically, I did *not* recommend shorting silver, either in the letter or on the hotline, because of its relative volatility and the industrial component in its price. If the economy is to pick up strongly, as the stock market has indicated, then silver has reason to hold up better than gold because of its industrial utility. During the precious metals rally from the 1982 lows, recall that I preferred being long silver rather than gold. As it turned out, silver more than tripled, providing four times the return of gold, which gained only 73%. During the current bear phase, it will be safer to trade gold from the short side than silver, for the same reasons.

JULY 11, 1983

Although gold has potential to $448, it remains in a major bear market and could enter a renewed collapse at any time.

Gold

The Fibonacci resistance level of $448 proved to be a ceiling for gold in April and May. In fact, the day the last issue was mailed, gold began a collapse that took it down 10% in 6 trading days. At that point, the wave (2) label sitting on the chart above the $443.75 level looked pretty good. On Thursday, a rumor that Brazil would default on loans caused a sharp one-day rally back to the $420s. A *sharp* rally on *news* in a *bear market* is not a reason to change one's opinion, but let's look at all sides of the gold picture and see what the technical position is.

The drop from $512 to $400 was virtually assured whether gold was in a bear or a bull market, and we were able to avoid that decline successfully. The long term chart illustrates what I consider the highest-probability outcome for gold over the next four to five years. As with the stock market, however, there currently are acceptable alternate counts.

The reason gold is finding support at $400 is that the apex of the preceding triangle is at that level. Triangle apexes typically provide support, partly because they often occur as fourth waves, which generally provide support for the next correction of one greater degree. Take a look at the daily chart of gold, which shows my interpretation of the June-February advance as an (a)-(b)-(c) rally in a bear market. The (b) wave is a symmetrical triangle (see text, p. 43) and defines the support level at $400. If this count is the correct one, gold is merely tracing out a series of 1's and 2's, and is about ready to collapse in a "third of a third." Now step back and take a look at the *vertical* nature of the *declines* on the daily chart of gold, and compare it to the struggling, *flat* shape of the *rallies*. This action is typical of persistent declines and is another technical negative.

Alternate Count

Due to the uncertainties in the daily wave count, it is possible to count gold as having completed a *five*-wave rally in the June-February period. A five-wave rally, of course, would guarantee an *a-b-c* correction followed by *new highs*. At this moment, all gold has completed from the $512 peak is a decline with two downward waves, a drop that can be interpreted as a completed a-b-c pattern. Moreover, the drop ended right on triangle support *and* at a 50% retracement of the June-February rally, both typical of a completed correction. *The $400 level, then, is the last stand for the gold bulls.*

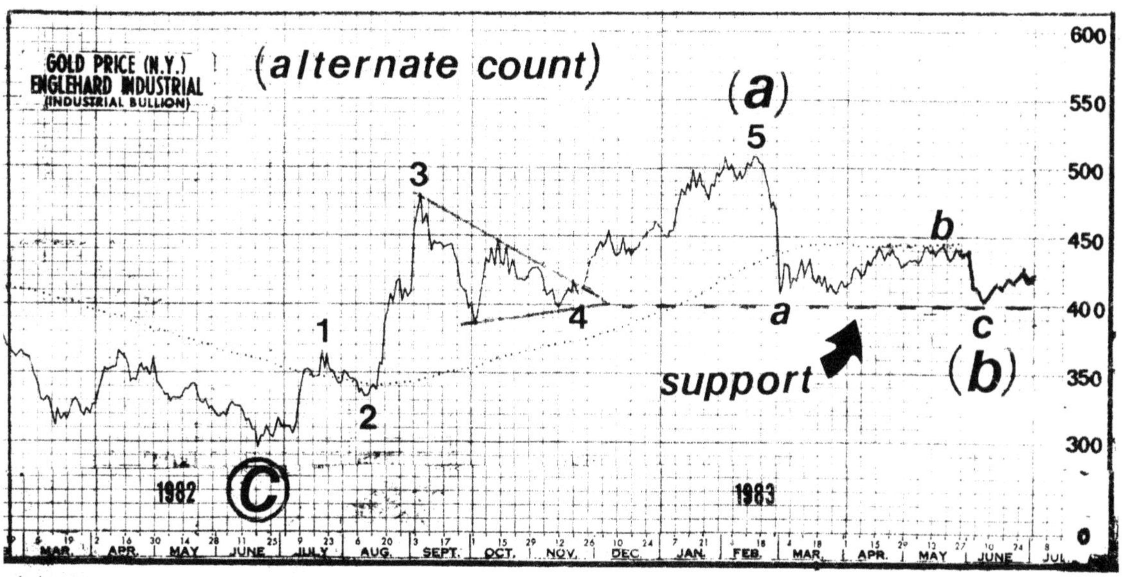

As discussed in the May issue, even if gold were to climb to new 1983 highs, the rally would probably best be interpreted as part of the Ⓧ wave that would separate two phases of bear market. Currently the Ⓧ label is at the February peak, but Elliott rules do not *guarantee* that it's over, since corrective-wave rallies can take many shapes. Still, it pays to go with the most probable interpretation based on typical market patterns.

Sentiment

Selling gold in February was made easier by the overwhelming bullish psychology at the top. The figures reported by Market Vane and by James Dines, as well as the wild outpouring of newspaper ads urging purchase of gold, constituted additional strong evidence that a top was at hand. At this point, it's not so easy. Market Vane's (61 S. Lake Av., Pasadena, CA) latest tally showed only 31% bulls among advisors. In other words, after a 20% drop, gold watchers are quite a bit more bearish than they were five months ago.

However, a crucial point, which I have stressed for months, is that the extreme nature of the bullish readings in January and February (6 straight weeks of over 80% bulls) has *major-trend implications*. A 30% reading will not be enough to offset the optimism in evidence at the top. So, the recent low number might provide a bounce, but not much more. And with bullish rumors flying, sentiment could revert to optimism quickly.

Just as important is the attitude of the press to the precious metals. If gold were *really* heading to $6000 by 1986, it is unlikely that the newswriters would be so eager to recognize a great bargain. The headlines on this page all appeared within the last two months. You know what kind of headlines have prevailed in the past when gold was truly at a bottom.

Tactics

As with stocks, the Wave Principle helps define the parameters of the situation, so our tactics are clear. The trading strategy we're using still seems best. Avoid gold as an investment. If you're short, keep a stop at $450 basis London fix, which is the breakeven point on our short sale. If you have already decided to buy for whatever reasons, keep in mind that a break of $400 would strongly suggest a fall to $300 within weeks. In other words, $395 is a sensible stop point for longs. Stay short ASA, which is now in its C wave down. Lower the stop to 74.

Silver

Here is last month's observation:

> Near term, it appears that silver has traced out a full five waves from late March, making a drop back to the $12-12.50 level basis the July contract very likely.

That day's opening marked top tick in the silver rally, and prices fell back as far as $11.10 before rebounding. I also commented, "If $12 is broken on the downside by a substantial margin, the bear market case will improve tremendously." It did, and it has.

Silver can still be counted in exactly the same way as gold from its peak price in February, that is, a series of 1's and 2's that point to dramatically lower prices. Often if the count for silver is unmistakable, an uncertain gold count can be resolved in favor of the one that parallels the one for silver. In this case, we have no such luck. The daily chart can be counted acceptably as a symmetrical triangle from February, which would portend a short sharp rally to new highs. Again, while a specific forecast would have a low reliability, the parameters are clear. *Silver should be viewed as a negative chart pattern unless it breaks the upper triangle boundary line.* If it does, the move would continue to about the $16-$17 level, since the post-triangle "thrust" would be expected to cover the same distance as the widest part of the triangle (see text, p. 44), which is $4.50-$5.50.

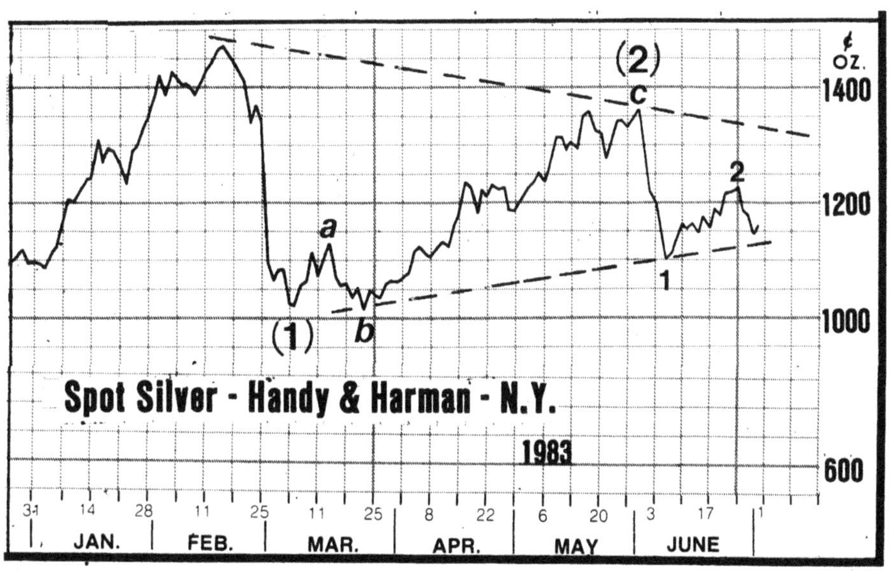

AUGUST 9, 1983

Gold remains in a major bear market. The preferred count points lower, but another rally back above $500 is still possible unless gold declines below $378.

Gold

Uncertainty is mounting, and three interpretations under the Wave Principle are valid at this time. The question of which is in force may be answered in days. Generally speaking, however, technical negatives still outweigh the positives. Here's a list:

1) Bearish Chart Activity:

– Rallies are very difficult, if not impossible, to count as "fives," indicating that the intermediate term trend, at least up until today, is still neutral or down.

– Rallies continue to trace out labored upward patterns, while declines have been sharp. Bear markets often progress in this manner.

2) Bearish Sentiment Indications

– The recent minor rally in gold has resulted in a rise in bullish advisory sentiment. Market Vane (61 S. Lake, Pasadena CA) tabulated only 30% "bulls" for one short week at the early July low. Sentiment jumped the next week to above 60% and has held there for three weeks.

– This summer, an offshore conference billed as the "first ever held exclusively on the precious metals" set an *all-time attendance record*, and the sponsor had to turn away "dozens of late registrants" due to lack of space. Such a high level of investor interest is typical of the early stages of a bear market, not the early stages of a bull market.

– There are more ads for precious metals investments on Financial News Network every day than there are for stock market services. The ads invariably refer to forecasts of $3000-$6000 gold by 1986.

3) Bearish Momentum Indications

– Despite "buy" recommendations on ASA by two of the most widely circulated newsletters in the U.S., the stock has still made no net progress for several weeks. The stop at 74 on our short sale is still intact.

– *For the first time since last year's bottom*, PIGS (the Prechter Index of Gold Stocks) has failed to confirm a minor new high in bullion. The price of gold in July moved above

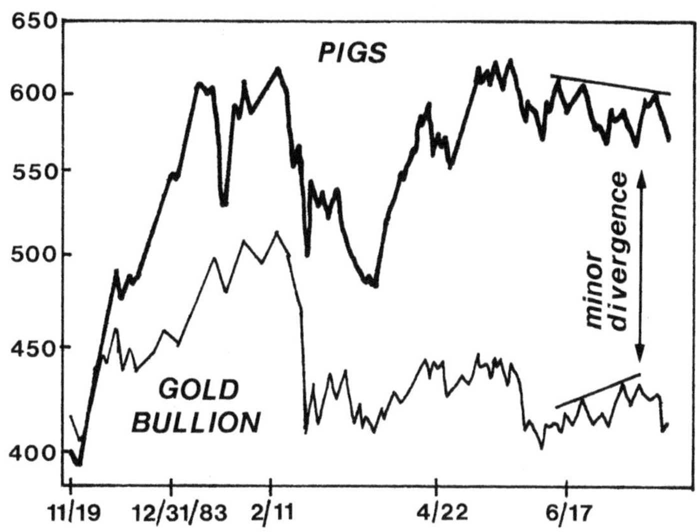

its June peak, but the index did not. This is only a minor divergence, but since it's the first, it's worth mentioning.

Preferred Count (Probability: 60%)

The preferred wave count is still as shown: a series of 1's and 2's of lesser degree, suggesting a severe drop just ahead. For reasons outlined below, a significant break of $378 would lend strong support to this interpretation.

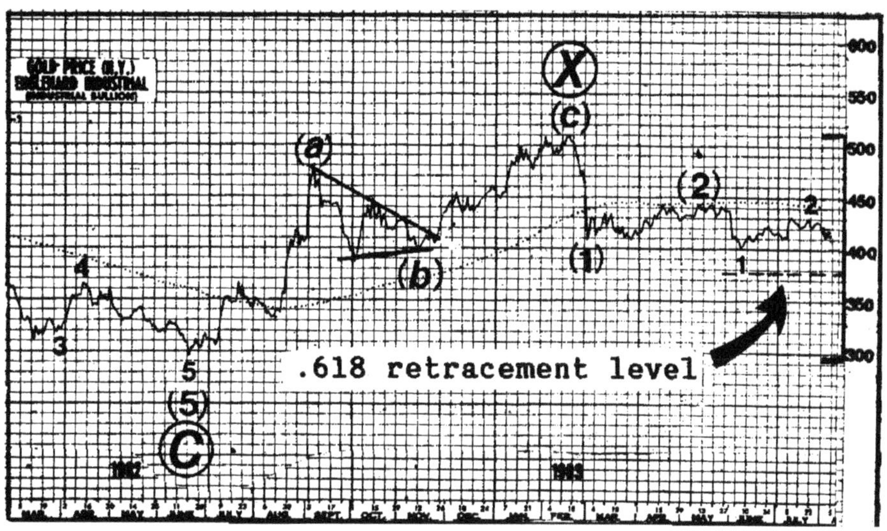

Alternate Count (Probability: 20%)

I began discussing an alternate count last month as a result of gold's continued sideways activity. That alternate is still alive, particularly since I've learned to become suspicious when

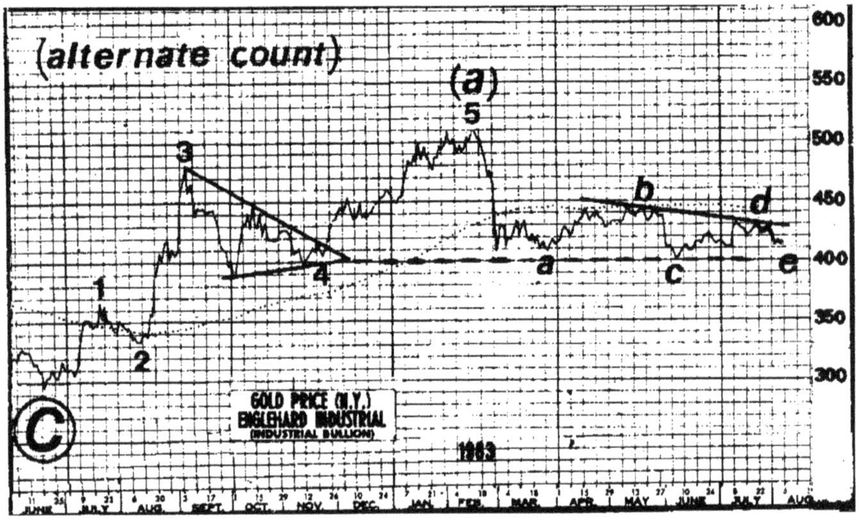

several 1's and 2's develop in a preferred count. Quite often when waves play out that far, the formation turns out to be a triangle. A "descending triangle" interpretation now carries an even greater validity than it did last month, mainly because the June-July rally retraced more than 61.8% of the previous decline. Retracements of that magnitude are common in triangles, but uncommon in second waves within extended third waves.

A triangle pattern can resolve in either direction (see text, p.43), unless its beginning can be pinpointed with certainty. Unfortunately in the case of gold, certainty isn't possible. The new low in late March allows the first declining wave to be counted as an a-b-c and thus as the first wave within a triangle. The "alternate count" chart shows the *most bullish* short term wave interpretation for gold. Without going into great detail, suffice it to say that an immediate move above $445 would confirm this count and project to $500+, with ultimate potential as high as $639, which marks a .618 retracement of the entire $850-$296.75 drop. This possibility is why I have a stop on our short position at $450. The "seasonal" pattern favors rising gold prices through the rest of the year, although everyone seems to know this fact. I've also noticed that Dennis Sanders (Box 3961, Davenport, IA 52808) has recently been projecting $650 gold by year-end, and his cycle work is about the best around. Meanwhile, the Wave Principle has yet to confirm a "straight-down" resolution to the pattern and is leaving its options open.

One For the Road (Probability: 20%)

Another acceptable interpretation would place an "a" at the early March low and begin a descending triangle pattern from there, which will count as wave "b". Wave "c" would then begin almost immediately and carry bullion down approximately the length of the widest part of the triangle, which is $40. From a peak at say, $418, that would bring the price down to $378, which also happens to mark a .618 retracement of the entire rise from $296.75 to $511.50. A drop that halted at that level could still lead to another large intermediate term rally within an ongoing wave Ⓧ. (Such a rally would also bring in the possibility of a huge Supercycle triangle from the $850 top, but let's take it one step at a time!)

Despite this long discussion, I have previously given all the reasons why the $511.50 top was a perfect one, so as yet I have no reason to be *expecting* much in the way of a rally. Developments over the next four weeks (if not the next four days) will probably clear up the wave picture. With regard to strategy, I would cover half the short sales at $379, just because it's a sensible place to take a profit.

Silver

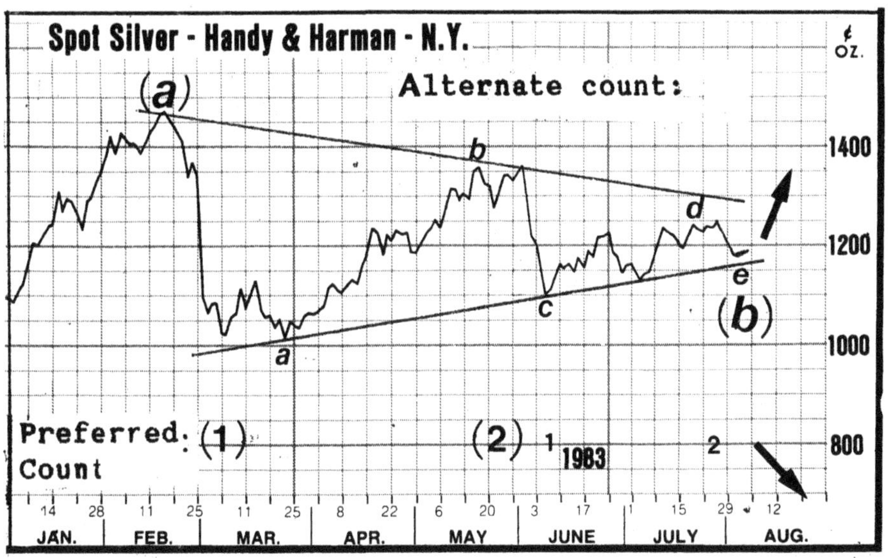

Silver is in basically the same position now as it was at last month's writing. Without reprinting word for word the analysis, I'll just repeat the conclusion: "*Silver should be viewed as a negative chart pattern unless it breaks the upper triangle boundary line.* If it does, the move would continue to about the $16-$17 level," based on the guideline of measuring post-triangle thrust. The accompanying chart shows the bullish alternate count, since the preferred count was illustrated in last month's issue. A break below $11 (spot) would project silver to $8.50 based on the same type of measurement. I prefer to bet on the downside unless the upper boundary line is taken out.

SEPTEMBER 6, 1983

In gold, the balance of evidence favors an immediate drop through the $400 "support" level.

Gold

On Friday (September 2), gold was virtually unchanged in price from the day last month's letter was written. In terms of general technical input, however, *gold looks even more bearish now than it did four weeks ago.*

While there has been an additional momentum negative in that the small August rally occurred on decreasing volume, the most condemning technical input during the past four weeks is from the investor sentiment area. Here's what's happened:

1) The debt crisis in Brazil reached the point that the government delayed payment of $1.5 billion in interest due foreign governments.

2) Several reports on the money supply were higher than expected.

3) Milton Friedman wrote an article for The Wall Street Journal making the case for a dramatic increase in price inflation next year.

Firms Mining Base Metals Turn to Gold

By Kevin Quinn
Staff Reporter of The Wall Street Journal

The big copper, lead, zinc and nickel miners are becoming gold bugs.

"The only projects being started are gold projects," says Richard Brown, exploration vice president at Asarco Inc., a big producer of base metals. "Everyone's hustling to get their fair share."

• Newmont Mining Corp., a copper concern, lists precious metals as its No. 1 exploration target. "They're darn profitable, and they're growing in importance to us," says Frank Ryan, a vice president. Newmont expects to increase gold production 60% within two years by developing a Nevada property.

• Inco Ltd., the world's largest nickel producer, recently announced plans for its first gold mine in Canada and may develop a Brazilian gold property with the Kennecott copper-mining unit of Standard Oil Co. (Ohio).

• Hanna Mining Co., a large iron-ore producer, has three promising gold prospects. It doesn't have a single base-metals exploration project this year.

• Phelps Dodge Corp., a major copper company, set up a "small mines" division in 1981 that last year examined nearly 200 prospects, mostly gold and silver properties.

"I don't know why gold is $400 an ounce," says Mr. Brown, the exploration vice president at Asarco. "But I know that it is and that it has stayed there for a couple of years. In this business, that's a sign of stability."

"The advent of $400 gold has opened a new window and placed a lot of deposits that weren't economic at $250 into economic range," Mr. Brown says.

4) Two U.S. marines were killed in Beirut, and the U.S. has ordered 2,000 more Marines to Lebanon.

5) The U.S.S.R. shot down a Korean Airlines jetliner carrying 269 civilians including a U.S. Congressman, in the first such action since the Hitler regime.

As a result of all these incidents, bullish sentiment toward gold (as reported by Market Vane, 61 S. Lake Av., Pasadena, CA 91101) has risen every week for *ten straight weeks*. Yet in the face of dramatic news and increased bullishness, *gold has gone nowhere*. In a bull market setting, it would have risen at least $100 an ounce by now, yet it hasn't budged. Not only is the stock market ignoring the disastrous news events, but gold appears to be doing so as well.

Meanwhile, the resurgence of bullish articles on gold in the media (see July 11 issue) is continuing unabated. "Stable Gold Prices Signal Time to Invest" was the headline on the front page of USA Today's "Money" section on August 11. The chairman of Jewelers of America described the trade show in New York as "one of the biggest buying shows on record. Jewelers don't think the price is going any lower, so they took out their pencils and bought." The jewelers aren't alone. In July, a multimillion dollar gold fund created in Canada was sold out in an unprecedented two weeks. Remember the technology-stock fund created by a major brokerage firm last spring at the fifth-wave peak? It was reportedly sold out in two days, and technology stocks have gone down ever since. *Extreme enthusiasm for any investment is an indication that the best has already been seen.*

On August 15, The Wall Street Journal came out with the most fascinating article to date in terms of revealing sentiment toward the price of gold. This article reveals a *technical* negative in that gold is being recognized as expensive (otherwise, why gear up to mine more of it?). But it also reveals a developing *fundamental* negative since the more the mines gear up to produce gold, the more downside pressure will be exerted on its price. The expectation for stable or higher gold prices revealed by every measure of mass psychology has gone on so long that another crash in the gold price probably lies directly ahead.

Wave Counts and Implications

The two wave counts that now appear most likely for gold are shown in the accompanying charts. (To reference the "bullish" count, see the August letter.) The preferred count shows nothing but lower prices ahead. The alternate count shown here was entitled "One for the Road" in last month's issue. The August rally has suddenly given this count a reasonably high probability. If gold has just completed a contracting triangle from early March, then several

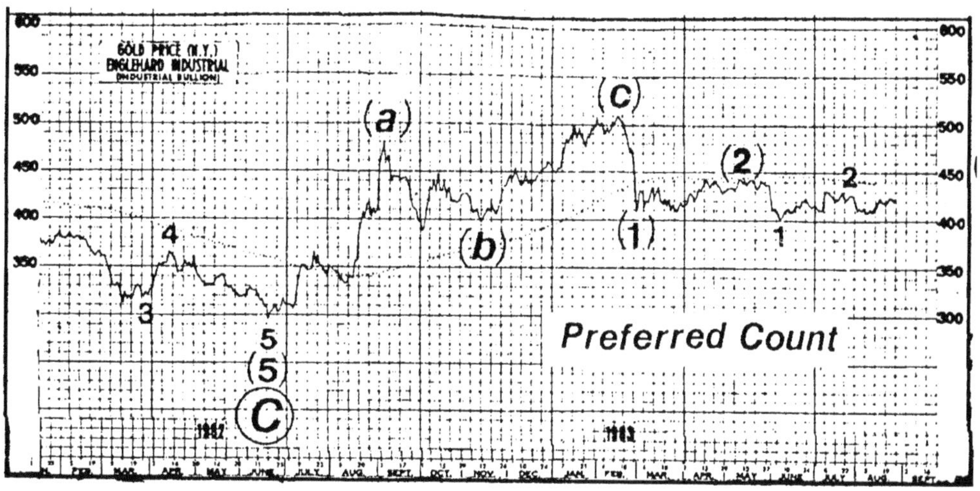

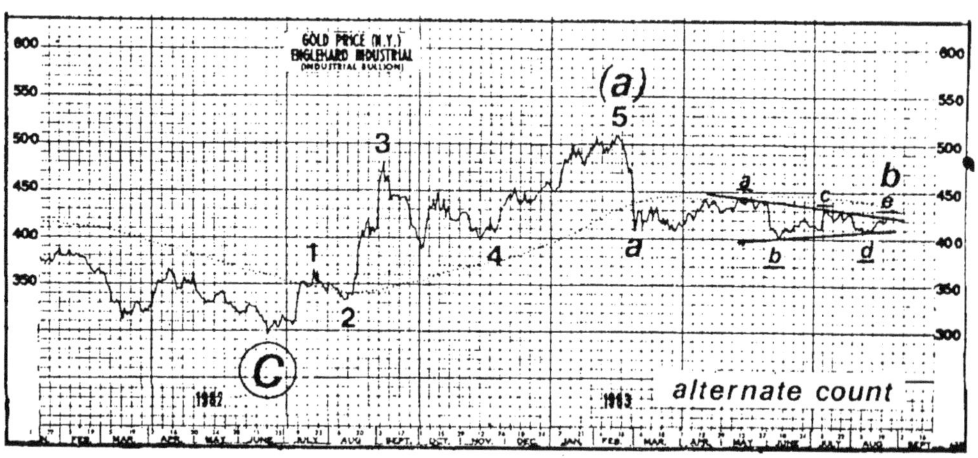

conclusions follow directly. First, since a triangle in this position must be a "b" wave, it implies that the upward correction from June 1982 is still unfolding. Wave (b) now in progress should fall at least to the $378-387 zone, since $378 marks a .618 retracement of wave (a) and $387 marks a drop equal to the widest part of the triangle (see text, p.44). If we could be sure, however, that wave (a) of the correction was a "three," as my preferred count shows, then the triangle would be marking only the *halfway point* of wave (b), which would be expected to carry back to or below the start of wave (a) at *$296.75*. Either way, this count implies that wave (c), from whatever level, will carry back above $511 some time next year before a more serious collapse can begin.

For now, look for a drop at least to $378-387, *with a high probability of a continuation to as low as $296.75* basis the London fix. The form of the decline should help us decide which of the two larger counts is valid and therefore whether to expect another intermediate-term bear market rally in 1984. As for the long term, there is more evidence with each passing month that gold will indeed fall at least to $179/oz. by 1987, and possibly as low as $105.

As for tactics, investors should remain out of the gold market. Traders can continue to hold short bullion with a stop at $450 and ASA with a stop at 74. Time premium is eroding in the puts I recommended in the 65-70 zone for ASA, but the stock still looks vulnerable and could make up for lost time quickly.

Silver

Investor psychology toward silver is even more extreme than that for gold, with 70% of analysts bullish, according to Market Vane. Moreover, the August rally carried to a new high for the summer but was *unconfirmed by gold*, a new negative in the momentum picture. What's worse, the new high in silver was made on a *lesser rate of change*, giving a typical divergence "sell signal."

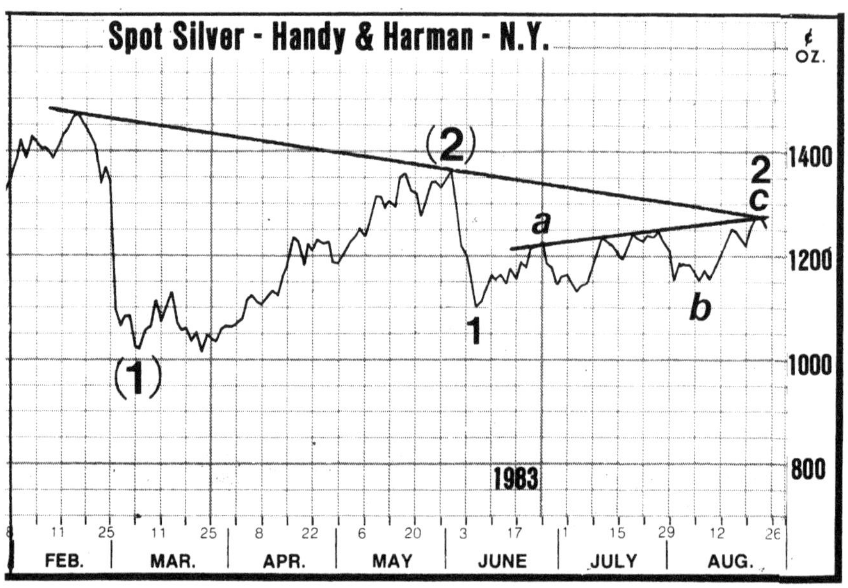

I explained last month that "silver should be viewed as a negative chart pattern unless it breaks the upper triangle boundary line." As you can see from the chart, it rallied *to* the line but never broke it. At the same time, it bumped against the *rising* resistance line connecting the tops formed since June. Compare that line with the *declining* resistance line in gold, which created the non-confirmation in August.

The wave count for NY spot shows a small five waves up during August, which can be counted as a final "c" wave in an a-b-c rally from June. As long as spot silver does not push through $12.77 (which can now be used as a stop for short sellers), I expect a drop to $8.50-9.00 from the current level of $12.20.

SEPTEMBER 22, 1983 – INTERIM REPORT

Gold looks no better than it did at the beginning of the month. Continue to hold 100% short, keeping the stop at $450. Our ASA short, by the way, may be starting to pay off.

OCTOBER 17, 1983

Gold remains in a major bear market, and each wave down further confirms the validity of our February "sell" at the $500+ level. I do not view the recent shakeout as a buying opportunity.

Gold

Last month's analysis concluded the following:

> *Gold looks even more bearish now than it did four weeks ago*...another crash in the gold price probably lies directly ahead. *Look for a drop at least to $378-387, with a high probability of a continuation to as low as $296.75* basis the London fix.

The lowest London fix so far was *$388.75*, so the "guaranteed" part of the decline is just about over. On that basis alone, I would suggest covering half your short sales in gold on the next selloff to new 1983 lows. Another reason to bank some profits is that now that the $400 level has been broken, many gold-watchers have issued "sell signals," and sentiment is down to only 36% bulls (up from 21% last week) according to Market Vane. With so many investors now jumping on our side of the market, it's time to buy back some of the gold they're now so eager to sell, down 25% from the peak. It's *easy* to sell gold now; it wasn't easy at the top.

Based on the two wave counts given in the September issue, the next direction for gold is less certain. Either gold will continue to decline to at least $296.75, based on either of the two counts given last month, or it will catch hold here in the $378-387 area and begin an intermediate term rally (in an overall bear market) back above $512. The accompanying chart shows the count that allows for either possibility in an ongoing upward correction from June 1982. The count shown here for silver is also applicable to gold and would not allow any intermediate term rally whatsoever. With reference to the long term chart of gold, the question remains whether wave X ended at $512 in February 1983, as I expect, or whether it has further rally potential before the next major A-B-C decline begins.

Based on the probabilities among these wave counts, I feel that *the bearish case for gold (another $100 down) is more likely.* A substantial break of $378 basis London fix would confirm it. Although I don't expect to see it, a move above $415 would indicate a final advance back above $512 prior to the resumption of the major bear trend.

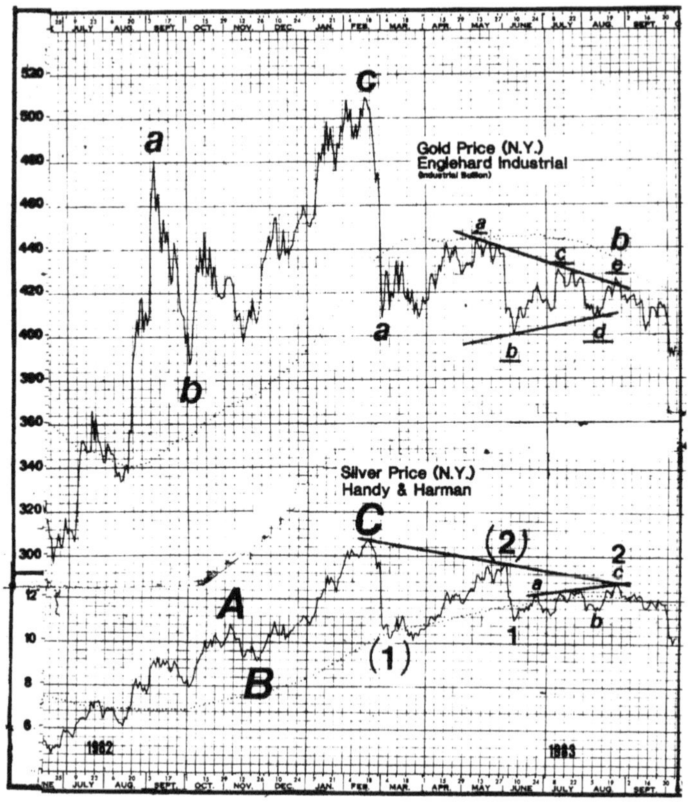

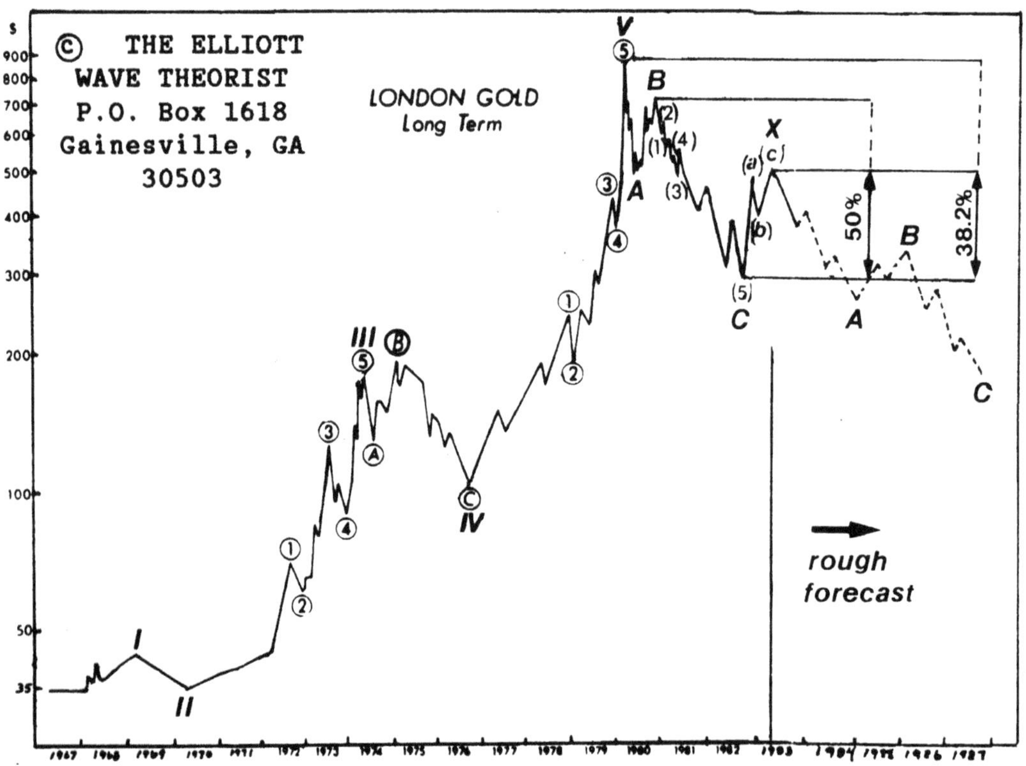

Strategy

For the remaining short position, lower the stop from $450 to $415 basis London fix. Gold is still the least attractive investment long term and has a high probability of continuing directly to $296, so I still want no part of the long side.

Sentiment

Here's what the nation's leading newspapers had to say about gold in the week prior to the latest collapse:

> 9/12/83 USA Today: "Gold Stocks Boast Big Gains." (Quote: "All indications are that these stocks will continue to perform well.") Note: ASA had closed that Friday at 67½ and has since fallen below 54.
>
> 9/14/83 WSJ: "Comex Lowers Margin on Gold, Silver, Copper."
>
> 9/16/83 WSJ: "Gold Mining Stocks Make Glittering Showing Despite the Lackluster Performance of Bullion." (Quote: "If the price of bullion cracks below $400, these stocks could be in for a drastic decline.") Note: The day *before* gold cracked $400, ASA closed at 56⅞, down 29% from its high of 80. If you had sold the day gold broke $400, you would have sold on what so far is the exact day of the closing low for ASA.
>
> 9/19/83 WSJ: "Many Analysts Raise Forecasts of Inflation: A Few See Real Surge."

The latest issue of Precious Metals Performance Digest, which does an excellent job of categorizing professional opinion on the precious metals, showed that in September, only *one* (1) market letter among the *fifty* (50) financial newsletters which they follow was bearish on gold, and that was *The Elliott Wave Theorist*. In other words, nothing had changed from the consensus opinion existing at the February peak. Talk about an ongoing minority view! In support of their observations came the October 10 issue of Barron's, which featured an article on the New York Society of Security Analysts' "World View of Gold" seminar held on Tuesday, October 4. For tens of "fundamental" reasons (i.e., guesses as to the actions of U.S., Soviet and Arab politicians), the speakers remained bullish on gold. Here is Barron's' summary of the sentiment at the meeting:

> At last week's meeting, Wall Street types and Transvaal types both were eager to explain why, despite its recent decline in price, rumors of pending bullion sales by debt-strapped countries and the IMF, and various and sundry other depressants, gold is — you guessed it — headed up.
>
> Whether it will or not, time will tell. But almost to a man, the speakers at last week's seminar were resolutely bullish on gold, despite its recent lack of luster. Nor were there any evident bears in the audience.

"But WHY?"

Most investors are uncomfortable with technical logic, and most demand current-event "reasons" why a market should move in one direction or the other. After the February "sell" recommendation, I received some inquiries along that line, so in the March 7 issue I ventured a guess as to what one explanation might later be of why gold wasn't soaring despite the precarious nature of third world debt. Here's an excerpt:

> I seriously doubt that the OPEC nations will default on loans to money-center banks. No country wants to lose its financial credibility entirely. And if you were an Arab sitting on a huge stockpile of GOLD and knowing you had to *sell something* to make up for the shortfall in your oil income....

On September 7, *six months later,* The Wall Street Journal ran this article:

Gold Falls $6.60 As Sellers Expect Big Portugal Sale

A Wall Street Journal *News Roundup*

Reports that Portugal may have to sell about 30 metric tons, or 964,500 troy ounces, of gold to repay a $300 million loan from the Bank of International Settlements pushed the gold price sharply lower yesterday.

Gold traders said they believe that Portugal will sell the 30 tons of gold during the next month, and several dealers sold heavily in anticipation of lower prices. On the basis of yesterday's Comex quote, the gold to be sold has a value of about $397.8 million.

The reasons always come out *later*! If you wait for them, you'll sell too late every time.

ASA

In the April issue, I showed a chart of ASA having completed five waves up into the January peak and then five smaller waves down into a low in March for wave "A" of an important correction. At that time, ASA puts were recommended as an excellent speculation going into the top of the B-wave rally in the stock. The next chart updates the wave count. Wave B took the form of a large triangle, and wave C finally broke down from its apex. The next important support is in the 49-53 area based on two guidelines

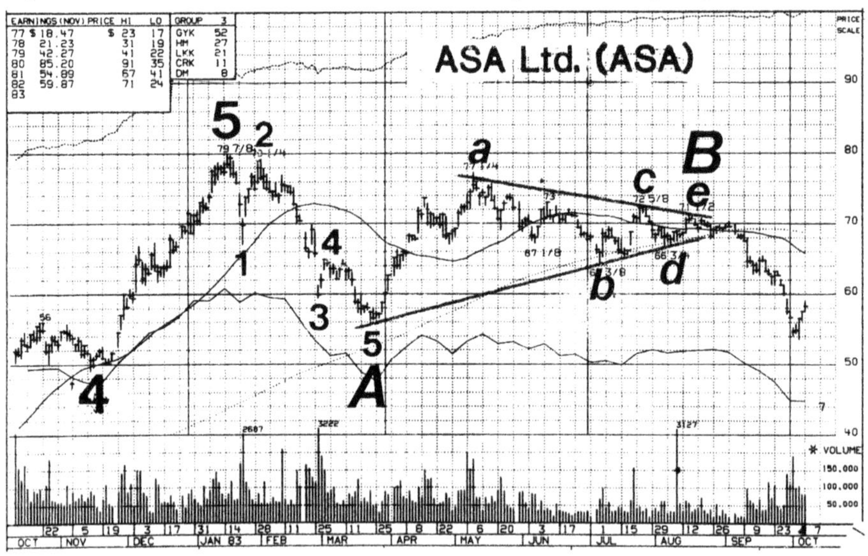

under the Wave Principle (the previous 4th wave low – see text p.55 – and the standard distance for thrust following a triangle – see text p.44). Therefore, you should plan to cover short sales and sell puts when the current decline enters that target zone.

Silver

Silver had just completed a rally to nearly $13 last month when Elliott analysis, sentiment, momentum and divergence all indicated a substantial drop directly ahead. The overwhelming evidence resulted in the conclusion that "I expect a drop to $8.50-9.00 from the current level of $12.20." Two weeks later, silver began a collapse which took it to $10, and the wave structure still appears incomplete on the downside. The chart here updates the one shown last month, and as you can see, wave 3 took a typically sharp drop (see text, p.67) but has not yet subdivided into five waves.

Short sellers can lower the stop from $12.77 to $11.50 basis spot. Even though the $8.50-9.00 level may be only a "first stop," I suggest covering shorts in that area.

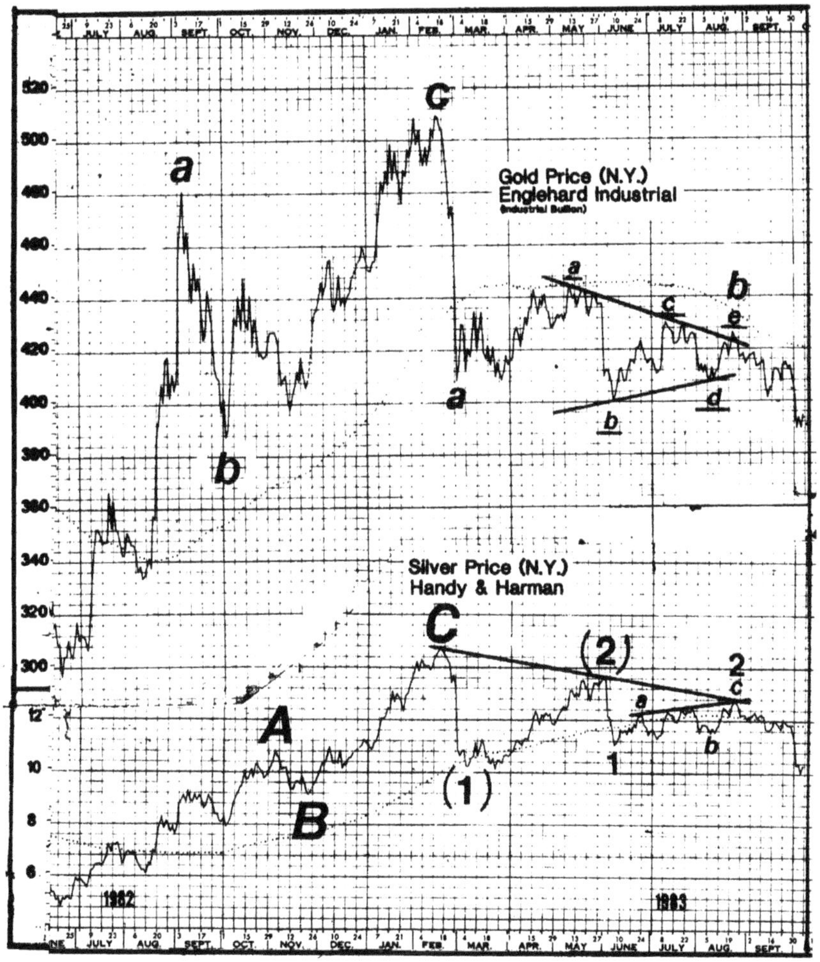

NOVEMBER 7, 1983

Gold and silver have finally hit their minimum downside targets of $378 and $8.50 respectively, completing a months-long trade on the short side. Although prices should rally short term, a break of the $368 level in gold would result in an immediate drop to $296.

Gold

Last week was a wonderful week, with *gold bullion, silver bullion* and ASA all hitting their long-awaited minimum downside targets simultaneously. It feels good to have taken profits after over eight months of declining prices. The minimum downside target for gold has been the $378-387 zone, which was finally entered on October 27, with a London fix of $384.50. The lowest price so far occurred on November 1, with an a.m. fix of $376 and a p.m. fix of $377.75. Strategy in the October 17 issue was as follows:

> The "guaranteed" part of the decline is just about over. On that basis alone, I would suggest covering half your short sales in gold on the next selloff to new 1983 lows.

Gold is now sitting right on the most important support point of its 13-year free-market trading history. Just look at the long term chart of gold bullion. The major uptrend line has three nearly perfect "touch" points and is in a position to create a fourth. Moreover, as this chart shows, support at the Fibonacci retracement point of $378 has been met precisely where the long term trendline cuts through the price action. If $378 is broken by as much as $10, it will be the final confirmation that the current bear market is of Supercycle degree, and therefore almost certain to carry through to its ultimate target of either $179 or $105 per ounce by 1987.

In the October issue, *both acceptable wave counts shown for gold called for its falling to the current level,* but from here, two possibilities arise. Gold could turn up now and climb in another bear market rally wave back above the February peak at $511.50, thereby completing a large countertrend advance from the 1982 low. The current drop in sentiment levels to only 20-30% "bulls" as recorded by Market Vane (61 S. Lake Av., Pasadena, CA) makes this outcome at least a reasonable possibility. However, if gold slips below current support, it will be expected to drop immediately at least to the 1982 low of $296.75/oz. Of one thing I am convinced: This long term trendline is *not* a valid trendline under the guidelines of the Wave Principle, and therefore *it is likely to be broken dramatically at some point before the current bear market runs its course.*

Trading Strategy: Even if $378 support is to be broken, the current short term wave count allows for a rally back up to just over the $400 level first. With that in mind, the following ideas should be profitable and relatively low-risk: If gold is still above $370 when you receive this letter, cover the remaining 50% short position; otherwise hold. Reinstate a 100% short position at $398 with a stop at $408 basis London fix, risking only $10. If that price level is not achieved, reinstate a 100% short position upon any London fix below $370. If gold gets above $428, it will probably signal that the intermediate term trend has reversed to the upside. In that case, traders can take a long position. Investors should avoid gold until the final low in 1987.

Last March, the outlook for gold allowed some speculation as to what "reasons" might come out later for weakness in precious metals prices. I suggested then that debt-laden nations might elect to sell gold in order to keep their finances in order. The "fundamentalist" gold bulls have steadfastly refused to believe that such action would be taken, but as the following article from The Wall Street Journal reveals, the governments of these countries are serious about wanting to remain respectable within the international banking community. In the long run, such actions will lead to another huge rise in the price of gold, but in the meantime, the gold market has had to clear the sales.

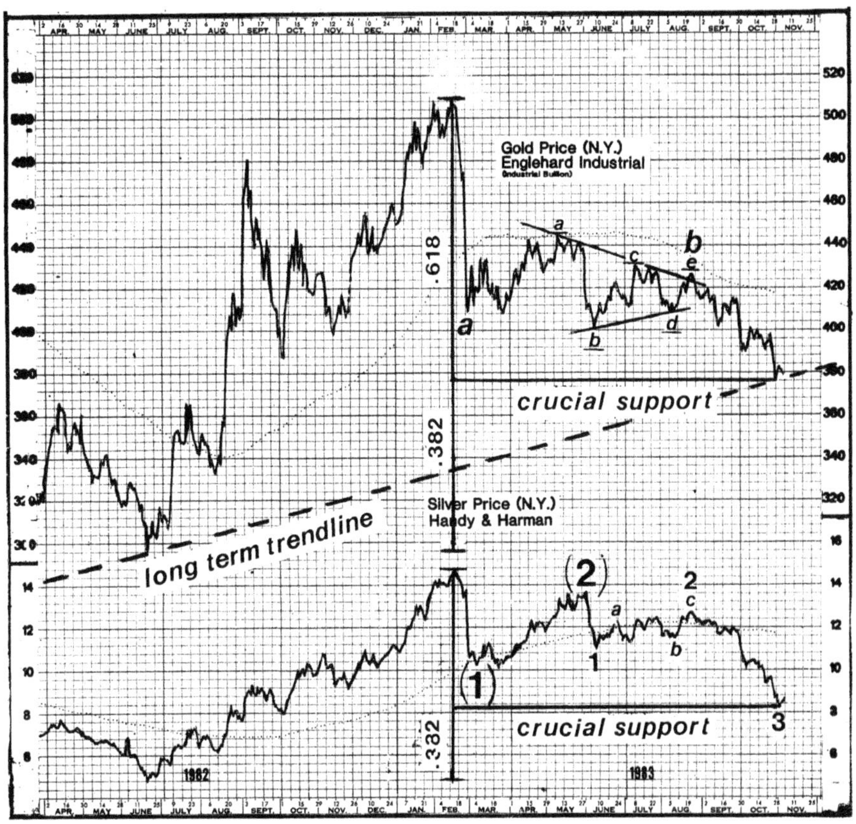

* * *

> **BRAZIL'S PRESIDENT DECLARED a state of emergency.**
>
> An aide to President Joao Figueiredo said the action was intended to create a "climate of tranquility" for congressmen voting on a controversial bill to cut wages. The government said the measure is vital to securing foreign bailout loans.

ASA

After holding short in ASA for several months, the October issue suggested the following: "*Cover short sales and sell puts when the current decline enters the target zone [49-53].*"

Since at 49½, ASA will have lost a Fibonacci 38.2% of its peak value and fallen back to the exact level of the previous fourth wave of one lesser degree (see text, p.55), I'd rather step aside for the time being, even though I feel that long term, ASA could fall to substantially lower levels. Short selling is a speculation, and the "easy" part of ASA's decline is over. It's time to look for another safe trade.

Question: with our minimum target having been met, do I therefore think ASA is a long term *buy*? Absolutely not! While a rally back to 60 is possible, the chart below, developed by Ian McAvity of Deliberations (Box 182, Adelaide St. Sta., Toronto, Ont. M5C 2J1) shows at least one good reason why it would be a dangerous "long." *Gold stocks in early September were valued at their highest level in at least nine years relative to bullion.* The decline since then has *not* been enough to get this ratio back into a more favorable position. And with *gold bullion* still historically overvalued relative to all other commodities (see chart in May 2 issue and further evidence in Sept. 6 issue), the risk in gold shares is still too high to warrant purchase.

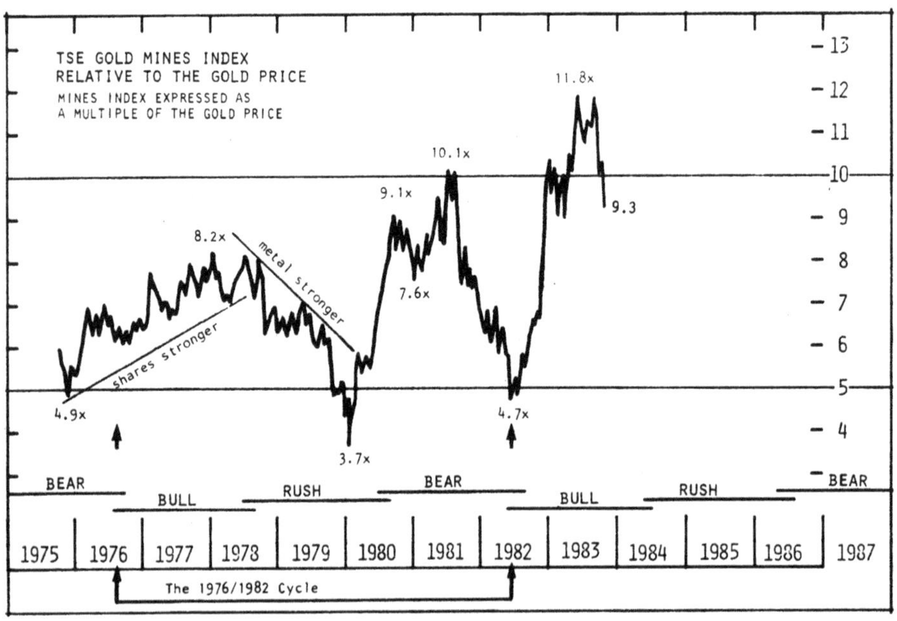

Silver

Now, *that* was a good trade. With silver still priced in the $12-13 range, Elliott analysis was able to forecast a "substantial drop directly ahead." The downside target zone of $8.50-9.00 seemed to be a long way down two months ago, particularly with the unrelenting drumbeat of pronouncements from all sides that the summer of 1983 had already provided the "last chance to buy silver before it goes to $50 an ounce." Last month's strategy read as follows:

> Even though the $8.50-9.00 level may only be a "first stop," I suggest covering shorts in that area.

Silver finally broke $9 basis London fix on October 27, with a close at $8.59, deep within the target zone. The lowest reading so far occurred three days later at $8.37, so all positions should have been covered as of November 1.

At this point, silver should rally back to the previous fourth wave level, which is the $10-10.60 zone. At that point, you can reinstate short sales with a stop at $10.80. Unlike the wave count for gold, *silver's wave structure is more confidently interpreted as requiring at least one more down wave in the bear trend which began last February*, as you can see on the daily chart. This fact alone increases the odds that gold is in for further price weakness.

DECEMBER 5, 1983

Gold bounced right off the Elliott support level and has hit first resistance at $405 basis London fix. Next resistance is $426. A move above $428 would signal a rally to above $500; a break of $374 would signal the beginning of a drop to below $300.

Gold

Based on our trading strategy, we covered 50% of our gold trade at $384.50 on October 27. As suggested in the November issue, "If gold is still above $370 when you receive this letter, cover the remaining 50% short position." The rest of that week, gold held above $370, so all remaining shorts were covered at an average London fix of *$381*.

As explained last month, "Even if $378 support is to be broken, the current wave count allows for a rally back up to just over the $400 level first." Since then, that rally has come to pass, with a gold robbery at Scotland yard providing the excuse for a price jump that was required by the technical position of the market. (Notice that the previous crises in Brazil, Lebanon, Korea and Grenada had no effect on the gold price; the wave structure had not yet completed on the downside.)

After eleven months of very high reliability forecasting, gold is now at a point of short term uncertainty. The parameters and alternative possibilities are clear, however, so a review should be helpful to establish perspective.

Long Term Wave Position

As I have been discussing since November 1979, the U.S. government's previous price-fixing policy toward gold lends some uncertainty to the long term wave interpretation. Silver, on the other hand, was freely traded in the late 1960s and clearly traced out first and second waves into the 1971 low. Gold traded in 1971 at the *same level* it did in 1967, raising the question of whether the Supercycle bull market actually began in 1971, four years after silver's. The tremendous collapse in silver since the $50 peak was fully expected, since it had completed five clear Cycle waves going into that high.

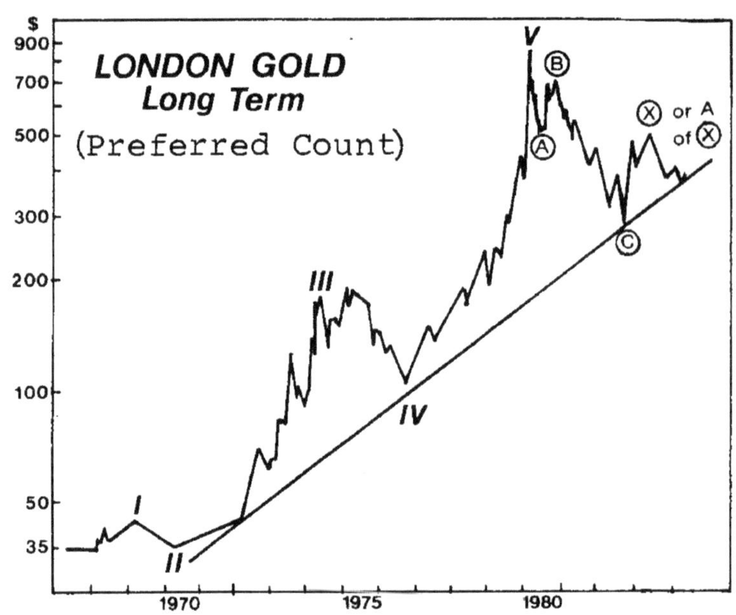

The wave structure will not *confirm* that gold's bull market started in 1967 unless it falls below the 13-year support line, the equivalent of which silver did long ago. Until then, it remains *possible* that gold began a Cycle wave advance to new all-time highs in June 1982. For that reason, it is worth keeping in mind that any move significantly above $639, a .618 retracement of the decline from $850 to $296.75, would be a strong indication in favor of the bullish long term wave count.

Intermediate-Term Wave Count

Alternate counts are possible now only because of the uncertain interpretation of the wave structure from June 1982 through February 1983. Is it *five* waves or *three*? It has been very rare for gold to be anything less than crystal-clear, but that volatile period is the reason that alternate counts on the intermediate term trend have been valid.

As you know, I have concluded that the balance of evidence strongly favors a complete five-wave count into the January high at $850. For this reason, the current bear market is most likely of Supercycle degree and should last into 1987. Corrections, of course, can take many shapes. While so far Elliott wave analysis has recognized every intermediate term turn in gold since the $850 high, it is still not certain exactly which corrective formation is occurring.

The best interpretation is still a "double zigzag" (see text, p.37) from $850, with the first Ⓐ-Ⓑ-Ⓒ having ended at $296.75 last year. So far, this ongoing count has served us well; the rally peak at $511.50 in February was easy to recognize, as was the low last month. Now the question is, was that decline part of the new Primary wave Ⓐ to the downside, or merely an interruption within wave Ⓧ, the rally between two Ⓐ-Ⓑ-Ⓒ formations?

Enough evidence is now available to state that the internal construction of the recent decline actually favors another move in bullion to above last February's high (see "Preferred Count"). Preliminary calculations show a target zone of $558-639, since (C)=(A) at $589, Ⓧ =.618 Ⓒ at $558, and Ⓧ =.618(Ⓐ-Ⓑ-Ⓒ) at $639. The peak would be expected to be met in 1984, which should be the last "rally" year in the 5½ year cycle if a Cycle degree bear market is in force. Short term, a London fix above $408 would suggest a continuation of the rise to $426, which marks the peak of wave e of the triangle *and* a .382 retracement of the decline from February. As last month's issue stated, "If gold gets above $428, it will probably signal that the intermediate term trend has reversed to the upside."

The bearish count shows everything from last February's high as part of a large declining wave that is about to enter an *acceleration phase* on the downside. Proof that this count is correct would come from a break of the low London fix to date at $374.25. Any break of that level would wipe out the long term trendline, confirm a bearish wave count *and* break the .618 retracement level of the June 1982-February 1983 advance.

Other Evidence

There appears to be a 9-month cycle in gold and silver, and November 1983 would have been a good point for that cycle to bottom (see chart, "Preferred Count"). That cycle implies three to eight months of rising prices.

On the negative side, Market Vane (61 S. Lake Av, Pasadena, CA) reported a dramatic surge in bullish sentiment after gold's one-week jump in price, to 64% "bulls," up from 29%. The string of low readings last month helped us call an upturn, but one high week is not enough for a strong signal to sell. The rapid change however, does reveal that goldwatchers are petrified of missing "the" major bottom. As long as psychology is in that state, I seriously doubt that "gold $4000" is in the cards for this cycle.

Trading Strategy

From here, at least the parameters are clear, with resistance at $408, $426 and $558, and support at $374.25 and $296.75. It actually doesn't matter whether you trade from the long or

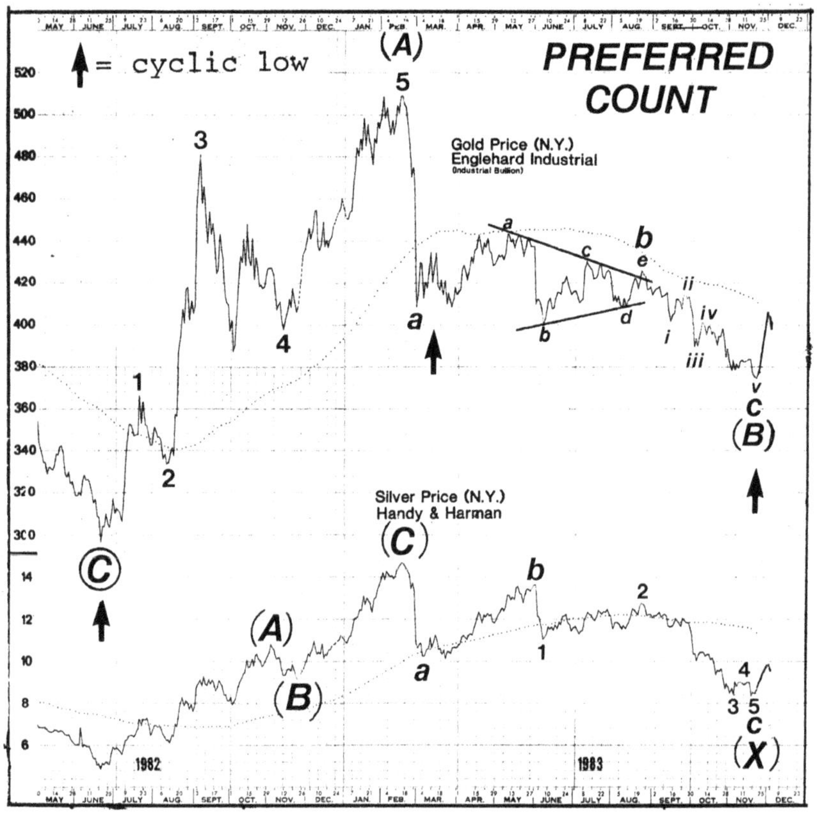
= cyclic low
PREFERRED COUNT
Gold Price (N.Y.)
Englehard Industrial
Silver Price (N.Y.)
Handy & Harman
1982
1983

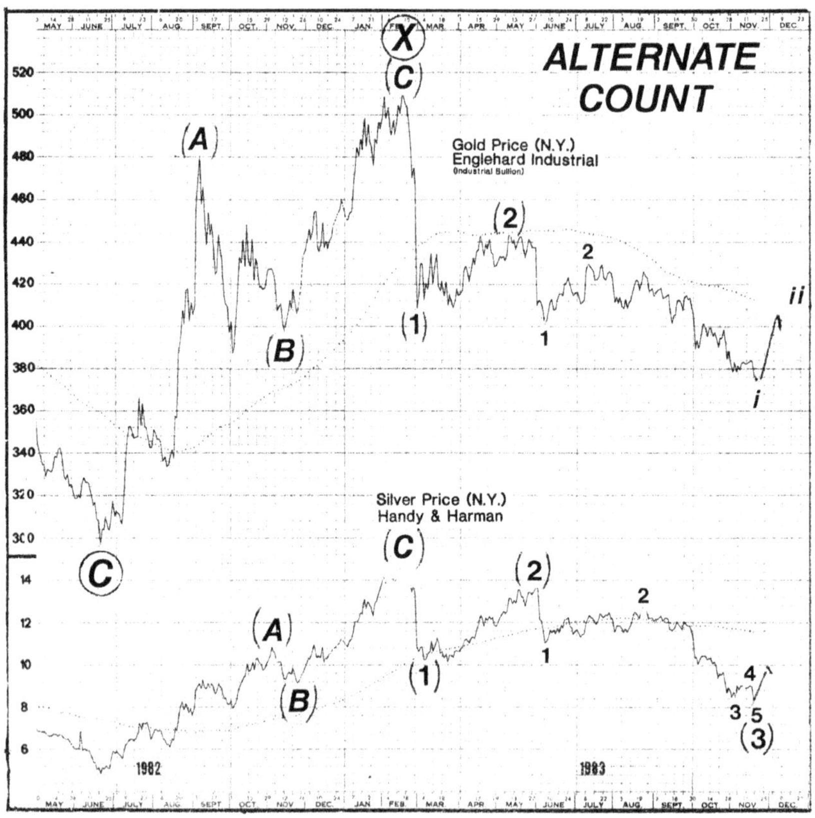
ALTERNATE COUNT
Gold Price (N.Y.)
Englehard Industrial
Silver Price (N.Y.)
Handy & Harman
1982
1983

the short side while gold is between $374.25 and $426, since positions can be traded around the support and resistance levels with little risk. A short sale held now with a stop at $408, and another at $425 with a stop at $428, would be as effective as going long now with $25 risk.

As indicated last month, the minimum requirement was a rise in gold to just over $400/oz.; that much has occurred. If you followed the trading suggestion in the November issue, you waited for the first London fix above $398 to move to a 100% short position, and placed a low-risk stop at $408. The actionable fix was $405.75 on November 30, which so far is the *exact high.* On that basis, you now have a short position with only $2.25 risk. (Limiting risk is the formula for consistent gains. On the Telephone Hotline, we bought at the low with a stop just $3 under, and closed out the trade at a $30 profit.)

However, because the rise from the November 21 low was a "five," the short side is now much less attractive than it might have been. Since our risk is so low, I'm willing to stay short with a stop at $408, but if stopped out, stand aside until a high-confidence signal is given. If stopped, reinstate shorts upon any break of $374.25; all participants go long on any London fix of $428 or above.

ASA

The target zone for ASA worked out perfectly, and all shorts were covered and puts sold. Last month's analysis allowed for a rally back to the 60 level, and the stock has since risen to 57, 14% from its low of 50. Several subscribers argued vehemently against selling out their put positions, since the metals were still "acting poorly" against the news. But according to the put/call ratios, that's just what the crowd was thinking, and the crowd is always wrong at the turns. Remember, *if you do not act when the opportunity presents itself, your next decision will always be an agonizing one.* A 60 put bought earlier this year was worth over $10 with ASA at 50. If the stock rallies back to 60, the put will be worthless. With ASA in the mid-50s, *now* what do you do? For my own part, the previous fourth wave peak was at 59, so ASA can be shorted again there with a stop at 62.

Silver

Last month's analysis was clear: "*Silver's wave structure is more confidently interpreted as requiring at least one more down wave in the bear trend which began last February.*" That final drop occurred when silver fell to a new low two weeks ago. As you can see on the charts on the previous page, silver has now completed a full three Intermediate waves from the February peak. That structure can be interpreted as an a-b-c, completing wave (X) of a double zigzag from the June 1982 low, which would indicate highs above $15 ahead. *Or, it can be counted as the first three waves of five to the downside. Either way, next resistance should be met at the $10.60 level basis cash, which is equivalent to $11 basis the March futures.*

The Elliott Wave Theorist, 1984

JANUARY 4, 1984 – INTERIM REPORT

Our last short sale in gold was entered at $405.75. Today's London fix came in at $374. I suggest covering 50% of current short positions, at a gain of $31. A full analysis will be presented in the January issue.

JANUARY 9, 1984

Gold and silver are poised to collapse. As long as $398 resistance holds, gold should fall to below $300/oz.

Gold

Last month, the balance of probabilities had shifted slightly in favor of another large intermediate term advance. However, I suggested waiting until such an advance was confirmed by a move above $408, preferring to stay short as long as that "stop" was not triggered, risking only $2.25 on our short sale entry. $374-387, which has been targeted as support since last August, has held gold for two months now, validating the Elliott wave computations. In deference to that support level, I suggested covering 50% of the short position last Wednesday on the London fix of $374. However, as pointed out in the November issue, "Of one thing I am convinced: This long term trendline is not a valid trendline under the guidelines of the Wave Principle, and therefore it is likely to be broken dramatically at some point before the current bear market runs its course." That trendline was broken in December, but the .618 retracement level held. Now, based on Friday's market action, it appears that the recent uncertainty around the $374 level is about to be resolved on the downside.

Wave Count

Based on the action in gold and silver futures on Friday, the wave count that classifies all 1983 action as part of an ongoing intermediate term decline is now the most valid. Remember, a break of $374, if it occurs Monday in London gold, will not be just a break of some minor support level. As explained last month:

> The bearish count shows everything from last February's high as part of a large declining wave that is about to enter an acceleration phase on the downside. Proof that this count is correct would come from a break of the low London fix to date at $374.25. Any break of that level would wipe out the long term trendline, confirm a bearish wave count *and* break the .618 retracement level of the June 1982-February 1983 advance.

The accompanying chart shows where gold sat as of Friday's p.m. fix. Notice that the 13-year support line and the .618 retracement support point converged right at the November

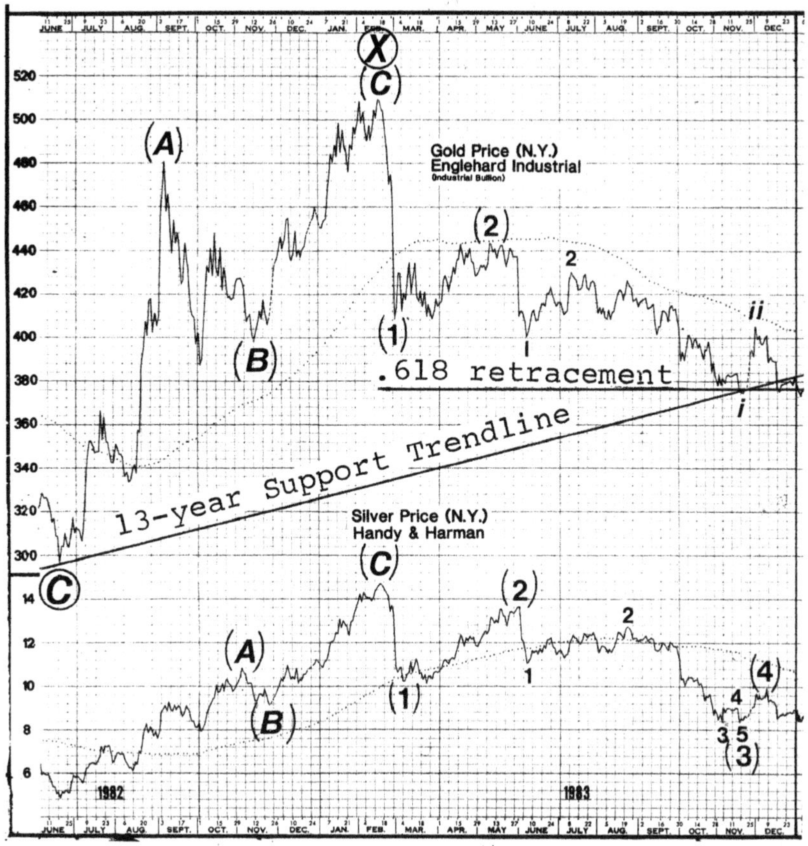

lows. Gold's response was dramatic but lasted only a week. With those lines giving way, the wave count on this chart (last month's "Alternate Count") is the most valid. It shows gold about to enter a "third of a third" wave, a point that often creates near-vertical price action (see text, p.67). I wouldn't be surprised to see a downside gap and a devastating week of decline given the current wave position in the gold market.

As added evidence, remember that after we covered at the low, last month's analysis called for ASA to be shorted again at 59, the probable rally peak in a bearish wave structure. The actual high was 58⅝, about as close to a perfect retracement as can be expected in an individual stock.

Review of Strategy

Our recent trading strategy in gold picked up an extra $23 on the way down. We covered shorts right on the October/November lows at an average price of $382.75 and moved back to 100% short at the exact rally peak at $405.75 on November 30. All the strategies for the past five years have been derived entirely from typical wave structure, behavior and targets. If anyone says your short side profits are "luck," just remember that last February at $500 gold, Gold Newsletter found only five "bears" among 28 analysts, and last September, at $410 gold, Precious Metals Performance Digest recorded only one "bear" (EWT) out of fifty market letters that specialize in gold and silver. And every one of them had "good reasons" to "buy gold now," ranging from world tensions to international debt to the rising money supply to the behavior of the consumer price index. The only factor they ignored was the trend in mass psychology toward the future, as revealed by the gold market's wave structure. It has occasionally felt like a long wait in building profits on the short side, but it certainly has beat losing money on the long side month after month, with stop-out after stop-out on the way down, while chasing each new rally that is "definitely signaling the start of the next bull market leg."

Current Tactics

As a minimum, let the 50% short position ride. Remember that there is a legion of "longs" out there who soon may be dying to sell you some gold. If we can recognize the next intermediate term bottom, we'll buy it from them. In fact, assuming that Monday's London fix will come in below $374, aggressive traders should return immediately to 100% short with a stop at $398. Any move by bullion above $398 would indicate something larger than just a minor second wave bounce on the way down. We'll address that problem if it arises.

Silver

The wave count for silver remains the same as before (see daily chart). The recent rally was wave (4), that peaked at $9.81 basis the London closing price, quite shy of the upside potential of $10.60. Silver is now in wave (5) to the downside. Because of the three-wave nature of the rise from June 1982 to February 1983, silver should eventually challenge, if not break, the June 1982 low at $4.90. Based upon the Wave Equality rule, if wave (5) is the same length as wave (1), it would fall to $5.38, a target that happens to be quite close to my original major downside objective calculation of $5.28 (see March 1982 issue). These targets indicate that substantial risk remains in the silver market despite the price damage suffered in 1983.

FEBRUARY 6, 1984

Gold's minor trend rally should peak soon and lead to a resumption of the bear market. Near term resistance is $388-$410 for gold, $10 for silver.

Gold

Gold remains in a major bear market. The break down through the 13-year support line occurred as expected last month, adding yet more evidence that the major trend is down. The near term trend turned up a week ago in response to the sudden increase in the number of "bears" in the gold market and the failure of gold stocks to make a new low along with bullion. The $150 drop from the peak at $511.50 was, for an Elliotter, a high confidence profit opportunity. The action around the long term trendline and Elliott support at $374-$387 has been less rewarding, but we've made some profitable trades even in this area. Gold will not

stay in this price range much longer. The wave structure is nearing resolution, so gold should move in a big way soon.

The chart of the long term gold picture illustrates the question at hand. The Ⓐ-Ⓑ-Ⓒ bear market decline which took place from January 1980 to June 1982 appears to be only the first ABC formation within a larger bear market. As I have discussed many times, normal Elliott wave guidelines (see text, p.55) still call for a low in gold in the range of the previous fourth wave of lesser degree, wave IV from 1974 to 1976. Calculations still point to either $105 or $179 as a final low before the entire decline has run its course. The only question at this point is whether wave Ⓧ, the rally separating two larger Ⓐ-Ⓑ-Ⓒ patterns, ended at $511.10 last February. If that peak was only part of wave Ⓧ, the structure would then require one more intermediate term rally back above $500 before the next bear wave begins.

Although it is more common to see an analyst present only the bullish or the bearish argument, I have always felt that it is more sensible, and of more value to you, to present all pertinent evidence and then sift through it, so we can arrive at an intelligent conclusion regarding our investments. Besides, each point I bring up has the potential to awaken a new thought in your mind as you form your own decisions. Let's go over the two most acceptable intermediate term interpretations in gold and discuss their probabilities.

Preferred Count

If the second Ⓐ-Ⓑ-Ⓒ decline began at the $511.50 peak, then the current congestion area will resolve on the downside, probably by the end of this month. The daily chart shows that a "third of a third" wave would be next, portending a collapse to below $300 in a matter of weeks. I prefer this count because the gold price appears to be following normal wave behavior in coming back up to "test" the long term support line that was penetrated last month. This is typical chart action. That line now provides resistance in the $388-$410 area. (As an aside, long term subscribers may have noticed that the 13-year trendline was broken at almost exactly the $388 level, the .618 retracement level for the entire 1976-1980 rise and a point that has had significance several times in the past three years.)

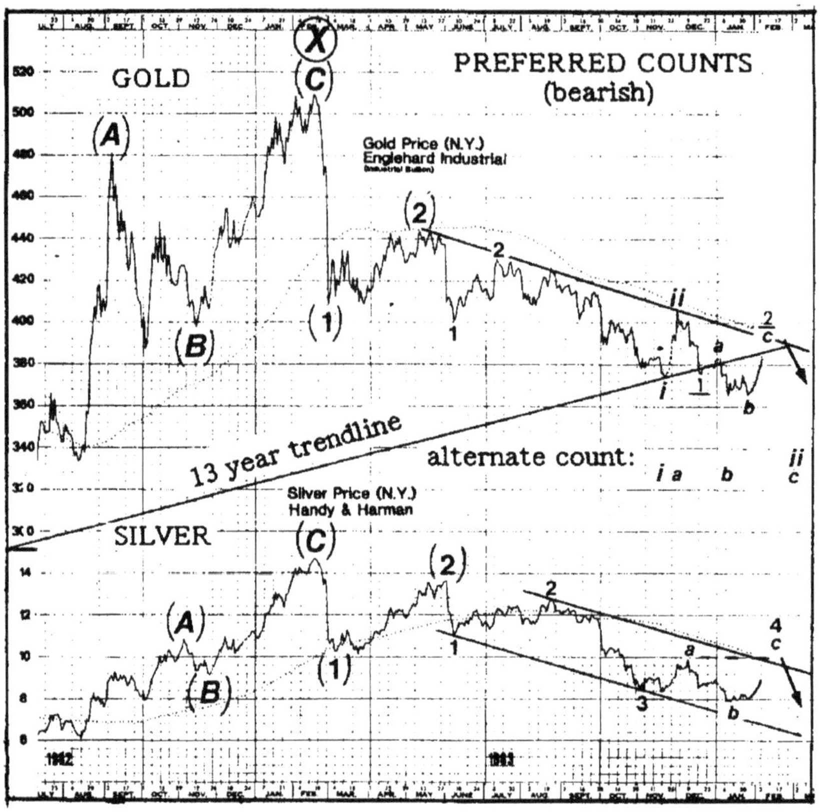

I've also noticed that once again the upside excitement is showing up most dramatically in the gold stocks, while bullion lags behind. This is the same condition that has preceded intermediate term drops in the gold price all during the past year. As of Friday, ASA had rallied above its early December peak, but gold bullion is more than $20 below its comparable level. That minor non-confirmation, if in remains intact, supports the case that ASA is in the process of completing an a-b-c rally, right against the downtrend line extending from the May 1983 top.

Furthermore, while it is true that the percentage of "bulls" dropped to a very low level last month, the last time that happened, a rally lasting only 1½ weeks was able to generate a "70% bulls" reading almost immediately. This abrupt turnaround revealed that while many might voice bearish opinions while the gold price is declining, there is as yet no widespread conviction that the trend is down. "Gold Jumps $5.50 an Ounce; Traders Say Turnabouts May Have Begun," says a WSJ headline from 2/2. It still appears that a legion of closet bulls awaits, dying to call that major bottom before everyone else. Remember, the piper has yet to be paid for the dramatically one-sided sentiment condition that existed not only at last year's top (see February and March 1983 issues) but also over the past six months, during which time Canada saw the creation of four new closed-end precious metals funds, which rapidly raised C$404 million from the public. Until this sentiment changes in an important way, the odds will be on the side of those who remain in harmony with the major trend.

Alternate Count

The 5½ year cycle bottomed in 1982 and is due to bottom again in 1987-1988, right when Elliott analysis also suggests a major bottom. Although the "up" side of this cycle is not expected to provide new all-time highs for gold, it may still have some rally power left in it during 1984. This should be the last year during which gold can launch a significant counter-trend rally, so for now, we have to stay on the lookout for one. This is one reason that wave Ⓧ could produce another big rally before the bear takes over again.

The wave count lends itself easily to this possibility, since a diagonal triangle may have ended last month, completing wave c to the downside in an a-b-c pattern from the $511.50 high. This count would imply a swift surge up to the $445 level (the "beginning of the triangle"; see text, p.30), a corrective wave pullback, and then a continuation to above last February's high. The peak could be no higher than $640, a .618 retracement of the previous Ⓐ-Ⓑ-Ⓒ decline. Whatever the price, a full five waves to above $511 would present a very high confidence short-selling opportunity.

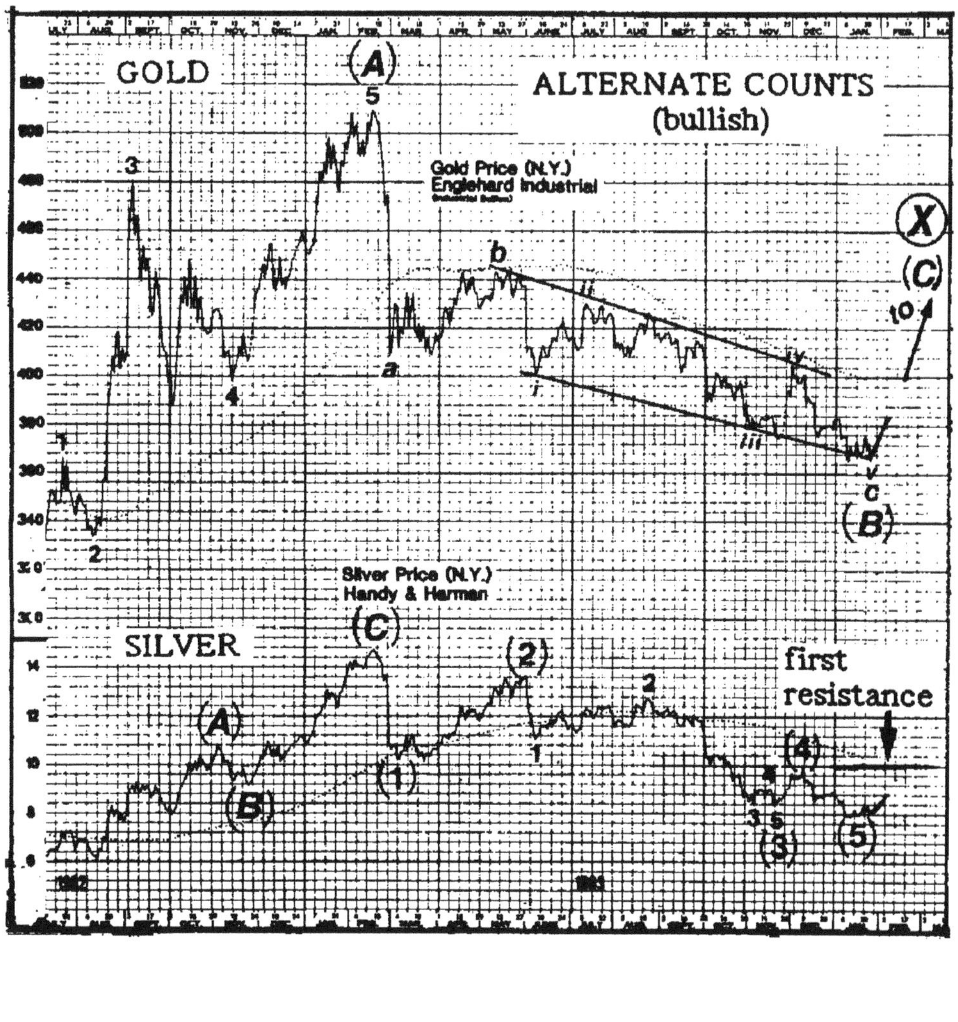

Tactics: Even if the alternate wave count turns out to be correct, a major bottom still appears several years away. Until the superbulls give up on $3000 and $6000/oz., gold is probably best avoided as an investment. However, as a trade, a five wave move above $410 will be a strong signal for an intermediate term rally to between $512 and $640/oz. prior to the next bear phase. If that event occurs, we'll do our best to get aboard after an a-b-c pullback and then ride the trend for $100 or so. For now, I would stay out or short with a stop at $415.

I made the case two months ago that ASA should peak near 59, the top of the previous fourth wave. It rallied to 58⅝ in December and hit 62½ last week. Based on December's strategy, you were short for only one day. I would sell short here with a stop at 64. There is also quite a good chance of its reaching the triangle apex at 69 (see chart), so that should be the highest possible point to enter the short side, with a stop at 72.

Silver

Silver's wave pattern has been quite clear for months. The January low at $7.90 was well above the worst case potential but sufficient to complete a full five Intermediate waves from the high a year ago. However, I prefer counting the action dating from early November as part of an a-b-c upward flat correction (see first daily chart). Either way, silver is likely to rally to just above the early December peak at $9.81/oz. basis the London daily closing price. In the alternate count, wave (4)'s peak level should provide resistance, and in the preferred count, wave c of the flat should carry to just above wave a, where the upper channel line comes through. If wave c were to be 1.618 times as long as wave a, a typical relationship in irregular corrections, silver would peak at $10.23. A sensible strategy would be to wait for the rally, then short silver in the $9.80-$10.20 range, placing a stop at $10.70 basis the London close.

MARCH 5, 1984

As of Friday's close, the precious metals forecasts from the February issue have been met, with gold in its target area of $388-410, silver in its target area at $9.80-$10.20, and ASA at precisely 69. The precious metals complex is now preparing to begin a severe decline. Gold should drop at least to $296, ASA to 39 by August.

Gold: Another Top at Hand

February's action in gold is strong evidence that my preferred count is the correct one. The expected short term rally has occurred, following the parameters outlined last month:

> The gold price appears to be following normal wave behavior in coming back up to "test" the long term support line which was penetrated last month. This is typical chart action. That line now provides resistance in the $388-$410 area.

The London price of gold is smack in the middle of the target range and has been trading right around $400/oz. since February 23. As you can see from the chart, the rally did take gold back up to "test" the 13 year trendline, which was broken in December, and in fact into the apex of *two* resistance trendlines. In my experience, such points have an exceptionally high degree of reliability in forecasting reversals. Even if the current rally in bullion is wave "c" of an a-b-c irregular flat correction, its maximum potential is $415, the point at which wave c would be 1.618 times as long as wave a (the November rally). For these reasons, I would remain out or short in the gold market, with a stop at $420 basis the London fix. If that stop is triggered, I'll reassess the situation, but as of now, I would not be inclined to rush in and buy.

Momentum

In the momentum area, divergences abound. As in last August, silver has gone above its previous rally high while gold has so far failed to do so. Gold stocks have soared, once again in apparent anticipation of $6000 gold, while bullion lags. These divergences reveal that the ongoing internal disharmony in the precious metals markets has not been resolved. If anything, this type of action is more typical of the early stages of a bear market rather than the late stages. Thus, not only is the market giving another short term "sell" signal, it is indicating that there is probably a long way to go on the downside before the major trend is exhausted.

Sentiment

One of the reasons I expected a short term rally last month was the low reading on Market Vane's sentiment gauge, which showed only 20% of services bullish on gold. Too many people had joined our "bear" camp, so it was time for a rally. However, at that time, I made this observation:

> While it is true that the percentage of "bulls" dropped to a very low level last month, the last time that happened, a rally lasting only 1½ weeks was able to generate a "70% bulls" reading almost immediately. This abrupt turnaround revealed that while many might voice bearish opinions while the gold price is declining, there is as yet no widespread conviction that the trend is down. "Gold Jumps $5.50 an Ounce; Traders Say Turnabouts May Have Begun," says a WSJ headline from 2/2. It still appears that a legion of closet bulls awaits, dying to call that major bottom before everyone else.

So far, that's just what has happened. In fact, this rally, currently four weeks old, has now resulted in a Market Vane reading of 84% bulls (silver 81%). This is the highest single week's reading since January 1983! Prior to that, you have to go back to the summer of 1980 to find comparable levels. Market Vane's tally is supported by the bull/bear ratings given in the latest issue of Precious Metals Performance Digest (10076 Boca Entrada Blvd., Boca Raton, FL 33433). Out of fifty (50) newsletters that forecast gold and silver prices, once again *The Elliott Wave Theorist* is the only newsletter listed as "bearish" on the long term outlook for gold! The last time this happened was in September, and gold hasn't seen those prices since. Based on these readings alone, gold should be trading below $300/oz. by summer.

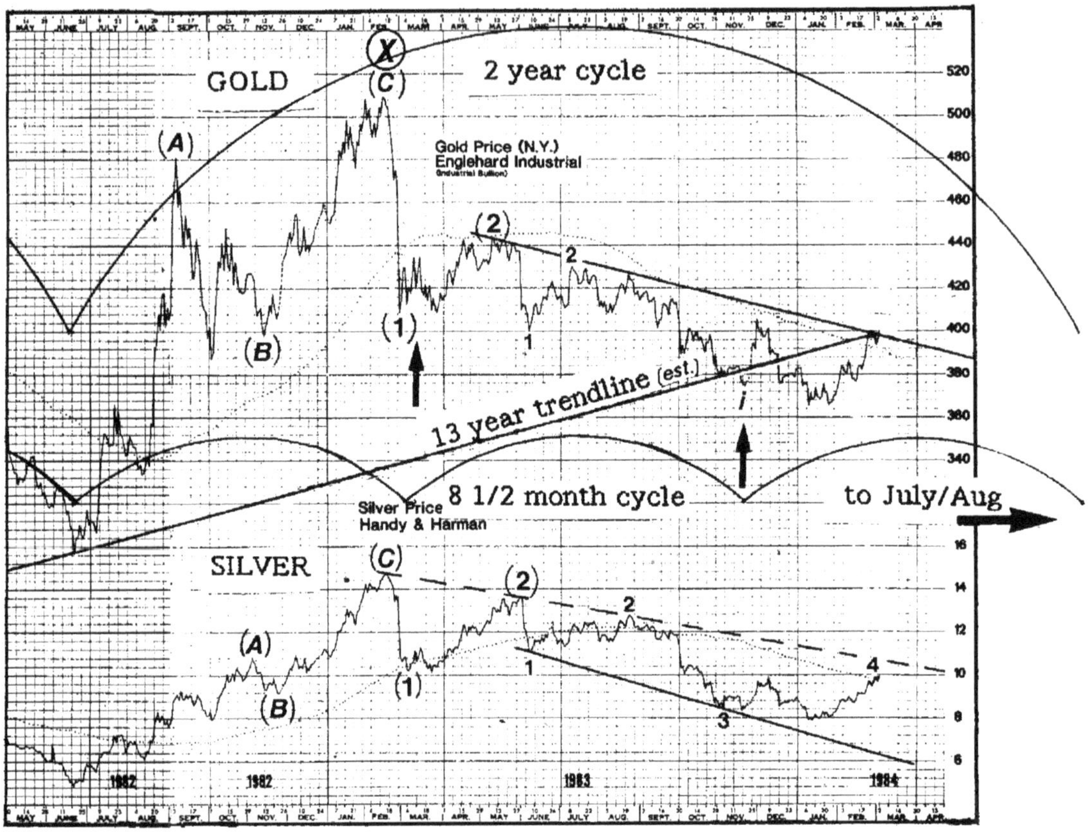
GOLD
2 year cycle
Gold Price (N.Y.)
Englehard Industrial
(A)
(B)
(C)
X
(1)
(2)
1
2
i
13 year trendline (est.)
8 1/2 month cycle
to July/Aug
Silver Price
Handy & Harman
SILVER
(A)
(B)
(C)
(1)
(2)
1
2
3
4
1982
1983
1984
520
500
480
460
440
420
400
380
360
340
16
14
12
10
8
6

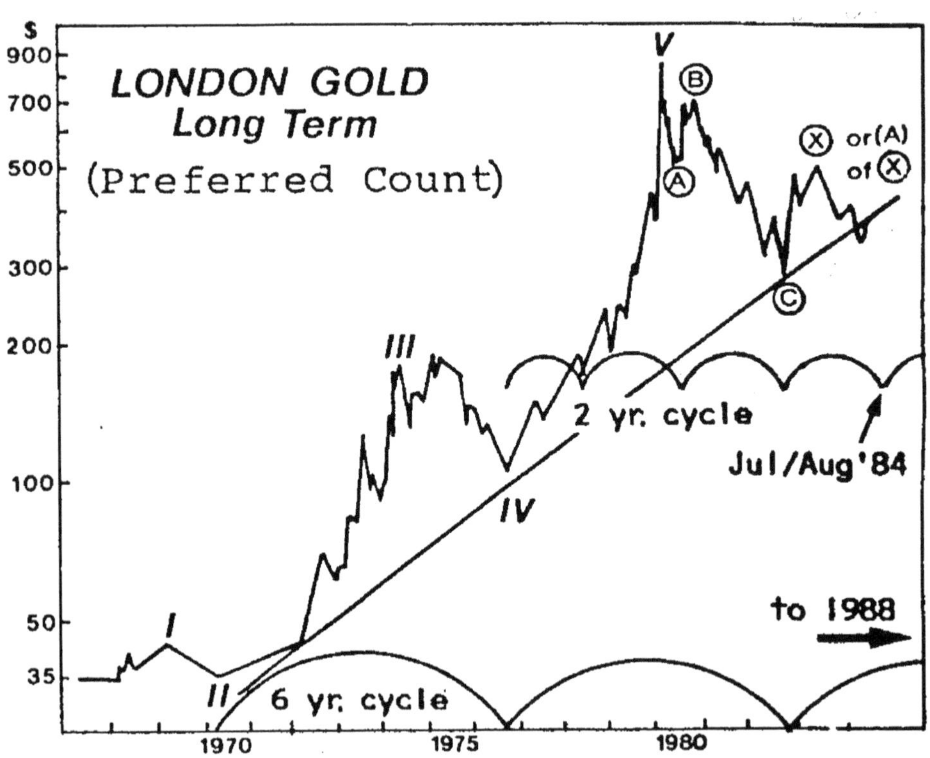
LONDON GOLD
Long Term
(Preferred Count)
$
900
700
500
300
200
100
50
35
I
II
III
IV
V
A
B
C
X or (A) of X
2 yr. cycle
Jul/Aug'84
6 yr. cycle
to 1988
1970
1975
1980

Time Cycles

In the December 5 issue of *The Elliott Wave Theorist*, I made the case for a "9-month cycle" (actually 8½ months) in gold and silver prices and argued that the upward phase commenced at the November lows, implying a period of rising prices for at least three months. Those three months are now up. The arrows on the accompanying chart of gold and silver have been left exactly where I placed them last November. Based on this cycle, this next important intermediate low for gold is not due until late July/early August 1984. What's more, it is evident that three of these 8½ month cycles combine to form one 2-year cycle, three of which in turn combine to form one 6-year cycle. The current position of the 2-year cycle is hard down and due to bottom with the next 8½ month cycle.

APRIL 3, 1984

Gold, silver and ASA all peaked exactly on the day that the March issue called for a top. The trend should remain down into July/August, with targets as follows: gold below $300; silver below $6; ASA below $40.

Gold

Last month's gold analysis was headlined, "Another Top at Hand." Gold, silver and ASA had just rallied to the target zones given in the previous month's issue, and overwhelming evidence from wave structure, cycles, sentiment and momentum measures all indicated a reversal of trend to the downside. On March 5, the day that issue was mailed, London gold registered its high fix at $406.85 (just below the upper end of its target zone at $410), London silver closed at $10.11 (just below the upper end of its target zone at $10.20) and ASA peaked at 69¾, just barely above our short selling point at 69. A week later, as Market Vane (61 S. Lake Av, Pasadena, CA) tallied its third week in a row of over 80% "bulls" on gold, newspaper articles such a "Guru Expects Hike in Metals," "Inflation Forecast Revised Upward by [Portfolio] Manager" and "Inflation Provides Golden Opportunity" were hitting the stands.

Today's new low for the reaction completes a five-wave count from the highs, virtually confirming that the intermediate term trend in gold has changed to down. A $15 bounce may occur soon, but if my analysis is correct, the early March peak should not be penetrated. Gold not only completed a clear irregular correction to the upside at that time, but it reversed quickly after briefly penetrating the 13-year trendline, which is offering heavy resistance.

The accompanying charts of gold and silver are exactly the same as those presented in last month's issue, with prices updated through Friday. If gold heads lower from here, there is no Elliott support until the June 1982 low at $296.75. That level is important only because if wave Ⓧ to the upside, which started at that time, is taking the form of a large flat correction, the (B) portion could bottom at that level before wave (C) carries gold back above $500/oz. Based on the 2-year and 8½ month cycles, the next intermediate term bottom isn't due until July/August.

Jim Tillman of Interstate Securities (Charlotte, NC) has taught me a lot about cycles over the years. I've mentioned his excellent and original work many times. His March 15 report to institutional clients had this to say about gold:

> Friday, March 9th, gold bullion, ASA and Homestake all gave the same signal - SELL - just when everyone except one advisor (Bob Prechter) is bullish on gold. I don't know what the others are looking at, but from a pure chart, cycle and momentum viewpoint, you have to have second thoughts about gold here.

As far as our strategy goes, depending upon your preference, you're either out or short in the gold market. Last month's stop level of $420 basis London fix can now be lowered to $407, making the current position a very low-risk trade. If $407 is exceeded at any time, the alternate count (see February 6 issue) allowing for a move above $500 will be in force. Although I don't expect it, if a rally above $407 does occur, cover all short positions and go long with a stop at $385.

ASA

ASA is tracing out a textbook double zigzag bear market, with wave X having peaked at 69¾, right at the apex of the wave B triangle within the first A-B-C zigzag decline. Last month's issue carried this chart, with the following comment: "For the first time since last year at this level, I once again recommend ASA puts. Use any close above 72 as a stop. The downside target is 39." ASA has started down on schedule. We can now lower the stop to 69¾, limiting our risk to near zero. A rally through 69¾ would probably have a dramatic effect on my opinion for the precious metals markets.

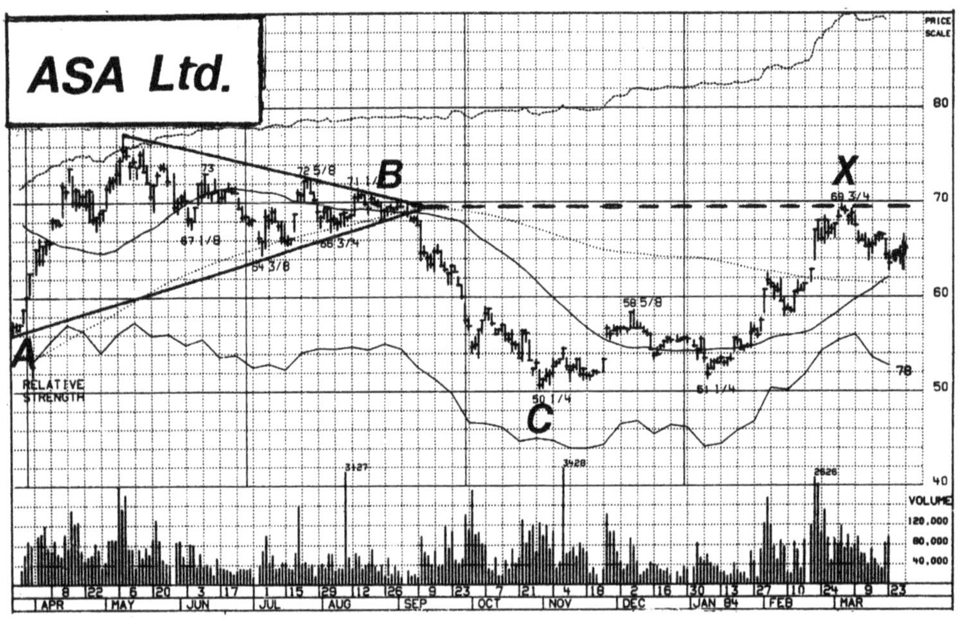

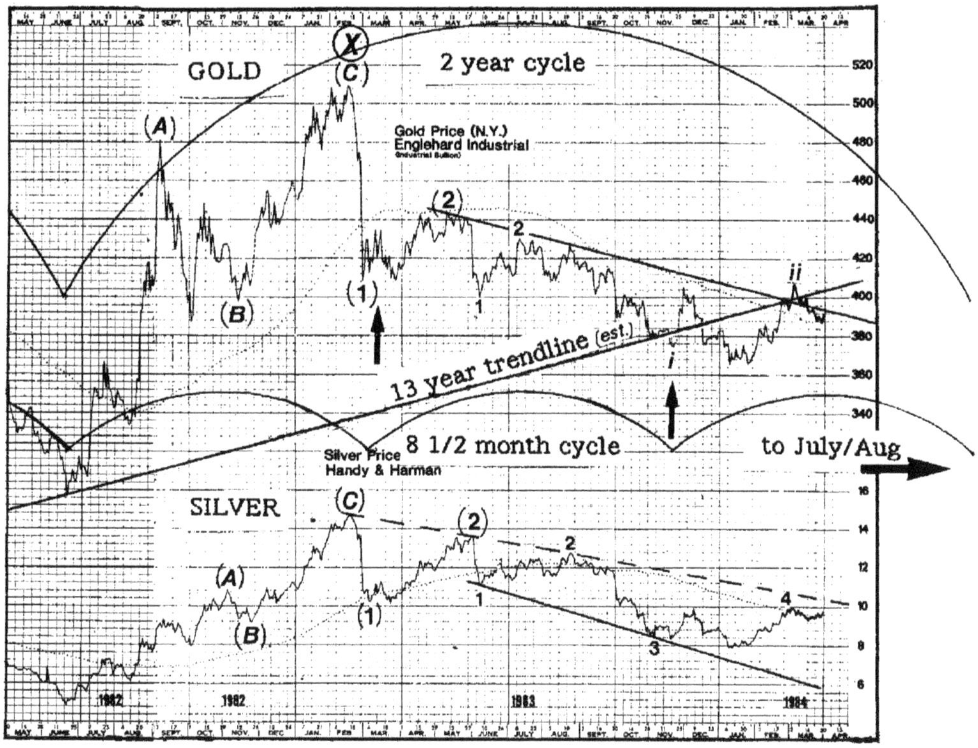

Silver

On the day of the silver top at $10.11 basis the London close ($10.50 basis July futures), *The Elliott Wave Theorist* made these comments: "It's an excellent opportunity to get 100% short (with a stop at $10.70)."

As I've often stressed, what is always of utmost importance is a good entry on a position. That way, if the analysis is right, we've caught the turn, and if wrong, our loss is minimal. At this point, we have a good entry, and the stop can be lowered to $10.25 basis the London close ($10.50 basis the July futures contract).

Silver stopped rallying beneath its 13-month downtrend line and, like gold, appears to have completed an irregular correction to the upside. This formation portends new lows ahead, with targets below $6/oz. If the downtrend continues, we can use subsequent price action to help pinpoint the most likely price for the final bottom.

APRIL 30, 1984

Gold and silver should head substantially lower into July/August. The sharpest phase of decline lies directly ahead. A move through $407, however, would force a change of opinion.

Gold

Gold remains in a major bear market from the all-time highs at $850. The Supercycle correction appears to be taking the shape of a "double zigzag," with the first Ⓐ-Ⓑ-Ⓒ phase ending in June 1982 and the Ⓧ wave countertrend rally peaking in February 1983 at $511.50. From that point, the second Ⓐ-Ⓑ-Ⓒ down phase appears to have begun. The only alternate count is that wave Ⓧ is still in progress. If it is, a low this summer would precede a final rally back above $500 before prices again began moving persistently lower toward the ultimate target of $105/oz. by 1988. At this point, both counts indicate lower prices for the months immediately ahead. Since an ongoing Ⓧ wave would probably be a "flat" (see text, p.38), the 1982 low at $296.75 appears to be a reasonable minimum downside target for the summer of 1984.

Short term, the wave structure from the high at $406.85 shows a five-wave decline and a feeble three-wave rally. This structure defines the short term trend as down. The intermediate term trend must also be assumed to be down unless the high at $406.85 is penetrated. If waves 1 and 2 have been completed, as they appear to have been, then wave 3, a sharper price decline, lies directly ahead.

Cycles

On March 5, gold completed an a-b-c irregular correction to the upside. That correction began at the November low, when the 8½ month cycle bottomed. The net gain for that cycle was a feeble 8.7%, the smallest gain for that cycle since the 2-year cycle bottomed in June 1982. That minimal gain supports the ongoing cyclic interpretation, since the third 8½ month cycle

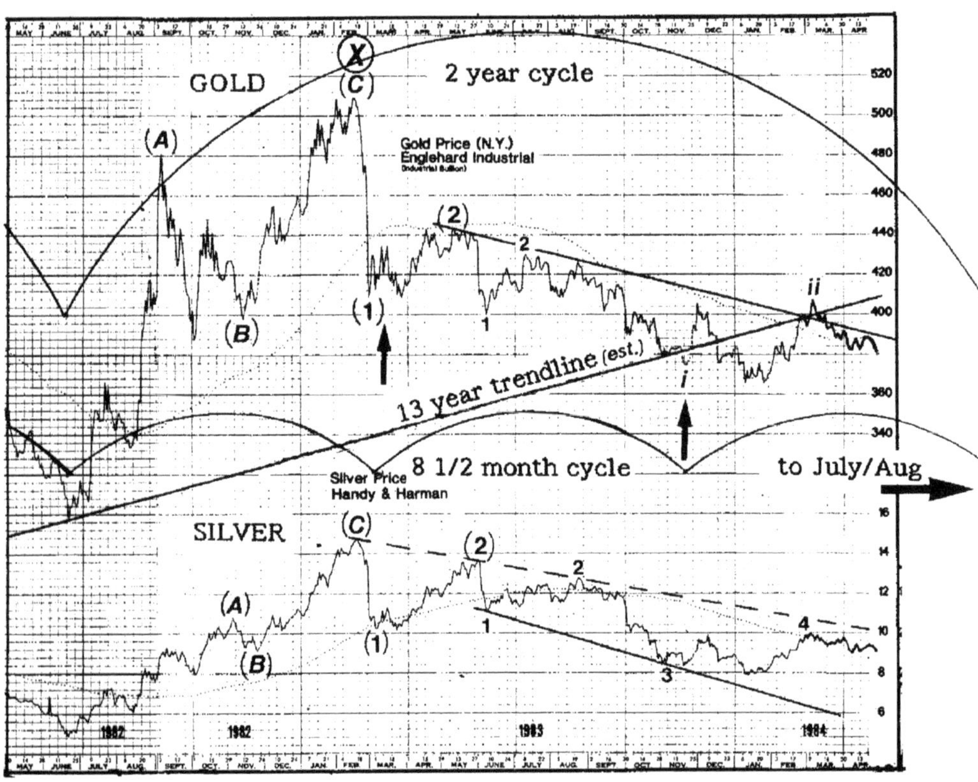

in the 2-year cycle should be the weakest. The 8½ month cycle has now peaked and is heading down hard with the 2-year cycle into the late July/early August time period. This combination of cycles is the most bearish since the June 1982 low.

Sentiment

The put/call ratio on gold futures contracts still indicates too much optimism. Meanwhile, bullish articles on the precious metals are still appearing in the major newspapers, including a feature article on April 23 in the WSJ explaining how you can buy gold in all sorts of ways (bullion, certificates, mining stocks, mutual funds, futures and options) and a feature on copper in Barron's on April 9, a week after the price peak. This kind of interest after a short term peak in any market is usually a danger sign, particularly when accompanied by apparently bullish events. In this case, the Soviets' stepped-up bombing in Afghanistan and a scary series of biological warfare articles being run in the WSJ are being ignored by the gold market. Even the flashy rumors, such as Volcker quitting and Reagan being shot, were able to get gold up only five or ten dollars on a bounce. It's not coincidence that the headline-grabbing Argentina default occurred on March 8, three days after the peak in prices. At the time, that default was being heralded as a reason to buy.

Momentum

At the March 5 peak, gold was stopped cold by the 13-year uptrend line, which now serves as resistance. At the same time, prices, which had shot briefly through the intermediate term downtrend line (see daily chart), ended up leaving only a spike on the chart. In other words, the upside momentum was not enough to penetrate that wall of resistance. On the other hand, downside momentum so far has been slow. A sharp break would be a good indication that the bulls have given up, and as yet that hasn't happened. Until it does, this area of technical input needs to be watched closely.

Tactics

Investors who are waiting for a good buy point should avoid gold at this time, since it should be trading below $300/oz. by August. As far as traders are concerned, our stop is now at the same level as our entry, so we are riding a no-risk trade on the short side. With respect to the stop, all participants should buy if the London price fixes above $406.85.

Examining the Bullish Case

This month, I received two letters asking how I could be bearish on gold when analyst X or Y was bullish. The answer is, I may not be right, but I must remain bearish because that's the stance that the technical evidence best supports. One letter enclosed a quote from another service, which proclaimed, "One thing is for sure. There is nothing at work in the market now to suggest a sharp decline in gold and precious metals prices. Clearly, the pressures are in the opposite – i.e., bullish – direction." In the markets, I'm almost never that certain about anything. So let's examine the bulls' argument.

The entire case, and the case I read every day in one service or another, is that the inflation rate is accelerating and therefore gold must go up. My first reaction to that line of reasoning is that it's a fundamentalists' black-box argument, which means that it ignores one important factor, people and what they are thinking. If gold prices rose and fell within an inanimate physical system, and accelerating inflation could be shown to cause a rise in prices, then accelerating inflation would always cause a rise in prices, period. However, the fact that people are involved rubberizes the equations. For example, even if accelerating inflation means more money around, there's no guarantee that that money will go into the gold market; it may go into the stock market or second homes. It may also be the case that indications of accelerating inflation are causing real interest rates to rise in a wiser-than-before credit market, thus choking off the usual effect of greater liquidity. The government is also made of people, and with the Federal government increasing its war on gold and silver owners, intangible assets may be given such a tax advantage over tangibles that for a few years at least, retirement and investment funds may virtually be forced into other vehicles, rendering impotent the bullish argument based only upon a mildly accelerating inflation. Most important, gold is overpriced historically relative to any representative basket of other commodities (see April, May and June 1983 issues). A bump upward in the inflation rate may not be nearly enough, relative to expectations, to cause the price to rise. If gold is being held up because of a widespread belief that the next round of inflation will be in the 25% range and it moves up slowly, then peaks in the 6% range, gold could actually decline as the too-mild acceleration in the inflation rate persistently disappoints its holders.

Despite my current opinion, gold may very well turn up soon. There are no guarantees in this business. If it does, however, the wave structure will get us aboard before we have suffered any loss whatsoever. In other words, if I turn out wrong, we know where our stop is. If the bulls turn out wrong, and they base their argument on something outside the market like the inflation rate, there is *no stop* except the point at which they give up on their indicator. That's a recipe for serious losses. Meanwhile, the gains racked up by Elliott wave analysis over the past four years are so great that an occasional stop-out (such as occurred last in January 1982 for a zero loss) is mighty cheap insurance.

Silver

Silver has fallen 10% ($1) since the "sell" point on March 5. A commodity as volatile as silver could retrace that decline in two days, but unless the early March peak at $10.11 basis London close is penetrated, the trend must be considered down. Traders should stay short. We can now lower the stop to the March 5 high, limiting our risk to zero.

Silver should fall at least to below $8 to complete the wave structure shown on the chart. A reasonable target is the $6 area, but I prefer to have more price structure to work from before trying to compute an exact target. For now, I'm more concerned with whether we're right to be "out or short." If silver falls under $8, we can relax and start looking for where the bottom might occur.

JUNE 4, 1984

Targets of "below $300" for gold and "below $8" for silver remain intact, but a move in bullion above $407 basis London fix would force a change in my intermediate term opinion to bullish.

Gold & Silver

The May issue took three pages to detail the precious metals picture, and there is as yet nothing to change that assessment. Elliott analysis recognized the top at $406.85 basis London fix on March 5. Traders sold short, and the stop has since been placed at $407, limiting risk to zero.

Although there are some uncertainties (see next paragraph), the balance of evidence in the precious metals markets remains bearish, and downside targets of gold $300, silver $8 and ASA 39 remain in effect. The May rally occurred in an environment of great fear, with an escalating war in the Persian Gulf, reports that Continental Illinois Bank is on the verge of collapse (the 80% drop in its stock price in 8 months isn't arguing with the reports), and more announcements from "third world" countries regarding non-payment of non-payable debts. In the face of all this news, gold has managed a rally of only $18 in five full weeks. The action in the rally has been spiky and nervous, with numerous daily reversals. The crisis environment, moreover, has pushed sentiment to 66% bullish on gold and 68% bullish on silver according to Market Vane. Meanwhile, ASA still sells at a fairly high premium to net asset value, indicating that the stock probably is not at a major bottom. Finally, as illustrated in the May issue, the 8½-month and 2-year cycles still appear to be pointing "hard down" into late July/early August.

The opportunities in the stock market and the historically high real rate of interest on government bills make gold one of the least attractive investments. I prefer to stay out of the gold market unless forced in by the price action. As far as trading goes, however, gold is once again at a critical juncture in the price pattern. As of Friday, the rally has retraced exactly 61.8% of the previous minor decline, a normal point for a countertrend rally to peak. The daily wave count, unfortunately, does not as yet confirm a new intermediate term downtrend, so the evidence from the Wave Principle allows for a resolution in either direction. The gold bulls are convinced that if interest rates decline, gold will soar. Now that Elliott analysis indicates a major top in interest rates, we must at least prepare for the possibility of a bullish outcome in the precious metals. Stay short for now, but if $407 is exceeded on a London fixing, go long immediately and place a stop at $380. As for silver, stay short. If the early March peak is penetrated, go long with a stop at $9.50 basis London close.

JULY 11, 1984

Gold is well on its way to the long-standing target of "below $300," while ASA is approaching its downside target of 39. Silver has fallen to its minimum target of "below $8," with maximum targets near $5. The precious metals' decline should end in late July/early August, presenting an intermediate term buying opportunity.

Gold

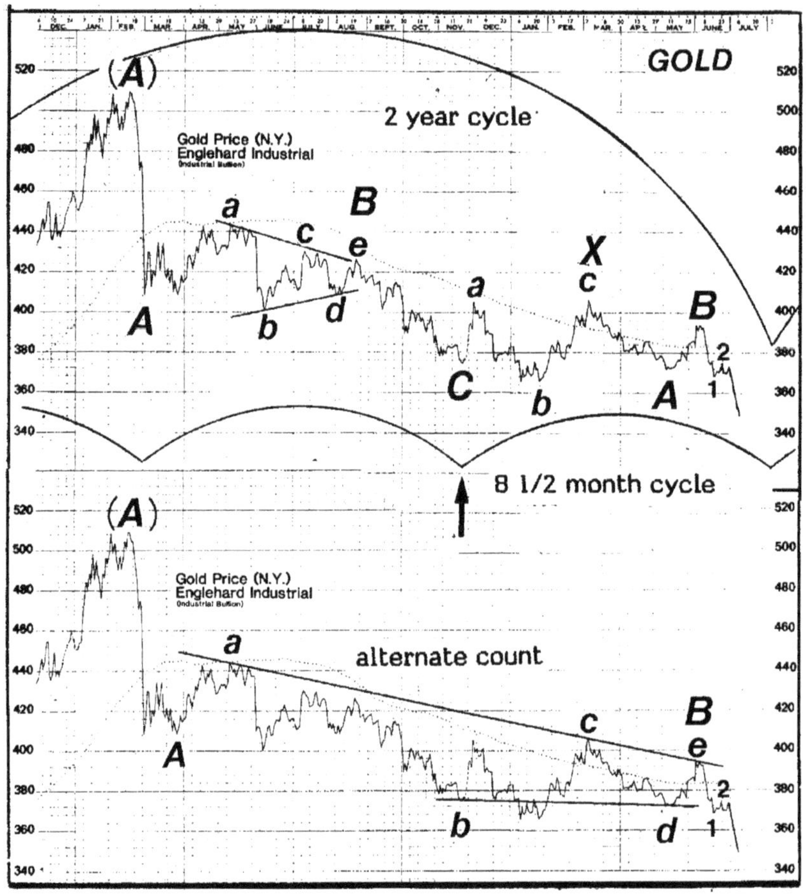

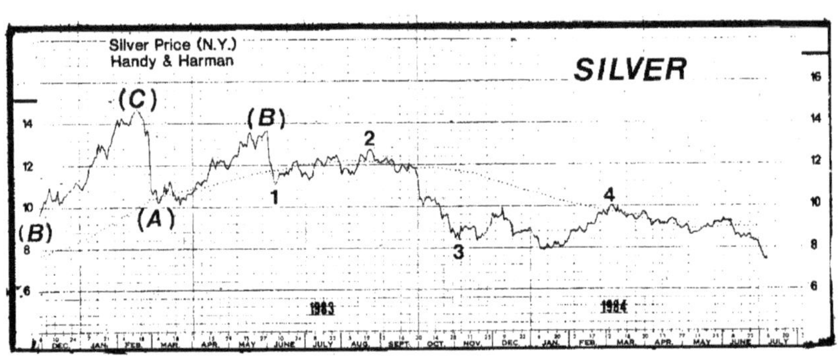

Elliott wave analysis has suggested being "out or short" in the gold market since the February 1983 peak above $500/oz. The downside target of "below $300" for the intermediate term decline remains in effect, as does the time target of "late July or early August" 1984. Our last minor "sell" point occurred on March 5, the exact day of the early 1984 rally top. If you followed the suggestion to short gold and buy ASA puts (or sell futures as we did on the Telephone Update), you've participated in one of the most profitable trades of the year. If you bought gold or gold stocks on that date, when one analyst was quoted as being "the most bullish on gold in my 15 years in the business," you would be down 16%-26% on your holdings and at least an additional 3% in lost interest, for an average 24% loss in only four months! If you annualize that figure, you'll see why most people lose lots of money in the markets.

The question is, will the downtrend continue? Most evidence says that it will, at least through the balance of July. As pointed out last month before the acceleration began, "the 8½-month and 2-year cycles still appear to be pointing "hard down" into late July/early August." In three to five weeks, gold should provide an intermediate term "buy" for the first time since June 1982. Let's look at the current technical picture.

Although the precise interpretation for the Elliott wave structure since the February 1983 high has been open to some fine points of interpretation, the structure has been typical of a bear market, and that was all we needed to know. At this point, while the preferred wave count used over the past year is still valid, the number of first and second waves of each smaller degree under that interpretation has become excessive and argues strongly in favor of a count involving a triangle. The wave count shown on the top chart on the previous page, was first suggested in the September 1983 issue and is currently the most satisfying of the acceptable alternates. The wave count on the bottom chart is also acceptable. The September 1983 issue made these observations:

> Since a triangle in this position must be a "b" wave, it implies that the upward correction from June 1982 is still unfolding. Wave (b) now in progress should fall at least to the $378-387 zone.... If wave (a) of the correction was a "three," then the triangle would be marking only the halfway point of wave (b), which would be expected to carry back to or below the start of wave (a) at $296.75.

All of these observations remain valid. The November low was $374.25, just $3.75 below the first-stop target, allowing Elliott analysis to forecast the minor rally back above $400. The intermediate term minimum downside target at $296.75 is still valid, ten months later. Most important is what the involvement of a triangle implies. Because a triangle in this structure must be in a "wave B" position (see text, p.41), the decline can only be tracing out a corrective wave structure, which in turn means that the bear market rally phase that began in June 1982 is still in force. [Note: This proved true. – Ed.]

For a year now, I have illustrated the possibility that the June 1982-February 1983 rally was only wave (A) of Ⓧ, where Ⓧ is a countertrend rally phase separating two Ⓐ-Ⓑ-Ⓒ declines. It is highly likely that after wave (B) of Ⓧ bottoms (probably in late July/early August when the 8½-month and 2-year cycles are due), gold should rise in wave (C) of Ⓧ to slightly above last year's peak. I wouldn't be surprised to see it hit the original computed target for wave Ⓧ of $547. That level could be reached in mid-1985, when the next 2-year cycle is due to peak along with the overriding 6-year cycle (see long term chart). From there, the second Ⓐ-Ⓑ-Ⓒ should take gold to its final target of either $105 or $179 by 1987-88. Below is an updated chart from the March issue that showed the positions of the longer term cycles. That interpretation still appears to be on track.

Interestingly enough, both intermediate term wave counts require the same resolution: a five-wave decline from the early June peak of $394.50 basis London fix. The third wave of

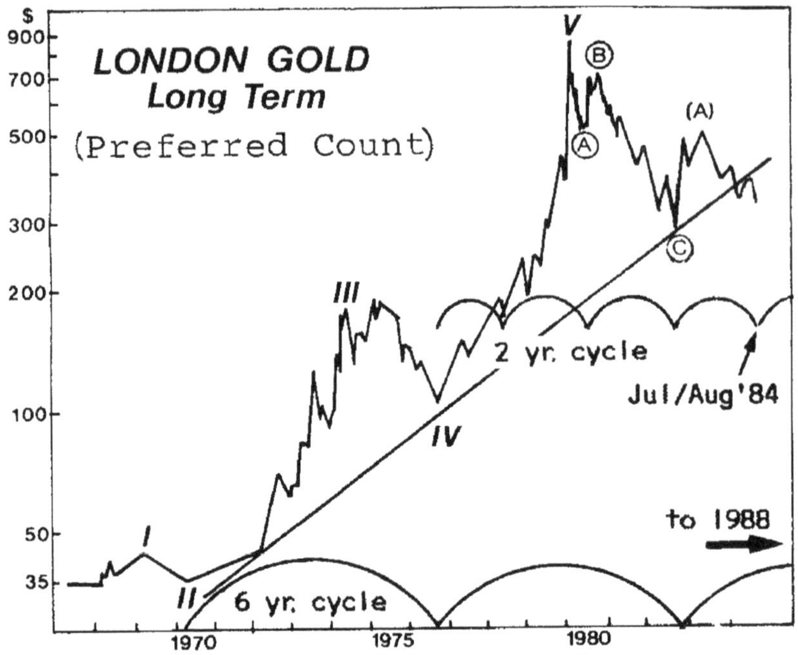

that decline is currently in force, and the fifth should be fairly easy to recognize. The upcoming low, if we can catch it, should provide the best long-side trading entry in over two years.

Sentiment

The record-setting bullishness in February 1983 is certainly exacting its toll. Sentiment is finally changing but is not yet at major bottom levels. Market Vane (61 S. Lake Av., Pasadena, CA) reports a drop to 31% "bulls" on gold, the put/call ratio on the gold stocks is rising, and ASA's price relative to its net asset value is declining. However, each of these measures has substantial room for improvement. A break below $300 for bullion should do it.

At this point, there are quite a few trend-followers who have just become bold enough to recommend selling gold short. Furthermore, as gold specialist Tony Henfrey (Gold Letter, Box 5577, Durban 4000, South Africa) points out, magazines are beginning to ask, "Is Gold Dead?" These are good signs of an impending bottom. However, there are two types of diehard "longs" remaining to be shaken out of the gold market. The first is the fundamental camp, which has been urging purchase of gold all through the first half of 1984 on the basis of an increase in the money supply (see discussion in the May issue). The second is the group that got long up to the eyeballs on the widely disseminated forecasts, still being advertised as late as last week, that gold will reach $3000-$6000 per ounce by 1986. (If it really is going there, it had better get its you-know-what in gear.) These groups

have very high expectations, and their discouragement should be correspondingly severe. The analysts who were predicting "limit moves in gold just ahead" due to inflationary pressures are getting their limit moves, all right. I wouldn't be surprised to see the Market Vane figures fall to record lows.

Tactics

Lower the stop from $407, where traders last sold short, to $370 basis London fix. Cover all short sales on any fix below $300/oz. and move to 50% long at that time.

ASA

EWT recommended purchase of puts in ASA when the stock hit 69 in March. With the stock recently falling as low as 49¾, puts have increased in value 200% to 1000%. Now that it's psychologically easy to sell short, ⅔ of the decline is probably over. Take profits now on enough of your position to pay for the initial investment, letting the rest ride. ASA's target remains 39. Sell all puts when ASA falls below 41.

Silver

The wave count for silver has been clear at each minor turning point since last year's top at $15/oz. As reiterated last month, "Silver should fall at least to below $8 to complete the wave structure shown on the chart." At this point, the fifth wave down from the June 1983 peak is in progress (see daily chart), and the $8 level has been penetrated. First support is near $7/oz. (where wave 5 equals .618 times the length of waves 1 through 3), while the most likely target is still near $5/oz. (where wave 5 equals waves 1 through 3 and matches the June 1982 low).

After ten years of stories about the "shortage" of silver, precious metals market letters have all of a sudden begun coming out with long research reports about the "silver surplus"! It is finally being suggested, 4½ years after the peak in silver and following a 90% drop in price, what some of the bearish "fundamentals" might be for silver: stockpiles are building, reclamation is improving, demand is down, and production is increasing. By the time the investing public digests and understands these arguments, silver should be at a good buy point.

JULY 24, 1984 — INTERIM REPORT

Gold appears to be in its fifth wave down. We have been "out or short" since the March peak at $407, but now it's time to formulate plans for covering short sales. Gold is approaching our long standing price target of $297 (+ or - $30) and our time target of "late July/early August." Just to put some money in the bank, cover half the position any time gold falls below $325 basis London fix. Lower the stop to $365 basis London fix.

AUGUST 6, 1984

Gold has finally hit a minimum downside objective, although risk remains to $270/ounce unless gold clears $360 on the upside.

Gold

An amazing number of people keep arguing, with little historical evidence, that if the Dow is going to 3700, it must be indicating a super inflation. I don't think inflation has anything to do with it. The best stock market rises in U.S. history have been during times of low inflation. Besides, wave V is an impulse wave under the Wave Principle, which indicates improving fundamental conditions. I can't imagine hyperinflation being the cause of a major stock market advance unless it's in the "B" wave position. The outlook for gold, which has been bearish for 4½ years and still calls for a low near $105 in 1987, continues to indicate that inflation will not be a major factor until at least that time.

Gold is now entering the time zone for a significant intermediate term bottom, based on the 2-year and 8½ month cycles. Unfortunately, enough downside risk remains that it is premature to recommend an aggressive long position. The "worst case" target has not been met, our sentiment indicator on gold still shows too little bearish psychology despite the $75 drop in prices in four months, and the decline from the June high is not yet a clear five waves down on the London fix chart (not shown). Furthermore, ASA has rallied back to resistance at 54 and still hasn't reached its most likely downside target of 39. For these reasons, I cannot yet safely recommend buying gold.

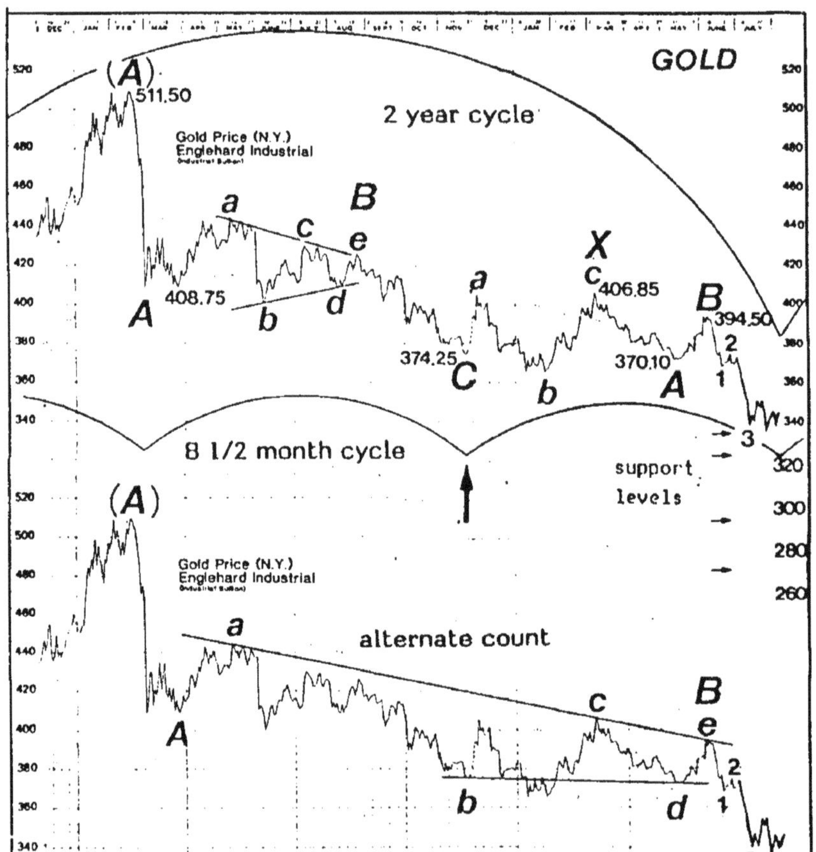

However, you should be aware that the wave structure finally allows for a bullish interpretation for the first time in months. As pointed out last month, "both intermediate term wave counts require the same resolution: a five-wave decline from the early

June peak of $394.50 basis London fix." The accompanying New York daily close chart shows what can be interpreted as a completed or nearly-completed "five," which in turn could mark the low of an (X) wave separating two (A)-(B)-(C) advances dating from June 1982. [Note: The point labeled (A) on the chart would be labeled (C) to fit this discussion. The October issue discusses the chart as labeled. The implications of the two labelings are identical in terms of price forecasting. – Ed.] Furthermore, using the preferred count, wave C is 1.618 times as long as wave A at $335.20, while by the alternate count, wave C is .618 times the length of wave A at $331. An interesting point about this interpretation is that if wave (X) bottoms near $332, the next (A)-(B)-(C) advance will be the same length as the first (a typical relationship in double zigzags) when it reaches a price of $547 basis London fix, which is exactly where I had computed the upside potential for wave Ⓧ two years ago (see July 12, 1982 issue). The low so far is $335 basis London, $332 basis the nearby futures contract. Secondary support lies near $323, since under the preferred count, the second A-B-C is .618 times as long as the first at $321.93, while under the alternate count, the widest part of the triangle points to a $324.50 target.

My main problem is that, although we're close to a low, it is impossible to pinpoint one single target, making the extent of downside follow-through uncertain. The lowest target using the preferred count is $269.70, where the second A-B-C will be the same length as the first. The alternate count's lowest target is $291.75, the point at which C will be the same length as A. This point would nearly match the June 1982 low at $296.75.

In sum, the potential support levels for an intermediate term bottom are $335, $323, $292-297 and $270, which are not much help in forecasting. A precise projection will have to await more evidence. However, uncertainty does have a bearing on strategy. Basically, my opinion on gold has changed from super negative in February 1983 to neutral/negative. I suggest covering half the short sales now. After all, gold has fallen $175 from the high last year, and taking profits is a sensible move. Cover the remaining shorts and go 50% long below $297. Move to 100% long at $271 with a stop at $260. If $360 is penetrated on the upside, cover all shorts and go long with a stop at $345. We took some profits on our ASA puts last month, but I would hold the rest for a target of 39, with a stop at 57. If gold turns up sharply, I will illustrate the long term count in the September issue.

Silver

The wave count for silver has been clear at every minor turning point since the 1983 peak at $15/oz. Here was last month's conclusion regarding price targets:

> First support is near $7/oz. (where wave 5 equals .618 times the length of waves 1 through 3), while the most likely target is still $5/oz. (where wave 5 equals waves 1 through 3 and matches the June 1982 low).

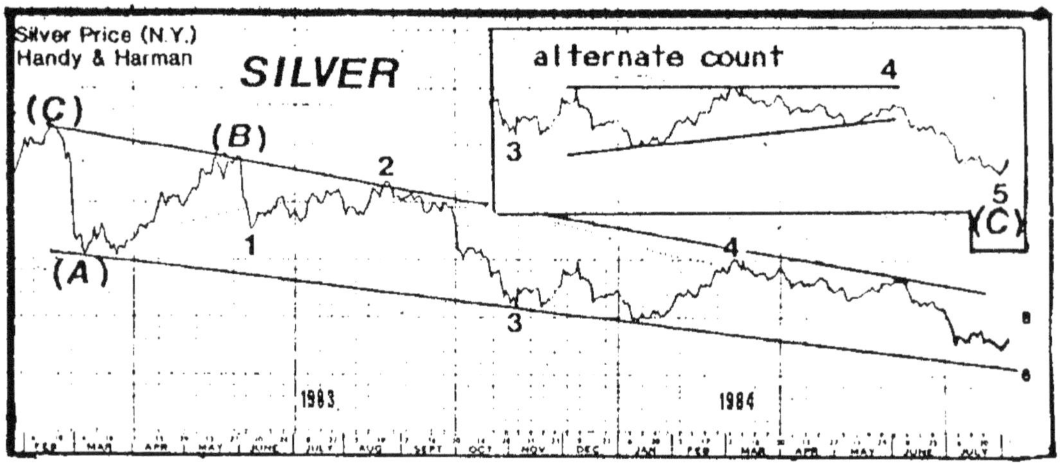

The first support level did quite a precise job in stopping prices, with the low London close so far at $6.92, from which point the current rebound began. Just as in gold, an alternate count does make it possible that silver has bottomed (see accompanying charts). Any move above $7.90 would probably confirm a new advance to above $15. However, the best interpretation is that the current rally is wave iv of 5 of (C), suggesting one more selloff to new lows prior to any significant upside move. Otherwise, the maximum likely upside on this countertrend rally is $7.60 basis London, which has very nearly been met.

My guess is that the recent bounce in the precious metals is a knee-jerk reaction to the bond market rally because of the widespread belief that lower interest rates are bullish for gold and silver. On the next decline to new lows, silver could be an exciting buy.

SEPTEMBER 4, 1984

Unless $370 basis London is exceeded, gold is still likely to fall to below $300/oz.

Gold

A common problem in this business is that analysts often feel pressed to give a "straight up" or "straight down" opinion even if the weight of the evidence is not strong enough to warrant it. The excuse I've heard from writers is that clients and subscribers demand it, so they give them what they want. I prefer having a strong opinion, but to fake it would merely make the next forecast more difficult, dilute the record of Elliott wave analysis, and generate losses for you. Last month, the evidence on gold was just plain inconclusive, and I said so:

> My opinion on gold has changed from super negative in February 1983 to neutral/negative. Gold is entering the time zone for a significant bottom, but enough downside risk remains that it is premature to recommend an aggressive long position. A precise projection will have to await more evidence.

I usually find that there is a good reason for neutral or inconclusive technical evidence. In this case, what has gold done in the four weeks following that observation? It's gone flat sideways! In other words, the technical work was right; gold was not about to make a dramatic move in either direction. One reason undoubtedly was Hard Money Digest's (3608 Grand Av., Oakland, CA 94610) observation last month that "An historic number of newsletters recommend the sale of gold with a full 56% disdaining the yellow metal." When the crowd decides it's OK to sell short in a bear market, the market is usually about to stage a rally attempt. As far as our tactics went, even the neutral evidence had a bearing on strategy:

> I suggest covering half the short sales now. After all, gold has fallen $175 from the high last year, and taking profits is a sensible move.

OK, so we've covered half the short sales. Did the action in August tell us anything? Here are some observations:

1) The upward structures on the hourly chart last month are almost all a-b-c's, which are typical of bear market rallies.

2) The advance in gold stocks and the struggling upward pattern in gold bullion appear to confirm that the 8½ month cycle did bottom right on schedule at our time target of "late July/early August." However, the unimpressive action since then indicates that the upward cycle pressure is being damped by what must be a strongly down long term trend. (The 8½ month cycle, by the way, was just confirmed as valid for silver by a computer study in the July '84 issue of Cycles magazine.)

3) According to Market Vane's (61 S. Lake Ave., Pasadena, CA) figures and our short term indicator, the sentiment picture for gold deteriorated as investors turned more bullish on the metal. This is a dangerous occurrence in the face of a sideways trend. On the other hand, the advisory services and financial media, which produced nothing but bullish articles all the way down from last year's top, are finally comfortable enough to forecast lower prices. On 8/25, with gold at its lowest price in over two years, the WSJ headlined, "Inflation's Diminishing Spectre is Auguring Weakness in Gold."

4) The momentum picture indicates that the deep oversold condition attained in July has now been relieved. This neutral status now makes it possible for gold to begin another wave of decline any time it wants to.

5) Gold appears to have tried to rally in a knee-jerk response to the powerful advances in stocks and bonds. But the contrast is striking, since gold's rally (at least so far) has been anything but powerful. While the DJIA is 150 points off its bottom, gold could hit new lows on two down days.

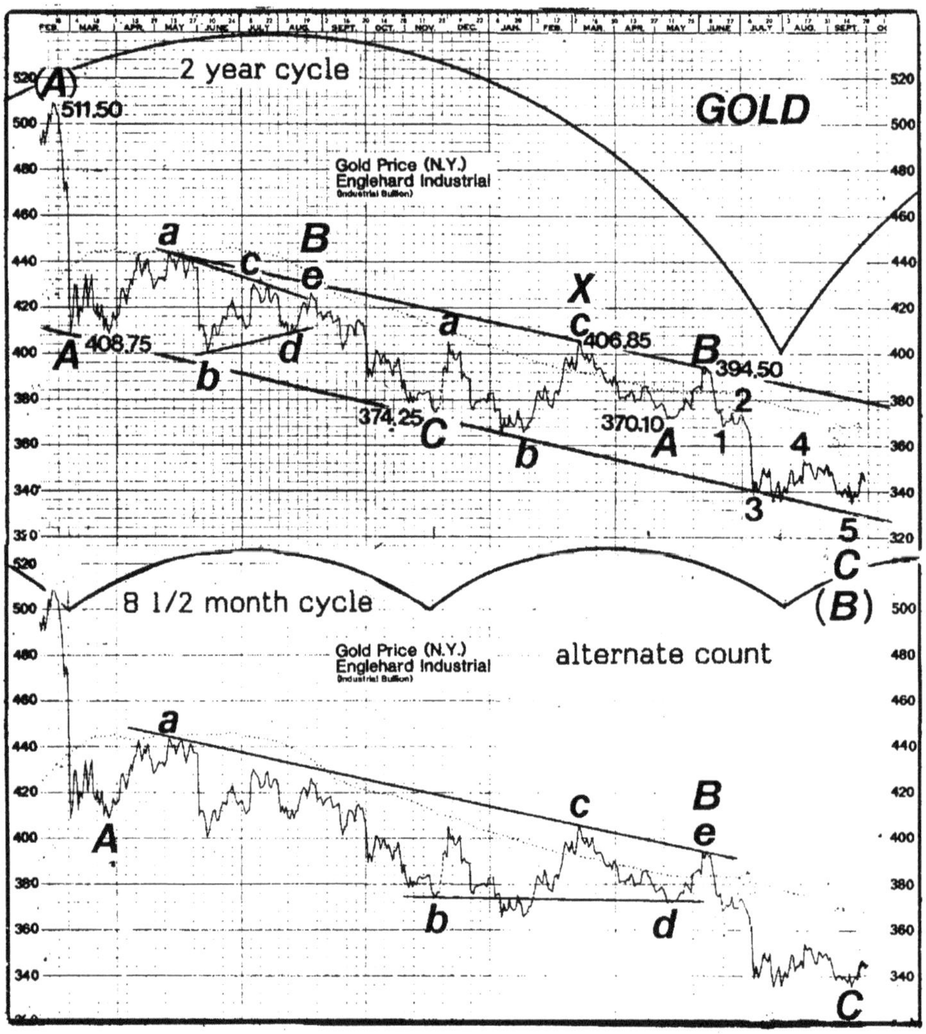

The bottom line is that I feel comfortable holding a 50% short position. Given the negative technical picture, gold is probably in wave 2 of a five-wave decline from the June high. Second waves can retrace much of first waves, so we should raise the stop to $370 basis the London fix. With the 8½ month cycle still officially "up," gold may try to rally or hold up as far out as November. The nearly parallel trend channel that gold has formed since March 1983 appears to allow for some rally as well.

A 100% short position isn't warranted because of the shift in media sentiment, the inopportunity of the cyclic time element and the leeway available within the downtrend channel. Still, another drop in prices during September would be consistent with the net technical evidence, and we're positioned to take advantage of it. I still plan to cover the rest of the short sales and go 50% long if gold hits $297. As far as ASA goes, we took profits in July on enough of the position to pay for the initial investment and are holding the rest for a target of 39, with a stop at 57.

Silver

No cigar this month. After forecasting support at $7 for the July bottom, I expected the August bounce in silver to fall short of $7.90 basis the London close, a close above which, I suggested, would "probably confirm a new advance to $15." As it happened, silver popped to $7.92, just 2 cents above resistance, and then fell back. While this minor penetration may prove significant, at this point I do not feel that silver has signaled a substantial new advance.

Take a look at the chart of silver. If the upper resistance line, which has held back prices ever since the 1983 top, can be penetrated, then silver will be off and running on a new advancing wave. That line cuts through at $8.40 early this month and $8.00 in early October. Unless that happens, silver remains an unattractive investment. Support levels are $7 (+ or - 10¢) and $5 (+ or - 20¢).

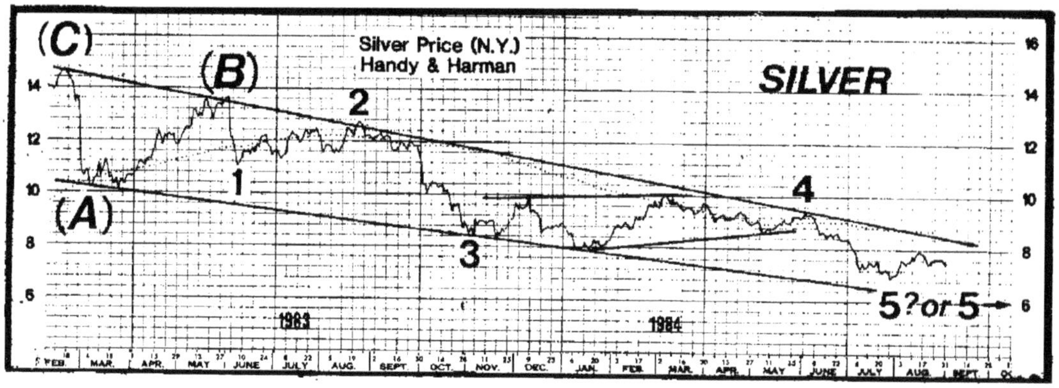

Long term, I am convinced that the fourth wave congestion period of the mid-1970s is rock-solid support. Any time silver enters the $3.90-$5.90 range, as it did in 1982, it is providing an opportunity to accumulate physical silver for long term investment.

OCTOBER 1, 1984

Gold is close to its first intermediate term bottom in over two years but should not be bought until it hits next support at $297 or takes out the stop at $360.

Gold

As you know, EWT has been bearish on gold's intermediate term trend for over a year and half. Now it appears time to assess the probabilities for a significant intermediate term bottom. The wave count used in the July and August issues has now been satisfied by a completed five waves down to end wave C. Under this count, the orthodox low for wave 5 on September 17 at $335.25 is a slight failure (see text, p.32) since it held above the July 9 low for wave 3, which occurred at $332.50. Besides the wave structure, the Fibonacci price relationships are in place for an acceptable bottom. The minimum downside target of $335.20 (see August 6 issue) was met at both lows. This is the point at which wave C equals 1.618 times the length

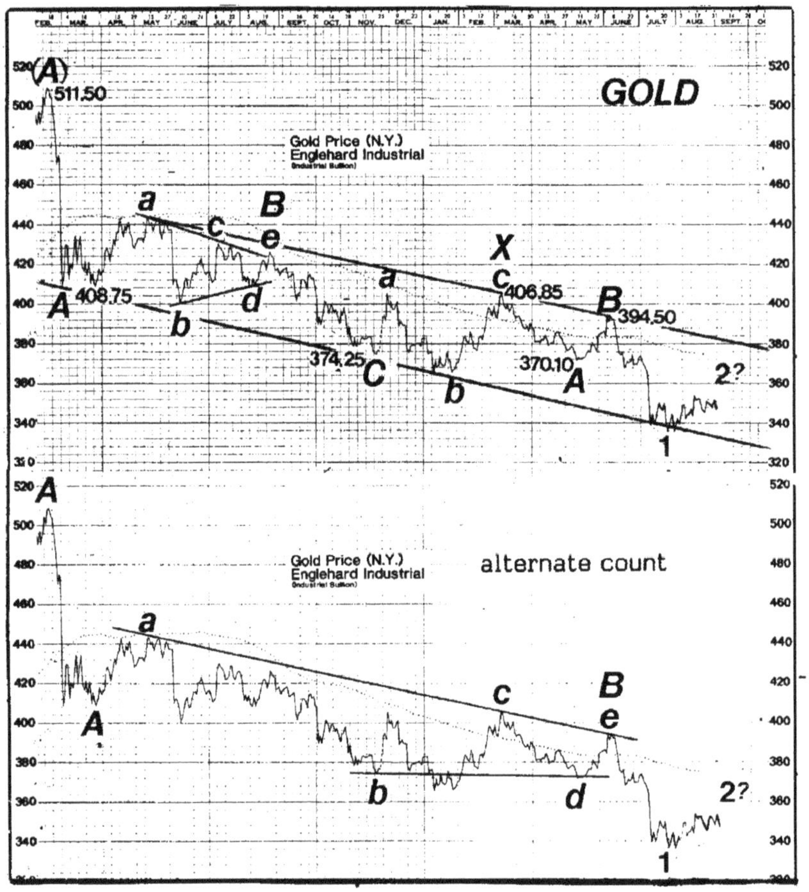

of wave A in the preferred count. Even the alternate count recognizes this area as support, since its wave C equals .618 times the length of wave A at $331. If gold heads up from here, then wave (B) of Ⓧ will have ended, and wave (C) will be destined to carry up to $547/oz. into the peak of the 6-year cycle, which is due in 1985.

The technical indicators support the case that gold may be making an intermediate term low.

1) The 8½-month and 2-year cycles bottomed on schedule in late July, and point "up" for at least the next two months.

2) On the momentum front, gold futures contracts hit new lows last month, while cash gold prices and gold stocks did not. This non-confirmation does not guarantee that a bottom has been seen, but it's typical of bottoms and must be considered bullish.

3) Investor sentiment darkened in September, with Market Vane's tally showing only 25% bulls just two weeks ago, the lowest percentage since January. This reading was generated, moreover, during a period of very mild decline for gold and a neutral performance from gold stocks, indicating that forces outside the market generated bearish sentiment. These conditions usually prevail near bottoms.

On the bearish side, while our own sentiment gauge did improve substantially as gold fell to $335.25, it is not yet indicating a "buy." In addition, ASA has rallied above its August peak, as has my gold stock index, but bullion has so far failed to confirm. Finally, a study of the chart of ASA shows strong trendline resistance at current prices, and it will take a move above 57 to break through it. The trading strategy below is formulated with these hurdles in mind.

Last month, I suggested covering half the short sales and turned from "bearish" to "neutral/bearish" on the intermediate term trend. We stayed 50% short through another new low in gold futures prices two weeks ago, but I can no longer comfortably recommend short positions, or puts on ASA. We took partial profits on our ASA puts in July, which would have been the perfect month to sell them all. Still, they were purchased when the stock was 69, so the remainder of the position closed out now should be moderately profitable.

The best strategy now is to cover all short sales in gold and put your profits in the bank. Go long either on a drop to the next support level at $297 basis the London fix, with a stop at $262, or on a rally up through the $360 resistance level, with a stop at $325.

It is almost certain that gold is not making a major bottom, which is unlikely to occur until 1987-88 at a price close to $105/oz., so I have no long term "buy" recommendation. Chances for an intermediate term rally have improved greatly, however, so be prepared.

Silver

All year, the wave structure for silver has been clearly readable. Last month, my count showed a possibly completed fifth wave in July, although caution was still warranted and support was reiterated at "$7 (+ or - 10¢)." The lowest London fix last month occurred on September 18 at $6.98. Obviously the Elliott support computations are still on target, and I'm beginning to feel better about the potential for a tradable bottom. For the first time since 1982, I'm willing to go long silver on a move above $8 basis the London fix, which would break prices above a 16-month downtrend line (see daily chart, below).

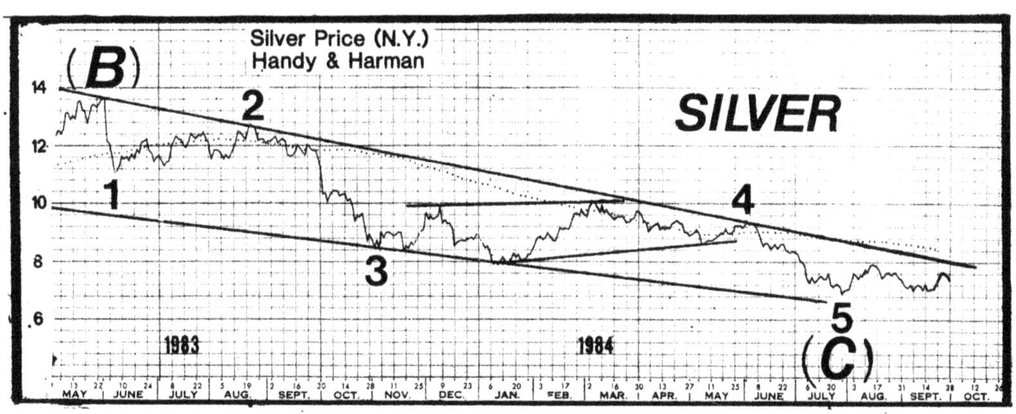

NOVEMBER 7, 1984

Gold is a trading "buy" for the first time in a year. As long as $320 basis London fix is not penetrated on the downside, a rally from here has the potential to be the best rally since the June 1982 low.

Gold

This month would be a good time to review the entire picture for gold for the benefit of new subscribers. Let's look at the long term outlook for gold and then zero in on the short term picture.

The bull market in bullion that took place between 1967 and 1980 traced out a typical five-wave Elliott structure (see long term chart). For this reason, the bear market which began in January 1980 when gold peaked at $850/oz. is not merely another interruption in the previous bull market. It is a bear market that must be of large enough degree to correct the entire 13-year advance that preceded it.

Long Term Price Target

Elliott's studies of typical wave behavior revealed that bear markets tend to bring prices back to the zone of the previous fourth wave of one lesser degree and usually to the lower extremity of that fourth wave (see text, p.55). This guideline may be a mouthful for those unfamiliar with the terminology, but take a look at the long term chart and you should understand the idea. Note that wave IV within the five-wave advance that preceded this bear market bottomed at $103.50 in August 1976. The peak price within wave IV occurred in December 1974 at $197.50. These two prices define the most likely range for the end of the current bear market.

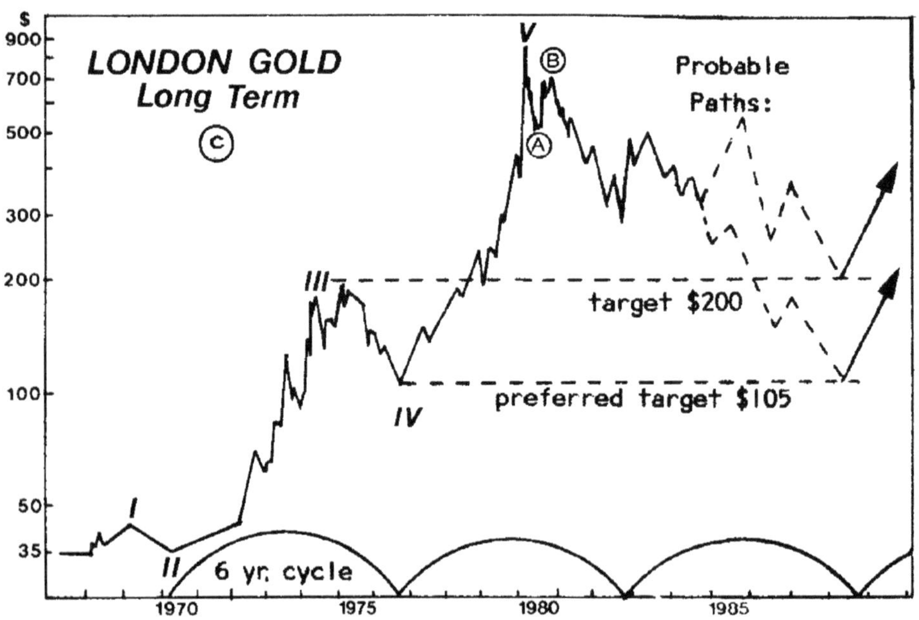

Elliott also discovered that Fibonacci ratio multiples within wave structures tend to have a strong ruling influence on the ultimate price extremities. I have found that when targets based on wave structure coincide with those based upon Fibonacci ratio multiples, reliability increases significantly. It is not coincidence that when I take the length of the first major drop in gold ($850-$474), and multiply it by 1.618, the resulting length taken from the September 1980 peak at $720 (a.m. fix) gives a downside target of $111.63, less than $10 from the lower boundary of the "previous fourth wave." This calculation would satisfy a typical wave relationship whereby wave Ⓒ = 1.618 Ⓐ. These two reasons establish "$105 (+ or - $5) as a sensible expectation. The lower of the two "probable paths" illustrates this possibility.

The second target I have been using is derived from a count that labels the drop from $850 to the June 1982 low at $296.75 as the end of the first zigzag in a "double zigzag" formation. That length, multiplied by .618 and taken from the possible upside target of $547.25 gives a downside target of $205, which is less than $8 from the upper boundary of the "previous fourth wave." These two reasons establish $200 (+ or - $5) as the second likely downside target. The upper "probable path" illustrates this possibility. (If the anticipated rally peaks at $517, the downside target would be $175, the "orthodox" top of wave IV).

I have not been able to come up with any other likely points of support. Therefore, we have three candidates for the ultimate low: $105 (if a 1985 rally peaks below $511.50), $200 (if it peaks at $547) and $175 (if it peaks at $517).

Long Term Time Target

The six-year cycle (measuring from low to low) in precious metals is well-documented. Studies using data on gold and silver stocks and gold prices in foreign currencies show that it has been present for a longer time than just the few revolutions that have occurred since the price of gold was decontrolled in the U.S. The 6-year cycle bottomed again in June 1982, right on schedule. Prices since then have acted exactly as they should in a bear market, undergoing a sharp initial thrust to the upside and then turning weak very early in the cycle. This phenomenon is called "left-hand translation" by cycle students. The next scheduled low is due in 1988.

I have used Fibonacci time multiples in the past but have found them, for forecasting purposes, insufficiently reliable. They occur enough times to be beyond coincidence but not enough to depend upon them in forecasting. However, it does fit nicely that applying the Fibonacci ratio to the time element in the gold market brings us to the same year as does the 6-year cycle. The bull market took 13 (a Fibonacci number) years to complete, running from 1967 to 1980. If the bear market were to take 8 (Fibonacci) years, or .618 times as long as the bull market, it would end in 1988.

The Intermediate-Term Outlook

Corrective waves may take many shapes. Elliott listed eight types of corrective formations and then observed that these may "double" or "triple" in extended sideways trends. Therefore, there is always a good deal of uncertainty on the intermediate term when dealing with major bear markets. The meandering Dow Industrial Average in the late '70s and early '80s is a good example. (So is the sideways trend of the past three months!) Fortunately, the bear market in gold, at least to date, has been a joy to follow because of its clear internal wave structure.

One phenomenon associated with cycles in bear markets is the typical occurrence of a rally into the time period for the ideal cyclic crest. The 6-year cycle is due to peak in 1985, so I fully expect the last strong bear market rally to peak in that year. Very weak cases can be made for targets of $639, a .618 retracement of the bear market to date, $573, a 50% retracement of the bear market to date, and $558, a .618 retracement of the $720-$296.75 drop. However, the most likely maximum upside target is $547.25, the peak of the previous fourth wave of lesser degree. It so happens that if gold holds in the $331-$335 area, which was computed in the August 1984 issue of *The Elliott Wave Theorist* as important "first support," then a rally to $547.25 would be the same length as the initial advance from June 1982 to February 1983. (In fact, measuring from the low so far, made on July 9 at $332.50, projects exactly $547.25!) For this scenario to evolve, gold should begin advancing this month.

As computed in the August 1984 issue, lower targets for the decline are possible, particularly $297 (+ or - $5). The next 8½ month cycle is scheduled to bottom in March/April 1984. If prices carry to new lows in that time zone, then the upside may be limited to $517 (+ or - $5).

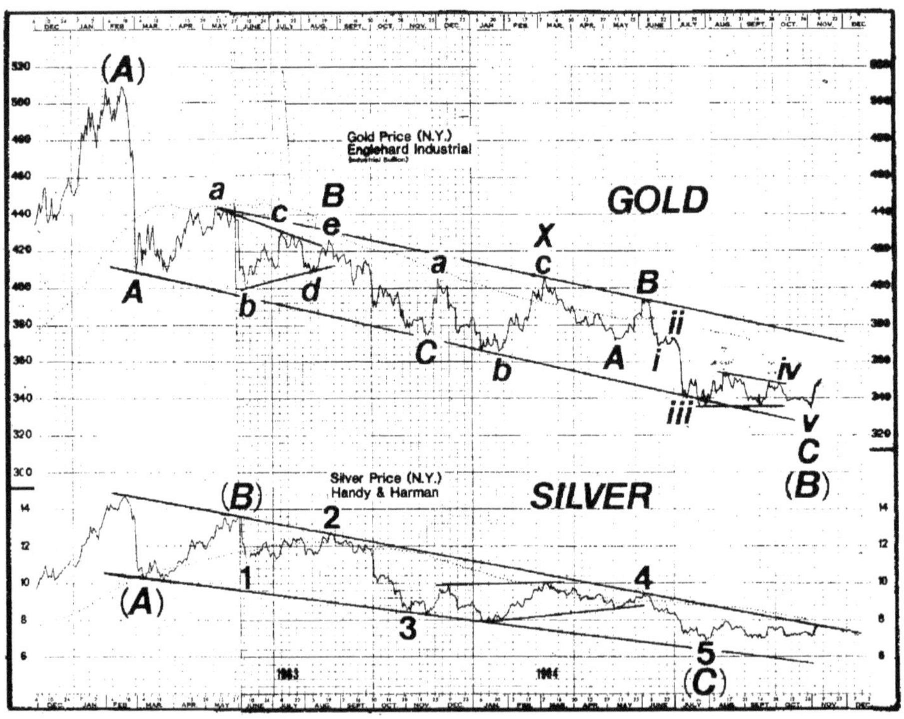

Despite some uncertainty on the particulars, it is possible to state the following with some degree of conviction:

1) The 1983-1984 decline is closer to a bottom than a top. Traders turning bearish at this late date, after a decline of $180, will find it difficult to make profits and keep them.

2) The last tradable intermediate term rally in gold, prior to the final decline in the ongoing bear market, should end in 1985.

3) The old high of $850 is in no jeopardy of being bettered in this cycle, and in fact, a move above $650 is extremely unlikely.

4) Gold is a trading buy at the Elliott support levels of $331-335, $295 or $270. A turn at one of these levels followed by a $30 move to the upside will confirm the beginning of an intermediate term rally.

5) A move above the 1983 peak of $511.50 is quite possible but will not signal a great new bull market. Gold will be a short sale soon thereafter for an ultimate target of $200 or below.

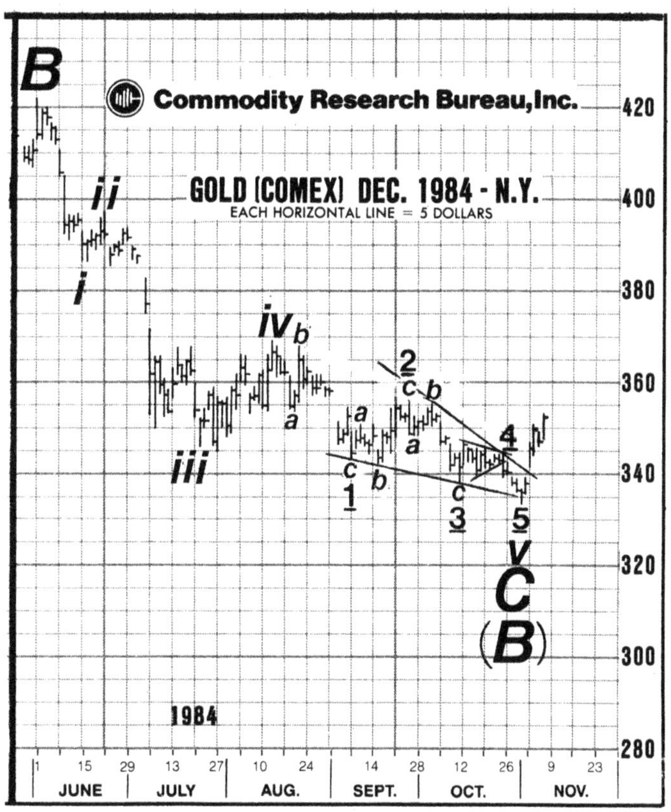

Long term investors should continue to avoid gold, as I have been suggesting for all but five months of the past five years. The best investment for 1985 should be the U.S. stock market, which will be in Primary wave ③, the most powerful part of the advance that began in August 1982.

Short Term Strategy

We covered half our short sales in September and half in October. My intermediate-term opinion changed from "bearish" to "neutral," and gold has fallen into line with the technical input by going flat sideways, in about as neutral a trend as I've even seen. However, that trend is probably about to change. Here is the bullish technical case:

1) In the July 11 issue of *The Elliott Wave Theorist*, I commented, "Both intermediate term wave counts require the same resolution: a five-wave decline from the early June peak of $394.50 basis London fix." It is now possible to count that decline as five waves in both the cash gold chart (as I did in the October issue) and in the chart of the December futures contract (see daily charts).

2) On the London fix chart, wave v is .618 times as long as wave i, which in turn is .618 times as long as wave iii. This interlocking Fibonacci relationship argues in favor of calling the decline from the June peak a single wave.

3) Gold has continued to hold in the $331-$335 Elliott support zone, which is based upon Fibonacci relationships in the larger wave structure from the 1983 top (see calculations, 8/6/84 issue).

4) The 2-year cycle has bottomed and is now pointing up.

5) Last week, gold futures contracts once again fell to new lows, and once again cash gold bullion did not. This is another in a string of bullish divergences.

6) Market Vane's sentiment tally for gold still shows a preponderance of "bears," which has persisted throughout the sideways trend of the past four months.

7) 14 months ago, I highlighted a newspaper article that detailed the tremendous rush by base-metal mining companies into the business of mining gold. That move was both a technical negative in that it revealed a too-bullish psychology and a fundamental negative in that the mines were gearing up to produce much more gold than before, which would be a long-term depressant on the price. Now that gold is nearly $100/oz. lower, the producers have a different outlook on the market, so at least psychology has changed. Here are some excerpts from a July 18 article entitled, "Gold Price Slide Threatens Canada Mines."

TORONTO (Reuter)—Canada's once booming gold-mining industry could be facing a series of mine closures if international bullion prices fall much further, analysts say. Industry observers said in interviews they feel the flurry of activity in the industry in recent years could come to a sharp halt this fall if gold prices fall much closer to $300 an ounce. In a wave of selling, international gold prices have fallen to about $346 an ounce. Analysts warn that more mines will be closed and exploration budgets slashed if gold prices don't improve soon. Until recently, Canadian gold-mining companies had been caught up in a Klondike-like rush, developing such new finds as the huge Hemlo Play in Ontario. Canada has been counting on new mining projects to stave off competition from the Third world and help it retain its position as the world's third largest gold producer, after South Africa and the Soviet Union. However, earlier this week Pamour Porcupine Mines issued a terse statement saying it was closing two large gold mines in Ontario after suffering a string of monthly losses. "Once gold gets down below $300 then you get into a pretty large list of mines that will be affected," one analyst said. Market analysts, who were assuming companies would be fetching over $400 an ounce for gold, are now sharply reducing earnings estimates for the industry. Gold-mining stocks have fallen sharply on Canadian stock markets and market-watchers say this does not bode

Here is the bearish technical case:

1) The 8½-month cycle is topping and will point down until March/April 1985.

2) Lower targets are still possible under the Wave Principle.

3) Gold bullion has failed to confirm the new high in most gold stocks, which occurred in late September/early October.

4) ASA is selling above net asset value.

With gold sitting right on support and the balance of technical evidence bullish for the first time in over two years, a "long" side strategy carries the least risk and the greatest potential for reward. I would like to recommend that all near-to-intermediate term traders buy gold now. In order to provide leeway for all the nearby support calculations from the August letter, place a stop at $320 basis the London fix.

Silver

If gold is bottoming, silver is also. For months, it has held the Elliott support level at $7, just as gold has held $331-335. In my opinion, it is acceptable to buy silver now, placing a stop at $7.00. The current psychological environment argues in favor of a silver bottom here. After two years of bullish sentiment among the hard-money experts, the mood has changed. The November 2 headline in Western Mining News, in reference to a recently-published Annual Review of the silver industry, reads, "[Major Brokerage House] Says Silver Likely to Remain Depressed." Major brokerage firms becoming negative on an investment doesn't guarantee a bottom, but you can bet that the investment in question has already declined significantly. Silver, of course, has lost over 50% of its value in the past 21 months.

DECEMBER 3, 1984

Gold will probably not begin a strong intermediate term rally until March/April 1985. Until then, or until it gets above $360, it's best avoided.

Gold

Last month I suggested buying gold with a stop at $320 basis the London fix. That stop has not been taken out, but the sharpness of the late November decline argues that a diagonal triangle is no longer in force, so that stop, which was based on a possible continuation of that pattern, is now irrelevant. As things have gone, we all would have been happier had I stayed with my previous strategy of waiting for $360 to be penetrated on the upside before buying.

Of the seven bullish technical points listed last month, fully five of them have been eliminated by the last week's short term selloff. It is no longer easy to count a five-wave decline; the Fibonacci relationships in the short term picture no longer apply; the $331-335 Elliott support level, which held for four months, was penetrated; the non-confirmations by the cash price on each new low in futures was negated by the new 1984 low in cash prices; and Market Vane's tally jumped to 70% "bulls" in mid-November. Of the four bearish technical points listed last month, all are still in effect. In other words, the balance has shifted back to the "bear" side.

One of the technical negatives listed in the November issue was that "the 8½-month cycle is topping and will point down until March/April 1985." I am reproducing the chart with the overlay of what have so far been reliable time cycles. As you can see, the 8½-month cycle will exert downside pressure on prices for another four months.

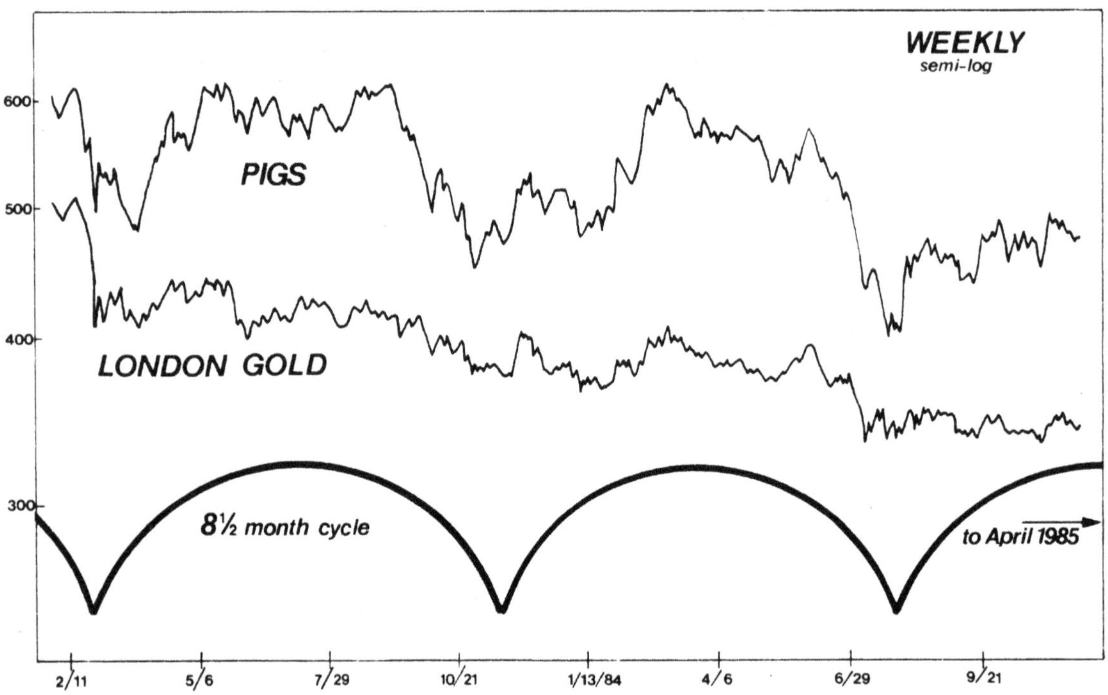

The second and third bearish points were bullion's failure to confirm the new rally peak in gold share prices and ASA's selling above net asset value. I have added a graph of PIGS (Prechter Index of Gold Stocks) to the gold price chart. It's worth studying for several reasons. The first is that the non-confirmation by bullion at the early November peak in gold stock prices is clear. Second, you can see that for the third time in the past two years, bullish sentiment toward precious metals has showed up in advances in gold stocks, with hardly a ripple in the price of bullion. Third, the most recent rise in share prices was the weakest of that period. Fourth, the rise in gold stock prices from July to November supports the case that during that entire time, the 8½-month cycle was indeed exerting an upward influence right on schedule. I had used the action in bullion (along with the orthodox wave ending points) to discern this cycle in the first place, but look how it jumps out at you when viewing the chart of gold stock prices! Because the most recent 8½-month cycle rally phase was the weakest of the past two years, a warning has been sounded. Unimpressive price action during the "up" phase of a cycle usually portends a severe drop in prices when the cycle rolls over. The rising 2-year cycle (see October issue) may keep the first three months of 1985 from being a disaster, but the message from this picture is to wait a while longer before entering the long side. Corrective waves are notoriously difficult to count, and latest developments allow for a number of possible interpretations, so I'm leaving the chart unlabeled until the count becomes more certain.

Strategy should be as follows: Traders should sell longs now, taking what is officially an $18 loss (about $13 based on when most of you received the November issue), one of the few small losses taken in *The Elliott Wave Theorist* in the past five years. Return to the short side with a stop at $360 basis London fix. As a fail-safe, move to 50% long if $360 is exceeded. Investors should continue to remain out of the gold market, awaiting the major market bottom due in 1988.

Silver

It is uncanny that after four perfect touch points against the downtrending resistance line of the past two years, silver was once again repelled after just touching that line at last month's rally peak. Since silver almost always moves in the same direction as gold, traders should take the 70¢ loss and await the next buying opportunity, probably in March/April 1985. Move to 50% long if the London price closes above $8.

The Elliott Wave Theorist, 1985

JANUARY 7, 1985

Gold has been very profitable on the short side. It should bounce almost immediately, but the ultimate bear market lows lie ahead.

Gold

After one month of looking for a rally, we moved back to a bearish posture again on December 3. That issue commented as follows:

> Of the seven bullish technical points listed last month, fully five of them have been eliminated; of the four bearish technical points listed last month, all are still in effect. In other words, the balance has shifted back to the "bear" side. Traders should return to the short side with a stop at $360 basis London fix.

Gold held up at $330 basis London fix for 4½ days after the December issue was mailed, long enough for traders to follow my recommendation to return to the short side. The subsequent drop in gold bullion and the smash in gold stocks has been substantial. Traders have another $30 profit on the short side, while investors have continued to stay out of gold altogether. I would always prefer not to have to change my mind, but as you can see, it produces better results than sticking with an opinion for ego reasons.

The rest of this discussion will be complicated. For those of you not interested in the fine points of wave analysis, I suggest you skip directly to "Strategy." But for those interested, I would like to take time to present an overview of the gold picture so you'll have an idea of the possibilities. Let's look at each count, starting with the long term picture.

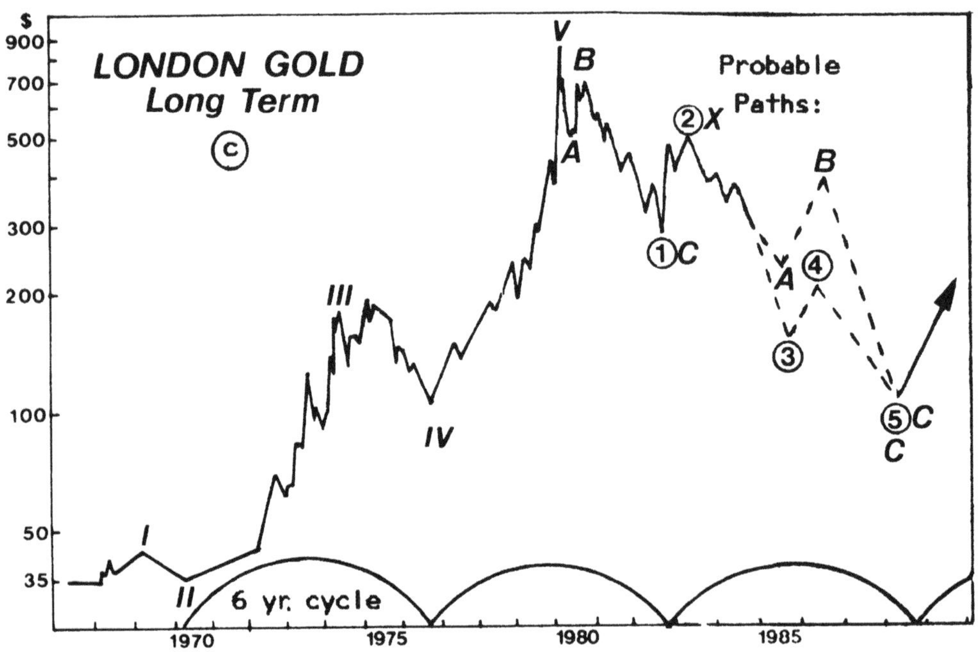

Preferred Count

Ever since the top at $512 in February 1983, I have presented two major possibilities on the wave labels for gold within its Supercycle bear market. There is no question that waves A and B took place in 1980. Following those two waves, the gold price may take the lower path shown on the long term chart (see dashed lines), completing a large C-wave decline of five waves, or it may take the upper path, completing a "double zigzag" bear market, which is counted A-B-C-X-A-B-C. The first labeling is supported by the fact that the ultimate target provided by the "fourth wave of lesser degree" method (see text, p.55) is $103.50, and a simple calculation of C = 1.618A yields a powerfully confirming target of $111.60. That's why I have compromised on a rough target of "$105 (+ or - $5)." The second labeling is supported by the fact that the average of waves A and C in the first zigzag is 1.618 times the length of wave B.

Notice that in terms of wave form, there is no difference whatsoever between these two labelings. It would merely be expected that wave "B" of the second zigzag in the double zigzag pattern would produce a stronger rally than a fourth wave in a five-wave sequence. These two concepts are so close in terms of outcome that I don't consider them alternate counts. They merely represent two ways of labeling the same phenomenon.

If this basic seven-wave count is in progress, then the smaller subdivisions, starting from the 1983 peak, can be counted two ways, as shown on the daily chart. I prefer the more bearish near term interpretation rather than the alternate, for several reasons:

1) The relationship between waves 1 and 2 is virtually the same as that between waves (1) and (2). Wave (2) is .238 times wave (1), while wave 2 is .212 times wave 1. (It is perfectly legitimate to mark the end of wave 1 at the early December low at $333.50 rather than the September low of $335.25. This change would make the second relationship even closer, at .231. However, I prefer the look of the expanded flat 2, which is the same as that of the expanded flat (2).) These ratios are quite close to the Fibonacci ratio .236, and a repeat performance in a lower degree is a very strong sign that one's count is correct.

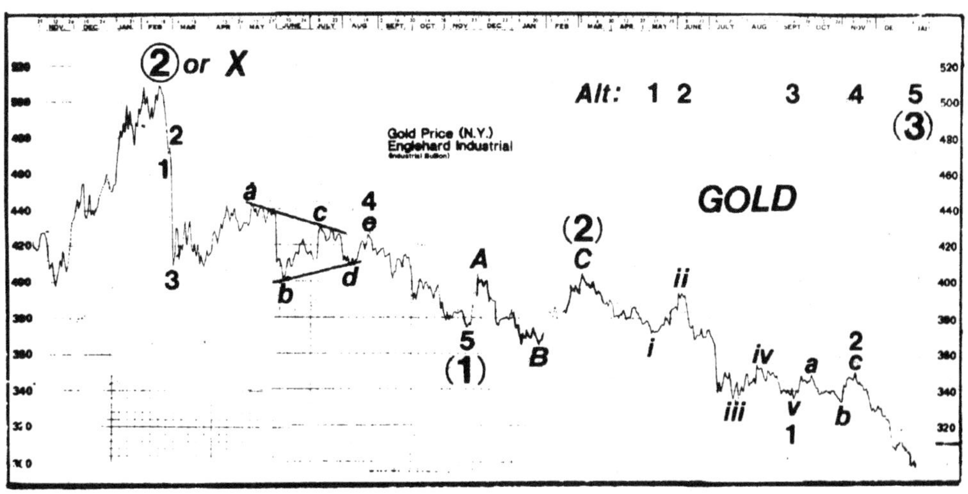

2) The 8½-month cycle, which was illustrated in the December issue, still points "hard down" into early April.

3) Open interest is still rising, a bearish sign.

4) It would be too "pat" for the market to create the widely-expected major "double bottom" at $297.

The drop from $350.45 in mid-November is completing a small five-wave pattern, as you can see on the chart, so a small rally should begin almost immediately. Resistance is $310 on the main count and $350 on the alternate. Following that bounce, the downside target intermediate term is near $220 if wave ③ of C is in force, and near $270 if wave A of the second zigzag is in force.

Alternate Count

The "double zigzag" concept, as I have explained many times, provides the major question of the year, since it is still not possible to be certain that wave X ended at the February 1983 peak at $511.50. That rally may have completed only wave Ⓐ of X, in which case the decline currently in progress is wave Ⓑ (see "Alternate Count" chart). This possibility is important to consider carefully because it would suggest a bottom very soon in the $269-297 range followed by a powerful rally back above $511.50 to complete wave Ⓒ of X. (Then the bear market would resume in earnest, either to the strongest target of $105 or a higher target near $180, the point at which the second ABC would be approximately .618 times

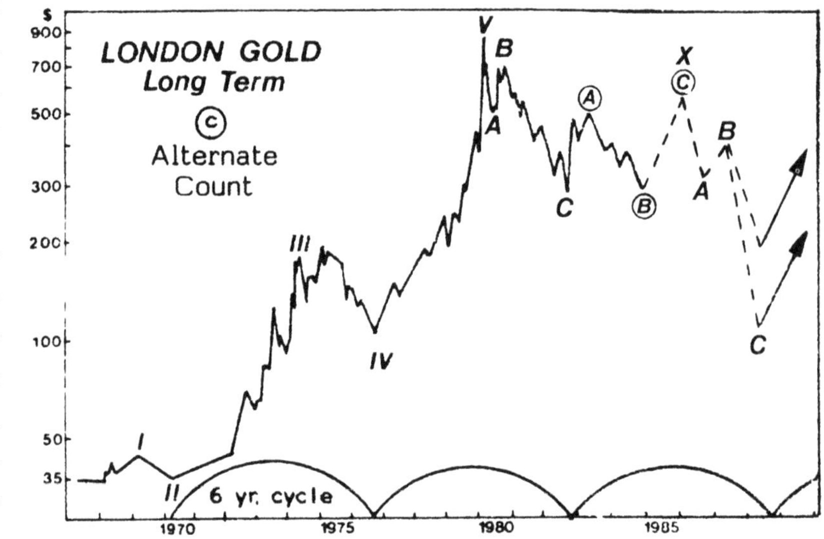

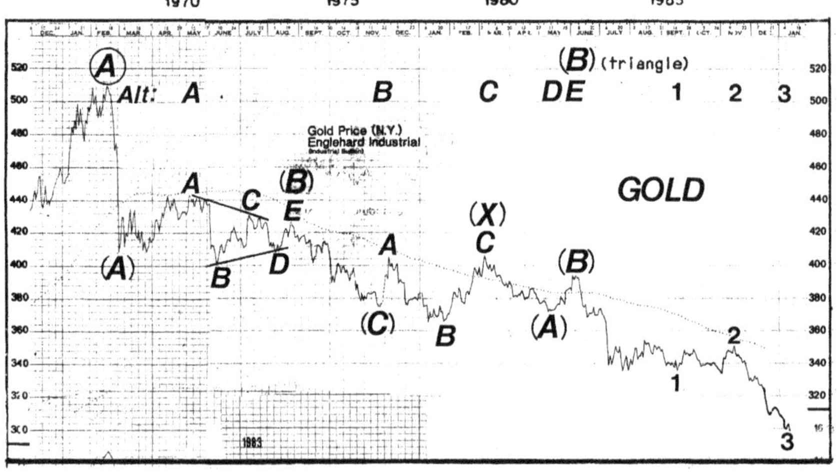

as long as the first.) So the trick in 1985 will be to decide whether a rally of that magnitude is likely, and if so, to time it. Let's look at the evidence.

The near term wave structure under the alternate count has been presented often in EWT over the past year. The second daily chart updates the (A)-(B)-(C)-(X)-(A)-(B)-(C) "double zigzag" count and the (A)-(B)-(C) simple zigzag count with a triangle in the wave (B) position. These counts are not really alternates either, since the outcome will be the same in terms of the form, which requires just a fourth and fifth wave to complete either way. The only difference is target level. As calculated in the August 6 issue, the first count still projects to $269.60 (the point at which the first ABC would equal the second), while the second would indicate a low at $291.25 (where C = A). No matter what the eventual outcome, I expect each of these levels to provide support for at least a minor rally. If the alternate count is the correct one, gold will bottom at one of these two support levels and begin a march to above $511.50 before the major bear trend resumes.

Support for this count comes mostly from the sentiment area. Market Vane reports only 20% "bulls" on gold, one of the lowest readings of the year. Unfortunately, low numbers have had a habit of changing almost immediately upon any strength in gold, so the question is still, "how much bearish conviction is there?" The best indication that some minds have changed was the cover of Business Week on December 17. That publication's reputation for providing a basis for contrary opinion makes their bold announcement of "THE DEATH OF MINING" a bullish sign.

Strategy

There is no doubt in my mind that a major bear market in gold is still raging and that it has at least three years more to run. Investors should continue to stay out of the gold market. There is better money to be made in the stock market or in money market funds.

Here's a trading strategy we can employ to take advantage of a situation where there are several alternatives. Traders should stay short and lower the stop to $320 basis London fix. This stop will guarantee a profit on the current trade and allow for my expectation of a small bounce back to $310. The alternate daily count (see second chart) would be expected to provide a bounce to $350 (the previous fourth wave; see text, p.55). Of all the variations, only the long term alternate count allows for a move above $360. Therefore, if you are stopped out at $320, return to the short side at $345 with a new stop at $360. Similarly, all counts but one indicate a continuation of the drop to at least $270, so cover shorts at $270 and stand aside.

Silver

The wave count for silver indicates next support at $4.90 because the fifth wave should not exceed the third wave in length. $4.90 is exactly the level of the 1982 low. Stand aside until gold has clearly bottomed or until early April, when the cycle low is due.

FEBRUARY 4, 1985

Gold's major bear market is still in force, and the long term target of $105/oz. by 1988 remains in effect.

Gold & Silver

The one-way bullishness among investors and advisors over the past five years on the long term prospects for precious metals is finally beginning to change, with headlines such as "Precious Metals Prices Likely to Continue Lower" (1/4/85) gracing a hard money newspaper and "Silver: 'I Wouldn't Put My Grandmother in It'" (1/14/85) (honest!) appearing in a major financial publication. As is typical of mid-trend psychology, it has now come to the point in the precious metals debate that "fundamentalists" and long term hard-money advisors are at each others' throats. Some warn of super deflation and a slaughter in gold, while others just as vehemently guarantee hyperinflation and $6000 gold just around the corner. As is to be expected, both agree that the longer-run outlook is "hardly in doubt." Whichever outcome (if either) turns out to be correct, certainly any investment manager who kept his clients fully invested in gold for the last half-decade as it lost 65% of its value, without taking pains to point out the safe and highly profitable alternatives in historically high real Treasury debt yields and in the U.S. stock market, should be politely reprimanded.

The January issue of EWT went into great detail on the gold market. None of those points has changed, since gold did little in January but drift sideways. My specific short term conclusion last month was as follows:

> The drop from $350.45 in mid-November is completing a small five-wave pattern, as you can see on the chart, so a small rally should begin almost immediately. Resistance is $310 on the main count and $350 on the alternate. Following that bounce, the down[trend should continue.]

The rally high on gold so far was $308 basis the London fix and $310 basis the February futures contract, right against first resistance. The minor wave structure in gold may allow for a final brief rally in the first half of February, but as yet I see few compelling reasons to purchase the metal. As argued last month, one of two conditions would make gold and silver an attractive purchase: either a continuation of the precious metals' decline into the 8½-month cycle low due early April or, as a fail-safe, an advance in gold above resistance at $360 basis London fix. Otherwise, they remain unattractive on the long side. Aggressive traders who are short gold should continue to follow the strategy set out in the January issue.

The case for a tradable rally soon (preferably out of the upcoming cyclic low, to give us an entry at good prices) is becoming stronger, as the quoted headlines suggest. I'll try to time that as best I can. However, the long term technical difficulties are still too great to expect a major bottom. As one example, the meager $10 rally in gold in mid-January caused the consensus of advisors to jump to almost 50% "bulls" according to Market Vane. This feverish desire to "call the bottom" has plagued the gold market for five years and does not reflect the kind of investor sentiment to be expected at a major bear market low.

MARCH 4, 1985

Gold is falling into a bottom of intermediate term significance. A tradable bottom should be made by early April.

Gold

Newcomers to the Wave Principle are often put off by the fact that it is not always possible to know precisely where the market is in all degrees of its wave count. However, because each market is almost always clear in most degrees of trend, an analyst can usually formulate a winning strategy around what he does know, while objectively placing stops to protect against the least likely outcomes. The gold picture last January provides a good example. There were numerous valid wave counts on gold bullion, all of which were outlined in detail in the January 7 issue. Despite the existence of various interpretations, all evidence demanded using this strategy for maximum potential for profit:

> There is no doubt in my mind that a major bear market in gold is still raging.... Investors should continue to stay out of the gold market. There is better money to be made in the stock market or in money market funds. Traders should stay short and lower the stop to $320 basis London fix. This stop will guarantee a profit on the current trade and allow for my expectation of a bounce back to $310. [A]ll counts but one indicate a continuation of the drop to at least $270, so cover shorts at $270 and stand aside.

At no time did gold's action call into question our basic outlook. Basis the London fix, gold rebounded to $308, just $2 shy of its bounce potential, completed a triangle for wave iv

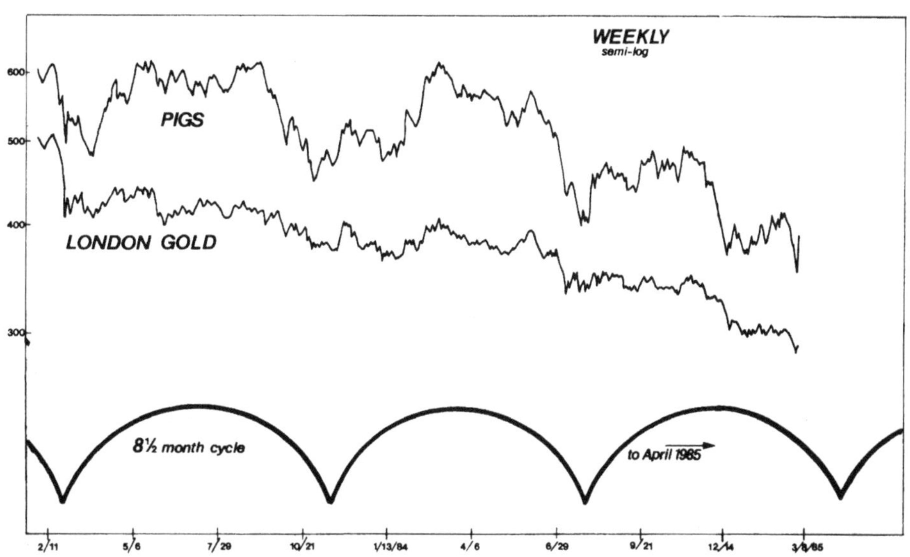

(see daily chart), which is an unmistakable sign of imminent breakdown, and then plunged into new low territory, paying us well for our hard work and patience.

The latest drop should erase the erroneous "massive double bottom" argument of the long term bulls who have been looking for various excuses to hold onto their gold throughout the past five years. For the basic chartist, there is no significant support now until $180-$200, so gold is now in an excellent position to begin changing the minds of long term investors from bullish to bearish. Prior to last week, Market Vane reported five straight weeks when advisory service "bulls" numbered between 40% and 50%, a high percentage for a mere $10 rally, but those are the psychological dynamics of a bear market. The developing panic of those who, for "fundamental" reasons, have been holding onto gold positions throughout this bear market should come to a head as the 8½-month cycle bottoms. Already, put transactions in ASA are extremely high, which is a warning sign to those holding short positions. We should see a bit more evidence of that dramatic shift in sentiment as the market nears its best intermediate term rally since 1982.

The 8½-month cycle, which helped EWT recognize the November 1983 low in gold and gold stocks, the March 1984 high, the June-July 1984 crash and recent weakness as well, will point to a low in the first week of April if prices remain weak until that time.

Wave Counts

The wave counts from the January issue have been vindicated. Not one of them showed a completed wave to the downside; all required at least one more collapse to new lows, and that has occurred. In fact, those same counts required the drop to be a fifth wave of some degree, and the evolution of the holding pattern into a triangle guarantees that the current drop is a fifth wave. For that reason, a bottom of some degree is rapidly approaching. The decline may be ending with the current drop per the alternate count, although my preferred count, which is the same as that in the January issue, indicates further weakness after a bounce. Our strategy will be constructed with these facts in mind.

For Wave Students

The question of the long term wave count for the bear market should soon be resolved. Additional erosion in the price of gold will weaken the case that the upcoming rally could have the power of the June 1982-February 1983 advance. The wave count that supports this case is that wave X, a "bear market rally" pattern dating from June 1982, is not over (see January issue). The recent drop, however, eliminated the possibility that wave X is a "flat" and has nearly eliminated one of the internal wave counts by exceeding the target of $291.25, which was based upon it. The only interpretation remaining is that wave X will be an "expanded flat." The current Ⓑ-wave decline, per the chart in the January issue, still subdivides into a "double zigzag" labeled (A)(B)(C)-(X)-(A)(B)(C). With that internal wave structure still targeting $269.60, any substantial break of that level will tell us exactly where we are in the bear market

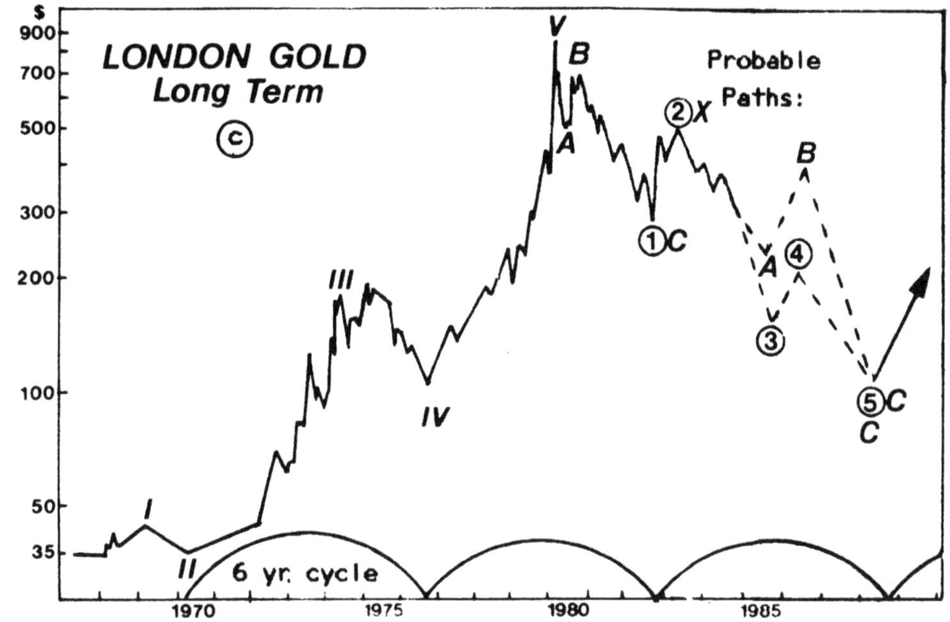

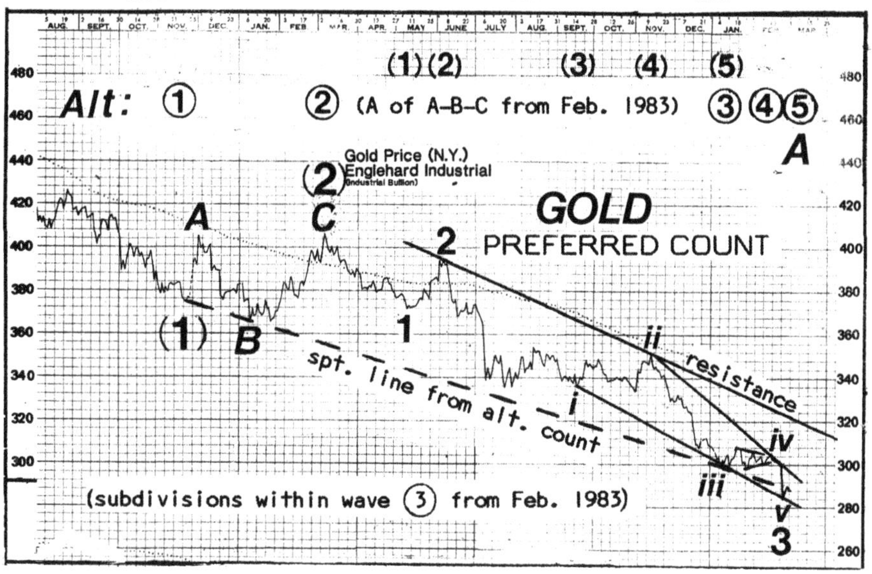

structure by eliminating this alternate count from the long term picture. If the situation warrants, I'll illustrate that count again in the April issue.

Strategy

Since a triangle always precedes the fifth wave in a five-wave sequence (see text, p.44), the current drop in gold is a fifth wave of some degree, as indicated by the accompanying charts. With the probabilities for further decline becoming less one-sided, it would be prudent for traders to take profits on half the short sales now. Keep the stop at $320 on the remainder. If gold completes a declining wave sequence (or perhaps a second wave correction of the next upward sequence) as the April issue goes to press, we'll look for a traders' buying opportunity. Investors should continue to stand aside, as we have throughout this debacle.

Valuation Study Supports Elliott Target

I have commented before, in watching gold stock prices hold up, that if gold bullion were really cheap, as the bulls claim, shouldn't the stocks have been decimated? Apparently gold is still dear, because the mines are generating hefty enough profits to keep share prices high. It will apparently take a substantial further drop to put the mines' profitability under enough pressure to bring the stock prices down.

While my forecast for an ultimate bottom near $105/oz. by 1988 has been met with some derision (perhaps deserved; time will tell), a new study by Paul Montgomery of Legg Mason, Wood Walker in Newport News, VA presents a very interesting picture with reference to the argument over whether gold at current prices is "cheap." Specifically, his chart shows the annual income provided by top quality bonds and expressed in constant (1967) dollars, which could have been purchased with 100 ounces of gold each year for the past 187 years. Based upon this measure, gold remains shockingly expensive. Of course, the reason that gold is currently valued at this level is the fear that the U.S. dollar will very soon become worthless, as have all currencies throughout history. The basic assumption that the dollar will ultimately be worthless is certainly correct, but the key to correct investment decisions is timing. If the resumption of rapid dollar destruction takes longer than the gold investors expect, their disappointment will result in more selling. And based on the above long term chart, the price of gold may still have a long way to fall. Montgomery points out that if corporate bonds stay at a 12% yield, and if inflation averages 4% per year, and if gold were ultimately to purchase an income stream equal to $400, which is generously at the upper boundary of the historical norm, gold would be priced at $112. Now where did I read that wave C = 1.618A at $111.60? Wasn't it in *The Elliott Wave Theorist*?

Silver

Silver is staying perfectly within its narrowing downtrend channel. As mentioned in the January issue, risk still exists to the $4.90 level. Whether or not that price is reached, silver

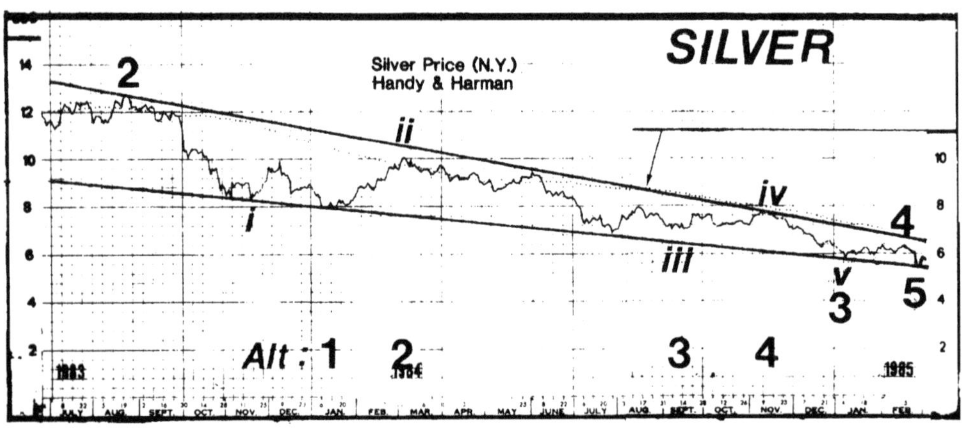

will be a "buy" when gold is a buy, and I expect that to be the case within a month. Don't buy silver unless the upper channel line, currently at the $6.80 level basis the closing cash price, is exceeded. If a "buy" is triggered, place a stop at $6.

APRIL 8, 1985

Gold and silver have made intermediate term lows and should advance throughout the second and third quarters of 1985. Although I don't expect it, a drop back below $295 basis London fix would turn the gold picture bearish again.

Gold

For several months, time cycles had been pointing to the start of the "best intermediate term rally since 1982" to begin the first week of April from approximately the $270 level. Last month the wave structures on the charts of gold and silver showed a potentially completed decline, and I began taking steps to prepare for a reversal. This is the way EWT saw it on March 4:

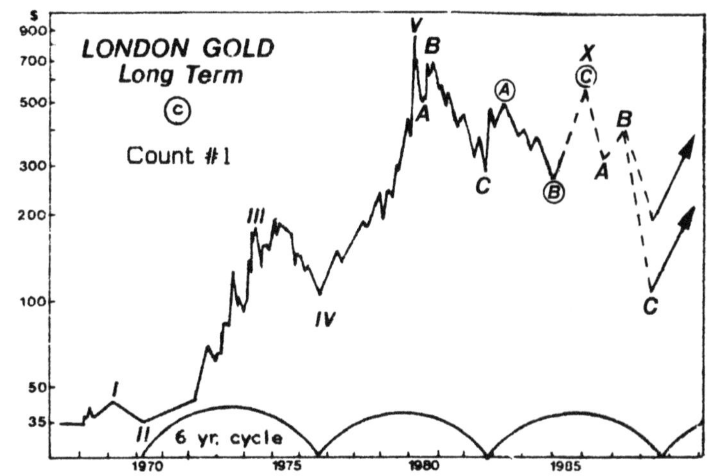

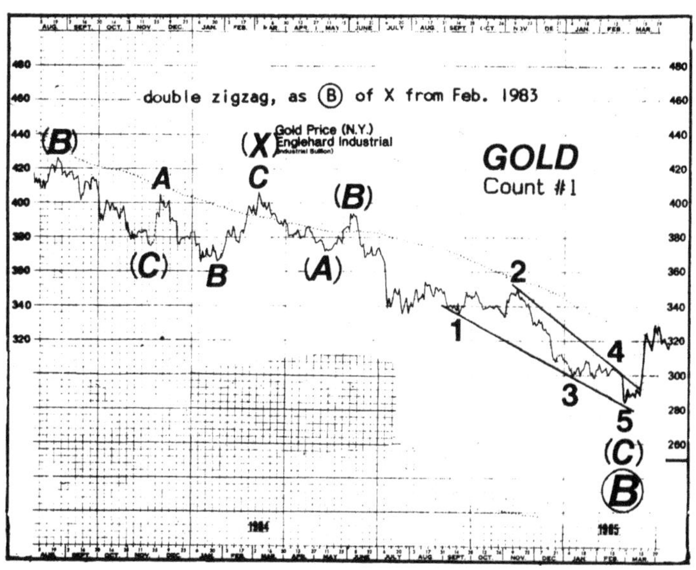

> The wave counts from the January issue have been vindicated. Not one of them showed a completed wave to the downside; all required at least one more collapse to new lows, and that has occurred. In fact, those same counts required the drop to be a fifth wave of some degree, and the evolution of the holding pattern into a triangle guarantees that the current drop is a fifth wave. [In addition], put transactions in ASA are extremely high, which is a warning sign to those holding short positions.

With the probabilities for further decline becoming less one-sided, it would be prudent for traders to take profits on half the short sales now.

The actual price low in gold occurred at $284.25 basis London fix on February 25. The cycle low didn't occur until March 18, when prices took off, but it still occurred two weeks earlier (and $14 higher) than expected. One thing I've learned over the years is to try to avoid "pride of opinion" whenever possible. Even though we had been looking forward to "the first week of April" for several months, the evidence on March 4 at least dictated covering half the short position. As a result, we covered half at $288.30 basis London fix, just $4 off the absolute bottom, while our protective stop at $320 (which was triggered at $333.25) took care of the rest. It is a tribute to the defensive utility of the Wave Principle that we showed a $20 profit on this trade even though neither the short sale, in December at $330.90, nor the recent exit (averaging $310.78) were particularly well-timed.

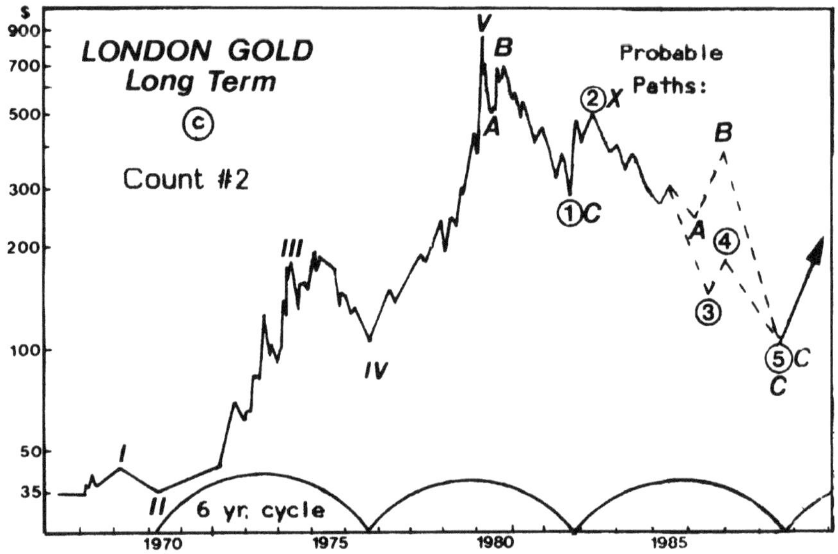

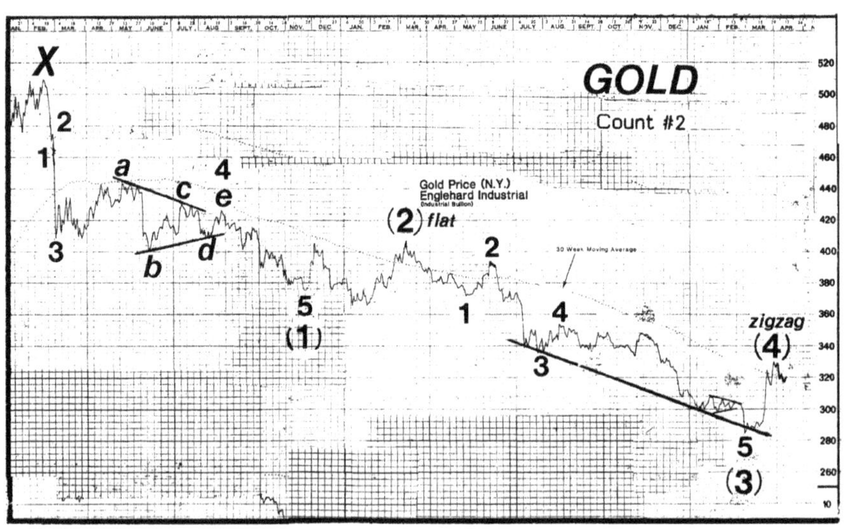

Cyclically, expectations with regard to gold have not changed. The upward influence of the 8½-month cycle, which is occurring in the final topping phase of the 6-year cycle (see chart), is expected to provide half a year of advancing prices. In other words, gold should be strong into late in the third quarter of 1985. The rally will be either wave B of the second A-B-C decline in the major bear market (see Count #2) or wave Ⓒ of X (see Count #1). In the first instance, gold would be expected to rally to $390-410. Under the second count, gold would be expected to peak in the $510-550 zone. We'll ride it as far as we can.

Alternate Count

There is still concern that gold could make one more new low. Count #2 is still viable because so far, gold has traced out only an a-b-c structure to the upside. That a-b-c, being a zigzag, alternates with the previous flat. Furthermore, open interest in gold plunged during the rally and some sentiment indicators have reached bearish levels.

Strategy

Traders can buy now with a stop at $295. If gold has truly turned, it should not retrace more than 62% or fill the gap. If gold breaks $295, return to the short side with a stop at $320. Investors should remain out of the gold market. I still expect the major bear trend ultimately to bottom in 1988 near the $105 level. Meanwhile, the opportunities in the stock market and the return on Treasury bills are too good to pass up.

Silver

The chart of silver in the March issue showed a completed wave count to the downside. At this point, the downtrend line that has held against every rally for two solid years has been broken and prices have settled back. Because silver has completed a satisfactory intermediate term declining wave sequence for the first time since June 1982 and because it has signaled a change in trend, I think it's a "buy" for an intermediate term trade to $10/oz. The $10 level marks the peak of the previous fourth wave of one lesser degree (a natural magnet for prices; see text, p.55) on the count as shown here. Although wave (C) can be shown to contain an extension within either wave 3 or 5, a study of "wave personality" (see text, p.67) strongly supports the case for an extended wave 5. The "wedge" shape of the fifth wave is also a strong sign of the end of the decline. Move to 50% long now and 100% long on a London close below $6.15. First resistance is $7.90. Use $5.80 as a stop.

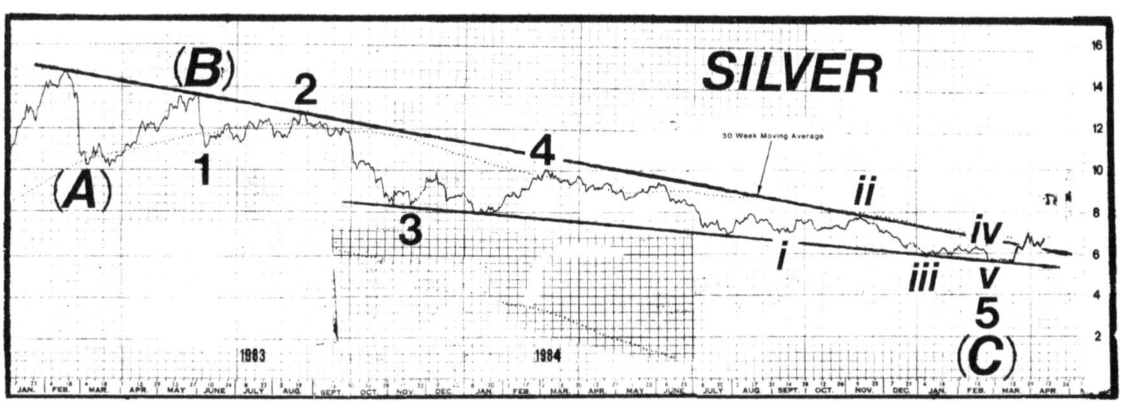

MAY 6, 1985

Gold is neutral/bullish. Silver fell back to our "buy" area on its London close of $6.12 on April 24. The 8-week cycle in precious metals is due to turn up by mid-May.

Gold

There are still two possible counts in the gold market, one indicating that an intermediate term low was seen in March and the other indicating that it will occur at the end of the next declining wave. These counts were detailed in a two-page discussion in the April issue, and nothing has occurred to eliminate either of them. It is still an acceptable strategy for traders to hold long positions, at least into early June. The very reliable 8-week cycle is due to bottom within the next ten trading days, so we'll see if there is any strength to the precious metals market when that cycle turns up again. Between now and May 25, use $284 basis London fix as a stop. After May 25, use $305. Investors should remain out of the gold market, awaiting the ultimate bottom near $105/oz. in 1988.

Silver

The April issue made two observations:

1) For the first time since the peak was registered in February 1983, silver completed a satisfactory intermediate term declining wave sequence in March 1985.

2) On arithmetic scale, the downtrend resistance line that had held for two years was broken on the upside in the March rally.

Last month I recommended moving to "100% long on a London close below $6.15." The selloff in April brought the London price of silver down to $6.12 on April 24, so we're now 100% long in silver. The downtrend line that now serves as support has declined a bit since last month, so the stop should now be placed at $5.70 basis London close. If silver turns up again and clears $7, raise the stop to $6.20.

Technical Note: On semilog (percentage-based) chart scale, gold and silver did not penetrate their downtrend resistance lines in the March rally. In fact, they climbed right up to touch those respective lines and have turned down from them. A move by the precious metals to above their March/April peaks would result in a penetration of this resistance and would be a significant event, probably confirming that an intermediate term reversal has been made. I'll show you those charts in an upcoming issue.

JUNE 3, 1985

Gold & Silver

Gold and silver are almost exactly unchanged from last month, so there is little new to say. The analysis presented in the April and May letters still stands. In a nutshell, the precious metals are experiencing bear market rallies. These rallies are probably not over yet. Investors should stay out of the precious metals markets. The ultimate low is expected to occur in 1988 at close to $105/oz. for gold. Traders can hold long, keeping the "stops" at $305 and $5.70 basis the London fix, respectively.

JUNE 24, 1985

The long term target for gold remains intact at $105/oz. by 1988.

Gold & Silver

For three months, gold has held within a sideways "trading range" pattern. Remember the 8½ month cycle (perhaps closer to 8 months), which had indicated a low by early April? The cycle that said then, "a rally is due soon" is now saying, "the decline should resume soon." The chart shown here will clarify its position.

Although the short term wave structure is consistent with the onset of another declining wave in the bear market, it is still possible that gold and silver could stage one more sharp rally, turning the upward zigzag correction into a "double zigzag" (see text, p.37). This interpretation labels all the price action since the March peak as a contracting triangle (see text, p.43), a mid-trend interruption. Since the triangle would have to be ending now, and since there is only a month remaining in the "up" phase of the 8-month cycle, the final rally in the "double zigzag" structure would have to begin almost immediately.

The April issue argued that the rally phase would end no later than the third quarter of 1985, and that assessment still makes sense. But the price potential that existed for a rally of $100-$200+ appears to have been wasted. Although the technical indicators make me want to sell short right now, let's let the Elliott wave parameters dictate strategy for traders. Upside

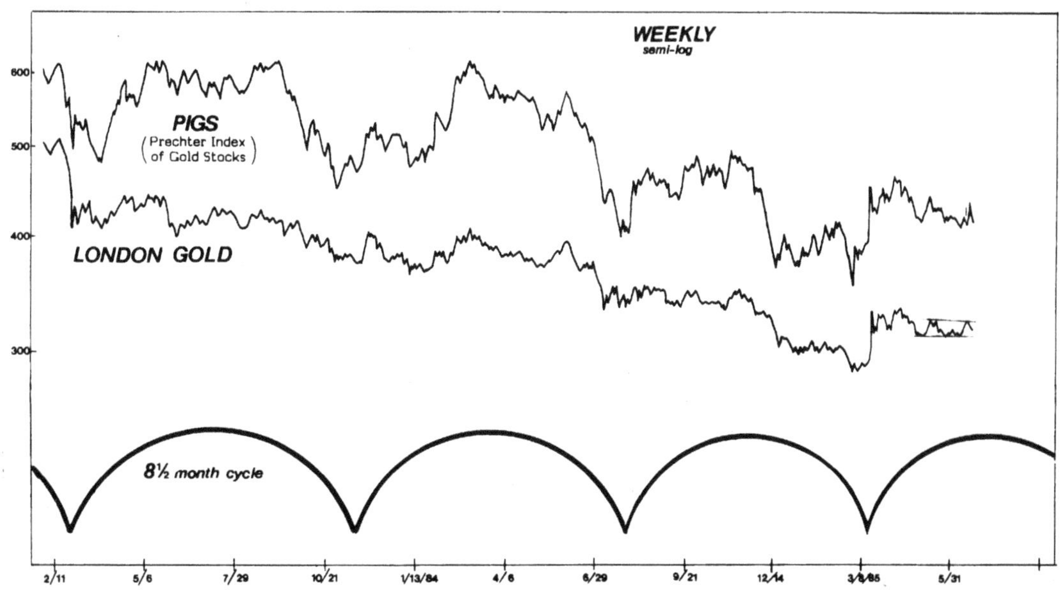

resistance is $350, the area of the peak of the previous fourth wave of one lesser degree (see text, p.55). Support for the apparent triangle is $311. Given these numbers, we should raise the stop on the long position to $310 basis London fix and plan to sell at $350. If stopped out, go short with a stop at $327. Investors should continue to stay out of the ongoing major bear market in gold, which has three years left to run. In silver, raise the stop to $6 basis London fix and plan to sell at $7.50. If stopped out, stand aside.

AUGUST 5, 1985

Gold and silver are in the final phase of the holding pattern/rally dating from March. A substantial decline is likely into October.

Gold & Silver

My gold trading strategy last month was worthless. It's unfortunate, because I think the analysis was basically correct. My conclusion then was summed up this way:

> Although the short term wave structure is consistent with the onset of another declining wave in the bear market, it is still possible that gold and silver could stage one more sharp rally. [S]ince there is only a month remaining in the "up" phase of the 8-month cycle, the final rally would have to begin almost immediately.

The metals bottomed a week later and have been in a short term rally since. While long term investors have remained comfortably out of the gold market throughout the bear market, traders took a $20 loss on the short sale as the rally perversely edged $1 above the stop (a problem in forecasting markets, not real-time trading). The silver trade on the long side also resulted in a loss.

The last "up" month in the 8-month cycle for precious metals is coming to a close (see chart, July issue), and the rally phase was anemic. As Richard Russell (Box 1759, La Jolla, CA 92038) pointed out, it is a poor performance when gold and silver are only able to "hold up" while foreign currencies climb powerfully month after month. Traders should sell short now. Use a London fix above $330 or above this week's high, whichever is higher, as a stop. Close out the trade if $360 is exceeded. Downside potential on the next wave is $180-$200. Investors stay out. The long term target remains at $105 in 1988.

AUGUST 8, 1985 — INTERIM REPORT

Our stop in gold was close, so the resulting loss was only $8. The pattern from March is still typical of an upward correction in a bear market. Using two Fibonacci multiple measurements, a top should be met at either $350 or $370 basis the December contract. Traders should accumulate a short position on strength above $340 and use $380 as a stop. The London fix should not exceed $360.

SEPTEMBER 3, 1985

Gold

It's time to do a major review of the gold market. The 2-year cycle bottom that EWT recognized over a year ago performed the function of slowing, for a time, the major bear trend in gold. From the late July 1984 cyclic low until today, gold is exactly unchanged. Now it appears that gold's sloppy sideways action is coming to an end. Where do we go from here? Let's look at the evidence.

Cycles

The mid-1984 issues of EWT tracked the progress of the 2-year cycle, which was due to bottom in "late July-early August" of last year. There is every indication that it did just that. The shorter trading cycle gave some valuable clues to the phenomenal underlying weakness of the major trend in gold. The first 8-month cycle decline within the upward portion of the 2-year cycle carried prices to new lows.

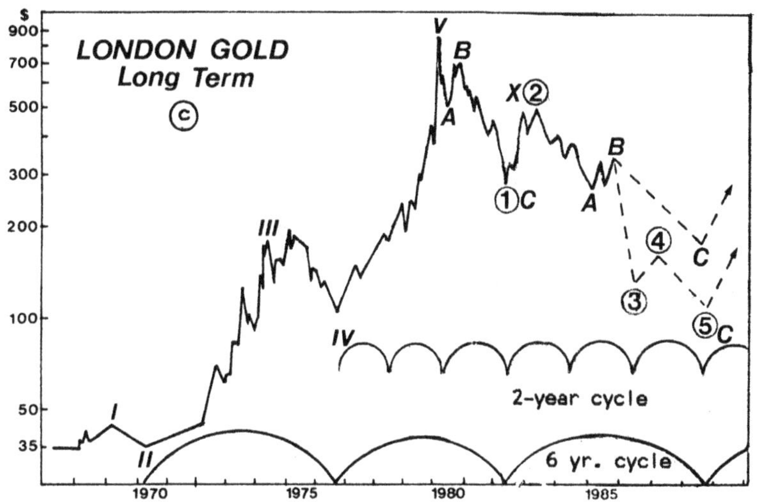

The second 8-month cycle has kept prices holding up in recent months, but that upside pressure is ending now. What about the position of the 2- and 6-year cycles? Fourteen months ago, the July 1984 issue made

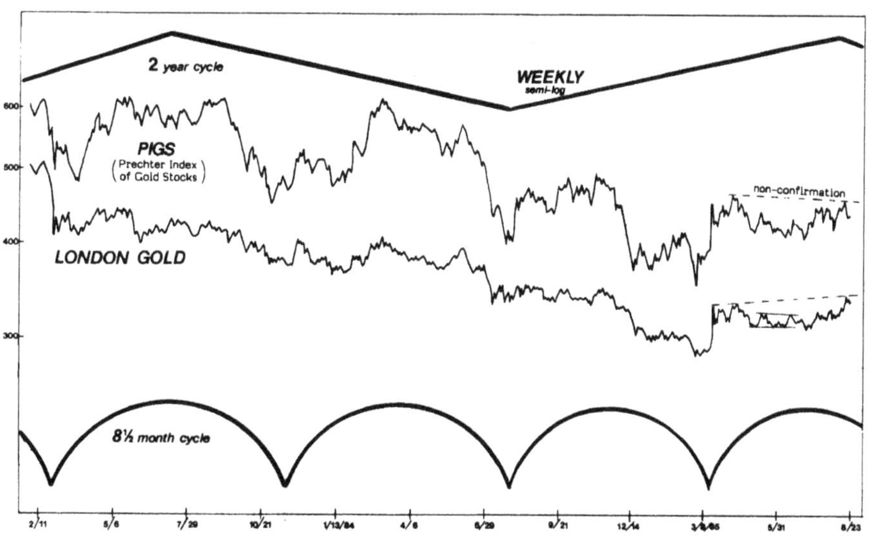

these comments on timing the end of gold's rally phase: "[The top] could be reached in mid-1985, when the next 2-year cycle is due to peak along with the overriding 6-year cycle." The April 1985 issue refined the time target by including the influence of the 8-month cycle and concluded as follows:

> The upward influence of the 8½-month cycle, which is occurring in the final topping phase of the 6-year cycle, is expected to provide half a year of advancing prices. In other words, gold should be strong into late in the third quarter of 1985.

If you study the charts presented here, you'll see that the 8-month, 2-year and 6-year cycles are coming into a peak, right on schedule.

Momentum

Generally at cycle peaks, there are indications of non-confirmation in upside price action. The current juncture is replete with them. Cash gold bullion exceeded its April peak, while futures contracts have not. Bullion has exceeded its April peak, while gold stocks have not. (The South African situation may be the "reason," but the technical fact remains.) Much more pronounced is the marked divergence between the trends of gold and silver. Silver last week couldn't even match gold in closing above its mid-August high, which in turn was substantially (30¢ cash, 60¢ futures) below its March peak! Platinum, meanwhile, had a two-day speculative jump that took it above its April high, while palladium fell substantially short. Even the powerfully rising foreign currency markets of the past six months stand in stark contrast

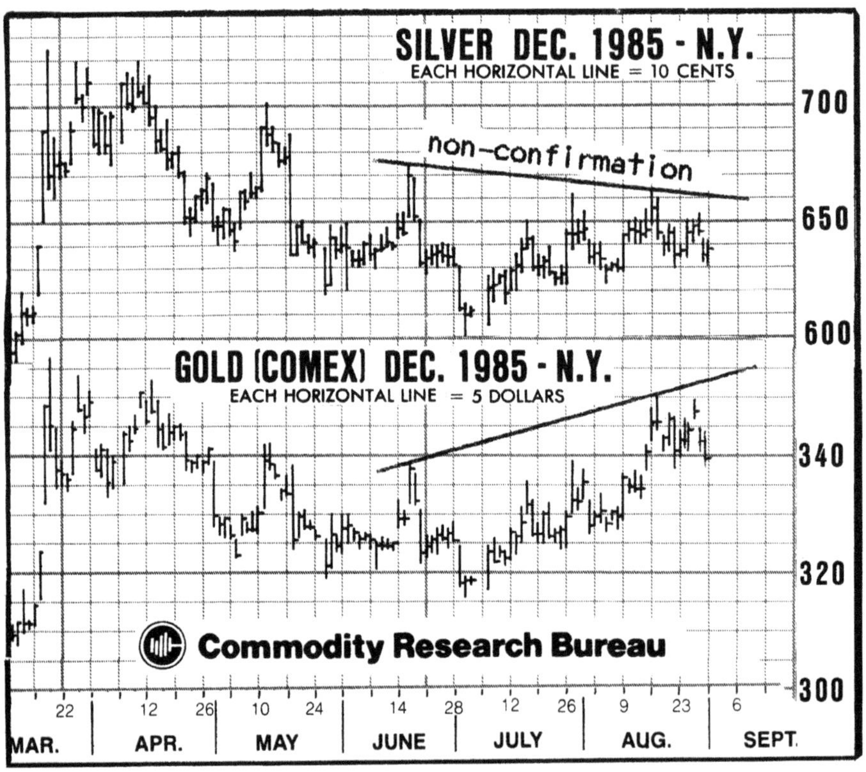

to the lethargy in the precious metals, indicating an even broader lack of unity among the inflation-hedge markets. This is a picture not of the beginning of a new bull market but of a last gasp upward thrust in a period of bear market consolidation.

Sentiment

Market Vane (61 S. Lake Av., Pasadena, CA 91101) tallied a big jump in the percentage of advisory services bullish for the precious metals, with gold rising to 78%, platinum to an amazing 93% and silver, which acts relatively poorly, to 62%. Meanwhile, several advisories rushed pull-out-the-stops "major buy" recommendations on gold and silver during the latest rally. That kind of conviction was not evident in the first a-b-c rally, and it rarely appears at market bottoms. It is typical of a cyclical top, whether that top is obvious from price action or not. This bear market shouldn't be over until the gold bugs stop the continual calls for a major bottom.

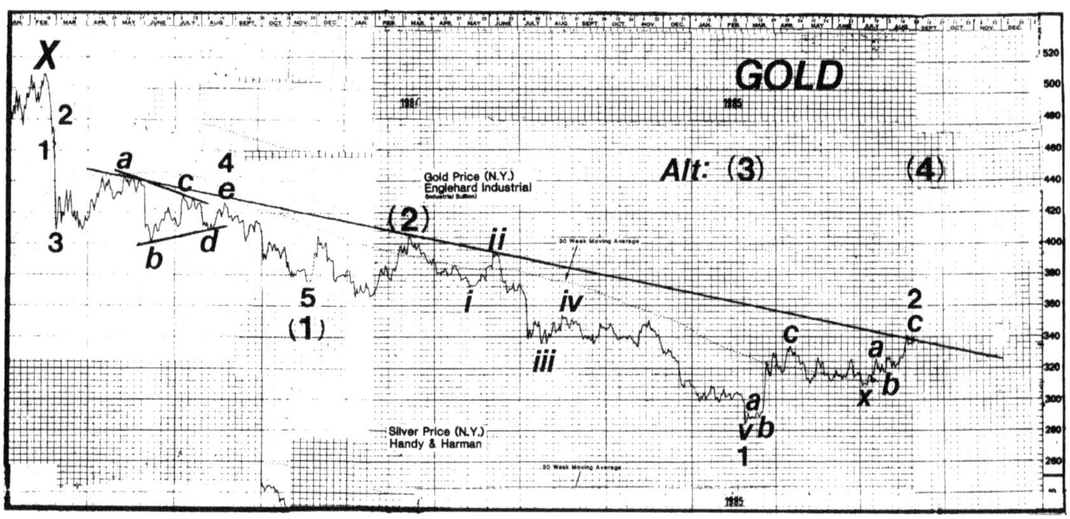

Wave Structure

The long term wave count remains the same. The major bear market in gold is tracing out either a zigzag or a double zigzag structure from the 1980 high. The long term chart shows the two acceptable labelings. Each implies identical action and even the same number of major waves, seven. The last uncertainty has been erased in terms of upside potential; there is virtually no possibility that wave X will contain another substantial rally. The July issue explained why:

> The April issue argued that the rally phase would end no later than the third quarter of 1985, and that assessment still makes sense. But the price potential that existed for a rally of $100- $200+ appears to have been wasted.

As a result, the "wave X" label was to remain at the $511.50 peak in February 1983, and in the July issue, the maximum upside potential for the rally phase was lowered: "Upside resistance is $350, the area of the peak of the previous fourth wave of one lesser degree. Support is $311." At the same time, the *short term* wave count was described as follows:

> It is still possible that gold and silver could stage one more sharp rally, turning the upward zigzag correction into a double zigzag (see text, p.37). The final rally in the double zigzag structure would have to begin almost immediately.

That rally did begin almost immediately, just one week later. The decline did find support near $311 (the low was $308.25). It is tracing out the second zigzag of a double zigzag, and resistance is powerful between $340 and $355 basis the London fix. The rally in gold to date has also fulfilled a Fibonacci multiple in that the second zigzag is just over 62% as long as the first, and it has carried right back to a downtrend line that has held back all rallies for over two years. This is a good place for a peak, whether the rally is counted as wave 2 of (3) or as wave (4) (see alternate count).

The wave counts for the foreign currencies, as David Weis has illustrated in the latest *Elliott Wave Commodity Letter*, could well be completed on the upside. The chart of the U.S. dollar also indicates that an a-b-c decline from the March high may be terminating. All of these wave counts are further evidence that the precious metals are in a precarious technical position.

What Next?

Short term, a host of signals for a top are in place. If you look closely at the daily chart of gold bullion, you'll see that one more minor new high is still possible over the next several days. Whether or not it occurs is irrelevant. If you look at the long term chart, you'll find no technical support for gold between $280 and $190, a vacuum. Fittingly, the next decline is most probably wave 3 of (3) of ③, a wave position that portends a persistent and perhaps dramatic decline. In fact, the wave structure and cycles provide a compatible picture right out into 1988: Wave ③ should end with the next 2-year cycle low, due in 1986, wave ④ should keep prices in a sideways trend for a few months thereafter, and then wave ⑤ should bottom in 1988, right on schedule with the 6-year cycle and the Fibonacci time target. The ultimate long term price target remains $105/oz. (+ or - $5), with interim support at $179 (+ or - $5) (which is an alternate but much less likely final target based upon the double zigzag wave count; see long term chart).

Strategy

The August 19 Interim Report was issued on what so far is the top day for gold. We're now short with a stop at $380 basis the December futures contract and $360 basis the London fix. If the December contract manages to exceed $365, add to your short position.

Silver

Silver has been the worst performing of the precious metals since March. Its maximum upside potential based upon the wave structure (and an alternate count) remains $10/oz., but it appears that time is running out for such a possibility. Here is a chart that was last shown in the December 1984 issue. I have no change in long term interpretation. At some time before 1988, silver should break below its June 1982 low at $4.90 to complete a double zigzag (A-B-C-X-A-B-C) pattern.

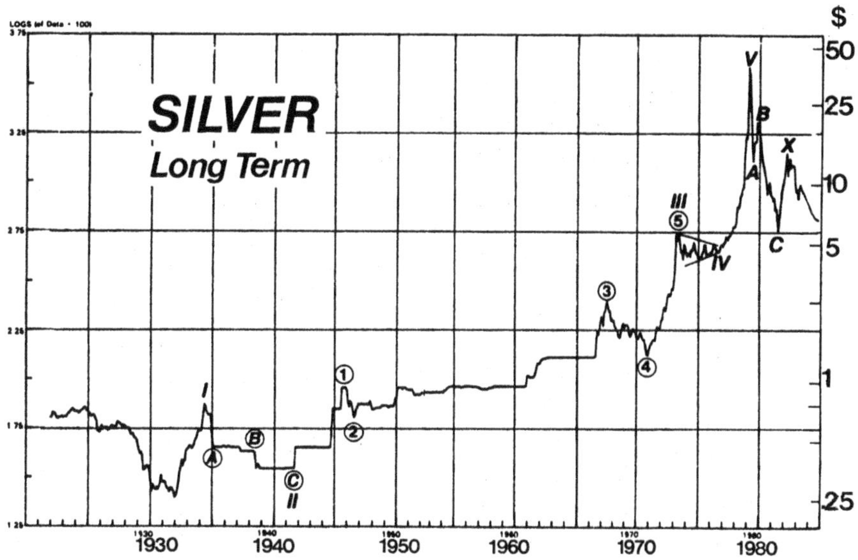

SEPTEMBER 30, 1985

Gold and silver resumed their bear markets in August and are scheduled to decline fairly persistently, along with mining share prices, for a full year. The long term target for gold is still $105/oz. in 1988.

Gold

The August 19 Interim Report was issued on the day of the top in precious metals prices. The leaping rally that preceded the high gave the illusion of strength, but technically it was very weak, and that's what I look for in a good short sale. The next nine trading days allowed plenty of opportunity to follow the recommendation to "accumulate a short position on strength above $340 basis the December contract." Of course, time will tell whether our long term assessment is correct. For the purposes of tracking this trade, I'll use the lowest possible entry price at $340. Place a stop at $350.

The September 3 issue devoted three pages to gold and silver, arguing the case that a new major wave to the downside was beginning. The precious metals gapped down again that very morning. The gold bulls had expected that the prices of North American gold mining shares would soar as investors switched from South African shares during the social unrest. Not only did they fail to go up substantially as ASA and the rest of the South Africans continued their collapse, the North American shares declined right along with them! To see why, take another look at the non-confirmation between gold stocks and bullion shown in the September issue. Fundamental reasoning always appears to make perfect sense but usually results in immediate losses. Market behavior is a better indicator of price direction.

Sentiment hasn't changed a bit. A full month after the rally high in gold and six months after silver peaked out, the headlines are still indicating a rush to call the "major bottom" in gold: "Gold's Recent Strength Indicates a Major Primary Trend Reversal," "Gold May Have Regained Some of Its Former Glitter," "Gold Bugs' Time is Close at Hand" and from Forbes, a cover story, "Is Gold the Only Answer?" Three of those headlines appeared on September 23. None of the arguments was technical. The rally-back attempt that has occurred in late September on news (the economic summit meeting, which brought the foreign currencies back to their highs) displayed little strength. In other words, the excitement over gold appears to be greater than what is warranted from the price action, a condition more typical of bear markets than bull markets.

The next 12 months should witness a substantial downtrend in gold, as it moves contra-cyclically against the stock market. Bullion's declining 2-year cycle is still likely to carry the price below $200/oz. in 1986. Long term investors should continue to stay out of gold, which has not yet completed its major bear market. The target remains $105/oz. in 1988.

Silver

The September issue pointed out, "Silver has been the worst performing of the precious metals since March." It still is, being the only precious metal futures contract that has already fallen below its July low. Silver's decline from the August peak remains intact and is holding inside a parallel channel. We shorted the August high on the Telephone Update.

NOVEMBER 4, 1985

Gold and silver remain in bear markets. Despite brief and dramatic short term rallies, the net result for November should be lower prices. A move above the August high would negate the bearish outlook for gold.

Gold

The August 19 Interim Report was issued on the top day in gold, and strategy got traders short between $340 and $350 basis the December contract. It is bothersome that this late in the 8-month cycle, prices are holding as well as they are, and there is currently a positive divergence between gold bullion and the gold stock average. This situation may imply just a short term rally or something more substantial. A short term rally into mid-November, halting in the low $340s basis the December contract and completing an a-b-c pattern from mid-September, would be the most "upside" I would want to see if the bearish case is to remain intact.

It is best to stick with current strategy because of what is possible; i.e., the potential reward is much greater than the risk. As a fail-safe, if the December contract hits $350, traders should reverse and go long, with a stop at $330. As you may have noticed, the 2½-year resistance line shown in the September 3 issue continues to contain all rally attempts. If the analysis in that issue remains correct, then gold sits in exactly the inverse position of stocks in terms of its wave structure, since it is entering Minute wave iii of Minor wave 3 of Intermediate wave (3) on the downside. Short term trading cycles (the 8-month and 8-week) are due to bottom between mid-November and mid-December, so they are theoretically in their "hard down" phases, at least for a short period of time. Investors should continue to stand aside, as we have done (with the exception of one entry-and-exit at the same price in 1981) throughout this major bear market.

Silver

Silver sports what appears to be a textbook descending triangle (see text, p.43). Usually the final rally of a triangle, wave e, is accompanied by the greatest bullish sentiment. You may recall that the early October lunge occurred on news that the Hunt family had disposed of the last of its silver. This was reported as a reason to be wildly bullish on silver, and the public rushed to buy futures, creating tremendous volume. The peak of the rally occurred the following morning. All those purchases now show a loss.

Descending triangles imply thrust, or short, sharp collapses. Using Elliott's measuring tool of "the widest part of the triangle," December silver should fall to near $5/oz. fairly rapidly. To complete the long term double zigzag pattern from the 1980 peak, cash silver would be expected to bottom ideally below the 1982 bottom at $4.90. The panics in tin and nickel prices that have jeopardized the London Metal Exchange may be conducive to a psychological environment of fear in the area of precious metals as well. A move in silver above the October peak would invalidate this analysis and indicate higher prices.

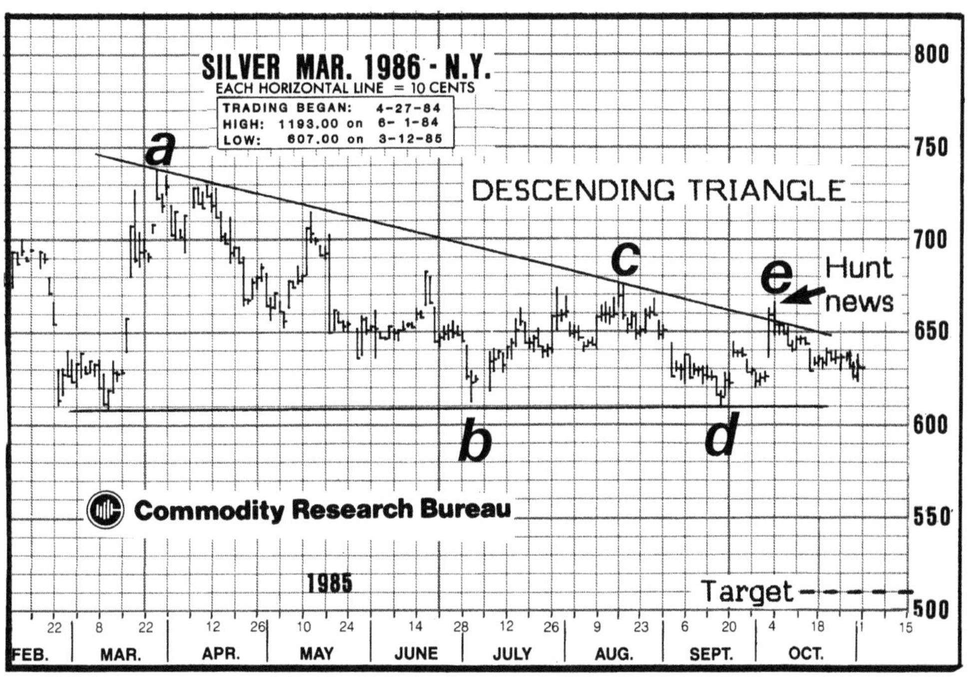

DECEMBER 2, 1985

Gold and silver, which have been edging lower, appear to be on the verge of an acceleration to the downside.

Gold

The technical situation in the precious metals remains negative on the intermediate and long term and has now returned to negative on the short term as well. Last month's neutral expectations were borne out quite closely, validating the analysis:

> A short term rally into mid-November, halting in the low $340s basis the December contract and completing an a-b-c pattern from mid-September, would be the most "upside" I would want to see if the bearish case is to remain intact.

Gold futures rallied into November 25, peaking at $333.40 and abruptly running out of steam just as cash bullion prices edged above their September peaks, completing the a-b-c wave pattern from mid-September. The positive technical signs that suggested a short term rally four weeks ago have fulfilled their meager promise and are no longer bullish. Here's a list:

1) The positive non-confirmation between gold bullion and the gold stock average did result in a three week rebound in gold stocks and a feeble rally in bullion. However, that technical positive has now been replaced by a technical negative in that futures contract prices in September failed to confirm the new two-month high in cash bullion prices.

2) The 8½-month cycle has bottomed, but no upside explosion has occurred, again bearing out our expectations. The 8-week cycle, which remains down into mid-December (see November issue) clearly has the overriding short term influence. Whenever a

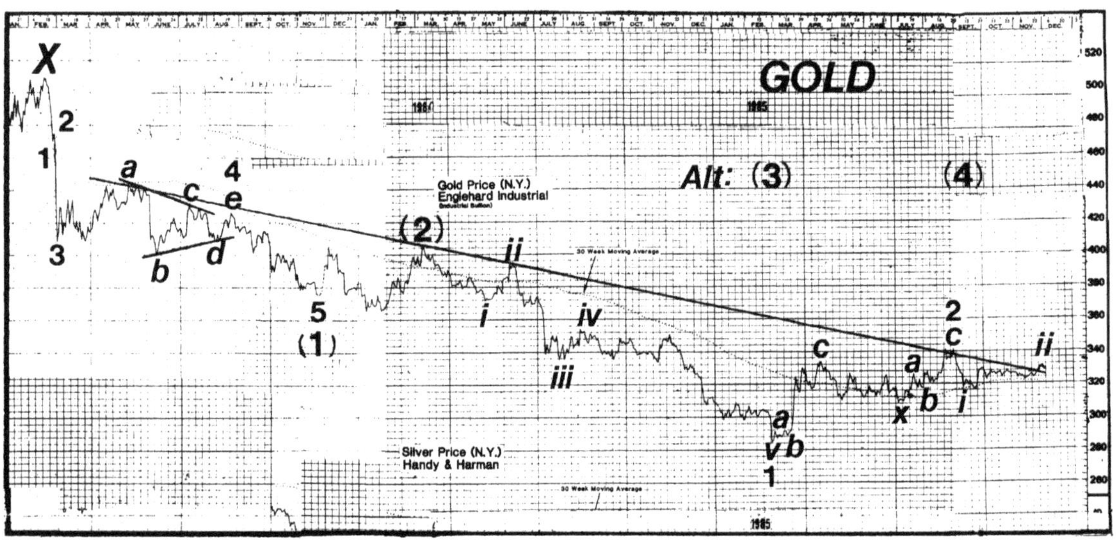

minor cycle overpowers a larger one, it is usually in the direction of the larger trend. In this case, the path of least resistance is down, and that's in line with the declining 2- and 6-year cycles.

3) The bearish sentiment that was in evidence a month ago has reversed dramatically on the measliest of rallies. According to Market Vane, advisors now number 72% bulls in gold, 82% bulls in silver and 90% bulls in platinum! This immediate return to all-out bullish fever has been typical of the precious metals market all the way down from the 1980 highs and is just more evidence that the mass investor psychology typical of a bear market is still operative. In support of Market Vane's tallies are the continuing articles and ads touting gold as a major buy. "Are You Ready For An Explosive Move in Gold?" headlines a full page ad on November 1. "Precious Metals: A Time to Buy," says the front cover of a major financial magazine dated November 26. The article debates not *if* a "major breakout" and "sustained bull rally" will occur, but merely when. For over three years, the stock market has climbed a Wall of Worry; for almost six years, the gold market has slid down (what I call) a Slope of Hope.

A major point of the bullish argument is that the huge fall in the dollar will cause gold to rise. Shouldn't the fall of the dollar already have caused gold to rise? In terms of everything but dollars, gold has been collapsing over the past several months; against dollars, which have been declining, all it has done is go sideways, a less-than-bullish performance. Once again, the actual facts are of less importance than their popular interpretation. You can bet that if gold were in a bull market, the dollar's performance would be filtered through a skeptical psychology and interpreted, along with gold's lack of response, as bearish.

The Wave Principle still supports a negative outlook for the precious metals. Ever since the peaks almost six years ago, both gold and silver have continually rallied in three-wave patterns, a required characteristic of a bear market. This phenomenon repeated in November, creating high probability conditions for another move to the downside. Intermediate term, the wave count presented in the September issue remains intact (see daily chart). As explained last month, "gold sits in exactly the inverse position of stocks in terms of its wave structure, since it is entering Minute wave iii of Minor wave 3 of Intermediate wave (3) on the downside." You saw what stocks did over the past ten weeks from a similar position in a bull market, and the potential remains for a similarly dramatic performance from the metals but in the opposite direction.

Cyclically speaking, the weakest price action should occur from November 25 into mid-December. From then into mid-January, the combination of rising 8-week and 8½-month cycles should provide a final period of relief before all cycles get in gear again on the downside. Strategy: Traders stay short with a stop at $350 basis the February contract. We shorted the August high, so we're in good shape. Investors stay out.

Silver

In silver, the three-wave November rally retraced a Fibonacci 60% of the five-wave October-November decline on the nearby contract. So far, the action is fulfilling the scenario outlined as a result of the "textbook descending triangle" that took place between March and October (see November 4 issue). The triangle ended typically, with a brief rush of buying on the news that the Hunt family had sold all its silver, and so far the peak registered then has not been challenged. The triangle still calls for silver to fall to "near $5/oz. fairly rapidly" in what Elliott called a "thrust," a swiftly unfolding five-wave structure. The best interpretation for the October-November sequence, then, is that the decline and rally are waves i and ii of the expected five-wave intermediate term decline. Under this analysis, the sharpest downside action, wave iii, lies immediately ahead.

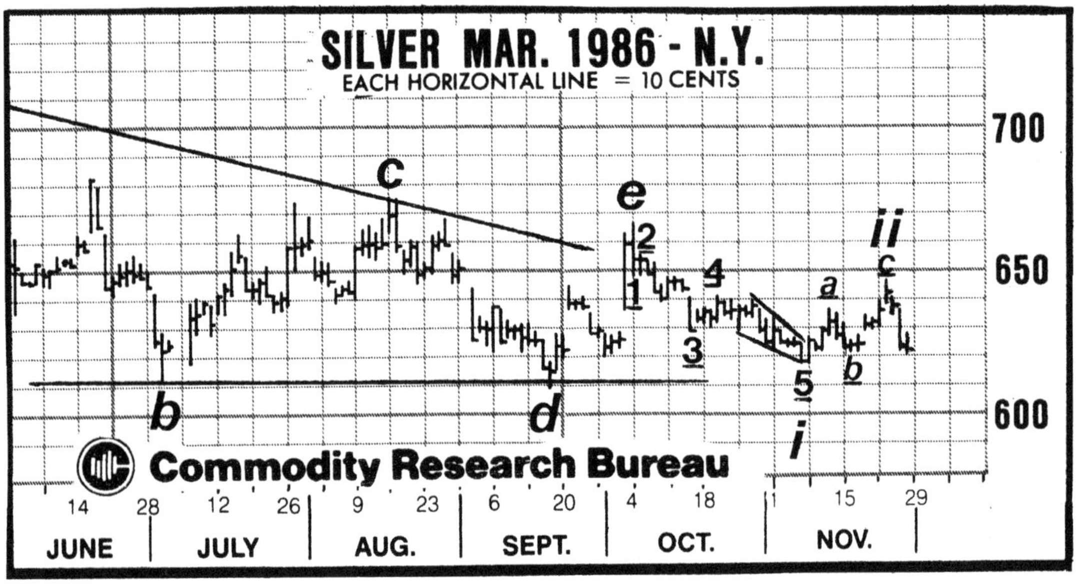

The Elliott Wave Theorist, 1986

JANUARY 1, 1986

Within the bear market trend for precious metals, short term cycles allow for continued choppy declines and rallies into late March, after which time gold and silver should accelerate to the downside in a four-month collapse.

Gold

The wave count shown in the December issue remains unchanged, so it might be useful to examine the cyclic influences on gold at the current time.

Gold and silver have behaved fairly contracyclically to stocks in recent years (a phenomenon identified years ago by James Dines). It just so happens that my projection of the time cycles for 1986 in the precious metals is almost exactly the inverse of that for stocks! Take a look at the chart. The 2-year cycle for gold remains down into August 1986. The 8-month cycle will be lending a weak upward pressure to gold in the first quarter, allowing the smaller 4- and 12-week cycles to dominate price action during that time. The combination of these smaller cycles indicates a decline into early January, a rise into late January, a decline into the first days of March and a rise into late March. All of these moves will take place during the context of a bear market, as defined both by the Elliott wave structure and the declining 6-year gold cycle. From late March, the 8-month cycle will be rolling over, causing the worst price damage in precious metals from April into August.

The brief rally in gold that occurred in December indicates that my earlier conclusion that an 8-week cycle was operative was incorrect. After studying last year's price action, it is clear that rally was the work of the 12-week cycle, which has recently re-established itself after being disrupted at the 8-month cycle bottom earlier this year. You may recall the discussion of that early bottom in the April 1985 issue. In that issue, the longer term cycles projected

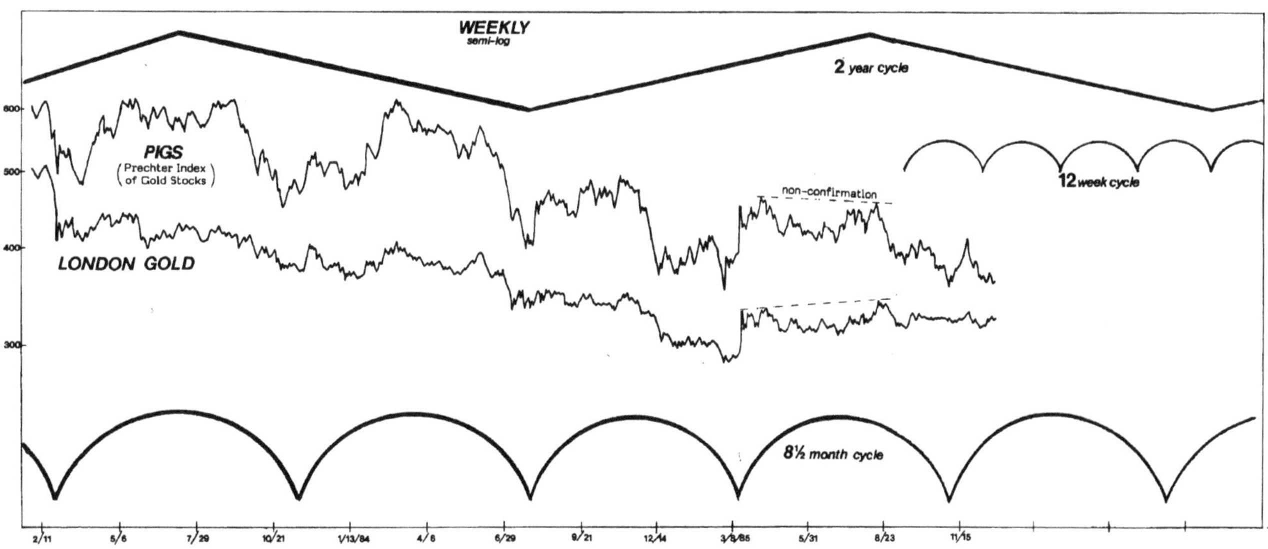

that "gold should be strong into late in the third quarter of 1985." As it turned out, the bear market rally holding pattern persisted until August 28, a pretty accurate cyclic assessment six months in advance.

We are currently still profitable from our short sale recommended right at the highs in August, and if all goes well, we'll be covering the position about a year from entry. Certainly investor and advisor sentiment remains too bullish to indicate a major low, with Market Vane reporting 52% "bulls" in gold and 48% in silver, despite silver's terribly weak performance. Shorter term traders should use the near term scenario outlined in the second paragraph (or follow the Telephone Update) for timing. Keep the stop at $350 basis the February contract, our approximate entry point, keeping risk near zero on this trade. If that stop is taken out, I do not want to go long.

Silver

Silver's wave structure over the past year is exceptionally clear. The chart traced out a textbook "descending triangle" (see text, p.43) from March to its "wave e" peak in early October (see illustration, November 4 issue). It then entered a five-wave "thrust," a swiftly unfolding pattern, to the downside. As you can see on the chart, wave i of the thrust ended in early November, wave ii peaked in late November on a Fibonacci 60% retracement, and as wave iii began, *The Elliott Wave Theorist* concluded, "the sharpest downside action, wave iii, lies immediately ahead." Silver has collapsed 60¢ an ounce in the last five weeks.

The 12-week cycle bottomed right on schedule but has resulted in the feeblest of bounces. This weak action in the face of a rising cycle is further evidence that silver is on its way to the triangle target of "near $5/oz.," with an excellent probability that it will break its June 1982 low of $4.90 basis London fix.

FEBRUARY 3, 1986

Although gold has rallied a bit further than expected, it has followed the intermediate term cyclical outlook presented in the January 1 issue. Most important, the wave pattern of the past year has finally clarified. The precious metals are now peaking and are poised to decline substantially for most of the balance of 1986.

Gold & Silver: Major Decline Ahead

After a year of uncertainty on the intermediate term, the gold picture has suddenly cleared up. At the last major selling opportunity on February 7, 1983, *The Elliott Wave Theorist* headlined the gold section, "Gold: Major Top Approaching." Six days later, gold peaked at $511.50, and the bear market which had begun in 1980 resumed. Since then, as long time readers know, it has remained a question as to exactly which corrective wave structure was unfolding, a large Ⓐ-Ⓑ-(1)-(2)-(3)-(4)-(5) [completing wave Ⓒ] zigzag from January 1980, or an Ⓐ-Ⓑ-Ⓒ-Ⓧ-Ⓐ-Ⓑ-Ⓒ double zigzag. Within the second possibility, it remained a question as to whether the wave Ⓧ rally had indeed ended at $511.50 or whether another rise into that area might occur to complete it. Now one interpretation has clearly established itself as the preferred count.

Eliminating Alternatives

In order for the zigzag interpretation to have been correct, gold should have developed a full five waves down from that February 1983 top. The rally from the February 1985 low has pushed far enough so that we must now label the 1983-1985 decline as an (A)-(B)-(C) (see long term chart), not a "five." This structure rules out the zigzag interpretation mentioned above because what would have been wave (3) of Ⓒ dating from February 1983 would have had to be a "five," and it wasn't. Now look at the weekly chart of gold prices. The best interpretation of the rally from February 1985 is that it is part of an upward corrective wave structure (i.e., a bear market rally), not a developing "five." Therefore, the idea that wave Ⓧ is still in progress is no longer attractive, because the rally for wave (C) of Ⓧ would have to be a developing "five," and it isn't. The bottom line is that my most recent preferred count on the short term wave structure was wrong, and the counts I was using in 1984 and early 1985 were correct.

The Preferred Count

1) The decline from January 1980 to June 1982 was a completed Ⓐ-Ⓑ-Ⓒ. This has been one of EWT's major assumptions all along, and it now appears conclusive.

2) The decline from February 1983 to February 1985 was a "three." It can be labeled internally either as a simple (A)-(B)-(C) zigzag, as in the accompanying charts, or as a "double zigzag." It doesn't matter which, since they have the same function. (For detail on the double zigzag labeling, see the September 1984 and April 1985 issues of EWT.)

3) The rally from February 1985 to the present is a "three." It can be labeled internally either as a simple a-b-c zigzag or as a "double zigzag" (see alternate count labeling on weekly chart). Again, it doesn't matter which, since they have the same function.

4) Since that rally followed an (A)-(B)-(C) decline, it must be labeled (X) and considered part of a developing double or triple zigzag to the downside (see text, p.37), which will unfold over the next two to three years to complete the bear market.

The fact that a triangle is in evidence within the 1985 rally phase is virtually conclusive evidence that the rally is a "three," since triangles never appear in the "wave 2" position. Interpreting the structure without using a triangle forces an a-b-c interpretation into the August high and still disallows consideration of a developing "five" (see Alternate count labeling on the weekly chart).

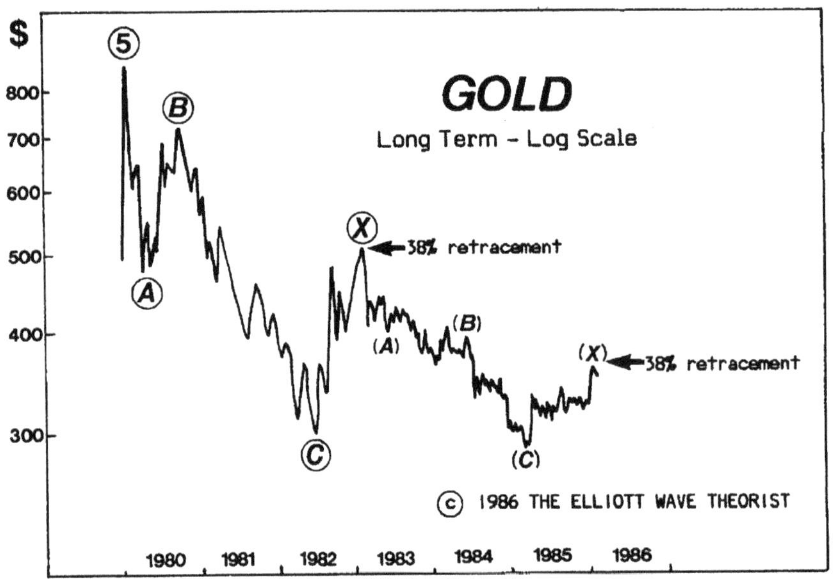

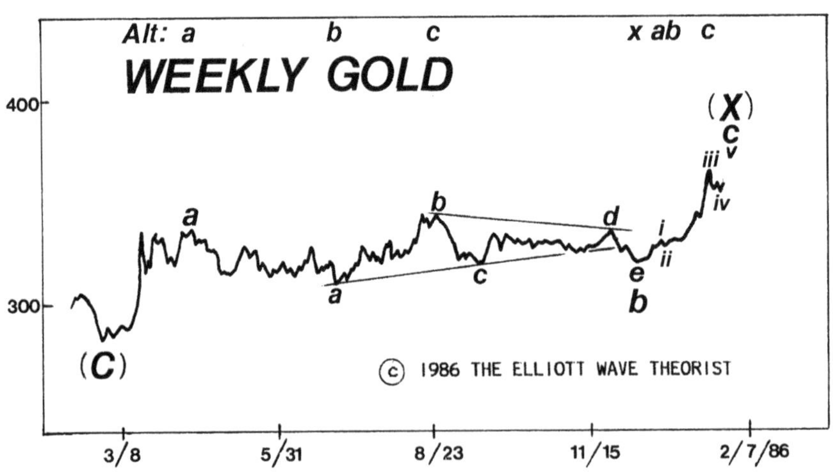

Targeting

The countertrend rally has either already ended or will do so on one more new high over the next few trading days. Almost every way I target the peak for this rally, it comes out the same. Just look at these Elliott wave computations in the rally from February 1985:

1) Using the triangle interpretation, c = a at $364.50.

2) Using the triangle interpretation, the widest part of the triangle (see text, p.44) projects wave c to $367.

3) Using the double zigzag interpretation, the second a-b-c equals the first a-b-c at $372.15.

4) A Fibonacci 38.2% retracement of the preceding (A)-(B)-(C) decline targets $371. If you will recall, Primary wave Ⓧ from June 1982 to February 1983 retraced exactly 38.8% of its preceding Ⓐ-Ⓑ-Ⓒ decline (see long term chart).

5) The apex of the wave (B) triangle that ended in May 1984 would be expected to provide resistance, and that level comes in at $370.

The computed target zone, then, is $364-$373. In giving the zone some leeway, we would certainly expect a price peak between $360 and $375 basis the London fix, an area that prices have already entered. I would abandon this interpretation only if London gold fixes above $410, because in the unlikely event that the current rally were to retrace 50% of the preceding (A)-(B)-(C), with c equaling 1.618a, gold could stretch as far as $394-$407.

Other Evidence

Cycles are right on schedule. Re-read this forecast from the January 1 issue:

> The combination of these smaller cycles indicates a decline into early January, a rise into late January, a decline into the first days of March and rise into late March.

Gold did pull back into "early January," bottoming on the first trading day, and has risen into "late January." The strength of this rally has been provided entirely by the 8½-month and the 12-week cycles, as illustrated in the January 1 issue. From here, the cyclic pressure is rolling over, so if a new high is to occur, it should occur this week. From here on out, except for one more weak rally attempt in March, the major cycles will begin taking over and propelling gold to new lows.

In the momentum area, volume expanded on the recent rally but not to the levels achieved in the March rally, either on a daily or weekly basis. Much more important, however, is the fact that the gold stock average is way below its April 1985 high, as is silver, while gold bullion is well above its corresponding high. These are glaring non-confirmations of the apparent uptrend. Such non-confirmations are typical of cycle tops.

Sentiment is loony. The Bullish Consensus recently reported between 70% and 95% bulls on gold, silver, platinum and copper. If you have a copy of the March 1983 issue of EWT, re-read the account of the terrifically bullish sentiment that accompanied the peak that year at $511.50. The investment world was convinced then that $3000 to $6000 gold was just around the corner, and it appears convinced now that a "major bottom" has occurred. Headlines in major financial publications in January include, "The New Gold Rush," "Metals: Ready for a Higher Orbit?," "Comeback Time for Gold?" and "Why Metals Look Bullish Despite Weak World Recovery." Such headlines have occurred throughout this one-year sideways/rally phase.

As one writer observed, "Traders now are scrambling to come up with reasons why cheap oil could even be bullish for gold," against historical precedent! Most gold watchers consider the recent long sideways trend as a base of accumulation; the sentiment that has accompanied the entire process argues much more strongly that it is a shelf of distribution.

Strategy

The cycles forecasted a January rally, but not its extent. On January 15, we were stopped out of gold at $350 basis the February futures contract. The short sale of August 19 (right at the peak of the first a-b-c pattern) was recommended just above $350 basis that contract, and the average entry price available from our strategy resulted exactly in a wash. As you know from watching the stock market, simple corrective patterns can turn into "double" corrective patterns, but their implication is still the same. Don't let that reality of the marketplace wear you out and keep you from participating when the real move comes.

Gold again appears to be a good short sale, since another (A)-(B)-(C) zigzag to the downside, of equivalent degree to the February 1983-February 1985 decline, lies directly ahead. Ultimately gold should fall below $200/oz., with $179 a minimum and $105 a maximum and most likely target. Traders should re-enter the short side and place a stop at $378 basis the London fix. If stopped out, short again at $394 or higher, and place a stop at $410.

Given the non-confirmation in the gold stock average (see chart, January issue), it is probable that the next decline in bullion will be accompanied by severe price declines in gold stocks, despite the recent widespread advertising that gold stocks are poised for a new bull market. Silver, by the way, is still terribly weak. It has been the beneficiary of widespread talk about how "cheap" it is relative to gold, so thousands of investors have bought it, while speculators have taken a long silver/short gold "spread." With each passing week, they lose more money, so something is rotten in the silver picture. Investors should remain out of the gold and silver markets; there is much better money to be made in the U.S. stock market.

MARCH 3, 1986

Silver has broken to new lows for the year, and gold should follow suit. Gold is poised to do what stocks and bonds did, but in reverse.

Gold & Silver

The January issue covered the cycles in gold, and the February issue detailed the wave count. Both of them are bearish. The brief February rally in gold brought the futures contract to an exact .618 Fibonacci retracement of the first five waves of decline from the January peak of wave (X) (see daily chart). This is the most common retracement for second waves.

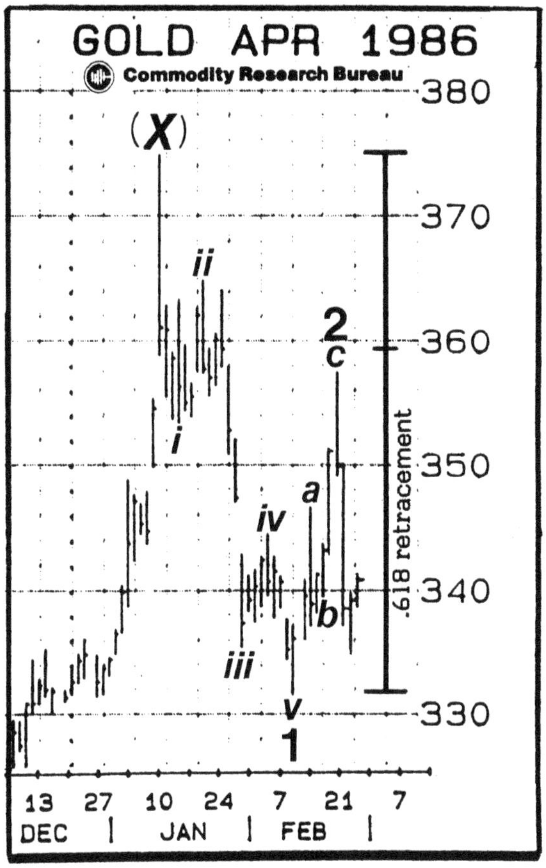

The sentiment report from February 25 (The Bullish Consensus, 61 S. Lake Av, Pasadena, CA) showed the majority of analysts still bullish on both gold and silver. In February, Gold Newsletter reported the results of its survey of "20 leading analysts" on gold and found 17 of them bullish on the metal for 1986, a whopping 85%. (EWT was one of the "three bears.") If you've been a subscriber for a while, you may recall the same survey in January 1983, which revealed a vast majority of bulls and just a few "minority bears," including yours truly. Six weeks later, gold collapsed from $511.50 to $400 in a matter of days. The end of the (X) wave rally in January 1986, which should (if counted correctly) be the point of maximum bullishness, coincided also with the reappearance of ads headlined, "Gold at $6000 per Ounce – Are You Ready?", articles headlined, "Gold to Soar in 1986" and "Platinum – Experts Looking For Further Gains in '86", and aggressive commentary such as, "Gold is in its most spectacular bull market in history," and anyone who doesn't see that is "blinded by static and inertial thinking!" Well, everyone, including me, is blind to the future, but the numbers reveal that the bulls are substantially more convinced of their clarity of vision than are the bears, at least at the moment. Sentiment on January 27, the day gold double-topped, was so positive that even the deflationary implication of a halving of oil prices couldn't break the bullish conviction. On the contrary, it strengthened it. The market rewarded the majority the way it usually does, by promptly crashing for two days, driving silver to new lows for the year. Here are the comments on silver from last month's issue:

> Silver is still terribly weak. It has been the beneficiary of widespread talk about how "cheap" it is relative to gold, so thousands of investors have bought it, while speculators have taken a long silver/short gold "spread." With each passing week, they lose more money, so something is rotten in the silver picture.

Since then, silver has collapsed another 50¢ an ounce on the futures market and has fallen below the shelf of support that has existed for eleven months.

We're still short gold. Traders can now lower the stop to the January highs basis the London fix for both gold and silver. The target remains $105/oz. for gold and below $4.90 (the 1982 low) for silver. As I have been saying for almost all of the past six years, investors should continue to avoid the precious metals and keep all investment assets in the U.S. stock market.

MARCH 31, 1986

Gold has played out its forecasted rebound rally phase, which was due to end in "late March," and is now poised for a virtually uninterrupted decline into August. I expect a crack well into the $200s by summer.

Gold

The precious metals have entered the time zone for the downside acceleration point projected three months ago. Since the metals have followed the script so well, there is every reason to believe that the forecast will continue to be followed. This was the projection, from the January 1 issue:

> The 8-month cycle will be lending a weak upward pressure to gold in the first quarter, allowing the smaller cycles to dominate price action during that time. The combination of these smaller cycles indicates a decline into early January, a rise into late January, a decline into the first days of March and a rise into late March. All of these moves will take place within the context of a bear market.... From late March, the 8-month cycle will be rolling over, causing the worst price damage in precious metals from April into August.

The accompanying chart shows how neatly the precious metals have fit into the cyclic outlook during the past three months. They now sit at the "rollover" point for the 12-week and the 8½-month cycles, with the 2-year and 6-year cycles already pointing down! The larger cycle chart is updated from the January issue. While a last gasp rally attempt in early April is not impossible, all cyclic forces point down relentlessly from now until August.

The wave structure is holding beautifully as well. Remember that .618 retracement mark shown in last month's issue? Gold futures rallied right up to it once again in late March, completing an a-b-c bear market rally (see chart). In fact, the Telephone Update called for the rally in April gold to peak at $359-$360; the spike high was $359.60. The chart here showing the wave count is from the February issue, with prices updated.

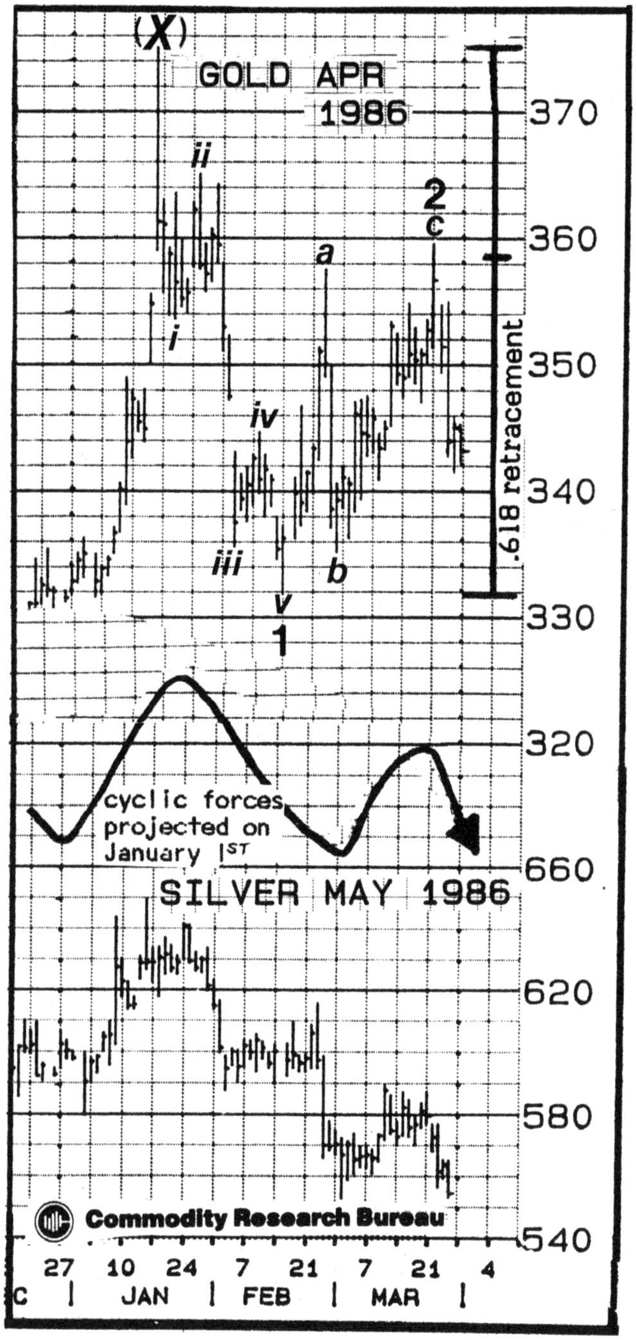

According to The Bullish Consensus, there were more bulls last week in the gold and silver markets than there were either in the stock market or the bond market, 72% and 60% vs. 59% and 56% respectively. Sentiment toward stocks and gold has been this way for most of the past three months, a tribute to misplaced contrarianism, which has degenerated into "fight the trend" madness. Since September, stocks have provided a 42% gain, while gold has gone absolutely nowhere, yet advisors have actually favored the gold market. (Meanwhile, silver is down 17%.) Investor sentiment thus at least fits my thesis that a cycle and wave top, not a bottom, is in the making. It isn't clear by looking just at prices, but a strong case can be made by studying the wave structure, cycle position and sentiment. Another sign that the precious metals have been in an attempted rally phase is the persistent strength in platinum, which has got to be the most talked-up precious metal since gold double topped in September 1980. The gold bugs can't get gold and silver moving, so they are concentrating on platinum. That wave count could use one more new high but appears vulnerable to a surprise decline. Investors should stay out of the gold market and continue to concentrate on U.S. stocks. Traders should stay short and keep the stop at the January highs basis the London fix for both gold and silver. Gold could fall close to $200/oz. by later this year, on its way to my ultimate target of $105.

The focus on "fundamentals" has brought out the case that falling oil prices are bullish for gold because they will cause a banking crisis. Considering fundamentals is usually just

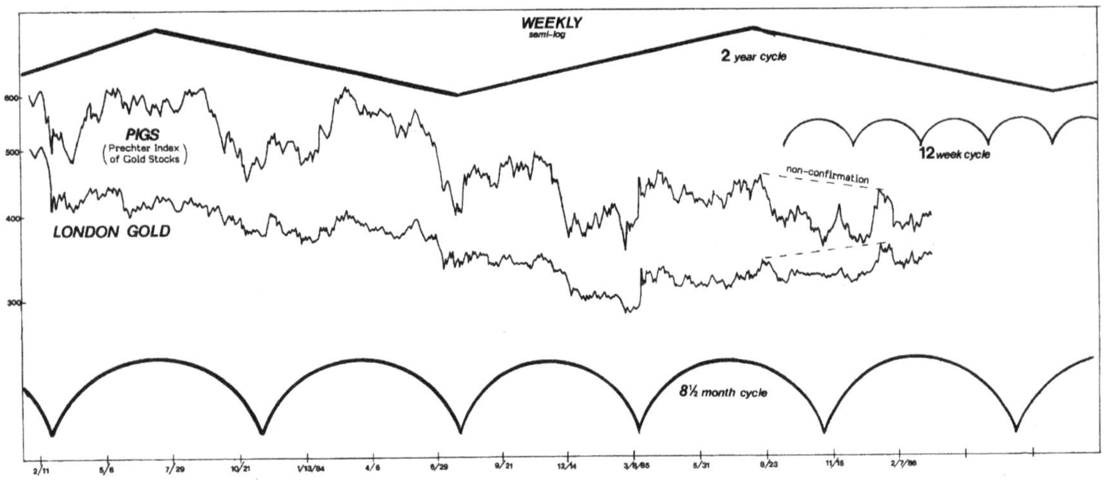

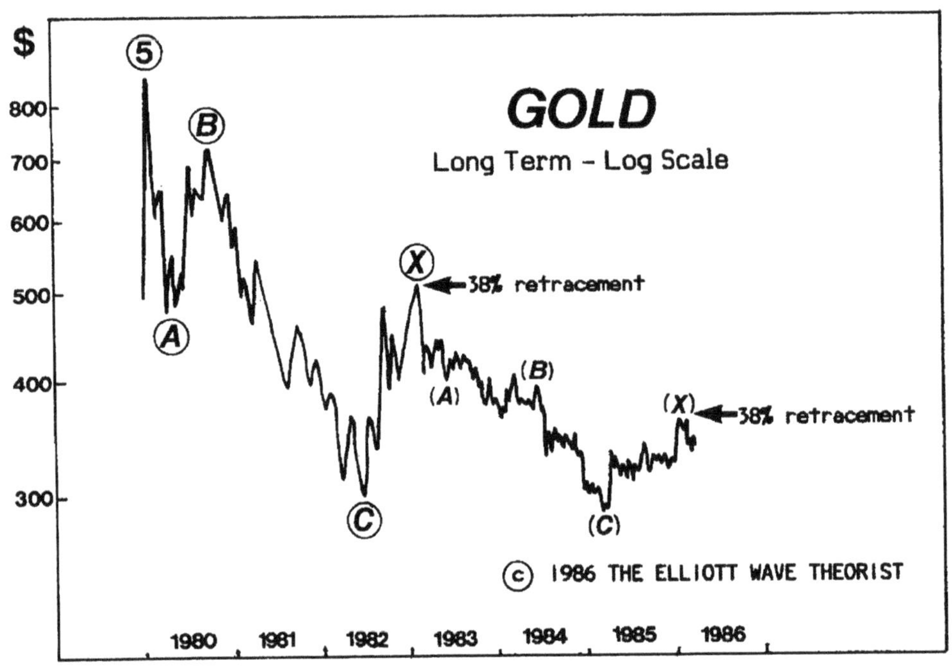

an excuse for rationalization, so let's try some ourselves. The following thoughts are courtesy of money manager and subscriber Sam Scholberg of Saginaw, Michigan. Since Russia sells oil, and oil prices have collapsed, what else can they sell in order to buy grain? Hint: they are one of the world's biggest gold producers. And since the Middle East sells oil, and oil prices have collapsed along with OPEC, what else can they sell in order to maintain the lifestyle to which they have become accustomed? Hint: the same stuff they accumulated during the twelve years of high oil prices. Finally, while the gold bulls labeled the idea that general price inflation could come down to zero "ridiculous," the fall in oil prices may just be enough actually to create a flat or declining Consumer Price Index in the months ahead. Once again, the preposterous is happening.

Silver

EWT has been more bearish on silver than just about anything. Last week, silver made a new closing low and has now fallen $1.15/oz. basis the May futures contract since the Hunts announced in October that they had sold all their silver. The frenzy to buy silver on that day was typical of thoughtless buying based on news and completed wave e of the triangle. There is a 60% bullish consensus on this terribly weak market, so the "give up" stage appears far away. Silver still has risk to below $4.90.

MAY 5, 1986

Gold stocks have dropped, along with silver, to below their 1985 lows, and a sudden collapse in the price of gold is possible at any time. Cycles still point to lower precious metals prices into August. If for any reason gold rallies to above $370 basis London fix, it will merely be providing a "last chance" short selling opportunity.

Gold & Silver

The April issue of EWT spent two full pages covering the precious metals' bearish technical position as revealed by waves, cycles, the non-confirmation at the last peak, and investor sentiment. From that date, silver collapsed another 55¢/oz., or 10%, and PIGS (the Prechter Index of Gold Stocks) slipped below an apparent "triple bottom," thus breaking the February 1985 low and bringing gold stocks to their lowest levels since late 1982. That index has now lost nearly 50% of its value since March 1984, a secret that the bullish analysts just aren't letting you in on. EWT also commented on platinum for the first time last month, concluding that it appeared "vulnerable to a surprise decline" after rising almost non-stop for 13 months. There has been no big decline yet, but platinum is down from that point, a big surprise to the bulls, who still number 70% of the crowd as of last week, according to The Bullish Consensus. As far as overall sentiment goes, there is hardly an advisory service covering gold that is not calling for a new bull market to between $400 and $800/oz. In fact, the gold bear market is so underbelieved that Barron's was able to sell advertising for an eight page special section on precious metals on April 28.

Meanwhile, of course, the price of gold bullion is unchanged from a year ago. Is this bullish for gold, as so many analysts contend? Silver has been collapsing, commodities from grains to oil have fallen dramatically from their all time highs, and the trend toward deflation is well established (brief inflationary interludes notwithstanding). So why hasn't gold fallen as dramatically? I think there is a reasonable answer. Market watchers have long noted that in the final stages of a bear market in stocks, the bluest blue chips are tossed overboard last, as the environment of panic finally persuades investors to give up even on shares of the USA's finest companies. Gold, as most investors know, is the "blue chip" of inflation hedge investments. It may well be that gold, in a similar way, will be the last inflation hedge investment to be sold by the long term hard money investors.

Time will tell. In the meantime, the technical position of the metals remains negative. The 12-week cycle points "hard down" into late May (May 27 is the ideal target date), suggesting a down May followed by a bounce into June. We should then see a resumption of the decline into at least August, when the 2-year and 8½-month cycles are due to bottom (please refer to charts in the April issue).

As far as the wave structure goes, gold has traced out a clear symmetrical triangle from either December or January. The implications of this pattern are unquestionably bearish for the intermediate term, but it leaves open the slim possibility of a rally first into the original "bounce" target area just above $370. I don't expect it. I am only mentioning it because if it does happen, it will not change my opinion; it will merely provide another shorting opportunity. Our official position for investors is out and for traders is short. Raise the stop temporarily to $400 basis London fix, then lower it back to the January peak if gold falls below $330. Whatever the ultimate low in gold, it is likely to underperform other investments, so unless and until gold begins tracing out bullish price structures, it is best avoided.

JUNE 2, 1986

The 12-week cycle in gold and silver is bottoming, so the metals should rally for several weeks, then resume their bear markets.

Gold & Silver

From the cycle highs in January, both gold stocks and silver futures have collapsed 26% in value, while gold bullion has slipped a mere $20/oz. The declines in these prices have been significantly more severe in foreign currency terms, since the US$ has been falling precipitously since early 1985, having lost over 30% of its relative value. Clearly the cycles have kept us on the right side of these metals markets. (It's ironic that the independent rating services show gold bulls as having been just as right as the bears even though gold stocks, silver and the silver/gold spread, which so many of them favored, have all plummeted.)

The May issue reiterated, "The 12-week cycle points 'hard down' into late May." The 12-week cycle is now in the time zone for a bottom. Several factors support this conclusion. A new low in prices was hit on May 20 for silver, and gold held above its April bottom, creating a non-confirmation. Volume at the time was light. Sentiment turned temporarily gloomy. In the wave structure, a triangle has formed on the chart of gold bullion, and the odds are 70/30 that it will resolve on the upside, producing a short term rally. Finally, silver completed five waves down from the January high, and the forecast for silver from the November 4 issue (and reiterated in the January 1 issue) has been fulfilled exactly:

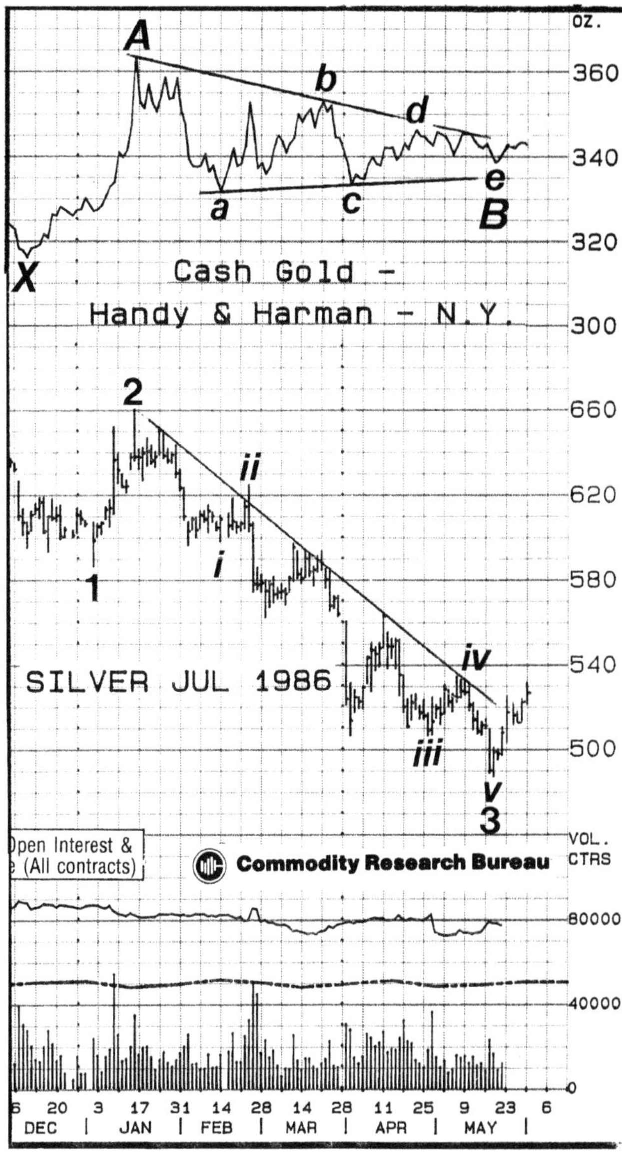

Silver sports what appears to be a textbook descending triangle. Descending triangles imply thrust, or short, sharp collapses. Using Elliott's measuring tool of "the widest part of the triangle," silver should fall to near $5/oz., ideally below the 1982 bottom at $4.90.

On May 20, London silver fixed at $4.85, and has since bounced 25¢. Another short selloff could occur over the next few trading days as part of the cyclic bottoming process.

The 12-week cycle is now expected to cause a rally in precious metals into the month of June. In silver, this rally will likely be wave 4 dating back to the October peak. Resistance is $5.30-5.60 basis July futures. In gold, it should be the last rally in the countertrend advance that began in February 1985. Traders should cover short sales now and reinstate them if London gold fixes above $365/oz., since the $365-$375 area is the rally target computed on page 9 of the February 3 issue. Because of their major trends, I am as bearishly biased in gold as I am bullishly biased in stocks, so trading strategy will reflect the desire not to miss the short side. If the upside target is not met, traders should return to the short side on a London fix below $332, which would signal a breakdown by taking out the low of wave c of the triangle shown on the accompanying chart. Investors should stay out of the precious metals, since the long term bear market still appears to be in progress. With the 8½-month and 2-year cycles pointing down into at least August, longer term traders who are comfortably short from much higher levels (particularly in silver) may choose to hold onto positions. All short sellers should use a penetration of $400 basis London fix on gold as a stop.

JUNE 30, 1986

Gold and silver remain in major bear markets. Gold will retain the Elliott wave potential to rally to $365-375 basis London fix unless $332 is taken out, in which case all trends will again point down.

Gold & Silver

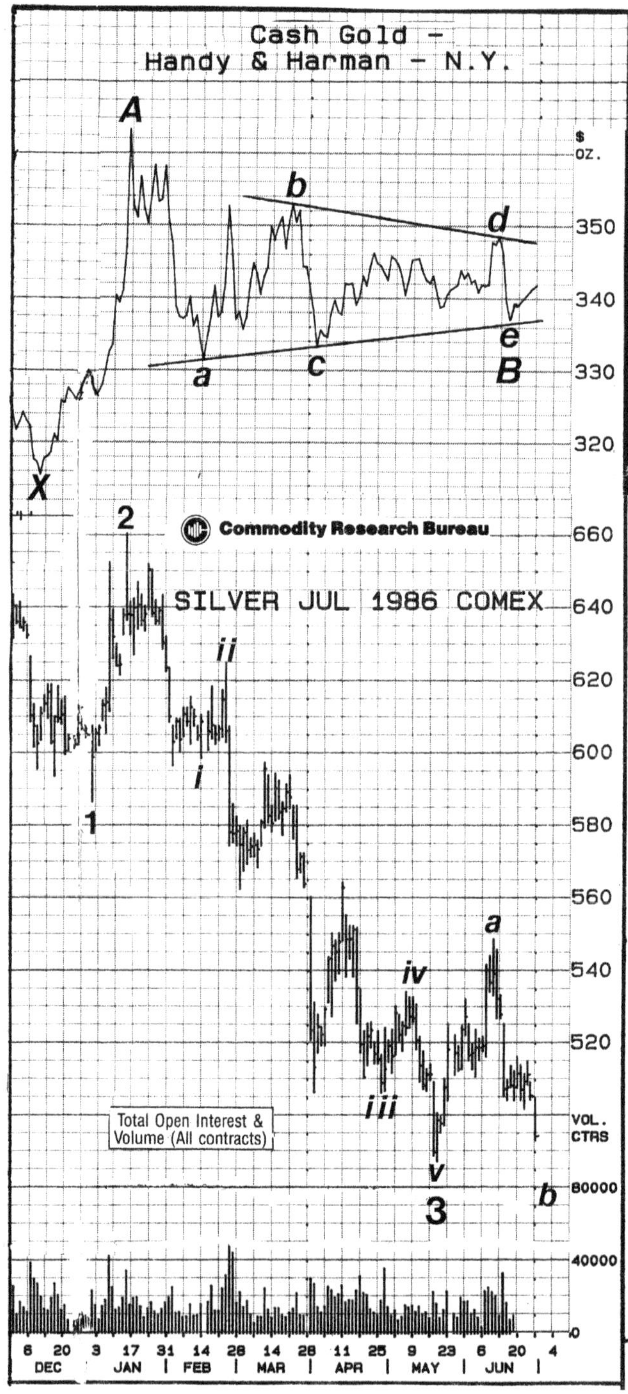

The last issue concluded, "The 12-week cycle is now expected to cause a rally in precious metals into the month of June.... In silver, resistance is $5.30-5.60 basis July futures." The silver rally peaked on June 11 at $5.48. (The chart shown is the July contract; add 5¢ to all numbers if you're following the September contract.) Alternation (see text, p.50) would suggest that silver is tracing out either an a-b-c flat correction or a triangle. If so, the "b" wave should be bottoming in a day or two, near the May low, and wave c to the upside would carry silver back once again to its resistance zone.

If such a rally occurs, it will provide the last chance for gold to rally to the $365-375 area basis London fix. If it does attain that price area, it will be a super short selling opportunity. The technical position of gold overall is so weak, however, that we cannot count on such a rally to the extent of taking a long position. As explained last month, this rally potential will be eliminated if the London fix slips below the "wave c" low of the triangle at $332. At that point, all trends will be pointing down. Remember, although the triangle pictured here may be bullish short term, it is conclusive evidence that gold is dead on the long term; a five-wave upward structure is not in force, and triangles always precede the final upmove in a sequence. Continue to plan to sell short upon either a London fix above $365 or below $332.

On the larger picture, time cycles up to two years in length remain down until at least August. Market sentiment is still characteristic of a bear market, with The Bullish Consensus reporting bulls among advisors jumping to 65% on gold and 70% on silver after a mere three weeks of rally. The wave structure is still bearish for gold on the major trend. We'll take a look at the long term charts again soon.

Julian Snyder (25 Broad St., New York, NY 10004), a brilliant student of long term market trends, offered this observation in his June 16 issue of International Moneyline:

> The current conventional wisdom is that the price of gold is holding up remarkably well in a generally deflationary environment. The reality is that the purchasing power of gold is dropping about as fast as the buying power of the dollar. When the value of an ounce of gold is measured in terms of the Japanese yen or the Swiss franc, it becomes clear that for the present, some kinds of paper money are a much safer haven for value than gold.

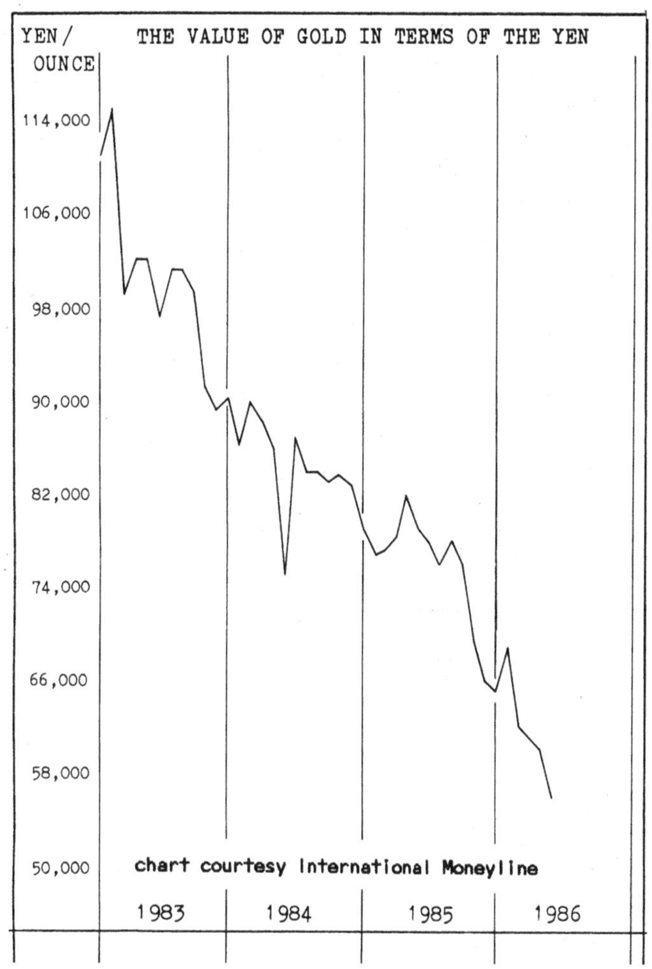

When looking at Julian's chart, I can only imagine what yen/silver must look like! If the dollar reverses its extended downtrend (and the outlook for bonds certainly allows for it), the dollar/gold ratio should decline. Even if the dollar does not rally, gold remains the most expensive of all the commodities, and I firmly believe that when it breaks to the downside, it will break big.

Reason magazine, August 1986

WHAT LIES AHEAD IN THE SPECULATIVE MARKETS

by Robert R. Prechter, Jr.

Although every financial issue of *Reason* has contained at least one analyst's fervent call for an upward explosion in precious-metals prices, gold for the most part has remained in a down or sideways trend since its peak in January 1980 at $850 per ounce. Silver, in turn, has been an unmitigated disaster, falling 90 percent from its $50 peak registered at that time. Is this the major bottom for precious metals? Is inflation ready to "resume," or "resurge"?

Although rallies may occur at any time, the evidence from the price structure argues strongly that the major bear markets in gold and silver remain in force. In support of this contention are (1) the lack of bearish conviction on the part of investors, a precondition for a major bear-market bottom, and (2) the position of time cycles in gold. In the past, the precious-metals markets have displayed a remarkable tendency to bottom at regular intervals. The next scheduled major low for gold and silver is not due until 1988. According to normal Elliott Wave parameters, moreover, gold still has potential ultimately to decline to the $100- to $180-per-ounce price range before the next major bull market begins.

If this potential appears ridiculously low to you, please consider the fact that all markets tend toward extreme overvaluation at tops and undervaluation at bottoms. There are some further points, too, that make such a target worth considering. Silver has already met its Elliott Wave bear market target zone of $3.50-$5.50, which itself appeared ridiculously low when it was originally suggested. Moreover, the prices of commodities, from grains to oil, have fallen dramatically from their all-time highs, and the trend toward deflation is well established (brief inflationary interludes notwithstanding).

So why hasn't gold fallen as dramatically as silver and commodities? Market watchers have long noted that in the final stages of a bear market in stocks, the blue chips are tossed overboard last, as the environment of panic finally persuades investors to give up even on share's of the nation's finest companies. Gold, of course, is the "blue chip" of the inflation-hedge investments. It may well be that gold, in reflecting a dynamic similar to that found in the stock market, will be the last inflation-hedge investment to be sold by long-term hard-money investors. Time will tell. Whatever the ultimate low in gold, it is likely to underperform the U.S. stock market, so unless and until gold begins tracing out bullish price structures, it is best avoided.

AUGUST 4, 1986

The 8½-month and 2-year cycles are bottoming in gold and silver and should provide a countertrend rally in the precious metals and related stocks. However, the extent of the rally will be limited and should ultimately provide a short selling opportunity as the bear market moves into its final 1-1½ years.

Gold & Silver

For over a year, EWT has continually forecast that the 2-year cycle pointed down in gold and silver until August 1986. From the last high for that cycle a year ago until last week, silver dropped 24% and PIGS (my gold stock average) 33% in an unrelenting year of erosion. It is now my opinion that the 2-year cycle has bottomed. The evidence is subtle, but if you study the long term cycle chart, you will see divergences between the new lows in gold stocks and silver futures versus the higher bottoms in gold and silver bullion. Also, while commodity futures prices in general have collapsed to below their 1985 lows, spot commodity prices have held up, resulting in a negative spread so large that it equals the positive spread that existed at the inflationary peak of early 1980! There is, temporarily at least, way too much willingness to bet aggressively on further deflation.

The price action projected for silver last month is working out:

> Alternation would suggest that silver is tracing out either an a-b-c flat correction or a triangle. If so, the "b" wave should be bottoming in a day or two, near the May low, and wave c to the upside would carry silver back once again to its resistance zone.

Silver took its time, but did bottom 5¢ from the May low and then bounced last week. The little upside gap in silver on Thursday, moreover, is a typical occurrence at a low (see chart).

Before projecting the most likely future course of precious metals prices, there is an important question to address. During the declining portion of the 2-year cycle, gold bullion actually managed to rise $10/oz., and platinum and collector coins have been going up persistently. Why? Either that strength in the face of downside cyclic pressure is extremely bullish, or something else is going on. Some have argued that the Treasury or Fed is fixing de facto the price of gold in the mid-$300s. Perhaps they are trying to do so, but the market ultimately is too big for that, as the experience of 1977-1979, when the government tried to keep gold down, shows. Even if an authority attempts to "engineer" gold into a flat trend over the next two years, the cyclic forces should eventually prevail. Similarly, given the corrective style wave structure in gold's rise from the low of early 1985 and the very high price of gold relative to commodities, I am inclined to reject the very bullish alternate count, which calls for a rise in gold bullion in a continuation of wave Ⓧ to above the February 1983 top at $511/oz. (see wave count chart, April issue). The subtleties in the precious metals area require a closer look at the cyclic forces in operation.

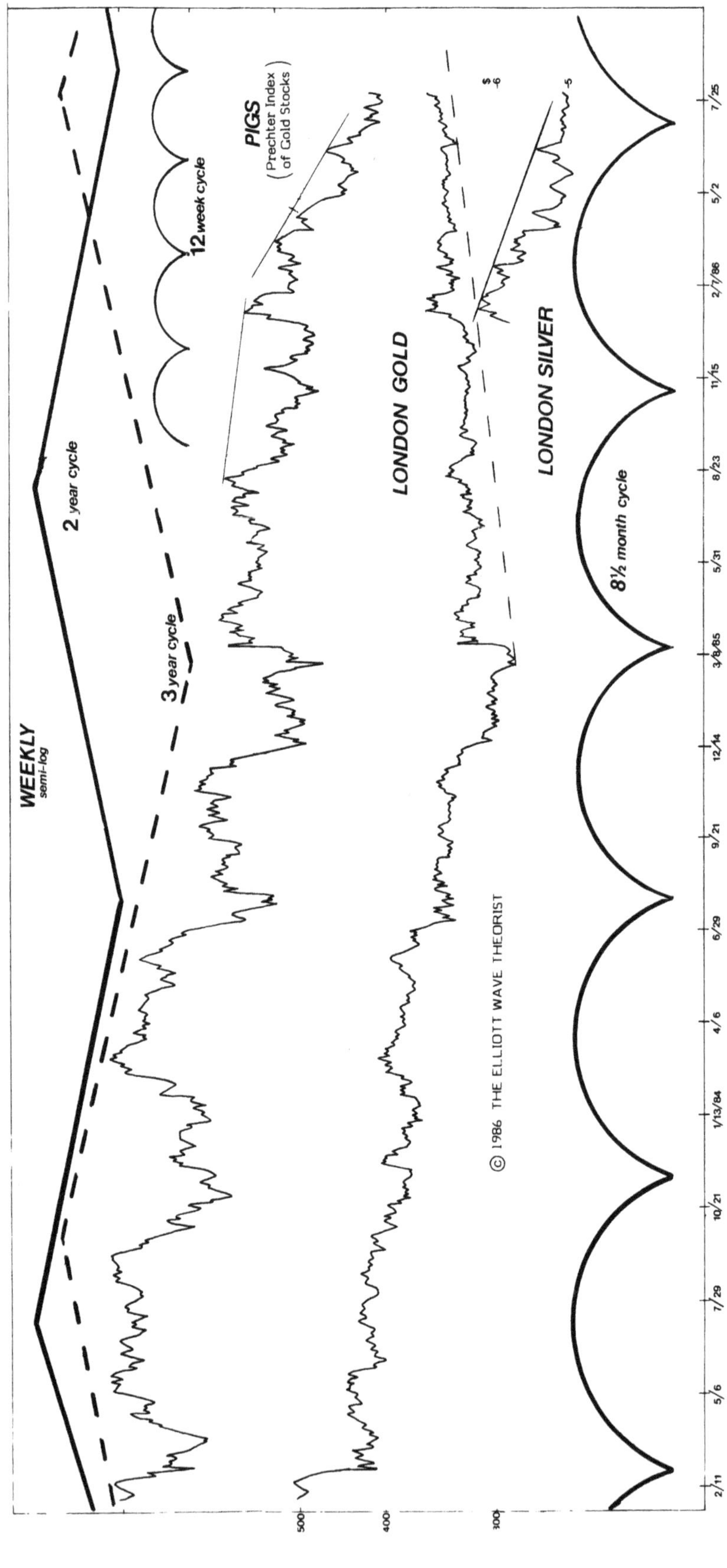
WEEKLY
semi-log
2 year cycle
3 year cycle
12 week cycle
PIGS
(Prechter Index of Gold Stocks)
LONDON GOLD
LONDON SILVER
8½ month cycle
© 1986 THE ELLIOTT WAVE THEORIST
500
400
300
2/11
5/6
7/29
10/21
1/13/84
4/6
6/29
9/21
12/14
3/8/85
5/31
8/23
11/15
2/7/86
5/2
7/25

A careful study of the price and momentum behavior in gold and gold stocks reveals the presence of a 3-year cycle (see dashed line on cycle chart). This cycle created price lows in 1970, 1973, 1976, 1979, 1982 and 1985 (the precise timing of the price lows in each of those years was governed by the shorter term cycles). Its existence was not immediately clear to me because of how well it fits into the patterns of the reliable cycles I have been tracking. The 6-year cycle bottoms concurrently with every third 2-year cycle and every second 3-year cycle, while the 8½-month cycle repeats roughly three times to create the 2-year cycle and four times to create the 3-year cycle.

Postulating this cycle makes sense of the entire precious metals picture. Gold bullion, platinum and collector coins have clearly been influenced more strongly by the 3-year cycle, which explains their relative strength. This cycle last bottomed in February/March 1985. That cycle is due to peak now, but the newly rising 8½-month cycle will probably cause continued strength into November for "right hand translation" of that cycle's top. Gold shares and silver, on the other hand, have been influenced more strongly by the 2-year cycle, which explains their relative weakness. That cycle is bottoming now. This situation implies a strong countertrend rally in these markets at least into November, then a period of distribution, creating "left hand translation" of that cycle's top. Ultimately, the 2-year, 3-year and 6-year cycles are all scheduled to bottom together in my long standing target year of 1988. The final 1-1½ years in both of these cycles should provide an

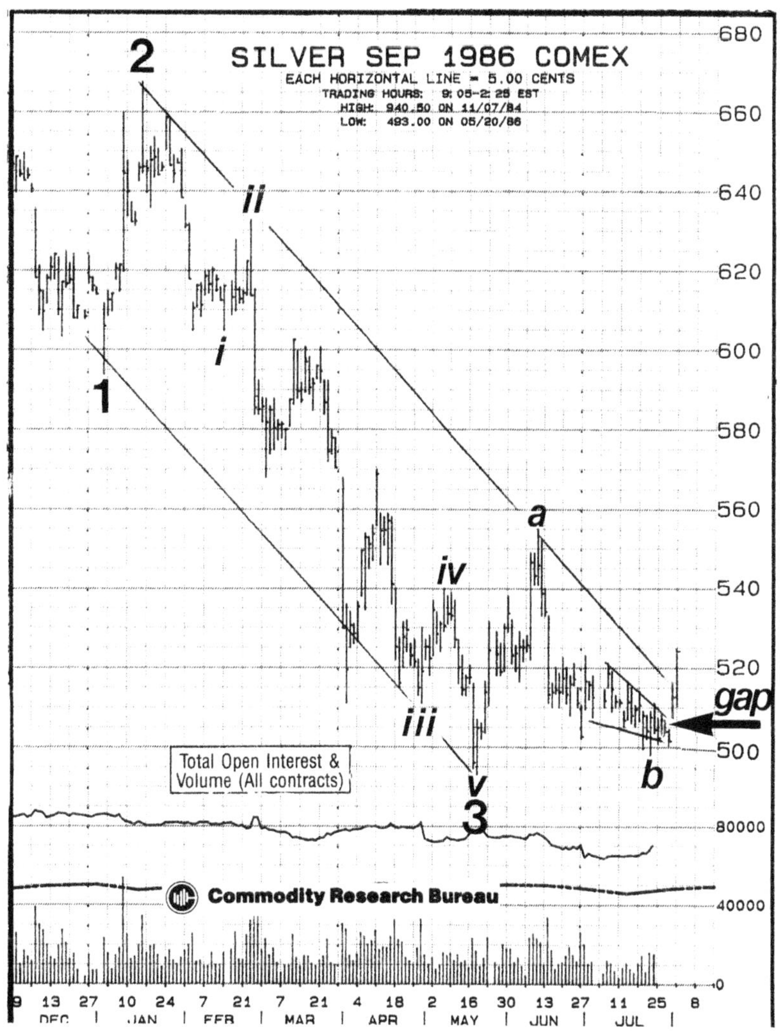

across-the-board bear market wave of decline for the precious metals. Thus, we should continue to avoid investing in gold and silver until 1988, when I expect terrific bargains to be available.

Just as I prefer to recommend "long side" strategy and avoid short selling in bull markets, I prefer not to take long positions in bear markets. Most of those who have tried to do so in the precious metals have repeatedly lost money for six years. The June 2 issue of *The Elliott Wave Theorist* suggested covering short sales in gold, and we are still in a neutral position. Let's stay on the sidelines, allow the 8½-month cycle to run its course, then look to sell short later. On the near term, the target for gold is still $365-375 basis London fix going into the 3-year cycle high and completing wave (X), as shown on the long term wave count in the April issue. If silver is in a fourth wave, as per my preferred count, it would rally to $5.60-5.70 basis the September futures, decline to a new low for wave 5, then rally back to the wave 4 peak in an a-b-c pattern. I would expect gold stocks to rally along with the very reliable 8½-month cycle, suggesting an up or at worst neutral market from here into November. All of this action would be expected to precede the rollover of the 2-year cycle. We'll keep up with the shorter term swings on the Hotline.

SEPTEMBER 2, 1986

The rallies in gold and silver occurred on schedule with the upturn in the trading cycles. The upward pressure remaining in these cycles should create little more than a topping process, if that, over the next 4 to 8 weeks. Gold's technical condition, from both a momentum and sentiment standpoint, is very weak, and supports the Elliott wave conclusion that a resumption of the bear market could begin at any time.

Gold

After forecasting for over a year that the 2-year cycle in gold and silver would turn up in August 1986, the August issue concluded, "the 2-year cycle has bottomed." The evidence was subtle but conclusive. From late July, gold stocks (not shown; see August issue) and silver experienced sharp rallies off their lows, while gold (which we covered in June) suddenly leaped out of its sideways consolidation. What is the technical picture now?

Looking out 1½ years, the most dangerous market on the board, technically speaking, is gold. Last month's issue went into great detail on the cyclic outlook for the precious metals, showing that gold and platinum were in the vicinity of their 3-year cycle highs. Both silver and precious metals stocks should benefit from their rising 2-year and 8½-month cycles, which will attempt to hold prices up until November. However, the 6-year cycle is down hard and will undoubtedly force these smaller cycles to be "left hand translated," creating an early peak in prices. The top in the metals complex should be completed some time in the next four to eight weeks. Ideally, the overall topping formation would contain one selloff soon, then a final rally, whether to a lower or higher peak. Then all trends will be down.

The most damaging evidence comes from wave structure, which has been of a corrective nature since the February 1985 low. In other words, the rise has been all or part of a bear market rally, not a new bull market. The long term wave count first presented in the April 1986 issue is still the preferred count (see chart).

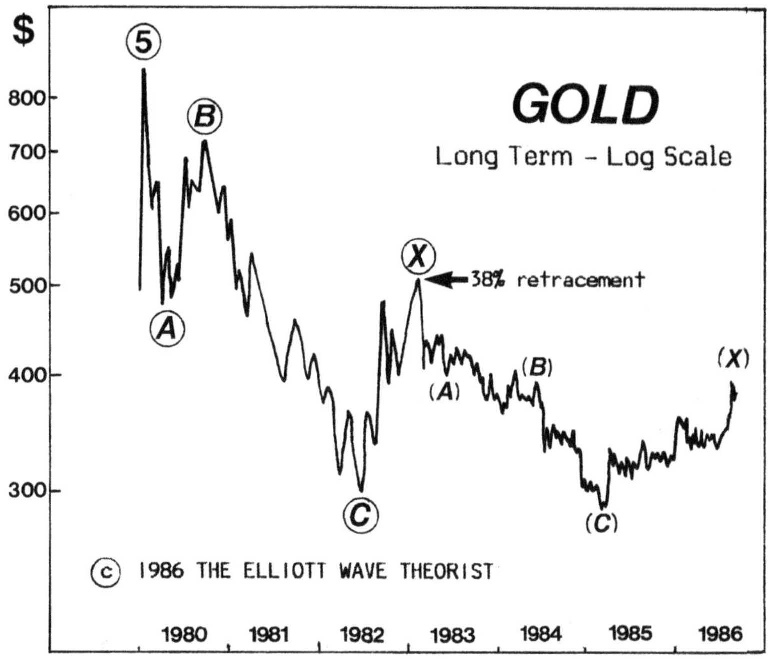

The internal count for wave (X) is that of a triple zigzag: three sharp, emotional rallies separated in this case by contracting triangles. One of those triangles was recognized as having ended in late June, which is why the July issue of EWT recommended covering short sales at that time. At this point, gold has completed or nearly completed the third zigzag to the upside. Furthermore, it has now pushed into price territory that leaves very little room to go. Since the rally passed the .382 retracement point of the previous (A)-(B)-(C) decline, it is likely to encounter next resistance near the .50 retracement level at $398 basis London fix. This target is further supported by the fact that 1.618 times the first zigzag added to the end of the first triangle projects $396 and by the resistance provided by the orthodox end of wave (B) (see long term chart) at $394.50. The London price hit $394.50 on August 11, so that resistance level has essentially been met. The highest target under the preferred count would be a .618 retracement at $424, which is supported by the fact that $418 would mark a .236 retracement of the entire bear market decline from $850 to $284.25.

The momentum picture is full of non-confirmations, with both gold stocks and silver failing to confirm gold's move above the January high. The sentiment picture indicates great vulnerability as well. Our 10-day put/call ratio for gold futures is now at its lowest level since January, when the last zigzag in gold was peaking and from which point gold stocks began their six month collapse. That peak occurred, typically, less than three months into the rising portion of the 8½-month cycle. Sentiment in platinum is now so euphoric that a major

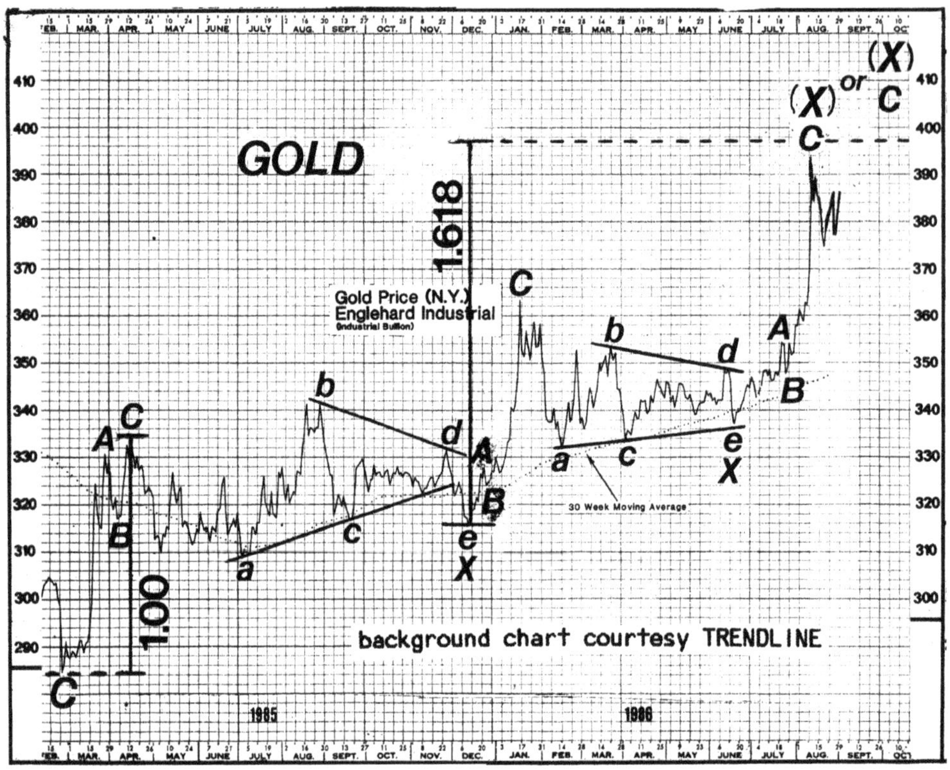

newspaper recently reported one brokerage company analyst's views that it could go to "several thousand dollars an ounce" from its current level at $600. Long time readers will recall the flurry of similar statements at $650-$750-$850 gold (it was at $475 two months after the top), at the exact top in cocoa, which EWT discussed in the January 9, 1984 issue, and at other major peaks. Last but not least, a list of fundamental arguments has suddenly surfaced to explain why gold rallied and why it should continue. Among these is the idea that continuing lower interest rates will be bullish for gold. Never mind that the great bull market of the 1970s occurred with rising interest rates; when a fundamentalist has made up his mind, rationalizations are a dime a dozen. It is not the reasons cited but the act of grabbing for them that has meaning to market analysis.

Traders have stood aside from the gold market during the past two months. I would like to move to 50% short now and 100% short if the London fix exceeds $417, with a stop at $440. Investors should remain out of the gold market and await the major bottom due in 1988.

Silver

Silver has followed the forecast quite closely for a year now. After bottoming within 5¢ of its projected low in July, the August letter made the following projection:

> Silver should rally to $5.60-5.70 basis the September futures, decline to a new low for wave 5, then rally back to the wave 4 peak in an a-b-c pattern.

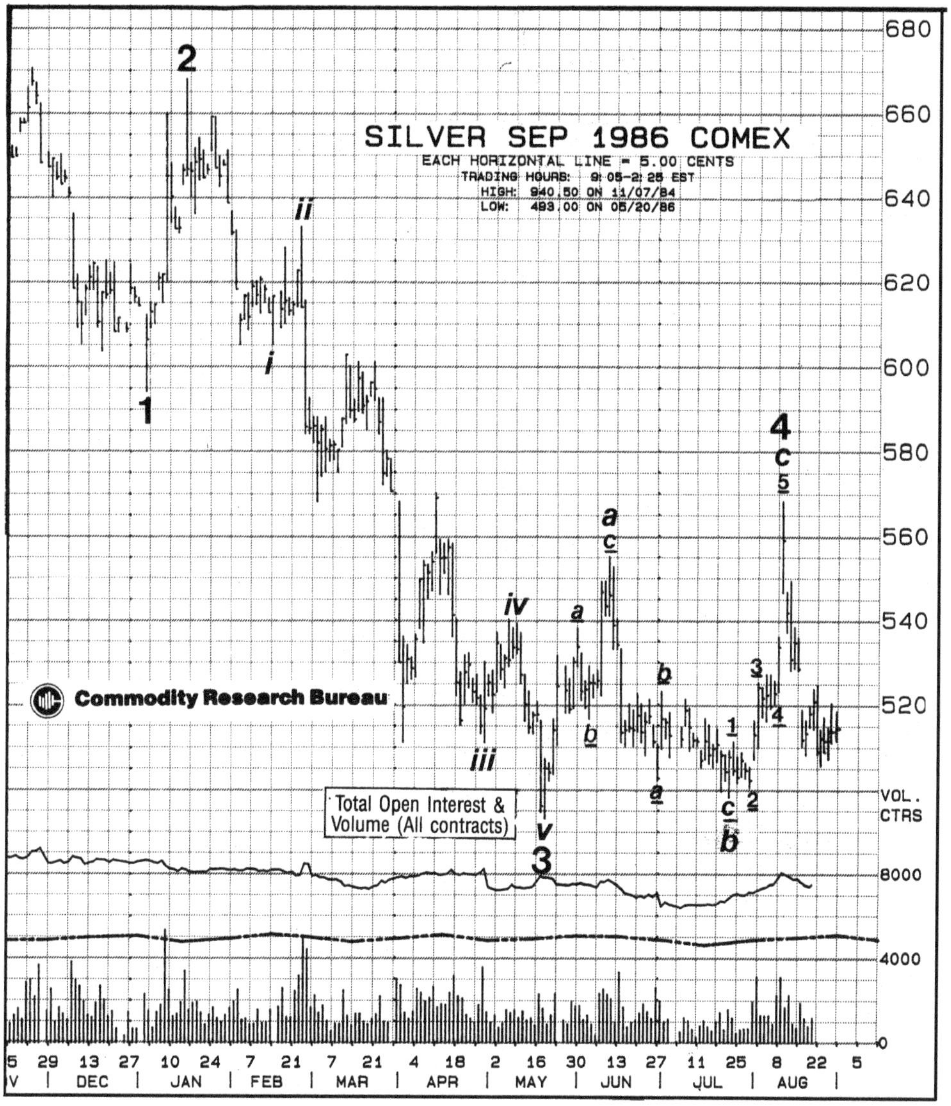

The rally then underway peaked at exactly $5.68 on a spike reversal and has since fallen to within 13¢ of a new low. As long as prices continue to follow that outline, the preferred count will be assumed correct. That count implies, as does the 12-week cycle in gold, that the metals will sell off soon, then undergo one last rally before rolling over in earnest.

SEPTEMBER 29, 1986

Gold and silver's bear market rallies are still scheduled to end no later than November, and they may have peaked already. A penetration of the September highs would allow a final rush in gold to the $510-550 zone, although the metals should be played only from the short side, as long side risk is extremely high.

Gold

EWT covered short sales in gold back in early June in anticipation of the 2-year cycle rally which was due in August. The August issue confirmed, "that cycle is bottoming now, implying a strong countertrend rally into November." The chart shows the jump that has occurred in gold and gold stocks since then. The cyclic update last month made the following projection:

> The top in the metals complex should be completed some time in the next 4 to 8 weeks. Ideally, the overall topping formation would contain one selloff soon, then a final rally, whether to a lower or higher peak. Then all trends would be down.

The technical negatives last month included documentation of the euphoric sentiment on platinum, which peaked exactly three trading days later, on September 5, then collapsed 19% in value, erasing half the previous four months' rally, in just one week. The September EWT formulated a short selling strategy to catch the 12-week cycle high in gold, but gold lagged platinum's top, just as it did at its bottom, and made life difficult. Unlike the stock market, where some good luck helped out, we had some weird bad luck with our $440 stop basis London fix. On what is so far the day of the high, September 22, gold alone (without platinum, palladium or silver) traded just high enough in London to provide an a.m. fix above $440, then sold off before New York opened. The closing London fix never cleared $440. The Telephone Update had seen what was coming and on the previous Friday concluded flatly, "Gold is thrusting out of a triangle, so should peak along with silver on Monday. Both are still short sales with stops at $450 gold and $6.20 silver, basis December." The peak did occur on Monday, and the stops basis the futures contracts held firm. Silver has since fallen 50¢ in value, while gold has pulled back.

Sentiment is still running 80%+ bulls in both gold and silver, and newspapers are reporting reasons why "no matter what happens," with the dollar, the economy, or interest rates, gold has to go up. Investors haven't bothered with this rally, but if you are a trader, hold short or return to short (if you do not get the Update and used the a.m. fix to get out), with a stop at $450 basis the December contract. If that stop is taken out, there will be an increased probability that gold is still completing its old Ⓧ wave, which began in June 1982. If so, it may have to clear the 1983 high at $511.50 before topping out. I was going to discuss that wave count, first postulated in the April 1985 issue, again, but due to lack of space, will do so next month if the rally continues.

As you have probably heard, the Japanese are buying gold to mint coins. The U.S. is due to start selling gold coins in October. The cycles have provided a bear market rally right on schedule, and gold is pushing for all it's worth to sell to the pre-announced buyers at the highest price it can manage. Momentum and sentiment are bearish for gold; only the 2-year and 8½-month cycles can keep it holding up for as long as another month or two.

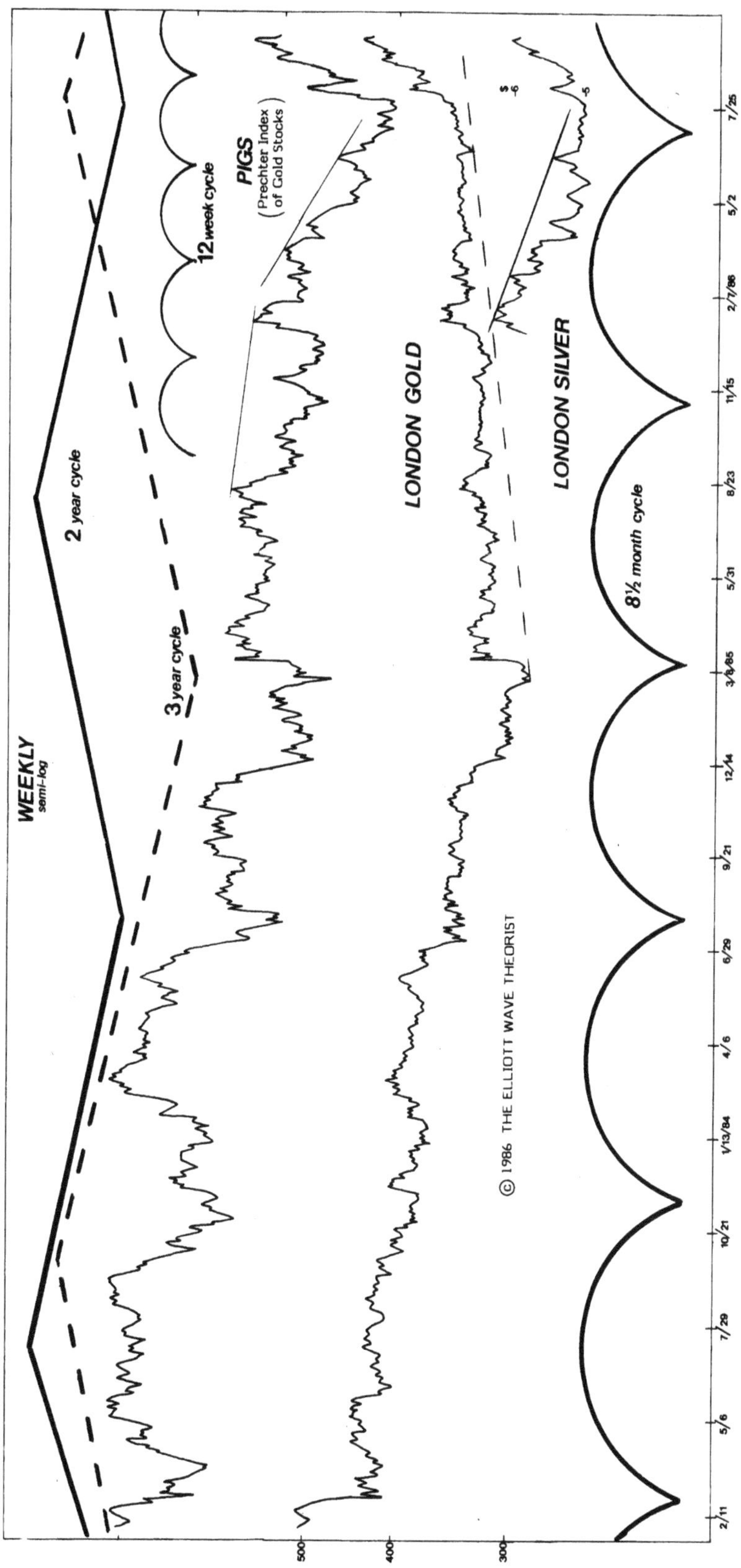
WEEKLY
semi-log
2 year cycle
3 year cycle
12 week cycle
PIGS
(Prechter Index of Gold Stocks)
LONDON GOLD
LONDON SILVER
8½ month cycle
© 1986 THE ELLIOTT WAVE THEORIST
500
400
300
2/11
5/6
7/29
10/21
1/13/84
4/6
6/29
9/21
12/14
3/8/85
5/31
8/23
11/15
2/7/86
5/2
7/25

Silver

For several months, the short term outlooks for silver have been correct in terms of form, although the projected fifth wave low in late August held 10¢ above the previous low in the December contract in a "truncated" fifth wave (see text, p. 32). That truncation had short term bullish implications for the rally that followed, and prices carried an additional 40¢ past $5.70. Silver should now begin a decline to new lows for the year.

NOVEMBER 7, 1986

The 8½-month cycle in gold is now in the forecasted time zone for a peak. Gold is building a top of major significance.

Gold: Major Top At Hand

Six trading days after last month's bearish analysis was mailed, the December gold futures contract "double topped" at $445 basis December and has since fallen to $400. Our short sale is still in effect, and the stop at $450 remains intact.

While the 12-week cycle, due to bottom this month, may cause a brief rally, the bigger picture is of much greater importance. The August issue estimated that upward cyclic pressure from the larger cycles would cause a "strong countertrend rally into November," and it's now November. In other words, gold in this time period is expected to be in distribution. What better time to distribute than when the new US gold coins are being sold by the truckload to the public? Further topping action is certainly possible this month, but our short selling strategy has already been implemented on the premise that the actual price peak would occur on the early side of the cycle. Put/call ratios have remained dangerously low on the recent selloff, indicating that the crowd views the recent 10% decline as no cause for concern. Lack of concern is no surprise, with gold fever running so high that every article extols the virtues of gold, Barron's is able to sell an 11-page special section called "Investing in Precious Metals" on October 20, and Australia enjoys a mining share frenzy, with prices jumping 2 to 20 times in price (thanks to subscriber Don Daisley for info and articles). This kind of activity is not typical of emerging bull markets but of tops. Remember when the public was buying technology stock funds in early 1983? They dismally underperformed the market from that point forward. Remember when the public was scooping up international stock funds six months ago? Those funds are down between 10% and 20% from their highs this year. Now the public is buying gold eagles like crazy. Joining the crowd rarely results in profits.

The next 8½-month cycle bottom is not due until April. I have no estimate yet for interim price lows in gold, but the long term target remains $105 in 1988, with "below $200" still a minimum expectation. This outlook may appear ridiculous to many people, but so did Dow 2000 four years ago.

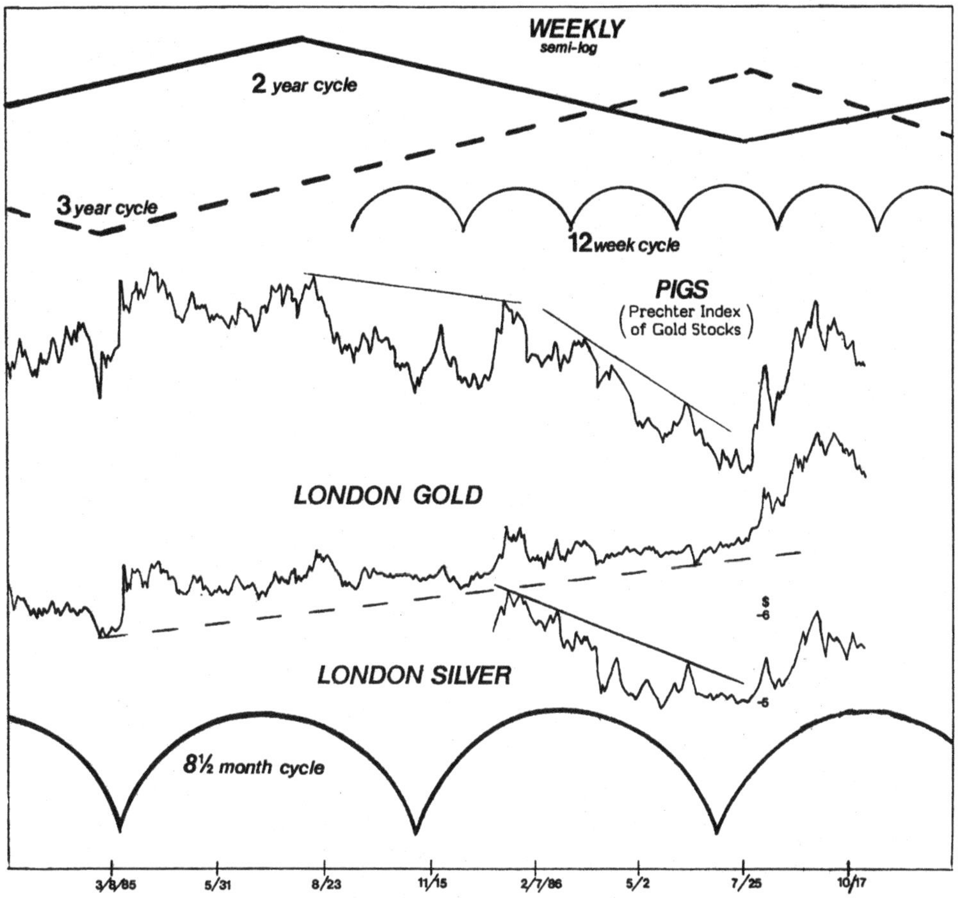

The new gold rush is on

THE AUSTRALIAN Tuesday October 14 1986

AUSTRALIA is still in the grip of gold fever. Stockbrokers haven't seen as much interest in the resources sector since the nickel boom of the 1960s.

"You can see why the share price of Australian gold stocks should move up even further."

U.S. Mint sells 10 tons of gold in Eagle coins

The Mint sold more than 320,000 ounces of gold — more than 10 tons — in the first day

American beauty: The American Eagle gold bullion coin is in great demand, even though it's not expected to have any numismatic value.

Precious Horde

"We've given up our main line, the investment quality rare coins just to handle the Eagle,'' [redacted] said. "I've got a list here that's 200 people if it's a nickel's worth, all waiting for two sets, three sets, whatever they can get their hands on.''

Focus on Gold.

Gold is red hot and shows no sign of cooling off.

"All three options are bullish for gold," he said. Reason: Foreign-denominated investments will yield less, and "that money has to find a home."

The Glitter Is Back

Gold Is Reasserting Its Claim as a Store of Value

With all this going on, it seems clear that gold prices can only go up, despite a sharp increase in U.S. production. The yield has

Shrewd investors know when the time is ripe to invest in precious metals. They also know the potential return on their investments can be multiplied with the power of leverage. In fact, many experts believe that now is an especially opportune time to invest.

Worried investors bid gold to $440

Other countries are readying entries for the gold-coin market. Soon there will be an Australian Nugget and a Golden Lion minted by Luxembourg. The word is that Brazil and the Philippines may enter the fray next year. But none of these will soar like the Eagle. ■

DECEMBER 1, 1986

Gold has begun a slide which will carry it to new lows for the decade.

Gold

Following the 2-year cycle bottom in precious metals and gold stocks, which occurred in the final week of July, EWT outlined these time parameters for the rally on September 2:

> [The] rising 2-year and 8½-month cycles... will attempt to hold prices up until November. However, the 6-year cycle is down hard and will undoubtedly force these smaller cycles to be "left hand translated," creating an early peak in prices. The top in the metals complex should be completed some time in the next four to eight weeks. Ideally, the overall topping formation would contain one selloff soon, then a final rally, whether to a lower or higher peak. Then all trends will be down.

The daily chart shows the rally finally ending in a "double top" exactly five weeks later. What about the internal price relationship in the rally? The most damaging evidence for the popularly accepted idea that a new bull market had begun, concluded EWT three months

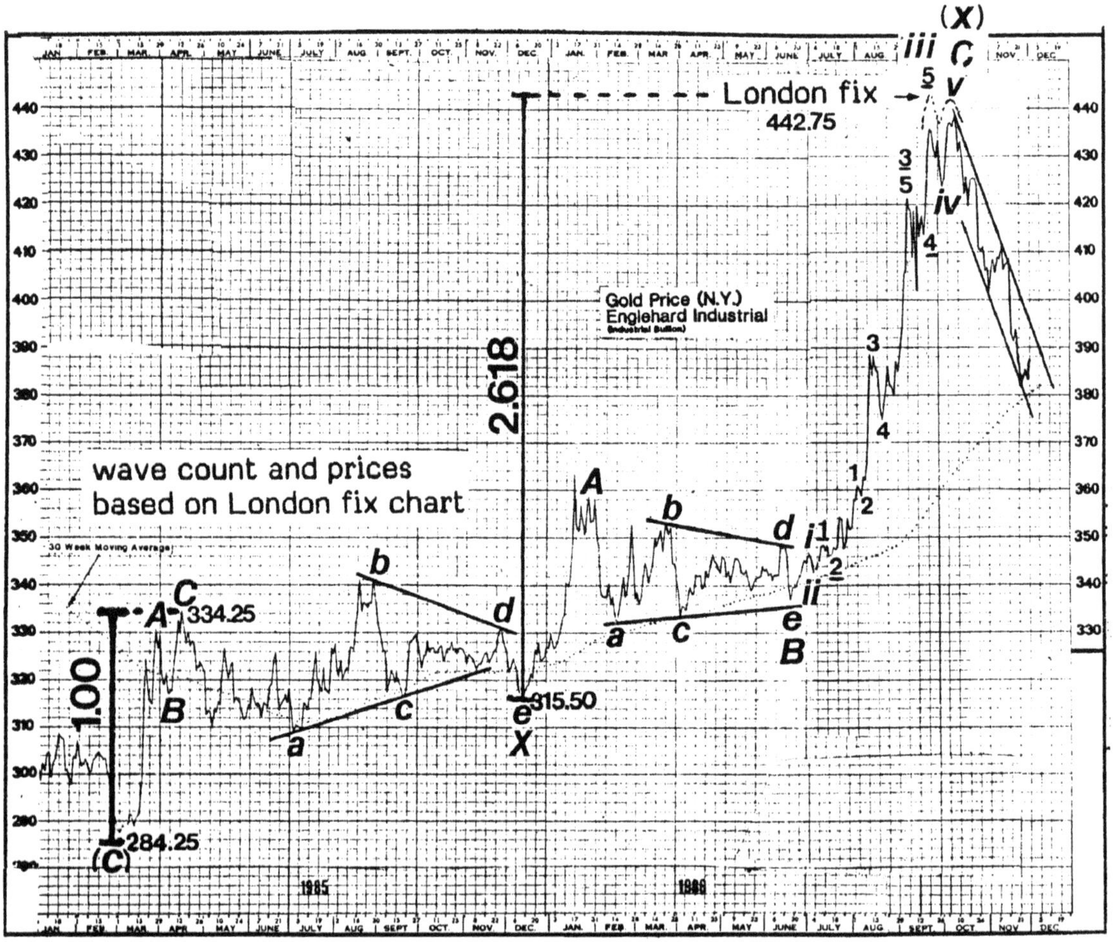

ago, "comes from wave structure, which has been of a corrective nature since the February 1985 low. In other words, the rise has been all or part of a bear market rally, not a new bull market." That issue contained a daily chart of gold and argued that if the internal wave count was correctly interpreted, the second rally phase should be in Fibonacci relationship to the first. A projection bar on the chart used the common 1.618 multiple to project a possible peak at $396. Prices paused after hitting that level (as usually happens) but then pushed through for a final lunge, registering top tick at $442.75. Why that level? It was not a random stopping point but one which created, within 1%, the rarer 2.618 multiple in the internal wave structure! In other words, the wave count, including the use of two triangles, was correct.

Traders sold short near the top, and remain so. Examine the chart and you'll see that each wave down from the top has the "1-2-3-4-5" look of an impulse wave, while the entire slide is nicely channelable between parallel lines. My gold stock average, despite the spirited rally caused by the cyclic upturn four months ago, last week fell back to a level unchanged from where it was the week gold bullion bottomed at $284.25 in February 1985.

Last month's issue listed numerous reasons why gold was not merely "correcting" in a new bull market, but beginning a decline from a "MAJOR TOP." Since then, more evidence has appeared. In Canada, the public is embracing the opportunity to finance exploration of small gold mines. Australia has been reporting a gold share "frenzy." Headlines such as "Gold Bulls Begin to Paw the Ring Again" and "Go For Gold" have appeared in the press. Meanwhile, as the price slips lower, the 10-day put/call ratio for options on gold futures contracts has budged only slightly and remains at half the level it reached in July when the metals were a buy. In other words, investors are still fixing their gaze upward, not downward. Newspaper quotations continue to reveal rationalizations in favor of higher prices. A university economist was quoted as saying that since the gold/silver ratio is a terribly high 70:1, "by that rule of thumb, silver prices are half what they should be." Observes EWT subscriber Lawrence Perkins, "It doesn't occur to them that gold might be twice what it ought to be, does it?" No, it doesn't. The week of the top, news that the new tax bill would allow IRA accounts to invest in U.S. gold and silver coins was interpreted as "very bullish" (news is always bullish at the top!). On the other side of the coin, the quoted bears have no teeth. As a counterpoint to "Eagle mania," one magazine cited a "bear" who forecast that gold would "stay between $375 and $450 during the next 12 months." All these observations reveal the symptoms of bear market psychology. Contrast this attitude to that in the stock market, where the main focus of debate is whether the averages will decline 10% or 20%.

Gold is on its way to below $200/oz., probably in 1988. Undoubtedly there will be stopping points along the way. There is minor support in the area of the triangle apexes at $320-350. There may be support at the previous lows in the $280-290 range. However, the dominant 8½-month cycle will not bottom until April, so rallies should be short-lived, take an a-b-c shape and generally provide short term traders with opportunities to sell short. Our position is 100% short for traders, who can now return the stop to $440 basis London fix, and out of the market for investors. We've done our work. Now we'll find out if we're right.

DECEMBER 1986 – SPECIAL REPORT

For the non-speculator, the one and only place to put your money to insure that it will hold *some* purchasing power relative to the total of goods and services available is into money itself: *physical gold*. I did not include gold in the above list of "investments" because gold is not an investment; it is money. Have you ever traveled abroad and taken a look at the local currency and wondered how the citizens of that country could take seriously what looks like "Monopoly money"? I've got news for you. You're using the same stuff. Monopoly money is the money over which some government has a monopoly. It is the currency of the realm only because the governments makes it illegal to use any other type. If a completely free market in money were available, I am quite certain that the market's choice would be gold, as it has been throughout the centuries wherever a free market for money has existed. This preference will undoubtedly remain until something better comes along. Sad to say, keeping money in the form of money does not add to productive capacity or prosperity. But in times of profligate government counterfeiting, there is no other choice but to hold something which will at least retain its value. However, since gold may drop in price in an initial deflationary stage, the best "parking place" for now is short-maturity T-bills. Later, when the financial crisis is at its nadir, a swift shift to gold will be essential.

The Elliott Wave Theorist, 1987

JANUARY 5, 1987

Gold, which rallied back above $400/oz. on Friday, is now poised to collapse suddenly in a third Elliott wave to the downside. Cycles in the precious metals continue to point down into April.

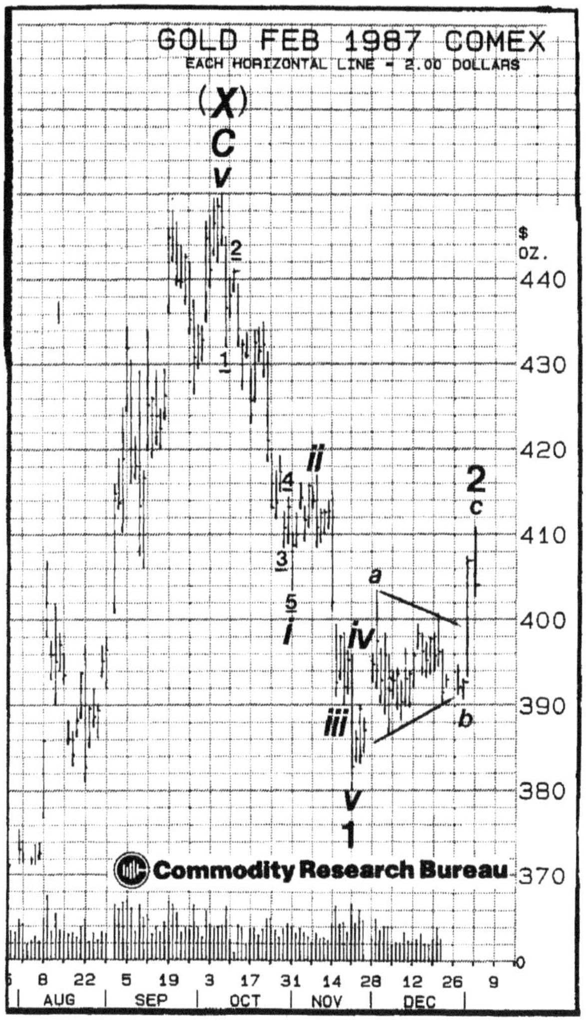

Gold & Silver

Gold is a disaster waiting to happen. The technical picture remains dismal and in fact has worsened over the past month. Take a look at the short term wave count shown on the chart of the February futures contract. Note the perfect five waves down, followed by a clear a-b-c countertrend rally. That countertrend rally basis London fix has now retraced 37.5% (just shy of a Fibonacci 38.2%) of the preceding decline, a perfect place for it to stop. On the larger trend, this can only mean that waves 1 and 2 of a substantial decline are in place. The next event should be a powerful and persistent collapse in wave 3. The put/call ratios on both gold and silver are in the basement and support the case for an immediate crash in prices.

The December issue noted that "newspaper quotations continue to reveal rationalizations in favor of higher prices" for gold, and gave a good example. Here's another:

> Some analysts suggested that if next week's meeting of the Organization of Petroleum Exporting Countries manages to prop up oil prices, traders might bet on rising inflation and resume buying precious metals. Oil prices are considered barometers of inflation, and precious metals, especially gold, are often held as inflation hedges.

Never mind that forcing the needle on a barometer does not cause a storm to brew. A forced rise in the price of oil against market valuation, if that were even possible, would not be inflationary; it would be deflationary because it would remove purchasing power from circulation and cause prices of other things to decline. Keep your eyes and ears open. Rationalizations are a sign of euphoria, no matter how studiously formulated.

The previous three issues of EWT spelled out the message from the intermediate term wave count, cyclic influences and market psychology, all of which turned extremely bearish as gold peaked in the $440 range. This issue will focus on relative valuation evidence indicating that the last place you want to be invested now is in the precious metals. But first, an update on gold coin sales in 1986:

> NEW YORK – Sales of gold coins skyrocketed to a record in 1986, thanks to several successful new issues.
>
> "It was a banner year for gold bullion coins," says David Ganz, a New York lawyer specializing in numismatics.
>
> Official gold coin sales soared 186%, to about 12 million ounces in 1986, from 4.2 million ounces a year earlier, according to the Gold Institute, a Washington-based trade group. The previous record, 9.9 million ounces, was set in 1979.
>
> Most of the gains stemmed from the smashing success of the American Eagle bullion coin and the Japanese Emperor Hirohito commemorative issue, numismatists say.
>
> The market's stellar showing stems partly from increased activity in gold, which appreciated about 24% from January levels. But the 1986 sales record was somewhat surprising, numismatists say, because trading activity and investor interest in gold was much greater in the high-inflation days of 1979, when the old record was set.
>
> Yet sales will continue to climb, many numismatists predict.

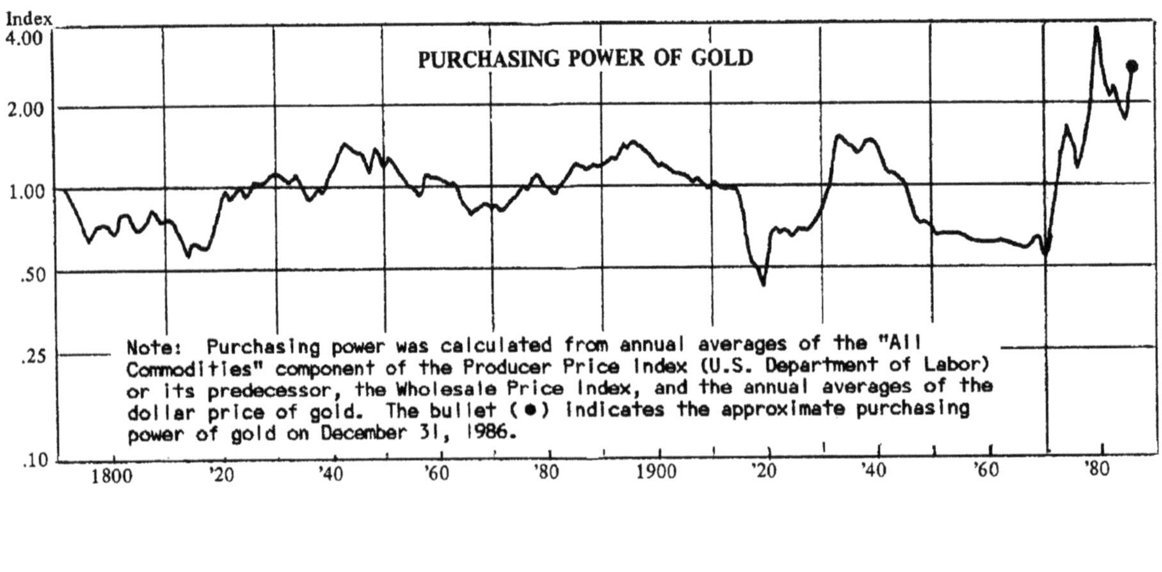

It is not coincidence that the world sales record set in 1986 rivaled that set in 1979, the year of the blowoff in gold bullion, because the recent advance was another blowoff. Even though the frenzy described above occurred at a lower dollar price, it occurred at a high price relative to commodities. In fact, as you can see by the chart above (courtesy American Institute for Economic Research, Great Barrington, MA), gold's purchasing power relative to commodities remains near its highest level of the past 200 years. In other words, gold is expensive. As you can see, a drop of 50%-75% would merely bring its relative value back in the range of the historical norm. In dollar terms, such a drop would be right in the $105-180 range targeted by the Wave Principle.

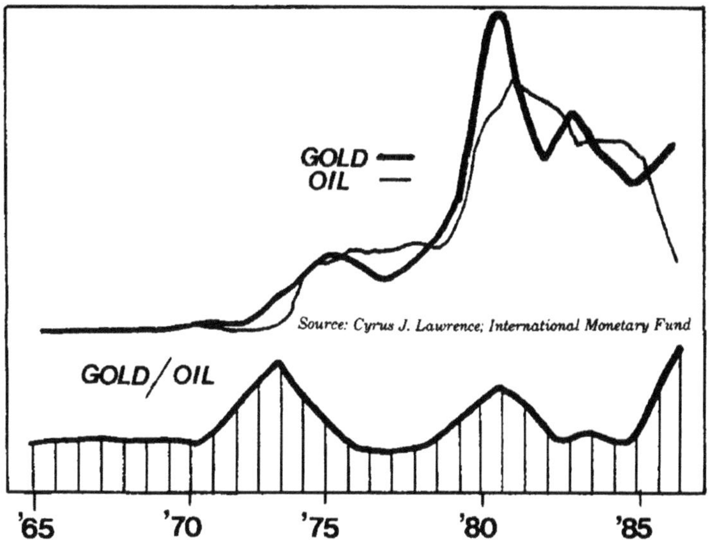

Here's another interesting chart, the ratio of the price of gold to the price of oil. According to this ratio, gold is at its most overvalued level relative to oil in at least the past 22 years, which is far as these figures go back. A high reading on this chart means that the odds are great that the price of gold will fall relative to the price of oil. As it happened, on each of the previous times that a similar ratio was reached, gold soon experienced a drop of 50% in dollar value. This time the ratio is even higher. An inflationist would point out that the ratio can be corrected by an explosive rise in the price of oil. True, but let's explore the odds of that occurring. Did you know that according to The Bullish Consensus, an unbelievable 95% of market watchers currently are bullish on the price of crude oil? That's a 19:1 ratio! Obviously, they all believe the OPEC meeting hype, when in fact bullish news is almost always coincident with market tops. With oil having risen a bit more into last week, that consensus figure has undoubtedly held firm for two straight weeks. Such a reading is as close to a "gimme" as Contrary Opinion can provide and is the type of one-sided bullishness that helped EWT call the top in platinum in early September. In other words, it is highly unlikely that oil will rise much in price and highly probable that it will collapse again.

If that conclusion is true, what does that say about the prospect for gold, which is already substantially overpriced with respect to oil? A 50% drop in dollar value as in the past would bring bullion to $200/oz. A coincidentally declining oil price would make my $105-180 target as sensible from a relative valuation perspective as the guidelines of the Wave Principle have long said it is on the basis of the expected developments in market psychology.

Investors should continue to stay out of the gold market. Traders should continue to hold 100% short with a stop at $440 basis London fix. Silver is not as overvalued as gold, but the technical picture is clearly bearish. I expect new price lows for the decade as silver accompanies gold into its next cyclic bottom due in April.

FEBRUARY 2, 1987

Gold probably completed a "test" of the October high on January 19 and should be resuming its downtrend.

Gold

The January issue provided over two full pages of discussion on the gold market. As an update on the price action, take a look at the chart below of daily futures prices. Notice the island reversal that occurred on January 19 at the $425-429 level basis the April futures contract. The gaps on each side of that reversal day occurred precisely at the .618 retracement level of the previous decline, a typical point of resistance to a countertrend rally. The wave structure is still bearish, the 8½-month cycle still points "hard down" into April and the relative valuation of gold shows it to be historically expensive relative to a basket of commodities, to oil (see January issue) and to silver.

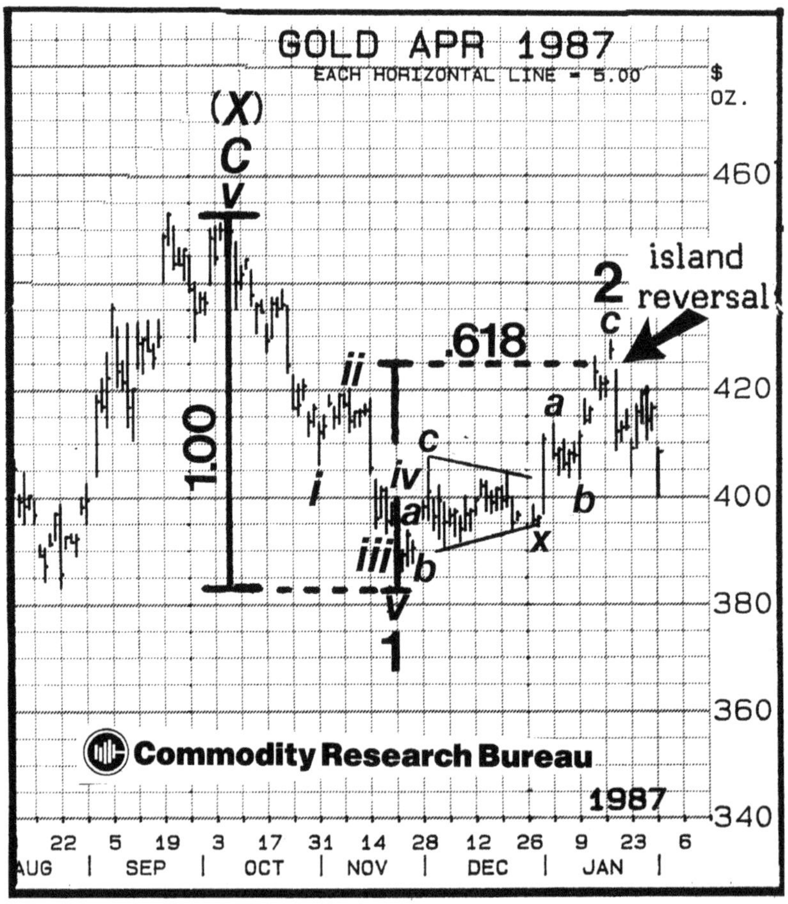

What about investor psychology? The November issue documented the euphoric sentiment toward gold in October, which happened to mark the price high for 1986. The main observation to make at this point is that sentiment hasn't changed. In fact, The Bullish Consensus reported last week that 74% of advisors were bullish on gold, 76% were bullish on silver and 80% were bullish on platinum! The January 26 issue of Barron's was able to sell 10 full pages of advertising for gold-related investments, an unlikely feat at a major bottom. The majority of letters I receive on gold feverishly question the bearish case. Predictions of increased inflation abound. The vast majority of shareholders of a major fund in Canada vehemently disagreed with management on a proposal to get out of precious metals. The concept that bearish sentiment of a "wave two" low is as dark as that at the preceding bottom is just as true, in reverse, at "wave two" rallies toward previous tops. Investors should stay out of the gold market, while traders should stay short with a stop at $440 basis London fix. First support is $360, but the long term target is still below $200/oz.

By the way, evidence is powerful that the dollar is spiking into a major low. Sentiment on the currencies last week showed over 90% bulls, with an exceedingly rare and very bearish 96% reading on the Swiss franc. Newspaper quotations from analysts reveal a general conviction that the dollar has "begun a free fall." One major article explored an analyst's reasons as to why the dollar has "no limit" on the downside. Now consider this. As gold has lost 10% of its dollar value since October while the dollar itself has been collapsing day after day, what will happen to gold if the dollar reverses?

MARCH 2, 1987

Gold's long term target remains "below $200/oz.," with specific targets still $179 (most likely) and $105 (worst case).

Gold

The discussion in the January issue included the valuation argument that gold is extremely overvalued with respect to the prices of commodities in general, silver and oil. Here are the observations made then about the gold/oil relationship:

> Gold is at its most overvalued level relative to oil in at least the past 22 years. On each of the previous times that a similar ratio was reached, gold soon experienced a drop of 50% in dollar value. An inflationist would point out that the ratio can be corrected by an explosive rise in the price of oil. True, but let's explore the odds of that occurring. Did you know that according to The Bullish Consensus (61 S. Lake Av, Pasadena, CA), an unbelievable 95% of market watchers currently are bullish on the price of crude oil? That's a 19:1 ratio! Obviously, they all believe the OPEC meeting hype, when in fact bullish news is almost always coincident with market tops. With oil having risen a bit more into last week, that consensus figure has undoubtedly held firm for two straight weeks. Such a reading is as close to a "gimme" as Contrary Opinion can provide, and is the type of one-sided bullishness that helped EWT call the top in platinum in early September. In other words, it is highly unlikely that oil will rise much in price and highly probable that it will collapse again.

This was the first comment EWT had made about oil in months. Exactly one week later, the price of crude oil stopped rising at $19/barrel. Here's what's happened since:

> **OPEC IS HAVING** increasing problems enforcing its December agreement to prop up oil prices. More oil companies are refusing to buy the group's oil at fixed prices, while some OPEC members are continuing to violate production quotas. OPEC's woes sent oil prices plunging to two-month lows of about $17 a barrel. Oil prices have plunged over 10% so far this month.

In recent days, crude oil has fallen as low as $16/barrel, stretching the gold/oil relationship to yet new extremes. The CRB Index of commodity futures prices has also fallen for five weeks, from what David Weis, editor of *The Elliott Wave Commodity Letter*, labels as the peak of wave 4 in a major decline. To an even greater degree than ever, the pull on gold from a valuation standpoint is toward substantially lower prices.

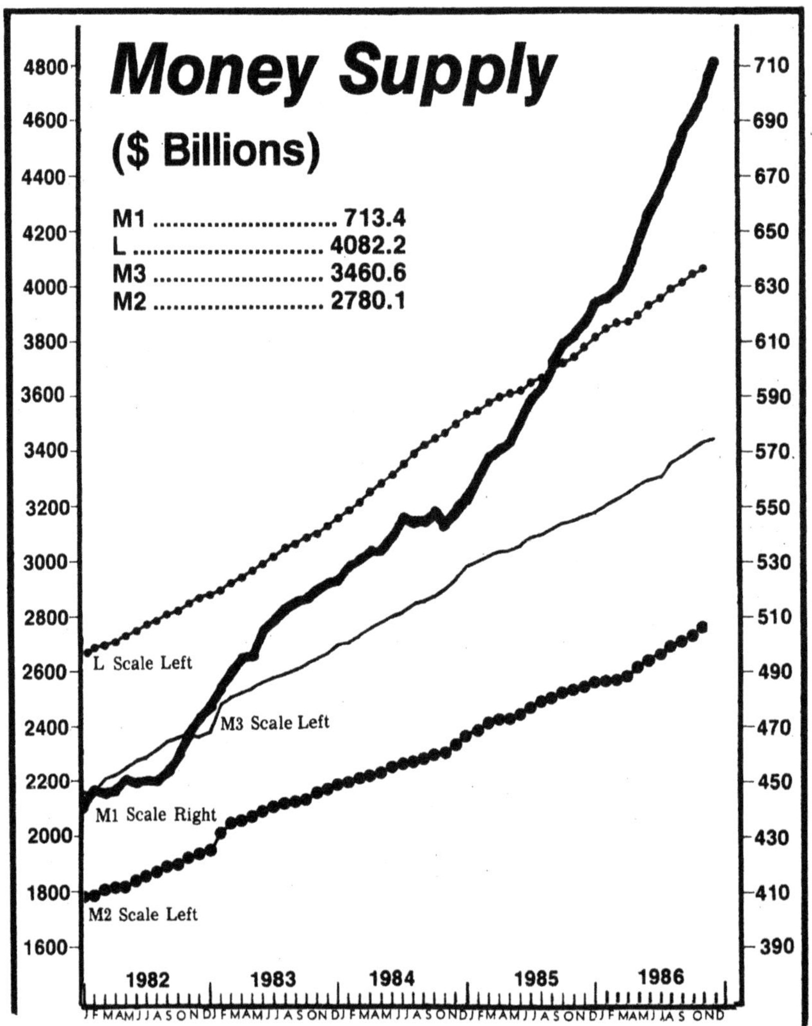

The strongest and most popular "fundamental" argument in favor of rising gold prices is this chart showing the growth in the money supply since 1982. It's certainly an amazing rise. However, it is *people* who spend and invest the money (a fact that "laws of physics" thinking ignores), and to date the net investment in commodities has been negative. So where is the money going? I doubt it is coincidence that the stock market, as measured by the Dow Jones Industrial Average, is up in percentage terms almost exactly the same amount as M1 from August 1982. As long as money is available, the current financial boom will remain intact. Perhaps it will be when the M1 line turns down that the crash in stocks and bonds will be upon us.

The long term gold picture has generated some fascinating mathematical relationships. Work was completed yesterday on a Special Report, and I hope to have that in the mail to you this week. Needless to say, the long standing target of "below $200/oz." is still intact, and the specific price of $179 looks better than ever.

MARCH 5, 1987 — SPECIAL REPORT
MATHEMATICAL RELATIONSHIPS IN THE GOLD AND SILVER MARKETS; FORECASTS AND PROJECTIONS

Ever since the blowoff top in gold in January 1980, *The Elliott Wave Theorist* has been using Fibonacci and Elliott wave relationships to project the turning points in the ensuing bear market. The initial forecast from early 1980 called for a decline to $477, a rally to just over $700, then a decline to $388 targeted for August 1981. All those came to pass. After a three-wave rally in late 1981, however, it became clear that gold was about to break below the $388 level, indicating that a more complex bear market structure was unfolding as a correction of the entire 1967-1980 bull market. In recent years, the ongoing preferred count has been that the bear market was taking the shape of a "double zigzag" (see text, p.37), which will ultimately be labeled Ⓐ-Ⓑ-Ⓒ-Ⓧ-Ⓐ-Ⓑ-Ⓒ. To date, all but the final declining wave in this pattern have taken place.

In targeting the ultimate low for gold, two guidelines have been employed. The first is that bear markets tend to bottom in the zone of the fourth wave of the preceding bull market of the same degree (see text, p.55). This guideline is just that; it is not a rule. However, whatever the market, it has proved helpful in approximately 90% of applicable instances in my experience. As you can see in Figure 1, wave IV in bullion began at the orthodox top of wave III in March 1974 at $179.50 and ended in August 1976 at $103.50. Until the wave structure indicates otherwise, those prices still mark reasonable minimum and maximum expectations for the ultimate bear market low. For this reason, I have continually reiterated that ultimately gold should fall "below $200/oz."

The second guideline deals with typical Fibonacci (see discussion, *Elliott Wave Principle*, Chapter 4) relationships between price lengths of waves, which allow forecasting to be even more specific. If the double zigzag interpretation is correct, then the second Ⓐ-Ⓑ-Ⓒ pattern will very likely be in Fibonacci relationship to the first. As mentioned as far back as the March 1983 issue, it so happens that .618 times $553.25, the length of the first Ⓐ-Ⓑ-Ⓒ , when subtracted from the wave X high at $511.50, gives a target of $169.59, less than $10 from the minimum downside target based on the "previous fourth wave" guideline. It has also been

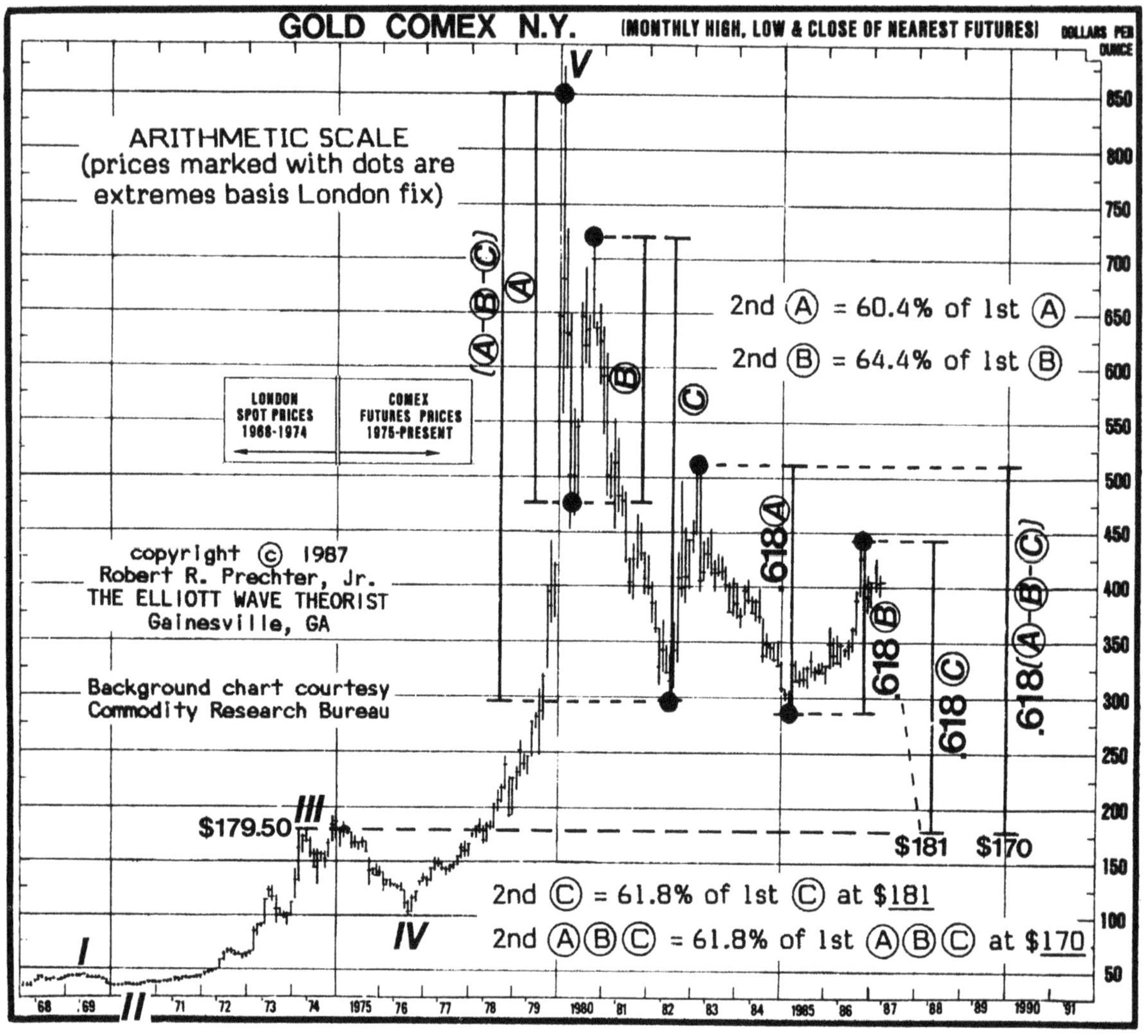

Figure 1

noted that if the ultimate decline from the first rally peak at $720 in September 1980 is a Fibonacci 1.618 times as long as the first wave of decline from $850 to $474, it would bottom at $111.63, this time less than $10 from the maximum downside target based on the "previous fourth wave" guideline. Thus, it became apparent some time ago that the ultimate target probably would not be just anywhere in the zone of wave IV but rather very near either the top or bottom end.

What has now come to light is a sequence of incredible relationships that powerfully support the validity of both the preferred wave count and the originally calculated price support levels as potential downside targets, with the upper level decidedly more strongly indicated. Long time readers may recall my postulation over three years ago that the net travel of the second Ⓐ-Ⓑ-Ⓒ pattern would likely cover .618 of the first, in typical double zigzag fashion. However, I had no idea that the internal wave lengths would end up mirroring the same relationship in what appears to be a design to produce that result! Take another look at Figure 1.

It is clearly the case that ever since the high for wave X in February 1983, the Ⓐ-Ⓑ structure thereafter has been in almost perfect Fibonacci relationship to the first Ⓐ-Ⓑ structure from way back in 1980! As you can see, the second wave Ⓐ decline covered 60.4% of the distance of the first and the second wave Ⓑ rally covered 64.4% of the distance of the first. If this pattern continues and the second wave Ⓒ decline falls a Fibonacci 61.8% of the distance of the first, it will carry to $181.18, within $2 of the minimum "previous fourth wave" target of $179.50.

These developments are remarkable enough, but substantially more is involved in the fascinating mathematical relationships of the wave structure. Long time readers will also recall my observation four years ago that wave X had retraced 38.8% (almost exactly a Fibonacci 38.2%) of the preceding Ⓐ-Ⓑ-Ⓒ decline.* In so doing, it brought prices to a peak of $511.50, which happens to be 60% of the peak price of $850. In other words, the two major

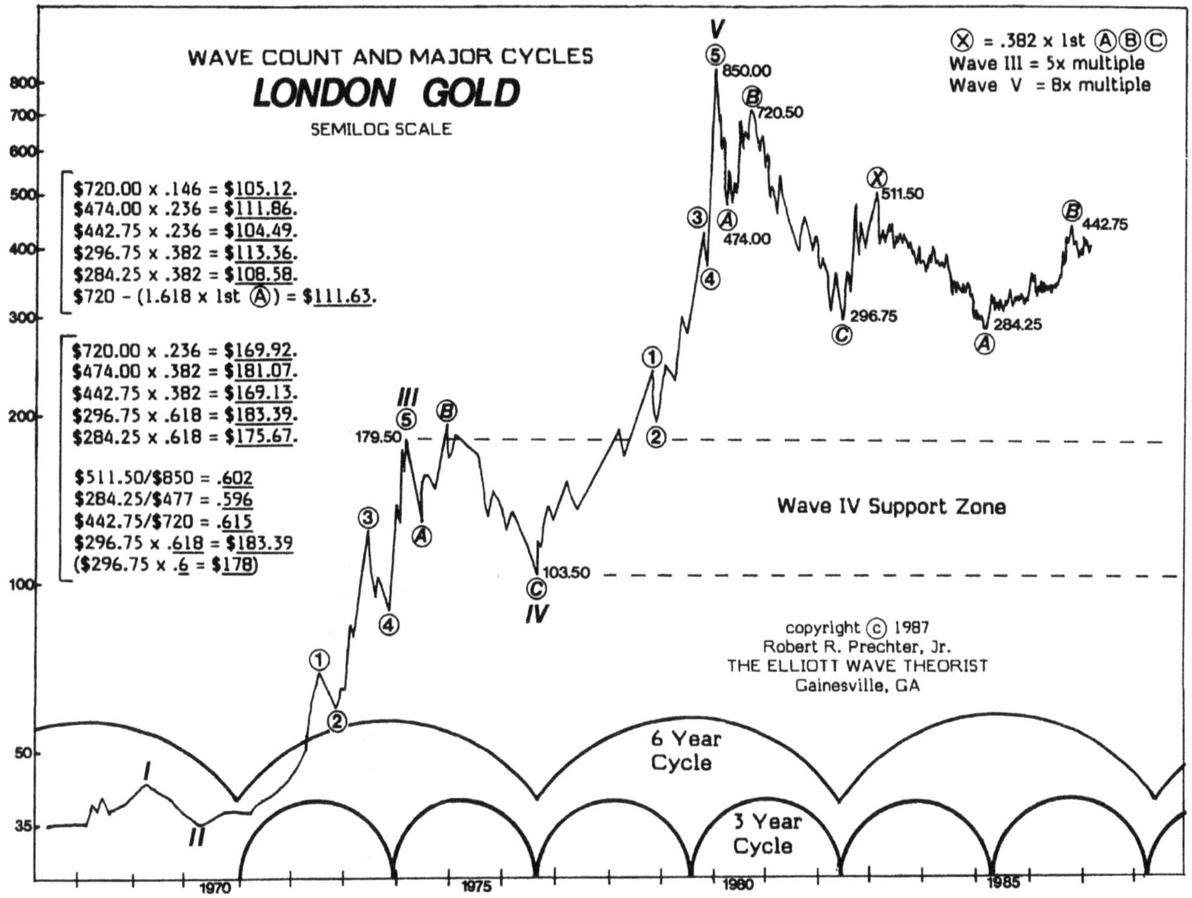

Figure 2

---

* This point also coincided with a 50% retracement of the preceding wave C, which EWT used in October 1982 to obtain an estimate of $508 for the X wave top which occurred four months later at $511.50. EWT projected the preceding decline to bottom at "$285-305," and it came in at $296.75. The bottom for the second wave A low was originally projected to "$269-297," and it came in at $284.25. – Ed.

top readings of $850 and $511.50, i.e., the starting points for each of the two Ⓐ-Ⓑ-Ⓒ waves, are related by a near-perfect Fibonacci ratio of .60 (3/5)! Now, because of this occurrence and the fact that each of the cross-related wave lengths are related by .618, it must then follow that all the corresponding turning point values of the bear market are in Fibonacci relationship, and that turns out exactly to be the case, as shown in Figure 2:

– The start of the second A is .618 times the start of the first, i.e., $511.50/$850 = .602.
– The start of the second B is .618 times the start of the first, i.e., $284.25/$474 = .600.
– The start of the second C is .618 times the start of the first, i.e., $442.75/$720 = .615.

The coexisting phenomena of these Fibonacci price length and value relationships could have begun only if the first Ⓐ-Ⓑ-Ⓒ decline were to have fallen a length approximately equal to .618 of its starting value, which it did: ($850-$296.75)/$850 = .65. (This drop, by necessity, brought the market to a price that was approximately .382 of the starting value: $296.75/$850 = .35.) In terms of forecasting, the sequence listed above brings us directly to the conclusion that if the end of the second Ⓒ occurs at .618 times the end of the first at $296.75, it will bottom at $183.39, again right at the minimum "previous fourth wave" target. (A .60 multiple, which more closely matches the first two calculations above, would yield $178.)

The sequence of price values ensures that, excepting the two wave Ⓐ starting points, Fibonacci multiples of all intermediate term turning point values within the bear market for gold yield both the original upper and lower target areas as results. Here is a list of the five that do so:

$720.00 x .236 = $169.92.	$720.00 x .146 = $105.12.
$474.00 x .382 = $181.07.	$474.00 x .236 = $111.86.
$442.75 x .382 = $169.13.	$442.75 x .236 = $104.49.
$296.75 x .618 = $183.39.	$296.75 x .382 = $113.36.
$284.25 x .618 = $175.67.	$284.25 x .382 = $108.58.

In other words, a drop to either area would provide a substantial web of Fibonacci price length and price value relationships for the bear market in gold. It must be stressed that all the interlocking price relationships projected for the bear market already exist in the long term wave structure for gold, since $103.50 and $179.50 marked key turning points in past price action. From an academic viewpoint, Fibonacci has unquestionably governed the price action, whether my forecast from here ultimately works out or not.

As my long time associate Dave Allman points out, it follows from the relationships in the above analysis that the percentage movements in the rallies and declines are virtually the same for the corresponding subwaves. As illustrated in Figure 3, the first Ⓐ-Ⓑ-Ⓒ pattern traced out the following sequence: a 44% decline, a 52% rally and a 59% decline, for a net fall of 65%. Wave X then intervened. The second Ⓐ-Ⓑ-Ⓒ pattern has begun with a 44%

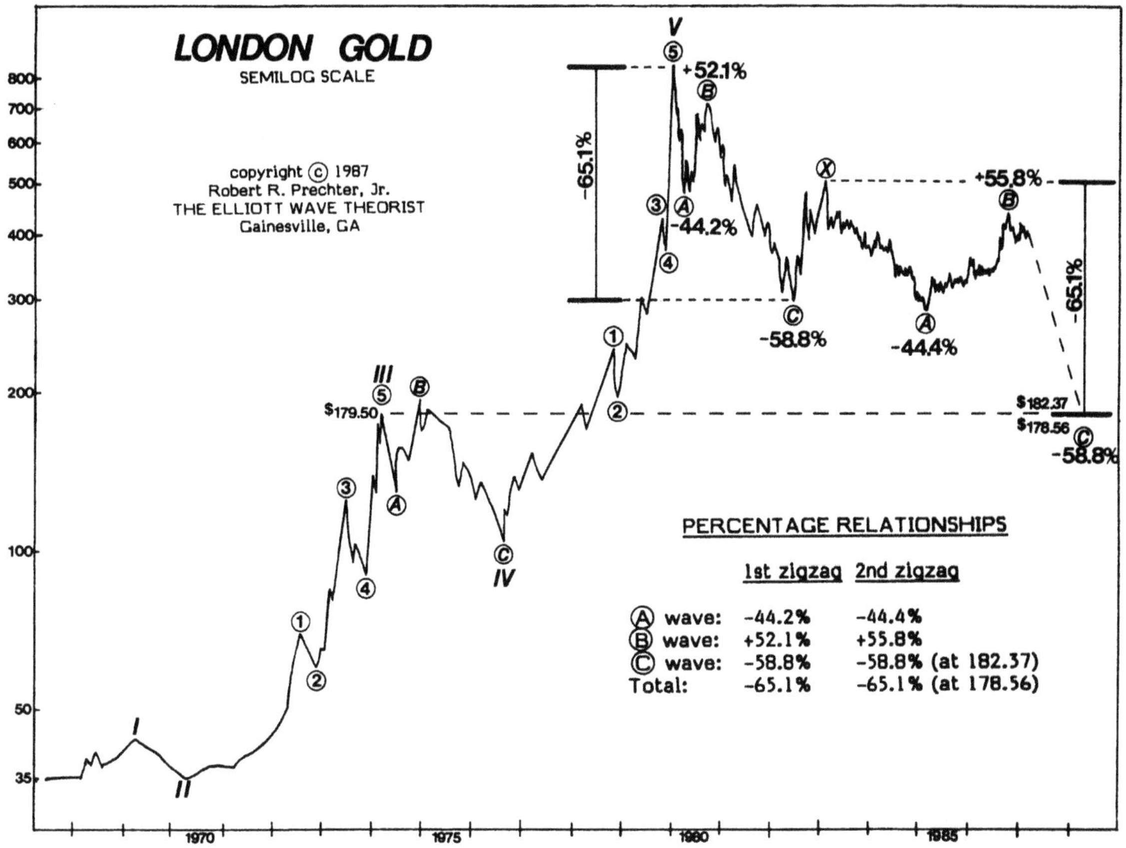

Figure 3

decline and a 56% rally. (If last September's $442.75 peak had been just $10 lower, it would have resulted in a 52% gain for the rally, precisely matching that of 1980's Ⓑ wave). The second Ⓐ-Ⓑ-Ⓒ pattern, then, is so far virtually an exact replay of the first in percentage price terms. What we have discovered, then, is that in terms of the price swings, the two sections of bear market are exact reproductions of each other on a percentage basis, with the second in Fibonacci relationship to the first on an arithmetic basis! If this relationship were to continue, the Ⓒ wave in progress would fall approximately 59%, resulting in a net decline for the second Ⓐ-Ⓑ-Ⓒ pattern of approximately 65%. These two ratios (to two decimal places) yield targets of $182.37 and $178.56 respectively, again, of course, right at the upper end of the "previous fourth wave" target zone.

From a practical standpoint, it is clear that time after time, the same price level emerges as a preferred downside target for gold, one that will most perfectly satisfy the network of Fibonacci price lengths, Fibonacci price values and equal percentages described above for all of gold's key bear market turning points. This level is $168-185, making the Fibonacci relationship originally postulated four years ago for the two sections of the double zigzag a firmer target than ever for the ultimate low in the price of gold, while further supporting the case for the double zigzag interpretation itself in the process.

Alternate Count (Probability 20%)

It is not unreasonable to make a case that wave X is still in progress, as I have indicated upon occasion for the past four years. It is becoming increasingly clear that if wave X is indeed still in force, it is probably tracing out a triangle pattern (see Figure 4 and text, p.44). Several points support this interpretation. First, the 1983-1985 decline is better counted as a three-wave structure than a "five," fitting the subdivision for a triangle leg. Secondly, note that while wave X [to February 1983] retraced exactly a Fibonacci .382 of the preceding Ⓐ-Ⓑ-Ⓒ (and ½ of the preceding Ⓒ), a phenomenon noted at the time, it is also the case that a .236 retracement would have occurred at $427, which is not far from where last year's rally, which would be labeled (c), peaked. (EWT discussed nearly this same point in the September 2, 1986 issue.) If the waves relate reasonably well to the 1982 low, then, they may be part of the same structure. As a projection, if wave (e) of a triangle ultimately peaks at the next lower Fibonacci ratio in the sequence, a .146 retracement of the first Ⓐ-Ⓑ-Ⓒ, it would top not far from $377.50, which is interestingly close to my original downside calculation of $388, which marked a .618 retracement of the 1976-1980 advance. It may be that ever since the break of that level, the market has coiled around it, ultimately to test it from underneath as resistance at the orthodox end of the "bear market rally" pattern, only then to turn down in the final phase of decline. If a triangle does form, we will, if necessary, recalculate the potential downside targets at that time.

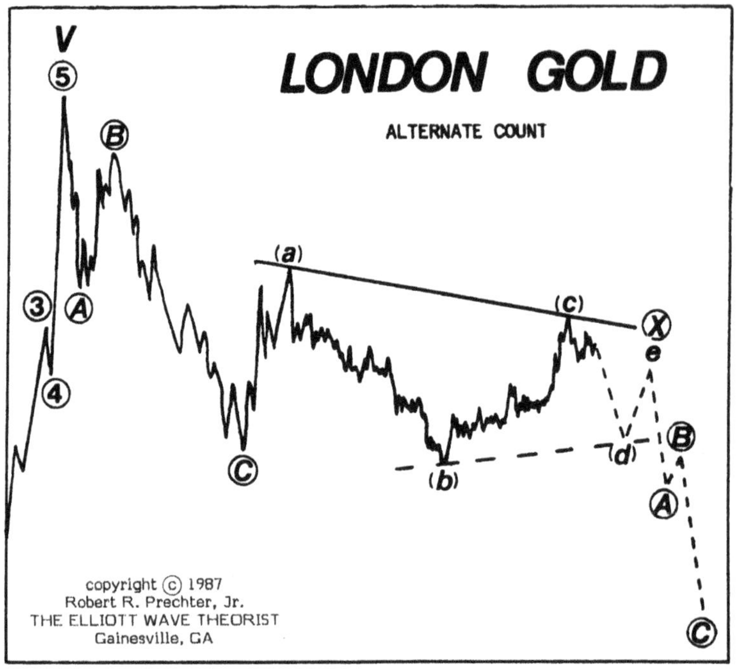

Figure 4

Silver

The wave structure for silver may be counted exactly the same way as that for gold: a double zigzag labeled Ⓐ-Ⓑ-Ⓒ-Ⓧ-Ⓐ-Ⓑ-Ⓒ, with all but the final wave Ⓒ completed (see Figure 5). Notice that wave X retraced just shy of a Fibonacci .236 (actually .217) of the preceding Ⓐ-Ⓑ-Ⓒ decline, much as wave X in gold retraced a Fibonacci .382 of its preceding Ⓐ-Ⓑ-Ⓒ decline. Notice also that the area of the fourth wave of the preceding bull market, wave IV, is $3.90-$6.40 basis the futures contracts, which, according to the guideline, should mark

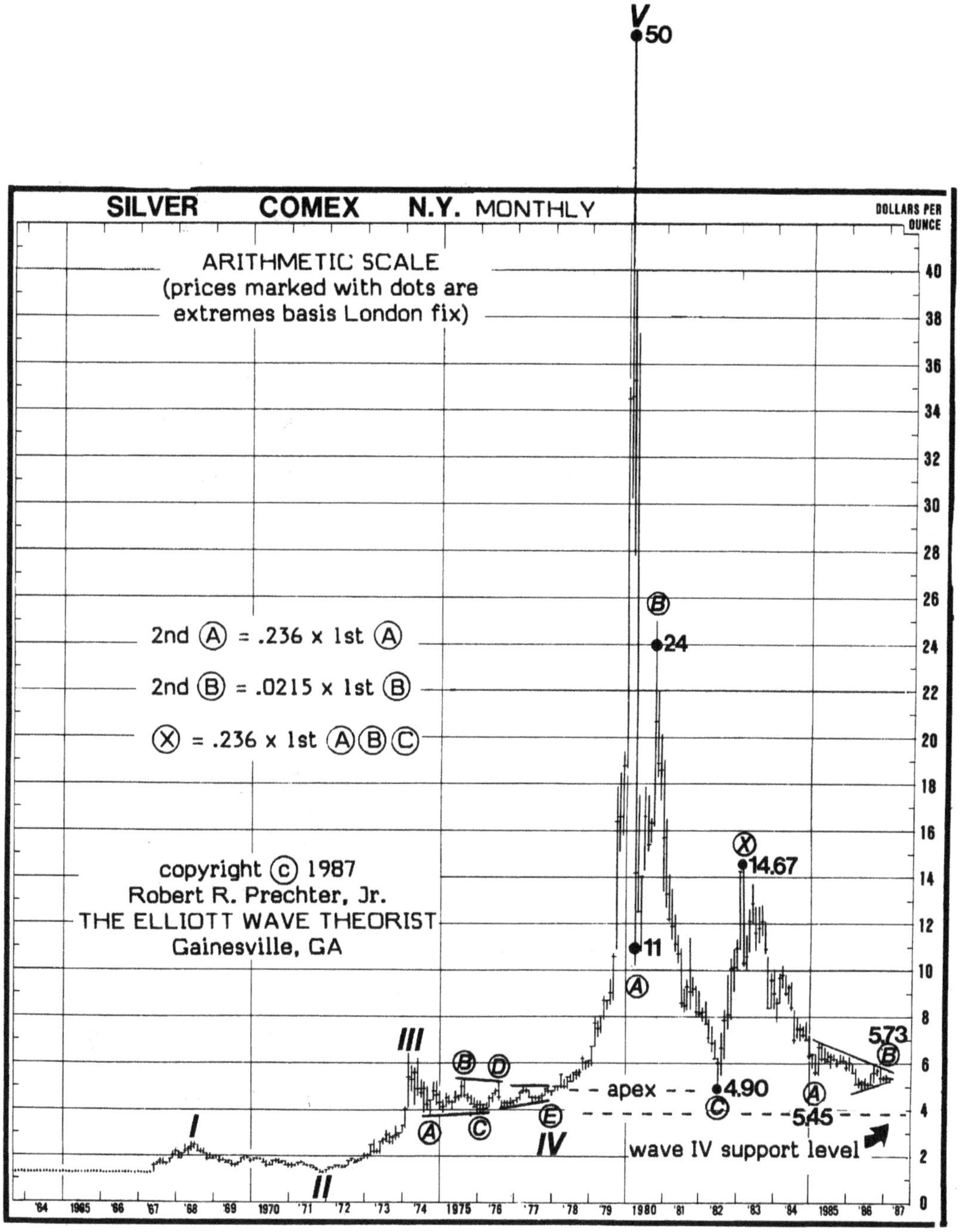

Figure 5

an area of support for silver. As you can see, wave IV was a contracting triangle, the apex of which was $4.90, the exact level of the bear market low for silver so far.

Let's examine the second Ⓐ-Ⓑ structure to date. I have been ignoring the meandering silver chart for most of the past two years, and, as is almost always the case when price action

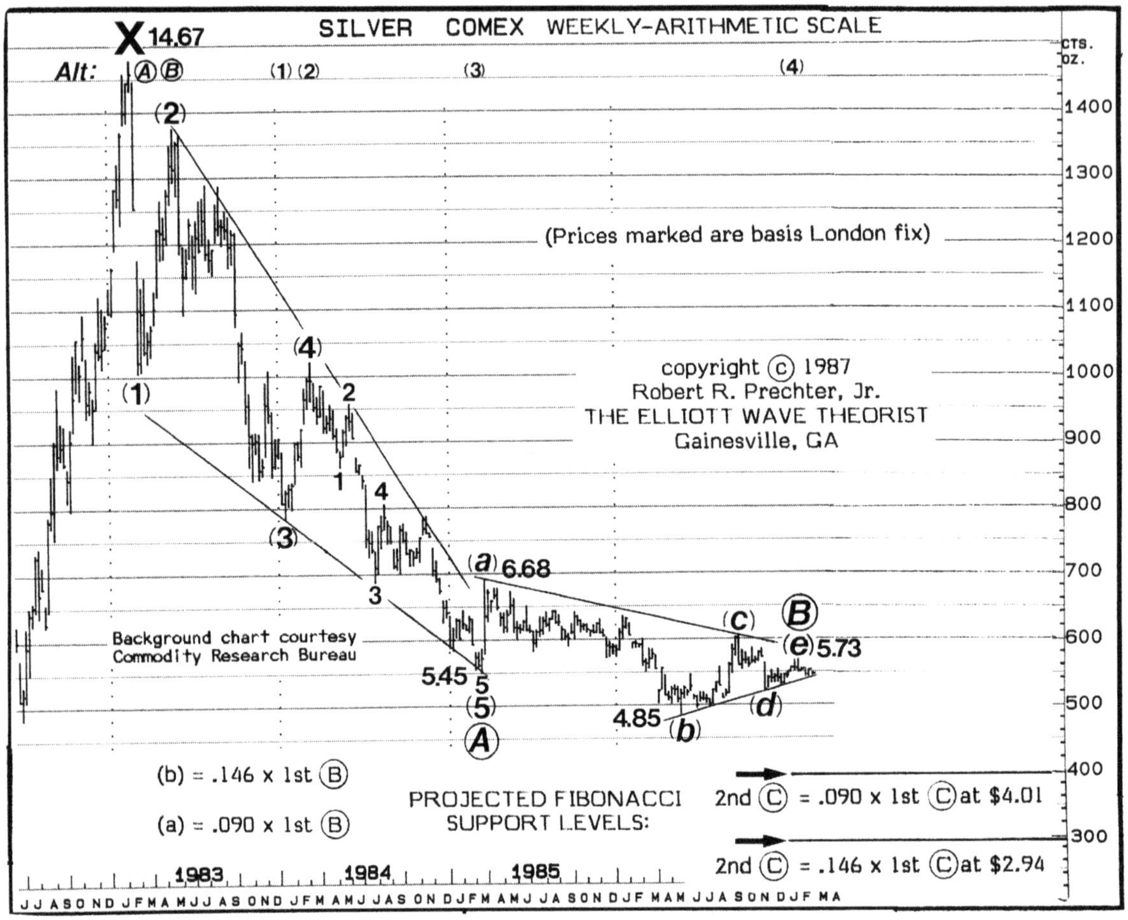

Figure 6

continually generates corrective wave patterns in both directions, this apparent meandering suddenly took the classic shape of a horizontal triangle. The preferred count in Figure 6 breaks no rules using the London fix prices, although on the futures contracts, wave (4) overlaps the price territory of wave (1) by a slight margin. The alternate count shown was the ongoing interpretation throughout 1983-1985, when EWT was following the silver chart closely, and is an excellent way to dispose of any quarrels regarding overlaps (see text, p.53). However, the other properties of the structure make the preferred labeling of far greater interest.

First, the turning points for the Ⓐ-Ⓑ structure coincide precisely with those for the Ⓐ and Ⓑ waves in gold. Notice the beauty of the contracting triangle in the wave Ⓑ position and how, despite the fact that silver appeared to be drifting lower over the past two years, the true structure was that of a bear market rally, beginning and ending precisely with the Ⓑ wave for gold and terminating at a net gain for silver of 28¢. Secondly, the Ⓐ wave by this count stayed perfectly within a descending channel with a wedge shape on semilog scale (not shown) and does so fairly nicely on arithmetic scale as well, as you can see in Figure 6.

Finally, this count reveals some remarkable Fibonacci relationships. While each cross referenceable subwave in the gold chart is related to its predecessor simply by the same Fibonacci ratio, .618, the waves in silver are related in the same way by different Fibonacci ratios. The second Ⓐ wave fell $9.22, or exactly a Fibonacci .236 (.618³) times the length of the first Ⓐ wave, which fell $39. Wave Ⓑ, being a triangle, has several measurement possibilities, but as it happens, every one of them carries a Fibonacci relationship! Wave (b), the longest wave within the second Ⓑ, travels .141 (.618⁴) times the length of the first Ⓑ; wave (a), the longest rally and therefore the maximum net advance achieved from the start of wave Ⓑ, travels .095 (approximately .618⁵) times the length of the first Ⓑ; and the net travel of wave Ⓑ (i.e., to the peak of (e)) is .0215 (.618⁸) of the first Ⓑ! If wave Ⓒ has begun, then, it may be expected ultimately to end within the "previous fourth wave" support zone and travel a distance which is a Fibonacci ratio of the first wave Ⓒ, which fell $19.10. If so, then only the ratios .090 and .0557 apply, yielding downside targets of $4.01 and $4.67 respectively. Using .146 yields a far less likely target of $2.94. The $4.01 target is almost exactly at the lower end of the previous fourth wave (which is $3.90 basis the futures and thus probably about $4 basis the London fix; exact figure not available for this study).

Figure 7

Alternate Count (Probability 20%)

It is entirely acceptable to label the decline in silver from the February 1983 peak as a developing five wave structure (see Figure 7). The parallel channel (see text, p.59) is quite clearly defined, the triangle occurs in the fourth wave position as required (see text, p.44) and wave (e) of the triangle bursts through the downtrend channel resistance line in typical fashion. This count is worth considering because it dovetails with the alternate count for gold. If silver were to fall in a fifth wave to complete wave Ⓐ, then rally in wave Ⓑ, gold at the same time could complete waves (d) and (e) of its wave X triangle. At that point, both metals would be ready for their final declining phases.

Since fifth waves tend to be related to first waves by equality or the Fibonacci ratio (see text, p.57), we can estimate a downside target for wave (5) under this count. Wave (1) fell $4.44. If wave (5) is to drop below the low for wave (3) and end in the zone of the previous fourth wave and be related by the Fibonacci ratio to wave (1), the applicable multiples would be .618 and .382, which target $2.99 and $4.04 respectively. These levels are almost precisely the same as the $2.94 and $4.01 targeted by the Fibonacci relationships expected from the preferred count! Please realize that in all these calculations, a dollar's difference in one or more of the wave lengths would have meant the disruption of this beautiful web of Fibonacci relationships.

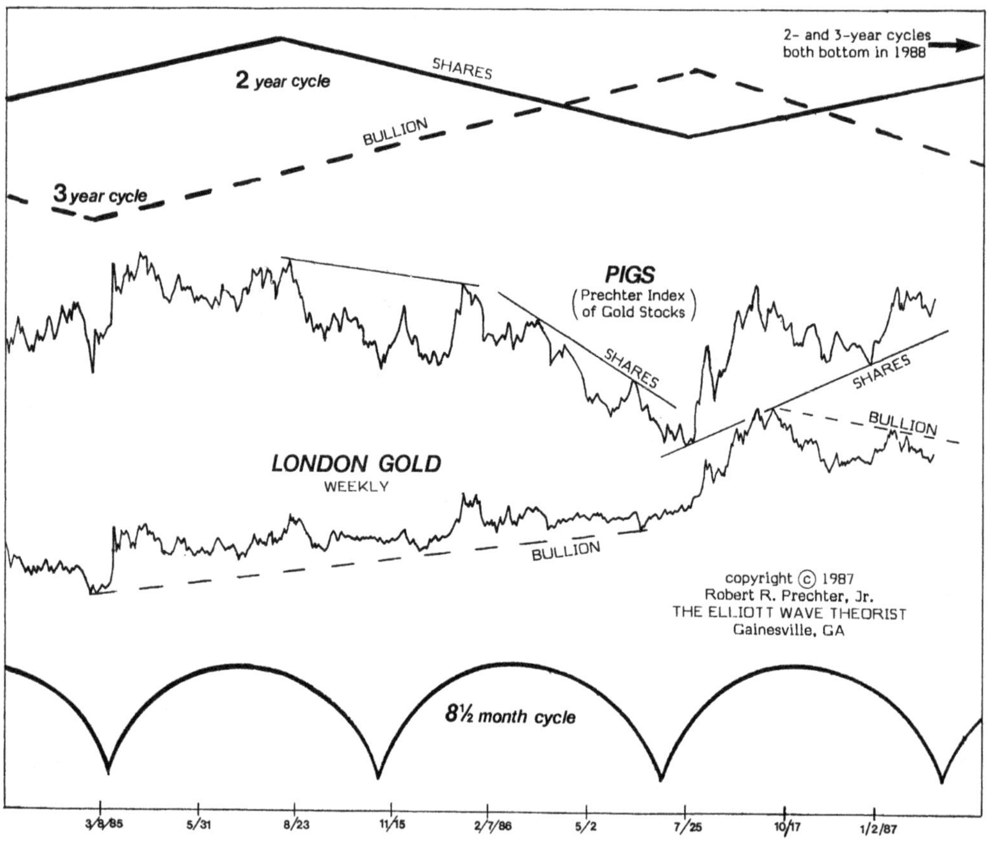

Figure 8

The Time Element

The 6-year cycle is still due to bottom in 1988 (see Figure 2), along with the 2- and 3-year cycles, which are operating exactly as expected according to the thesis put forth in the August 1986 issue, which explained the situation as follows:

> For over a year, EWT has continually forecast that the 2-year cycle pointed down in gold and silver until August 1986. From the last high for that cycle a year ago until last week, silver dropped 24% and PIGS (my gold stock average) 33% in an unrelenting year of erosion. It is now my opinion that the 2-year cycle has bottomed. The evidence is subtle, but if you study the chart [note: Figure 8 has been updated for this report], you will see divergences between the new lows in gold stocks and silver futures versus the higher bottoms in gold and silver bullion. Also, while commodity futures prices in general have collapsed to below their 1985 lows, spot commodity prices have held up, resulting in a negative spread so large that it equals the positive spread that existed at the inflationary peak of 1980! There is, temporarily at least, way too much willingness to bet aggressively on further deflation.
>
> Before projecting the most likely future course of precious metals prices, there is an important question to address. During the declining portion of the 2-year cycle, gold bullion actually managed to rise $10/oz., and platinum and collector coins have been going up persistently. Why? ...A careful study of the price and momentum behavior in gold and gold stocks reveals the presence of a 3-year cycle (see dashed line on cycle chart). This cycle created price lows in 1970, 1973, 1976, 1979, 1982 and 1985 (the precise timing of the price lows in each of those years was governed by the shorter term cycles).
>
> Postulating this cycle makes sense of the entire precious metals picture. Gold bullion, platinum and collector coins have clearly been influenced more strongly by the 3-year cycle, which explains their relative strength. This cycle last bottomed in February/March 1985. That cycle is due to peak now, but the newly rising 8½-month cycle will probably cause continued strength into November for “right hand translation” of that cycle’s top. Gold shares and silver, on the other hand, have been influenced more strongly by the 2-year cycle, which explains their relative weakness. That cycle is bottoming now. This situation implies a strong countertrend rally in these markets at least into November, then a period of distribution, creating “left hand translation” of that cycle’s top. Ultimately, the 2-year, 3-year and 6-year cycles are all scheduled to bottom together in my long standing target year of 1988.

> The June 2 issue of *The Elliott Wave Theorist* suggested covering short sales in gold, and we are still in a neutral position. Let's stay on the sidelines, allow the 8½-month cycle to run its course, then look to sell short later.

As the 3-year cycle rolled over in gold bullion (and platinum) last September/October, we sold short (with a stop) with the expectation of 1½ - 2 years of decline, and we still hold that position. The 3-year cycle is right now entering its final down year, so a dramatic collapse in the price of bullion could occur at any time. Since the 2-year cycle influences gold stocks more than bullion, as indicated above, gold stocks should hold up or decline less severely than bullion through the spring of 1987, when the next 8½-month cycle tops out. From there, the 2-, 3- and 6-year cycles will all be pointing down powerfully and jointly into 1988, providing a final across-the-board bear market wave of decline for all precious metals related investments. Thus, the message from the time cycles is that we should continue to avoid investing in gold and silver until 1988, when terrific bargains should be available. The third 8½-month cycle bottom from here will occur in August-September of the target year, although catching the low in "real time" will depend upon a number of things, not the least of which will be the wave count and price level.

Alternate Timing (Probability 5%)

I cannot exclude the possibility, particularly if the alternate counts for gold and silver unfold, that the bear market will last way beyond 1988, say, into the next 6-year cycle low in 1994. Obviously this is not a likely outcome, but in the interests of a complete discussion, I have included this thought.

Valuation

Recent issues of *The Elliott Wave Theorist* have demonstrated that gold is historically overpriced relative to oil, silver and a basket of commodities (please review if necessary). Merely bringing these relationships back into line will require a 50%-75% drop in the dollar price of gold. Such a decline would bring the price of bullion within the Elliott wave target range.

Investor Sentiment

The euphoria that accompanied the September price peak and the October "orthodox top" in gold prices was thoroughly documented in *The Elliott Wave Theorist*. I mentioned the heavy coin sales, record extremes of bullish forecasts among advisories, the one-sided commentary in the press and the extremely low readings on the put/call ratio. The consensus opinion from professional quarters is that gold prices will rise to between $500 and $800/oz. over the next year or two, and the latest readings still reflect that optimism, as you can see in Figure 10, courtesy of Davis/Zweig Futures, Inc. (P.O. Box 5345, NY NY 10150).

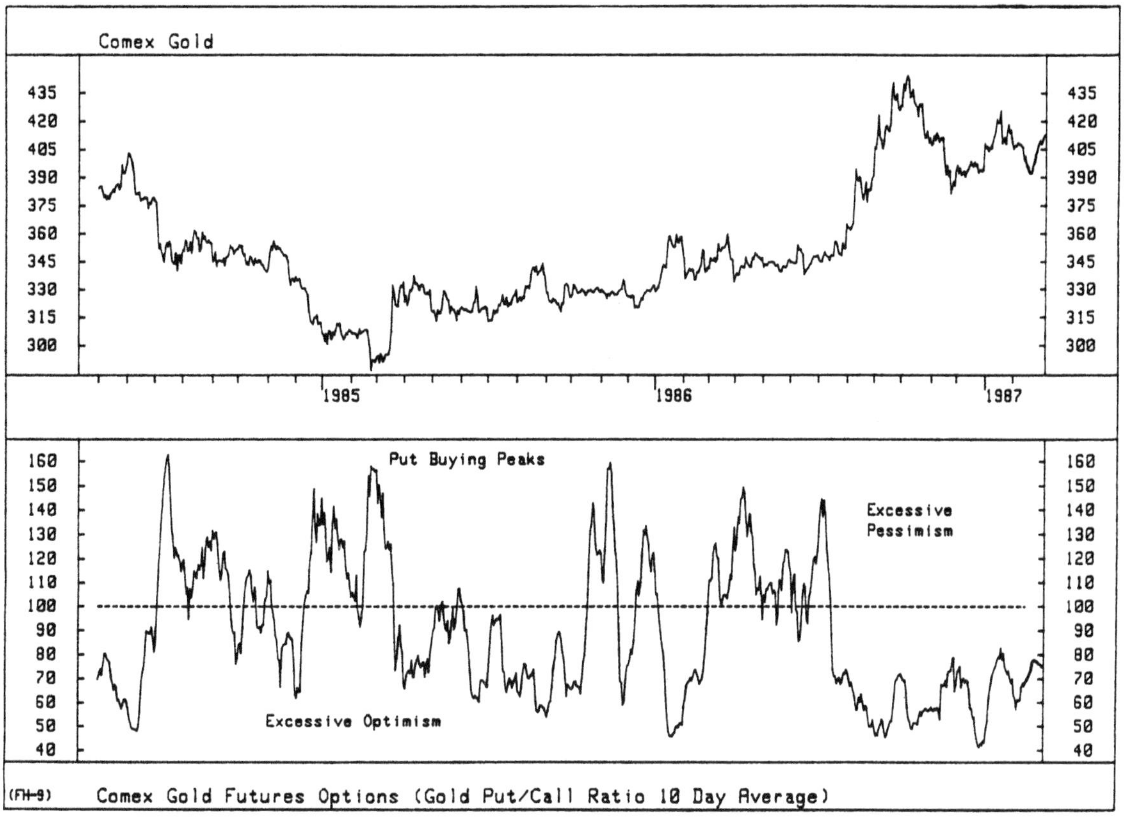

Figure 10

Summary

Strategically speaking, investors and traders should stay out of or short the precious metals markets until either one of the downside target levels is met, our stop is taken out, or a clear five wave structure of Intermediate degree indicates that a new bull market has begun. The highest probability downside target for gold bullion basis London fix is \$177, + or - \$9. The second most probable target is \$108, + or - \$7. For silver, the highest probability target is \$4.02, + or - 5¢. Valid but slightly less likely targets are \$4.67 and \$2.97, both + or - 5¢. As for timing, 1988 appears to be the year to buy precious metals. As always, wave form will take precedence over price and time targeting. If a satisfactory wave structure completes itself, the bear market will be over at that point, no matter what level is achieved. I'll keep you posted.

Upon studying the percentage movements in the silver picture, no relationships such as those revealed by gold appear. However, long time readers may recall my downside target estimation for the first wave C in silver based upon the conjecture that the percentage drops for wave Ⓐ and Ⓒ would be equal, which targeted \$5.28, which turned out to be a fairly close estimate of the ultimate bottom that occurred at \$4.90. Applying the 62.8% drop of the second wave Ⓐ to the second wave Ⓒ gives a rough estimate at \$2.13, which appears low.

MARCH 31, 1987

Gold is expected to stay below its September 1986 peak, although a slight penetration would be acceptable under the analysis presented in the March Special Report. The long term downside risk in metals and commodities is very large.

Gold

What is more astounding than the lack of true bullish conviction toward stocks despite a persistent multi-year bull market is the recent crystallization of extreme bullishness toward commodities, despite over six years of a major bearish trend. For students of market psychology, this is probably the most important lesson that 1986-1987 will have to offer. Peter Hackstedde of The Bullish Consensus reported last week that in the "inflation hedge" markets, he found 76% bulls on gold, 85% on silver, 94% on copper, 85% on platinum and an average of 90% for the foreign currencies! Given the price action, the readings this week should be even higher. To put these numbers in perspective, that reading on silver was the highest since January 1983, just weeks before it crashed from its peak at over $14.50/oz. But that's not all. Analyst and broker Peter DeSario of E.F. Hutton in Stuart, FL, reports that the composite bullish consensus on all non-financial commodities was 69.2% last week, the highest reading in over three years. Peter adds that every time the composite consensus toward inflation hedges has reached the low 60s or higher in the past six years, a substantial decline in commodity prices has occurred within weeks, often immediately. This week's reading could well be a record.

This general conviction that commodity price inflation is back, despite so much evidence to the contrary, is indicative that most investors and traders are still trying to make a profit out of the bull markets that occurred in the last decade. It will undoubtedly require the final cyclic downswing, scheduled from mid-1987 through mid-1988, to wipe out the deep-seated bullish conviction on this sector of investments.

The expected scenario for gold bullion, gold stocks and the dollar appears to be playing itself out as projected. It is still probable that the September 1986 peak in gold bullion was the top; for this reason, we're still short with a stop at $440 basis London fix. As for gold stocks, the following assessment was reiterated in the March 5 Special Report:

> Since the 2-year cycle influences gold stocks more than bullion, gold stocks should hold up or decline less severely than bullion through the spring of 1987, when the next 8½-month cycle tops out.

The performance of gold stocks recently has reflected the power of that cycle, whose influence is still likely to extend into spring. I was asked for a fundamental explanation of why this skewed relationship should occur. Since fundamental "cases" can always be made in favor of any position, I can oblige as follows: Gold is historically overpriced with respect to all other commodities (see January 1987 issue). The income for gold mines is dependent greatly on the value of their product. With gold bullion merely holding in the $400/oz. range, profits for gold mining enterprises are high. Thus, the stocks can rally as gold goes nowhere. Add to that the conviction among investors that gold will not fall, and the stocks can boom.

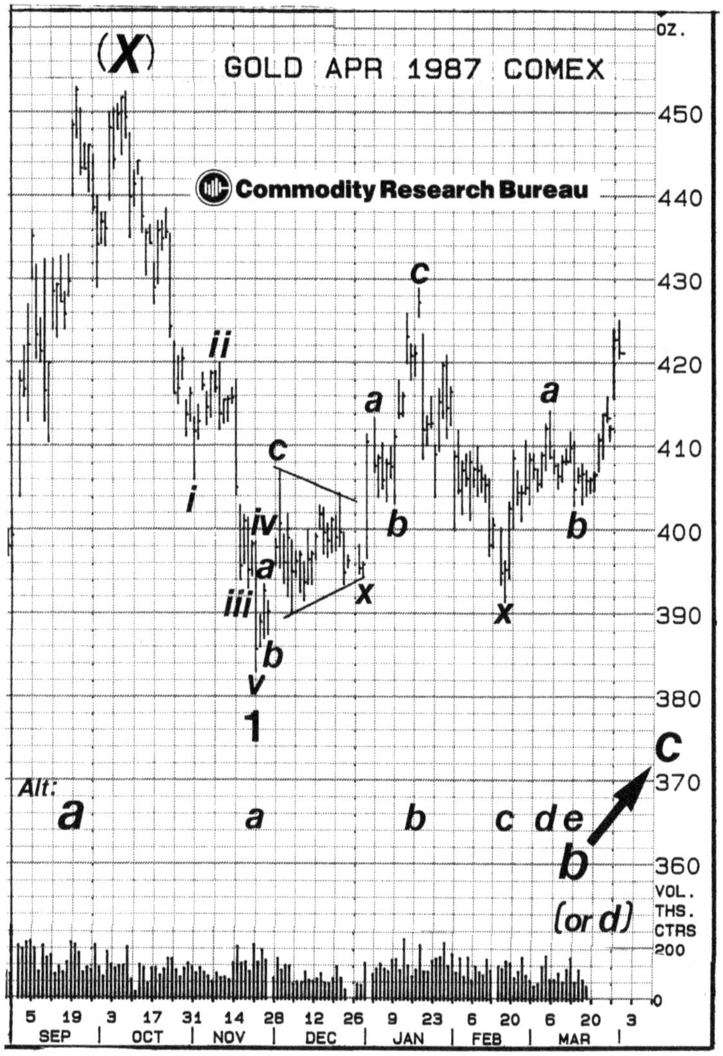

The 8½-month cycle in precious metals bottomed on March 20. That cycle theoretically points up through spring, although a price peak may be registered at any time, since the 8½ month rhythm is battling a host of other cycles that point down. The wave structure in gold is best counted as a wave 1 down into the November low, with wave 2 still in progress (see accompanying chart). The best alternate count is that of a triangle from September, which will lead to a rally taking gold back to or above the September peak before the next major downturn occurs. Even in this case, a failure of wave c to exceed the peak of wave a is highly likely, since as you may recall, the September peak exceeded the Fibonacci projection by several dollars. I have kept risk low on every trade ever recommended in *The Elliott Wave Theorist*, so stubbornness will not keep us short if our stop is hit. Nevertheless, the technical evidence is too negative to allow for any buying. There should be a more attractive opportunity when the long term cycles bottom in 1988.

As a last word on the historically high relative valuation of gold, it is notable that the world is literally in a "gold rush." Mining concerns around the globe are digging furiously, buying up claims, modernizing and expanding. This wouldn't be happening if gold were not highly priced. And in the long run, increased production will be a depressant on the price.

APRIL 27, 1987

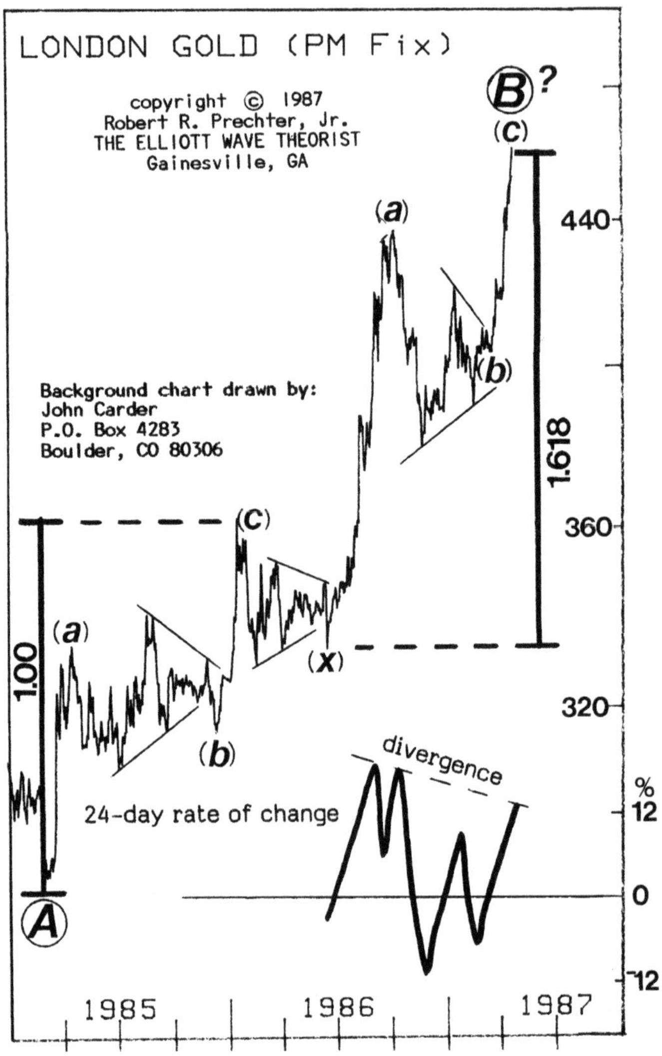

Gold and other precious metals are peaking, and the dollar is bottoming, all on a major trend basis.

Gold

"Now that gold has made a new high, don't you have to conclude that the major trend is up?" That's the question I've been hearing over the past two weeks, and it does deserve an answer. So here's the answer: absolutely not. Gold is still undergoing a bear market rally, and the fact that it tacked on an extra 5% above last September's peak is no reason to begin projecting it to $2000/oz. What changes my mind about a market is a change in its technical condition. Gold's technical condition does keep changing ...for the worse. An analogous situation, with the same intensity of general disagreement, existed all during the bond market's topping phase over the past twelve months. It took awhile for the market's action to prove the validity of the technical indicators, but ultimately the piper was paid.

Price level alone should only occasionally be the catalyst for a decision, and then usually for stops on a trading position, to minimize risk. For instance, our "stop" on short sales at $440 basis London fix moved us to the sidelines on the opening of April 14. The price paid for our error was at most (allowing for the worst entry) $15 basis London fix and as little as $5 basis the June 1987 futures contract. I hate taking losses, even small ones. However, everyone makes mistakes in the market. The real questions are, "How many do you make?" and "How much do you lose when you make them?" The key to making money consistently is to keep losses small when you're wrong and to let profits ride when you're right. That's been my goal, and it has served us well over the years.

Let's review the outlook from last month's issue:

> The 8½ month cycle in precious metals bottomed on March 20. That cycle theoretically points up through spring, although a price peak may be registered at any time, since the 8½ month rhythm is battling a host of other cycles that point down. The wave structure in gold is best counted as a wave 1 down, with wave 2 still in progress. The best alternate count is that of a triangle from September, which will lead to a rally taking gold back to or above the September peak before the next major downturn occurs.

That triangle and the subsequent advance are shown on the accompanying chart. The extremely high level of valuation, the bearish wave structure and the unbelievably dangerous condition of investor sentiment have been detailed in EWT for several months. Now we can add something that has been missing from the picture: a significant momentum divergence. Despite the widespread orgiastic desire to own gold recently, the latest advance has so far failed to generate a better "overbought" condition than the rally of 1986's third quarter, as you can see on the bottom of the chart. Moreover, my ongoing interpretation of the internal wave patterns once again reveals a Fibonacci relationship in that the second a-b-c zigzag, at Friday's a.m. fix, has now traveled 1.618 times as long as the first (see bars on chart). By the way, if stocks are in a "wave 2" position similar to that of January 1983, it may be important to note that gold collapsed 20% in value in February 1983.

The recent explosion in silver (the "poor man's gold") is likely a signal that the speculation in the precious metals complex is climaxing. EWT made the following comment way back on August 4, 1986, just as gold stocks and silver were lifting off:

> Gold shares and silver, on the other hand, have been influenced more strongly by the 2-year cycle, which...is bottoming now. This situation implies a strong[er] countertrend rally in these markets....

Although the advance lasted longer than originally expected, the relatively better performance in gold shares and silver relative to platinum and gold bullion have confirmed the cycle analysis given in that issue. From here **on out, the 2-, 3- and 6-year cycles in precious metals are either down or topping, and all are due to make a final low in 1988.**

Investors should stay out of the gold market; there are better and less risky places for your money. Traders sell short now with a stop at $480 basis London fix. The best alternate count allows gold to exceed its 1983 peak at $511.50 basis London fix before declining again. That count has been addressed numerous times in the past; we'll detail it again if events warrant. For kamikaze traders only: Short a far out contract of silver if the nearby contract exceeds $10, and stop out the position if it exceeds $11.

JUNE 1, 1987

With all markets in apparent "runaway" trends at the time, **the April 27 issue of The Elliott Wave Theorist called for short term lows in stocks and bonds and peaks in gold and silver. All occurred exactly on that day. "Tests" of those turning points occurred on May 20, and they appear to have been successful. Gold, gold stocks and silver have been losing ground since** April and have only just begun declines which should last over a year.

Gold

With gold and silver hitting new highs and in apparent "straight up" mode in late April, the technical situation on April 27 nevertheless argued that a top was in the making:

> [T]he relatively better performance in gold shares and silver relative to platinum and gold bullion have confirmed the cycle analysis given in [the August 4, 1986] issue. ...The recent explosion in silver (the "poor man's gold") is likely a signal that the speculation in the precious metals is climaxing. ...From here on out, the 2-, 3- and 6-year cycles in precious metals are either down or topping, and all are due to make a final low in 1988.

The strategy for gold traders was to "sell short now with a stop at $480 basis London fix." Most futures contracts peaked on a blowoff that morning, although the June contract and London gold edged $1-3 higher on the "test" of the top, which occurred three weeks later on May 20. The peak London fix at $479.95 was amazingly close to our stop, but the short sale is still intact. By the way, most metals watchers were too bullish to have noticed the fact that the gold stock average topped out on April 14 (on the "a" wave low in stocks). It has since fallen over 20% on a closing basis. (If the Dow were down 20% from its high, it would be considered a disaster.) Remember in the August 1986 issue, when EWT argued for a precious metals rally based partly on the spread between spot and future commodity prices, which indicated "way too much willingness to bet aggressively on further deflation"? Well, the markets are now saying that the *inflation* scare is over. The technical situation for precious metals in April and May was one of the most bearish I have ever seen in markets, not unlike that of bonds in March. Now we'll have to see if our observations pay off. Although I don't expect it, if gold manages to make a new [near-term] high, we may have to see the February 1983 peak at $511.50 taken out before selling short again.

Silver

After staying quiet on silver strategy for two years, EWT viewed the situation on April 27 as demanding a short sale. That morning was the exact high to date, although the blowoff was so violent that our conservative strategy wouldn't have worked. Throughout the month-long silver rally, our office received many questions asking why we weren't recommending buying and what the difference was between a bear market rally and a bull market. Well, it

Silver's boom melts in a flash

Days like Monday are what make silver traders wish they'd chosen a less nerve-racking line of work — say, a career in bomb disposal.

Spot silver — for immediate delivery — and futures — contracts for the future delivery of silver — shot up in early trading in **New York** and **Chicago**: investors worried about the free-falling dollar flocked to precious metals in the morning — especially to cheaper silver. Silver went from $9.66 to $11.25 an ounce, silver futures up their full 75-cent exchange-imposed limits, to $9.795 an ounce for May. Then in about six minutes, by 11:30 CDT, futures prices dropped $1.50 — from the up limit to the down limit. Panic and rumors turned a retreat into a rout. Spot silver closed at $7.80.

"It was like everyone trying to get out the door of a burning building at the same time," said **Walt Breitinger**, an **A.G. Edwards & Sons Inc.** commodities broker. Word at the Chicago Board of Trade was that a few traders were throwing up in the bathrooms after losing hundreds of thousands of dollars.

APRIL 29, 1987 • USA TODAY

Grassroots silver buying has kept the lobbies of coin shops and bullion dealers packed for weeks. And while silver's Monday meltdown may have spooked them on Wall Street, it hasn't fazed them on Main.

At **Gold & Silver Emporium** in **Encino**, Calif., waiting lines 50 customers long have been the rule for three weeks. There, silver's slither — from $9.66 to $11.25 and down to $7.80 an ounce Monday — sparked heavier buying, which continued Tuesday as the price slipped to $7.65. "People are taking it as a correction. They seemed thrilled to get in for less," said Vice President **Charles Surasky**. "It's just absolute madness," said **Peter Hug**, corporate vice president for **Guardian Trust Co.**, a **Toronto** bullion wholesaler that's seen daily silver trades shoot from 400 to 4,000 in the past four weeks. "My phone blew up. We had to put a new circuit in."

Silver mania has made **First Union National Bank's** new metals brokerage service a hit in **Charlotte**, N.C. The first ads aren't even out, yet the service is fielding 50 calls a day, most for silver bars.

The crowd scene in **Arizona Stamp & Coin** is "highly reminiscent of '79 and '80," when gold and silver mania swept an inflation-ravaged land, said **Neil Powell**, owner of the **Tucson** shop. **Sims** agrees, but still is worried by the size of Monday's price slide: "It's possible the silver boom got to be news just in time to be history."

took over a month for the "spot" silver contract (April) to climb from $5.50 to $11.25, and just 15 minutes to retrace over 70% of that rise. That's a reasonably good display of the difference; it's a matter of risk.

How has the public taken the news of the dramatic reversal? Has it scared them to death, say, as the measly 7.9% correction in the Dow has scared them out of stocks? Quite the contrary, as you can see from the article reproduced here.

With that scene in mind, it may be timely to review the description of crowd "personality" during the first decline in a new bear pattern (from page 68 of *Elliott Wave Principle*):

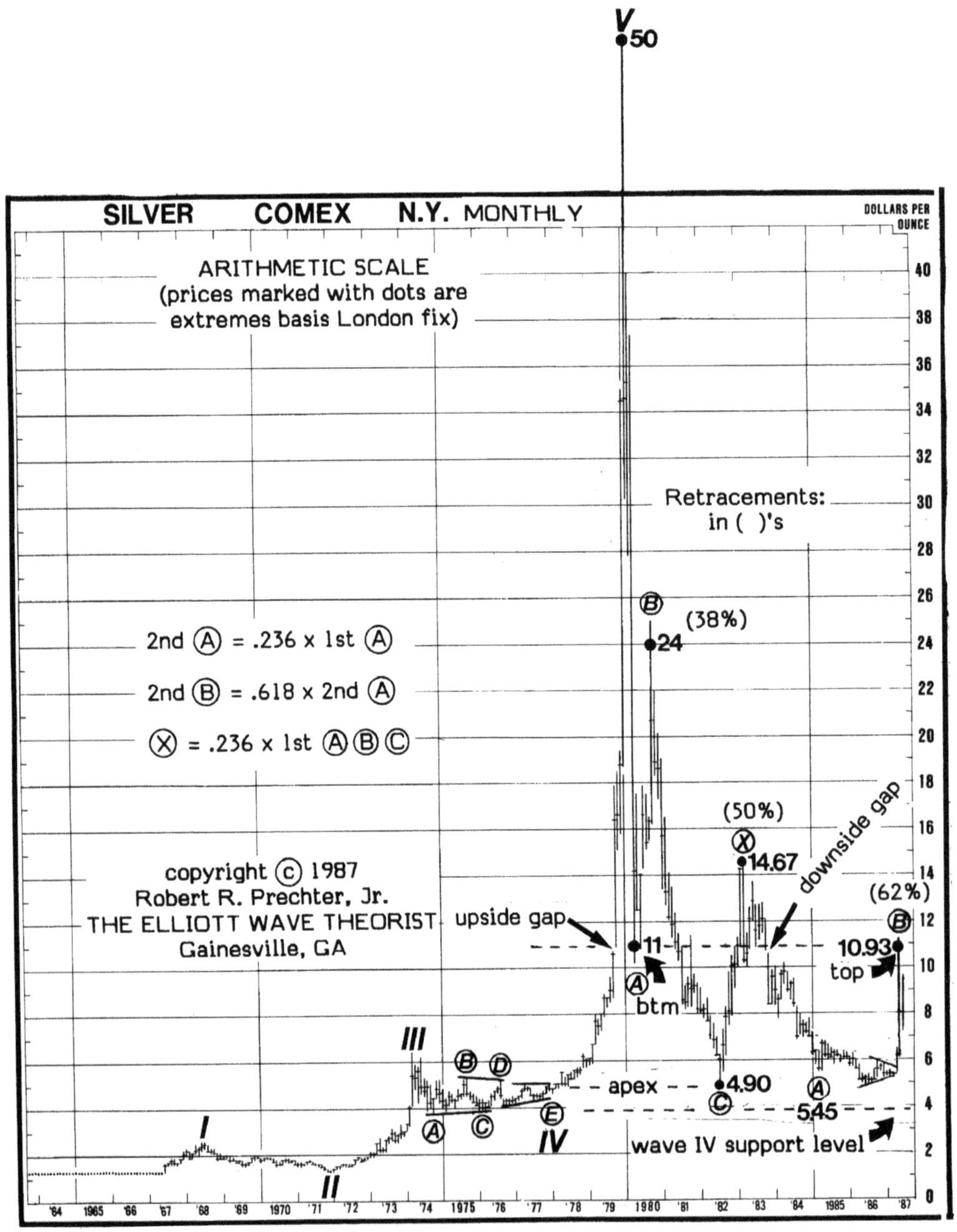

"A" waves — During A waves of bear markets, the investment world is generally convinced that this reaction is just a minor pullback pursuant to the next leg of advance. The odd-lot public surges to the buy side, despite the first really technically damaging cracks in individual stock patterns.

The big picture in silver, like that for gold, strongly suggests that the third major bear market rally since the January 1980 peak is over. The chart shown here is from the March Special Report, with prices updated. The count is the same up to the final label for wave Ⓑ. Wave Ⓒ should now carry silver prices to new lows for the decade. The best alternate count, labeling the entire structure from the 1980 low at $11 as a triangle, is also bearish. Further, as subscriber Joe Rasillo pointed out in a letter 1½ weeks before the top, a peak near $11 would mean that the bear market rallies were proceeding through an orderly Fibonacci ratio progression of retracing approximately 38.2%, 50% and 61.8% of their preceding declines, while making lower peaks each time. The recent top also occurred right at silver's most important support/resistance price level (see chart), where dramatic turns or gaps have occurred. The peak was only slightly above the top of the previous fourth wave within wave Ⓐ, a normal point of resistance for partial retracements (see text, p.55). As disorderly as manic crowd behavior may appear on the surface, it is truly anything but. (Ironically, $10 was EWT's original upside target for silver when wave Ⓐ first ended; see March and April 1985 issues!)

JULY 6, 1987

Gold's technical condition remains weak, and the outlook, particularly past mid-August, is extremely bearish.

Gold — An Overview

Few people know that my first major investment was in gold stocks. In February 1972, I purchased shares in West Rand Investment Trust (which later merged with Orange Free State Investment Trust to form Anglo American Gold Investment Co.). The South African golds quadrupled in the two years thereafter, and I sold out. Even then, it was only 1974, and the long term gold rise still had over five years left in it. Despite a limited experience with investments, I did understand one thing clearly: That was a bull market.

Financial trends are varying and cyclical. It is all well and good, for instance, to recognize that in the long run, U.S. stocks have made an excellent investment. However, to have come to that conclusion, and to have acted accordingly, in 1928, 1968 or 1972 would have resulted in catastrophic loss. The gold market is no exception. There are times to own gold and times when it should be avoided. 1974 was a good year to sell it. So was 1980. February 1983 was another. Evidence is powerful that the 1985-1987 rise is providing yet another selling opportunity. Six categories of analysis continue to support a bearish view for the price of gold.

Price Patterns

As you know, the Wave Principle is a detailed description of the price and volume patterns that typify bull markets and their corrections and bear markets and their countertrend rallies. Suffice it to say that the price patterns dating from the 1982 low are decidedly more typical of an ongoing bear market than of a new bull market. Similar considerations allowed EWT to identify the countertrend rally peak in gold on September 23, 1980, on the day of the top, and that of February 15, 1983, a week before it occurred. The Wave Principle's message now is that gold is very likely ending its third major countertrend rally within the ongoing bear market that began in January 1980. Ultimately, the downside potential, based upon various guidelines of price behavior (see previous issues), is still to below $200/oz.

Time Cycles

Time cycles do not define market movement as does the Wave Principle, but it is clear that fairly precise cycles (i.e., specific time periods between highs or lows) do exist in the behavior of markets. Cycles can alternate in dominance or even disappear, but until momentum oscillators and price action confirm such aberrations, the probabilities of successful analysis will increase when recent cyclic behavior is extrapolated into the future. For example, throughout

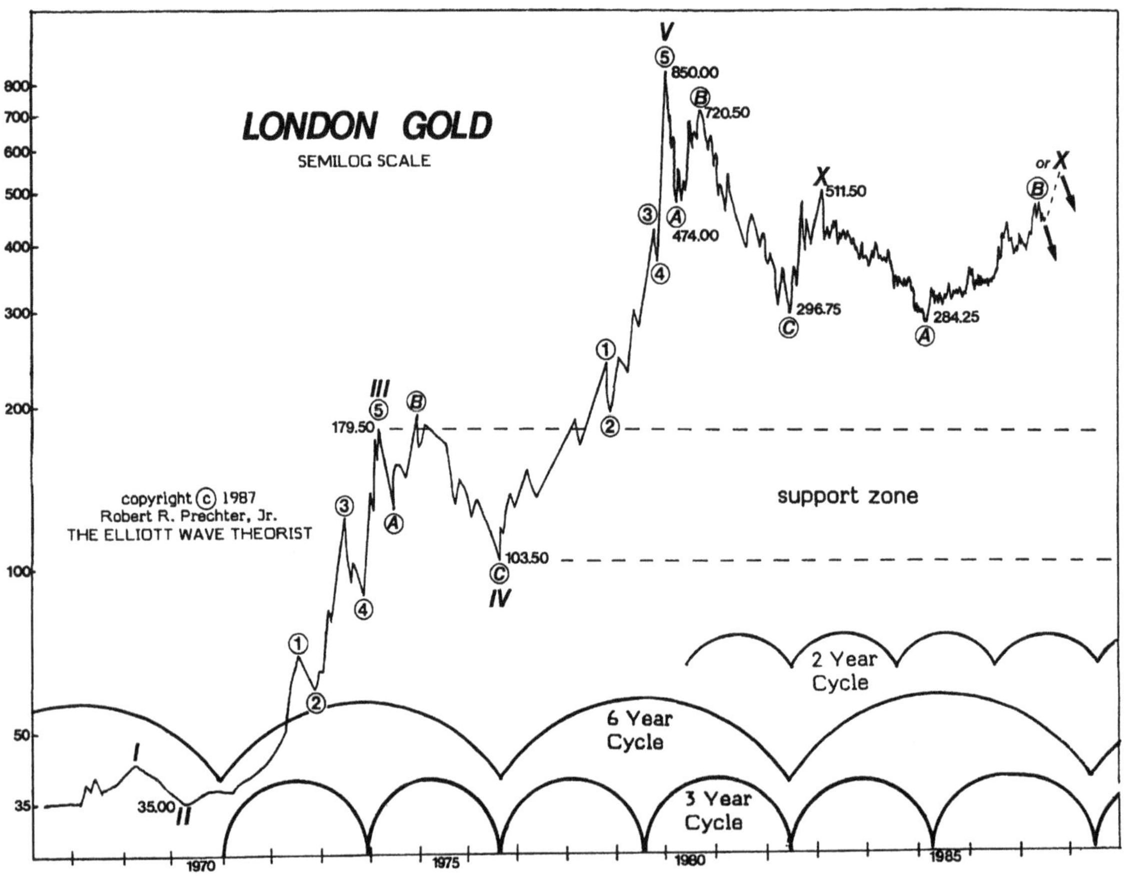

the first half of last year, time cycles indicated that a major rally for precious metals would begin by the first week of August, 1986. *The Elliott Wave Theorist* maintained that opinion throughout the first seven months of the year because a clearly visible 2-year cycle had existed in the price action for a number of years (see chart). Moreover, during that time, the trends of gold stocks and silver remained down while gold drifted sideways, revealing that that cycle was exerting the expected influence and thus was still operative. In the final week of July, almost precisely on schedule, that cycle turned up, and the gold stocks and precious metals began a rally worthy of the name. The ideal peaking time for the 2-year cycle is late July, but I have expected an early price peak since the other relevant long term cycles in gold already point toward lower prices until the summer of 1988. In sum, the cyclic outlook supports the bearish interpretation of the price structure.

Rate of Price Change

The jump in the price of gold from July to October 1986 was swift and powerful and carried to $440/oz. After settling back into November/February, gold ran up once again to new highs at $480/oz., but the rate of price change was slower than that of 1986's third quarter. This development is not a guarantee that a top is in place, but its occurrence is quite typical of cyclic tops. The February 1983 peak occurred in the same manner, after an advance that was slower than the preceding June-September 1982 rise. The subsequent decline was literally a collapse. If in coming weeks gold manages a third rally peak on even less power, the technical situation will become even weaker.

In addition to the above observation, it is also the case that when gold bullion eked out a slightly higher peak on May 20, gold stocks were significantly below their April peaks. Technicians call this situation a bearish "non-confirmation," which is an indication that a trend is becoming selective, a typical precursor to trend change.

The past year's action in silver also suggests that the brief precious metals boom has ended. For months, while other precious metals climbed higher, silver lay dormant. Finally on March 23, it launched a one-month surge, climbing from $5.50 to $11.25 on the nearby futures contract. In frenzied trading on April 27, silver then collapsed, retracing 70% of the preceding one-month rally in 15 minutes. On June 22, it had fallen to an 80% retracement of its rally. The violence of the blowoff, the rapidity of the initial retracement and the extent of the subsequent weakness are all characteristic of action within an ongoing larger bear market.

Investor Sentiment

The extent of the buying panic in precious metals during the recent rally can hardly be overstated. From September 1986 through May 1987, Market Vane of Pasadena CA tallied numerous weeks of 75%-95% "bulls" among advisors with respect to the precious metals. Newspaper coverage and commentary was one-sidedly bullish. The public frenzy for gold and silver, according to some observers, was as strong as it had been in late 1979 and early 1980, at the major top. Lately, coin salesmen have reported in major newspapers that the average investor sees the recent drop in the silver price as a bargain buying opportunity. Ironically, the wild rush by silver vendors and magazine writers to capitalize on the rally took a couple of weeks to implement, so their ads and articles finally hit the newspapers in May and June, after a top of some significance had been recorded. In another reflection of bullish sentiment, one futures exchange, after eliminating its gold contract from trading in February 1985, right at the low for gold, reintroduced the contract on June 15 in recognition of the huge public demand. To date, the put/call ratio on gold futures has remained in low territory, indicating a deep lack of willingness to bet on the downside. All of these occurrences reveal a type of behavior and attitude among investors which is typical of tops and the beginning of important declines, not the early stages of a prolonged bull market. For comparison, recall EWT's comment at the February 1983 peak that Jim Dines' tally of bulls and bears showed a higher percentage of bulls than at the 1980 major top. For contrast, witness the continuing argument and skepticism with regard to the stock market, which has more than tripled since its 1982 low and yet in the past three years has not generated a single week of 80% bulls among advisors! When the real top in stocks is at hand, you can bet you'll see enthusiasm. Just remember this simple rule: When the majority is staunchly bullish, all their money is invested, and there is hardly anyone left with buying power to propel prices higher. According to the sentiment indicators, that is the situation with regard to the gold market today.

Valuation

The 1985-1987 "bull market" in gold has occurred almost exclusively in dollar (U.S., Canadian and Australian) terms. In Swiss francs, Deutsch marks and Japanese yen, there has been no bull market. Evidence is quite powerful that the dollar has been stretched to the limit temporarily and is due for a 12- to 18-month countertrend rally, which could well serve to value gold downward in dollar terms.

Even if the dollar were not to rise relative to foreign currencies, gold could fall substantially in dollar value simply because it is historically overpriced relative to other things denominated in dollars. According to a study by the American Institute for Economic Research (see January issue), in order to bring the price of gold in line with its average value relative to a standard basket of commodities over the past 200 years, gold would have to decline in relative value by 50%. If both of these forces work toward equilibrium, a substantial drop in the dollar price of gold will certainly occur.

Supply-Demand

As discussed above, wave pattern, cycles, momentum status, valuation and the state of investor sentiment all strongly suggest that the "demand" side of the equation has been fully satisfied and is running out of power to move prices. What about the "supply" side of the equation? Numerous recent research reports indicate that the dramatically expanded mining efforts around the world over the past five years (as a result of the extreme relative overvaluation of gold; expansion wouldn't be occurring if it were cheap) are now scheduled to begin providing as much as a 30% increase in the world's stockpile of precious metals in just five years. This potential increase does not take into account possible stepped-up selling by those countries that are deeply in debt. Satisfied demand plus increasing supply usually leads to a falling price. I see little reason why this time should be different.

Alternate Count

What if gold goes to another new high? Will that change my outlook? If you read the preceding sections, you will find that price action alone has the ability to affect only two of the six categories of analysis presented above, so the odds are that my opinion would not change. In fact, such action might well be welcomed as another silver-platter (pardon the pun) selling opportunity. From an Elliott wave standpoint, there is still an outside chance that gold bullion will attain a new high in the culmination of wave Ⓒ of X of the alternate count (as last illustrated in the April 1985 issue). It's "last shot" at achieving the $510-$550 range before heading downward again will be available during the next six weeks as the stock market battles its downward cyclic pressure. Gold stocks and silver, which have fallen 24% and 39% in value from their respective closing peaks, have virtually no chance of making new highs.

A more pertinent question might be, what if Prechter is completely wrong and gold is on its way to the moon? One answer is that the Wave Principle is an excellent tool for forcing changes of opinion when an analyst is wrong. That's one reason why, according to Commodity Traders Consumer Report, *The Elliott Wave Theorist* (in stocks, bonds and gold combined), errors and all, has the highest profit per trade among all short term timing services for the four-year period that CTCR has been tracking trading advisors. I hope to be alert enough to catch most advances of importance. Frankly, however, if my outlook is to prove incorrect, it is not likely to be as a result of continuingly rising gold prices but rather that the cycle low scheduled for 1988 will provide only a temporary rally as a precursor to further decline. The more gold falls over the next year, particularly if it drops far enough to satisfy Elliott wave expectations, the more bullish the implications will be. If the decline into the summer of 1988 is moderate, it will be much less likely that the major bear market dating from 1980 has ended. I have a definite idea of what ensuing action would likely be in that case, but we'll cross that bridge if we come to it.

Short Term Outlook and Strategy

The 8½-month cycle, which last bottomed on March 20 (see March 31 issue), is now in its topping phase and is not due to bottom until early December. Investors stay out of the gold market. Traders remain short and keep the "stop" at $480 basis London fix.

AUGUST 10, 1987

Gold, which last month had cyclic potential to hold up until August, is likely to begin declining in earnest as wave 3 to the downside gets underway.

Gold

EWT recommended selling short gold at the spike top on April 27, and the evidence continues to indicate that that strategy will pay off. The subsequent "tests" of the highs on May 20 and August 4 appear to have created a "triple top." The wave structure (see near term chart) shows a clear five waves down for wave 1, and an a-b-c expanded flat (see text, p.39) for wave 2. Cycles, momentum, sentiment, valuation and supply-demand factors also remain extremely bearish on a long term basis.

With regard to sentiment, readings last week revealed a continuing widespread enthusiasm for the precious metals. EWT has been reporting since September 1986, the month gold first hit $440, that the 10-day average of the put/call ratio showed way too many investors bullish to make a long position attractive. It has been almost a year since then, and despite the flood of bullish commentary on gold, its price is virtually unchanged. Note the contrast between markets. Stocks have *gone* up, and fear and caution have increased in recent weeks. Gold has merely *held* up, and bullishness has increased. Last week Market Vane (Box 90490, Pasadena, CA) tallied 85% "bulls" for gold, 86% for silver and an unbelievable 96% for platinum, even

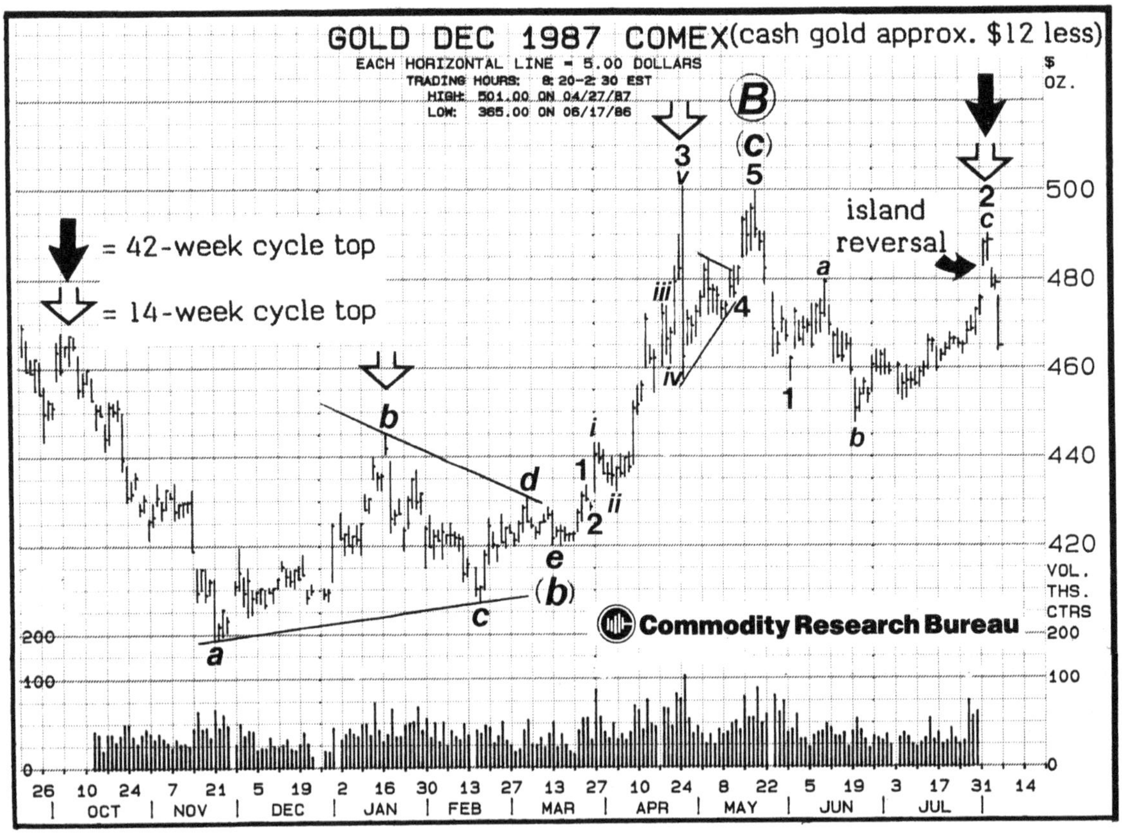

though these markets were below their 1987 highs (platinum is below even its September 1986 high). Traders are of the same mind as the advisors. The chart shown here of our long-quoted 10-day put/call ratio (courtesy Ned Davis Research) shows that it plunged in July to its lowest level in at least three years. Meanwhile, P/E ratios on gold stocks are sky high, in the 70:1 range, in contrast to the 15:1 ratios at their 1980 peaks. These P/E ratios reflect the same level of extreme overvaluation that accompanied the "nifty fifty" glamour stocks in January 1973 just before that list embarked upon a two-year crash. The bold-faced headline of an article in a major magazine last week read, quite accurately, "Gold Fever."

Cycles in gold argue that a top of importance was met last week. As you can see in the chart, gold tends to peak approximately every 42 weeks (near bond market bottoms), with a subdivision into three cycles of 14 weeks. Declines of varying importance follow, but this time gold could not manage a new high for the cycle at the top and even left an island reversal on the futures chart (see daily chart), both extremely bearish developments. Unless last week's high is exceeded, the message from this cycle is, "stay bearish."

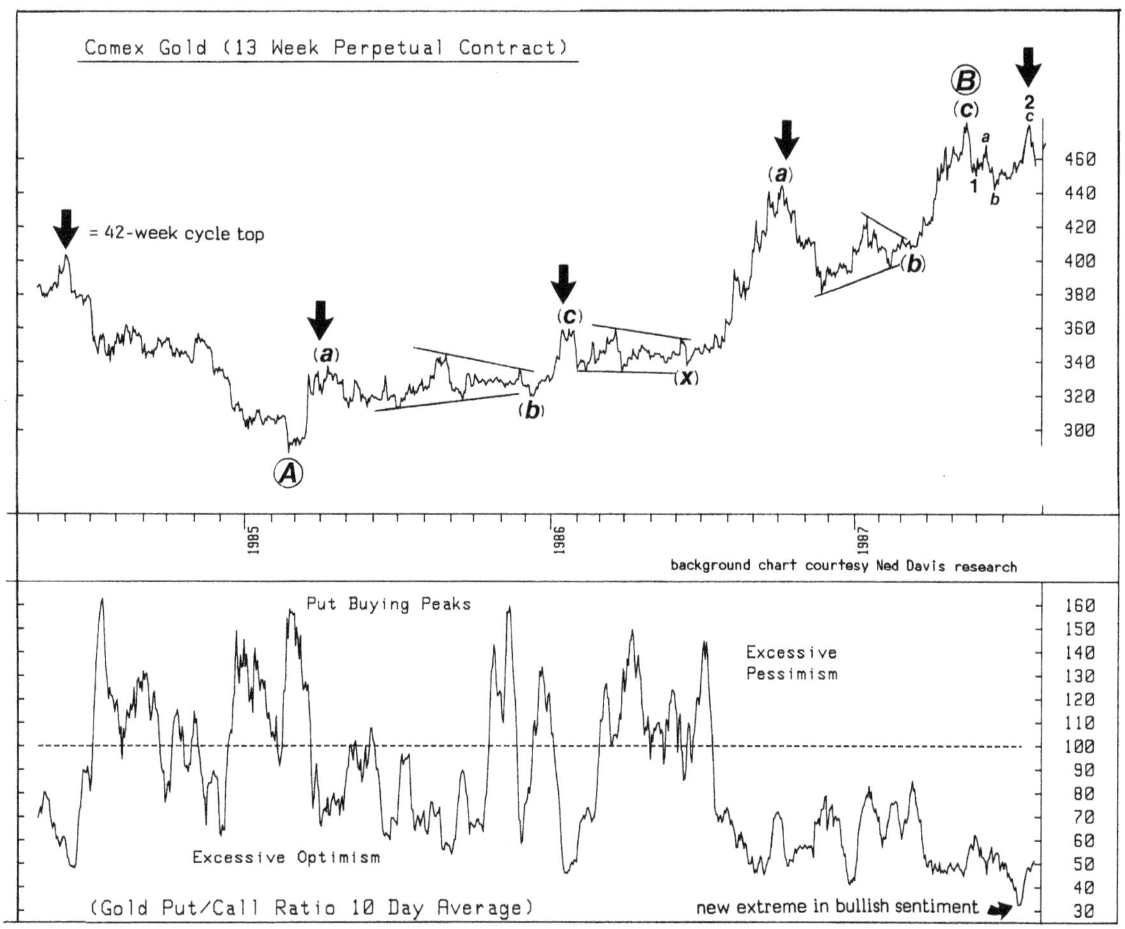

Investors should stay out of the gold market. Traders should remain 100% short. Keep the stop at $480 basis the London fix because if $480 is exceeded, the alternate count shown last month still allows for a final lunge into the $510-$550 range (although time is running out). If stopped out, sell short again at $530, with a stop at $560. The long term price projection for the bear market dating from January 1980 is still to below $200/oz. With that target in mind, you may enjoy these excerpts from a recent newspaper article on gold:

August 11, 1987 NUMISMATIC NEWS

What's happened to the demand for U.S. gold bullion coins? Sales by the Mint to its primary distributors for the week ending July 24 were only 10,000 troy ounces and total sales of the 1987 pieces in the first 30 weeks of the year amounted to only 754,500 ounces.

This is an average of 25,250 ounces a week for the first 30 weeks of 1987. If sales continue at that level through the remaining 22 weeks, the total for the year will be 1,307,800 troy ounces.

This is just over half the Mint's original projection of 2.3 million ounces on an annual basis (and only a third of industry projections of four million ounces). It is less than half of the Mint's revised projection of 3.1 million ounces following the huge demand during the first three months of sales at the end of last year.

Sales were almost two million ounces (1,869,250 according to the Mint's preliminary figures) in less than 12 weeks after their introduction.

When demand fell almost vertically to only a fraction of that level after the first of this year, industry spokesmen and coin dealers commented that the first quarter of the year is generally slow for precious metals.

Now, well into the third quarter, there is no sign of an upturn.

Industry experts and dealers offered a variety of explanations for the doldrums in gold coins, most of them citing other major elements in the current economic cycle.

"I think the great variety of offerings of gold and silver pieces is just burning people out," he added, "there's so much on the market they just can't afford it all.

"We're buying tons back, not many U.S. Eagles but Krugerrands, Maple Leaves, ducats and four ducats, silver bars, Mexican pesos by the thousands, all kinds of silver bars, circulated silver, and throwing a lot of it right into the melting pot," Hendrickson said.

The aftermarket for recent U.S. precious metals commemorative issues has also been affected, Hendrickson commented, citing as an example the steady decline of the Statue of Liberty proof $5 from well over $300 to the $250-$275 range in the last two or three months.

"People apparently just can't afford to sit on all these things; at the same time interest rates are up a little and they're giving up some of their gold and silver," Hendrickson said.

New York Times

It is hard to find an executive in the gold mining business in North America who does not believe that life right now is too good to be true.

The price-earnings ratios of gold stocks have been awesome in recent months, with some reaching as high as 70 times earnings.

"Our direct operating costs are $131 an ounce, so gold will be very profitable for us even if the price goes down to $200 to $225 an ounce, which nobody is predicting," said Reid of Silver State. "Whatever happens, I don't see the price going low enough for us to cut back."

Despite the gold market's euphorically bullish psychology, the reality is that gold sales dried up dramatically six months ago, as the next article from Numismatic News reveals. The orgy of public coin buying that the newspapers reported (see November 1986 EWT) apparently did coincide, as EWT argued, with the end of the period of dramatic price appreciation. If measures of investor sentiment were showing worry during the recent sideways trend, such news might be taken as a sign of a bottom. With "blue sky" prices widely expected, however, this news merely shows that everyone who might have wanted to buy gold has done so. The owners of those satiated gold accounts have since merely been sitting around, waiting for gold to soar and make them rich. If the situation described in this article is accurate, supply, as EWT forecast several months ago, may soon begin to overcome demand. Such conditions are generally the precursors to bitter disappointment and long bear markets.

Consider this: If gold declines by 50% in dollar value, an investor will be able to purchase twice the amount of gold with the same number of dollars when it ultimately bottoms out.

AUGUST 31, 1987

Gold's wave structure is a series of first and second waves from the peak, so is setting up for an acceleration of its decline.

Gold

The most recent two-week 4-point drop in bonds was the first in six months that was not accompanied by a rally in gold. Gold acts "heavy," and its wave count is best interpreted as a series of first and second waves to the downside. Traders should stay 100% short with a "stop" at $480 basis London fix. Investors stay out.

In case you haven't been following other inflation hedges, the price of oil this month plummeted 17½% in just three weeks. Now for a lesson in psychology. When was the decision made to begin night trading in bonds? Right at the top! That's when demand is heaviest. Now we find that night trading in gold was approved in August and the same for oil has been under discussion in recent weeks. 24-hour trading in the stock market will probably be introduced in 1988 or 1989....

OCTOBER 5, 1987

Gold is still in a topping phase, and the long term outlook is bearish. However, until a sharp break occurs, potential for one last jump into the low $500s remains.

Gold

Gold is virtually unchanged from its price a year ago, so our avoidance of it in favor of stocks has been well rewarded. Like the stock market, gold has a highly reliable long term outlook (in this case, bearish; see prior issues) but is at a crossroads on a short term basis. Our short sale is still intact, with a stop at $480 basis London fix. Until a substantial downside break confirms the bearish interpretation, it is acceptable to count the sideways action from May as a corrective pattern, which includes a triangle. If a rally occurs from the end of the triangle, it will carry into the low $500s, finishing off the entire advance from February 1985 and completing wave X, whose original target from 1982 was $540. The chart shown in the July issue is reproduced here, and nothing has changed.

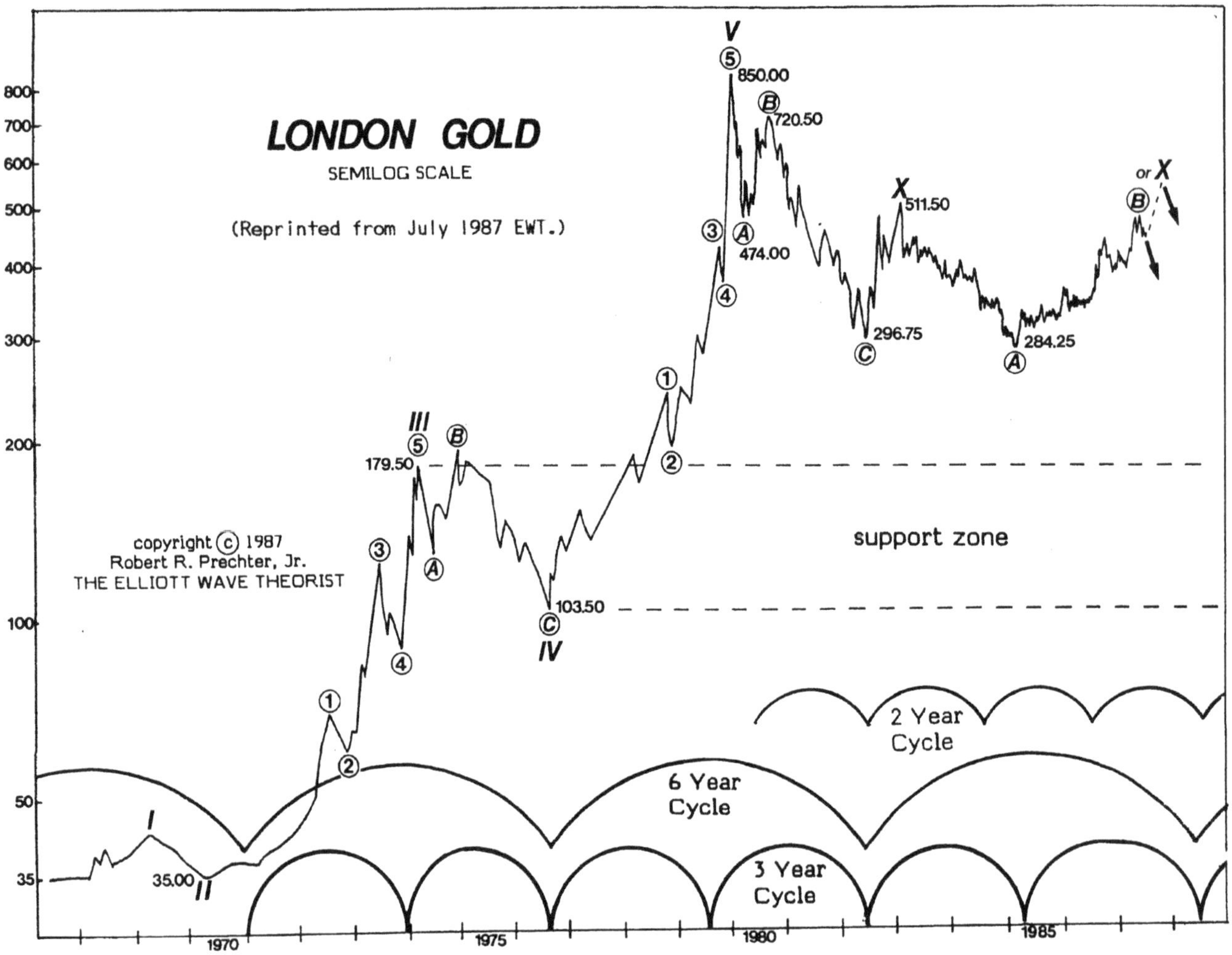

OCTOBER 22, 1987 – INTERIM REPORT

Followers of the letter also had some misfortune this month, as the price of gold took out our stop basis the London fix by less than $2 before promptly falling back into its trading range. The larger picture for that metal is still very bearish. In terms of wave pattern, a "post triangle thrust" (see text, p.44) has occurred, and the hourly chart shows five waves down and a partial rally back today, a bearish combination. For the first time, not only traders but also longer term investors, if so inclined, should move designated funds to 100% short gold. If the London price fixes above $482, cut back to 50% short, then move to 100% short at $540 with a stop on the entire position at $570.

NOVEMBER 2, 1987

Gold is completing a top formation and is vulnerable to a persistent decline into 1988.

Gold and Silver

Cycles are strongly down into mid-1988. Momentum is giving "sell" signals. Investor psychology has been too bullish for a year. Bullion remains expensive relative to commodities. Supply is increasing as the mines expand production. Gold stocks have finally crashed from their terrifically overvalued levels, and platinum and silver are weakening. Six weeks ago, an observant subscriber sent this note: "Each month for the past year, my bank has sent me a flyer for 'tax free' bonds, government bonds, 'high yield' bonds, etc. with my bank statement. This month I received information about a gold fund instead. Somewhere around here is a top." The gold market appears to be where the bond market was in early March and where the stock market was in mid-August. Stay short gold per the strategy in the October 22 Interim Report.

NOVEMBER 30, 1987

Gold is in a long term topping formation, but its short term outlook allows for further rally.

Gold

It is frustrating that gold is the only precious metal that held up in the past few months. Since April 27, when EWT recommended shorting the spike rally, silver futures have collapsed from $11.25 to $6.25. A similar move in gold would have it trading a month ago at $268! Gold stocks (see chart) also fell 40%, and the metal bugs' favorite, platinum, has been persistently weak. These drops have occurred despite both the decline in the dollar and the stock market crash. Nevertheless, gold has merely gone sideways.

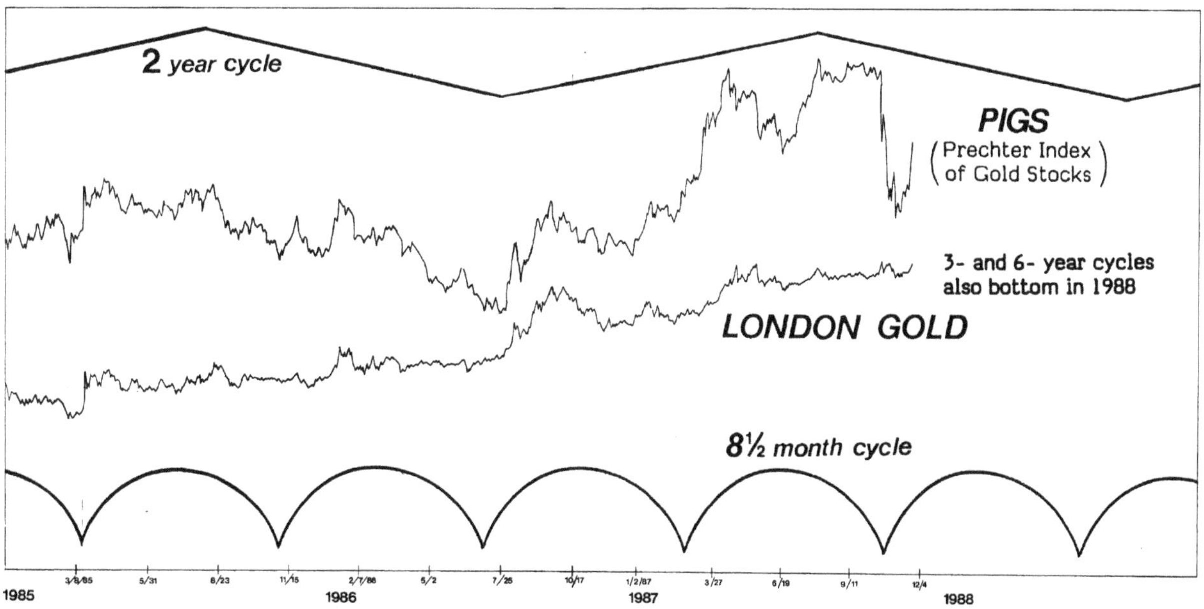

If gold manages another new high, it will be unconfirmed by gold stocks and by every other precious metal, providing another long term technical negative. Such a negative would come at a time when the last 8½-month cycle in the 2-, 3- and 6-year cycle complex is peaking. A reasonable analogy would be the 16-week cycle low in stocks that occurred on August 19, just before the last high preceding the change from bull market to bear. The accompanying chart shows an update of the 2-year and 8½-month cycles. Notice how precipitously gold stocks fell when the 8½-month cycle entered its final down phase in October. The sharpness of the drop is due to the fact that the 2-year cycle has rolled over and is now adding its influence to the downside. For this reason, the current 8½-month cycle rally should peak early in what cycle analysts call "left-hand translation." Since gold held up during the down phase, it will have an opportunity to jump to a significant new high in the up phase. However, its severe overvaluation may ultimately result in a "better late than never" collapse when the 8½-month cycle rolls over into the lows for the 2- and 6-year cycles. A final low in precious metals is still due in the second or third quarter of 1988, so plan your purchases for that time period.

The long term wave count is still as shown in the October issue. Continue to use the recent trading strategy of covering 50% on a London fix above $482 and moving back to 100% short on a fix above $540, with a stop at $570. If stopped on any portion, traders should move back to 100% short on a break of $455 basis the nearby futures contract. That level would indicate a break of the intermediate-term trendline dating from June 1986.

The time is rapidly approaching for another in-depth discussion of the long term wave structures in both gold and silver. Stay tuned.

Wave Goodbye to Gold?

Why a Technician Is Bearish on the Metal

By ROBERT PRECHTER

IN April 1987, anyone looking for evidence of a top in the metals had to be excited. Gold had already hit one peak in September 1986 at a London price of $443 an ounce and, after dropping to $380, was lunging again for the highs. Silver was finally enjoying a frenzied surge, the type that often accompanies the peak of a buying spree in the precious metals. Normally conservative "value" buyers had been talking about price earnings multiples of up to 200 on the gold stocks, which were already selling at unhealthy ratios of 70:1. Overall, technical readings for the metals were continuing to worsen and, on April 24, the short-term indicators argued urgently that a top was hours away.

On Monday morning, April 27, the metals opened on the upside in panicked trading, with gold reaching $477. At the same time, I found out later, a friend of mine who had been waiting a long time to sell his physical silver called his bullion firm to get a quote. "You can get $10.75 for it," he was told, as the price of the nearby silver futures contract was exploding, ultimately hitting $11.25 an ounce.

As my friend was rushing to his dealer's with the bullion in his car's trunk, however, the trend suddenly reversed. Selling poured into the market, driving prices down. Twenty minutes later, silver futures had collapsed to $7.20, off an amazing 36% from the morning's peak.

My friend's coin dealer honored the morning quote, so my friend was happy. Temporarily, so was I, because I had "known better" than to buy gold that morning with the crowd; I was calling for a top. But something funny happened on the way to the bank. While silver fell 44% (see Figure 3), platinum slid 27%, and gold stocks—after holding up until October—finally plunged 40%; my main object of focus, gold bullion, held stubbornly in the upper $400s-low $500s, where it remains to this day.

Many people have taken gold's ability to continue rising, albeit slowly, as a sign of strength. That it is. But is it a sign of *technical* strength? Does the market's condition imply a significant further rise, and should we embrace the increasingly popular conclusion that gold is in a new bull market or on its way to $850, $2,000 or even $6,000 an ounce?

For eight years, my analysis has argued that gold's January

Figure 1

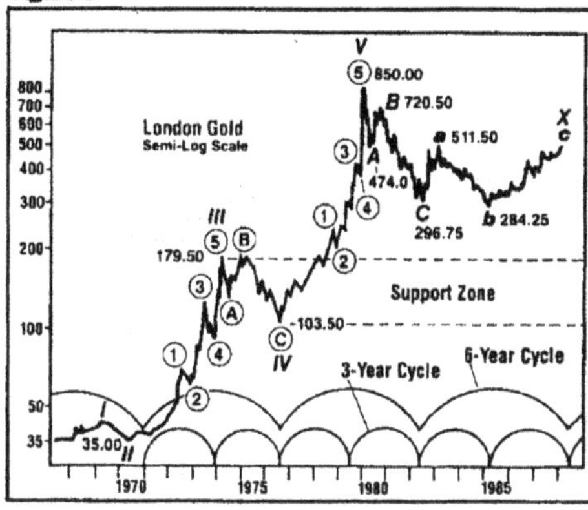

Figure 2

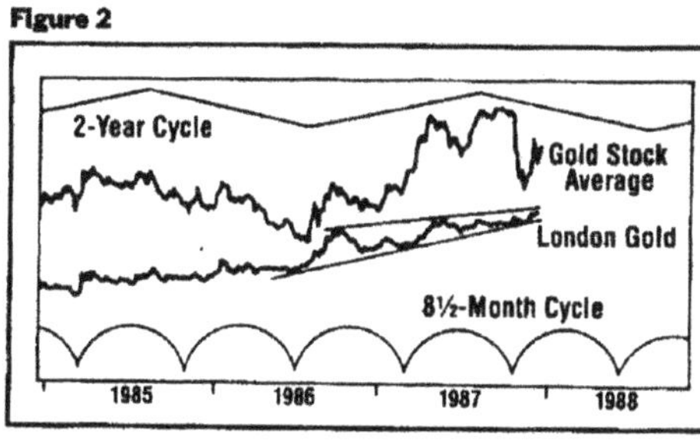

1980 price of $850 marked a bull market peak of great significance, and that a major bear market was in force. Within that bear market, three powerful intermediate-term rallies have occurred, one in 1980, one in 1982-83, and the current one dating from 1985. The first two were sharp and relatively easy to call. The latest one began earlier and has lasted longer than time cycles would have suggested. However, longevity per se is not an argument for a trend's continuation. Often, it is precisely time that lulls investors to sleep, providing assurance that the trend in force will continue. Recall, for instance, that the bond market (which had provided such bullish technical readings in the summer of 1984) flashed terrible warning signals in early 1986. Nevertheless, it took 10 months, from April 1986 to February 1987 (with the Dow Jones 20 Bond Average hitting a new high), for bonds to complete their top formation. The technical piper was finally paid with a 25% wipeout in eight months.

Sometimes during a mostly sideways trend, the technical condition of a market will improve rather than deteriorate. For instance, when the stock market traveled net sideways from February to September 1985, the price pattern and psychological state of the market improved to their most bullish conditions since the 1982 low, and combined to indicate an explosive rise ahead. However, as gold has struggled to move 15% higher in the past 15 months, its technical condition has remained long-term bearish. In fact, I view gold today as in a position similar to that of bonds in early 1987. Let's look at some of the factors.

• **Elliott Wave Pattern.** R.N. Elliott observed that bear markets tend to bring prices back to wave four of the preceding five-wave advance of the

Figure 3

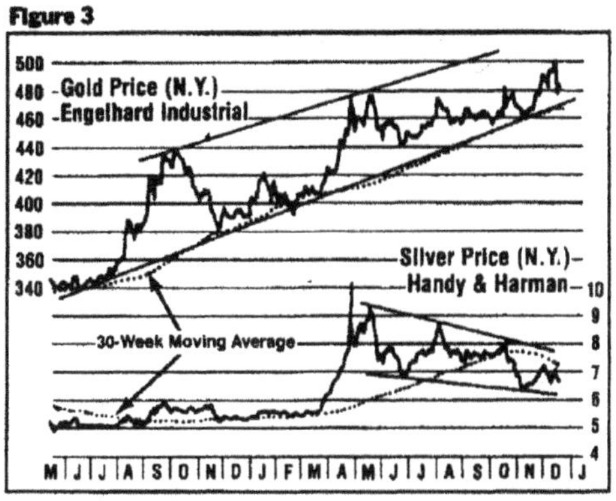

same degree, or relative size. Figure 1 shows that wave IV covered a price range of $100-$200 an ounce. Until the price pattern on the upside forces a change of opinion, that area remains the most reasonable ultimate downside target for bullion's price before the long-term bear market breathes its last. Within the bear market, the initial declining phase took an A-B-C shape. The action since then is best labeled an X wave—one that separates two A-B-C patterns. The second rally within that pattern is ending in the shape of a *wedge* (see Figures 2 and 3), which usually carries bearish implications. Thus, the countertrend rally dating from 1985 appears nearly over, and another major phase of decline, taking the A-B-C shape, should begin fairly soon.

• **Time Cycles.** The two-, three- and six-year cycles are due to bottom later in 1988 (see Figures 1 and 2). Silver, platinum and gold stocks already have succumbed to their downside pressure. The 8½-month cycle, which last bottomed in early November and shows up most clearly in the gold stock average, would be expected to create an *early* peak in gold stock and bullion prices since the larger cycles are pulling down hard at the current time. Thus, beginning in early 1988, virtually all cyclic pressure will be downward, at least into summer.

• **Momentum and Breadth.** Gold bullion was the *only* component of the precious metals complex that made a new high recently. Figure 3 illustrates how silver, in a well-established decline since April, merely built a series of lower "shelves" as gold was touching each of its new highs. Platinum did the same. Gold *stocks* (Figure 2), for the second time since April 27, failed to confirm the new high in bullion, but this time by a *significantly wider margin.* In addition, gold's rate of ascent from 1985 (Figure 1) is *slower* than it was in either the 1980 or the 1982-83 advances. Furthermore, its rate of ascent *within* this rise has been slowing ever since it first hit $440 an ounce in September 1986. All these signs don't guarantee a top, but they are typical of one.

• **Investor Psychology.** The overwhelming desire to own precious metals, which existed at the various peaks over the

Figure 4

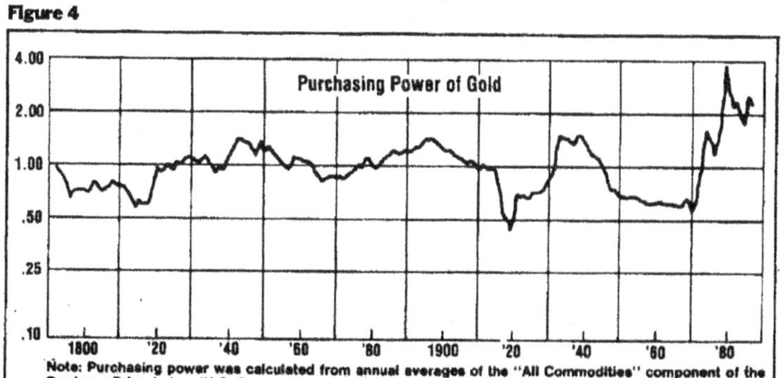

Note: Purchasing power was calculated from annual averages of the "All Commodities" component of the Producer Price Index (U.S. Department of Labor) or its predecessor, the Wholesale Price Index, and the annual averages of the dollar price of gold. Updated through Dec. 31, 1987.

Robert Prechter publishes The Elliott Wave Theorist *in Gainesville, Ga.*

past 15 months, has subsided. Nevertheless, the strings of weeks revealing 75%-85%-95% "bulls" in The Bullish Consensus' poll of precious metals advisers have a long-term negative implication that has yet to be realized. Until psychology turns clearly bearish, indicating an important bottom, that negative implication remains.

• **The Dollar.** Remember the change of perspective that occurred in the stock market last August-September? The majority had been skeptical of the bullish outlook through the first seven months of the year. Then, it suddenly became fashionable to argue not *whether* the Dow would hit 3000, but *when.* The focus on the dollar now is not *when* it will bottom, but *whether it ever will.* That psychology is appearing at the same time as a slowdown in upside momentum for the foreign currencies and an Elliott Wave count indicating that the end of the dollar's 2½ years of weakness is very near. If the dollar finds a major bottom in coming weeks (as our Elliott Wave Commodity Forecast projects), gold's price in dollar terms will be adversely affected.

• **Valuation.** According to a 200-year study by the American Institute for Economic Research (Chart 4), the value of gold today is extremely high relative to that of a basket of commodities. This relationship can be rationalized, but the fact remains that gold is about the most expensive of all basic things. Merely to return gold to the center of its historical range would require a drop of 50% relative to commodity prices (or a doubling of commodity prices while gold holds steady).

• **Supply/Demand.** Gold exploration has increased dramatically in recent years. This activity, first, confirms that gold is expensive. Otherwise, why would mining operations so proliferate? Secondly, if these mining operations are successful, the supply side of the gold equation will exert a negative influence on the price.

To conclude, the technical condition of the gold market continues to indicate too much danger to justify a substantial investment. Long-term investors may find their money better spent in purchasing gold at lower prices later. On the short term, the "X" wave pattern of recovery, dating from 1982, is nearing completion. Normally, the second rally (the "c" wave) in such a pattern will register a high *above* that of the first, which in this case would suggest a London fix above $511.50 at the peak. If the top occurs below that level, it will merely reflect even greater weakness in the pattern. More important, the advance is living on borrowed time. When a market holds up for a long period into declining cycles, the ensuing drop is often dramatic. Even with a dramatic drop, however, the ultimate Elliott Wave price target is so much lower than current levels that it's doubtful that the next six-year cycle low will mark the end of the bear market. It will certainly be followed by another significant rally (perhaps wave B of the second A-B-C pattern), however, so some purchases may be justified then, depending upon the condition of the price structure and technical indicators at that time.

One goal of market analysis is to make money. The more important goal is to recognize investment situations bearing a high degree of danger, so that disasters can be avoided. An analysis of bonds last March revealed high risk. An analysis of stocks in early October revealed high risk. And an analysis of gold today reveals the same thing. ■

The Elliott Wave Theorist, 1988

JANUARY 4, 1988

Gold continues to build its long term top. The peak should be registered (if it hasn't been already) in the $500-550 range basis London fix, to be followed by a sharp decline.

Gold

Many people have taken gold's ability to continue rising slowly as a sign of strength. That, it is. But is it a sign of *technical* strength? I.e., does this action imply significant further rise in the future, and should we embrace the increasingly popular conclusion that gold is in a "new bull market" or "on its way" to $850, $2000 or $6000/oz.?

For eight years (interrupted by a brief return to a bullish opinion in August 1981 at $388), EWT has argued that the January 1980 peak at $850 marked a multi-year top and that a major bear market was in force. Within that bear market, three powerful intermediate-term rallies have occurred, one in 1980, one in 1982-83 and the recent one dating from 1985. The first two were sharp and relatively easy to "call." The latest one began earlier, and has lasted longer, than expected. However, longevity per se is not an argument for the continuation of a trend. Often it is precisely time that lulls the investor to sleep, apparently providing assurance that the trend in force will continue. Recall, for instance, that the bond market, which had been so powerfully bullish in the summer of 1984, flashed terrible warning signals in early 1986. Still, it took ten long months, from April 1986 to February 1987 (with the Dow Jones 20 Bond Index hitting a new high), for bonds to top out. Nevertheless, the technical piper was finally paid with a 25% wipeout in eight months.

Sometimes during a mostly sideways trend, the technical condition of a market will improve rather than deteriorate. For instance, when the stock market traveled net sideways from February to September 1985, the price pattern and psychological state of the market improved to their most bullish conditions since the 1982 low and combined to indicate an explosive rise ahead. However, as gold has struggled to climb 15% higher over the past fifteen months, its technical condition has remained long term bearish.

R.N. Elliott observed that bear markets tend to bring prices back to the "previous fourth wave of one lesser degree." As you can see in the long term chart, wave IV covered price territory between $100 and $200 per ounce. Until the price pattern on the upside forces a change of opinion, that area remains the most reasonable ultimate downside target area for the dollar price of gold bullion before the long term bear market breathes its last.

Within the bear market, the initial declining phase took an A-B-C shape. The action since then is best labeled all or part of an "X" wave, a structure that separates two A-B-Cs, the second of which could begin at any time. Normally, the current rally would be expected to register a high above that of the 1982-83 rise, i.e., above $511.50. It is unlikely to be much higher than $547, the original target calculated during wave Ⓐ of X in 1982-83. If the top occurs below $511.50, it will merely reflect even greater weakness in the pattern.

The 8½-month and 2-year cycles point down until later in 1988, as illustrated on the chart in the December issue. Gold stocks, silver and platinum have already succumbed to their downside pressure. Gold bullion should do so, whether it lunges to one more new high or not. It is worth remembering that when a market holds up a long time into declining cycles, the ensuing drop is often dramatic, as if to get prices back to where they "should have been in the first place." Nevertheless, it is doubtful that the next 6-year cycle low will mark the end of the bear market, although it will certainly generate another significant rally.

As the December issue indicated, "If gold manages another new high, it will be unconfirmed by gold stocks and by every other precious metal, providing another long term technical negative." As it happened, gold bullion was the only component of the precious metals complex that managed to make a new high, on December 14. Gold stocks (see chart, December issue) failed to confirm the new high in bullion by a wide margin. Silver (see chart in this issue) and platinum have built a series of lower "shelves" since April 27 while gold struggled to each of its new highs.

Gold's rate of ascent from 1985 is slower than it was in either the 1980 or the 1982-83 advances, much as the June-August rise in stocks last year was slower than the January-April rise. Furthermore, its rate of ascent within this rise has been slowing ever since it first hit $440/oz. in September 1986. All these are signs of a market that is topping.

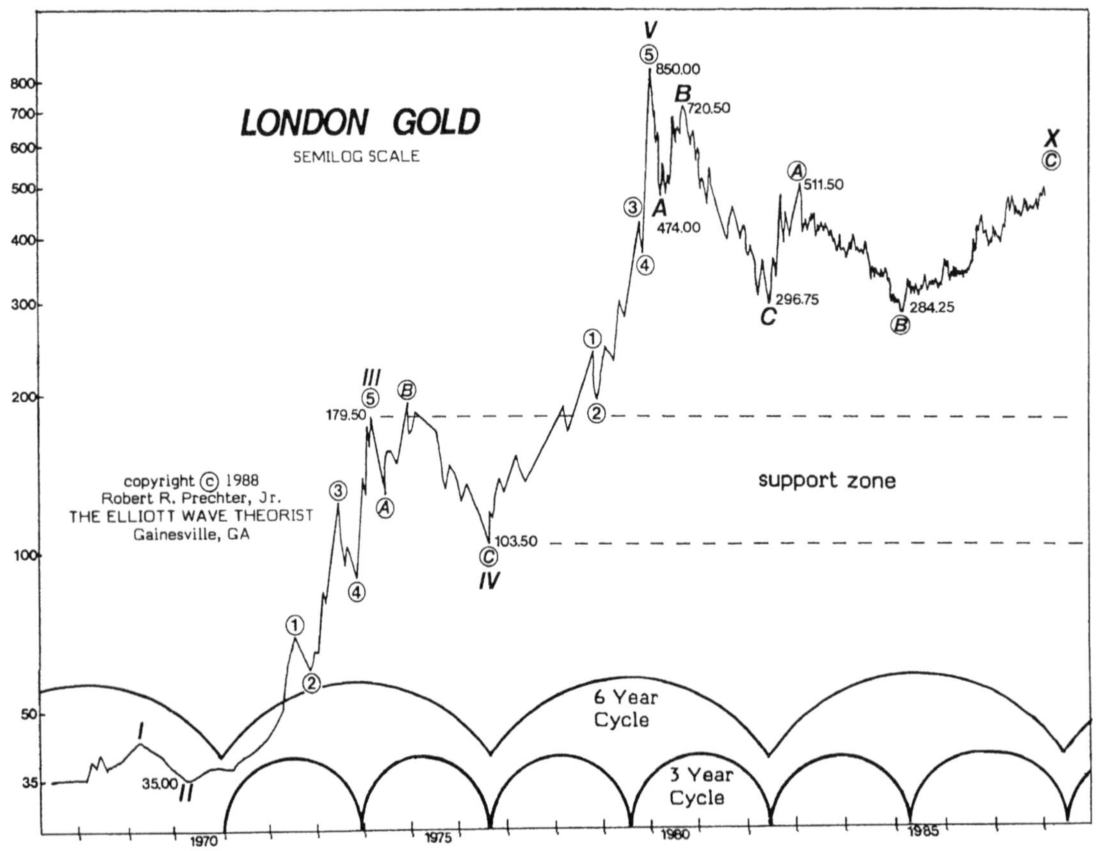

The overwhelming desire to own precious metals that existed at various peaks over the past fifteen months has subsided. Nevertheless, the strings of weeks revealing 75%-85%-95% "bulls" last year in The Bullish Consensus poll of precious metals advisors have a long term negative implication that has yet to be realized. Until psychology clearly turns bearish, indicating an important bottom, that negative implication remains.

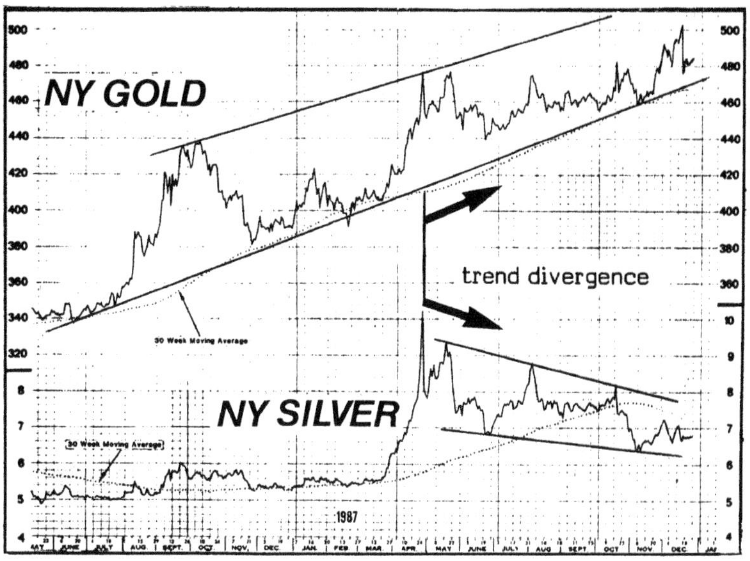

The next chart, last shown in EWT a year ago, has been updated through 1987. According to this 200-year study by the American Institute for Economic Research (Great Barrington, MA), the value of gold today remains extremely high relative to that of a basket of commodities. This relationship can be rationalized, but the fact remains that of all basic "things," gold is about the most expensive. Merely to return gold to the center of its historical range would require a drop of 50% relative to commodity prices (or a double in commodity prices while gold held steady).

To conclude, the technical condition of the gold market continues to indicate too much danger to justify investment. Long term investors may find their money better spent in purchasing gold at lower prices later.

One goal of market analysis is to make money. A more important goal is to recognize investment situations that contain a high degree of danger, so that disasters can be avoided.

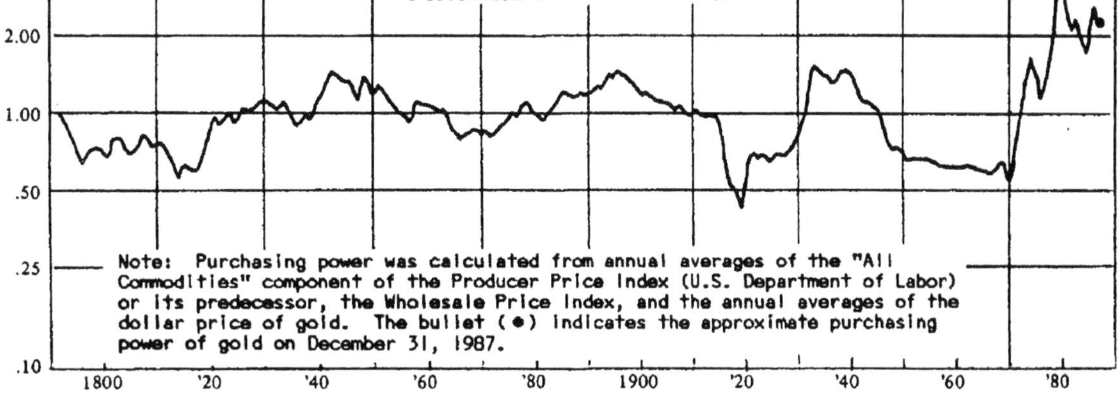

An analysis of bonds last March revealed high risk. An analysis of stocks in early October revealed high risk. An analysis of gold today, in my opinion, continues to reveal that it is in the "high risk" category among available investments. Investors should remain out of the gold market. Traders and investors so inclined are already 50% short, with plans to move to 100% short on a London fix above $540, with a "stop" at $570. If $540 is not achieved, traders will move to 100% short on a break of $455 basis the nearby futures contract.

FEBRUARY 1, 1988

Gold has cracked its long term uptrend line, virtually confirming a top. Short term, the 5- and 8-week cycles may provide a rally back to the breakdown point, but the larger trends are down.

Gold

To the technical warning signs of the past ten months (during which time gold stocks, silver and platinum have fallen significantly) we can now add a price breakdown in gold bullion, complete with a gap, which has brought gold below its six month price shelf at $465 and below its uptrend line dating from mid-1986 (see chart). With two short term cycles due to bottom this week, gold may attempt a rebound, particularly since markets often return briefly to a "breakdown" point before resuming a decline. However, with waves, cycles, sentiment, momentum, valuation and supply-demand factors all bearish on the intermediate and long term trends, and with the dollar having staged what appears to be a major reversal (see EWCF), this is no time to change our strategy. Investors should stay out of the gold market, and traders should hold 100% short.

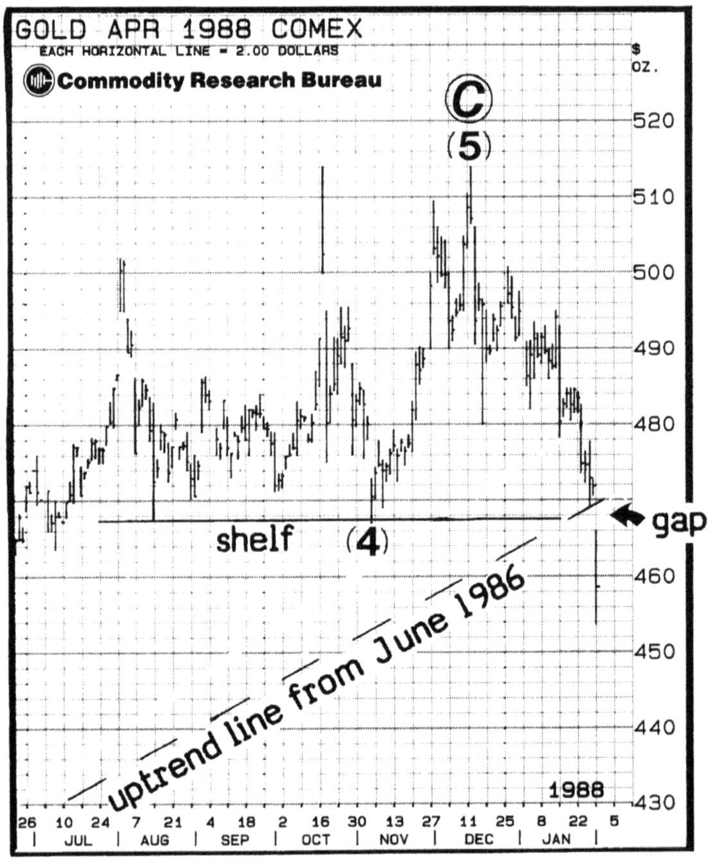

On the long term picture (see chart, January issue), wave Ⓒ of X has probably ended. A break below $425 basis the nearby futures contract will confirm it. That wave Ⓒ could not register a peak above that of February 1983 is either a very bearish failure or an argument in favor of the case that wave X will be a triangle, per the alternate count in Figure 4 of the March 1987 Special Report. The advance from February 1985 may be counted as a triple zigzag (see text, p.37), given the many phases of that uptrend that can be classified as triangles (see past three years' issues). Even in that case, gold needs to fall another $100/oz. to complete wave Ⓓ. I will update the long term wave status in an upcoming issue.

FEBRUARY 29, 1988

Gold is nearing the completion of a five-wave decline in wave (1) from the December peak. Any countertrend bounce should find resistance in the $450-$470 range basis the nearby futures contract. The next significant move will be an acceleration of the decline in wave (3).

Gold

As you can see from the chart, the wave structure in gold from the December high is a textbook example of a developing five wave structure. Wave 3, which is ending now, was the extended wave. Within it, wave iii was extended, as is typical. Wave ii was a zigzag (see text, p.36), while wave iv was an irregular flat (see text, p.39), satisfying alternation (see text, p.50). Within wave iii, the breakdown gap occurred precisely at the "third wave of the third wave" (see text, p.67), the exact center of the structure. Wave 3 channels beautifully between two parallel lines (see text, p.59). Wave v is to date equal to the length of wave i, a typical occurrence satisfying Elliott's "rule of equality" (see text, p.57). Finally, the entire five wave structure is occurring within a larger channel, as you can see by the dashed lines on the chart.

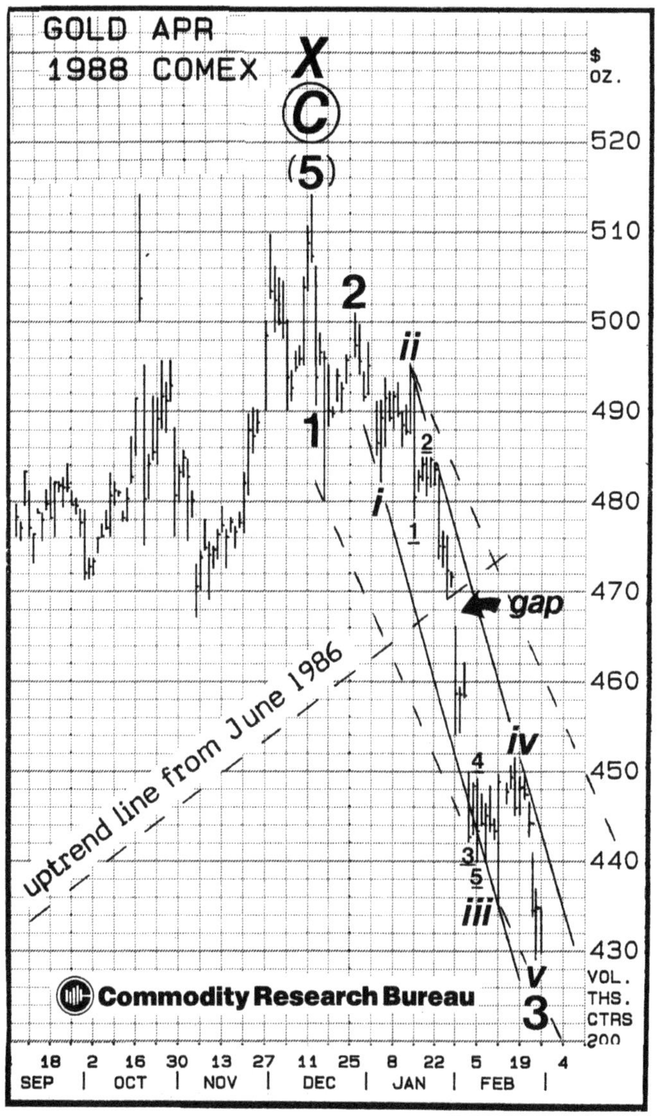

The peak of wave Ⓒ of X will not be confirmed until five waves down are complete. So far, only three waves have occurred, so an alternate count of a-b-c down is acceptable, though clearly an alternate.

In support of the case that the major trend is still down is a report from The Bullish Consensus showing that the percentage of advisors bullish on gold last week was 43%, indicating a complacency which is usually absent at a major low. The fact that the minor cycle lows of early February were able to generate only a feeble three-week consolidation is also bearish. On the near term, bullish momentum divergences are occurring, and the 10-day average of the put/call ratio on gold futures has hit its highest level since early July 1986. A wave (2) rally should take care of this sudden willingness among traders to bet on the downside. Regardless of the short term possibilities, however, it is well to keep in mind that all time cycles of 8½ months and longer point down into the third quarter of the year.

If wave 4 causes a rebound back to "the previous fourth wave" (see text, p.55) at $451 and if wave 5 equals or is 1.618 times the length of wave 1 in typical fashion, the larger wave (1) should bottom in the $410-430 range basis the April futures contract. Traders are 100% short. Cover half the position below $416 and move back to 100% short at $449 with a stop at $490. I neglected to mention last month that investors [so inclined] were holding 50% short from strategy given in the October 22 Interim Report and reiterated in the January issue. Hold 50% short and move to 100% short at $449 with a stop at $490.

The last collapse in gold stocks occurred, with some delay, along with the collapse in the general stock market last October. Since the outlook for the stock market is still bearish, gold stocks, which have been drifting back toward their October lows, still carry a substantial risk.

MARCH 28, 1988

Gold has rallied right back to the resistance area targeted in the March issue. The next move should be down.

Gold

The March issue provided this assessment:

> Gold is nearing the completion of a five-wave decline from the December peak. On the near term, bullish momentum divergences are occurring, and the 10-day average of the put/call ratio on gold futures has hit its highest level since early July 1986. A wave (2) rally should take care of this sudden willingness among traders to bet on the downside. ...Any countertrend bounce should find resistance in the $450-$470 range.

A short term rally began the day that issue was mailed and has now brought London gold to $453.95, an exact Fibonacci .382 retracement of the December-February decline (futures came within \$2). The put/call ratio has retreated rapidly back to neutral/bearish, and the oversold condition has been relieved. As a reflection of long term sentiment, it may prove significant that in late 1987, three major gold funds were designed and developed, and plans were made to extend gold futures trading to nighttime sessions (due to begin soon).

The wave count from the March issue has been amended slightly, as you can see by the chart. Note that the Elliott channel, when drawn from the exact Minor wave turning points (see text, p.62), is virtually perfect, with the "third of a third" gap occurring as the price action re-entered that channel.

Traders are still 100% short, and investors moved from 50% to 100% short on the rally to \$449 basis the April contract. Hold short and keep the stop at \$490 basis London fix.

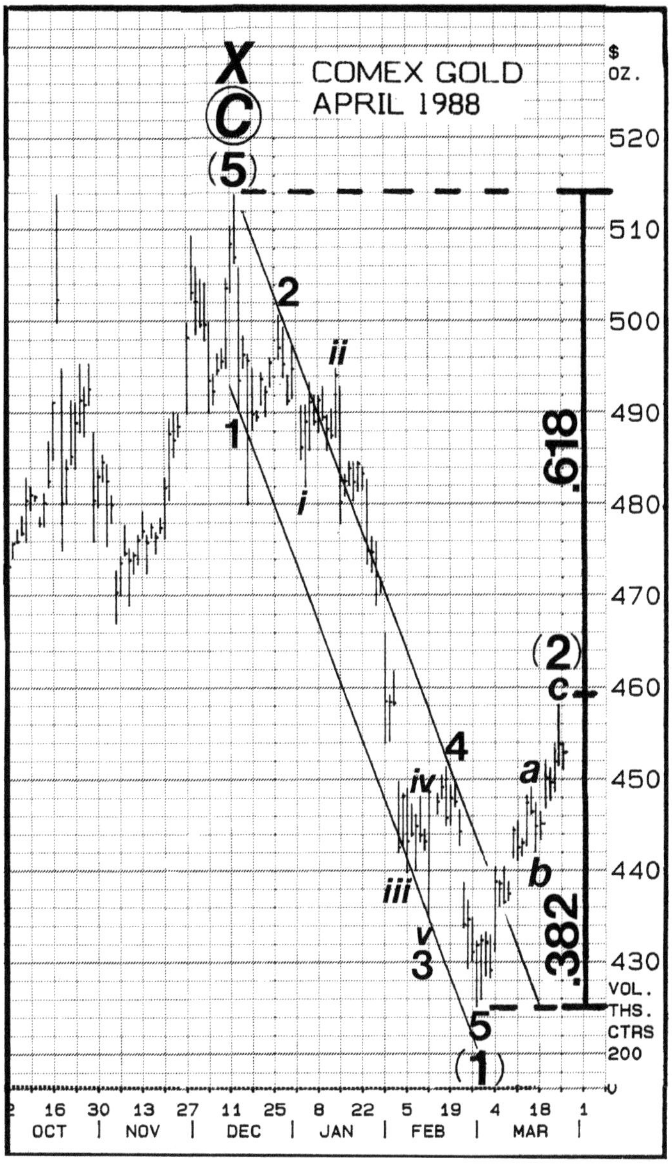

MAY 2, 1988

Gold is on the verge of another sharply declining wave of Intermediate degree.

Gold

Despite all the sound and fury of the past two months, gold has been repelled exactly at the .382 retracement level of the December-February decline. The March issue, published the day of the bottom, recognized the end of a five-wave decline [of Minor degree; it turned out to be the wave (1) low at Intermediate degree] and projected "a wave (2) rally" to the "\$450-\$470 range" basis the April contract (equal to \$455-\$475 basis June), which has marked upside resistance ever since.

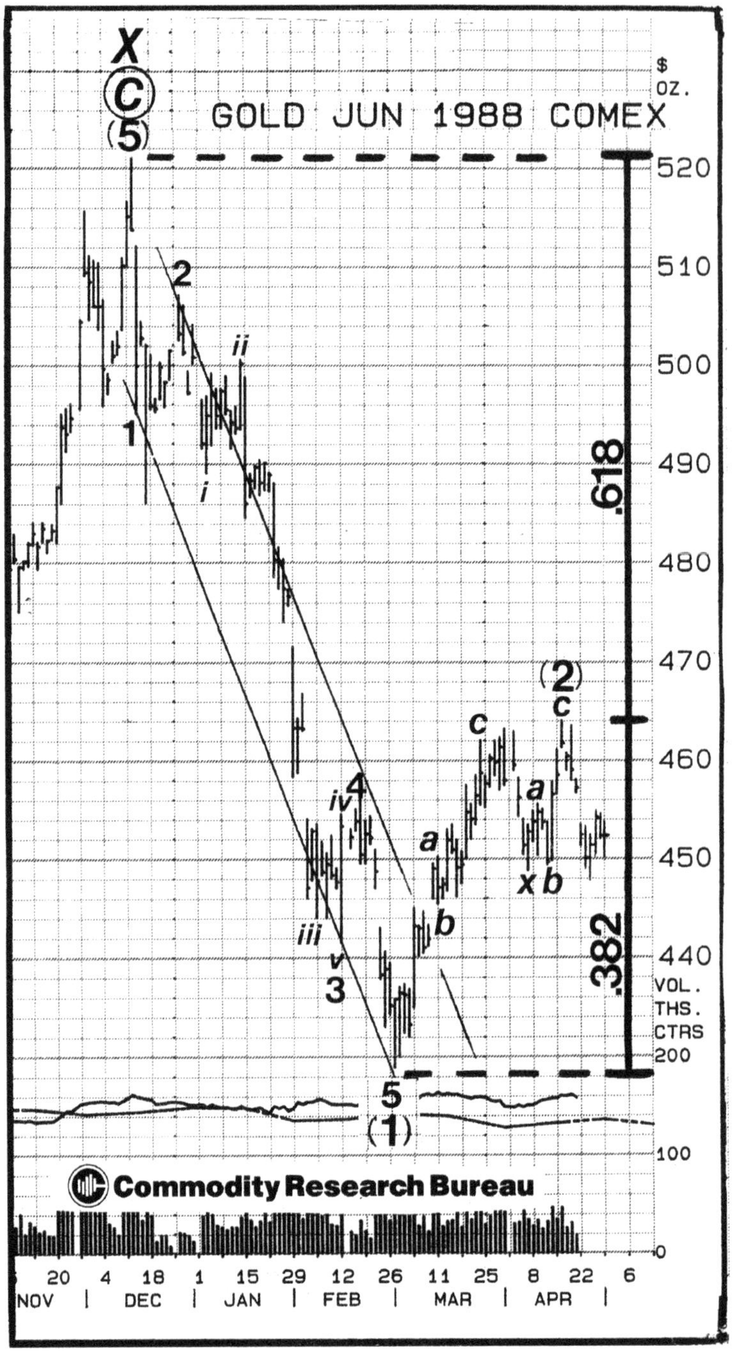

The London fix peaked on March 30, while futures prices peaked on April 18, setting up a non-confirmation at that second high against "cash" gold and all the other precious metals, which were below their prior peaks. Furthermore, the gold price has now held up long enough that the 10-day put/call ratio is at its lowest level since the major top in December. All of this is going on while the U.S. is skirmishing in the Persian Gulf, a situation that hasn't exactly caused a runaway move in gold on the upside as would have occurred if the market were bullish.

Second waves are followed by third waves, and third waves usually contain the most dramatic action, so be prepared for a drop in the gold price that makes headlines. All participants should hold 100% short with a stop at $490 basis London fix. If the London price fixes below $420, lower the stop to $460.

Silver's long term bear market is still in force as well, and its price is ultimately likely to go much lower than anyone currently expects. In the meantime, the most conservative target for 1988 is near $5/oz. Gold stocks, despite their drops from last year's highs, are still overvalued, and a drop in gold will surely impact their prices.

JUNE 6, 1988

Gold and silver are staging final rallies in their six-year partial recovery patterns.

Gold & Silver

Last week, on its fourth attempt, gold moved above the .382 retracement level of the December-February decline. A .618 retracement would be met at $472 basis London fix, so our stop can be lowered to $480 basis London fix.

The long term picture will be resolved either by a move above $511.50 or below $423. As long time readers will recall, the big picture on gold is best interpreted as an Ⓐ-Ⓑ-Ⓒ rally from June 1982, the entire pattern being wave X within an ongoing bear market from the 1980 all-time high of $850/oz. With the technical indicators so bearish last December, wave X seemed best interpreted as a developing contracting triangle (see text, p.43), by which wave Ⓒ would have been peaking. If, on the other hand, wave Ⓒ is to complete a simple Ⓐ-Ⓑ-Ⓒ flat correction (see text, p.38), as explained in the January issue, it would be expected to top above wave Ⓐ, which peaked at $511.50 in February 1983. Throughout 1988 so far, that possibility has remained open. If wave Ⓒ is still in force, its upside target calculated six years ago when the countertrend phase began is still $547 basis London fix.

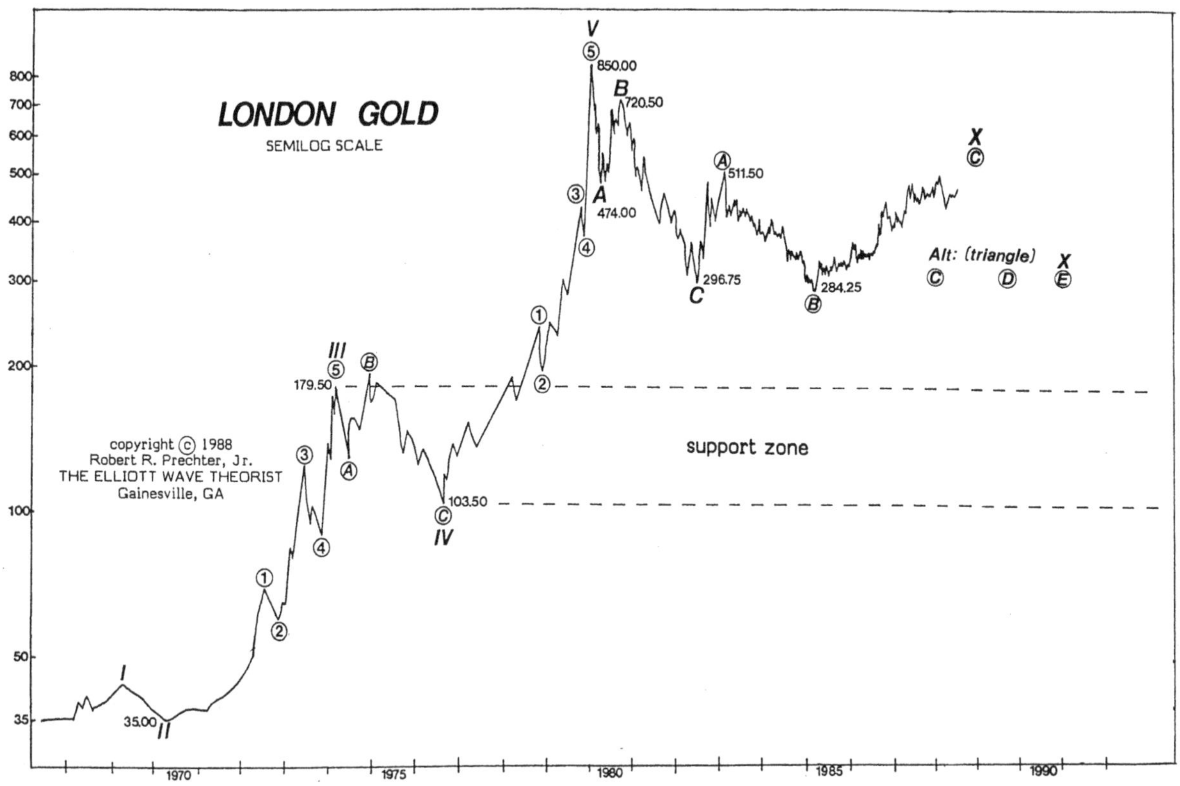

Meanwhile, silver is tracing out a most interesting long term structure (see chart). EWT's last look at the major trend patterns in silver appeared a year ago in the June 1987 issue,

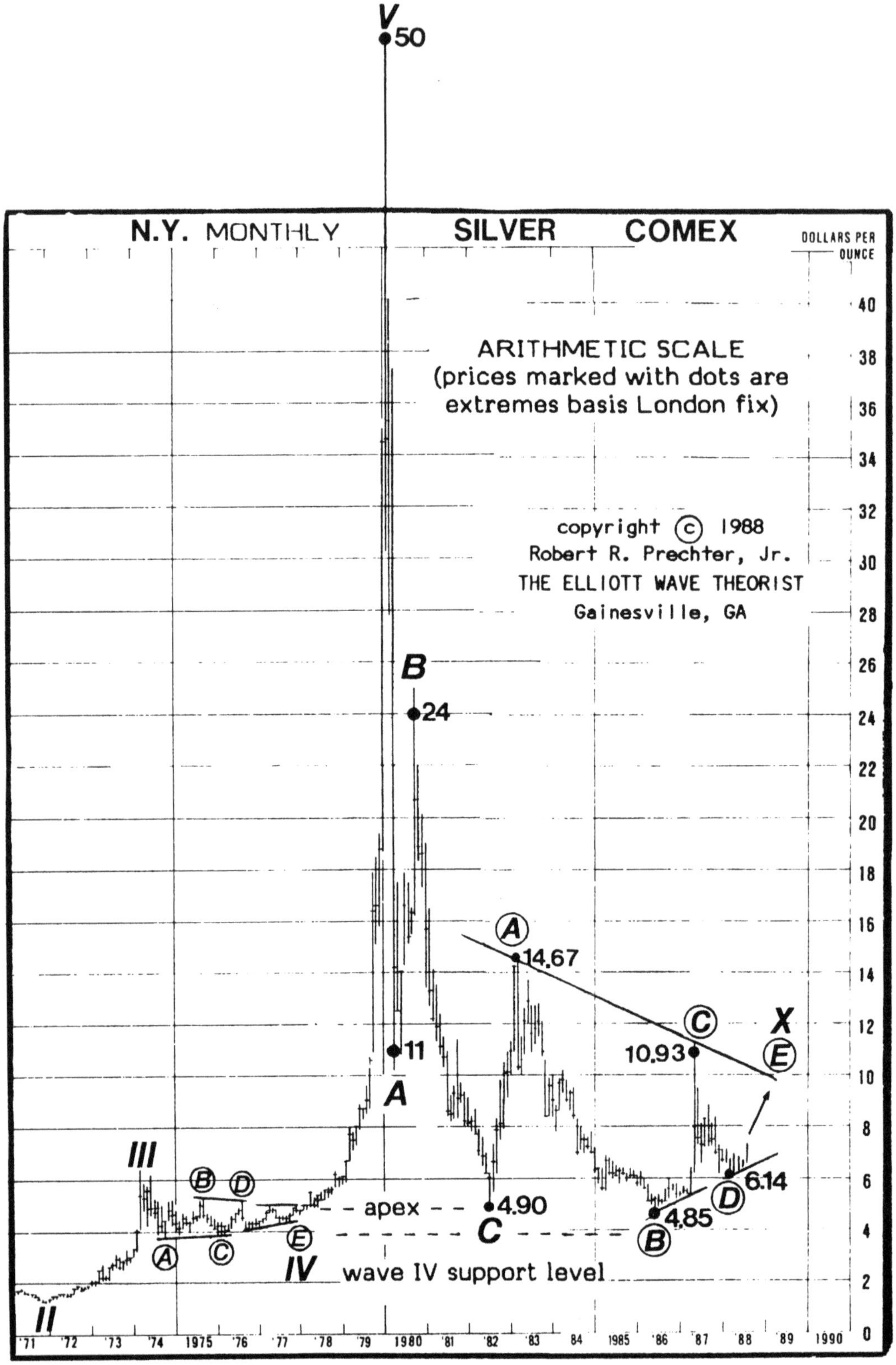
N.Y. MONTHLY
SILVER
COMEX
DOLLARS PER OUNCE
ARITHMETIC SCALE
(prices marked with dots are extremes basis London fix)
copyright © 1988
Robert R. Prechter, Jr.
THE ELLIOTT WAVE THEORIST
Gainesville, GA
V
50
B
24
11
A
Ⓐ
14.67
Ⓒ
10.93
X
Ⓔ
III
Ⓑ
Ⓓ
Ⓐ
Ⓒ
Ⓔ
apex
4.90
C
4.85
Ⓑ
Ⓓ
6.14
IV
wave IV support level
II
'71 '72 '73 '74 1975 '76 '77 '78 '79 1980 '81 '82 '83 84 1985 '86 '87 '88 '89 1990
0 2 4 6 8 10 12 14 16 18 20 22 24 26 28 30 32 34 36 38 40

showing the position of the peak at $10.93 (basis London fix) in the overall picture. It is likely that all developments since June 1982 have been part of the same wave, a contracting triangle. If so, then silver is now in wave Ⓔ of that triangle. The entire triangle will be labeled "X", denoting a completed countertrend recovery phase dating from 1982. This triangle, as is the case with gold's Ⓐ-Ⓑ-Ⓒ pattern, will be followed by another 1980-1982 style A-B-C pattern to the downside. This interpretation argues that both metals have been in a "bear market rally" since 1982, and that it is near an end. It was still right to sell silver at the prior peaks, since the subsequent highs have been lower. Gold, however, can still manage another price high as its multi-year recovery phase terminates.

According to the financial press, the "fear of inflation" has returned. Examine the price rises into 1980 and you'll understand why the fear of inflation runs so deep and why, as a result, inflation has been curtailed at successively lower levels since then. This latest psychology is normal for an "E" wave, when the last buyers step forward to invest. It is not, however, normal for a 6-year cycle bottom, which has been scheduled for mid-1988. Therefore, if gold registers a new high in coming months, the influence of that cycle will have to be reconsidered.

If stopped out of short positions, all participants should return to 50% short above $511.50 or below $445, and 100% short above $540, with a stop at $560, all figures basis London fix.

JULY 5, 1988

Gold's technical condition is extremely bearish, implying a collapse well below $400/oz.

Gold

The June issue explored both the bullish and bearish possibilities for gold, showing that even EWT had second thoughts at the wave (2) high. Nevertheless, our analysis forced us to stay short. Gold's single zigzag merely turned into a double zigzag, labeled a-b-c-x-a-b-c (see chart, and text, p.37), creating a false breakout that promptly led to a swift drop back toward the lows for the year. If London gold falls below $420, lower the stop from $480 to $460 basis London fix.

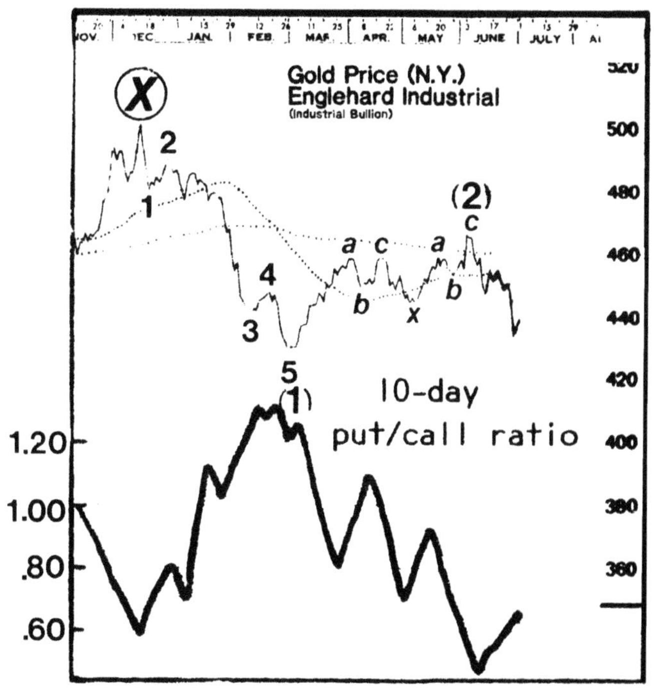

Testifying to the power of the bullish psychology toward gold is this chart of the 10-day moving average of the put/call ratio on gold futures contracts, which hit its lowest level of the year on June 13 and which, despite gold's decline in June, remains at extremely bearish levels. The public last month expected gold to go up, as you can see by the clipping at the top of the page, so a trap has been set, which, according to the best wave count, should catch bulls, not bears.

WALL STREET JOURNAL

THE GOLD OUTLOOK brightens, some say, as inflation jitters return.

Gold, the traditional inflation hedge, isn't performing as well as many experts expected. But renewed talk of inflation has some predicting a spurt of gold buying. About 1,500 people attended recent gold seminars by GoldCorp Australia; only a few hundred had been expected.

AUGUST 1, 1988

Gold and gold stocks are poised to enter a third wave to the downside.

Gold

Gold is another market for which August 1988 (+ or - 1 month) has been an ideal target for a cycle bottom. That bottom is approaching, but as yet the wave structure from the peak last December is incomplete. As you can see on the first chart, the best interpretation is that from the June high, waves 1 and 2 are in place, indicating a sharp decline for wave 3 directly ahead. Once five waves down have unfolded from the June high, covering short sales will probably be warranted.

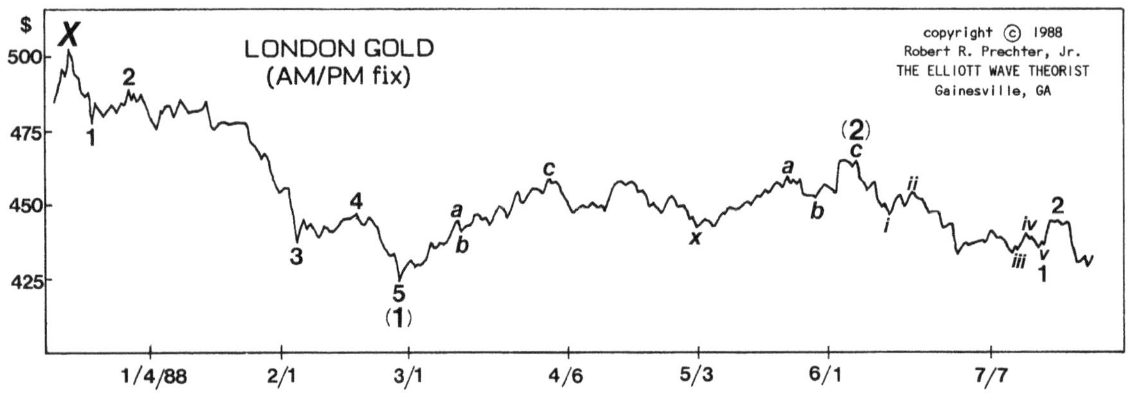

Supporting the short term bearish case is the chart of PIGS (the Prechter Index of Gold Stocks), which reveals a classic contracting triangle (see text, p.43) following last year's collapse. A triangle is a continuation pattern, indicating that another impulse wave to the downside is required. If you examine the chart closely, you will observe that the decline from the end of wave e so far shows five waves down yet did not carry the index to a new low. This development strongly argues that the drop from the end of wave e was only the first wave down within a larger five wave impulse. A small recovery for wave two occurred last week. It appears that wave three is next, so this chart agrees with that of gold bullion.

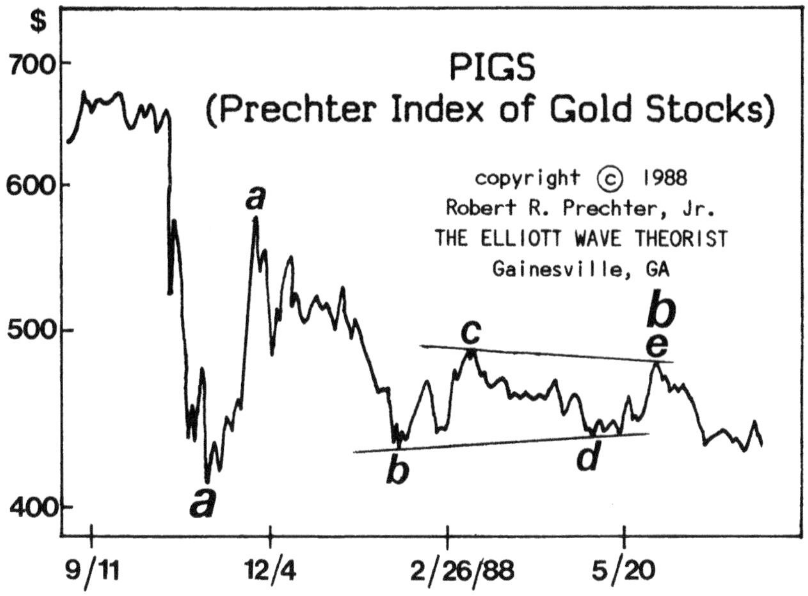

Both investors and traders should remain 100% short, keeping the stop at $480 basis London fix. If London fixes below $420, lower the stop to $460. If it fixes below $400, lower the stop to $440.

AUGUST 24, 1988 — INTERIM REPORT

Ironically, gold is in a similar position to bonds. Its 10-day put/call ratio has risen to its highest level of the year. No one wanted to sell short at $500 last December, but the crowd suddenly *does* want to be short at $430. All participants should cover short sales now. The September issue will elaborate on wave structure and strategy.

SEPTEMBER 6, 1988

Gold and silver appear to be bottoming. The as yet unfulfilled bear market rally target of $547 for the major countertrend rally pattern in gold dating from 1982 is likely to be achieved before the next major drop.

Gold

The Interim Report suggested covering short sales in gold, based on three factors. First is the long standing expectation of a 6-year cycle low in the summer of 1988. Second was the sudden surge in put buying, which pushed the 10-day average to its highest level of the year. Third was the chart of PIGS, our gold stock average, which is approaching the end of its declining wave structure. Although we did not reap the gains I had hoped, it is of some comfort that while most gold and gold stock players showed losses in 1988, we made some money at the game. Still, bullion closed Friday essentially unchanged from the month EWT turned bearish exactly two years ago.

Wave Count

As you can see on the daily chart, the wave structure in cash gold (while still possibly a bearish (1)-(2)-1-2) is best counted as an a-b-c pattern from the December high, with wave c subdividing into a diagonal triangle (see text, p.30). That count suggests one more drop to below the low of wave a at $423.75. The pattern in PIGS suggests the same thing, having followed last month's script exactly:

> PIGS reveals a classic contracting triangle (see text, p.43) following last year's collapse. A triangle is a continuation pattern, indicating that another impulse wave to the downside is required. If you examine the chart closely, you will observe that the decline from the end of wave e so far shows five waves down yet did not carry the index to a new low. This development strongly argues that the drop from the end of wave e was only the first wave down within a larger five wave impulse. A small recovery for wave two occurred last week. It appears that wave three is next.

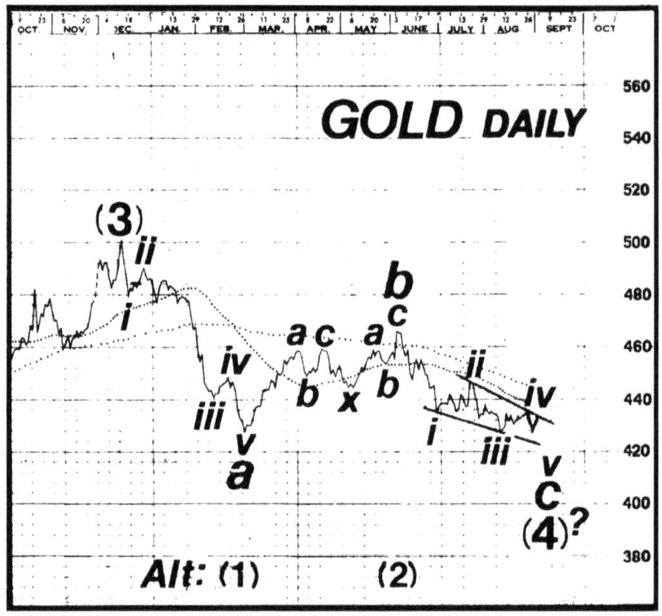

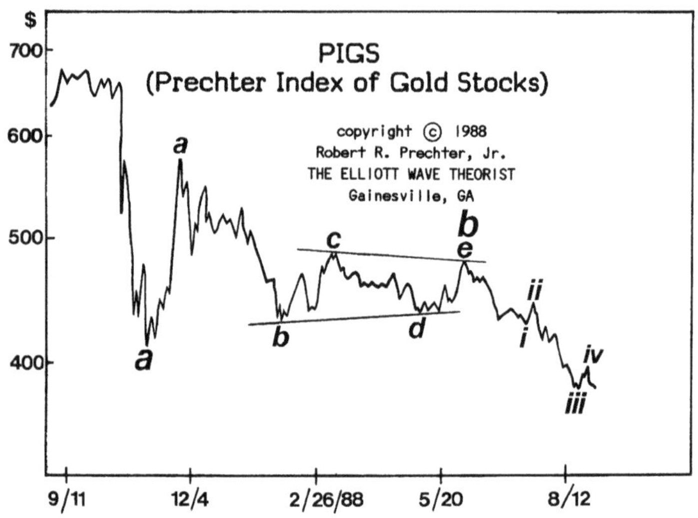

Wave three did unfold immediately thereafter, bringing our stock index below the 1987 low, as projected. Wave four is now in place, and wave five is in progress. The index should register its final low within days. The selling pressure in this index is coming mostly from the South African gold stocks. North American stock prices have declined recently also but are holding above last year's lows. Thanks to an astute subscriber who sent charts of various gold stock funds, we can see why. In seven funds weighted toward or composed entirely of North American gold stocks, the Elliott wave count shows five waves up from the 1987 low followed by an a-b-c pullback to near the previous fourth wave, a classic setup for further gains (see top graph). You can see the difference between that and those funds holding South African gold stocks in the middle graph. Metals bullion funds are also making new lows, as the bottom graph reveals. Ironically, it is a technical positive in the overall gold picture that South African stocks and metals bullion funds are breaking their prior lows while most North Americans are not. This divergence of trends is creating a bullish non-confirmation in the momentum picture.

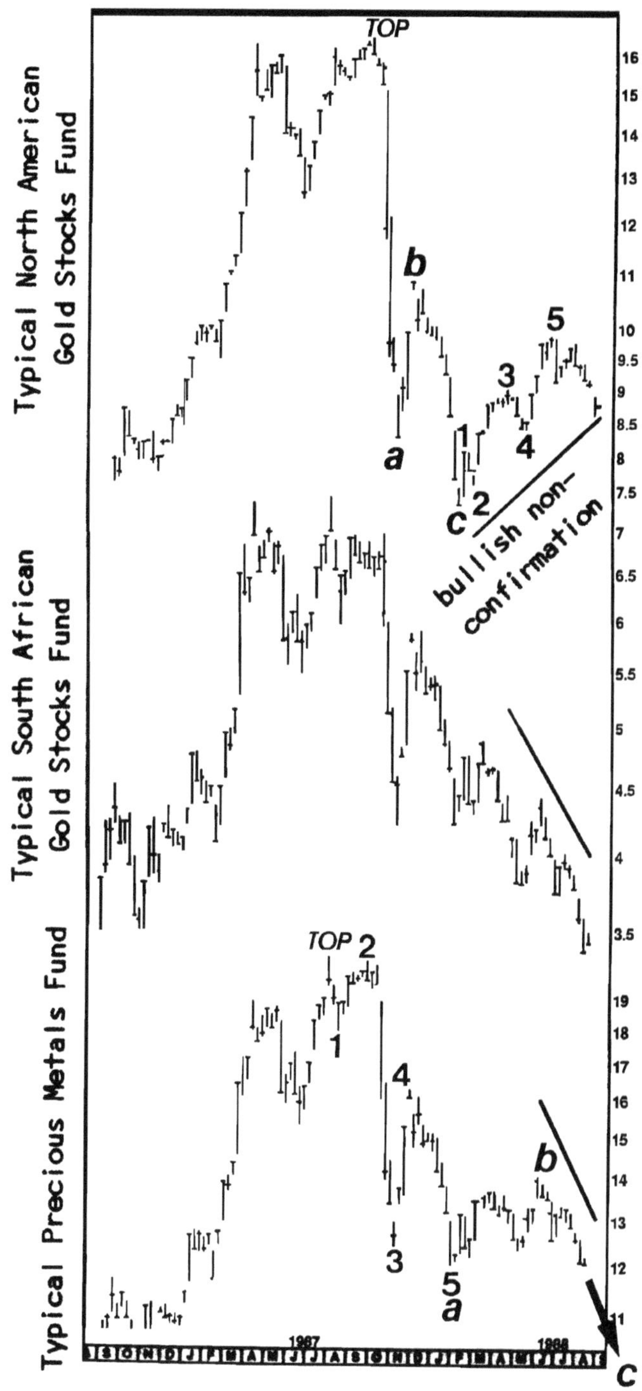

Source: Growth Fund Trends

Long Term Picture Resolving

As EWT has explained in past issues, the long term wave count would be well served by a rally to above the 1983 peak of $511.50, in order to complete wave X, subdividing Ⓐ-Ⓑ-Ⓒ, from the 1982 low. Our long standing target of $547, first formulated in 1982, is still a reasonable target (see discussion, June issue). Now look how the Fibonacci relationships stack up:

– If wave c of (4) is indeed in progress and is .618 times as long as wave a (see daily chart), it will bottom at $416.

– If wave (4) bottoms at a .382 retracement of the net travel of waves (1)-(3), it will bottom at $419.

– If wave (5) travels .618 times the net advance of waves (1) through (3) in the rally from 1985, a typical relationship (see text, p.107), and if wave (4) bottoms in the $416-

419 range computed above, wave (5) will peak at \$551-554, just a few dollars from the long standing target of \$547.

It would not be unreasonable for any such rally to peak in the November-January period, when stock market cycles are scheduled to bottom. "Brokerage Firms Give Gold a Hard Sell," says a 9/1 headline. Can you imagine how bullish sentiment will be toward gold if it rallies over \$100/oz. to a new high?

9-Year Cycle

Recent issues of EWT have promised to examine the position of the long term cycles in this time frame, so here goes. Several months ago, Campbell Gorrie, the astute editor of Investment Insight (GPO Box 3704, Sydney 2001 Australia), observed that a 9-year cycle may be operating in the market for gold bullion, with prior lows in 1967, 1976 and 1985. With only two revolutions having occurred, and with the trend projected to be down into August, I decided to defer judgment to see how prices behaved. Since they have held up well, the case for a 9-year cycle has strengthened (see chart).

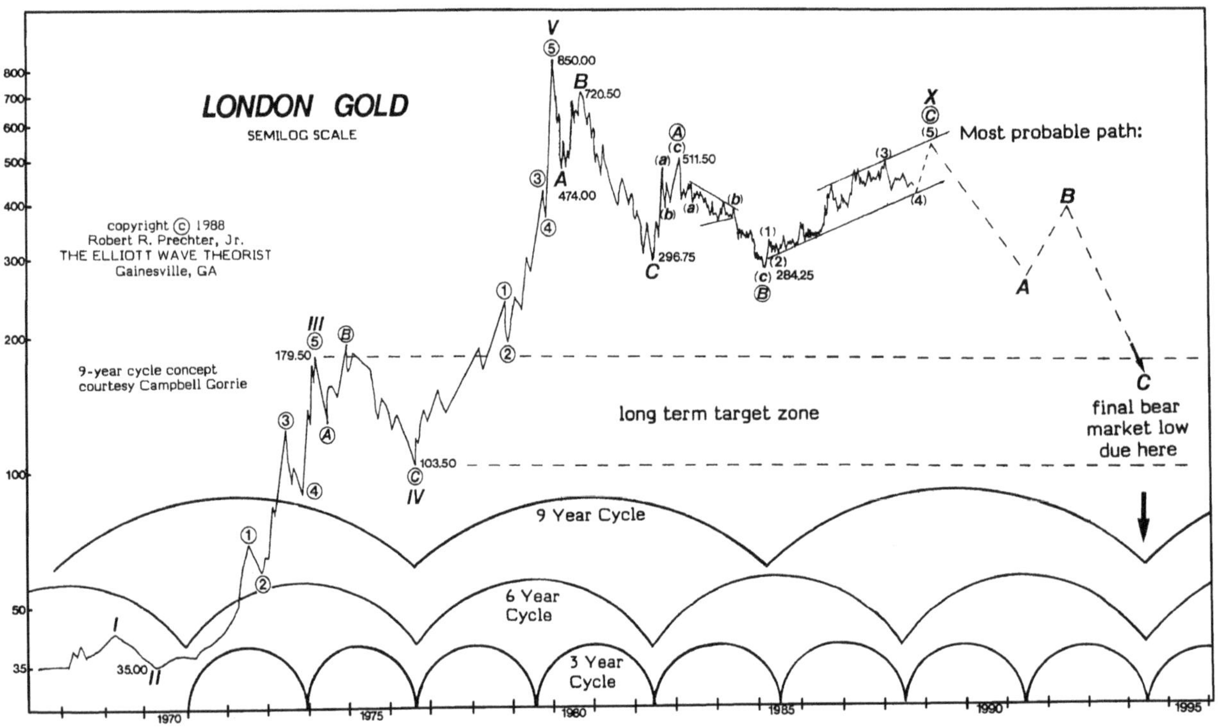

A 9-year cycle in gold has fascinating implications. If gold bullion peaks near \$547 in coming months, the 9-year cycle may turn down then, an early peak being consistent with the Elliott wave conclusion that overall, a major bear market is in force from 1980. The 3-year cycle will then bottom in 1991, completing wave A. The next 3-year cycle will cause a rally for wave B and a decline into 1994 for wave C, thus completing the second A-B-C of the double zigzag dating from 1980. [Note: The change in degree for the initial Ⓐ-Ⓑ-Ⓒ decline, now labeled A-B-C, was in deference to Elliott's implication that X waves are the same degree as the component waves of the preceding and ensuing three-wave patterns. I later concluded that Elliott had erred and introduced the labels W, Y and Z to mark those three-wave patterns and to identify the degrees properly. – Ed.]

The 1994 low (due in the summer, if prior cycle timing holds) will be caused by the 3-, 6- and 9-year cycles bottoming together for the first time in 18 years. The prior instance (in 1974-76; see chart) saw gold lose 50% of its value, and that was in a bull market. The 9-year cycle by itself brought gold down 67% from 1980 to 1985 in a bear market. The next drop will have both the 6- and 9-year cycles behind it, and occur within a bear market, so the percentage decline from an interim peak should be the largest yet. The year 1993, by the way, will mark the point at which gold will have been in a bear market for a Fibonacci 13 years, balancing the 13-year bull market from 1967 to 1980. In conclusion, EWT's long standing downside target range of $103-$197, apparently, will be achieved in 1993-1994, many years later than my original expectations.

Strategy

With both PIGS and bullion for the first time all year in a position to complete intermediate term wave counts given one more new low, it appears reasonable to buy these markets. (It will be our first purchase since the summer of 1986). Both investors and traders should move to 100% long given a London fix below $423.75, with a stop at $400. If you are short and London fixes above $464, make the September low a "stop and reverse" point. Reverse to 100% short on a fix above $540, with a stop at $580. Stock players should buy North American gold stocks or the funds listed on page 8, with a stop at the 1988 lows. Sell them if London gold fixes above $540.

Silver

If gold does achieve $547, silver should complete the rally for wave Ⓔ, as projected in the June issue, by rallying to near $9/oz. A rise to that level would mark the termination of the entire countertrend pattern from 1982 precisely coincident with that for gold.

SEPTEMBER 21, 1988 – INTERIM REPORT

The pattern of prices on the daily gold chart has quickly returned to bearish implications with the past two down days by eliminating the possibility that a diagonal triangle was ending. Our tight parameters will limit the loss on this trade to 5%. Traders should return to 100% short with a stop at $445 basis the nearby futures contract. Cover at $365. Investors should stand aside in what appears to be a long term bear market with more to go on the downside.

OCTOBER 3, 1988

Gold remains in a major bear market, but the sentiment picture suggests a low nearby. Support is near $365.

Gold

The potentially completed a-b-c decline on the daily chart of gold last month was proven wrong. Our strategy bought on weakness, however, as the market dropped to a new low for the year, so when our stop was hit, the loss amounted to only $20. Our gold stock index (PIGS) is completing wave v of c on the chart shown in last month's issue, and the gold stock funds listed then have shown just about as deep a second wave pullback as can be allowed, so owners of those should continue to use the 1988 low as a stop.

The Bullish Consensus reports only 12% bulls on silver, the lowest reading ever, so there is far too much danger being short that market now. The biggest surprise last month was that a similar indication, the highest put/call ratio on gold futures contracts in well over a year, produced no rally. Any time an indicator gives me a clearly false signal, I throw it out. Then I try to learn something for the price paid. Peter Hackstedde (Downwave Digest, Box 91450, Pasadena, CA) made this observation:

> The commercials (the big money) are holding net long positions of record proportion in gold, while the put/call ratio is extremely high. They are also holding net short positions of record proportion in silver, while the put/call ratio is [very low]. An explanation comes when we consider the gold/silver price ratio, currently at 65 to 1. Historically this ratio averages about 35 to 1. I think what we're seeing is the public betting that the spread will narrow and the commercials taking the other side of the trade. The big money is playing the role of the "house," and they have a far better track record.

Thus, spread factors may be affecting the put/call ratios. The public may own puts in gold and calls in silver, and the commercials may be hedging their long gold/short silver futures positions with the same purchases, neither necessarily with a strong opinion on the direction for gold. From now on, the gold put/call ratio will be ignored unless it is supported by the same action in silver's put/call ratio, which would imply a one-sided attitude toward the precious metals complex.

The long term wave pattern now more strongly supports the case that Cycle wave X, shown in the chart in last month's issue, is taking the form of a contracting triangle. Wave Ⓒ ended last December, and wave Ⓓ is in force now. A typical Fibonacci relationship would suggest that wave Ⓓ be .618 times as long as wave Ⓑ (see PRC manual), which is why the trading parameters were outlined as they were in the September Interim Report. Traders should keep the stop at $445 basis the nearby futures contract, and cover at $365. Investors should continue to stand aside.

OCTOBER 31, 1988

Gold

The short term technical condition of gold is mixed. The long term outlook still suggests a bear market in progress. Investors should continue to stand aside. Traders should remain short with a stop at $445 basis the nearby futures contract.

NOVEMBER 28, 1988

Gold

Last month's assessment was, "The short term technical condition of gold is mixed." Indeed, it has stubbornly held up despite the fact that oil has plummeted in recent months, gold stocks have tested their lows and silver has just hit its lowest level in 1½ years, having fallen nearly 50% from its 1987 high. What matters now is that the mixed technical picture in gold is rapidly approaching a resolution.

For wave students: The bearish case is still that gold is tracing out a (1)-(2)-1-2, as per the first daily chart (top). If so, the latest rally should stop in the $425-$445 zone, which is right about where the uptrend line dating back to the 1985 low (see chart, September issue), which was broken in September, now provides resistance. The idea that wave Ⓓ of a large triangle is in force (see discussion, March 1987 Special Report) will be negated by a move above $480, which would eliminate the case that the current rally is an "x" wave (see text, p.37) within a double or triple zigzag decline.

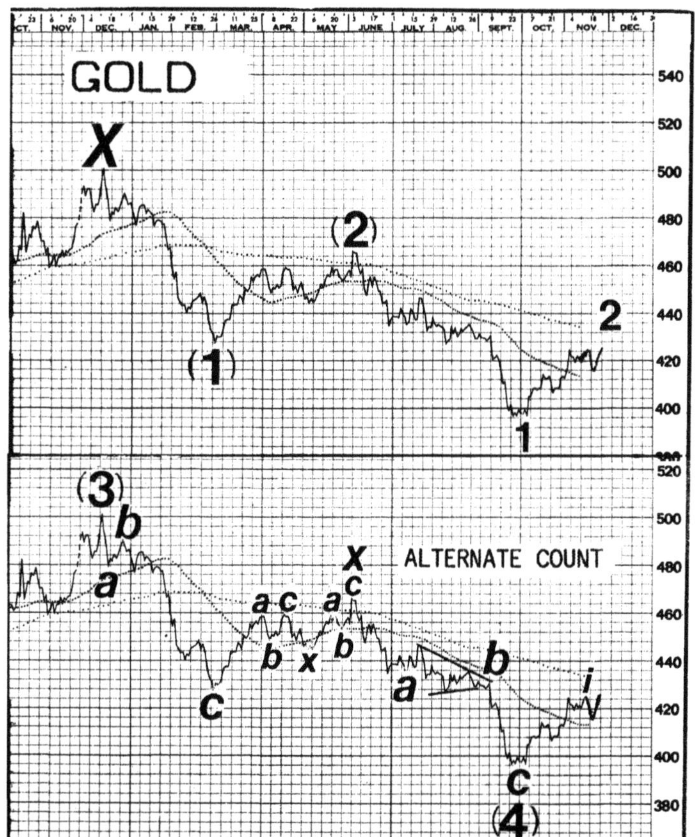

Given the extent of the recent price recovery in gold, the decline from December 1987 to September-October 1988 must still be considered a possibly completed corrective pattern, per the second daily chart (bottom). The decline ended when the second a-b-c was equal to the first on the weekly futures chart. The 6-year cycle, long scheduled to bottom in the third quarter of 1988, certainly may have seen its low in late September-early October. Reasonable upside potential for the countertrend rally pattern dating from the 1982 low is still $547, as explained in the September issue. However, based upon the .618 relationship also explained in that issue, the peak could occur as low as $530, so resistance should be expressed as a range of $525-$550.

The Elliott Wave Theorist, 1989

JANUARY 2, 1989

Gold's short term technical condition is neutral, but the long term outlook remains bearish.

Gold

The December issue reiterated, "The bearish case is still that gold is tracing out a (1)-(2)-1-2; if so, the latest rally should stop in the $425-$445 zone." One week later, on December 5, a peak price for the London fix was registered at $430.40.

Our stop on traders' short sales, at $455 basis the nearby futures contract, should be lowered to $430.40 basis London fix if $400 is broken. Traders should take profits under $370. Although prices *could* fall a lot further, $365 is the most reasonable stopping point if wave Ⓓ of a triangle dating from 1982 is unfolding.

The rally for wave Ⓔ would then provide a final short selling opportunity prior to the beginning of the second A-B-C decline in the bear market pattern dating from the 1980 high. Please refer to the September issue for a look at the long term picture and downside forecast. This picture will be updated if gold bullion falls below $400 again. The 9-year cycle in gold bullion prices (as shown in the September issue) indicates an ultimate bottom in 1994.

Half the gold funds suggested in the September issue have been stopped out. The rest have retraced so much of what appeared to be five wave advances that it is increasingly unlikely that gold stocks have seen their lows, despite the supposed bottoming of the 6-year cycle. Investors should remain *out* of the gold market and exit any gold funds, staying in Treasury bills. The alternate count, that an impulse wave to $525-$550 is in force, is increasingly unlikely.

JANUARY 30, 1989

Gold is about to break its 1988 low, and we're still short.

Gold

The long term picture in gold continues to weaken. There is little question now that the wave Ⓒ label at the 1987 high is correct. As you can see by the dashed lines on the chart, the only question remaining is whether waves Ⓓ and Ⓔ will occur to complete a triangle for wave X or whether X is over. From a practical standpoint, it hardly matters. If the bear market remains in force, as EWT continues to argue, *the 1987 high will not be exceeded for years*. A move above it would confirm a new bull market from 1985.

As the January issue stated, "Although prices *could* fall a lot further, $365 is the most reasonable stopping point if wave Ⓓ of a triangle dating from 1982 is unfolding." That target,

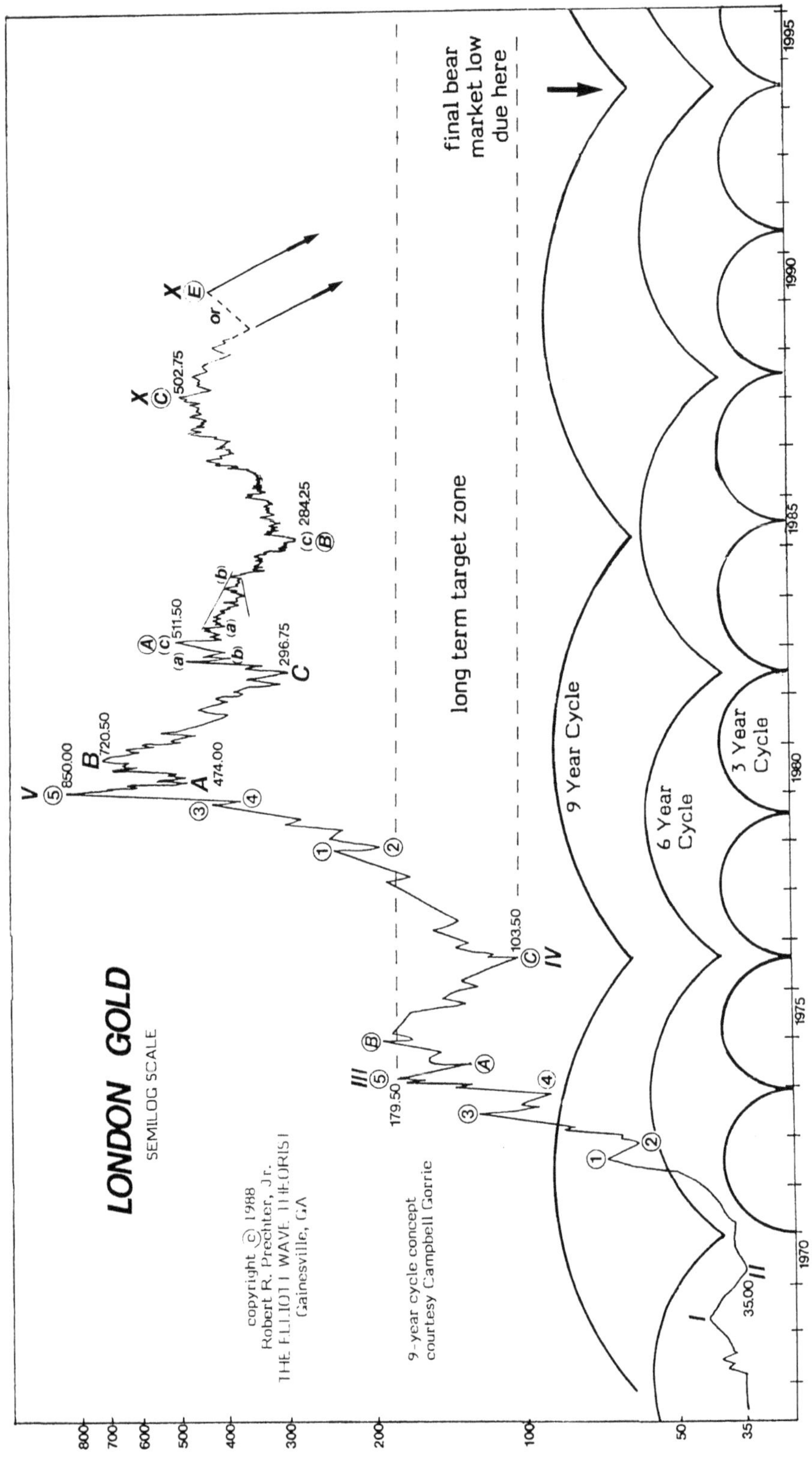

LONDON GOLD
SEMILOG SCALE
copyright © 1988
Robert R. Prechter, Jr.
THE ELLIOTT WAVE THEORIST
Gainesville, GA
9-year cycle concept
courtesy Campbell Gorrie
long term target zone
final bear
market low
due here
9 Year Cycle
6 Year
Cycle
3 Year
Cycle
850.00
720.50
474.00
511.50
296.75
284.25
502.75
179.50
103.50
35.00
or
800
700
600
500
400
300
200
100
50
35
1970
1975
1980
1985
1990
1995

plus or minus 5 points, not only marks the point at which wave Ⓓ of a possible triangle will be .618 times as long as wave Ⓑ (the 1983-1985 drop) but also marks a .618 retracement of the 1985-1987 rally. *Despite this neat calculation, the wave structure has all the earmarks of a 1-2, 1-2 from the December 1987 high.* In fact, the two brief rally retracements were *almost exactly the same*, 53% and 51% respectively. For this reason, we will attempt to hold onto some short sales if a "third wave" style rout occurs.

Traders are still 100% short. Prior strategy lowered the stop to $430.40 basis London fix. Traders should cover 50% under $370 and the rest if after February 16 gold fixes between $350 and $370 and is making a new low for the year. Investors should remain *out* of the gold market, collecting T-bill interest. Over the next several years, prices are still expected to fall *below $200/oz.*, with $180 and $105 (+ or - $10) the best specific targets for the early 1990s.

FEBRUARY 1989 — SPECIAL REPORT

Gold

Since 1980, *The Elliott Wave Theorist* has made a case that gold has been tracing out a major bear market pattern. The best interpretation of the wave status has been that the first phase of bear market ended in June 1982 at the termination of an A-B-C decline. From there, gold began an intra-bear-market recovery pattern (to be labeled "X"). The partial recovery pattern, which has retraced a Fibonacci 38.2% of the A-B-C decline, is either an Ⓐ-Ⓑ-Ⓒ that ended in December 1987 or an Ⓐ-Ⓑ-Ⓒ-Ⓓ-Ⓔ triangle that requires one more rally (though still peaking *below* the December 1987 high of $502.75). From the recovery pattern's end, gold is expected to trace out a *second* A-B-C decline into the early 1990s to complete a "double zigzag" bear market pattern from the 1980 peak of $850/oz.

R.N. Elliott observed over fifty years ago that *corrections tend to terminate in the area of the fourth wave within the preceding five-wave sequence of the same degree.* This guideline indicates that gold will fall at minimum to *below $200/oz.*, the highest price within wave IV, as you can see in Figure 1. Using the London fix as a basis, the peak within wave IV was $197.50 and the low for wave IV was $103.50. It so happens that potential Fibonacci relationships within the bear market, as listed in Figure 1, strongly support this area as a downside target. In fact, the strongest points indicated coincide closely with the orthodox beginning of wave IV at $179.50 and its low at $103.50. Figure 1 also reveals that gold has found support or resistance very close to the $100, $200, $300, $500 and $800 levels, each a multiple of 100 times the first five Fibonacci numbers. If gold drops to a Fibonacci ⅛ of its all-time high and a Fibonacci ⅕ of its 1983 and 1987 recovery pattern highs, it will have returned to the anchor point of the progression. For that reason, and because prices usually fall close to the *low* of the previous fourth wave, the strongest possibility for an ultimate bottom is near the *lower* end of the

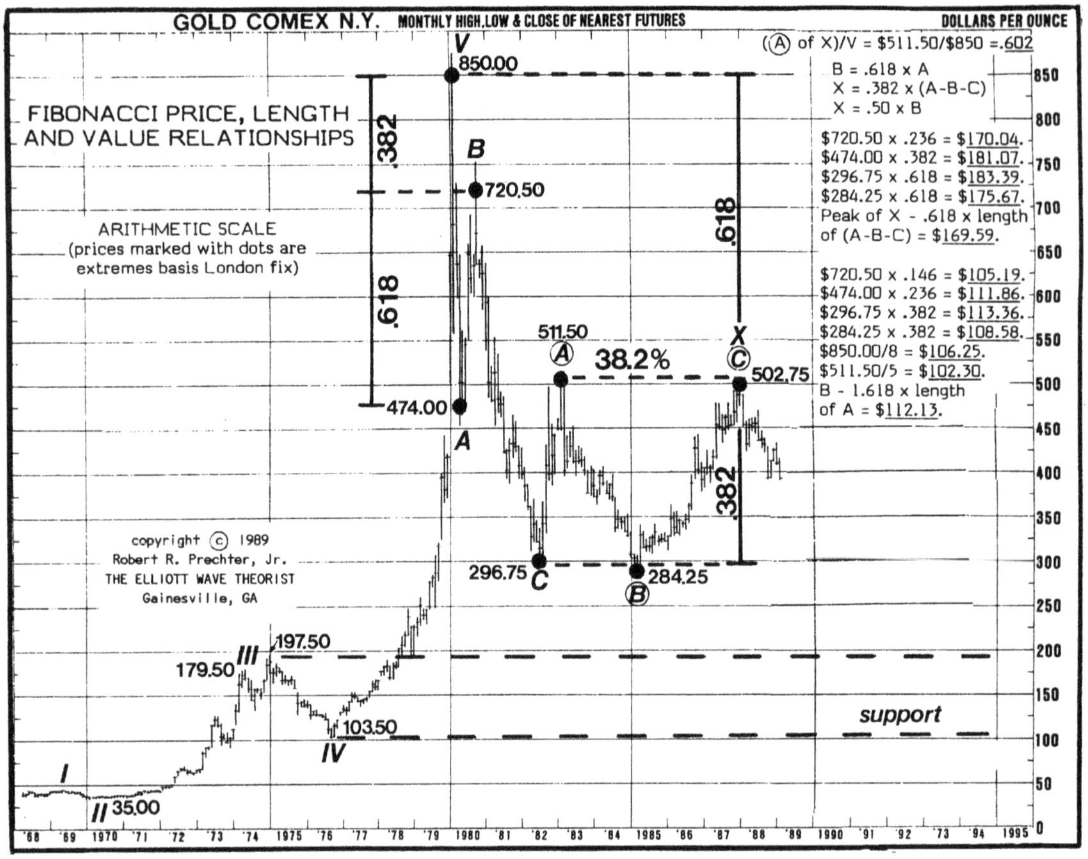

Figure 1

$103.50 - $197.50 range. This projection appears outrageously low relative to current generally held expectations, particularly since such expectations are for *higher* prices, not lower ones at all.

As is so often the case with corrective patterns, the best alternative interpretation carries precisely the same long term message, although the internal labeling is less than compelling. Figure 2 shows that it is acceptable to count wave A as an overlapping five-wave structure called a "leading diagonal triangle." The wave B rally under this interpretation stopped so far within $2 of a perfect Fibonacci 38.2% retracement at $502.75, and right at the peak of the previous fourth wave, which topped at $511.50. A 61.8% retracement to the $630-$640 range would be a maximum, leaving open the slim possibility that the wave B rally is not over yet. Nevertheless, the net evidence favors the conclusion that the peak is in place. A 38.2% retracement is the most common retracement percentage following leading diagonal triangles, and cycles (see below) indicate that time is running out for any such move to the upside. Thus, *regardless of the interpretation of the form within the bear market, the Wave Principle indicates that a bear market rally pattern is yielding, or will soon yield, to another major phase of decline.*

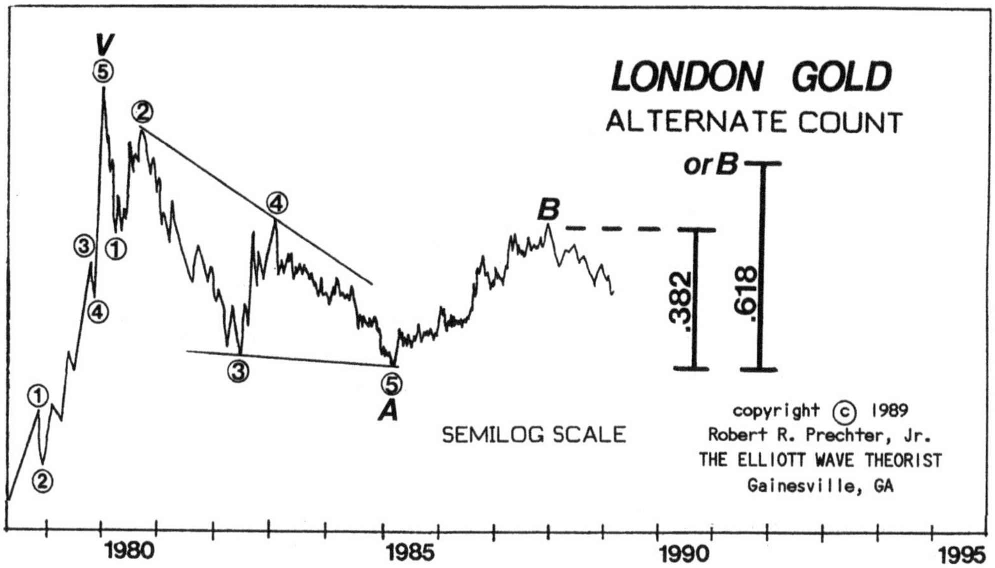

Figure 2

In terms of timing, all intermediate term turning points in the gold price movement from 1967 forward can be accounted for with just two long term time cycles, a 12-year cycle and a 9-year cycle (see Figure 3), the latter of which is a component of the larger 27- and 54-year cycles (not shown). Although the bullion price was fixed by the government before that time, the price action of gold *stocks*, which habitually bottom and top within a year of the gold bullion price, confirms these cycles. The chart of Dome Mines in Figure 4, for instance, reveals a major decline into and rise out of December 1957, within a few months of the last time the two cycles in gold bullion would have been scheduled to bottom together. The reason this observation is so important is that *both cycles seen in Figure 3 are due to bottom together again in 1994* in their first joint low of the free market pricing period of the last two decades. [Note: The 9-year cycle in Figure 4 projects to 1993. — Ed.] Even the "leapfrogging" downside pressure from these two cycles resulted in a 66.6% decline in the value of gold from 1980 to 1985. Merely an equivalent percentage drop from the December 1987 peak would bring gold under $180. However, this time the cycles will be working together all the way into the bottom, providing support for the Elliott wave conclusion that a low closer to $100 is likely. Gold holders, then, may suffer almost as much as stockholders into the early 1990s.

As you can also see in Figure 3, Fibonacci time periods appear to be operating in the gold market. The 13-year advance from 1967, when wave I began, subdivides into two periods of 8 and 5 years at the December 31, 1974 peak at just under $200/oz. That date marked the top of wave Ⓑ of IV upon the legalization of gold holdings for Americans and preceded the largest correction of the bull market, a 50% drop. Since the peak in 1980, turning points have come at Fibonacci intervals. 2 years later saw a low, 3 years later a high, 5 years later a low,

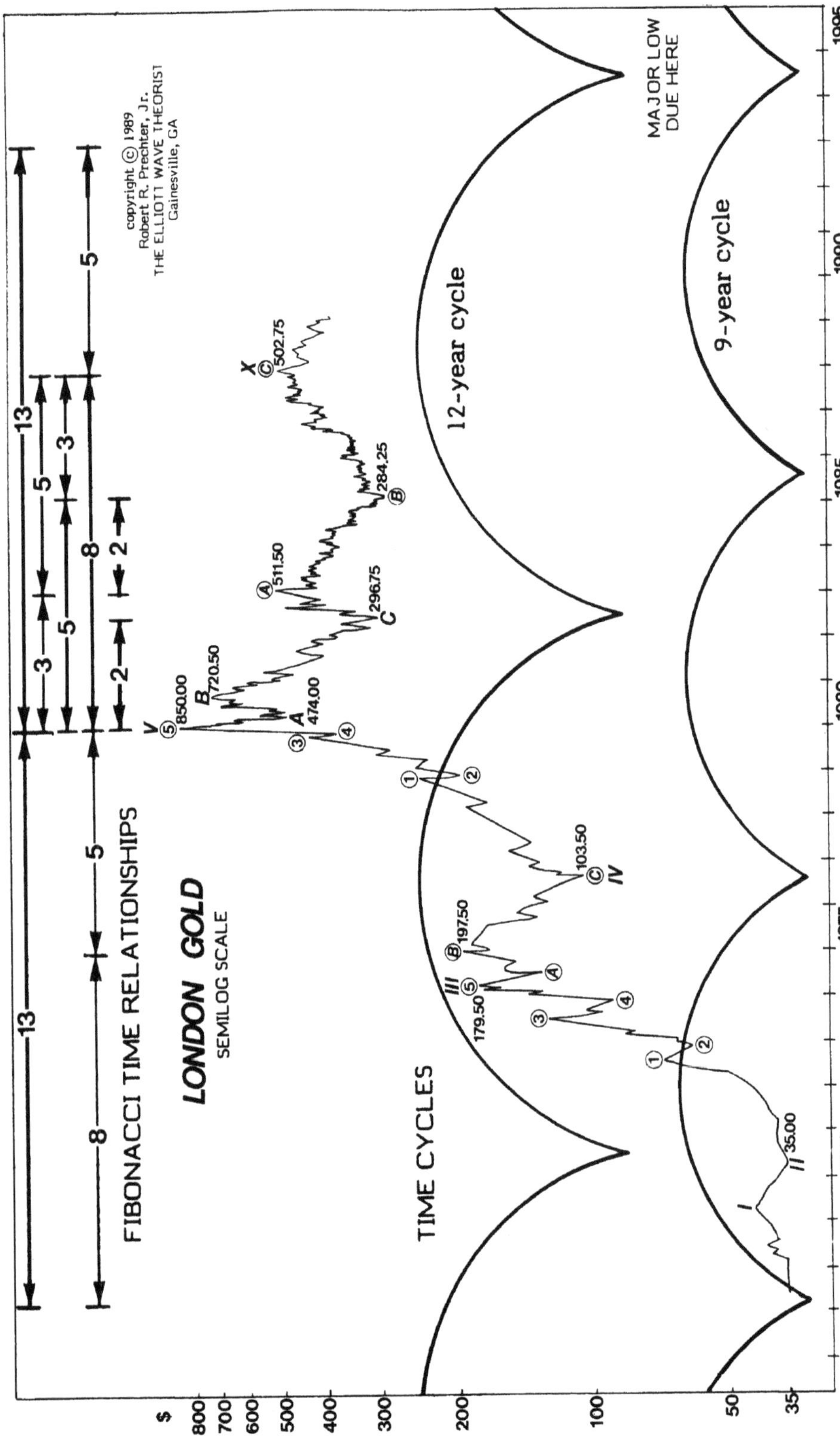
FIBONACCI TIME RELATIONSHIPS
LONDON GOLD
SEMILOG SCALE
TIME CYCLES
12-year cycle
9-year cycle
MAJOR LOW
DUE HERE
copyright © 1989
Robert R. Prechter, Jr.
THE ELLIOTT WAVE THEORIST
Gainesville, GA
13
8
5
3
2
850.00
720.50
474.00
511.50
296.75
284.25
502.75
197.50
179.50
103.50
35.00
$
800
700
600
500
400
300
200
100
50
35
1970
1975
1980
1985
1990
1995

Figure 3

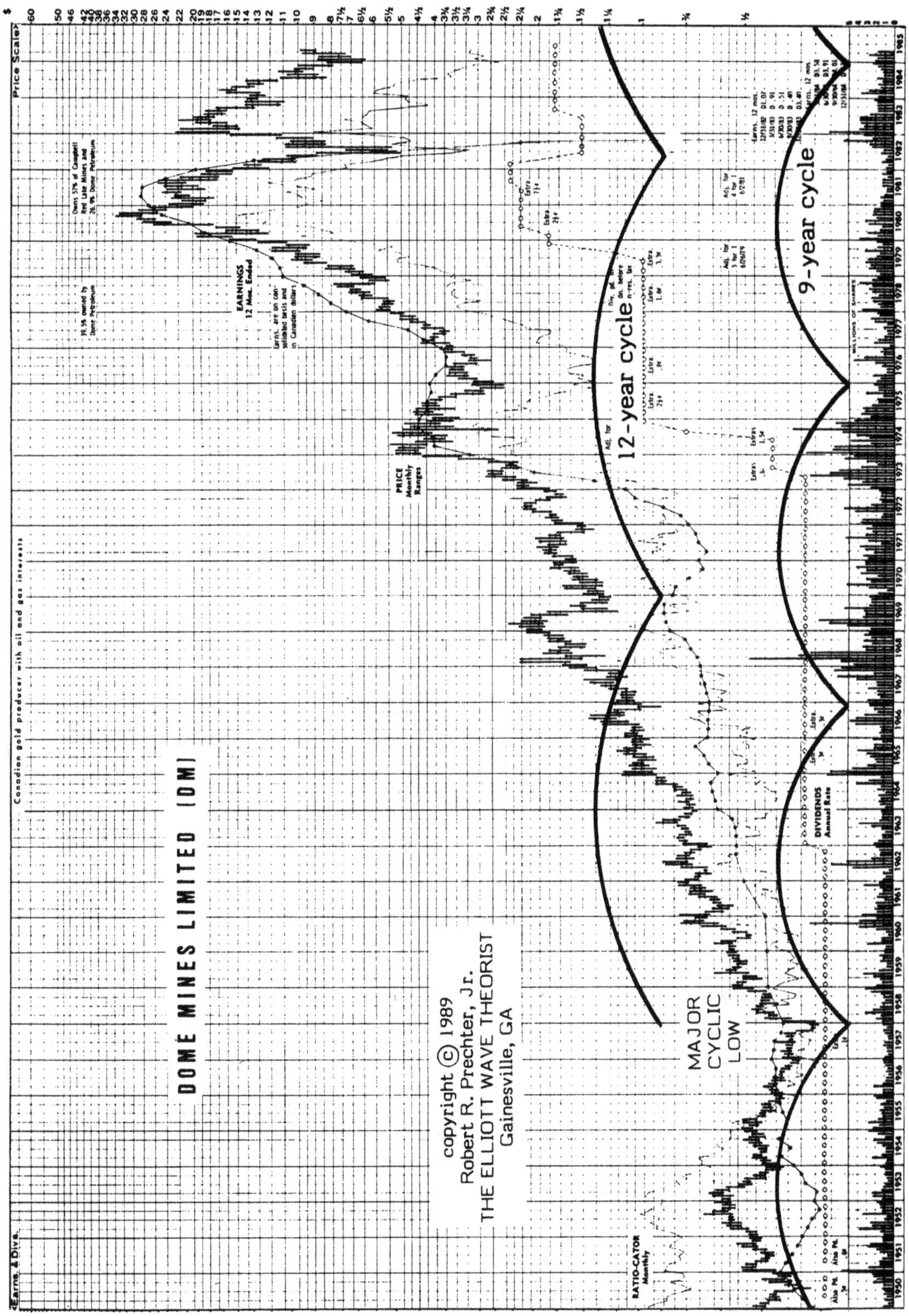
DOME MINES LIMITED (DM)
copyright © 1989
Robert R. Prechter, Jr.
THE ELLIOTT WAVE THEORIST
Gainesville, GA
MAJOR
CYCLIC
LOW
12-year cycle
9-year cycle
Price Scale
Earns. & Divs.
EARNINGS 12 Mos. Ended
PRICE Monthly Ranges
DIVIDENDS Annual Rate
RATIO-CATOR Monthly

Figure 4

and 8 years later a high. *13* years from the 1980 peak is 1993,* suggesting a turning point, most probably a low, some time between December 1992 and December 1993. [Note: Gold fell persistently until March 1993. – Ed.]

Taking all relevant time studies into account, then, it can be concluded that *gold will experience an extremely low valuation bottom in 1993-1994 + or - 1 month.* It is possible that two bottoms will occur, not unlike the stock market lows of 1932 and 1933, the first marking a Fibonacci time period low and the second a "test" on the cyclic bottom from which prices will explode on the upside.

With respect to the larger financial picture, the recovery pattern in gold dating from June 1982, together with the stock market boom that began in August 1982, reflect a period of financial reliquification of the economy. Gold's 1987 price peak, together with the 1987 and 1989 (est.) peaks in the stock market, are clear evidence of a topping process which is signaling *the end of the reliquification phase.* The outlook for both stocks and gold supports the case that the next phase for the economy should be *an across-the-board deflation.* [Note: From this time, the Dow Jones Transports collapsed 50 percent, the Value Line index fell back to its 1987 low, a recession occurred in 1991 and S&P earnings had their largest contraction since the 1940s, lasting until 1993. It was, however, only a Primary degree correction. – Ed.]

Perhaps you have heard the idea that gold is not only an inflation hedge but also a "*deflation* hedge" (translation: it will never go down). This thesis, touted in recent years, is based upon the fact that gold *stocks* soared during the 1930s. Such a conclusion naively ignores the fact that the Federal government during those years supported a fixed price for gold at $21 per ounce. While the deflation raged from 1929 to 1933, the *relative* value of gold was soaring simply because its dollar price was fixed. Gold mining companies benefitted, and their stocks went up. Today, that situation does not exist. In fact, the free market has brought gold to a point of extreme overvaluation in terms of a basket of commodities according to the 200-year chart of that relationship shown in Figure 5. The Federal government shows no desire to enforce its "legal" statutory price, which, by the way, is all the way down at $42.22 per ounce, not exactly encouraging to the idea that government might fix the price artificially high. While it is always difficult to predict what government will do, it is clear that there is no reason to expect gold bullion to rise in price in a monetary deflation. Even price fixing would only keep it flat. *If* its price is fixed artificially high prior to the winding down of a deflation, which in this day of floating exchange rates is unlikely, one might argue that gold stocks could do well, but global unrest and the potential for a government seizure of the mines will make investment in them extremely risky.

---

* And 21 years from 1980 is 2001, which marked another significant low in gold. – Ed.

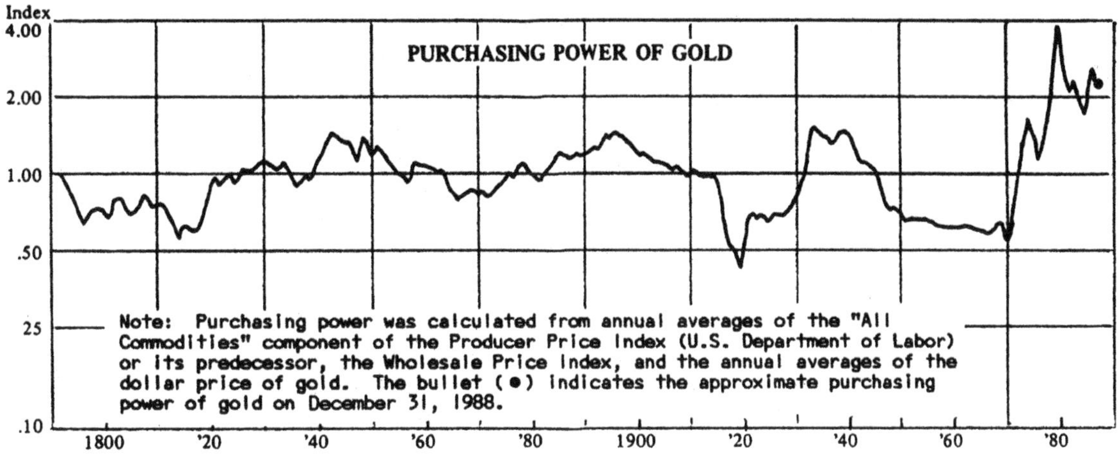

Figure 5

With regard to risk, it must be pointed out that the low end of the target range for gold cited above need not *necessarily* be a downside maximum, as it would be if the market were for stocks. As *Elliott Wave Principle* pointed out, commodities form "contained waves," i.e., do not necessarily continue to build in bull markets of degree higher than Cycle. Degree building occurs continually in *stock market* waves because the history of mankind is a history of progress; commodity prices need not reflect spiraling valuation throughout history. Thus, although the downside target is based upon the most strongly indicated support levels within the preceding wave structure, it is not imperative that that structure define the limits of the bear market. Nevertheless, an 80% drop in the price of gold from its 1987 high would be just about right to reflect the expected deflation and correct part of its current overvaluation relative to commodities. It is not necessary that all the overvaluation be corrected. After all, although its current premium is due to embedded inflation fears, some premium value on hard money will be warranted if global financial conditions worsen. In terms of planning upcoming purchases, the time considerations cited above should carry as much weight as those for price. If *both* are satisfied at some point in the future, the odds that a low is at hand will approach certainty.

If the cyclic outlook is correct, from an extreme price low in the early 1990s, the 9- and 12-year cycles will then provide an immediate and powerful advance lasting four to six years [Note: It lasted three years. — Ed.], then a period of sideways or declining values into the years 2003-2006.

Silver

The long term wave structure in silver (see Figure 6) also reveals a continuing bear market. Unlike gold, silver has already undergone a collapse of over 90% and has achieved the price area of its previous fourth wave, wave IV, which ranged from \$3.50 to \$6.50. Nevertheless, its bear market pattern appears incomplete. The recovery phase dating from 1982 has taken the shape of a contracting triangle, whether completed upon the rise to \$8 in 1987 or requiring a final rally, still to a peak *below* that of wave Ⓒ. Either way, the larger formation, like that for gold, argues for another A-B-C decline from the end of the triangle.

As shown additionally in Figure 6, there appears to be a 5- and 10-year cycle complex in silver, which suggests that the next important lows will occur in 1992 and 2002. This outlook complements the cyclic pictures already presented for the stock market and gold. The fact that commodities form "contained waves" (see discussion above) allows for the price of silver ultimately to go substantially below its previous fourth wave, and the prospects for a depression make extreme low prices for this industrial metal probable. Despite all the arguments presented in books, ads and editorials, then, silver is hardly likely to climb to "over $200/oz." in the next five years. A deep undervaluation would be less of a surprise.

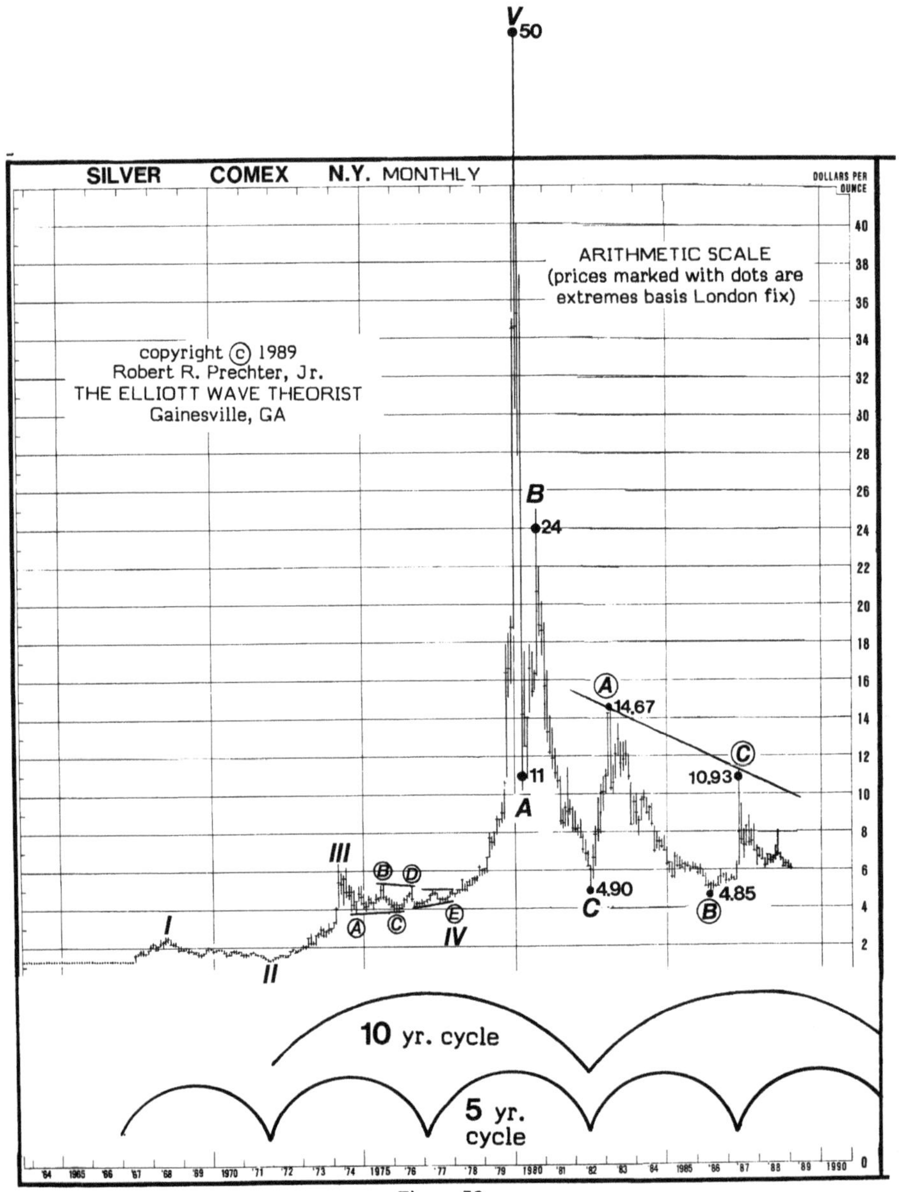

Figure 6

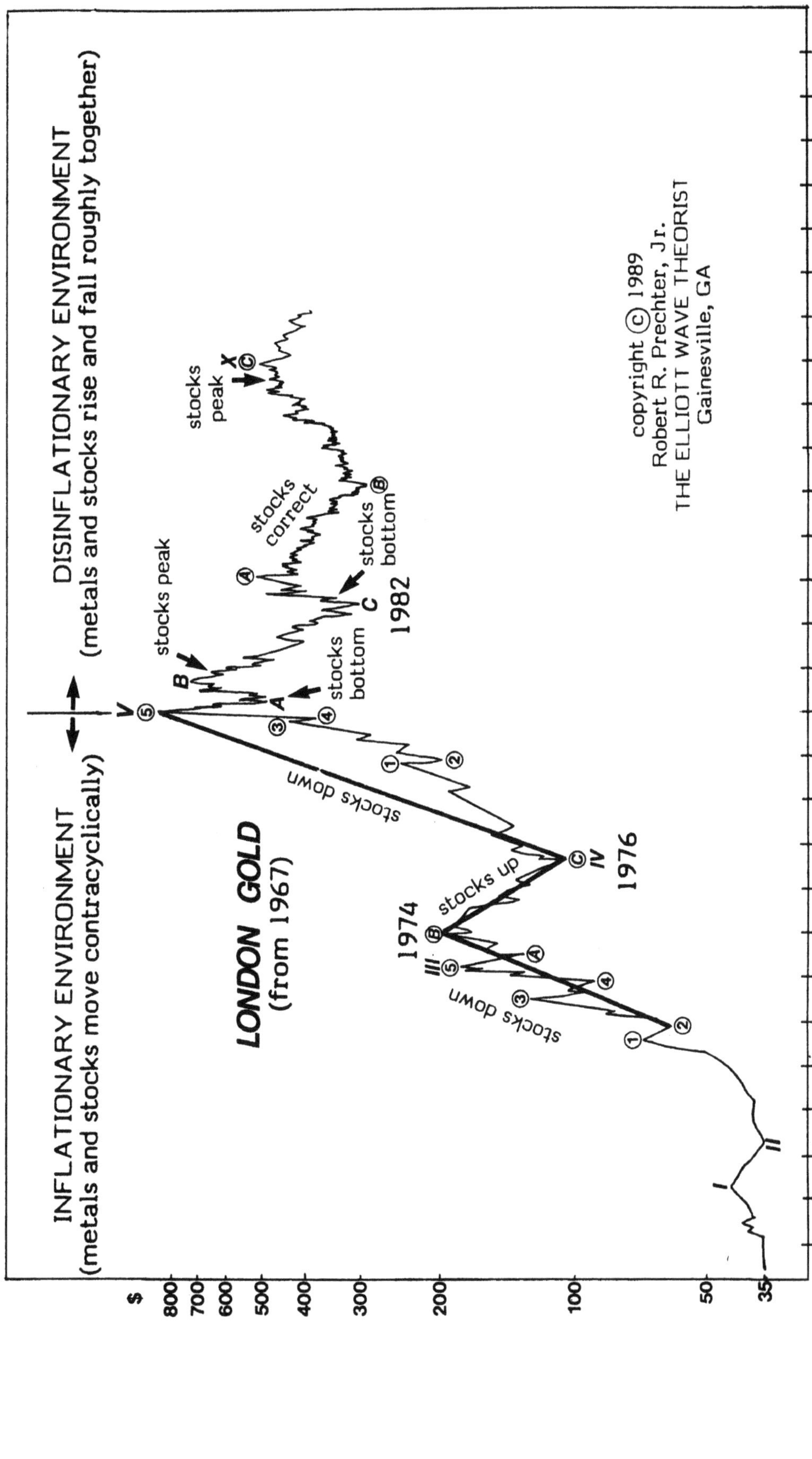
INFLATIONARY ENVIRONMENT
(metals and stocks move contracyclically)
DISINFLATIONARY ENVIRONMENT
(metals and stocks rise and fall roughly together)
LONDON GOLD
(from 1967)
stocks down
stocks up
stocks down
stocks peak
stocks bottom
stocks correct
stocks bottom
stocks peak
1974
1976
1982
copyright © 1989
Robert R. Prechter, Jr.
THE ELLIOTT WAVE THEORIST
Gainesville, GA
$
800
700
600
500
400
300
200
100
50
35
1970
1975
1980
1985
1990
1995

Figure 7

Underlying Inflation vs. Deflation

For some time, *The Elliott Wave Theorist* has been making the case that the world is in a transition phase from inflation to deflation, with deflation continuing to gain the upper hand. Major deflations, following an initial period of economic boom, are ultimately extremely destructive, and the next one should be no exception. But how, some people have asked, can precious metals, commodities and stocks go down *together*, as the wave structures call for? Aren't stocks and commodities contracyclical? Such behavior appears to be contrary to the observations made during the extremely inflationary environment of the 1970s, which most remember well. An examination of longer term trends, however, suggests a fluctuation relationship between contracyclicality and confluence (see Figure 7). Specifically, *when the main trend is inflations, commodities and stocks tend to be contracyclical year by year, yet ultimately end up at higher levels after several decades. However, in a post-inflationary environment, all markets tend to move together year by year, as liquidity ebbs and flows*. When liquidity returns, even briefly it boosts all markets. Thus, unlike the 1970s, when roaring inflations into 1974 and again into 1980 were *destructive* to stock market values, each inflationary phase of the 1980s has provided a *lift* to securities prices and the economy. It is the periodic *deflations* during that time that have been destructive.

What is perhaps most fascinating about he charts of the precious metals is their reflection of the fact that liquidity is now of prime importance with regard to the health of the stock market and the economy. Note that when gold and silver bottomed in March 1980 and June 1982, stocks bottomed as well. With regard to tops, shortly after gold and silver peaked in September 1980, stocks peaked and fell 24%; shortly after gold and silver peaked in 1983, stocks peaked and dropped 16%; shortly after silver peaked in April 1987, stocks peaked and dropped 35%. Gold since peaked in December 1987 and is down 20%.

Art and Collectibles

Prices for art, collectibles and memorabilia of all kinds, from paintings to gold coins to Art Deco to baseball cards to classic cars to old records, have experienced a bubble concurrently with those in real estate and the stock market. Its extent is reflected by the collage below. These items should sell for substantially less sometime in the 1990s. Drops of over 50% in the top end and as much as 95% in the lower tiers would not be a surprise.

MARCH 13, 1989

Gold remains in a decline of major proportion that will not end until 1993 or 1994, probably at ⅕ its December 1987 value and ⅛ its all time high value.

Gold — A Slope of Hope

We all know that bull markets climb a Wall of Worry. Bear markets, as I opined once before, slide down a Slope of Hope. "Now You Can Worry About Inflation," says one headline. "Inflation Is Here," says another. "Jump in Inflation Rate A Shocker," says a third. If these assertions are true, why is gold about 3% off a 2½ year low? Why did Sears close its doors nationwide for three days to lower prices? Why is silver scraping bottom? Is it really going to happen that news about inflation will come out *before* the markets go up this time? Did calling the markets suddenly get easy?

The price of gold historically turns up *before* inflation is obvious and turns down *before* an inflationary phase is over, often by a year or more. The downturn that began in 1987 indicates that inflation will recede.

The wave structure on the daily chart for gold (not shown) shows an A-B-C (i.e., countertrend) rally for three weeks right back to the previous fourth wave. Waves A and C are of equal length. Meanwhile, *the put/call ratio has fallen to its lowest level since June 1988* on a 10-day basis. June 1988 was the month of the wave (2) peak at $465 basis London fix. In other words, *there is as much bullish sentiment among traders now as there was when gold was testing its post-1985 high nine months ago.* The articles about inflation having returned or being in prospect, then, have done their usual job in creating a bullish market sentiment. The weak response in the form of a $16 rally appears to indicate that the path of least resistance is still down.

Long Term Cycles

The Wave Principle continues to indicate that gold remains in a major bear market pattern from the peak at $850 in 1980. The December 1987 high, moreover, is best labeled wave Ⓒ, indicating, as EWT said last month, that it "will not be exceeded for years." These conclusions were reached despite the fact that the "6-year cycle" had long indicated some kind of rally from about August 1988. A rally did begin in September 1988, but its structure was not impulsive, so we stayed short. Gold has since fallen to a new low. Where was the famous 6-year cycle?

Upon studying the long term chart of gold bullion, it became apparent that all lows that had occurred since 1967 could be explained by an interplay between two cycles, the 9-year cycle, which Campbell Gorrie postulated last year, and a 12-year cycle, which last bottomed in 1982 (see chart). The "6-year cycle," widely recognized among gold watchers, was then revealed as only an *apparent* cycle, a byproduct of these two cycles of longer duration. This was an exciting discovery.

It was immediately clear that if the idea of dominant 9- and 12-year cycles was correct, then their prior coincident lows had to have occurred in *1958*. One impediment to a complete analysis all along has been the limited data due to the government's price fixing of gold at $35/oz. prior to the 1970s. However, the prices of *gold mining stocks* were not fixed, and recent history shows that they usually bottom within a year of major bottoms in bullion. A check of the long term chart of Dome Mines confirmed the new analysis. As you can see by the inset on the chart, a major low occurred in *December 1957*. That low was preceded by *five years of decline* and launched a huge bull market. Of utmost importance is that the 9- and 12-year cycles are, for the first time since 1958, once again scheduled to bottom together, in 1994. This concurrence strengthens the conclusion reached in the September issue that the final bear market low will be due in that year.

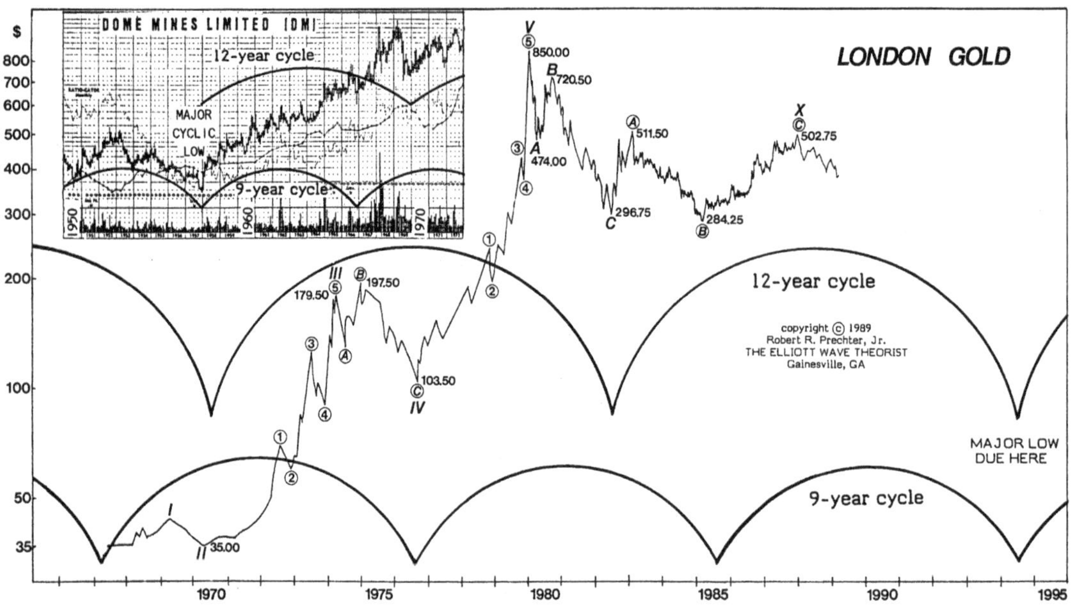

These two cycles provide additional information. They explain why gold climbed for such a long time after the 1985 low, giving us a year's worth of headaches. More important for now, however, is that they also indicate *extreme weakness in the bigger picture*, since despite a powerful upward influence from *both* cycles from 1985 through 1988, gold could not exceed its 1983 peak and could not even hold up through the end of the period of jointly rising cyclic pressure that lasted through mid-1988. The 9-year cycle, in fact, isn't due to join the 12-year on the downside for another several months. The price peak in December 1987 indicates "left hand translation," i.e., an early peak, which is classic bear market behavior.

No major cycles of lesser duration than nine years are evident in the price structure. Thus, *there is no reason to expect more than shallow and/or brief price recoveries as gold falls relentlessly from its 1987 high right into a final low in 1993-1994.* The ultimate price target is still below $200/oz., with $105 the most reasonable target based on calculations made years ago and again featured in the February Special Report.

Traders are still 100% short. The $365 level (+ or - $5) is still support if a wave Ⓔ rally to $400-$500 is to occur. However, the wave structure on the daily chart continues to reflect a market that could accelerate on the downside. Our strategy has been designed, as indicated in the February issue, "to hold onto some short sales if a 'third wave' style rout occurs." Traders are planning to cover 50% when London fixes below $370. Hold the remaining half of the short position. Keep the stop at $430.40 basis London fix. Investors should remain *out* of the gold market, collecting T-bill interest.

APRIL 3, 1989

Trends for gold remain down. $365 basis London fix is still important support. A clear break of that level will indicate a developing downside acceleration.

Gold

Rising Inflation is a Global Trend

"Inflation, inflation, inflation!" That's what all the headlines have been shouting for a month. Defiantly, gold slips to new lows. Which do you believe? Which did you believe in April-June 1987, immediately following the peak in silver at $11 and its secondary top at $9.50? The headlines below show what articles and ads had to say then. Today silver is making two-year lows, down nearly 50% from its 1987 high. The ads and articles shouting "inflation" are likely to be wrong this time, too.

June 11, 1987

"Silver's Increase is not a Temporary Phenomenon"

SILVER

IS EXPLODING! DON'T MISS OUT

Silver has again begun to outperform all other precious metals

Silver Is Waking Up!

Speaking of the 1987 high, remember when the crowd gave us such grief for being bearish on gold back in 1987 as it edged to new highs late in the year, well after the peak in silver? Gold *stocks* peaked as well, in August of that year, but the bulls said their crash in October was a "fluke." Well, our gold stock index has been devastated in the past year and a half, falling nearly 50% into last December's low. The rally since then appears to have completed a fourth wave (see next chart), with another drop due for wave 5. An even more bearish alternate count would label the decline as an ongoing double zigzag (see text, p.37), labeled a-b-c-x-a-b-c, with the second a-b-c having just begun.

Long term wave patterns and cycles still point to lower prices for gold bullion as well. Both were illustrated in detail in the March issue. Although the wave structure allows for a third wave rout (which is why part of the short sale position will be maintained), the support point near $365 under the alternate "triangle" count for the post-1982 wave X recovery must be respected.

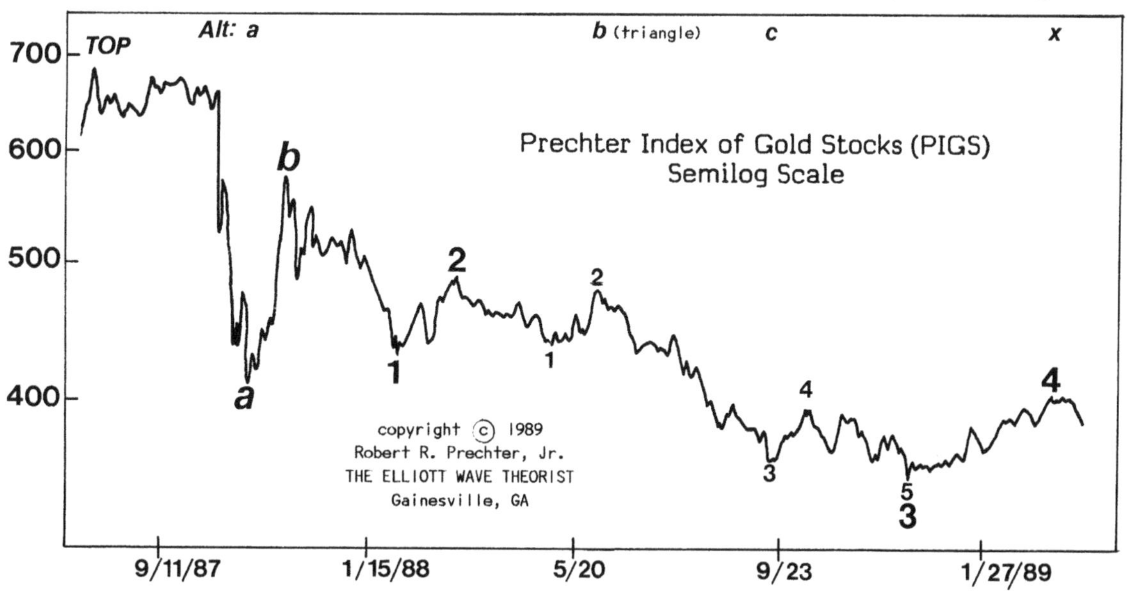

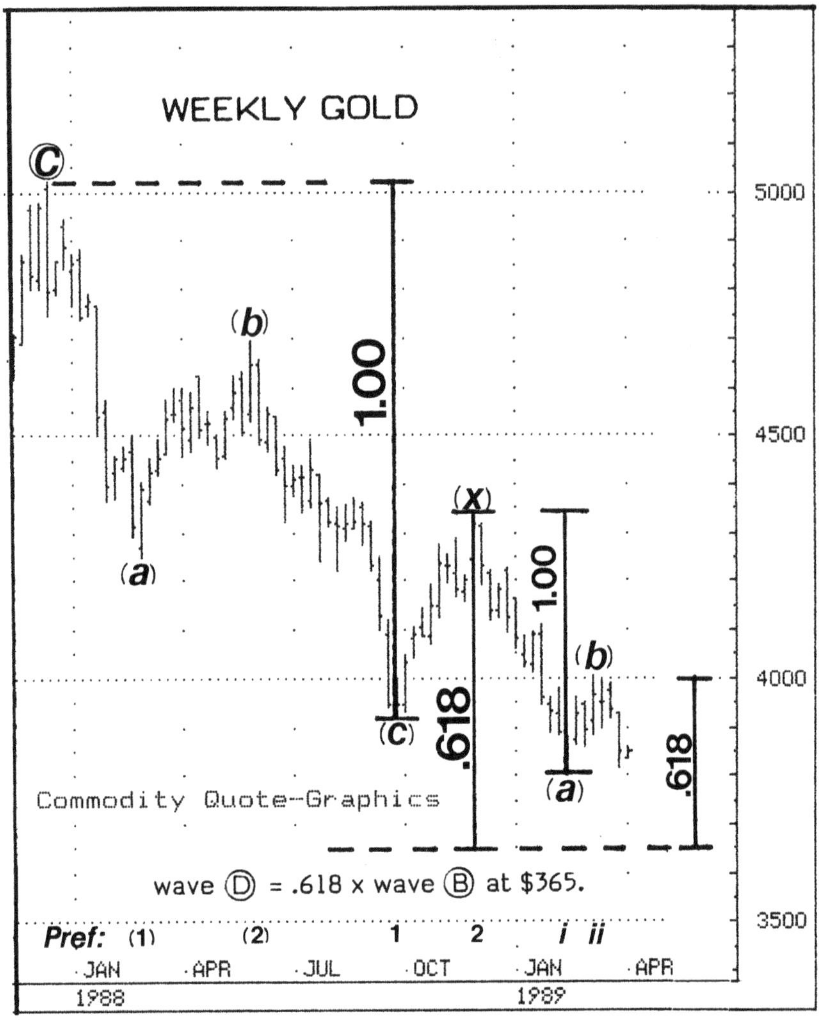

Fully three major and typical Fibonacci relationships within wave patterns indicate that if gold is in wave Ⓓ of a triangle dating from 1982, it will bottom near $365 basis London fix. As discussed and illustrated in the February issue, that is the point at which wave Ⓓ will be .618 times as long as wave Ⓑ (see PRC manual). As the weekly chart reveals, it is also the point at which the second (a)-(b)-(c) in the double zigzag pattern from the December 1987 high will be *.618* times as long as the first *and* the second wave (c) will be *.618* times as long as the second wave (a). If this level breaks significantly, the preferred count labeling the declines from 1987 as waves (1)-(2)-1-2-i-ii (see bottom line of chart) will become almost certain, and gold will be in a third-wave free fall.

Our strategy remains the same. Investors should remain *out* of the gold market. Traders are still 100% short. Cover half on a London fix below $370. Keep the stop at $430.40 basis London fix.

MAY 1, 1989

If gold breaks $365, a downside acceleration is likely.

Do you recall 1987, when EWT interpreted the indicators in the gold and silver markets as bearish? Silver peaked in April and crashed, yet gold rallied grudgingly right into the final month of the year. It was enough to turn the last doubters bullish. Yet throughout those final months of gold's three year rally, our indicators remained steadfastly in "sell" mode. In fact, each new high pushed them further into that mode. Now we know why. Gold and gold stock holders have paid quite a price for ignoring those signs, and there are still few indications of a major bottom in place. It is probable that later this year, stock buyers will find themselves in a similar situation.

Gold — The Slope of Hope Steepens

All the inflation that headlines claim the world is experiencing was mysteriously accompanied last week by new 1989 lows for both gold and silver. The wave count in gold from the 1987 high is more compellingly than ever best interpreted as a series of first and second waves of smaller and smaller degree, implying a collapse in prices dead ahead (see chart). Supporting this case is the 10-day average of the put/call ratio for gold futures, which has just plummeted once again to its lowest level since June 1988 when the wave (2) peak was registered. Second wave peaks following major tops usually mark the extreme in bullish sentiment, so if current psychology matches that of June 1988, it is optimistic indeed and likely to be incorrect. The extent of investor interest still present in the gold market is reflected by the thriving ripoff schemes involving the purchase of precious metals on 20% margin with huge fees being pushed via telephone by fast talking salesmen as described in a 4/24 Wall Street Journal article by Stan Angrist. At major bottoms, such schemes don't fly because investors aren't interested.

Notice that our long standing potential support level of approximately $365 basis London fix is the same level being hit in May by the multi-month support trendline on the daily chart. There are now several reasons, then, that this level will mark either a stopping point prior to a rally of $100/oz. or so to complete a triangle pattern from 1982, or a downside acceleration. The preferred count supports the latter outcome, but our strategy takes both into account. Investors should stay out of the gold market. Traders are still 100% short; lower the stop to $420 basis London fix. Following a London fix below $370, cover half and lower the stop on the remaining 50% position to $390 basis London fix.

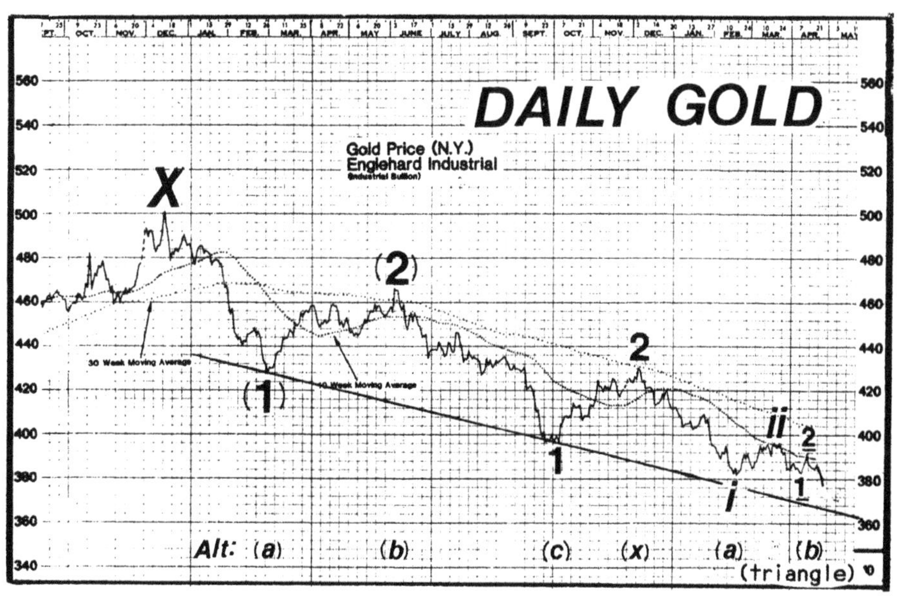

MAY 30, 1989

Gold and silver, after declines lasting 1½ and two years respectively, are finally in position to stage a rally. This potential will be eliminated if they fall 5% below their recent lows.

Gold & Silver

Can you recall all the bullish media commentary toward gold and silver in 1987 and 1988? Last week, London silver hit $5.08/oz., less than half its peak price of two years ago and less than 25¢ from a new low for the 1980s. Our Prechter Index of Gold Stocks also touched a new post-1987 low last week, the minimum required drop given the wave count in the April issue. Gold has reached our minimum downside target of $365/*oz.* basis London fix, in place for months. The actual low so far was $359.27, on May 22, satisfying the Fibonacci relationships discussed in previous issues. Some pessimism has finally crept into the precious metals picture as well. The Bullish Consensus for gold touched a fairly low 30% twice in May, and the bottom fishers in silver, as well as the bullish buyers of the silver/gold spread, appear finally to be giving up.

At this point, the Elliott wave picture for silver allows for a sharp rally, probably peaking in the $8-$10 range, to complete wave Ⓔ of a descending triangle dating from June 1982. A significant break of $4.85 basis London fix will eliminate this count. Thus, silver is delivering exactly the same message as gold, which now allows for a wave Ⓔ rally into the $440-$500 range to complete its corresponding triangle. The overall Elliott wave message for the metals now is that a major rally is in prospect for the first time in months, but another 5% decline will eliminate this possibility and suggest a "third of a third" crash in progress (see wave count in the May issue). These long term charts for gold and silver illustrate the short term crossroads at hand. The ultimate low for the precious metals is not due until 1993 + or - 1 year (see March issue).

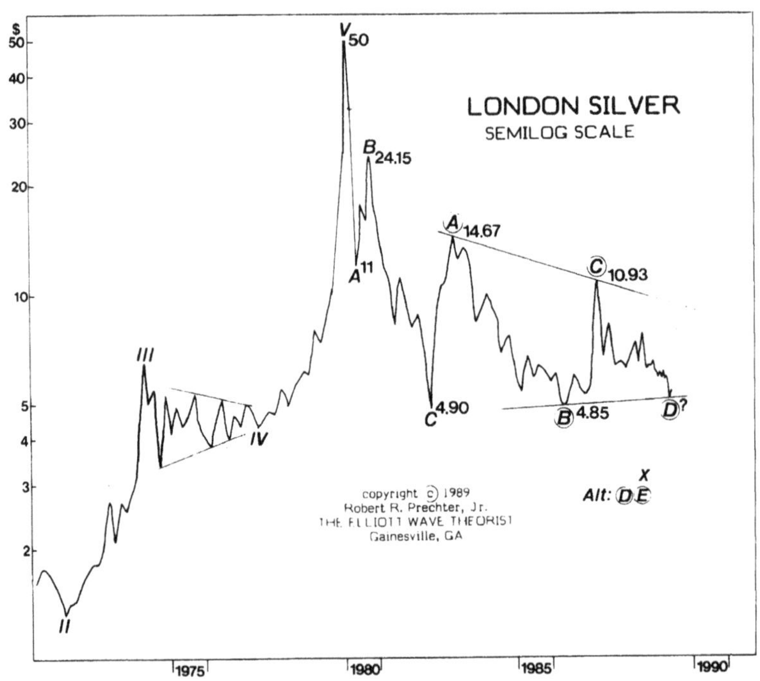

Traders covered half their short positions on May 19 immediately after the London price fixed at $366. The stop has been lowered to $390 on the rest. If a low risk trade becomes available, we should take it. Cover the remaining 50% of short positions if the nearby contract is below $370 but has not traded below $348

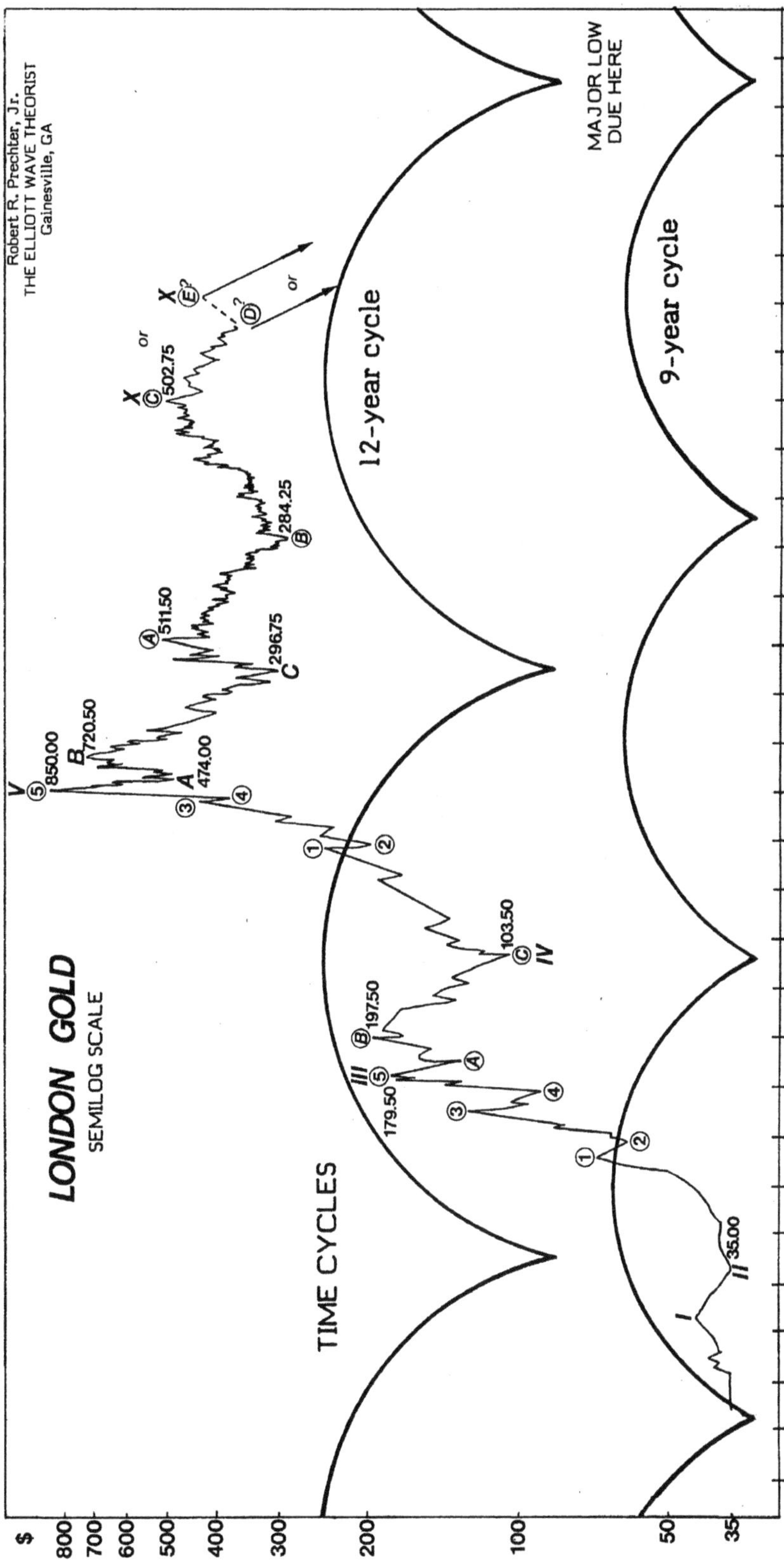
LONDON GOLD
SEMILOG SCALE
TIME CYCLES
Robert R. Prechter, Jr.
THE ELLIOTT WAVE THEORIST
Gainesville, GA
12-year cycle
9-year cycle
MAJOR LOW
DUE HERE
850.00
720.50
474.00
511.50
296.75
284.25
502.75
179.50
197.50
103.50
35.00
or
$
800
700
600
500
400
300
200
100
50
35
1970
1975
1980
1985
1990
1995

[by the time you receive this issue in the mail], and move to 100% long with a stop at $348 basis London fix. If stopped, reverse to 50% short with a stop at $380 basis London fix. Since silver has twice the upside percentage gain potential as gold, it is worth attempting a trade in that market as well, for the first time in years. Move to 50% long below $5.25 and 100% long below $5.06 basis the nearby futures contract and use $4.80 basis London fix as a stop. Investors should stay out of the precious metals market.

JULY 1, 1989

Gold rallied from our support level of $365 + or - $5 and will retain rally potential as long as the June low is not broken.

Gold & Silver

Now that a $150 decline in the price of gold from a year and a half ago has borne out our expectations, I have a point to stress: I am a "gold bug." To state the reason simply, paper money created by a state is doomed ultimately to depreciate substantially, if not catastrophically, in value, based upon the natural incentives and forces associated with governments. The incentives are overwhelming for governments to use the issuance of paper money as a hidden method of confiscating assets, one which is, conveniently for politicians, poorly understood by most voters and subjects.

By extension, it is not reasonable to advocate a "gold *standard*," i.e., the state's issuance of paper money tied to a "price" for gold. My reasoning could fill pages, but a cursory glance at the past fifty years' monetary experience in the U.S. should be sufficient evidence that a gold standard is only as good as the political promises behind it, reducing its ultimate value to that of a paper standard. It could be argued, in fact, that a gold standard of this type is *more* dangerous than one of paper, since it imbues citizens with a false sense of security and allows critical long range planning to be built upon potentially dramatically incorrect assumptions concerning the stability of the monetary measuring unit.

The only sound monetary system is a private one. The only sensible monetary unit, until a better one is discovered and chosen, is the one that has been continually adopted by the free market, and that is gold. Prices should be denominated not in dollars or yen or francs, but in grams of gold. Paper certificates could certainly be issued against gold deposits, but the acceptance of such paper would then be an individual decision, and risks of loss through imprudence or dishonesty would be borne by individuals through conscious choice. Most critical to the understanding of the wisdom of such a system is the knowledge that private issuers of paper against gold have every long run incentive to provide a sound product, just as do producers of any product for the market.

Thievery and imprudence will not disappear among men, of course, but at least such tendencies would not have the potential to be institutionalized as they are when government controls the currency. From a macroeconomic viewpoint, occasional losses resulting from dishonesty or imprudence would be limited in scope, as opposed to the national (and perhaps ultimately, global) disasters that state controlled money has facilitated throughout history.

That being said, it is also true, and of critical importance to wise investing, that markets come in both "bull" and "bear" types. Six categories of analysis, as detailed in issues of EWT, supported a bearish view for the price of gold back in 1987. None of these has reached "bell ringing buy" status even now, so further waiting is required. How much waiting? Fibonacci time lengths shown in the February Special Report support the case that an important secondary peak occurred in December 1987, which was a Fibonacci *8* years (off by only two weeks) from the major top in January 1980. A Fibonacci *13* years from 1980 indicates a turning point in *1993*, just one year from the projected low based on time cycles.

When the time comes to be heavily invested in gold, I expect to be recommending only non-numismatic gold coins, not collectibles and not gold stocks. The reason is that the next economic downturn, as A.J. Frost and I discussed in our book, *Elliott Wave Principle*, will probably signal the onset of the deepest economic depression since the 1930s. The premium that most people will be able to pay for rarity and quality in coins, art, or any collectible item is likely to shrink dramatically. Further, as the crisis deepens, governments will become increasingly willing to confiscate assets, and paper assets such as domestic stock certificates may be an easy target. I would not wish to place my assets in foreign gold mining shares when global social conditions were destabilizing. There are a dozen ways that you could lose the value of such assets, from foreign conquest to domestic takeover to flood, strike or explosion. In fact, the more difficult the situation becomes for mines, the more valuable your bullion style coins will be, since mining difficulties will constrict the flow of new supply, or at minimum raise fears that it will.

Anyone with a reliable method of analysis and stop placement should always go with his analysis 100%, since "diversification" into non-performing assets is counterproductive to profiting through investments. The successful analyst can always change his mind and must work to remain alert for reasons to do so.

At present, EWT's long term opinion still stands: gold is in a bear market that will ultimately hit bottom between $100 and $200 per ounce. On an intermediate-term basis, the target of $365/oz. was achieved, and last month's issue recommended that traders cover short sales and buy. We are also holding a 50% long position in silver and will move to 100% long below $5.06 (it got within 4¢ on Thursday and Friday) basis the nearby contract.

Although the internal subdivisions on the a.m./p.m. London gold chart are sometimes less than perfect, a five wave rally *is* in place in London gold from the June 13 low. This development is consistent with the start of a larger advance, which would be confirmed by a move above $380 basis London fix. Until that happens, however, that rise can be counted as wave "c" of an a-b-c upward flat correction, peaking right at the apex of a preceding triangle (see alternate count on the chart), allowing for another breakdown in prices. Indicators are neutral. While this situation disallows a strong forecasting conviction, it is consistent with the case that *any rally will be a bear market rally, not the beginning of a substantial bull market wave.*

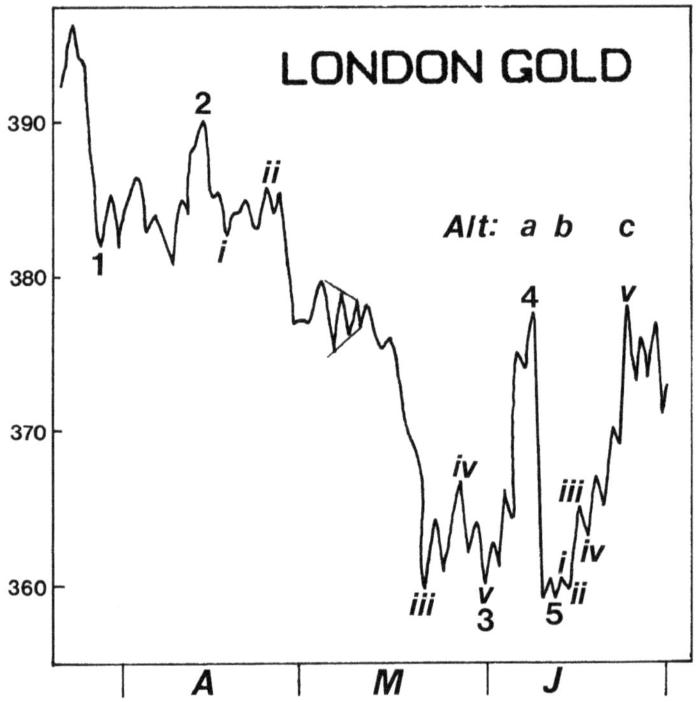

With long term cycles exerting the greatest influence on gold prices, and with wave structure quite clear, we haven't needed to add short term time cycles to our precious metals input this year. Nevertheless, it is interesting to note that Don Weisman of AcuTrend (Box 34, St. Cloud, MN 56302), who has been doing a good job with the metals for quite some time, has a model that projects a rally over the next month or so.

Investors should remain out of this long term bear market. Traders should place a sell stop and reverse to 50% short at $356 basis the nearby futures contract. If gold moves above $400 basis London fix, raise the stop-and-reverse to $370 basis London. If you return to 50% short, move to 100% short at $377 with a stop at $385, both basis London fix. Traders should keep the stop in silver at $4.80 basis London fix.

JULY 29, 1989

Gold, by going sideways, has dissipated its bullish potential enough that traders should join investors on the sidelines once again.

Gold & Silver

Gold has rallied since meeting our downside target, but the length of the meandering since then has given the advance from the June low less of an impulsive look. The odds have increased that gold is in a corrective rally of only Minor degree. Traders should sell long positions now, at approximately breakeven, and join investors on the sidelines. Silver positions should also be closed out.

AUGUST 28, 1989

We are still out of the gold market, which continues to languish.

Gold & Silver

So far, our decision to stand aside from the precious metals markets has been correct. Both gold and silver may still be forming triangles from the 1982 low, allowing for wave Ⓔ, a final sharp rally, to occur. Silver still presents the better risk/reward ratio, as it is close to the level of its May 1986 low, where a stop can be placed. Gold could rally $100, but silver has potential to double to the $8-$10 range as long as $4.85 basis London fix is not broken significantly. The current price is only 30¢ above that level. Traders can buy with a stop at $4.80 basis London or $4.75 basis nearby futures, whichever is hit first. Sell above $8.

OCTOBER 2, 1989

Silver has completed its intermediate term base pattern and still has rally potential to the $8-$10 range. Gold is likely to follow, but it has less upside potential in percentage terms. Long term, both metals remain entrenched in bear markets.

Gold & Silver

Last month, *The Elliott Wave Theorist* suggested that gold traders use *silver* as their vehicle this time, since the risk/reward ratio was better. Silver (see chart) appears to have completed a three-month basing pattern. That pattern can be labeled as a diagonal triangle (see text,

p.30), which probably marked the end of the 2½ year decline for wave Ⓓ as shown on the long term chart in the September issue.

In case you missed it, the article reproduced here, which appeared as silver was bottoming, well summarizes typical thinking at a low in a commodity. All the factors mentioned therein are "fundamentals," which presumably were understood by the market and already factored into prices. It is worth noting now because it supports the case for respecting the low as a legitimate turn. Look for a mysterious improvement in "fundamentals" if silver makes it to $8-$10 in wave Ⓔ.

The wave structure in silver off the low shows five waves up with an extended fifth wave (see chart). Wave v is 1.618 times as long as the net travel of waves i through iii, a typical relationship (see text, p.107). A .618 retracement for wave 2 would bring the December contract back to $5.23, in the range of wave 2 of the extension, the normal zone of support.

Silver sinks, remains a tarnished investment

USA TODAY
SEPTEMBER 6, 1989

Silver is sinking toward a three-year low, and analysts say the metal still doesn't shine as an investment bargain.

Tuesday, silver closed at $5.063 an ounce, off 1.3 cents. It hasn't fallen below $5 an ounce since July 1986. The metal is close to the level at which it has tended to bottom throughout the 1980s.

But instead of representing a bargain for investors, analysts say silver could stay bogged down for a while. "There isn't any indication that there's much upside potential in silver for the foreseeable future," says [redacted], president of [redacted] Capital Management in Toronto.

Among the factors weighing against silver:

▶ **Oversupply.** Annual demand worldwide for silver rose 5.5% during 1988 to 443 million ounces. But warehouse stocks of the three principle commodities exchanges — Comex, Chicago Board of Trade and London Metals Exchange — also are rising, says John Lutley, executive director of the Silver Institute.

What's more, silver mining has picked up. And because silver is a byproduct of mining for gold, copper and other metals, increased production in those areas adds to the glut.

▶ **Slowing demand.** The photographic film and electronics industries — which account for 65% to 70% of U.S. silver demand — could be facing a slowdown. "That would take a big bite out of silver demand," says [redacted], chief economist at [redacted] Research Corp.

▶ **Technical factors.** Prudential-Bache analyst [redacted] says silver often moves in tandem with gold, which could be headed for lower prices because of oversupply. "There's been some talk about (the Soviets) selling gold, and all these markets respond to each other," she says.

The bottom line, says [redacted], is that silver has been falling for a while, "and there's nothing to suggest the trend will change."

Silver slides

Quarter—end spot closing price per troy ounce, N.Y. Comex:

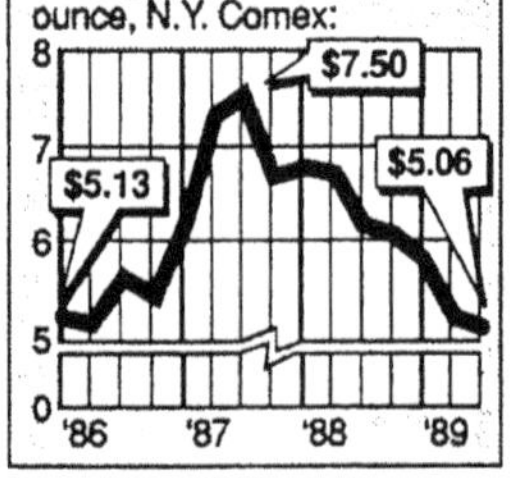

Source: USA TODAY research

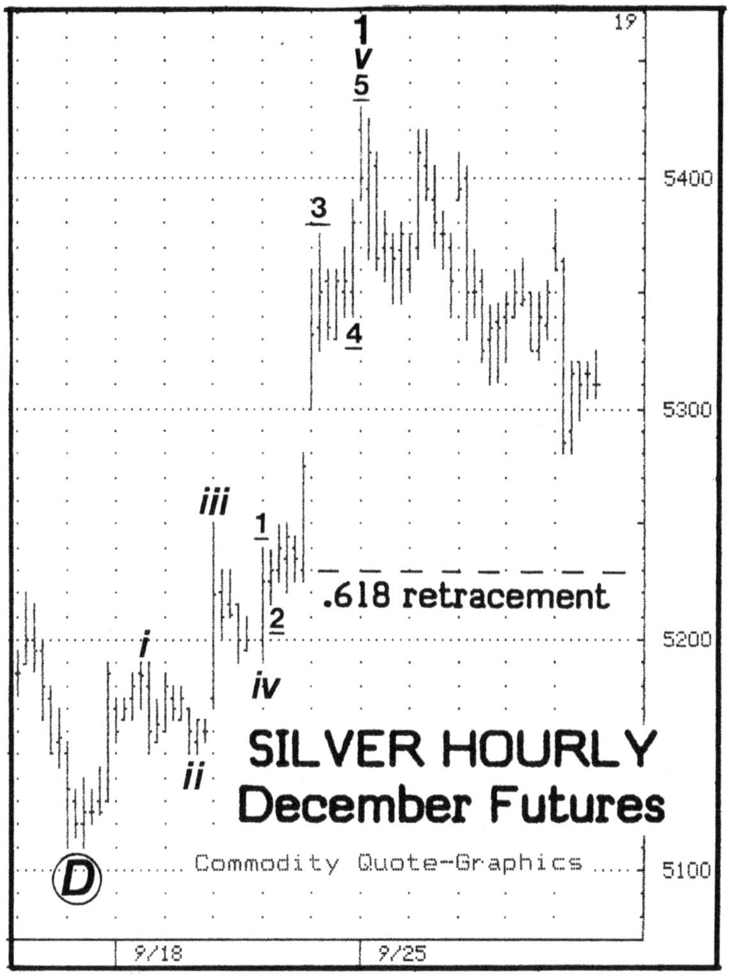

Traders in the metals are 50% long silver. Traders and investors should raise the stop to $5.11 basis the December silver futures contract (now the most active) and move to 100% long at $5.26. Sell above $8.

If gold is in a corresponding wave Ⓔ, it should rally about $100/oz. to the mid-$400s, as per the projection line shown on the long term chart in the June issue. One surprise is that sentiment has turned bullish very quickly on gold. This event may dampen the rally, but it can equally be argued that such psychology should be expected in an "E" wave, which in this case, after all, is the final move in a seven-year net upward recovery pattern! The irony of triangles in bear markets is that when the "E" wave begins, *most analysts view it as a rise from a base when in fact it is the final rally in a top*. If a clear wave Ⓔ unfolds, we will be presented with the best short selling opportunity since January 1980.

OCTOBER 18, 1989 – INTERIM REPORT

Gold and silver have wasted their bullish cyclic potential and appear to be poised for another wave of decline. Traders should move to 100% short gold with a stop at $390 basis nearby futures.

OCTOBER 30, 1989

Gold and silver may have near term rallies, but their longer term outlook is bearish.

Gold & Silver

The current technical situation in gold and silver would best be resolved by a short term rally followed by an intermediate-term decline. In silver, even though a new low occurred in the December contract, stopping out our position, no new low occurred in the "continuation" chart, so the diagonal triangle wave count into a low shown in the last issue is still acceptable, allowing for a rally. Furthermore, there exists a bullish non-confirmation in that while the nearby silver futures contract made a new low, that for gold did not. Those are the short term bullish considerations.

As for the intermediate term, gold stocks over four months ago rallied right on schedule with the upturn in the 8½-month cycle, and it is now time for them to peak. In the past when that has happened, bullion has joined stocks in declining in the "down" portion of the cycle.

The only change in strategy given in the Interim Report was a short sale recommendation for traders in gold. Traders should keep the stop at $390 basis nearby futures. If that level is penetrated, wave Ⓔ in the triangle pattern from 1982 will likely be in force, per the chart in the June issue, and gold will have potential to near $450. If stopped, return to the short side either at $450 or $360 basis nearby futures, whichever is touched first, and place a stop $30 above that level. Another acceptable strategy is to be long gold with a "stop and reverse" at $360. Investors should stay out.

DECEMBER 4, 1989

Gold is rallying in wave Ⓔ of a triangle dating from 1982 and should peak in the $400s prior to several years of decline.

Gold & Silver

One of clearest chart patterns, in my opinion, is that for gold. As readers for the past year know, the best description for the post-1982 wave structure has been a developing *contracting triangle*, first postulated in March 1987. Last year, EWT projected the ideal low London fix for wave Ⓓ to be approximately $365/oz. based upon the typical Fibonacci relationship between waves "D" and "B" in triangles (see PRC manual). The lowest fix, on September 15, was $355.75. At the low, silver was in exactly the same position, while sentiment toward that metal was as negative as it gets at Primary wave lows, as the analysis in the October issue reported. Since then, gold and silver have enjoyed their best rallies in two years. As you can see on the smaller chart, reprinted from the January 30, 1989 issue, our long term graph has continually displayed two dashed lines, one depicting a continuing decline and the other projected along the probable path for waves Ⓓ and Ⓔ. The market is following that path, so the alternative line can now be eliminated.

The first A-B-C decline within the major bear market took a Fibonacci 2 years (see long term chart), while the partial recovery pattern, wave X, appears to be on schedule to last a

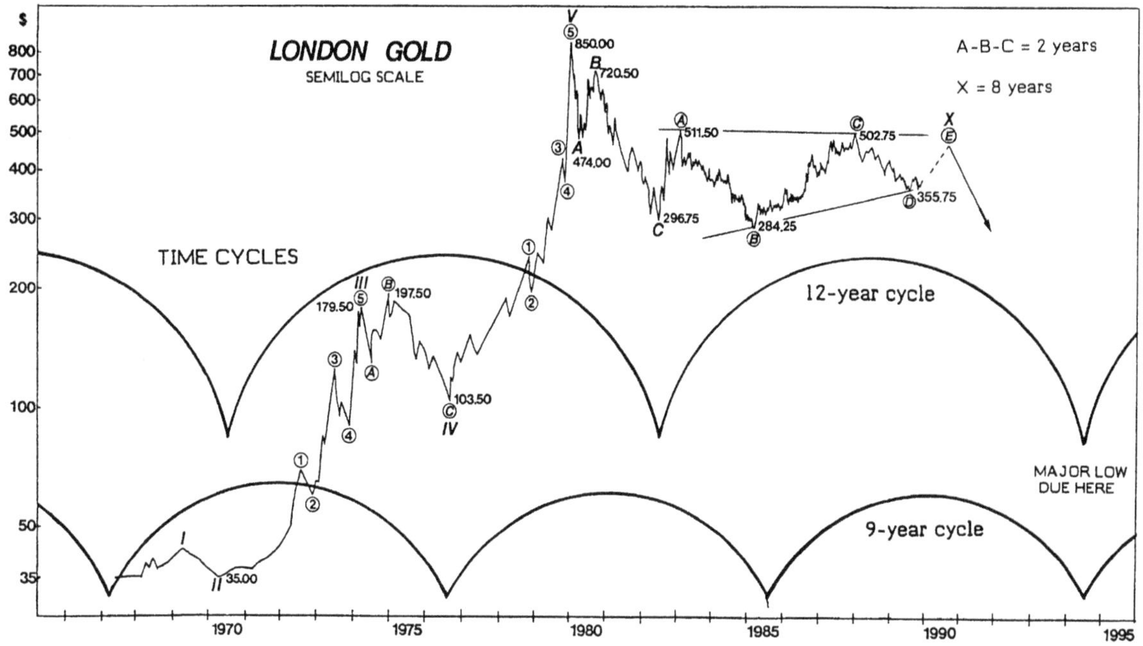

Fibonacci 8 years. The triangle structure is a partial recovery within a larger bear market, so the entire pattern must be understood as a recovery phase, and wave Ⓔ is its final move. It is for this reason that the sentiment on gold has quickly reached an extremely bullish fever, with the Bullish Consensus (Box 90490, Pasadena CA) hitting 75% last week, its highest reading since August 1987. Hardly anyone is missing his chance to announce a major bottom and to urge the purchase of gold. Analyses calling for $800/oz. and $3000/oz. are proliferating. This quick reversal of sentiment is classic "E" wave behavior. The crowd is getting fully invested and will have just enough time to pat itself on the back before a bear market phase equivalent to that of 1980-1982 commences and ultimately carries the price of gold to between $100 and $200 per ounce. Cycles (see bottom of chart and analysis in the February Special Report) indicate a low due in 1994. *1993* would terminate both a Fibonacci 3-year decline and a Fibonacci 13-year bear market.

It was terribly annoying that the very last sharp selloff in gold and silver ruined our nice "long" positions and produced instead a $20 loss in gold. It was an example of how good analysis can be frustrated when it comes to devising a strategy to make money from it. For future reference, we should keep in mind that when a pattern ends in the futures market, stops should be based on the continuation chart, not the nearby contract. From the end of its pattern, silver made a new low on the latter, but not the former. [Note: The short sale for traders recommended in the October Interim Report was apparently stopped out at $390 for a small loss. — Ed.]

Wave Ⓔ should provide an excellent trade, the best short-selling opportunity since gold topped at $720 in September 1980. Although "E" waves can be brief, the conservative approach

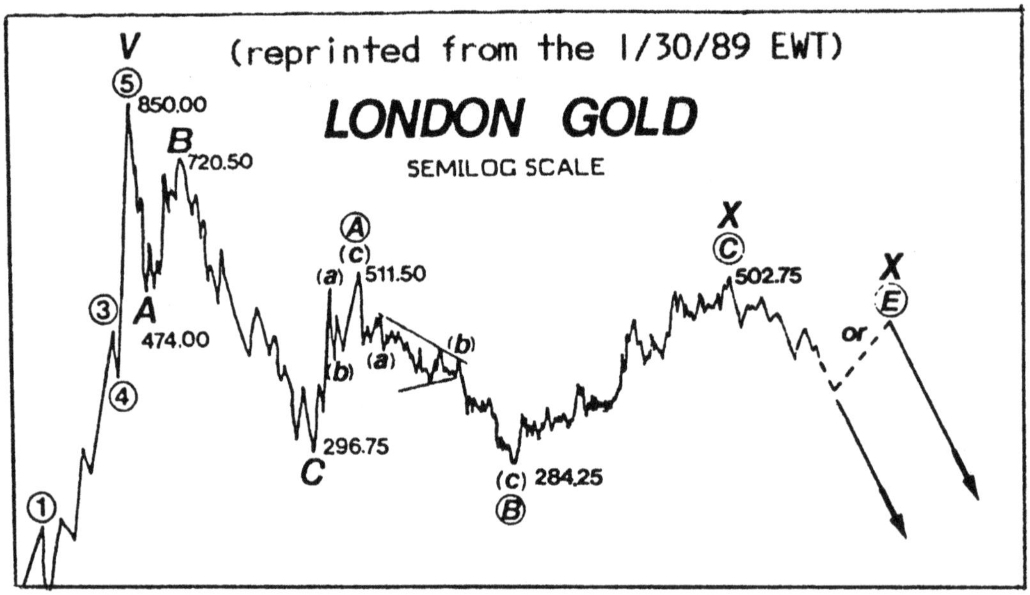

is to wait for a rally of normal size before taking action. If wave Ⓔ is a typical Fibonacci .618 times the length of wave Ⓒ, it will peak at $496/oz. basis London fix. A .382 relationship would target $443 and a .50 relationship $469. Traders should move to 50% short at $440, 100% short at $465 and 200% short at $495 with a stop at $515, all basis London fix. Investors should stay out of gold. Silver still has potential to the $8-$10 per ounce range in its own wave Ⓔ, prior to a resumption of the major bear market.

Alternate Count?

An alternate count that some analysts are using for gold involves treating the $720 peak in September 1980 as the "orthodox top" (see text, p.30). This would, it is argued, allow an Ⓐ-Ⓑ-Ⓒ wave count from there into the 1985 low. While this wave count cannot be ruled out, there are several reasons why it should not be taken as preferred. First, it is unlikely that a market that was as strong as gold in the 1970s would end in a fifth wave failure of such magnitude ($130). Second, the rally to $720 satisfied all requirements for a corrective wave rally, with its a-b-c structure and .618 retracement. EWT's call for a corrective wave peak was mailed the day of the high of that rally on September 23, 1980, so this analysis is clearly *not* being made only in retrospect. Third, the wave structure in the 1983-1985 decline was and is better interpreted as a "three," which is a requirement of triangles. It is *not* easily interpreted as a "five," as would be required in wave Ⓒ of the supposed Ⓐ-Ⓑ-Ⓒ correction. Finally, the peak in 1987 fell short of the peak in 1983, which is necessary for the triangle interpretation. First waves of new bull markets have a tendency to clear such peaks. Gold *stocks*, on the other hand, did make their orthodox fifth wave peaks at the $720 high in bullion (see October 3, 1980 issue), a reasonable occurrence given the late start by gold stocks in bullion's 1976-1980 advance. If the price of gold exceeds $511.50 basis London fix, then the alternate count will gain a good deal of credence. However, betting on that outcome at this stage is not the best way to approach a correct ordering of the probabilities.

DECEMBER 25, 1989

Gold

The two pages of wave and cycle analysis on the exciting long term position for gold in last month's issue remain valid. Within wave Ⓔ, wave (a) appears nearly complete. It should take several months for waves (b) down and (c) up to take place. Traders are still planning to move to 50% short at $440, 100% short at $465 and 200% short (twice a normal futures position) at $495 with a stop at $515, all basis London fix. This is a reasonable strategy with respect to our expectations but does carry risk. The exact resistance calculations were given in the December issue ($443, $469 and $496) for those who prefer to trade at each level with close stops.

The Elliott Wave Theorist, 1990

JANUARY 9, 1990 – INTERIM REPORT

Gold is consistent with waves (a) and (b) of Ⓔ having been completed, with a neat 38.2% retracement by wave (b) in London-fix prices ending at last week's low at $394.95. Look for a wave (c) rally to the resistance levels listed in the January issue. Silver has the same wave count. It is quite common for silver to have its biggest rallies during the final upmove in an advance in gold, which the next rally should be. The potential for a sharp rally will remain as long as $5.02 basis the nearby contract is not taken out.

FEBRUARY 5, 1990

Gold is struggling to put in a respectable wave Ⓔ rally and so far is on track with expectations.

Gold & Silver

Wave Ⓔ in gold, its last bear market rally of the post-1982 recovery pattern (see long term chart, December issue), still appears to be on track. The majority, despite what is so far a measly rise of only 18%, has announced a new bull market. This conviction is typical of psychology in an "E" wave. Evidence of the breadth of bullish sentiment is supported by the Bullish Consensus figures, which reveal that advisors have been averaging 80% bulls, a 4:1 ratio, for four weeks, an extreme typical of the *end* of a long rise, not the beginning. *In fact, out of 32 futures contracts, gold is #1 in advisors' bullish enthusiasm.* Cycles clearly indicate a peak in the first half of 1990 and a low in the fourth quarter. (In fact, stocks, bonds and gold all have cycle lows due in the fourth quarter.)

There is far too much long term danger to invest in the metals. Short term support, if a flat correction is in progress, is $395-400. A break of that support area would argue that the wave Ⓔ rally is over. Calculations for resistance levels given in December were slightly off; the correct levels for Fibonacci multiples of wave Ⓒ are $439, $465 and $491, so traders should move to 50% short above $435, 100% short above $460 and 200% short (twice a normal position) above $488, with a stop at $520, all basis London fix. Those wishing to reduce risk may use the resistance levels for reference and keep stops close.

Silver has yet to signal a major breakdown by falling below $4.85 basis London fix, and as EWT explained in the January Interim Report, "It is quite common for silver to have its biggest rallies during the final upmove in an advance in gold." Therefore, a frenzied rally in silver to the $8-$10 range is still possible some time in the next few months. Such a rally would further lock in the long term bullish conviction that the precious metals are "the place to be."

FEBRUARY 26, 1990

Gold is still on track in its wave Ⓔ rally. Any further rise will begin triggering our short-selling strategy for traders.

Gold & Silver

One of the most popular opinions among analysts today is that gold has begun a new bull market. In my judgment, the probability of that having occurred is close to zero. EWT has been calling for a bear market rally, however, and that rally has occurred. Recent developments are adding interest to the picture.

During February, our gold stock index fell over 18% after peaking within two weeks of the ideal high for the 17-month cycle (see chart). Gold bullion hardly budged in price.

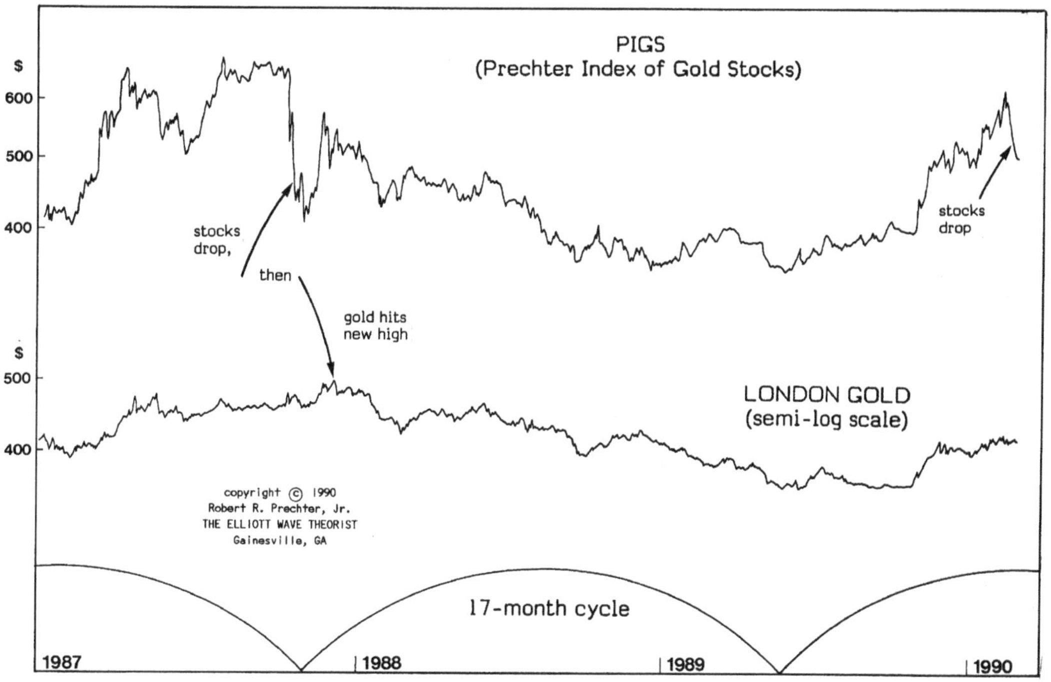

The last time this type of development occurred was in 1987, and in that year it was followed by another rise in gold bullion to its final high. It would be ideal for this progression to repeat. If it does, our short-selling strategy, in place for months and still requiring higher prices, will be triggered nicely. The next 17-month cycle low is due in the fourth quarter. Silver is running out of time to launch a rally, but the possibility will remain for a few more months as long as the 1986 low at $4.85 basis London fix remains unbroken.

APRIL 2, 1990

The 17-month cycle illustrated in last month's EWT appears to have provided the peak for wave Ⓔ in gold at $423.75 basis London fix. The bear market has probably resumed, although the uptrend line at $360 has not been broken yet. Although there is a slim chance for a bounce back into the $400s, gold's bear market rally appears to have topped in February.

Gold

These comments began last month's section:

> One of the most popular opinions among analysts today is that gold has begun a new bull market. In my judgment, the probability of that having occurred is close to zero. EWT has been calling for a bear market rally, however, and that rally has occurred.

Since the price of gold just fell $60/oz. in five weeks, retracing most of its nine-month advance, wave Ⓔ of the contracting triangle (see text, p.44) dating from 1982 may well be over. Rarely does an "E" wave trace out a flat correction as would now be required for further rally. It usually traces out a zigzag, which is in place on the chart. Moreover, the action of both gold stocks and bullion appear to confirm the validity of the 17-month cycle, which was shown last month in a topping phase. Also keep in mind this description of the psychological environment from the February 5 issue, the day of the top in gold stocks and two days before the peak in bullion:

> The majority, despite what is so far a measly rise of only 18%, has announced a new bull market. This conviction is typical of psychology in an "E" wave. Evidence of the breadth of bullish sentiment is supported by the Bullish Consensus figures, which reveal that advisors have been averaging 80% bulls, a 4:1 ratio, for four weeks, an extreme typical of the *end* of a long rise, not the beginning. In fact, out of 32 *futures contracts, gold is #1 in advisors' bullish enthusiasm.* Cycles clearly indicate a peak in the first half of 1990 and a low in the fourth quarter. ...There is far too much long term danger to invest in the metals.

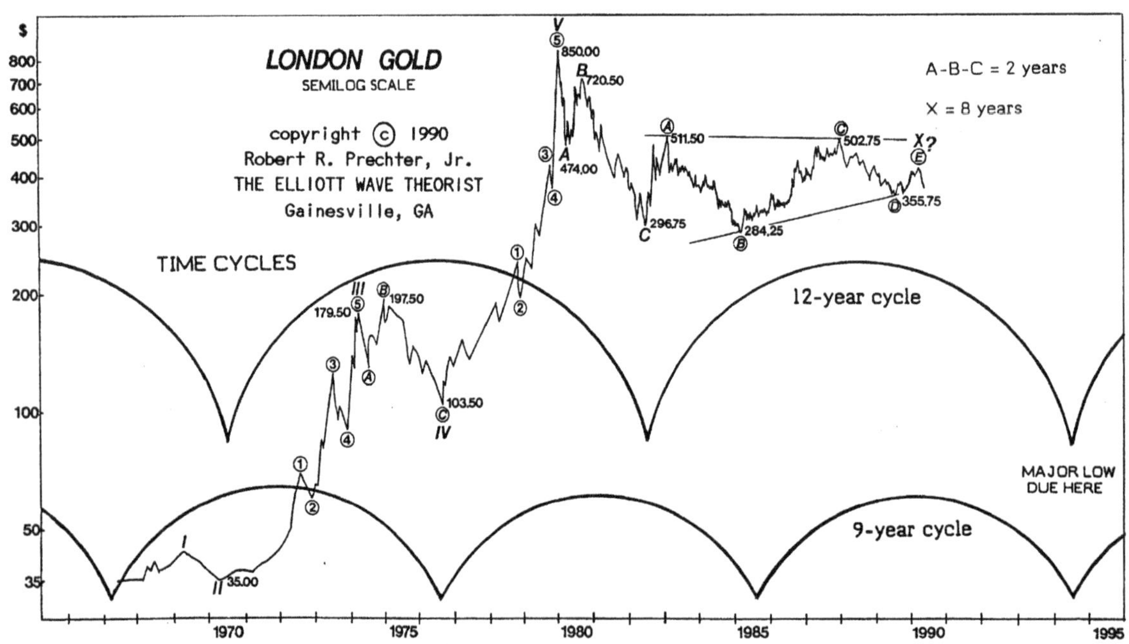

A poll of 200 investors taken in February by The Public Register was similarly revealing. Their one-year outlook for most markets was typical, i.e., that in 12 months they would be almost exactly where they are today. As EWT pointed out long ago, such pronouncements are not validly conceived predictions at all, merely extrapolations of present conditions or trends. Investors' outlook for silver, however, was for a move to $10/oz., a 100% gain from current levels! That lopsidedly bullish outlook is likely to be as right as the public's bullish outlook for real estate two years ago and that for secondary stocks six months ago.

That the bullish enthusiasm in February was a typical reflection of the psychological state of mind of the investment crowd at the end of a long term bullish phase is a subtle point. The bullish phase in this case is not a one way advance but an Ⓐ-Ⓑ-Ⓒ-Ⓓ-Ⓔ *sideways* pattern that nevertheless constitutes an *upward* correction. The fact that investors did become so bullish last month is testimony to the power of R.N. Elliott's observation that pattern, not level, reveals the state of psychology in a market.

Gold's technical condition has been so bearish in recent months that EWT's only plans were to have traders sell short at high levels while investors stayed on the sidelines. Unfortunately, and despite the majority's call for $1000 and $2000 gold, bullion's performance since the bottom last year has been so weak that it even fell $15 short of its first Fibonacci resistance level!

The bear market rally for gold is probably over. However, it is still within the realm of possibility that wave Ⓔ is tracing out a complex pattern that will take it to the mid- to upper $400s. It is still within the realm of possibility that *silver* will undergo a rally for wave Ⓔ (see chart, September 1989 issue), since the critical support level of $4.85 basis London fix has not yet been broken. For this reason, keep our short selling strategy in place for now (see details in the February issue). A drop below $360 will break the uptrend line from 1985 (see chart). All participants should continue to avoid the "long" side of the gold market.

APRIL 30, 1990

Short term rallies notwithstanding, gold's major bear market remains in force.

Gold & Silver

The February 1989 Special Report argued that the bear market in gold beginning in 1980 would bottom in 1993 or 1994, the former suggested by Fibonacci progressions and the latter by cycles. Subscriber Steve Rock points out that two of the Fibonacci relationships that point to 1993 indicate May 1993. That is the month at which the February 1985 low (the low for the 1980s) would divide the bear market into Fibonacci proportion. It is also the month at which the second phase of decline dating from the February 1983 peak would take a Fibonacci 4.236 times as long as the first phase of decline (labeled A-B-C as the top chart shows).

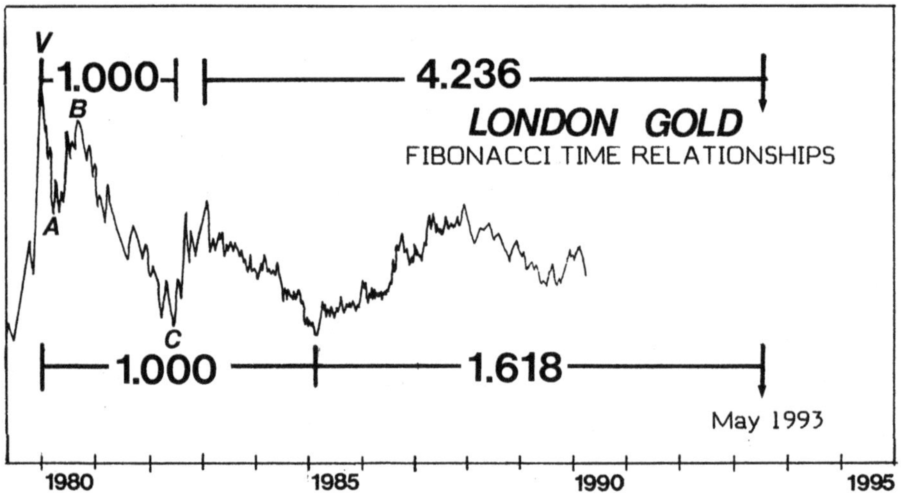

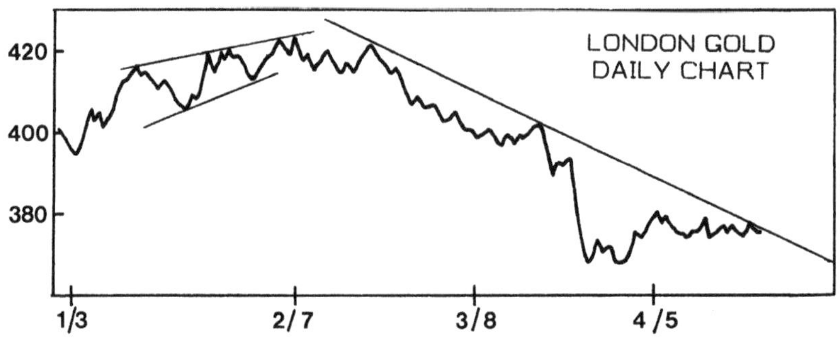

The sideways action in gold over the past eight years has allowed analysts and investors, under the impression that a large base is forming, to stay bullish for the long term. As documented in EWT, bullish opinion reached another extreme in January and February of this year despite the measliest of rallies. Notice that this psychology occurred at a point *below* the peak of December 1987. This is a common occurrence. EWT documented a similar occurrence in February 1983, when the percentage of advisory services bullish on gold hit an all time high despite the price being more than $300 below where it was in 1980. As another example, the peak attendance (4732 people) for an NCMR conference occurred in November 1980. Investors were signing up for that hard-money-oriented conference in August and September, when gold bullion was peaking at $720/oz. in its "B" wave, eight months *after* the all time high at $850.

With the tools of time forecasting indicating no bear market low until at least three years from today, there is every reason to continue to avoid investing in gold. Gold's day will come. When it does, it may present the best investment opportunity of the 1990s. For now, however, the downside target remains "below $200/oz.," with the highest probabilities for a low near $105 and $179 respectively (see February 1989 Special Report).

On a short term basis, the sideways action in gold over the past month has relieved the oversold condition and brought prices right to a declining trendline, as you can see on the a.m./p.m. London fix chart. (Notice also the neat diagonal triangle into the peak; see text, p.30.) This development is short term bearish. Meanwhile, silver has declined to within 9¢ of the $4.85 level basis London fix (see discussion in the February 1989 Special Report). A break of that level will confirm that silver's Ⓔ wave peak occurred at $5.89 in November 1989.

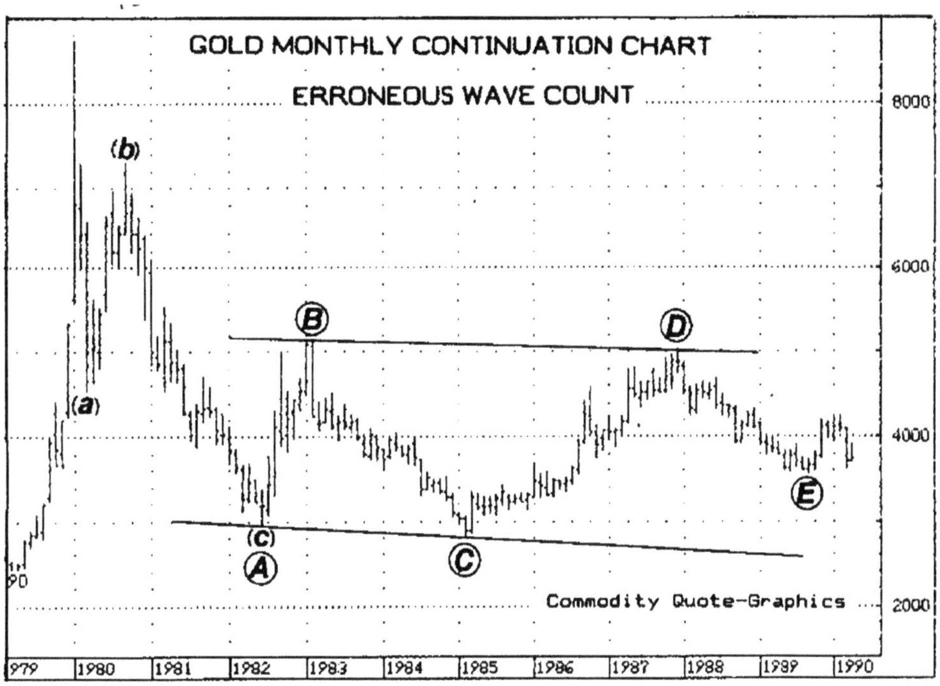

Erroneous Count

As an aside, it might be worthwhile to address why gold is *not* tracing out a triangle from the 1980 peak (see chart). Some wave labelers, probably desiring to find a reason to stay long term bullish, have suggested this wave count, which is clearly erroneous. Besides being one of the ugliest supposed triangles I've ever seen, it violates the definition of a triangle. Briefly stated, no triangle pattern can allow wave "C" to move beyond the price level of the end of wave "A" except an expanding triangle (see illustrations in text, p.43), which itself requires wave "B" to move beyond the price level of the start of wave "A." In this case, then, all types of triangles can be eliminated as acceptable interpretations of the price action from the 1980 peak.

MAY 28, 1990

Gold & Silver

Gold made another new low for the year last week, while silver did not. This is the first non-confirmation in awhile and could allow for a short term rally. However, the big picture continues to be that of an ongoing bear market. Silver again coyly held within 9¢ of its 1986 low at $4.85 basis London fix. Potential for a rally to $9 remains as long as that level holds. A break of that level will confirm that the second major bear market decline for precious metals is in force, with the target for gold still below $200/oz. I lean toward expecting a breakdown because the 17-month cycle in gold (see chart, March issue) remains "hard down" until October.

Special Section: Collector Coins

Gold and silver's price trends have continued to confound the precious metal bugs, who for the past ten years have continued to argue that $1000 gold and $50 silver are "just around the corner" and that inflation is due to take off again "any time now." It hasn't happened. It isn't likely to do so soon, either, short term rallies notwithstanding.

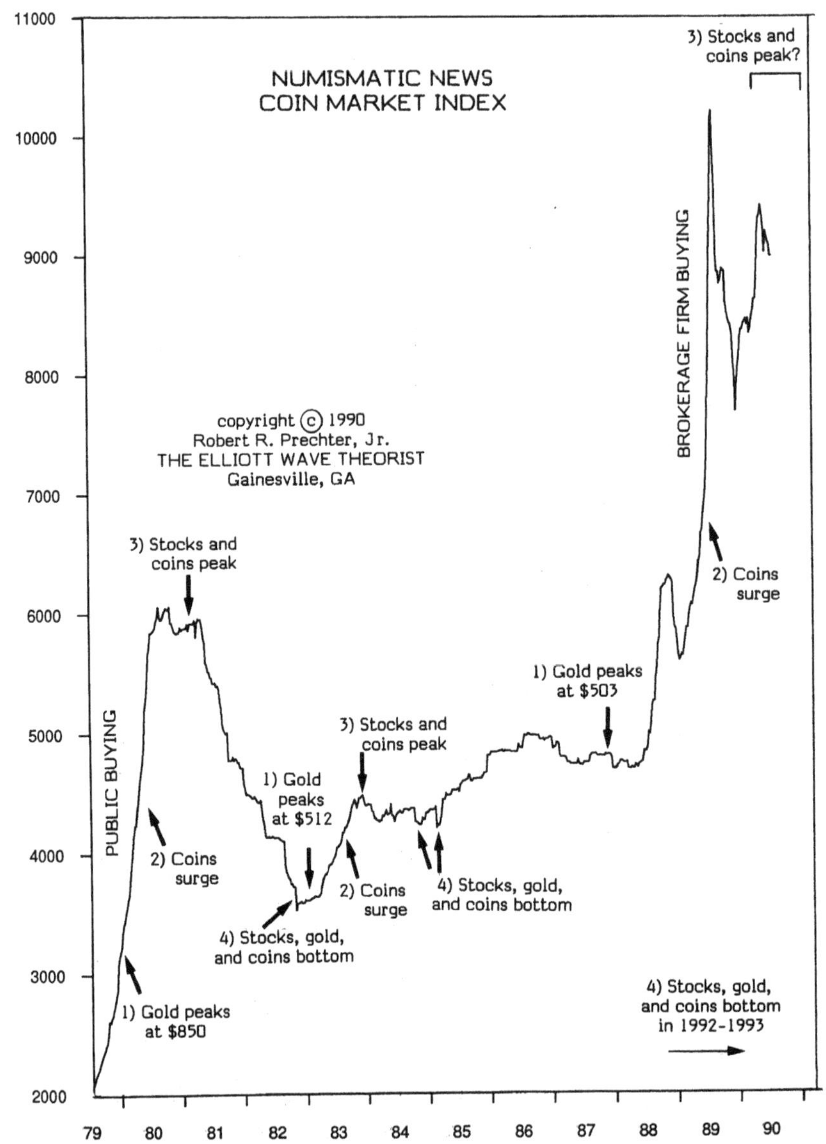

This chart, constructed from data courtesy of Numismatic News, Iola, WI, supports the case that prices for collector coins are often less a function of the underlying metals prices than of the prevailing psychological environment for standard investments. Coin prices over the past decade have surged powerfully after the peak in gold and silver prices, when the stock market was rising. The sequence in this disinflationary decade, in fact, appears to be as follows:

0) Stocks and gold rise.
1) Gold peaks.
2) Collector coins rise.
3) Stocks and coins peak together.
4) All three markets bottom together.

Thus, collector coin prices enjoy some benefit from rising bullion prices but react much more strongly to an ebullient climate for investment as reflected by a rising stock market. Ironically, those who waited for gold to decline in price ended up paying much more for their coins.

The reason this analysis is so important now is that coins have recently enjoyed a surge in prices beginning after gold peaked in December 1987 and coinciding with the rising trend of the stock market. The coin market is way overbought, and signs of a stock market top are building rapidly. Collector coins, then, have registered or are about to register a major peak in prices.

Perhaps the biggest clue that the bull market is ending is the fact that the brokerage industry has finally embraced the concept of coins as an investment. Their decision to act comes after two decades of dramatically rising coin values to the extent that, according to Salomon Brothers, rare U.S. coins over the past twenty years have produced the highest average annual return among all major investments, including the most prized art. How deeply have brokerage firms gone into coins? According to *Coin World*, on February 8, Merrill Lynch filed with the SEC for formation of a $50 million publicly offered limited partnership in rare coins, with an option to push the ceiling to $75 million. Merrill's first fund, offered in 1986, generated $7.25 million. The second brought $25 million and closed its offering over a year ago. In addition, Kidder Peabody's Futures Management Corp. expects to invest $100 million in its rare coin fund in 1990, adding to the $42 million it already has in it. Shearson Lehman Hutton is becoming involved in that market, and as *Coin World* put it, "the success with the Kidder fund has other Wall Street investment firms sitting up and taking notice." This is the same type of deep commitment some brokerage firms made to "nifty fifty" fundamental stock analysis in late 1972-early 1973, to real estate in 1979 into the mid-1980s and to junk bonds in 1985-1986. All this buying is in anticipation of wide public demand. In similar situations of the past, anticipated demand turned out to be a false hope. The casual assumption that demand would be *forthcoming* was simply based on years or decades of public demand *preceding* such decisions. Note that most of the brokerage firm buying came during the near vertical surge in prices in 1988-1989. That is when it became clear to coin investors that brokerage firms were committed to coins as an investment, and prices were adjusted accordingly. How many dollars and how many years of such investment were discounted by that surge? Needless to say, all the new coin market players stress the desirability of holding coins *long term*.

I have been waiting patiently before issuing this commentary, watching the behavior of both the stock market and the gold bullion market, each of which is related to some aspect of collector coin investment psychology. If the progression depicted in the chart remains true, a joint peak in stocks and coins is the next event to occur. At this point, I would estimate that collector coins in general (along with stocks) have between zero and eight months left in their major appreciation. Although I hesitate to place wave labels on this type of index, which often peaks when it is moving most vertically, it appears that *coins are in the fifth wave up from the 1982 low*. The risk in this market now due to cyclic forces in commodity prices, inflation/deflation and the economy is tremendous and increasing. If the gold bullion price declines into 1993, then collector coins will receive a "double whammy," and a loss of 50%-90% would not be out of line. Consider that a 75% decline would merely bring coin prices back to where they were when the gold price first achieved $350/oz. in 1979.

There are times when action is so prudent that it must be encouraged. Any investor overly weighted in collector coins should strongly consider *selling* his collection at today's lofty prices. If you're truly a collector, you should delay your purchases for two to three years. This is only one analyst's opinion, of course; the final decision is up to you. [Note: See follow-up dated July 1995.]

JUNE 29, 1990

Gold should be avoided completely as an investment. If it rallies further in wave Ⓔ, an excellent short sale will be provided. Silver may bounce, but its long term bear market is not over yet, despite the recent decline to its lowest level in 14 years.

Gold & Silver — A Slope of Hope

A few years ago, I coined a phrase that balances the idea of the famous "Wall of Worry" that bull markets climb. Bear markets, I suggested, slip down a "Slope of Hope." Well, for the precious metals, the Slope of Hope is steepening. Those preaching inflation, and the 86% of the public (according to a recent poll) that fears it, are not watching inflation's key leading indicators, the price of gold and silver. Those who think that gold is a "hedge against deflation," as some have asserted, are quite unlikely to have been satisfied by recent action either.

As anticipated last month, silver finally broke down through its long term support shelf at $4.85 basis London fix. This event further reduces the chances that gold bullion could still be in wave Ⓔ of its triangle and supports the case that the February peak will not be challenged in coming months. (For a look at the long term picture of gold, see the April issue.) This new evidence nicely fits our ongoing cyclic analysis that "the 17-month cycle in gold remains 'hard down' until October." As far fetched as it may seem to most observers, the 17-month cycle indicates that the price of gold should accelerate to the downside over the next four months. This chart, which was last shown in the March issue, updates prices to the present and shows an idealized picture of the downside pressure now being exerted on prices by the 17-month cycle. As you can see by the wave labels, the count for the London fix agrees with this picture in that a sharp decline in a "third of a third wave" appears imminent. Dan Ascani's conclusion in the latest *Elliott Wave Commodity Forecast* [now *Futures Junctures*] that "the wave structure in platinum argues strongly that the 1988 low will be taken out, probably soon," certainly fits the picture for gold and silver. It would not be surprising to see the $300 level in gold broken before year-end. The ultimate target, due to be met in 1993, is still "below $200/oz.," with $105 the most likely stopping point.

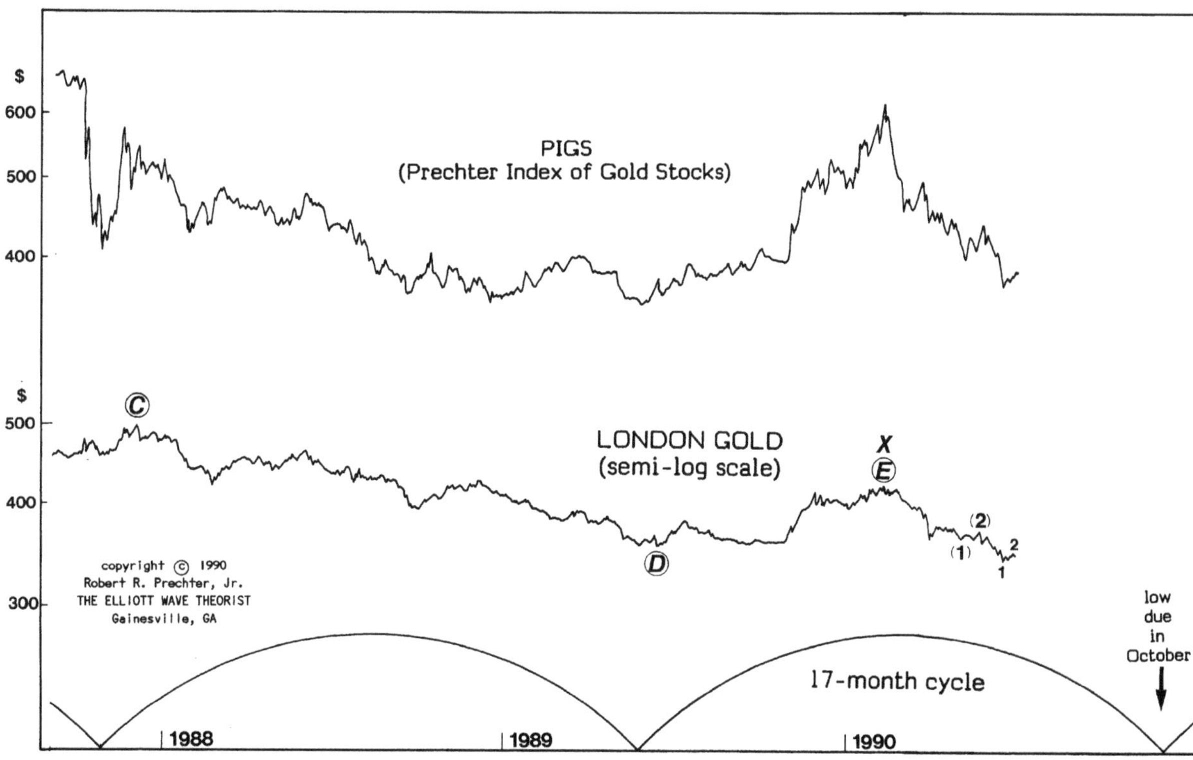

JULY 27, 1990

Gold is nearing the end of its countertrend rally.

Gold & Silver

The daily chart of London gold presents the best wave count for gold from the 1987 high. The wave ② rally currently underway is just a few dollars from its first resistance area at $375 basis London fix, which marks the peak of the previous fourth wave and a .382 retracement. The "downside acceleration" that appeared likely given the position of the 17-month cycle (see chart, July issue) has not yet materialized, but with three months of downside pressure left to go and the wave count shown here, this market is still best avoided as an investment. In fact, traders should short gold now with a low-risk stop at $380 basis London fix.

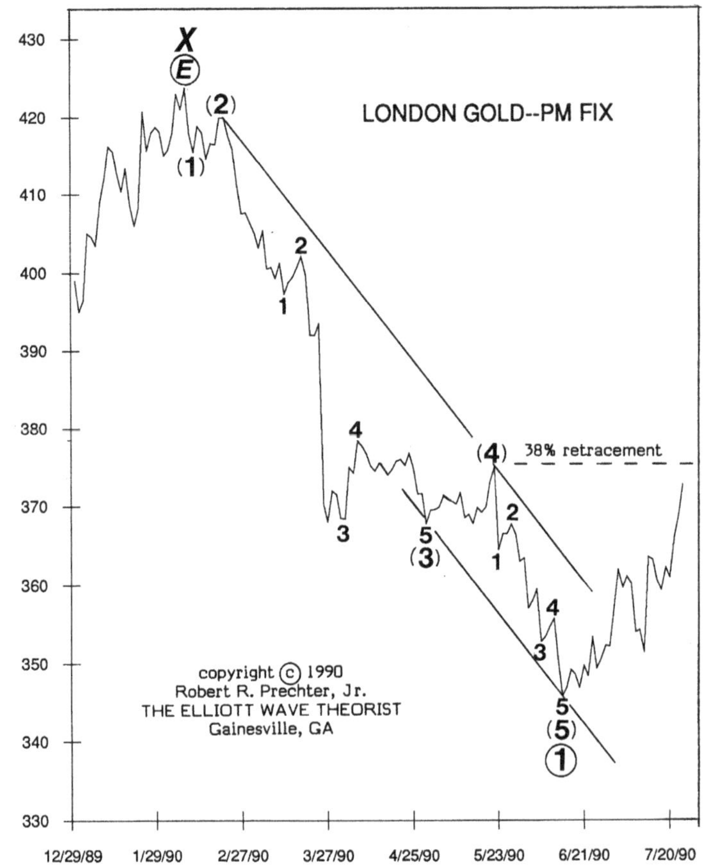

THE A.J. CORNER

I spoke with A.J. Frost last week, and he's still sticking with his two main predictions, to which he has held since 1987, that gold will ultimately soar to $1000/oz. and that the Dow will peak at 3249 before the next collapse takes place. As for the latter forecast, the Dow is less than 10% away, a great call already as far as I'm concerned. I've asked A.J. to contribute to a book project I'm working on, a real treat for you that will be announced by year end. [Note: This was the book, *The Elliott Wave Writings of A.J. Frost and Richard Russell*, which was published in 1996. – Ed.]

AUGUST 1, 1990

"Collector Coin Prices Nearing a Major Peak," by Robert Prechter for the August 1990 issue of *Coin World*

Supporting the case that the bull market for collector coins is ending is recent "internal" market action. It is classic behavior at an overall market peak for segments of a market to

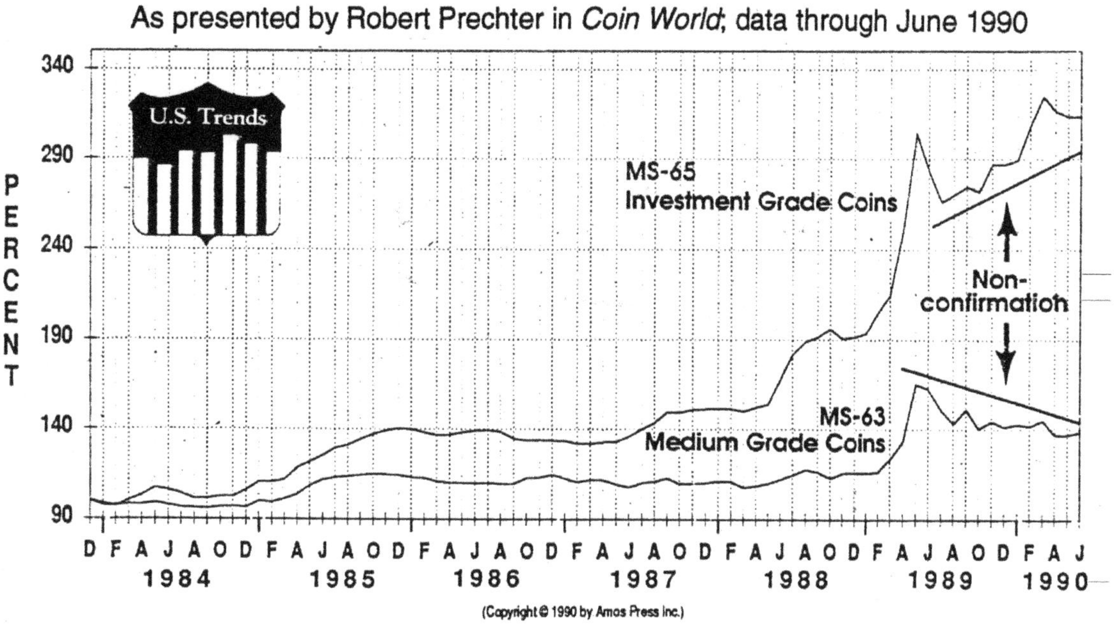

CHART REVEALS trend of lower grade coins diverging from higher grade coins in the last year.

begin moving counter to the previous trend, while others continue in the prior direction. For example, it is typical in the construction of a stock market top for secondary stocks to begin heading lower well before the "blue chips," or high grade stocks. The accompanying chart, published regularly in *Coin World*, reveals that over the past year, the trend of low grade coins has diverged from that of high grade coins. In technical parlance, the index of low grade coins has "failed to confirm" this year's new high in the index of high grade coins. As *Coin World* Trend Editor Keith Zaner described the action in a recent article: "The rare coin market is definitely divided. Collector coins are doing extremely well but the common date[s] are weak." This behavior is analogous to what happens when a stock market is peaking after a prolonged rise.

AUGUST 31, 1990

Gold's recent runup is part of a "last gasp" in a top-building process that extends back to 1987. Silver is within pennies of new lows for the decade after sporting the single highest bullish consensus other than petroleum products a week ago. At some point gold, probably held in a foreign depository, will be the alternative of choice[, but not now.]

Gold & Silver

The rally in gold since mid-June drove the ten-day average of the put/call ratio on gold futures contracts to its lowest level since we've been keeping the indicator, a very bearish reading. In fact, despite war news from the Middle East and a frenzied rally, gold bullion fell short of last February's peak, and gold stocks didn't even get close. The bullish attitude among traders toward silver was so strong that The Bullish Consensus a week ago revealed 77% bulls. Only oil and gas futures had higher percentages, and those for obvious reasons. Silver performed so poorly that last week, three days after its brief rally peaked, it fell right back to the area of its lows. The summer rise in gold can be nicely counted as a "five," so another short term rally could ensue to finish off what may actually be wave Ⓔ of the triangle we've been tracking. Regardless, with technical indicators this weak, investing in gold for the long term is out of the question. Traders were stopped out of the last trade for a $15 loss. If gold climbs, move to 50% short at $428 and 100% short at $478 basis London fix, with a stop at $505.

The Gold/Silver Ratio

Last week a subscriber wrote to request comment on the gold/silver ratio. Now is a perfect time to highlight this picture. In the 1970s, there was a belief that gold and silver had a traditional ratio of valuation. This belief has emptied the pockets of numerous traders who have, for ten years, continued to bet that silver would begin outperforming gold "any day" because the spread was so wide. As you can see by the chart, which EWCF editor Dan Ascani prepared, the ratio was 16:1 in late 1979 and early 1980. It has since risen to over 80:1, a Fibonacci five times multiple of the multiple. Most fascinating is that the change in multiple forms a beautiful ten-year-long Elliott wave, complete with a diagonal triangle fifth. As Paul Montgomery pointed out when presenting his study of the bond/stock yield ratio, such constructs cancel out many "fundamental" considerations such as, in this case, the inflation rate, the absence or presence of war fears, etc., and leave a trail of changing investor preference due almost exclusively to psychological factors. Such changes are precisely the province of the Wave Principle. While other wave counts are possible, the odds are high that the gold/silver ratio is peaking out.

Because the price pattern for gold suggests that a bear market is in force, it is more prudent to assume that the ratio will fall as a result of gold declining rapidly rather than silver advancing rapidly. As you are aware, EWT's long term downside target for gold is to "below $200/oz.," with the most likely stopping point near $105. Consider this. If the ratio were to return to its level of early 1980 and silver did not budge, gold would fall to below $80/oz.! A return to 16:1 may be unlikely, but the ratio could certainly return to a middle range between, say, 30:1 and 40:1. Gold's target could

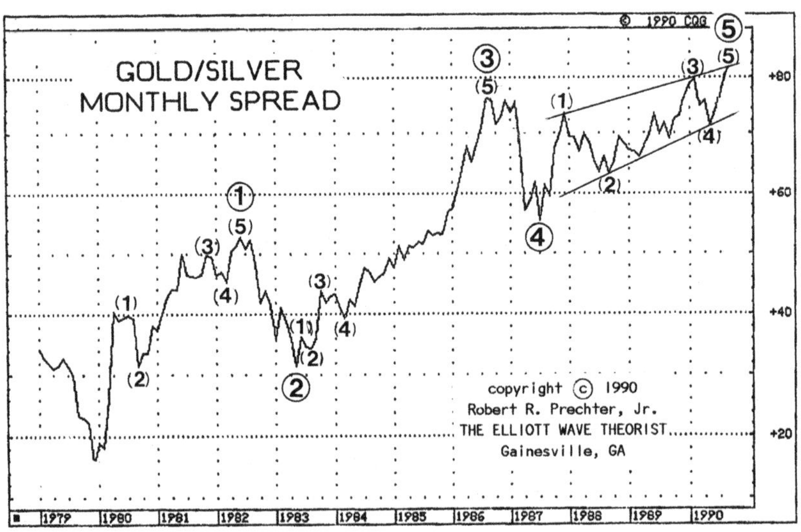

then be met if silver falls only another $1. All that is required is a change in perceived relative value, which according to R.N. Elliott's rules is about to begin.

SEPTEMBER 28, 1990

Gold should continue its rally until it reaches the mid-to-upper $400s. After that, its trend should be down for three years.

Gold

The September issue noted numerous bearish sentiment indicators and non-confirmations with regard to gold, and to date little has happened to change that assessment. If a bear market began at the peak of wave Ⓔ last February, then the summer 1990 rally was merely a deep wave (2) retracement. However, there is another wave count to consider, and if it works out, traders will be allowed an excellent short-sale entry. As last month's issue mentioned, the rally that began this summer "may actually be wave Ⓔ of the triangle we've been tracking." "E" waves of triangles, as EWT has explained in the past, usually occur on news. There was little news at the February peak, but now the conflict in the Middle East is presenting a classic news background for a wave "E" rally in a triangle of eight years' duration. Take a look at the chart and you'll see this labeling.

Certainly the attendant technical evidence supports the conclusion that the summer rally fits either of these interpretations, which have in common that the rise is all or part of a corrective-wave advance, not the start or resumption of a true bull market. True bull markets display strong breadth and agreement among components. Corrective wave rallies are selective. Consider that since wave Ⓔ began, gold stocks have lagged badly, retracing most of their initial gains, volume in numismatic gold coins hasn't budged, and silver has fallen to a new 14-year low! What does such action more likely indicate, a real bull market or a corrective-wave advance?

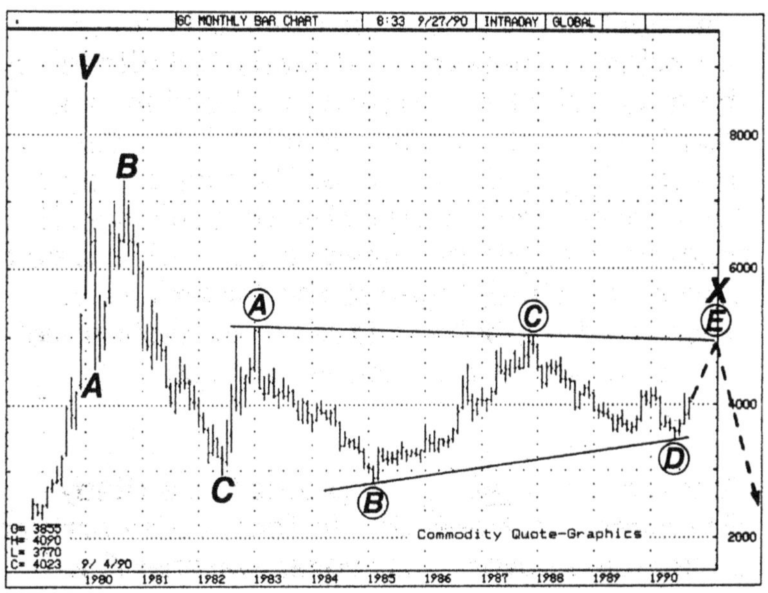

For wave students: The summer rally in gold best counts as a "three" on the daily chart (not shown) and thus fits both interpretations: wave (2) or part of Ⓔ. The rise was short for a complete wave Ⓔ, so the most sensible conclusion is that if wave Ⓔ is in progress, it will develop into a double zigzag (see text, p.37), which will soon carry the gold price to a new high for the year. Ideally, that final rise would occur on even more dramatic news, such as actual fighting in the Mideast.

Two targeting methods (see PRC manual) will help provide good short selling entry points if wave Ⓔ is still unfolding. First, "E" waves of triangles are often related to "C" waves by .618. Next, the second a-b-c in a double zigzag is often equal in length or related by the Fibonacci ratio to the first. The two best targets under this analysis, then, are $448, where the two zigzags will be equal (if wave x, the intervening decline, has ended) and $481, at which level Ⓔ = .618 Ⓒ. These targets are based on London fix prices, but using nearby futures provides similar figures. Traders, then, should move to 50% short on a London fix above $445 and 100% short on a fix above $478, with a stop at $505. Investors should continue to avoid the precious metals.

OCTOBER 26, 1990

Gold should be avoided completely as an investment. If it rallies further in wave Ⓔ, an excellent short sale will be provided. Silver may bounce, but its long term bear market is not over yet despite the recent decline to its lowest level in 14 years.

Gold

Investors should continue to avoid gold. Even holding T-bills (not to mention stocks) has vastly outperformed holding gold (not to mention silver) for the past ten years. The big opportunity for traders will be on the short side in a month or two *if* gold rallies further in wave Ⓔ (see chart in October issue). If it doesn't, fine; that will be another down market we will have avoided.

Special Section: Silver — Five Major Peaks in a Decade

I can recall the 1980s' tops in silver quite vividly. Each had its own story. Take a look at the chart showing the long term wave picture in silver. This developing pattern has remained quite readable throughout this time despite silver's behaving in what might appear to the average market watcher to be a highly deceptive manner. You might enjoy relating the scenes with the corresponding price spikes on the chart.

Wave V

As silver rose into its first peak at $50/oz., a trading acquaintance of mine told me that he was tired of trading options, that he "needed more excitement," so he started trading silver futures. He got more excitement, all right. He started shorting about $20 too early and wiped out his net worth in two weeks. On the exact top day, another trading friend came back to the office from lunch looking a bit pale and related a story of seeing a man walk into his friend's coin shop, plunk down $50,000 in bills and demand, "Turn that into silver!"

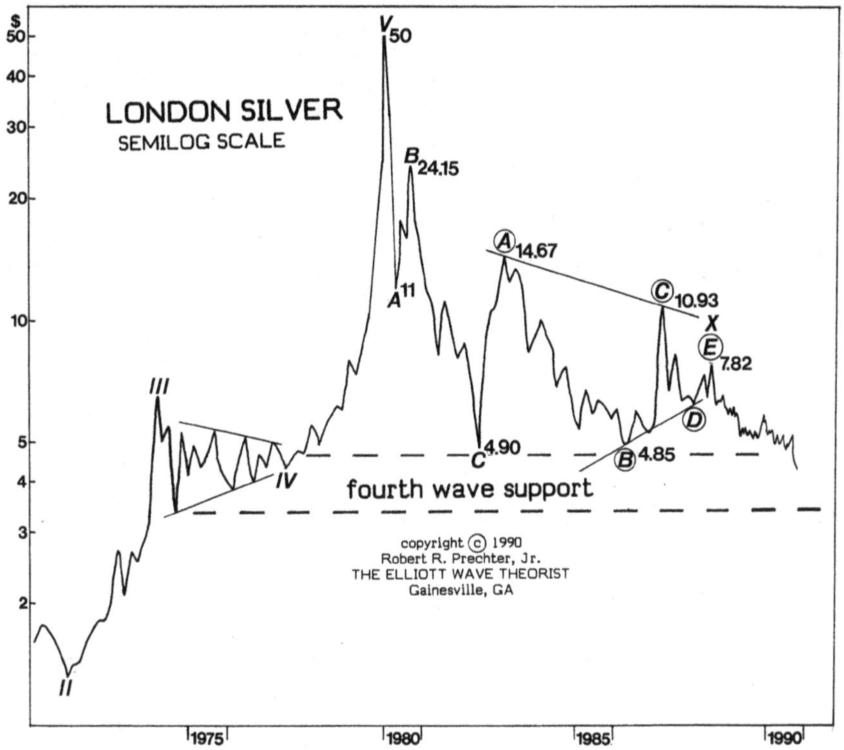

The proprietor checked the quote and said, "I'll have to charge you $52 an ounce." The man answered, "I don't care what the price is; just turn that paper into silver!" He had bought literally the minute of the top and had the distinction of paying a higher price than is shown on any chart. The January 6, 1980 issue of EWT described the price action in gold (and by extension, silver) as a "blowoff."

Wave B

The next important rally peak occurred at $24/oz. in September 1980. Three months prior, in June, the famous National Committee for Monetary Reform had held its summer conference in Montreal, and I made my first major presentation as *The Elliott Wave Theorist*. There were 1000 attendees, and it was disconcerting to this newcomer to watch 997 heads shake slowly as I argued that gold was going to peak soon in its bear market rally and fall below $400/oz. and that the place to be was stocks. On September 23, 1980, EWT issued an Interim Report on the exact top day in the metals indicating that the rally in gold, which had met its upside target at $710, was over.

Wave Ⓐ

The third rally peak, which occurred in February 1983, was accompanied by the most bullish investment advisory sentiment ever on the precious metals, a classic "B" [or "X"] wave psychology (see text, p.68). The February 1983 EWT issued a "sell" on gold, and it crashed a week later, along with silver. The February and March 1983 issues chronicled the event.

Wave Ⓒ

In April 1987, yet another major bear market rally in silver was culminating in a frenzied surge. Even then, silver sold for an apparently depressed ⅕ of its peak price seven years prior, so it looked like a "bargain." Normally conservative "value" buyers were talking in press interviews about price/earnings multiples of 200 on gold stocks, which were already selling at terribly high ratios of 70:1. Once again, it was classic corrective-wave psychology. Overall technical readings for the metals were continuing to worsen, and on April 24 the short term indicators argued urgently that a top was hours away. That weekend, EWT issued a short-selling strategy for gold and silver. As it turned out, the one for gold was eight months (though only $25/ oz.) too early. But silver was about to kiss the sky goodbye, at the peak of wave Ⓒ of X. On Monday morning, April 27, the metals opened on the upside in panicky trading, with gold reaching $477 in London. At the same time, an acquaintance of mine who had been waiting a long time to sell his physical silver called his bullion firm to get a quote. "You can get $10.75 for it," he was told, as the nearby silver futures contract was exploding in price, ultimately to $11.25/oz. As my friend was rushing to his dealer's with the bullion in the trunk of his car, however, the voracious precious metals buyers were running out of money. Suddenly the trend reversed, and selling poured into the market, driving prices down. Twenty minutes later, silver futures had collapsed to $7.20, off an amazing 36% from the morning's peak. It never saw those highs again. (In case you're wondering, my friend's dealer honored his morning quote.)

Wave Ⓔ

The last rally worthy of the name culminated in June 1988. That month's issue of *The Elliott Wave Theorist* showed once again the detailed wave count for silver, arguing that despite the "inflation" headlines in the press, the rally was merely wave Ⓔ in a multi-year contracting triangle. As that issue stated, "This latest psychology is normal for an "E" wave, when the last buyers step forward to invest." Even those buyers have now lost 50%, though that's better than the 92% loss for the guy who paid cash at the $50 top.

How Low?

The buyers at each of the above-described peaks have regretted their actions ever since. [EWT said originally in November 1979, "Silver can be expected to drop back to between $4 and $6 some time in the next decade," which it did.] As EWT said again in 1988, "Silver's price is ultimately likely to go much lower than anyone currently expects." The downside support zone of $3.78 - $5 was clearly marked back then on the chart (see dashed lines on the chart). Although silver hasn't fallen below the bottom of that zone, the fact that it has finally broken below the apex of the triangle that formed wave IV in the 1970s is an ominous sign.

As you can see by the chart, silver has recently cracked to $4.20, a price it hasn't seen since 1976. What's more, if the Elliott wave count for gold that EWT has been illustrating for years is correct, then the ultimate low for silver can only be imagined. According to our long-standing target, gold still ultimately needs to fall to below $200/oz., probably close to $100, in order to complete the Supercycle bear market that began in 1980. Time cycles still indicate that the bear market will not end until 1993. It is hard to imagine silver advancing significantly with its higher-class cousin doing so poorly. As you can see by the semilog chart, there is still lots of room on the downside on a percentage basis, a fact that is not evident on the standard arithmetic charts, which make silver appear as if it is near zero already. The price of $3.78 registered on July 12, 1974 is the low of the "previous fourth wave" support zone, but is not necessarily a target. We will rely on wave form to tell us when the bottom is at hand.

NOVEMBER 30, 1990

The long term outlook for gold is bearish, and a major decline could begin at any time.

Special Section: Gold

The long term wave structure and cycles remain very bearish for gold into 1993, so investors should continue to avoid the precious metals. The near term picture has just gotten very interesting.

As far back as the February issue, EWT had concluded, "Cycles clearly indicate a peak in the first half of 1990 and a low in the fourth quarter." The outlook was refined in the July issue, which included a chart labeled, "low due in October." Gold has made a low in mid-October, but the rally so far has been extremely anemic. In fact, our gold stock index has failed to participate in the rally and has now fallen to its lowest level in over four years. In examining the long term price pattern in gold, it appears that a very rare and beautiful Elliott wave pattern is taking place.

In the late 1970s, silver created a nine-wave triangle, one in which the "E" wave itself traced out a triangle. [See illustration accompanying the 9/1/95 issue, from Chapter 1 of *Elliott Wave Principle*. — Ed.] The same picture can now be identified in gold, as you can see by the long term chart. The details of wave Ⓔ are shown on the daily chart.

EWT has been making the case for several years that the partial recovery pattern dating from the 1982 low was tracing out a triangle. Wave Ⓔ appeared to end last February, but little happened apart from further sideways action. This sideways extension of the count may explain why. One additionally interesting fact is that the swings of the triangle appear to be zeroing in on the $388/oz. level. Very long time readers will recall that that level was EWT's forecast for a low back when gold peaked in 1980. $388, which marked a .618 retracement of the 1976-1980 advance, was hit to the dollar in 1981. It led to a rally that failed after several months, confirming that the old uptrend was dead. It now appears that the entire partial recovery pattern from 1982 is trying to register its orthodox peak near the $388 level. This price would precisely mark the .618 division of the bear market that is now in force if its ultimate target is indeed $103.50, as EWT has argued all along based strictly upon the normal stopping point in bear market wave patterns! The 1976-1980 advance was a fifth wave, which is

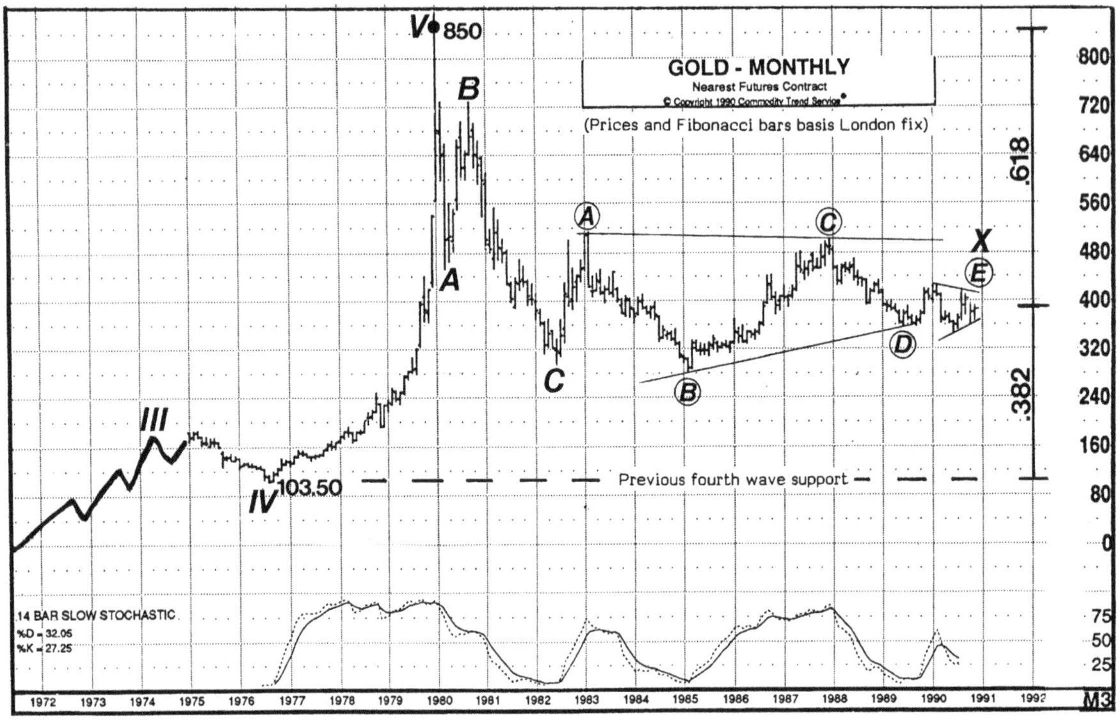

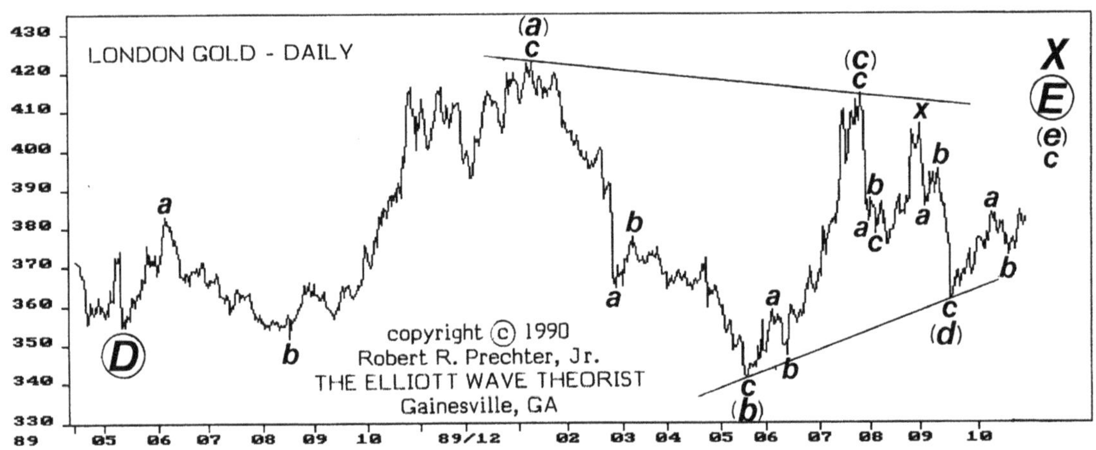

precisely what this bear market should fully retrace, so the $388 level has as much meaning as it did a decade ago and even more validity in dividing that distance into Fibonacci proportion.

There are additional interesting relationships in place. In terms of time, the year 1990, as the February 1989 Special Report pointed out, is a Fibonacci eight years from the 1982 low, five years from the 1985 low and three years from the 1987 high, making 1990 [i.e., now] an ideal year for the end of a pattern. From here, a Fibonacci *three* years down in the second major A-B-C decline of the bear market would be in 1.618 time proportion to the Fibonacci *two* years down in the first major A-B-C decline from 1980 to 1982. Notice also the symmetry in the fact that wave Ⓑ fell to a new low relative to the start of the large triangle wave X, just as wave (b) fell to a new low relative to the start of the small triangle wave Ⓔ.

If the 17-month cycle did bottom in October, and if it is topping already, then the left-hand translation is extreme, which is in turn very bearish. When silver moved out of its late-1970s triangle on the upside at \$6/oz., there was no stopping it as it soared virtually non-stop to \$50/oz. What a surprise it would be to the majority, which is focusing on Mideast tensions, if gold, after a Fibonacci eight years of "holding up" from 1982 and a Fibonacci five years of "holding up" from 1985, now resumed the relentless bear market that began a decade ago.

The updated chart of the gold/silver ratio argues once again that a five wave advance from 1980 is near an end and supports the case for a major decline in the price of gold. Investors should stay out. The downside potential is so well indicated that it seems worth a \$30 risk. Traders should move to 100% short immediately with a stop at \$418/oz. basis London fix. Our previous analysis that wave Ⓔ would rise to about \$481, at which level it would be a Fibonacci .618 times the length of wave Ⓒ, is still valid and will immediately revert to the best wave count if the \$418 level is exceeded. If stopped, return to 100% short at \$475.

The Elliott Wave Theorist, 1991

JANUARY 4, 1991

Gold is in a wave Ⓔ rally, the final rise in a triangle pattern dating back to 1982. Though it is not expected, a rise above the 1987 peak at $502.75 would negate the long term bearish analysis.

Gold

The analysis presented in last month's Special Section on gold remains valid. If gold is in wave (e) of the smaller triangle beginning June 1989, the current rally should peak below $418 basis London fix. If gold is in wave Ⓔ of the larger triangle beginning June 1982, gold should peak below $512. The long term picture remains bearish, and major cycles point to a great buying opportunity in 1993-1994. Traders keep the strategy from last month, holding 100% short with a stop at $418 basis London fix.

JANUARY 25, 1991

Gold probably ended an 8½-year partial recovery pattern on January 14, fulfilling the expectations presented in the Special Section on gold in the December issue.

Gold

The December issue of EWT presented a Special Section on gold, which concluded that from the 1982 low, gold was about to finish a contracting triangle (see text, p.43), the "E" wave of which was itself a contracting triangle. "E" waves typically occur on *news*, some fundamental justification for buying that traps investors at precisely the wrong time. Fears of the onset of war in the Gulf accompanied the early January rise in the price of gold, and that just happens to be the wave that EWT was labeling wave (e). As the January issue stated, "If

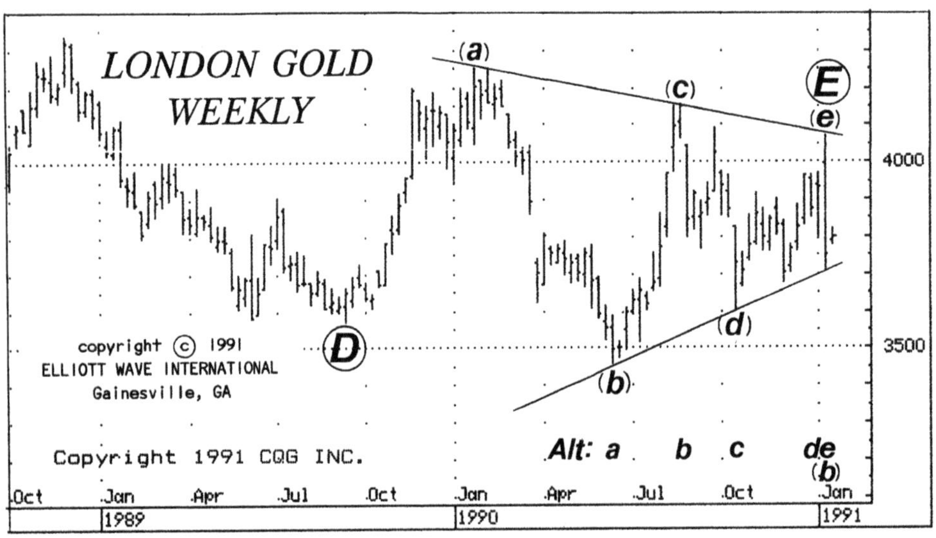

gold is in wave (e) of the smaller triangle beginning June 1989, the current rally should peak below $418 basis London fix." The chart above is an updated version of the one shown two months ago. The day of the peak, this headline appeared in USA Today:

Investors seeking safety in gold coins

Nervous investors, fearing war in the Persian Gulf, flocked Tuesday to American Eagle gold coins. The U.S. Mint reported that it sold 25,000 ounces of the coins within a 24-hour period that ended Tuesday. That's compared to 32,950 ounces sold during all of December.

Investors rushed into gold, believing they were entering a "safe haven." When the Alliance attacked Iraq on the evening of January 16, gold briefly rose a few dollars overseas, but the next day it collapsed. If the last rally in gold is over, the typical investor, who has shifted from high yield bonds to stocks to foreign stocks and now to gold, will soon discover that he is once again in another bad investment, with what's left of his money evaporating rapidly once again.

Keep in mind, however, that the outlook for declining prices will not be confirmed until gold falls below $350. Until then, the chart can be labeled as still being in the larger wave Ⓔ, which leaves open the possibility that gold will reach the mid to upper $400s before turning down in earnest.

The peak in London prices at $403.70 on January 16 is now a benchmark high. Traders can lower the stop on our 100% short position from $418 to $404. If that level is exceeded, the pattern will then suggest a bullish intermediate term picture. If traders are stopped out, return to 50% short at $440 basis London fix and 100% short at $475, with a stop at $505.

The June 29 issue of EWT illustrated the 17-month cycle along with the label, "low due in October." That low came on schedule on October 16. After four months, there has been little net progress, suggesting that longer term cyclic influences are down, which further suggests that the cycle is likely to peak early. It may already have done so. That conclusion will be confirmed if gold falls below the level of the October low at $365 basis London fix.

MARCH 1, 1991

The final period of rise in gold into December 1987 was technically speaking a fools' market, and our warnings appeared off base for a number of months. However, silver (the "secondary" market to gold) started down in April of that year, way ahead of its blue chip cousin, and, though it took awhile, those who bought gold in the $450-$500 range have paid the price for trend following. Gold is in a bear market that will continue until 1993-1994 and end near $105/oz., though a brief countertrend rally should begin now.

Gold

It's time for a rally in the precious metals, but first let's review the bigger picture. EWT updated the bearish long term outlook for gold in the Special Section from the December 1990 issue. The triangle thesis presented then has proved out perfectly, as the peak made on the fear of war on January 16 ended wave (e) of Ⓔ (see updated chart) right on the trendline. At the time, the International Herald Tribune announced, "Gold Rush Underway in Taiwan," quoting a dealer saying, "if war breaks out, the demand for gold will rise further." The prior day was the top. Despite war, recession and uncertainty, gold keeps slipping further down the Slope of Hope and is now $150 below its 1987 high.

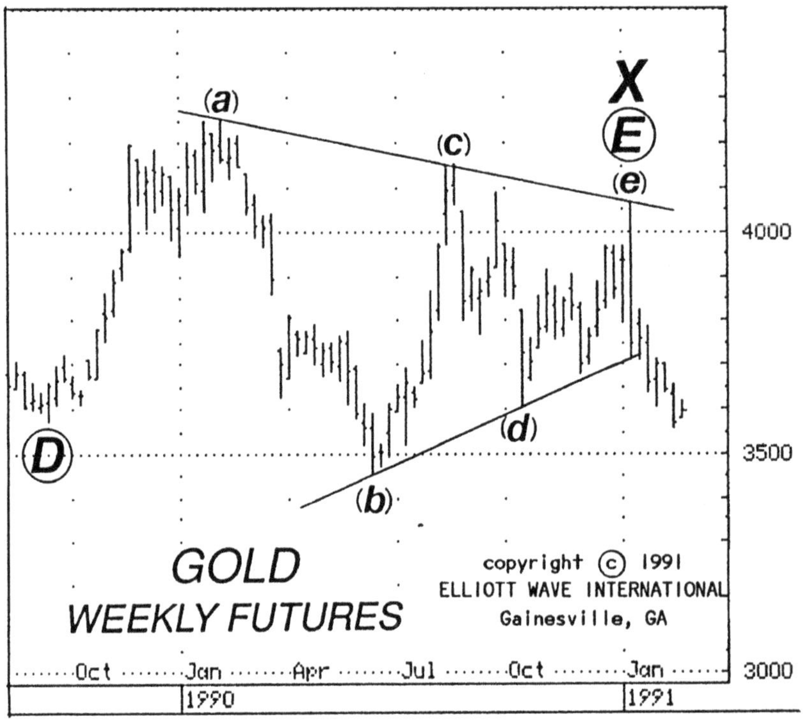

Gold is not due to register a major bottom for several years, so no long term investment is warranted. Our traders' short position was entered well enough that we should stay short and keep the stop just above the "war fears" wave X high at $404 basis London fix.

Silver

The Special Section on silver in the November 1990 issue remarked as follows:

> Silver has recently cracked to $4.20, a price it hasn't seen since 1976. If the Elliott wave count for gold...is correct, then the ultimate low for silver can only be imagined.... As you can see by the semilog chart, there is still lots of room on the downside on a percentage basis, a fact that is not evident on the standard arithmetic charts, which make silver appear as if it is near zero already.

Silver, which was already down over 90% from its high at the time that was written, has lost another 15% of its value in four months, touching $3.55 this week. As Jim Dines recently commented, "I'm absolutely certain that silver will bottom some day within 3½ dollars of its current price."

Update on Collector Coins

The Special Section on collectible coins from the May 28 issue flatly stated, "the collector coin bull market is ending. Any investor overly weighted in coins should strongly consider *selling* his collection at today's lofty prices. If you're truly a collector, you should delay your purchases for two to three years." At the time, many chart watchers viewed the proximity of the long term uptrend line (see next chart) as a reason that coins were a "buy." In fact, collector coin prices have had the steepest drop since the blowoff in 1989, have decisively broken their multi-year uptrend line, and have lost 40% of their value in the past year. Many coins are now selling at ⅓ their peak 1989 values. If you're a collector, I hope last year's warning proved useful.

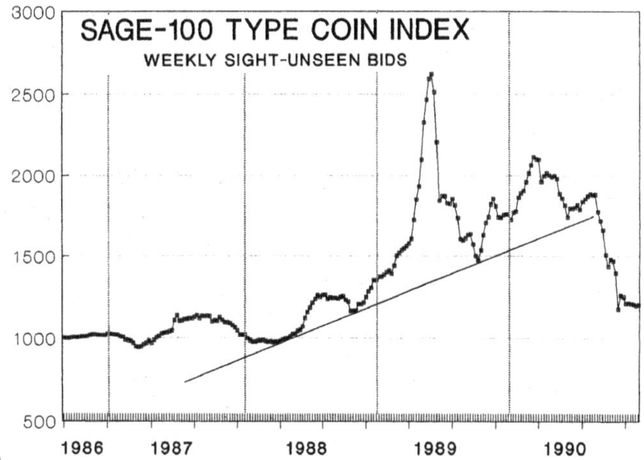

MARCH 29, 1991

Gold is on the verge of another, more dramatic, slide.

Gold & Silver

The March issue argued that "a brief rally, the largest in six weeks" was "due to start now" in gold and silver. Gold rose $12 basis the London fix ($16 in futures), and silver jumped over 60¢. Both rallies were "the largest in six weeks," silver's the largest since 1989.

These rallies occurred within the context of a bear market, and the major downtrend is about to resume, if it hasn't already. Both gold and silver have peaked so far right at the level of their previous fourth waves on the daily charts (not shown). The ten day moving average of the put/call ratio on gold futures options has retreated to a low level. Extremely important is the fact that the "up" phase of the dominant 17-month cycle in gold, which bottomed in mid-October, has so far resulted in exactly zero net progress, merely a holding pattern. When prices go sideways during the rising phase of a cycle, they almost always fall precipitously in the declining phase. The 17-month cycle is now running out of time on the upside and is not due to bottom again for over a year.

It now appears that gold is about to fall far enough to wipe out any potential for an upside resolution of the long term triangle pattern which was detailed in the Special Section in the December issue. Investors should stay out of gold. Traders should stay short and keep the stop at $404 basis London fix. If gold falls below $340, lower the stop to $380 basis London fix. The long term target is still below $200/oz.

APRIL 26, 1991

Gold remains vulnerable to a major drop. Resistance is at $370-380. Silver may reach a major bottom within several months.

Gold

The outlook for gold remains bearish. The January peak at $403.70/oz. completed the contracting triangle that dates back to 1982, as illustrated in the Special Section in the December issue. From there, gold traced five waves down on the daily chart (not shown) into late February, completing wave 1 of a new downtrend. Since then, gold has traded sideways, finding resistance exactly at the "previous fourth wave" (see text, p.55) at $370 basis London fix. Three weeks ago in early April, the ten day average of the put/call ratio on gold futures contracts hit its lowest level since last September, when gold was above $400/oz. Thus, the sideways trend of the past two months has encouraged buyers, a typical setup prior to a third wave down. Gold could drift back up to $370-380 in a more complex wave 2 rally, but the ultimate downside target is still below $200/oz., ideally near $105. Investors should stay out; traders are holding short with a stop at $404 basis London fix.

Silver

The picture in silver is getting interesting. For the first time since the peak at $50 over eleven years ago, the wave structure is approaching the point that it is worth watching for signs of a major bottom. The long term chart updates the count from the November EWT, now indicating a nearly completed corrective pattern from the 1980 peak. The weekly chart shows the detail of the last decline and reveals that, ideally, one more selloff lasting a few months would do it. There are two other acceptable labelings of the bear market with virtually the same implications. The "Alt." labeling on each chart

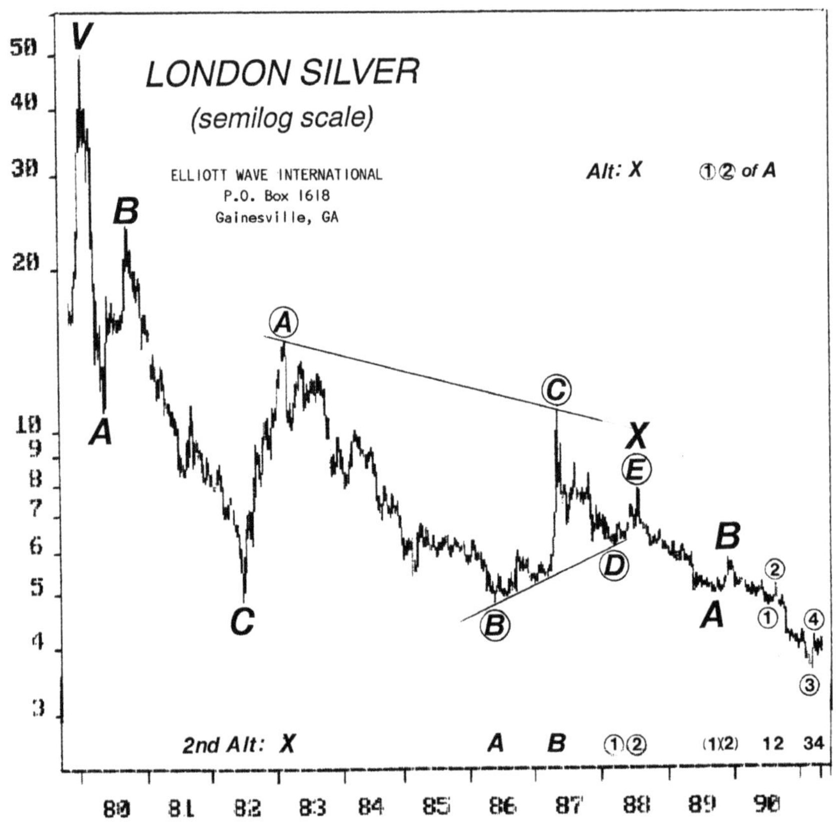

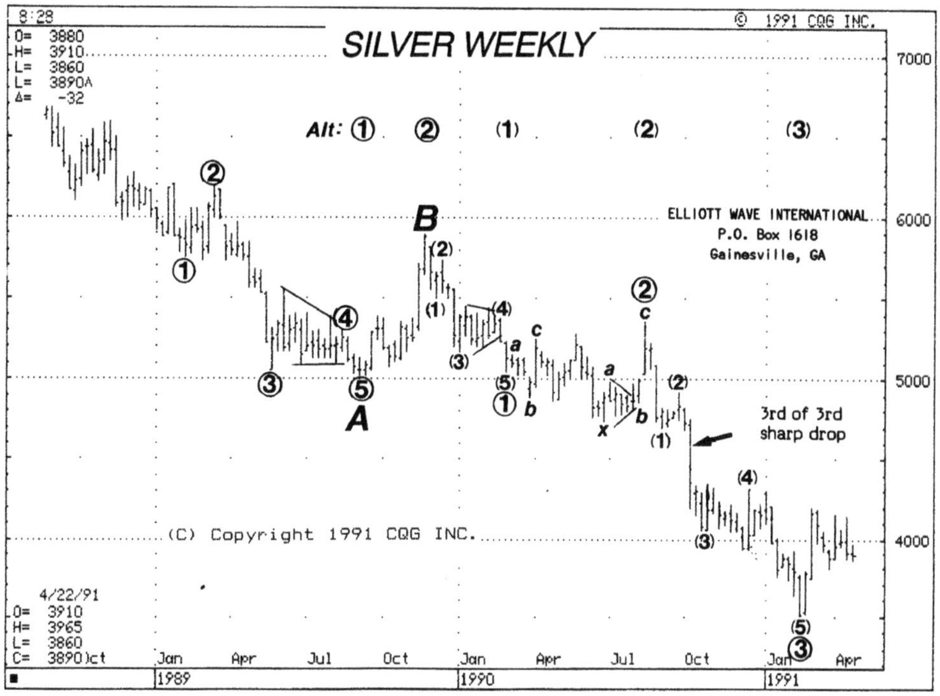

is a count that indicates substantial further decline ahead, an interpretation which of course fits the outlook for gold and may indicate that our years-ago projections to as low as the $2-$3 range for silver may come to pass. Let's look at some additional evidence.

Gold/Silver Ratio

Remember when it was assumed that 16:1 was the "normal" ratio between the prices of gold and silver? Who would have believed in January 1980 that in eleven years it would exceed 100:1, as it did recently? Many people have bet continually that the 16:1 ratio would return as a result of a big rally in silver. However, the driving force behind the change has been a psychological shift in relative value governed by R.N. Elliott's Wave Principle.

This chart of the gold/silver ratio was last presented in the December issue and is shown here with exactly the same wave count, which has progressed to the point that wave (3) is over and wave (4) is in progress. As you can see, another rise for wave (5) will finish off over a decade of relative weakness in silver vs. gold. Look how neatly this chart supports the case that the bear market in silver will end with one more wave down. Thus, it is possible, even if gold is to fall to its target of below $200/oz., that silver will begin a new bull market. Keep in mind, however, that it will be risky to buy silver outright. As stated on August 31, "It is more prudent to assume that the ratio will fall as a result of gold declining rapidly rather than silver advancing rapidly." Gold will have to fall rapidly to achieve the expected 50%-70% further loss in value over the next three years. During that time, silver might build a long base, perhaps involving a first and second wave to the upside, without great upside

progress. A safer speculation would be to take a "long silver, short gold" position at some point in coming months, to be held for the next several years.

MAY 31, 1991

Gold and silver have some potential for a brief rally, but they should fall to new lows in coming months.

Gold

Gold is down nearly 30% from its 1987 peak, and silver is down 65%. Based upon both PIGS (the Prechter Index of Gold Stocks) and the PBX gold stock index, gold stocks have fallen 44% since their peak in February 1990. PIGS, in fact, is now at its lowest level in almost five years. It has been right to be on the bearish side of the precious metals market.

Declines are what create buying opportunities. Are gold, silver and gold stocks attractive investments as a result of their price declines of the past 16 months? Upon examining the technical aspects of the precious metals markets, the picture reveals long term bear markets still in progress along normal lines.

There are several reasons why gold and gold stocks probably have more to go on the downside following a short term rally. They are illustrated on the chart. First is that PIGS has traced out a contracting triangle since the fourth quarter of last year, and it should resolve on the downside, probably bringing the index to below 300. Secondly, the 17-month cycle,

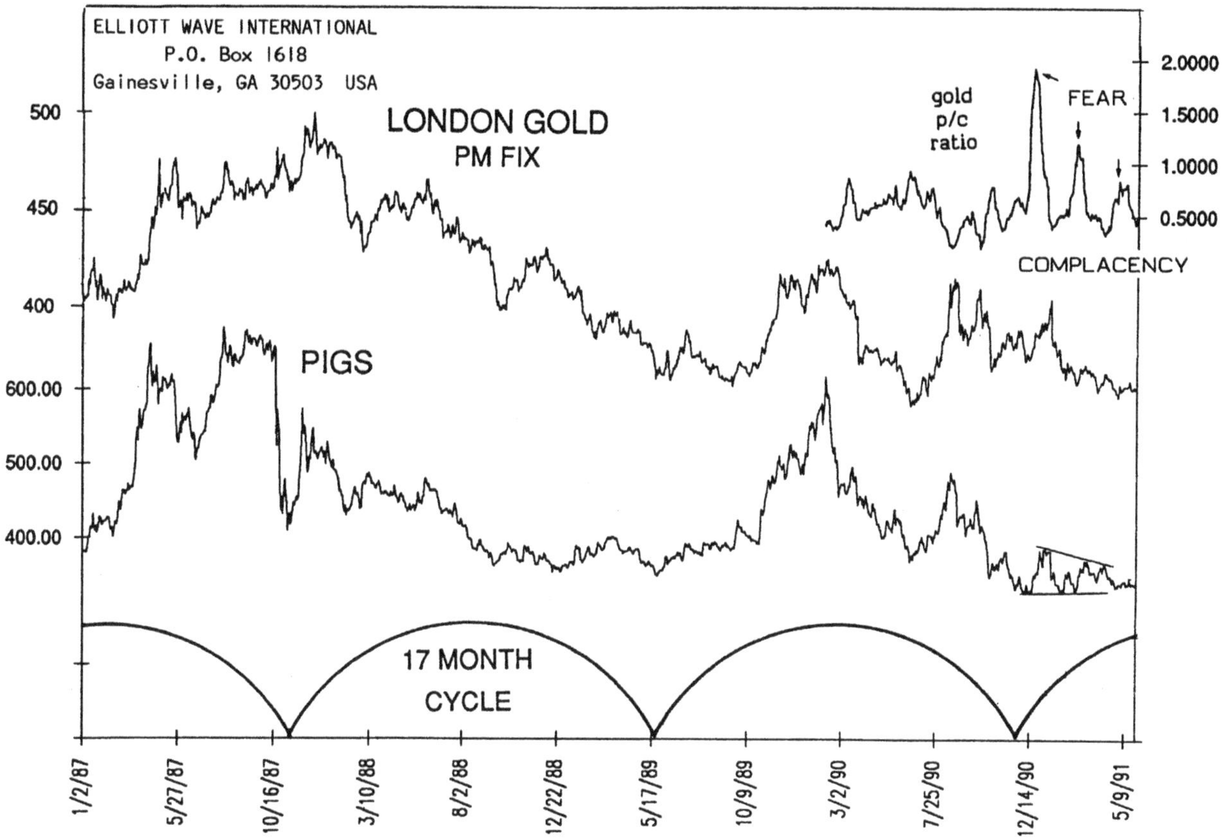

which has so accurately forecasted and tracked gold stock action (and to a lesser degree, the price of gold bullion) for years, has actually been trying to *rally* the market for about seven months. It is due to roll over this summer and lead to its next bottom in or near April 1992. This cyclic pressure will serve to make the downside the path of least resistance. Thirdly, the ten day average of the put/call ratio on gold futures contracts is back into low territory, meaning that traders are now lined up to enjoy the next rally in gold, which further means that it isn't likely to happen now. Of particular interest is the profile of gold's put/call ratio during the past year. The chart shows that the three occurrences of *bearish* investor psychology in recent months have traced out a series of lower peaks. In other words, traders are becoming disenchanted waiting for a downside break. The occurrences of *bullish* investor psychology, however, have reached similar levels each time, indicating that traders are becoming increasingly comfortable with long positions. To summarize, traders have concluded that this year's action is a *base*. Technical factors suggest that it is a *shelf*, from which prices will fall.

Investors should stay out of gold. Traders are still short, with a stop at $404 basis London fix. There is a good probability that the rally that just started will carry for several days, bringing London gold into resistance at $370-380 as outlined in the May issue. Those who did not sell short higher may therefore be provided a low risk entry. When gold finally bottoms, probably in or near 1993 (see analysis in the February 1989 Special Report), we'll be buying aggressively.

Silver

The May issue of EWT updated the long term picture in silver, so please review that issue for full details. The recent short term action in silver has fit right into the pattern outlined last month. According to the ongoing interpretation, silver began a wave ④ rally at the February low, which will take the shape of an (a)-(b)-(c) or a triangle. The daily chart, updated to the present, shows that this interpretation has, if anything, gained in probability due to the appearance of a contracting triangle, which can only be labeled as wave (b). After another brief burst to the upside for wave (c), silver should once again fall to new lows in wave ⑤.

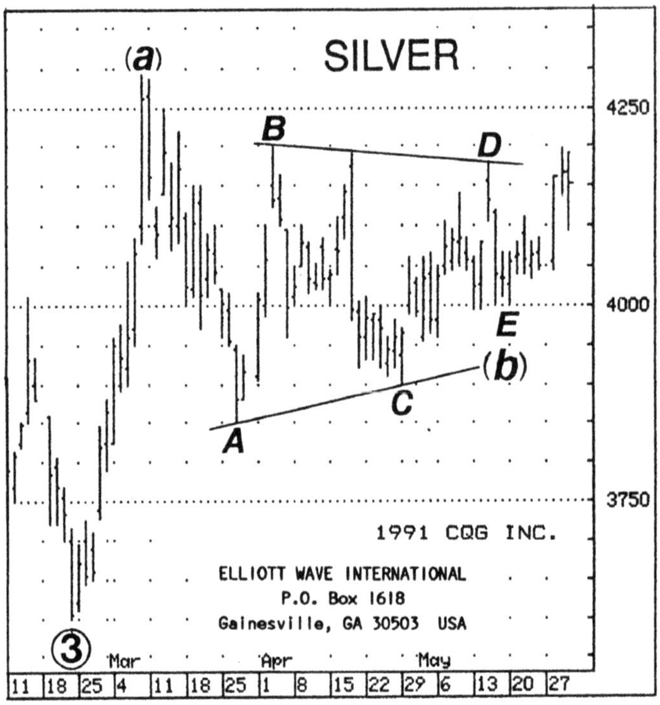

Sentiment toward silver, moreover, hardly seems washed out. Most analysts have jumped on the chance to call a major bottom. Investors appear confident about the prospects for silver as well. For example, Goldman, Sachs & Co. in May issued "silver notes" sold in $100,000 denominations. These are a fancy instrument that simply allows an unleveraged bet on higher silver prices. According to a table in a May 20 Wall Street Journal article by futures industry expert Stan Angrist, if silver remains unchanged from the issue date price of $4.06, an investor will lose 2.5% of his money. If silver goes up 10%, his return will about equal that from a T-bill. The net result of buying one of these notes is no different from buying five fully paid futures contracts, except that the cost of transacting in the note is *ten times as much*, or $2500 instead of about $250 commission for the futures contracts (and even that isn't charged until the position is closed out)! The amazing thing is that a spokesman says, "The offering was so well received that it might be increased to $60 million" worth of notes before the May 29 cutoff date! If a major bottom had just occurred in silver, this note issue, it seems to me, wouldn't have been this well received.

JUNE 28, 1991

The short term rallies in gold and silver projected by EWT occurred on schedule. Both metals should now fall to new lows for the year.

Gold & Silver

The June issue made the case for a "short term rally" in the context of a major bear market for the precious metals. Here was the outlook for gold: "There is a good possibility that the rally which just started will carry for several days, bringing London gold into resistance at $370-$380, as outlined in the May issue." Gold did begin a rally shortly thereafter, and the peak price so far is $372.75 basis London fix, right into resistance.

The gold put/call ratio remains low, "bulls" are near 70% according to The Bullish Consensus, and interest in calling a major rally has increased. Overall, there is no reason to alter the long term analysis presented in the June issue indicating lower gold prices for the remainder of the year. Traders should stay short with a stop at $404 basis London fix.

At the same time a month ago, the chart of silver showed waves (a) and (b) completed, with wave (c) lying directly ahead. As the June issue put it, "after another brief burst to the upside for wave (c), silver should once again fall to new lows." As you can see by the chart above, wave (c) took place right on schedule, propelling the price up to $4.646 basis London fix, right to a confluence of technical resistance: both a downtrend line and the point at which waves (a) and (c) were approximately equal in length. The rally prompted numerous brokerage firms, newspapers and analysts to issue buy recommendations for silver. Now it's time for the fall to new lows. Any move above $5 will negate this analysis.

The extent of the rally prompts a change in wave count. The channel and the nearly equal rallies within it argue that silver is in the process of tracing out a five-wave decline from the peak of wave Ⓔ. That in turn will constitute wave A of the second A-B-C pattern (see long term chart, May issue). This conclusion fits the outlook for gold much better and indicates that the next low in silver, while it will lead to the biggest rally in two years, will still not mark its final bottom.

There are some bullish factors in the gold market. First, after 94 years of operation, the Spokane exchange, which traded penny gold shares, closed a month ago due to lack of volume. Second, the board of trustees of the Kemper Gold Fund voted to close and return the money to its shareholders. During 1988-1990, the $62 million fund could raise only another $11 million. Third, total money in gold mutual funds dropped by 25% last year to $3 billion. These events reflect disinterest in the gold market. Whether they reflect the *final* washout is doubtful, however, given the long-term outlooks from wave structure and cycles.

JULY 26, 1991

Gold and silver hit our upside targets over a month ago amidst an orgiastic dissemination of bullish opinion. Both metals have started down again and should hit a new low for the year within weeks.

Gold & Silver

The technical condition of the gold market requires strong language. *Rarely has there been this much excitement about buying a market after so little convincing has occurred in the form of rising prices.* Have you read any opinion on gold in recent weeks that has *not* advocated its purchase? Financial newspapers have devoted dozens of column inches to gold and have interviewed as many bullish analysts. Gold is an "obvious" buy. As Joe Granville used to say, "If it's obvious, it's obviously wrong." As you can see by the first excerpt below, *grains,* which are scraping multi-year lows, are generally considered an "obvious" short sale. Not surprisingly, Peter DeSario is identifying *bullish* factors in many agricultural commodities for the *Elliott Wave Commodity Forecast.*

The bullish conviction toward gold is evident not merely from anecdotal evidence. In July, the ten-day put/call ratio on gold futures contracts fell to its lowest level since the August and September 1990 tops in the $408-$417 area (basis London fix), which in turn were the lowest readings in two years' worth of data. This event is of particular importance given the intermediate term analysis of the put/call ratio presented in the June issue (see updated chart), showing the complete dissipation of willingness on the part of traders to buy puts when gold declines. This is classic market psychology for a cycle top. It just so happens that the 17-month cycle, which last bottomed in or near November 1990, was projected in EWT's June issue "to roll over this summer." It appears to be doing just that. At the same time, the 46-week cycle is also topping, portending a "double whammy" into their combined lows, due near March 1992.

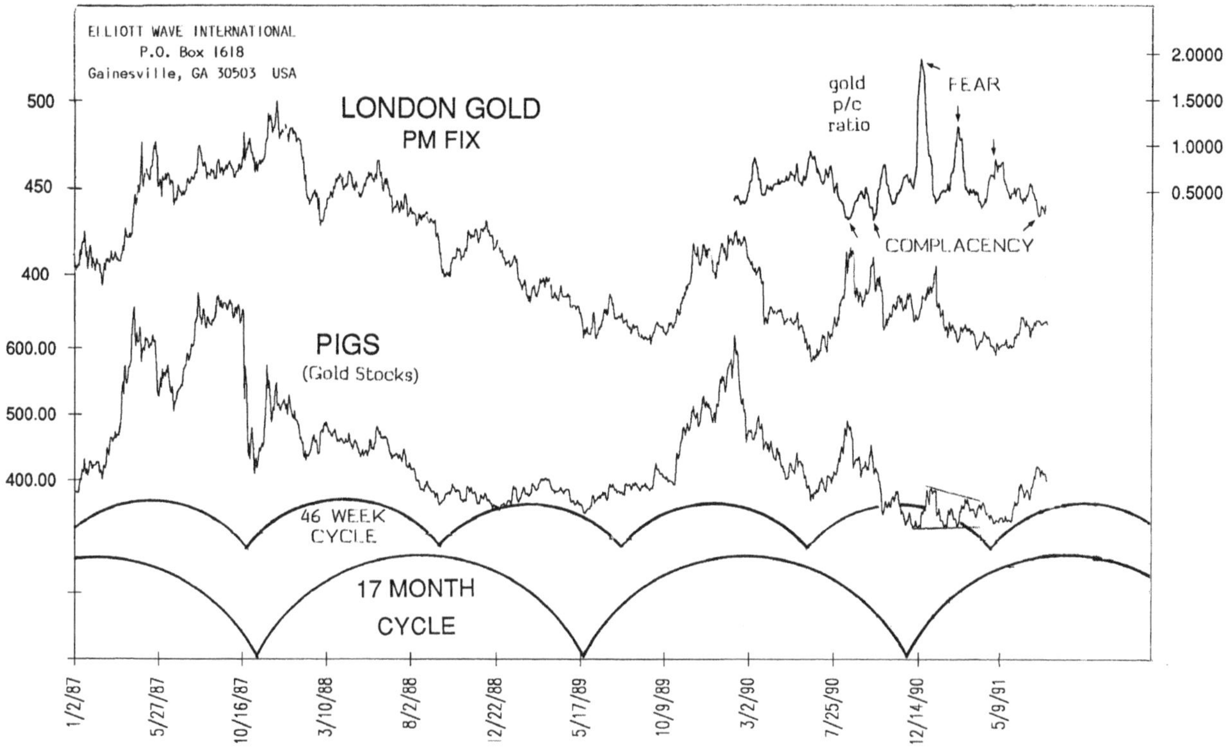

Gold Fever Is Biting Even Non-Bugs These Days Who Believe Metal's Price Is About to Take Off

The hot plays in futures markets in the second half of this year will be metals for the bulls and grains and soybeans for the bears, analysts and traders say.

Singing Bullish Refrain

THE WALL STREET JOURNAL

JULY 15, 1991

Some prominent gold bugs are singing their siren song again: The price of this eternal "store of value" is about to take off.

But this time, some non-bugs have joined the choir. These investors, with no known penchant for gold, say they also think the metal is about to have another fling in the sun.

One of those investors [redacted] is among the biggest commodity traders on Wall Street.

Gold fever has also bitten Comstock Partners, which manages Dreyfus Capital Value Fund and Comstock Partners Strategy Fund. Comstock is telling aggressive clients to invest 15% of their assets in gold stocks.

Unlike true gold bugs, who can be spotted by their stratospheric predictions—such as more than $3,000 [redacted]—Mr. [redacted] says a "significant move" for gold would be to $550 an ounce.

[redacted] newsletter, agrees that investors want the perceived safety of gold. He predicts the "ultimate outcome of the financial excesses of the last decade" will be higher gold prices.

The great hope of gold fans is runaway inflation, which devalues the dollar and other investments that compete with gold.

N.Y., in late May made his first gold recommendation in 1½ years. His reasoning: The federal government's deficit problems will spark a rise in inflation that could send gold up to about $500.

action may pick up in the pits if, as some traders predict, bull markets develop in precious and base metals, whose fortunes are expected to improve as the U.S. economy recovers.

Gold Fever

Gold stocks are attracting some money managers, who say the supply-demand equation looks favorable to them.

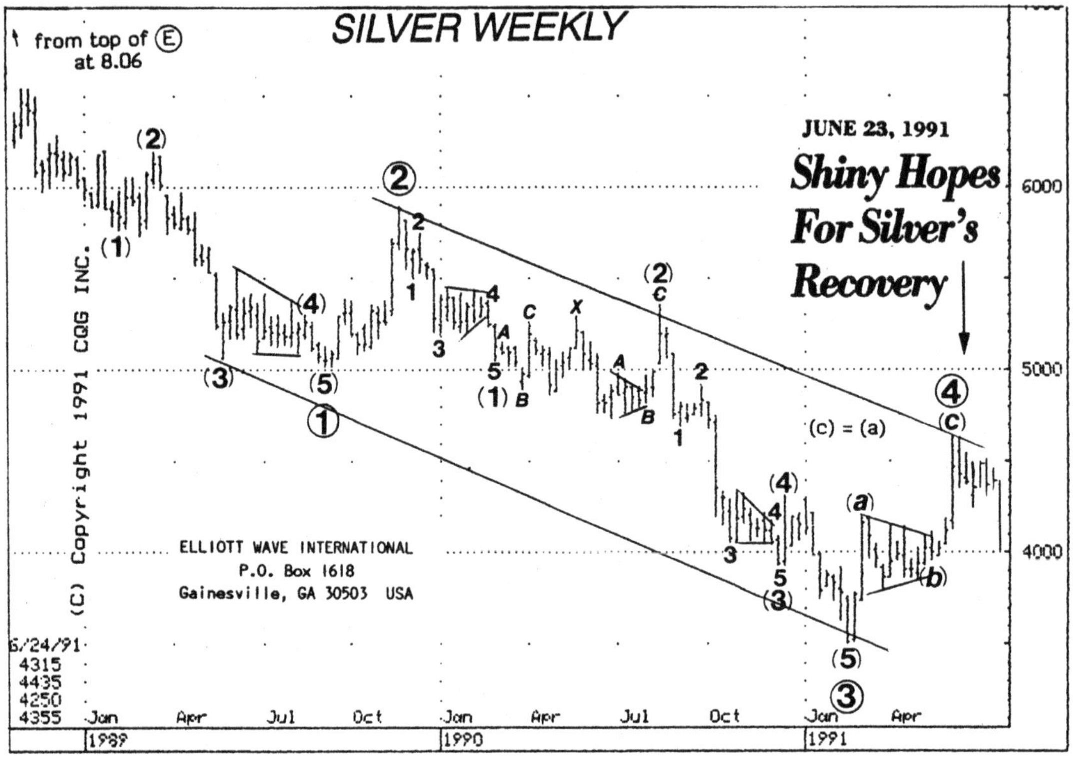

The rally to "$370-$380" forecasted in EWT two months ago was fulfilled. Gold has probably already begun another wave of declining prices in the long term bear trend which reasserted itself following the partial recovery peak in December 1987 at $502.75/oz.

Silver, after completing its wave (c) with perfection, has remained below the downtrend line illustrated in the July issue and has begun to collapse again, in wave ⑤ (see chart). It should follow gold to a new low for the year. Gold stocks have followed the stock market, bottoming last October and rallying back toward (but falling short of) the highs of summer, 1990. With both the stock market and bullion in a technically bearish condition, gold stocks, which have already slipped 10% off their highs made during all the excitement, should fall at least to near their 1990 lows.

Traders have been holding 100% short, and the rally gave those not so positioned the opportunity to sell. Keep the stop at $404 basis London fix. If gold falls below $350, lower the stop to $380. Investors stay out. The ultimate downside target is still below $200/oz., with an ideal target near $105.

A.J. Corner

From a reader: "As you know, your colleague, Jack Frost, is on record expecting $1000 gold. If gold is indeed headed for $1000, what series of events would turn you bullish?"

Answer: I get this question about once a month, so perhaps it's time to answer it. I haven't printed A.J.'s bullish count for gold over the past few years because I have disagreed with it.

Without detailing the entire case, A.J. believes that the 1985 low was the end of gold's bear market, and that the rally into 1987 was wave one of a new bull market. Wave two has been in force, with wave three due to emerge any time. If he turns out right, it will be a pleasure to detail his case and talk about how well he called it. As for changing my position, it will take either an overwhelmingly bullish technical condition near a low *or* a move by the price of gold to above the 1987 high at $502.75 (I wrote a Barron's article on gold at that time) to negate the bearish case, which was updated in the Special Section of the December 1990 issue of EWT. As for A.J., he says that under $300 would suffice to change his mind.

AUGUST 9, 1991 — SPECIAL REPORT

Gold and silver are making new lows. Gold is still in a declining cyclic phase that is expected to last into [1993-]1994.

AUGUST 29, 1991

Gold and silver declined as expected and after a brief bounce should fall to new lows for the year.

> **The hot plays in futures markets in the second half of this year will be metals for the bulls and grains and soybeans for the bears, analysts and traders say.**

Gold & Silver

Remember the above comment from a July 15 newspaper? The August EWT took exception, citing the opposite outlook based on technical factors. Here is a headline from August 5:

BARRON'S **August 5, 1991**

Grains Soar, Metals Sink

The clear technical signals of two months ago paid off nicely in reflecting intermediate-term tops in the gold and silver markets. The most important observation to make now is that both gold and silver fell from their June peaks in five waves. This structure indicates that the larger downtrend has resumed. In the detailed chart of silver shown in the August issue, the latest five wave decline is wave (1) of ⑤. This count suggests a short term bounce of about 5% in the metals, the outlook for which is supported by the ten-day put/call ratio on gold futures contracts, which is back to a level that has marked short term lows. The same ratio for silver is neutral, which tempers the power of the high put/call ratio in gold. It should take months for waves (3), (4) and (5) to unfold, so the longer term outlook remains bearish. Investors are out; traders are 100% short with a stop at $404. If gold falls below $350, lower the stop to $380 (all basis London fix).

SEPTEMBER 27, 1991

Gold and silver have bounced as expected, and should now resume their bear markets.

Gold & Silver

The next chart and headline are from an article I wrote for the Barron's issue of January 4, 1988. Analysis at the time indicated that a top in gold was occurring. To date, the 12/87 peak at $502.75/oz. has not been challenged. Analysis in the January 25, 1991 issue of EWT concluded that an 8½-year-long triangle in gold had ended with the rally peak at the onset of the Gulf War. As that issue stated, "The peak in London prices at $403.70 on January 16 is now a[nother] benchmark high." The persistent fall from both of these peaks supports EWT's ongoing decade-long wave interpretation.

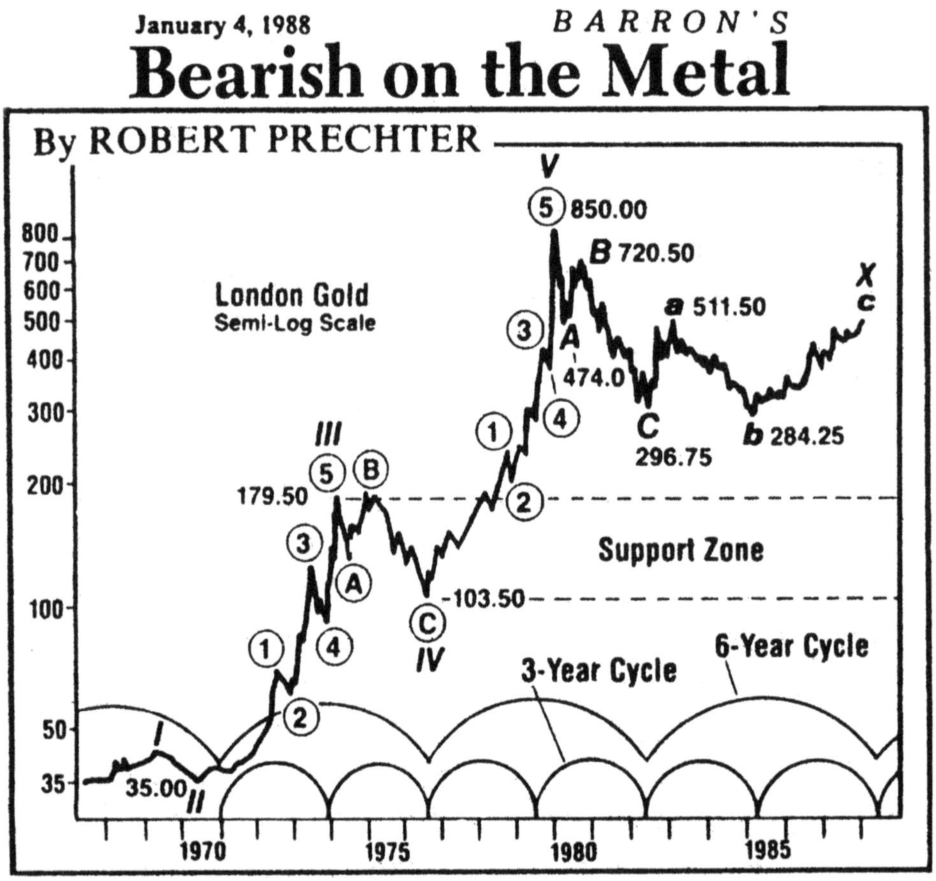

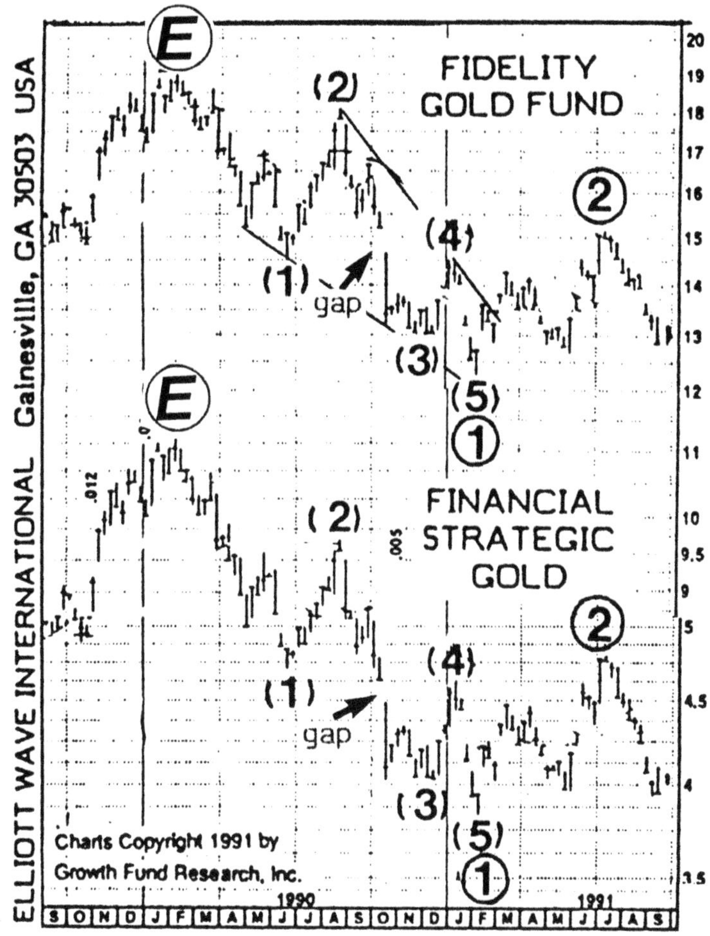

Take a look at the next charts and you'll find more evidence that a new set of impulse waves to the downside began at the wave Ⓔ top in January. These charts depict two gold stock funds. Notice the beautifully clear five wave declines and a-b-c rallies. Note the typical gap in wave 3 of (3) of ① on both charts. The next stage for gold stocks should be wave (3) of ③ to the downside, which should contain an even larger down gap. For more charts, please review the August issue.

Last month's issue called for "a short term bounce of about 5% in the metals." Silver rallied from $3.845 to $4.325 (basis December), about 12.5%, while gold has edged up about 3.5% so far. These bounces are over or nearly so. Traders should remain 100% short. Our stop was lowered to $380 basis London fix on last month's strategy. If gold falls below $320, lower the stop to $350. Investors stay out.

NOVEMBER 1, 1991

Gold and silver are peaking after the expected short term rally.

Gold & Silver

The September issue of EWT called for "a short term bounce of about 5% in the metals" and concluded last month that "the bounces are over or nearly so." Silver had already peaked, while gold has since risen just far enough to reach the 5% rally target.

At this point, a bearish non-confirmation of five weeks' duration exists between silver and gold, with silver the weaker market. The ten-day average of put/call ratios on gold futures, which had gotten moderately bullish at the price low in September, has now retreated to typical "top" levels once again. Silver's put/call ratio never did budge, so technical signs of a major low are virtually nonexistent.

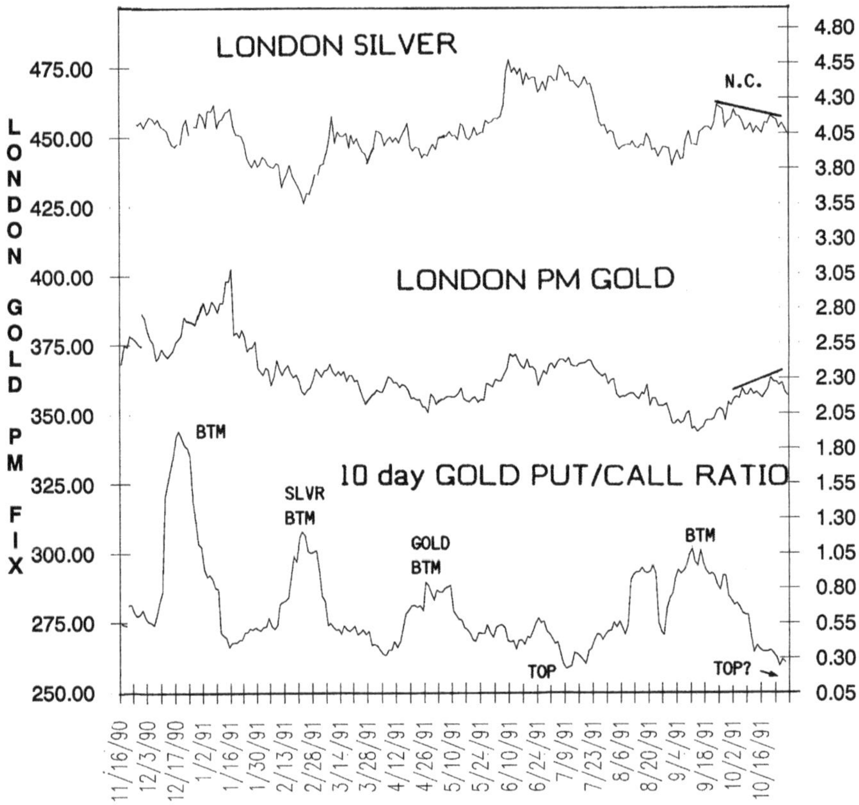

The only cause for pause in expecting an immediate decline is that the rally in gold has taken the shape of a "five," implying that it *is only wave "a" of a larger rally*. Sometimes in such situations, wave "c" is very short. To be safe, traders should maintain the stop at $380 basis London fix on the 100% short position. Investors should stay out of the gold market.

NOVEMBER 27, 1991

As expected, gold reached a slight new high for its rally. Gold and silver are now poised to undergo a downside acceleration.

Gold & Silver

The November issue called for a slightly higher high in gold's rally, but no higher peak in silver. That's what happened.

The put/call ratio on gold futures remains low. Silver has continued to languish, compounding the bearish upside non-confirmation against new rally highs in gold (see chart, November issue). ASA has retraced 2/3 of its summer decline. Despite arguments heard daily that gold is a "great buy," is "undervalued" and "provides an alternative to overpriced stocks," its technical condition suggests that it may be on the verge of a collapse. Traders are short with a stop at $380 basis London fix. Investors are out.

The Elliott Wave Theorist, 1992

JANUARY 3, 1992

Gold and silver must begin accelerating to the downside now if the wave count is to remain bearish. Even a slight rise from here (3%) would turn the metals picture near term bullish.

Gold & Silver

Gold did little after its January 1991 drop, although the minor turning points in July (top), September (bottom) and December (top) were successfully revealed by the extremes in the put/call ratio. That ratio was so bearish in October-November that the December issue called for a crash. December trading in fact produced the largest single "down" day for gold since the collapse following the wave Ⓔ peak a year ago. With time cycles pointing lower at least into February, the expected crash may indeed be underway. At this juncture, however, the wave count has certainly reached a point that requires *immediate resolution by market action.*

As you will recall, the long term picture from the 1980 peak indicates a bear market in progress. That bear market is taking the form of a double zigzag, to be labeled A-B-C-X- A-B-C. The first A-B-C ended in 1982. Wave X took the shape of a contracting triangle, labeled Ⓐ-Ⓑ-Ⓒ-Ⓓ-Ⓔ. Wave Ⓔ itself ended in a smaller contracting triangle, as you can see on the chart. The final attempt at an advance coincided with the outbreak of war with Iraq. From there, the wave structure can be counted as completing wave (1) down and an expanded flat correction for wave (2) up, as shown on the daily chart. The slight failure of wave C of (2) to exceed the peak of wave A is extremely bearish. The latest decline, even though it hasn't quite taken out the 1991 low, has pushed the gold price back below its triangle trendline, which extends back to 1982.

Next Best Count

The drop from the January 1991 peak, as shown by the "Alt." labeling on the chart, may have taken the shape of an (a)-(b)-(c) and finished off a much longer wave Ⓓ. That low was then followed by the five-wave September-December advance, signaling the start of a more significant rally. By this count, the latest drop would have to halt immediately, hold above $350 basis London fix, and lead to a rise above the December high.

Indeed, some worry is beginning to creep into investors' minds with regard to the precious metals. The put/call ratio has picked up in recent sessions, and headlines at the December top, such as "Gold Looks Good, Inflation or No" (12/12), have yielded to "Silver's Steady Decline is Battering Investors, and a Sustained Rally Isn't Expected Next Year" (12/30). Gold must begin falling in wave (3) immediately or the market will signal that it is continuing the triangle that was presumed complete at the January 1991 high. The net result would be a prolonging of the sideways trend of the past eight years before the start of the second A-B-C zigzag decline.

DECEMBER 30, 1991

LONDON—Holding the dubious distinction of worst commodity performer since the early 1980s, silver is expected to remain depressed in 1992.

Investors who bought silver when it was fashionable a few years ago are taking a big beating, bullion dealers say. At $3.89 an ounce, silver's price is down by 92% from its 1980 peak, compared with 87% for coffee and 72% for sugar. Only a few investors bought silver when it peaked at $50 in 1980, bullion dealers say, but many purchased it at prices of $15 to $35 an ounce.

Silver

The article above details one of the disaster markets that the Wave Principle helped us avoid. Like gold, the best wave interpretation is still the bearish one. The rally in the first half of 1991 took the (a)-(b)-(c) shape typical of countertrend moves, and the decline immediately following that rally was a clear "five." Since then, silver has drifted lower and has remained below its 3½-year downtrend line and therefore within its declining price channel. A rise above this downtrend line, particularly in concert with a rise in gold to above its December peak, would change the picture from bearish to bullish, at least for several months.

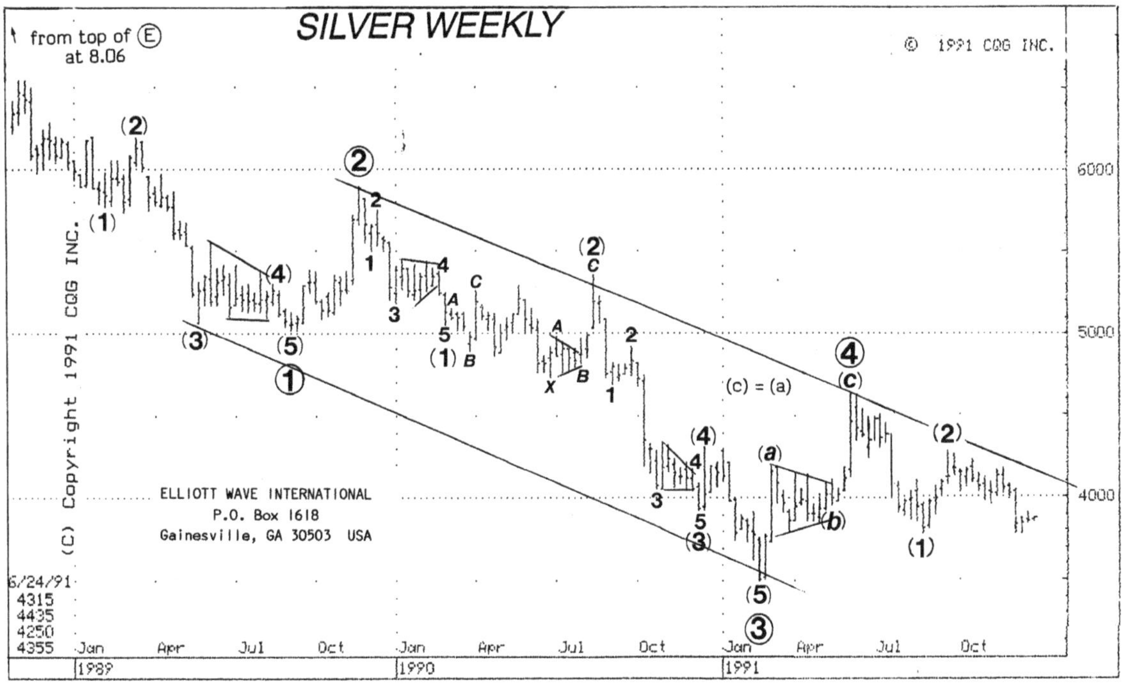

Investors should stay out of gold and silver. Traders should stay short gold and lower the stop to $370.75 basis London fix.

JANUARY 17, 1992 – INTERIM REPORT

Silver signaled its rally just days after the January issue was mailed. Gold has been a weak sister, yet to confirm a trend change.

JANUARY 31, 1992

Gold and silver responded to the short term bullish factors of a month ago; their rallies are likely already ending.

Gold & Silver

The January issue of EWT recognized some [minor] bullish technical factors in the precious metals markets. Just pennies from its low at the time, silver has since had its best rally since the first half of 1991. Gold made a low that Monday and rallied in sympathy with silver, though so weakly (just $13 basis the futures contract) that our lowered stop for traders' short sales wasn't even approached.

While silver rallied "above its downtrend line" (see chart, January issue), EWT explained that for the entire precious metals picture to turn bullish on an intermediate term basis, gold had to get above its December high as well, and to date, that hasn't happened. At this point, the put/call ratios are back in low territory and an a-b-c pattern to the upside is in place on the gold chart. As has occurred with every bear market rally for twelve years, silver's rally generated newspaper headlines predicting higher prices. In this case, a major article appeared on January 20, written precisely as both metals peaked for the month. While the requirements for a bullish intermediate term picture are still valid, it is highly probable that the precious metals rally is over. Investors should stay out of gold and silver. Traders are still short gold, with a stop at $370.75 basis London fix.

FEBRUARY 28, 1992

Although another near term selloff is likely, gold is showing signs of an approaching bottom. If the $330/oz. level holds, gold should rally from a March low into the mid-$400s.

Gold & Silver

Our bearish stance toward gold and silver during the past several years has served us well. At this juncture, there are several reasons to consider a slight change in wave count. The long period of choppy action between $350 and $420, the slightly lower lows and lower highs during that time, the short price distance of the "E" wave triangle of 1989-1990 (see December

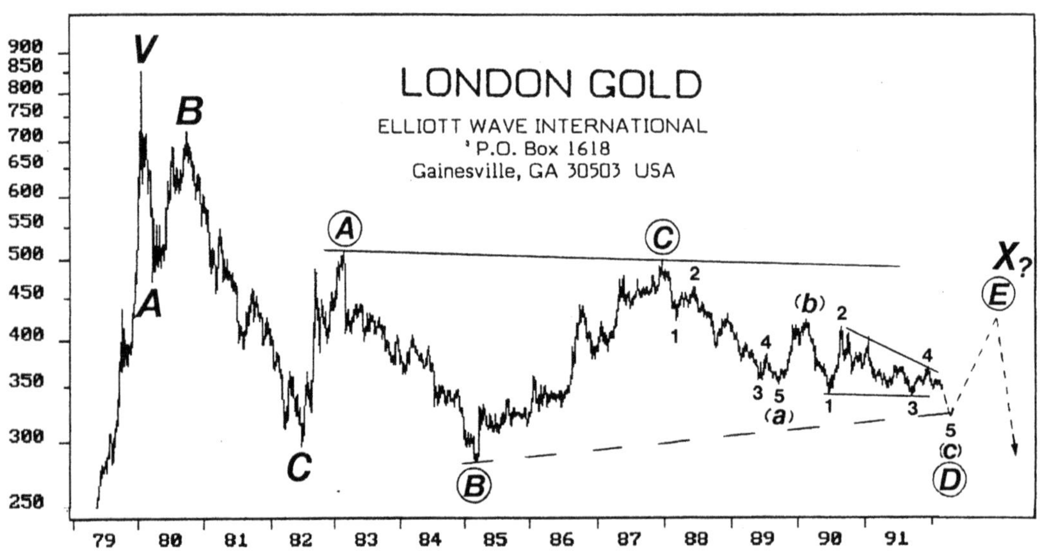

1990 issue) and the rising put/call ratio in gold in recent weeks despite little net price action, all challenge the conclusion that wave Ⓔ ended a year ago.

The chart shows one way to label the action of the past four years, with wave Ⓓ subdividing into a lengthy (a)-(b)-(c). Wave (c) is a developing diagonal triangle with one low remaining to finish the pattern. By this count, wave Ⓔ would then generate a rally to at least $420/oz. but no higher than $500.

The long-observed 17-month cycle, which last bottomed in October, 1990, is due to bottom again in March. Traders should cover short sales now. Traders and investors should buy gold in the $340-$350 range basis the nearby futures contract with a stop at $330 basis London fix. Figures show that traders in silver currently prefer calls over puts by a huge margin, so that metal should perform worse than gold over the near term, regardless of direction.

MARCH 27, 1992

As long as the $330 level holds, gold is making a bottom that should lead to a rally of $100/oz.

Gold & Silver

Here is reproduced the ending portion of the long term chart from the March issue, showing EWT's forecast for a short term drop in gold, halting in the $340 area, + or - $10, to complete wave 5. As explained last month, "Wave (c) is a developing diagonal triangle with one low remaining to finish the pattern."

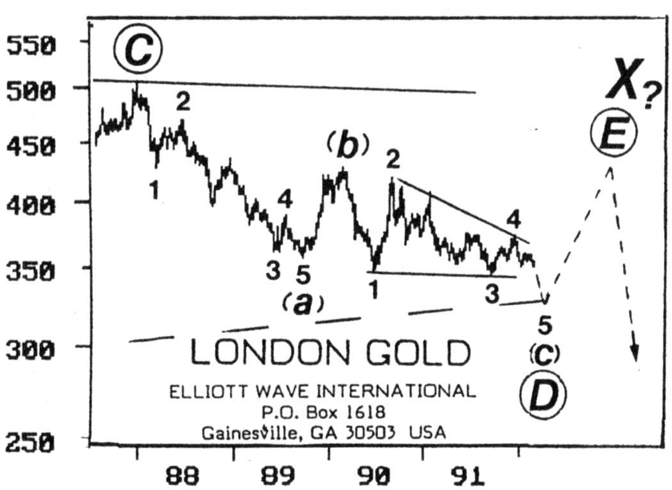

Gold Bugs Sing Blues as Price Hits Lowest Level in Nearly Six Years

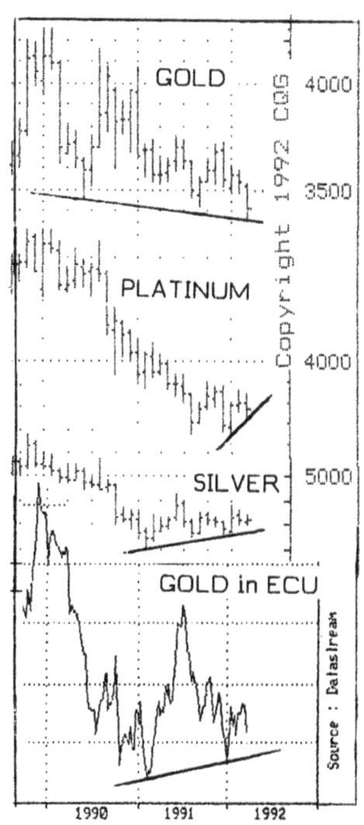

A sharp drop in gold did occur, following the line and bringing the price right into the target zone. Major newspapers, which have ignored gold for a year, suddenly ran articles about the four-year decline. The 17-month cycle, which was "due to bottom in March," should now turn up, carrying the price of gold "to at least $420/oz. but no higher than $500."

The price of gold in ECU (European Currency Units), by the way, has not fallen below its early 1991 low. As you can see by the chart, a non-confirmation exists between gold in U.S.$ and gold in ECU. The new low in gold was similarly unconfirmed by silver, which at a recent low of $4.02 held above its August and December lows of $3.82 *and* well above its low of $3.55 registered in February 1991. At the same time, platinum held above its low of January. Such non-confirmations are common at bottoms.

The above evidence supports the case for a low. However, the current "buy" recommendation is based primarily on the fact that the price pattern offers a well defined opportunity with $20 risk. The probability for a low in gold is itself not very high, just a bit better than 50/50. The chief bearish factor is that long term time cycles (see February 1989 Special Report) are in hard-down mode right into 1993-1994. Remember that a drop below $330/oz. basis London fix will negate the bullish potential, and may indicate a "third wave" style crash in progress. The current opportunity is for a potentially profitable trade only; it is *not* time for major accumulation.

Might gold stocks make a good speculation here? Perhaps. The latest selloff in those issues appears to have come from the end of a year-and-a-half long contracting triangle. Triangles in bear markets are followed by a thrust, one final drop to new lows. However, gold stocks present risks that gold itself does not. These risks will be particularly high in this decade, given the outlook for world economic contraction and social unrest. Here are two articles, one from a year ago and one from last November, that convey the risks:

South African Gold Mine Closed After 69 Die in Ethnic Violence

WELKOM, South Africa, Nov. 11 — In the wake of the worst mining violence in South Africa's recent memory, 2,500 dispirited black miners were sent home today and gold production curtailed at a major mine here after 69 men were killed and up to 180 more injured in a week of factional clashes.

The fighting, in which residents of the mining camp dormitories attacked each other with knives, staves, hammers, sharpened iron bars, chunks of concrete and clubs fashioned from tree branches, added a new dimension to the political violence afflicting South Africa.

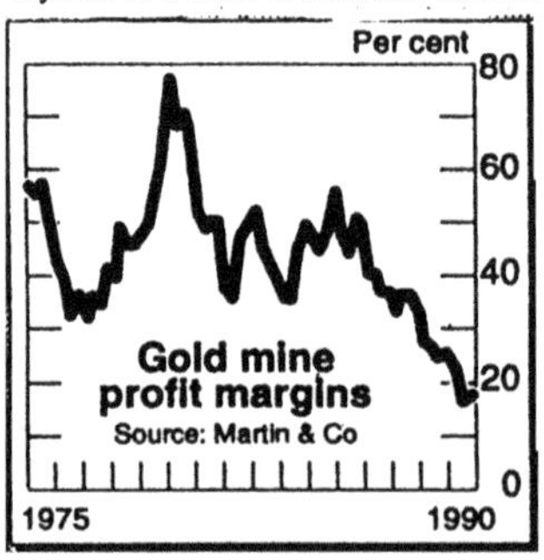

FINANCIAL TIMES

APRIL 16 1991

The industry faces its worst crisis since gold was discovered on the Witwatersrand more than a century ago.

Indeed, the more production problems mines experience, the more valuable the gold bullion *already produced* becomes. In other words, choose your stocks carefully or stick to bullion. Traders and investors are now 100% long. If $330 basis the June futures contract is broken, investors should move back to cash and traders to 50% short with a stop at $350.

MAY 1, 1992

Gold

The near term support zone of $340 + or - $10 has held so far. The net bullish factors detailed in the April issue remain in force. Traders and investors bought gold "in the $340-$350 range." If $330 basis the June futures contract is broken, all participants should exit positions. The long term picture still calls for gold to fall well below $200/oz. Cancel any other strategy.

Silver

Silver appears to be tracing out a contracting triangle that fits nicely into a declining parallel trend channel dating back to 1987. The February 1989 Special Report forecasted a 1992 cyclic low for silver. A breakdown in silver from this triangle will be a fifth wave thrust, possibly setting up the first long term buying opportunity in silver in twenty years. If silver does break down from here, our gold trade will likely be stopped out. A bearish stance is warranted for the next several months as long as $4.45 is not exceeded. The slope of the trend channel suggests an ultimate low in silver below $3/oz.

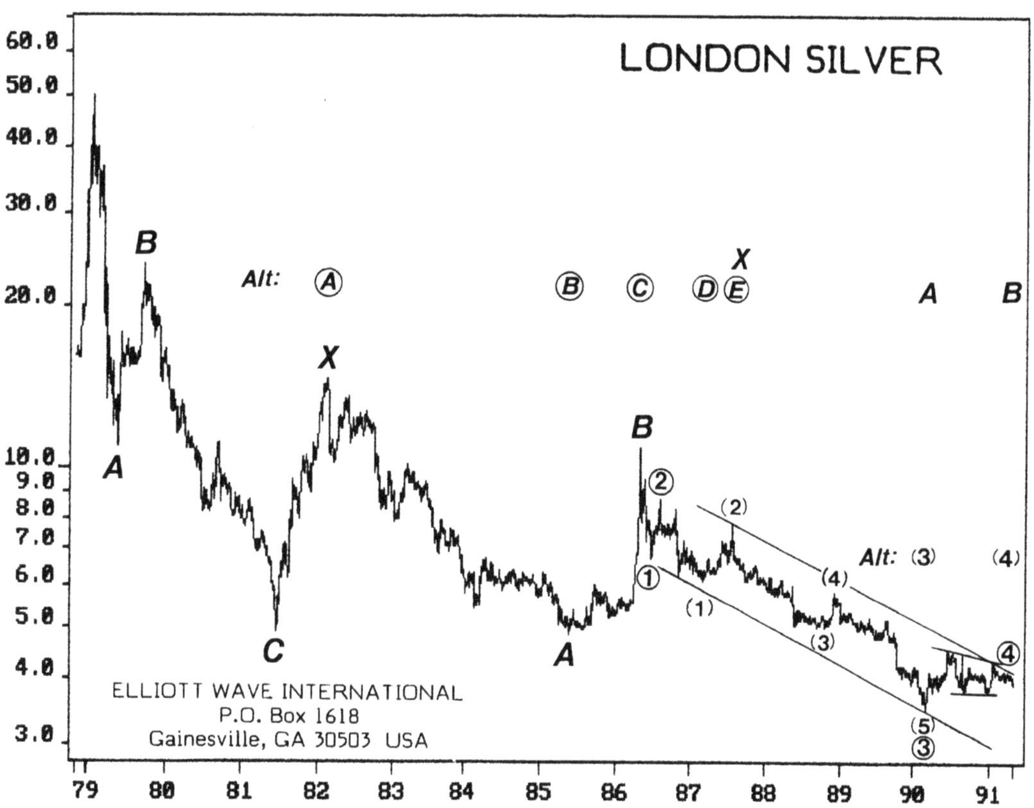

MAY 29, 1992

Gold appears to have completed a bottoming pattern, although a break of the May low will negate the bullish potential. Silver should rally briefly, then fall to $3.50 or lower. A move above $4.41 will negate that bearish outlook.

Gold

The gold market has been very lethargic. In the meantime, the put/call ratio has fallen back to neutral territory, keeping the overall probability of a trend change less than ideal. The wave structure from late March to mid- May appears to have been a diagonal triangle. Such patterns almost always mark the conclusion of the prior larger trend, which in this case was down. A break of the May low would be significant, so those who bought gold "in the $340-$350 range" should raise the stop to $334 basis the nearby contract.

Silver

The put/call ratio for silver futures has fallen to the area of its lows for the past year. At the same time, silver may be completing its contracting triangle dating from February 1991, as you can see by the chart. Ideally, wave e of the triangle should carry to $4.29, + or - .02, at which level it would be .618 times as long as wave c and satisfy internal relationships as well. For the triangle's position in the bigger picture, see the long term chart in the May issue.

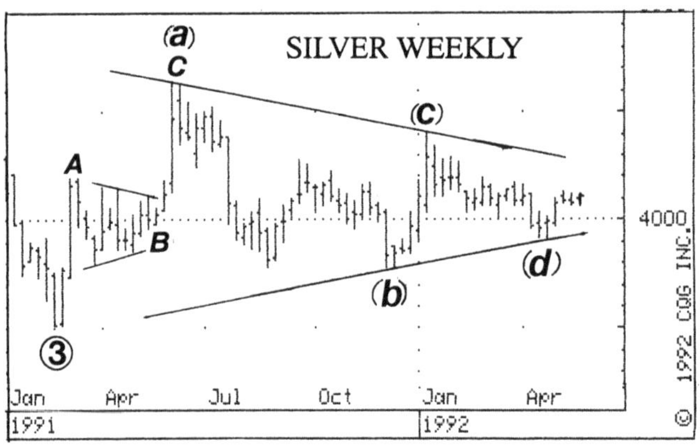

A thrust (see text, p.42) should bring silver to new lows, implying a drop of at least 60¢/oz. from its current level. Traders should move to 50% short silver now and 100% short above $4.25, with a stop at $4.42. Cycles are due to bottom in August-October.

Gold/Silver Spread

The Elliott Wave Theorist argued in the April 1991 issue that the gold/silver spread was in Primary wave ⑤ from its 1980 low. The ratio has now fallen from the upper channel line at 99 down to 81, returning precisely to the lower support line dating back a decade. As long as this line holds, our contradictory positions of long gold, short silver could work out. If the line breaks, then at most, one of them will succeed.

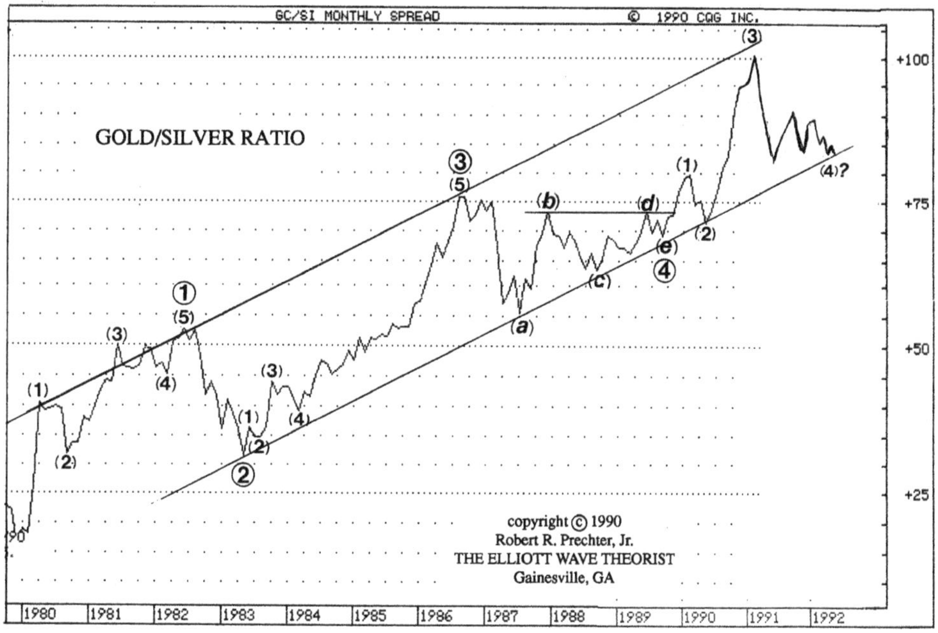

JUNE 26, 1992

The technical outlook for gold is mixed.

Gold & Silver

Gold and silver have been as sluggish as bonds. Gold has edged higher, and silver has languished, keeping both of our trades intact. The wave structure remains friendly for gold, although a break of the May low would eliminate the bullish implications. Traders should keep the stop on our long position at $334 basis the nearby futures contract. Traders in silver remain 50% short, with plans to move to 100% short at $4.25, with a stop at $4.42, all basis the nearby futures contract.

For profits, stocks, bonds better than gold

Gold stocks' shine may not last

JUNE 9, 1992

S African gold profits 'lowest since 1960s'

Sentiment in the gold market is mixed. The put/call ratio is *very* low, indicating trader bullishness. However, newspaper articles continue to knock the metals, as you can see by the headlines above. Another interesting development deserves mention. "Commercials," i.e., those in the business of gold production, are more often right about trends than the public. It is worth noting that Newmont Mining bought gold heavily in the futures market in May, particularly in light of its correct judgment in *selling* futures four years ago. The public, which is now shunning gold as an investment, is nevertheless buying jewelry in record amounts. At the major top in early 1980, the situation was the opposite. Much of the public was buying gold and silver products as investments, while lining up for blocks to sell their coin collections and the family silver. Simply stated, the public is a "trend follower" when dealing with investments, yet a "bargain hunter" when dealing with goods. The current situation, then, appears to be more indicative of a bullish situation than a bearish one. It's a very interesting picture, if a fuzzy one. Our *major trend* bearish stance on gold of the past twelve years has certainly been correct, as the industry is finding out.

JULY 31, 1992

Gold rallied nicely, as expected, but is due for a correction soon. Silver should collapse to new lows in August (or September at the latest), probably to near $3/oz., there registering a final bottom for its twelve-year bear market.

Gold & Silver

Our "long gold, short silver" stance has paid off. Gold *rallied* $25/oz. from the week of May 11 while silver *fell* 35¢/oz. in the same period, in one of the most dramatic divergences of trend ever for these two metals.

Silver is approaching its most exciting juncture since January 1980. The long term wave count (see May issue) indicates the approaching end of a twelve year "double zigzag" decline.

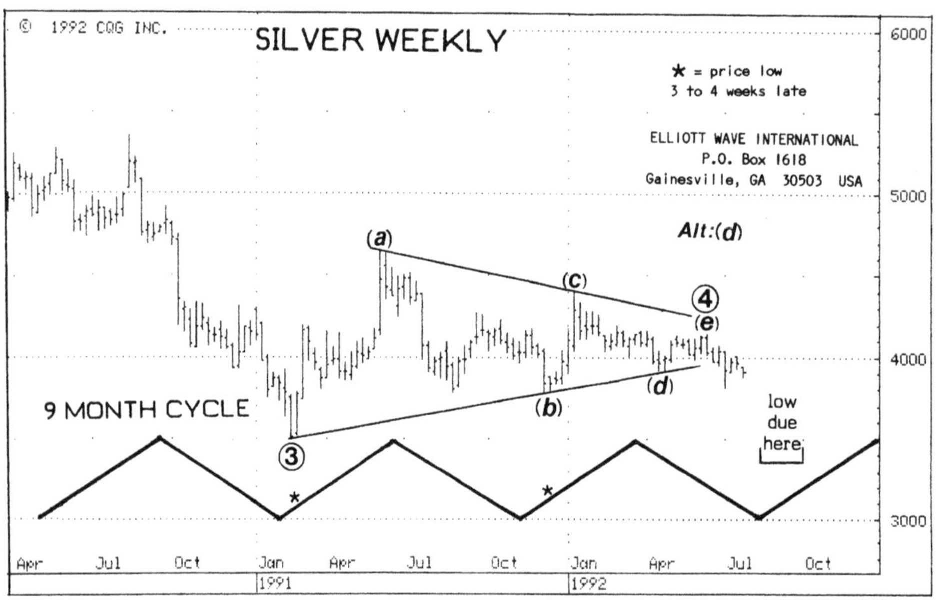

Wave ④ of the last "C" wave traced out a clear triangle, as you can see on the chart. Wave ⑤, a thrust to the downside, should carry the price of silver at least to a new low, and likely close to $3/oz.

Timing indicators suggest that the final low in silver will occur within weeks. First, thrusts are usually "swift and short." Second, the 9-month cycle postulated by the Foundation for the Study of Cycles (Irvine, CA) is ideally due to bottom in early August, as you can see on the chart. In actual practice, the last two price lows occurred three to four weeks after the low of the cycle was due. Thus, the time between now and early September is highly likely to see the final low in silver.

Gold has met a long term downtrend line and is nearing the peak of its first rally phase, so it should undergo a correction soon. The sentiment of advisors has gone from bearish to bullish short term and neutral long term, so a near term pullback and then an upside acceleration would be a contrary opinion.

Two months ago, many analysts were predicting that the price of gold would skid to $320 an ounce or maybe even to $300—the lowest price since the mid-1980s. But now gold is rising gently, and many of the same gurus are singing a different tune. They claim that after several false starts, gold is finally on course to higher ground following years of dismal investment performance.

The correction in gold should occur during wave ⑤ in silver, after which time silver should join the rally in gold. As long as the May low in gold is not broken, it should ultimately carry to near $470/oz. basis London fix to complete wave Ⓔ of its triangle dating back to 1982. If the May low does break, then the interpretation that wave Ⓔ ended in January 1991 will resume preferred status.

Traders and investors should raise the gold stop to $341 basis the nearby futures contract. Traders should stay 50% short silver. Move to 100% short at $4.25 basis the nearby futures contract, with a stop at $4.42. Cover below $3.20.

AUGUST 28, 1992

Gold has resumed its major downtrend. *Silver is approaching the final low in its 12+ year bear market.* The ideal scenario would provide a bottom in the $2.90-$3.50/oz. range within three months.

Gold & Silver

The August issue reprinted an article that described the sudden transformation of many former gold bears into bulls. The wave count, however, indicated that the rally had just ended. Our conclusion was, "Gold has met a long term downtrend line and is nearing the peak of its first rally phase, so it should undergo a correction soon." Gold broke down the next day, and quickly fell to 75¢ above its May low basis London fix.

The drop was a *much larger retracement* of the preceding rally than is normal for second wave pullbacks in new uptrends. What's more, as you can see on the daily chart of the December futures contract on the next page, the decline traced out a clear five waves. Therefore, even

though the May low has not been broken in the cash market, such a break has become likely. For now, we will return to the conclusion that wave Ⓔ ended in January 1991 and that there will be no significant rally prior to gold's continuing its descent to our ultimate downside target below $200/oz.

Silver presented a fascinating picture last month. Here is the summary from August:

> Silver is approaching the most exciting juncture since January 1980. The long term wave count (see May issue) indicates the approaching end of a twelve year "double zigzag" decline. Wave ④ of the last "C" wave traced out a clear triangle, as you can see on the chart. Wave ⑤, a thrust to the downside, should carry the price of silver at least to a new low, and likely close to $3/oz.

Silver has been falling ever since. The Elliott wave pattern requires five waves down from the peak of wave (e). The decline should bring prices to below $3.50 (the wave ③ low) before the multi-year bear market ends. The ten-day average of the put/call ratio for silver futures has suddenly jumped to a very high level, exceeding its peak of February 1991 at the bottom of wave ③. This indicator, therefore, confirms that a bottom of *larger degree*, just as we are anticipating, is indeed approaching.

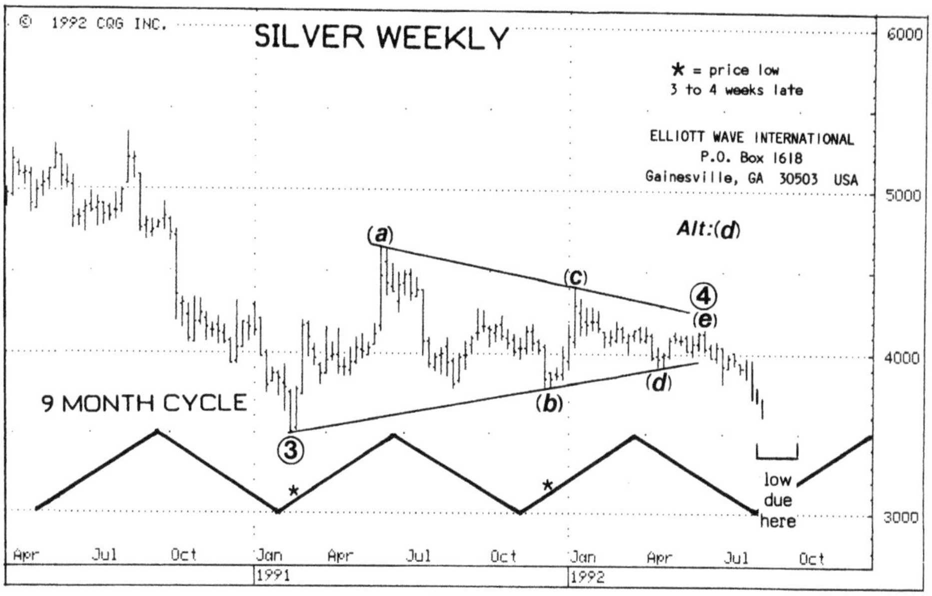

The 9-month cycle originally called for a low in late August-early September, but the wave structure indicates a couple more months of decline. The timing bracket on the chart from last month still leaves the window open into November, when the apex of the wave ④ triangle will be met (see text, p.43). To sum up, the bottom should be registered within three months, at least below $3.50, and ideally just below $3/oz., based on the projection suggested by the width of the triangle (see text, p.42). We'll use wave structure in attempting to identify the low on the Hotline.

Investors and traders were stopped out of gold for a small loss of $10. Traders are still short silver. Lower the stop to $4 basis London fix and *cover all shorts upon a London fix below $3.50. From thereon out, we should think only of where, when and how much to buy.* Traders should move to 50% short gold now and to 100% if it hits $350 basis London fix, with a stop at $357 basis the December futures contract. Investors should keep funds in the European money market. Between $2.90 and $3.50/oz. for cash silver prices, long term investors should accumulate a comfortable amount of junk silver coins for possible emergency use later in the depression.

SEPTEMBER 25, 1992

Gold rallied precisely to targeted resistance. The outlook is now bearish as long as $355 is not penetrated on the upside.

Gold & Silver

The daily chart of December gold futures last month projected an a-b-c rally to the $351-$355 resistance area. Prices rallied to a peak of $354.50 on September 18, as you can

see by the updated chart. The next move should be a downside acceleration. Long term cycles in gold indicate that its final bottom will occur in 1993 or 1994 (see analysis in the February 1989 Special Report). Any move above $355 will challenge this idea and reinstate the probability that gold will rally into the mid-400s in wave Ⓔ of a long term triangle, as discussed in detail in the March issue.

Silver is still approaching the final bottom in a bear market that has so far lasted over twelve years. There are several reasons why it may carry into a Fibonacci 13th year. As you can see by the weekly chart, silver is still working its way down in wave ⑤. The best conclusion is that wave (3) of ⑤ is extending. This interpretation implies that our downside target in the $2.90s will indeed be achieved. A diagonal triangle (see text, p.31) resolution, requiring only *one more wave down to the minimum target level of* $3.50, cannot be ruled out, but either way, a final low would be expected in coming weeks. However, complicating the timing element is the fact that the 9-month cycle almost certainly bottomed in late August-early September, coinciding with the "cycle low due here" label we've had on the chart. The 9-month cycle suggests a rally lasting another two to four months, then a decline into its next scheduled low in May-June 1993, a time period that happens to coincide with a cycle low for gold. If silver follows this scenario without falling below $3.50 first, we will plan to buy it then.

Gold traders moved to 100% short when the London price fixed at $350.75, exact top tick so far. Our average short sale entry is $347 basis December, and our stop is very close at $357. If the stop is hit, reverse to long with a stop at $340. *Silver traders should cover shorts now.*

If silver does fall below $3.50, it will be time to begin buying bags of silver coins for use later in the depression. *I recommend buying at least one bag now, just in case the low is in.* When the financial system breaks down, even if normal sources of money are inoperative only

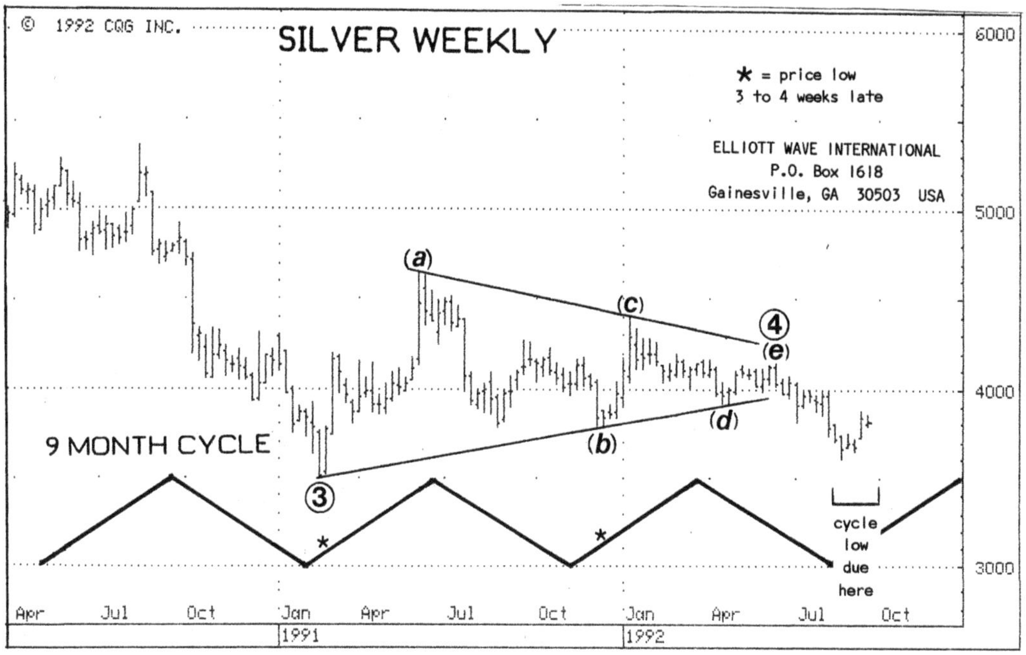

temporarily, having some tangible purchasing power could save your life. Premiums for "junk silver" bags are very low these days, as warehouses fill up and disinterest reigns. $1000 face value bags, containing 715 fine ounces of silver, are now going for under $3000 (with silver at $3.85). You may wish to ask about pre-1935 silver dollars or Kennedy half dollars as well. Dealers will almost always be able to obtain a current quote for you while you're on the phone. Quotes reflect that minute's price for silver, so timing can be important, but cash purchasers shouldn't fret too much about whether the price is $3.95 or $2.95 per ounce. It's not $45, $35, $25, $15 or even $8, and those levels are where most other people own it. Here are three sources for pre-1965 U.S. silver coins (and other coin investments as well) that I personally believe to be honest dealers with good prices. Call them for quotes and info. [Note: Sources omitted; see *Conquer the Crash* for updated sources. —Ed.]

We do not know that silver will not fall to much lower levels (another $2 would be a huge percentage drop). However, there are two things we do know: (1) at $3.50/oz., silver has fallen 93% from its 1980 high and (2) *not until now* has the Wave Principle *even once* suggested that the final bear market low was nigh. If you're an investor or speculator, this is the kind of opportunity you await, and await it we have, avoiding every dollar of decline from $50/ oz. to today.

OCTOBER 30, 1992

Gold also peaked precisely at our target and has begun a major collapse. It's due to bottom next May.

Gold & Silver

After three years of slow erosion following the 1988-1989 slide, gold is once again getting *very* exciting. Here is the analysis from the October issue:

> The daily chart of December gold futures last month projected an a-b-c rally to the $351-$355 area. Prices rallied to a peak of $354.50 on September 18. The next move should be a downside acceleration.

Gold at the time was still at its highs. As explained then, a further rally of *only 50¢* would have negated the outlook. It was one of the lowest risk short-sale entries we've ever had.

Take a look at the daily chart and you'll see that gold, after holding up for about a week, began falling sharply, leaving *four gaps* along the way. The declining structure is of *five* waves, indicating that the larger trend is down. Put/call ratios haven't budged yet, so traders' sentiment is still too bullish. Near term resistance is now at $345.

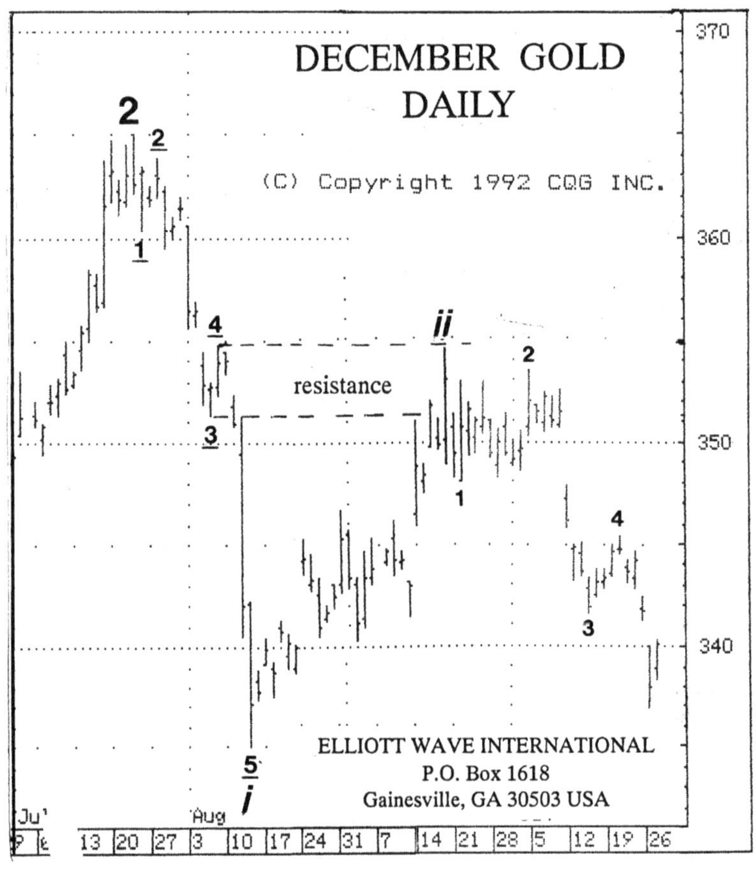

Long term, gold is still expected to fall to below $200/oz., with $105 an ideal target. The next two intermediate term cycle bottoms for precious metals are due in May-June 1993 and February-March 1994. Either of these could mark the final bear market low, although the first one is more likely to see the low for silver, the second the low for gold.

Traders are holding 100% short gold with a stop at $357 basis the nearby contract. We are positioned for what should be a Fibonacci 8-month collapse, from September to May, possibly ending a Fibonacci 13-year bear market. Investors are out of precious metals except that those preparing for depression bought a bag of pre-1965 "junk" silver coins last month within pennies of the 19-year low in price. Buy another if silver falls below $3.50/oz., and delay any final purchases for the cycle low expected in the second quarter of 1993, when it should be selling for under $3.

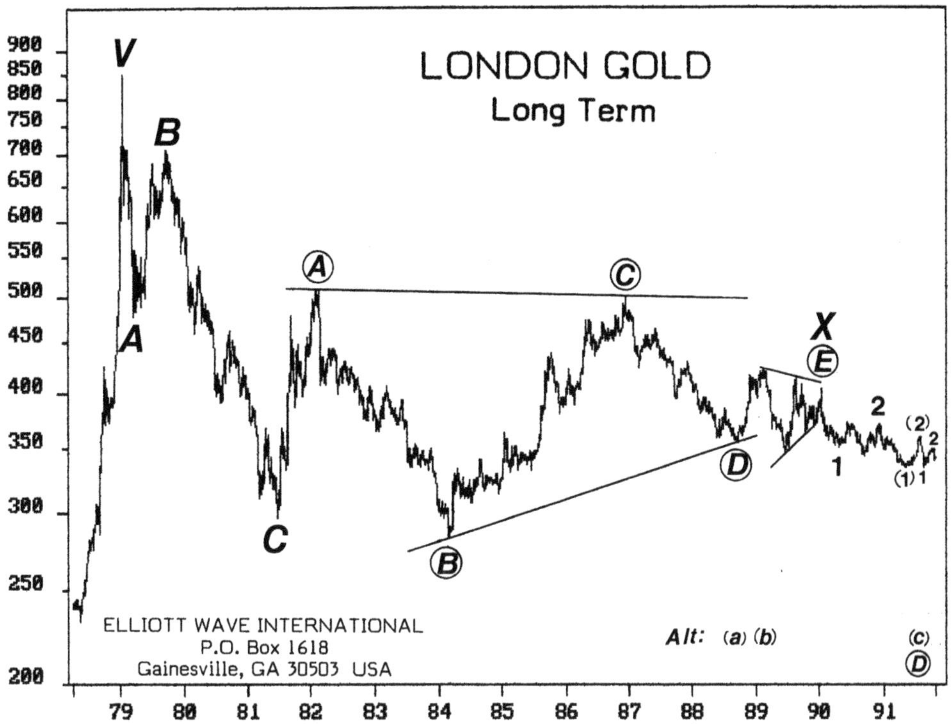

The 12+ years of decline in silver have brought out the bears. One EWT reader reports that at a local fair he attended, a man in a collectibles booth commented that "a couple of years from now, silver won't even be a precious metal." *This sentiment is the opposite of the national silver fever that EWT battled at each rally peak from 1980 to 1987.* Capitulation among formerly committed silver investors should be even more evident at the final low. Look for major newspaper articles on the subject in coming months. Be patient and ready to buy.

NOVEMBER 25, 1992

Gold is bouncing in a small second wave, and is likely to accelerate on the downside within a few weeks. Silver remains on target to fall below $3.50/oz., possibly then registering its final bear market bottom.

Gold

The declines in gold dating from last summer continue to unfold in five waves, supporting projections for lower prices. Near term resistance was identified last month at $345 (the peak of wave 4; see text, p.57), and gold has indeed stayed below that level. The long term chart in the November issue showed a series of first and second waves down. A final small second wave should precede a downside acceleration. That wave, labeled 2, began on November 9. A "third of a third" sharp drop, probably featuring a large gap, is due some time in coming weeks. The low put/call ratio supports the continuing bearish outlook.

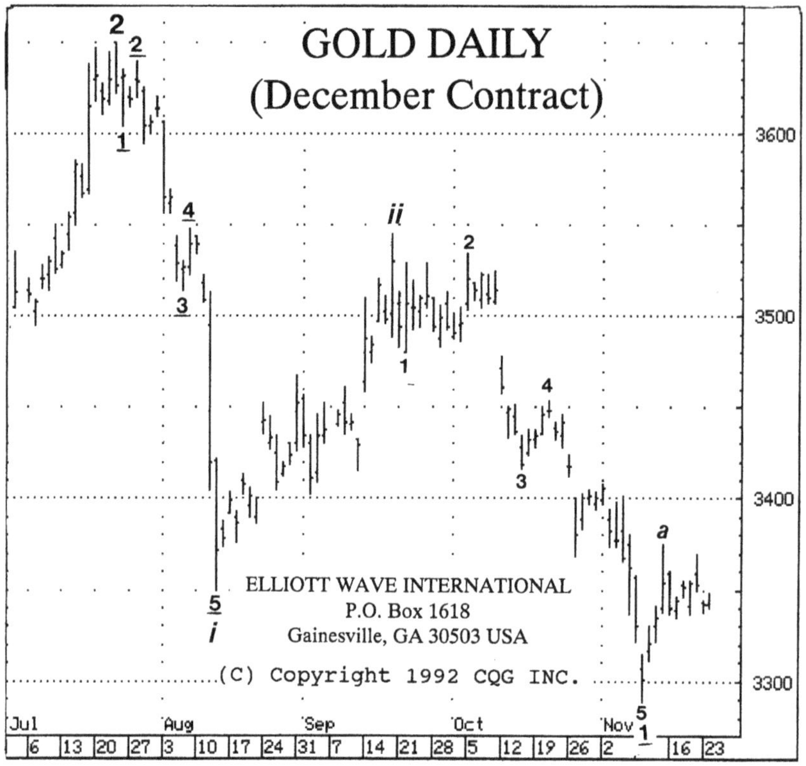

Investors are out of the gold market. Traders are short. Lower the stop to $348 basis the nearby futures contract.

Silver

For almost 13 years, *The Elliott Wave Theorist* has tracked the bear market in silver. After all this time, wave structures indicate that silver is finally approaching its long awaited low. The next chart shows the bear market structure from the top in 1980.

Since February 1991, every intermediate-degree move in silver has been three waves. This fact allows only two acceptable wave counts for waves ④ and ⑤ from that time. The first is the interpretation that EWT has been showing all along, that wave ④ was a contracting triangle (see text, p.41). This means wave ⑤ began in May 1992, from which point prices have indeed fallen significantly.

The second count labels wave ④ as a zigzag rally ending in May 1991. The three-wave structures since then mean that wave ⑤ must be a *diagonal triangle* (see text, p.31). Subwave (5) of the pattern is now unfolding, as you can see by the labeling shown here.

Both interpretations support the case presented in EWT over the past year that silver must fall at least below its wave ③ low at $3.50 before the final bottom is registered. The currently low put/call ratio argues that the forecasted drop is in force now. Because the diagonal triangle count allows the next low to be the last, those wishing to buy bags of junk silver should do so whenever the price of silver falls below $3.50 (see October issue for dealers).

The financial replay (with numerous minor differences) of the 1920s and 1930s has produced a number of remarkable similarities. As you can see by this chart (courtesy of The Investor's Edge, 1043 17th St., Santa Monica, CA 90403), the bear market of the past dozen years in silver mirrors the last great bear market, which took place from 1919 to 1932. The sharp rally following the bottom in 1932 is exactly what EWT is expecting after the low that is imminent.

The next 9-month cycle bottom is still due in May. That month could mark a higher low, but if wave ④ was a contracting triangle, silver will register its final bottom then, probably below $3/oz. Either way, a great speculative buying opportunity for futures traders is probable soon. Stay tuned to the Hotline.

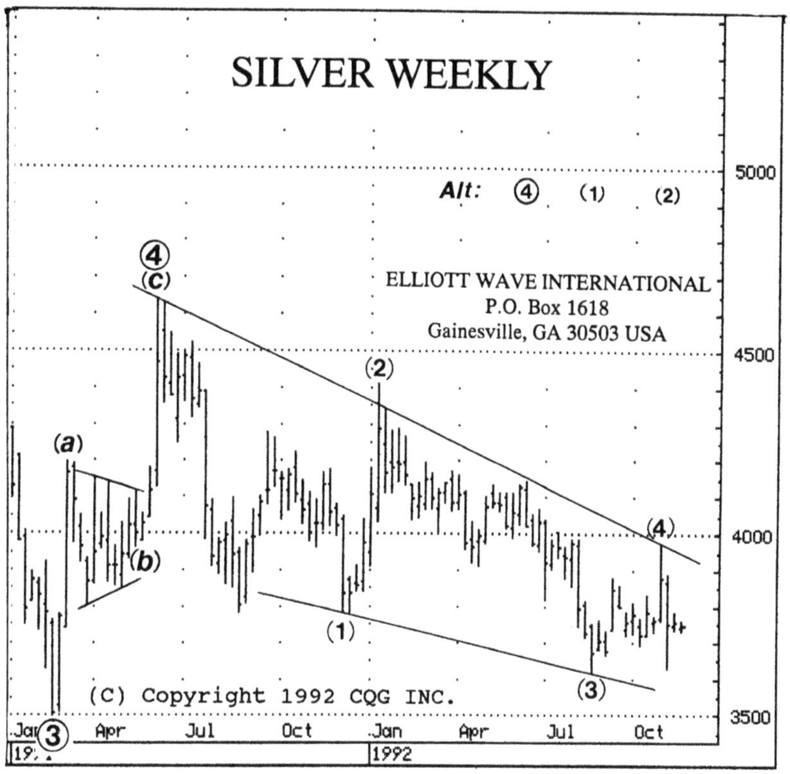

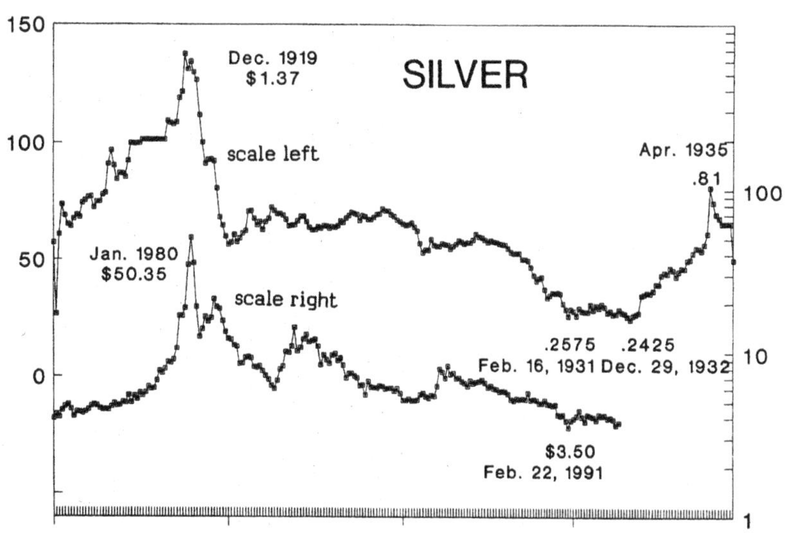

DECEMBER 31, 1992

Gold is poised to accelerate its downtrend. Silver is nearing the end of a 13-year bear market but should at least break $3.50/oz. before it bottoms.

Gold & Silver

Precious metals enjoyed a bull market of 13 years' duration from 1967 to 1980, spanning almost exactly the bear market in stocks labeled Cycle wave IV. *The Elliott Wave Theorist* has long pointed out that a Fibonacci 13-year bear market in gold and silver would project a low in 1993. The February 1989 Special Report showed that time cycles forecasted a low for silver in 1992 and a low for gold in 1994, supporting the case for weakness until those years. The charts from that publication are shown below, exactly as presented nearly four years ago, with the Fibonacci time bar added to the silver chart. That report summed up the evidence this way: "Taking all relevant time studies into account, it can be concluded that *gold will experience an extremely low valuation bottom in 1993-1994, + or - 1 month.*" Silver's time studies projected a low in 1992-1993. These observations have kept us correctly bearish on the precious metals throughout this time.

The difference in time cycles for the two metals suggests that silver will bottom before gold. That's why recent issues of EWT have focused on projecting a low for silver in coming weeks or months. Moreover, the minimum downside target for gold is still below $200/oz., with a maximum and best target near $105. In terms of price, it's far too early to consider buying gold.

From *The Elliott Wave Theorist*, February 1989

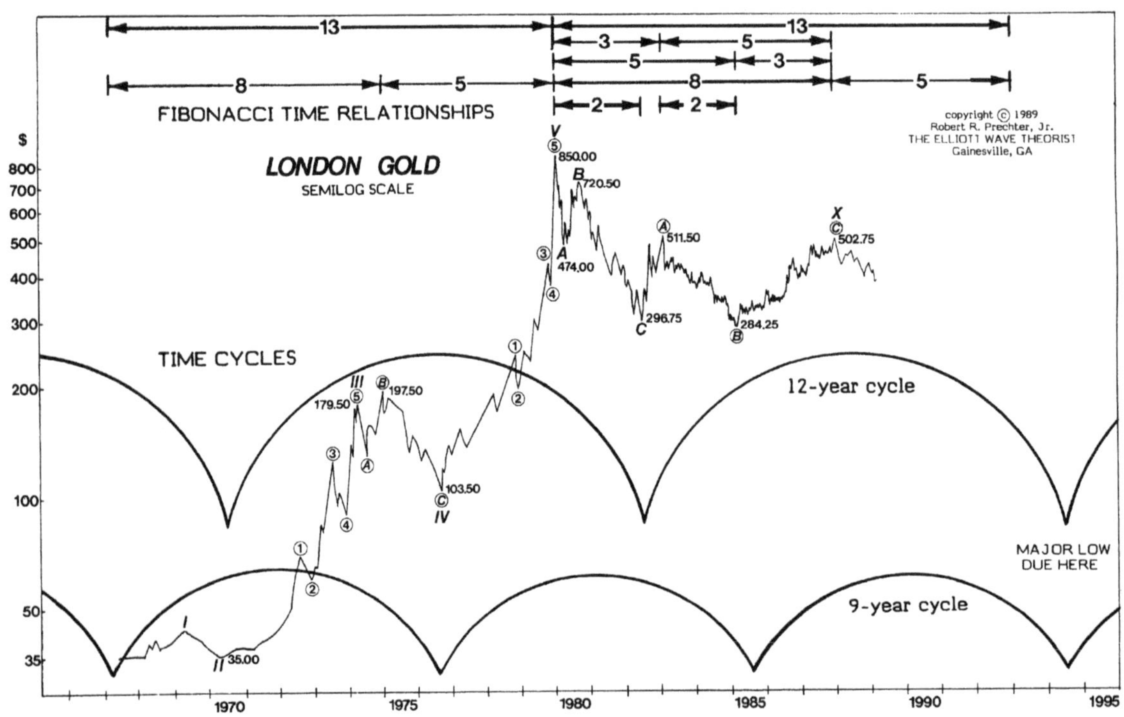

From *The Elliott Wave Theorist*, February 1989

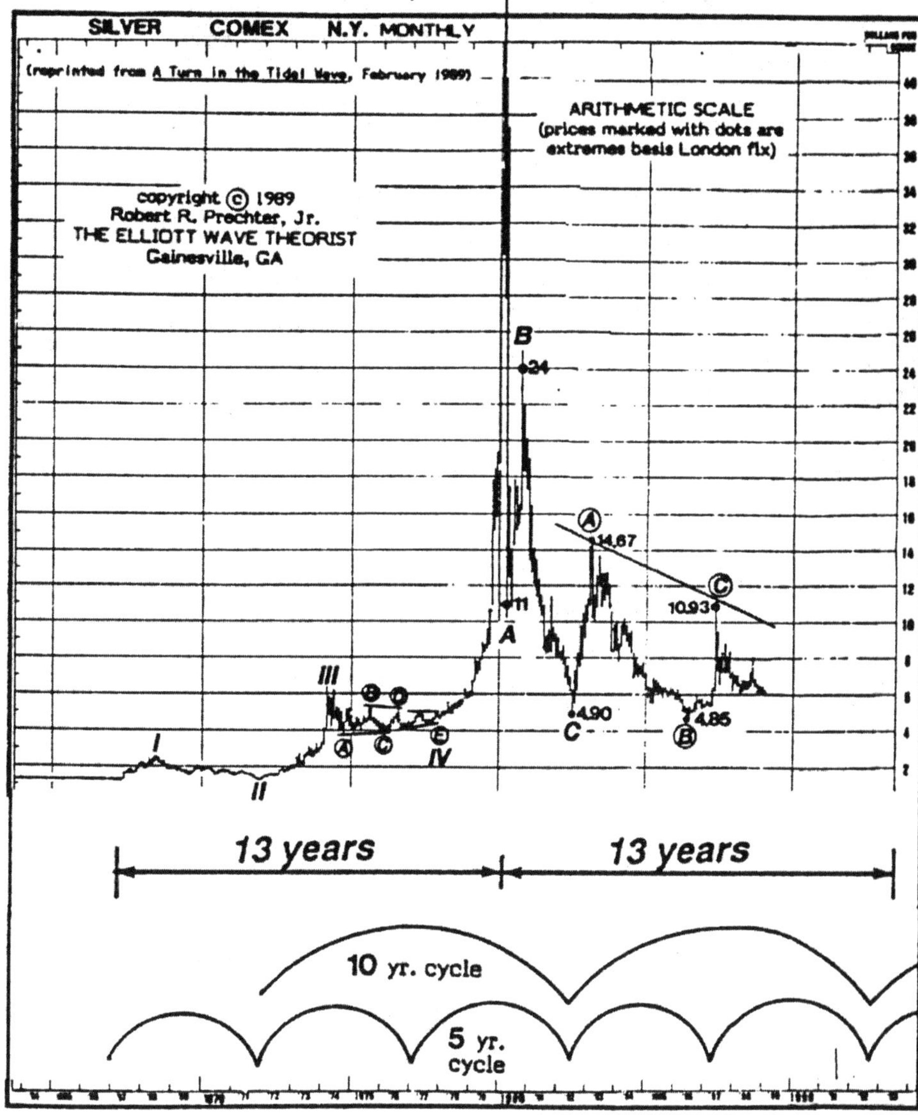

If the precious metals bottom in 1993-1994, then they are likely to experience at least a 5-year bull market, into 1998, and as much as an 8-year bull market, into 2001. The most satisfying outcome would be a 5-year bull market followed by a 5-year deflationary bear market into the year 2003.

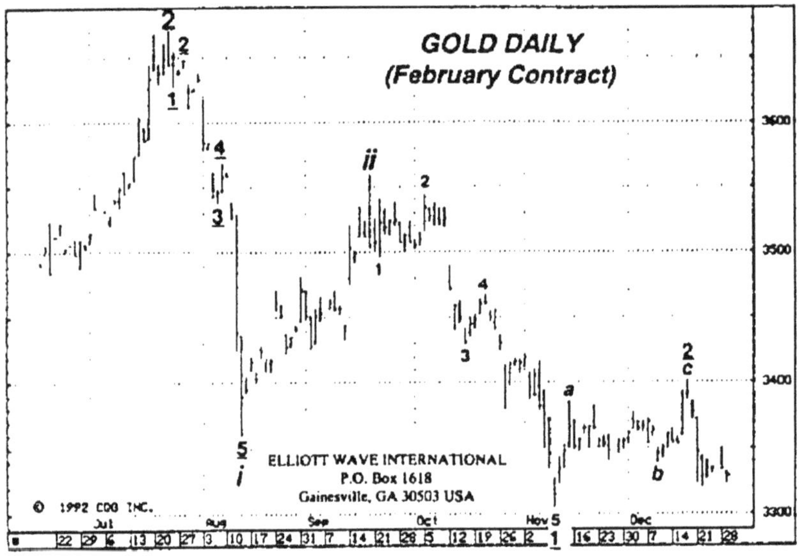

Near Term Outlook

As you can see on this daily chart, the latest rally in gold, wave 2, was composed of three waves, confirming that it was counter to the main trend, which is down. With the developing series of first and second waves now as low as Minuette degree, a near-vertical drop, probably featuring a large gap, is likely to take place early in the new year.

The ten-day average of the put/call ratio is fairly high for gold, so keep in mind that a move above $348 would negate the bearish outlook. The same ratio is at a *record low* for silver, which still appears on track for a drop to at least below $3.50. For a detailed discussion, see the December issue. Cycles indicate a low in May-June for both precious metals.

Way Back Then

The Wave Principle has been of immense value in planning my professional life. The perfect expression of the Wave Principle in the pattern of gold prices in 1972-1974 was what first convinced me of its validity. Even as a novice, I was able to track the waves in that explosive price rise, riding the uptrend and then exiting a coin position the day after wave Ⓑ peaked at $200/oz. on the last day of 1974. At the same time, as forecasted years earlier by A. J. Frost, stocks had clearly registered their low for Cycle wave IV, and that fact portended a great bull market ahead. These two markets were crystal clear at the time (little did I know then that markets aren't always so clear), and, mostly because of my enthusiasm for the new discovery and partly because of the conclusion that the upcoming bull market in stocks would make a good career, I went to Wall Street and, after months of trying, landed a job that year. That was a very useful decision. It also led to some outrageous and fun times that I will never forget. One of these days, I'll tell you about them.

The Elliott Wave Theorist, 1993

JANUARY 29, 1993

The wave structure in gold favors a continued decline as long as $348 is not exceeded on the upside.

Gold & Silver

There is some evidence that the bear market in gold is maturing. For instance, the Comex (Commodity Exchange) of New York, which relies heavily on gold and silver futures trading for its income, is allowing itself to be acquired by the Chicago Board of Trade due to falling revenues. The Dutch central bank sold 400 metric tons of bullion reserves in the last two months of 1992, indicating a bearish mindset within a government body, a sign of a maturing trend. Newspapers and magazines mostly report disinterest among professionals and the public. Gold stocks have fallen 40% more in value in just the past year and a half. Nevertheless, all that this evidence reflects so far is that *we have been right in recognizing the bear market and staying out of it.*

A thorough perusal of Elliott wave and cyclical evidence still leads to the conclusion that despite potential rallies, the long term trend in the price of gold is likely to remain down. Elliott wave price projections still call for an ultimate low under $200/oz., with an ideal target near $105. Intermediate term cycles continue to point down until May, and long term cycles are still due to bottom in "1993-1994," of which period quite a bit remains. Valuation studies indicate that gold has fallen only to the very upper end of its historically typical range of valuation relative to commodity prices (see chart in the February 1989 Special Report). Reaching the lower end would require gold near $100/oz. even with no further decline in commodity prices.

Sometimes the final months of a bear market are the worst, and they often take place following a period of very slow decline that some advisors view as "basing" in a "low valuation area," such as we are hearing today. It would be risky to abandon our cautious approach at this time. Near term, there are two points to watch. A fall below $320 would constitute a dramatic break of both the moderately sloping support trendline that has been in force since last August and the slightly steeper line dating from September 1991, thus indicating the start of a downside acceleration. As stated in previous issues, a move by gold above $348, while not conclusive, would challenge our near term interpretation of the wave structure and suggest that wave Ⓓ had just ended.

Silver is a different story. It is *actually* cheap, which is why EWT, after waiting for twelve years, finally recommended that those wishing to be prepared for the worst of the depression begin by buying one bag of "junk" silver coins at today's low prices. Silver is *very* likely to complete its long term bear market some time in the first half of 1993, for all the reasons given in recent issues of EWT. Its next cyclic low is due ideally in May, and its wave structure appears to require at least one more drop, to below $3.50/oz. Little has happened in the past month, so there is nothing to add to this opinion.

FEBRUARY 26, 1993

Gold should be considered as still in its bear market unless the nearby futures contract moves above $348. *Silver is about to fulfill our long-standing forecast that the bear market would ultimately carry to below $3.50/oz.*

Perspective

The last watershed year for the major markets was 1980. You might be interested to know that EWT, then less than a year old, prepared readers for a major confluence of trend changes at the time, with gold and silver approaching their tops at $850 and $50, short term interest rates at 16% and inflation fears at fever pitch. Here is an excerpt from an article that appeared in Futures magazine (then Commodities magazine) in January 1980.

January 1980 Commodities

"Elliott counts suggest important tops in silver, gold, the major commodity market indexes and short-term interest rates," says a well-known Elliott wave analyst Robert Prechter in a recent special report of his newsletter, *The Elliott Wave Theorist*.

"If my wave count is valid, silver can be expected to drop back to between $4 and $6 per oz. sometime in the next decade," Prechter says. "The Elliott outlook for depression in the late '80s may go hand in hand with such a price collapse."

On interest rates, Prechter points out that charts of both the prime rate and 90-day T-bill yields show channelable five-wave advances with an exhaustion break of the upper trendline on the surge in rates after the Federal Reserve's Oct. 6 actions. The fifth wave in T-bill yields is even subdivided into five clear waves, he says of his charts.

"This count should mark the end of the three-year rise in short-term interest rates," he concludes. "Even if this is only an intermediate top, a normal Elliott pullback based on the prime rate back to 11½% and T-bill yields back to 9%."

The conjunction of five waves on various interest rate charts, according to Prechter, "all seems to point to the same conclusion: The world is about to begin a phase of general disinflation."

Gold & Silver

Recent weeks have witnessed a surprising flood of bullish predictions for precious metals. Gold stocks have rallied about 25%, retracing a modest ⅓ of their declines from June 1991. During February, options-on-futures players loaded up on calls and shunned puts, particularly in silver. So far, however, neither gold nor silver has budged on the upside. In fact, silver fell last week to within ½¢ of its bear market low. *Our long-standing forecast that the bear market would eventually carry silver to below $3.50 appears*

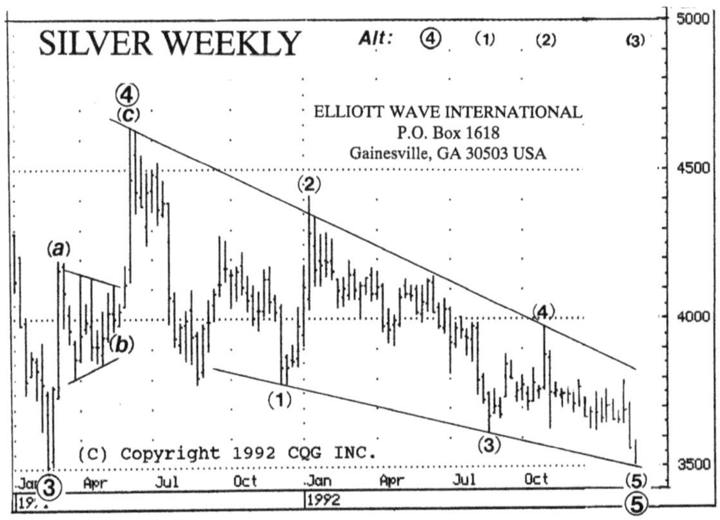

about to be fulfilled. Gold has remained stagnant, penetrating neither level ($320 or $348) that would signal follow-through in that same direction. The put/call ratio has fallen substantially in gold as well, however, so a continued bearish stance remains reasonable as long as $348 is not exceeded.

While for years EWT has projected a low for gold in "1993-1994," silver has been expected to bottom ideally in May 1993. If silver is finishing off a diagonal triangle from June 1991 as shown in the chart, the target zone for the low of $3.20-$3.49 *will probably be met in March.* If it ended a contracting triangle in June 1992 at 4.15, wave ⑤ will probably take until May and fall further, to below $3.

Employing Strategies

Time and price scenarios provide excellent guidelines to long term action. In this case, for instance, they implied throughout the past 13 years that one should not buy silver at $50, $25, $15, $8 or $5, or before 1992. However, when the period for opportunity finally arrives, strategy must be employed to gain the optimum advantage.

As an example, the Futures magazine article from 1980 cited above correctly forecasted an approaching peak in gold after 13 years of rise but estimated the upcoming top at $482/oz. (for a total gain of 1377%). In the final weeks of its fling, gold rose an additional 76% before reversing violently, so that forecast was significantly off. The same article forecasted that the next bear market bottom would occur at *$282.50*, a perfect forecast in that the 1985 low of *$284.25* basis London fix (*$281.20* basis futures) has marked the exact low for gold for the past 13 years. Thus, sometimes time and price targets are met perfectly and sometimes they aren't. That means using a bit of strategy as a major trend approaches termination.

One's investment situation determines strategy. *Cash investors, for instance, could average purchases in silver below $3.60.* EWT has suggested that subscribers wishing to be prepared for the worst the depression has to offer take advantage of the approaching bottom by buying bags of "junk" silver coins at low prices. We recommended buying one several months ago near the last low, while waiting for "below $3.50" to buy the rest. That opportunity appears to be imminent. *In fact, with the nearby contract having hit $3.505, let's buy a second bag now.* (Please refer to the October 1992 issue for names and addresses of dealers.) As for futures trading, some people can afford to risk more than others. Certainly *if* silver falls into May, thereby placing both price and time guidelines at an optimum point, EWT will not hesitate to recommend a speculation. That doesn't mean that a futures trader has to miss the turn if it comes earlier; he just has to pay attention to the short term behavior of the market. You can do it on your own or utilize our telephone hotline messages.

Jim Dines (Box 22, Belvedere, CA 94920) has a silver stock average made up of ten issues: Agnico-Eagle, Asarco, Avino, Coeur d'Alene, Equity Silver, Hecla, Industrias Penoles, Northgate, San Andreas and Sunshine Mining. Sunshine, just out of bankruptcy, is the only pure silver play and therefore is probably the most leveraged issue. *You should investigate these issues with your broker and devise a strategy for accumulation.*

MARCH 26, 1993

Silver is building a major bottom in its 13-year bear market. Gold may stage a short term rally, but long term, the bear market has more to go.

Gold & Silver

Silver is groping for its final bear market bottom. The wave structure, as shown in the long term chart, has completed all or nearly all of the required subdivisions from the 1980 high thirteen years ago. The final resolution may have occurred in February, as illustrated in the February 26 issue of EWT. The second best count (shown in the "Alt" line on the chart last month) allows for one more new low, which fits the projected bottom for the 9-month cycle, which is still due in May. Regardless, EWT has been suggesting the accumulation of physical silver near recent lows. See the March issue for a list of silver stocks and some trading and investing suggestions.

Gold is a different story. As you can see by the two charts, it remains historically overvalued against a basket of commodities and against silver, which recently sold for 1/100 of the price of gold, way below its one time "norm" of 1/16. Gold's time cycles are due to bottom later than

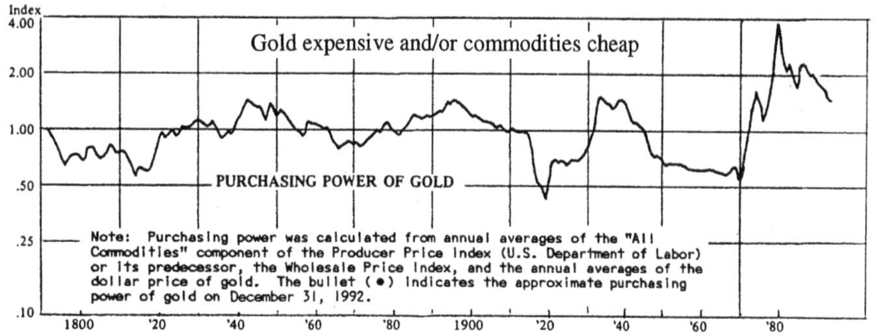

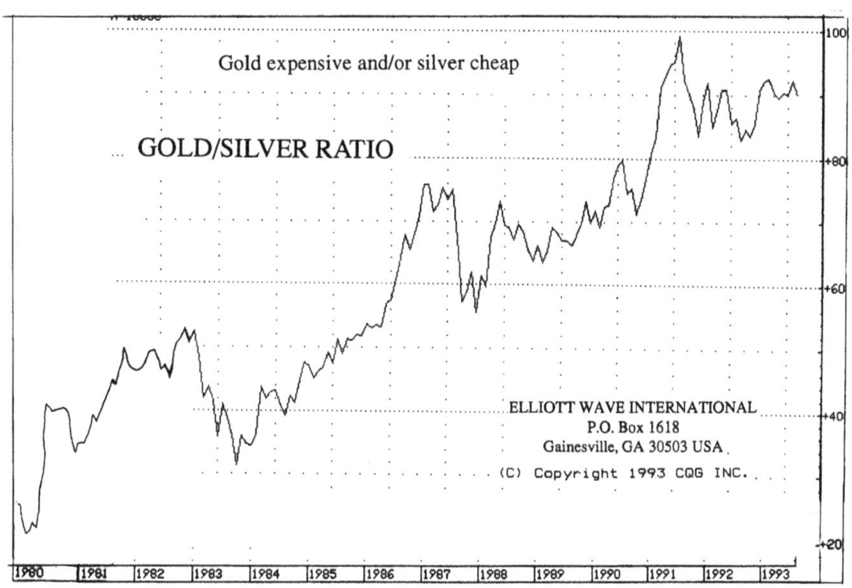

silver's, in 1994 rather than now. What's more, gold's long term downside target is far lower than today's price, while silver has met its bear market target. For all these reasons, I prefer silver to gold.

One of the most useful services EWT has provided its readers in the past six years has been to keep you out of precious metals and precious metals stocks. Most gold and silver stocks have collapsed 50%-80% over that time. For example, Hecla eroded from 27 to 7, Echo Bay Mines from 30 to 4, Sunshine Mining from 10 to 7/16, Coeur D'Alene Mines from 36 to 9 1/2, Vaal Reefs from 15 to 2 5/8 and Winkelhaak from 36 (it was 59 in 1984) to 4 3/4. That's devastation. Gold stocks have been touted ferociously in recent weeks, and small rebounds have taken place. (When the newspaper says they're up "a whopping 25% on average," they mean that a stock that went from 30 to 4 is now at 5.) Nevertheless, there is a strong Elliott wave case that the bear market in gold and gold stocks has not yet ended. In fact, it would be normal for some base building to occur even if these stocks *are* bottoming. Silver and silver stocks appear more attractive, so that is the preferred alternative for those wishing to make an investment in precious metals.

APRIL 30, 1993

Gold and silver have begun to advance from intermediate and major degree bottoms, respectively. The stronger performance by silver is exactly as forecast. A brief pullback in the precious metals is expected to occur into May or June.

Gold & Silver

July 31, 1992: "*Silver is approaching its most exciting juncture since January 1980.*"

August 28, 1992: "*Long term investors should accumulate a comfortable amount of junk silver coins between $2.90 and $3.50/oz.*"

November 25, 1992: "*For almost 13 years,* The Elliott Wave Theorist *has tracked the bear market in silver. After all this time, wave structures indicate that silver is finally approaching its long awaited low.*"

January 29, 1993: "*Silver is* very *likely to complete its long term bear market some time in the first half of 1993, for all the reasons given in recent issues of EWT.*"

February 26, 1993: "*One's investment situation determines strategy. Cash investors could average purchases in silver below $3.60. EWT recommended buying one bag of "junk" silver coins several months ago near the last low; with the nearby contract having hit $3.51, let's buy a second bag now. You should investigate this list of silver stocks with your broker and devise a strategy of accumulation....*"

March 26, 1993: "*The final resolution may have occurred in February, as illustrated in the February 26 issue of EWT. Traders and investors (particularly those who would be willing to buy gold) should go 100% long silver below $3.50; if silver hits $3.90 first, move to 50% long. Silver recently sold for 1/100 of the price of gold, way below its one time norm of 1/16, [so] I prefer silver to gold.*"

After 13 years of bear market (see long term chart in the April issue), EWT turned long term bullish on silver and silver stocks in late 1992-early 1993. The price low has almost certainly been registered, .01 above our recent target of "below $3.50," in a truncated fifth wave (see text, p.29). The rally in silver is tracing out clear *impulse waves* (i.e., "fives") from its February low on the daily chart, indicating that a new larger uptrend has begun. As expected, silver is already outperforming gold substantially, having rallied 23.9% so far to gold's 9.6%.

The long term chart of gold bullion reveals a recurring cycle of 3 years, 7 months' duration that began at the November 1978 low. This "3½ year cycle" bottomed again in June 1982, December 1985, June/September 1989 and now in March 1993, precisely when it was due. Off that bottom, gold is advancing in five waves, and the Philadelphia Exchange's Gold and

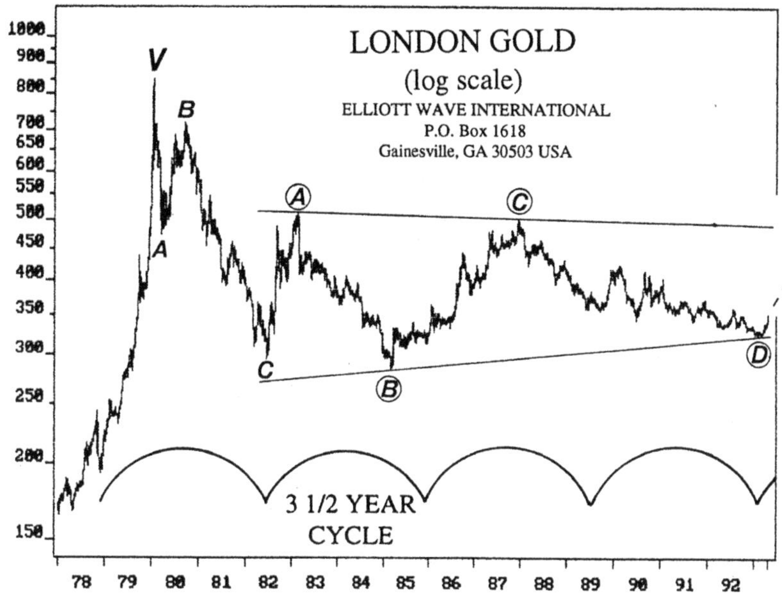

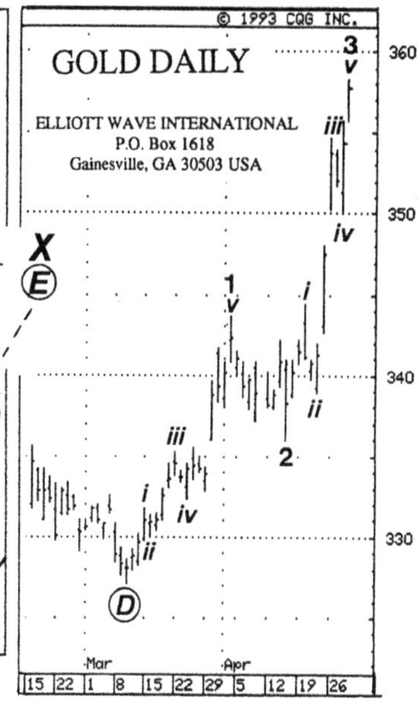

Silver Stock Index (symbol XAU), which bottomed way ahead of the metals, is also moving impulsively, as you can see by the second and third charts.

The daily charts of both gold and silver require one more brief pullback and rally high before starting the largest correction since the rally began. The 9-month cycle low due in May/June for the metals suggests a *brief period of softness* into a "wave 2" buy spot some time during the next two months. Ideally, silver should pull back to $4.08, gold to $350.

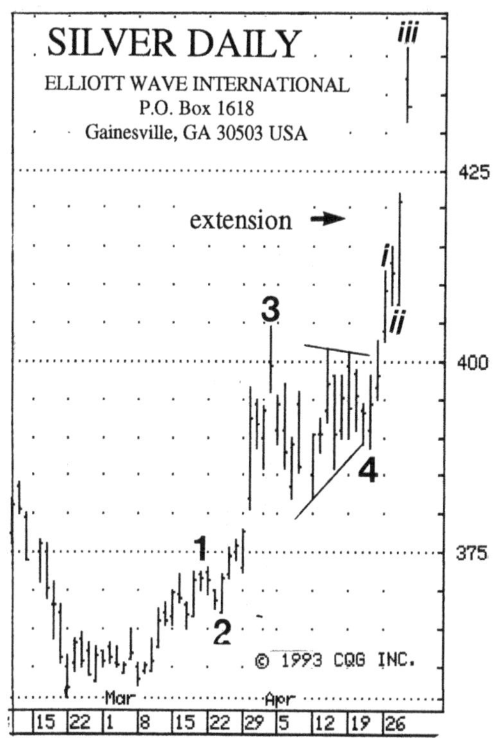

In terms of the Wave Principle, gold is now advancing in wave Ⓔ of the triangle that began in 1982, as you can see on the long term chart. "E" waves are often about 61.8% of the length of "C" waves in triangles, so $461 is a good estimate for the upcoming peak. Thus, gold should enjoy a strong rise, but silver's rise should be stronger. "E" waves are always accompanied by extreme psychology, so bullish sentiment should be powerful by the time this rally peaks. The position of the 3½-year cycle emphatically supports that expectation.

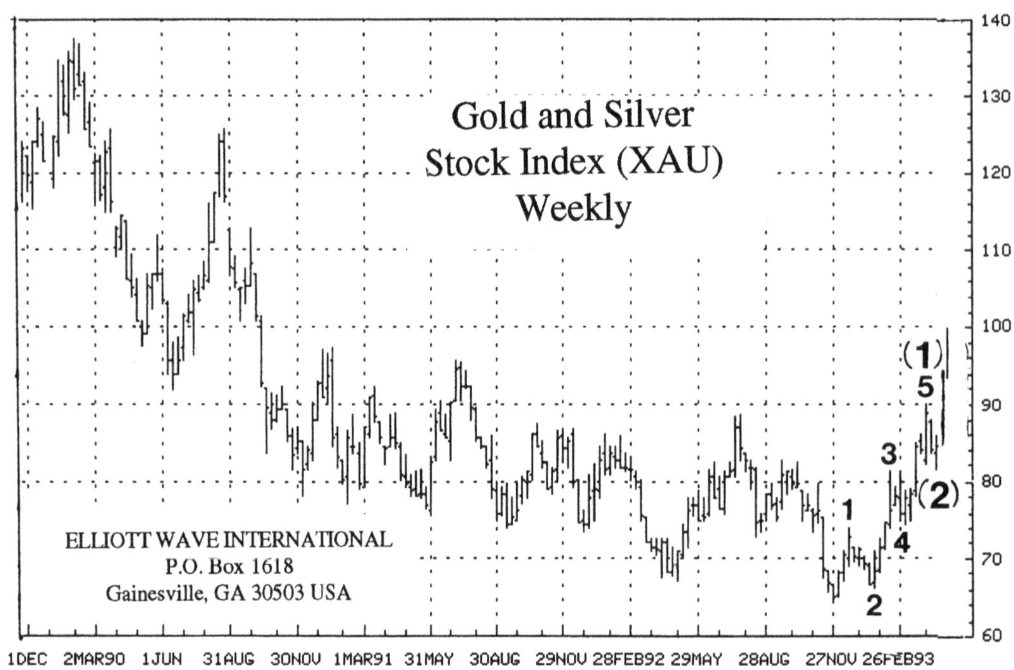

When gold ends wave Ⓔ, silver should be completing the first wave of a new bull market. After that peak, gold will experience its second and final A-B-C decline to its ultimate bear market bottom, while silver undergoes its wave ② pullback to a higher low.

Silver in Terms of Swiss Francs

The bear market in silver relative to Swiss francs appears to have ended as well. The long term chart shows a clear triple zigzag bear market.

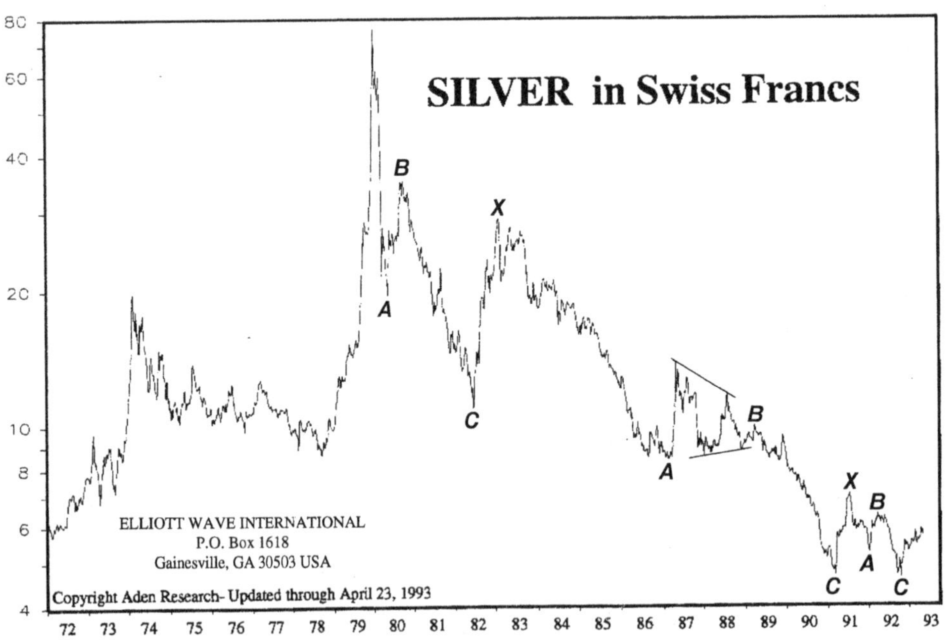

MAY 28, 1993

The upside target for gold remains $461. Silver and silver stocks are expected at least to triple before the uptrend that began in February terminates.

Gold & Silver

For months up until March 1993, the precious metals were asleep. Sagging lower month after month, gold and silver had been deleted from investors' buy lists. Gold was down 61.6% from its all time high. Silver was down an amazing 93%. Precious metals stocks were on the bargain shelf. While most eyes were on the stock and bond markets, *The Elliott Wave Theorist* was taking a different stand, preparing readers for a new major bull market in silver. From its low in February, *silver advanced 34.7% in three months, more than the stock market has risen in the past three years!*

"Nothing in gold's fundamentals has changed since a month ago, when the price languished at a seven-year low of $325 an ounce." —The Economist, May 1, 1993. That comment, which was written with gold in the $350s (it has since hit $385), is quite correct. Central banks still hold lots of gold. Producers are mining at a strong rate. Interest rates remain low compared to levels common in the past 20 years. "These facts about gold," says the article, "make soaring prices unlikely." It might be reasonable for a reader to ask whether fundamentals usually signal an important top or bottom in a market. Of course, they do not. (If they did, reading the newspaper would make us all rich.) Fundamentals lag the social psychology that produces them and are therefore far more predictable than predicting. Forecasting is best achieved using technical analysis, i.e., the analysis of market behavior, than by studying events and conditions outside the market. Ironically, yet quite necessarily, gold's fundamentals will almost certainly appear more bullish at its peak than they did at its bottom.

Sometimes turns in markets are accompanied by a "cover," a fundamental story that serves to dismiss the importance or validity of the turn. The cover for the recent turn in the precious metals is the popular assertion that the rally is phony because fund manager George Soros bought a pile of gold shares simply to manipulate the price of gold, either because he wanted to make a quick buck selling the stock or because he was short bonds and wanted a rising gold market to spark fear in the bond market. This is the man who made $1b. last year shorting the British pound, hardly a market that most people consider manipulable. It is more likely that he just recognized another turn.

Elliott Wave Analysis

As opposed to the static fundamentals, the clearly completed bear market pattern in the price of silver announced earlier this year that bearish psychology had played its last card in that market. (See EWTs from August 1992 forward.) At the same time, gold was ready for a significant bear market rally. As shown in *The Elliott Wave Theorist* last month, charts of silver, gold and the precious metals stock index showed rising impulsive (as opposed to corrective) wave patterns, indicating a new uptrend in force. As you can see by the accompanying charts, they have continued to rise in clear "fives," sporting a completely different look from the choppy, overlapping, corrective rallies of the preceding five years.

The peaks of wave (1) in silver and wave (a) in gold are near, so the largest correction since the rally began is due to begin soon. However, it is likely to be mild and/or brief. Precious metals bull markets are typically quite relentless, and those who try to sidestep corrections (particularly in the stocks) usually get left behind. Silver has support at $4.51 and $4.25 basis nearby futures and should hold above

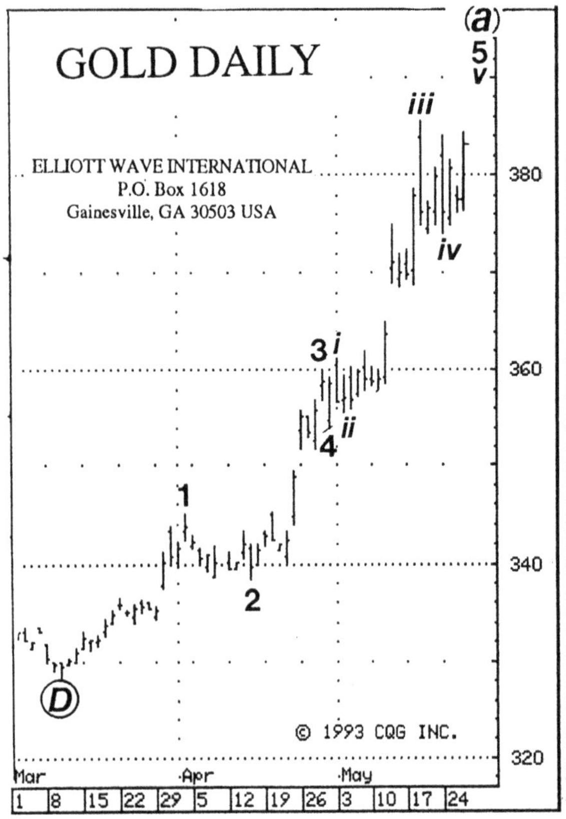

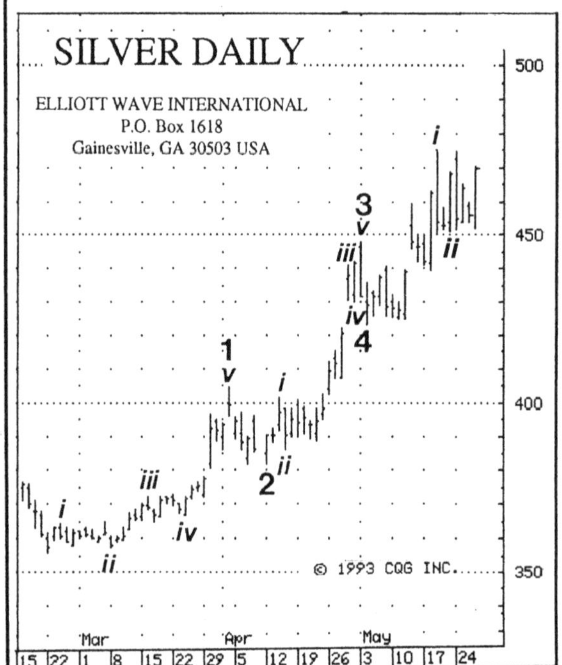

that lower level. Gold has support at $374 and $358 (+ or - $3). After a correction, gold should stage wave (c) to near our target of $461/oz., and silver should trace out waves (3), (4) and (5) to wherever it's going. As EWT has argued for months, silver should perform far better than gold, a triple or more in price being well within reason.

JUNE 25, 1993

Gold and silver pulled back in wave (2), as expected, and are now poised to rise powerfully in wave (3).

Gold & Silver

The April 30 issue of *The Elliott Wave Theorist* made a forecast that is critically important at this time: "The 9-month cycle low due in May/June for the metals suggests a *brief period of softness* into a wave (2) buy spot some time during the next two months."

That issue called first for "one more brief pullback and rally high," both of which occurred in May. The May 28 issue then recognized that "the peaks of wave (1) in silver and (a) in gold are near, so the largest correction since the rally began is due to begin soon." At the time, the daily chart of gold futures required one more new high in wave v of 5. That new high occurred the very next day, as you can see on the first chart. Silver had already peaked, right at the top of a very orderly trend channel, as you can see on the second chart.

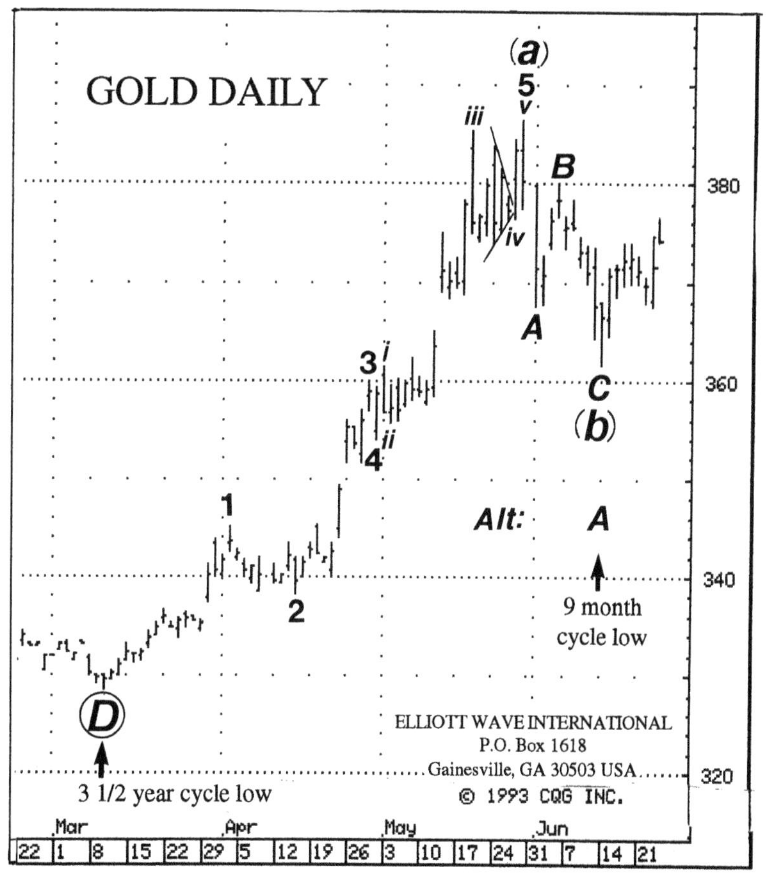

The month of June has indeed witnessed "a brief period of softness" and "the largest correction since the rally began." Gold futures bottomed at $361.70, right on projected support at "$358 + or - $3." Silver dipped briefly below support at $4.25, then reversed. Gold retraced 39.7%, and silver 49.6%, of its initial rise, quite close to

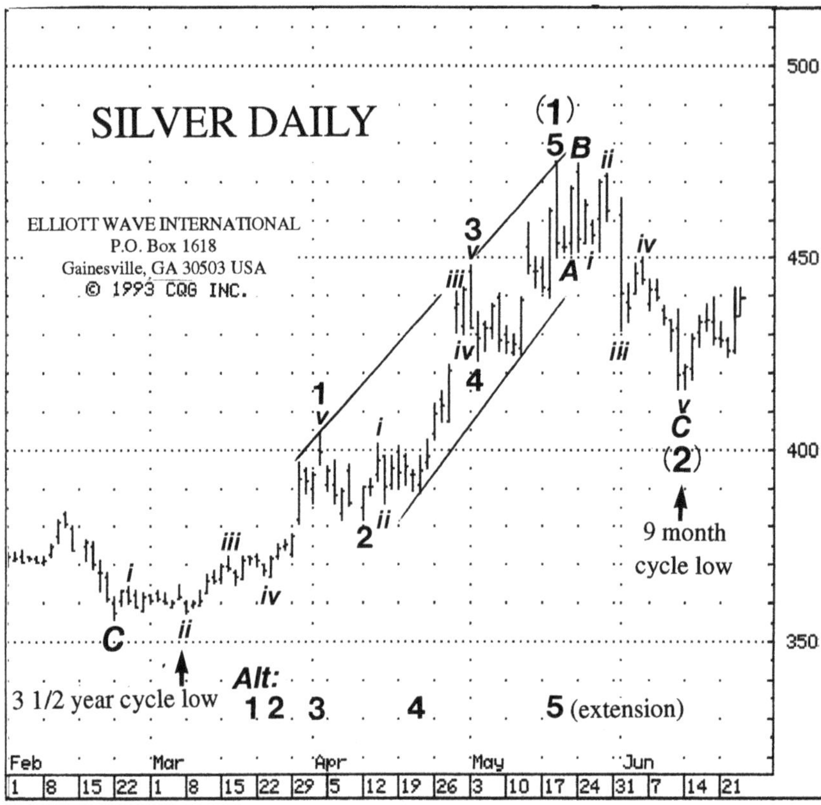

the classic 38.2% and 50% retracement percentages that occur so often in markets. Moreover, as you can see on the updated charts, these corrections have taken an a-b-c shape, which is exactly what was required to fulfill the outlook for wave (b) and (2). There is a remote possibility that silver could fall as low as $4.07 based on the support level suggested by the count labeled "Alt." on the chart, but the key point to make is that sufficient corrective action has taken place. The charts now show clear five wave advances and three wave pullbacks, the classic picture of a new bull market in progress.

Per the quote at the start of this section, the three wave pullback has occurred into the expected time for the 9-month cycle low. This is good news, because both waves and cycles now carry precisely the same bullish message. The wave structure calls for a third wave up in silver (and a "c" wave up in gold), the most powerful part of any impulsive sequence. Cycles call for an immediate upturn in the 9-month cycle, which will add its strength to the powerfully rising 3½-year cycle that bottomed in March (see illustration in the April 30 issue). Both studies suggest explosive upside potential directly ahead and lasting probably into the fourth quarter of 1993.

The upside target for gold remains $461, while silver is still expected to "triple or more in price" from its $3.50 low. Indeed, third waves are usually longer than first waves, and fifth waves in bull markets in commodities are often longer than third waves (see text, p.145). Thus, the current upside potential for silver in waves (3), (4) and (5) is itself greater than a triple and certainly continues to support EWT's forecast that silver will outperform gold and probably every other investment in 1993. For anyone who has so far missed the boat, this wave (2) pullback is providing a last chance to enter at reasonably low prices.

Precious Metals Stocks

The Gold/Silver Stock Index (symbol XAU) topped one peak shy of our expectations, requiring a slight change of wave count. Nevertheless, from the May high, the correction has followed the right script, taking an a-b-c shape and bottoming in the area of wave iv of 3, a normal stopping point when wave 5 is short. It is unlikely that this index will correct further, but if it does, it should fall no lower than the area of wave 2, between 82 and 90. The XAU is right in sync with silver: ending wave (2) and beginning wave (3).

The March 1993 issue listed nine silver stocks from the Dines Silver Stock Average for you to investigate and purchase according to your criteria. Needless to say, they have risen strongly on average since. In speaking with Jim Dines recently, he offered some updated thoughts on the precious metals issues. The following is a current list of attractive issues from the Original Gold Bug: Agnico-Eagle (AEAGF), Anglo-American Gold (AAGIY), Avino (AVO), American Barrick (ABX), Coeur d'Alene (CDE), Equity Silver (EST/A), Hecla (HL), Minoroco (MN-RCY), Placer Dome (PDG), Sunshine Mining (SSC) and United Keno Hill (UKH). Some of these are Canadian; some trade on the Vancouver Exchange; some are highly speculative. Make sure, as before, that you review these with your broker and make purchases that suit you and your financial situation. If you want frequent updates on these stocks, I recommend The Dines Letter (Box 22, Belvedere, CA 94920).

EWT'S SILVER CALLS, 1979-1993

11/18/79
1 "The evidence argues persuasively that at the very least we are reaching an interim peak in the inflationary spiral. Elliott counts suggest important tops in silver, gold, the major commodity market indexes and short-term interest rates... If my wave count is valid, silver can be expected to drop back to between $4 and $6 some time in the next decade."

6/10/80
2 "...we can assume with conviction that the ultimate low for silver has *not* been seen, and that after the B wave has run its course, another decline should get underway, taking silver to lower lows... I expect silver's ultimate low to be in the vicinity of $4-$6 per ounce, the area of the 1974-1976 "trading range." As for the B wave currently underway, the *minimum* target would be the peak of the fourth wave of lesser degree, or $17.50."

10/3/80
3 "My guess is that silver has peaked along with gold and that its zigzag B-wave rally has ended... Therefore, prepare for a final C wave down to lows significantly under the last low at $11 per ounce, probably closer to $4-$6 per ounce."

3/15/82
4 "Wave A of silver's bear market fell from $50 to $11, or 78%. If wave C also falls 78%, it will bottom at $5.28. Just as a wave C low at $5.28 would be 48% of wave A's low at $11, so the B wave peak at $24 was 48% of the high at $50. Here's where the Fibonacci ratio enters, since 48 is 61.5% of 78. In other words, the percentage distance between the two highs will be equal to the percentage distance between the two lows *and* equal to 61.8% of the percentage distance between both the first high to low and the second high to low, only at the $5.28 figure." [Note: It bottomed at $4.90.—Ed.]

10/4/82
5 "Silver appears to have climbed in five waves off its low, so once this correction ends, silver should rally to a new high."

11/8/82
6 "My upside target for silver is $17, plus or minus $1. Interim resistance is at $11."

11/29/82
7 "The recent formation can be counted as an a-b-c irregular correction. If this count is correct, silver's next move is up strongly."

2/7/83
8 "While gold may or may not climb to new highs on its next rally, silver's pattern virtually demands another wave (or even two) to new highs."

SILVER
(Monthly)
log scale
50
25
10
5
1
2
3
4
5
6,7
8
9
10
11
12
13
14
15
16
17
18
19
20
© 2004 Elliott Wave International
1980
1982
1984
1986
1988
1990
1992

3/7/83

9 "Silver...has completed its full A-B-C bear market rally and is due to follow gold down to *below* last year's low at $4.90 per ounce."

8/4/86

10 "Gold shares and silver have been influenced strongly by the two-year cycle, which is bottoming now. This situation implies a stronger countertrend rally in these markets."

4/27/87

11 "The recent explosion in silver (the "poor man's gold") is likely a signal that the speculation in the precious metals complex is climaxing."

6/1/87

12 "The big picture for silver strongly suggests that the third major bear market rally since the January 1980 peak is over."

9/6/88

13 "Silver should complete the rally for wave E...by rallying to near $9/oz. A rise to that level would mark the termination of the entire countertrend pattern from 1982 precisely coincident with that for gold."

2/15/89

14 "The long term wave structure in silver also reveals a continuing bear market. Unlike gold, silver has already undergone a collapse of over 90% and has achieved the price area of its previous fourth wave, wave IV, which ranged from $3.50 to $6.50. Nevertheless, its bear market pattern appears incomplete. The recovery phase dating from 1982 has taken the shape of a contracting triangle, whether completed upon the rise to $8 in 1987 or requiring a final rally, still to a peak *below* that of wave Ⓒ. Either way, the larger formation, like that for gold, argues for another A-B-C decline from the end of the triangle."

10/26/90

15 "...silver has recently cracked to $4.20, a price it hasn't seen since 1976. What's more, if the Elliott wave count for *gold* that EWT has been illustrating for years is correct, then the ultimate low for silver can only be imagined... The price of $3.78 registered on July 12, 1974, is the low of the "previous fourth wave" support zone but is not necessarily a target. We will rely on wave form to tell us when the bottom is at hand."

5/31/91

16 "Silver should once again fall to new lows."

9/25/92

17 "Silver is still approaching the final bottom in a bear market that has so far lasted over twelve years... If silver does fall below $3.50, it will be time to begin buying bags of silver coins for use later in the depression. I recommend buying at least one bag now, just in case the low is in."

2/25/93

18 "Our long standing forecast that the bear market would eventually carry silver to below $3.50 appears about to be fulfilled... We recommended buying [a bag of "junk" silver coins] several months ago near the last low... With the nearby contract having hit $3.505, let's buy a second bag now... You should investigate the following silver mining issues and devise a strategy for accumulation...."

3/25/93

19 "Silver is groping for its final bear market bottom. The wave structure...has completed all or nearly all of the required subdivisions from the 1980 high thirteen years ago. The final resolution may have occurred in February."

4/29/93

20 "The price low has almost certainly been registered, $0.01 above our recent target of "below $3.50," in a truncated fifth wave. The rally in silver is tracing out clear impulse waves, indicating that a new, larger uptrend has begun."

JULY 30, 1993

Silver is on the verge of a powerful upside acceleration in wave 3 of (3), and gold is about to jump above $400/oz. in wave 3 of (c).

Gold & Silver

The May 28 issue of EWT projected a June pullback in gold to $358 + or - $3 and in silver to $4.25. Those pullbacks occurred on schedule, tracing out the required a-b-c formation and fulfilling classic retracement percentages (38.2% and 50% respectively) of the preceding advance. The June 25 issue came to this conclusion:

> The charts now show clear five-wave advances and three-wave pullbacks, the classic picture of a new bull market in progress. The three-wave pullback has occurred into the expected time for the 9-month cycle low. The wave structure calls for a third wave up in silver (and a "c" wave up in gold), the most powerful part of any impulsive sequence. Cycles call for an immediate upturn in the 9-month cycle.... Both studies suggest explosive upside potential directly ahead.

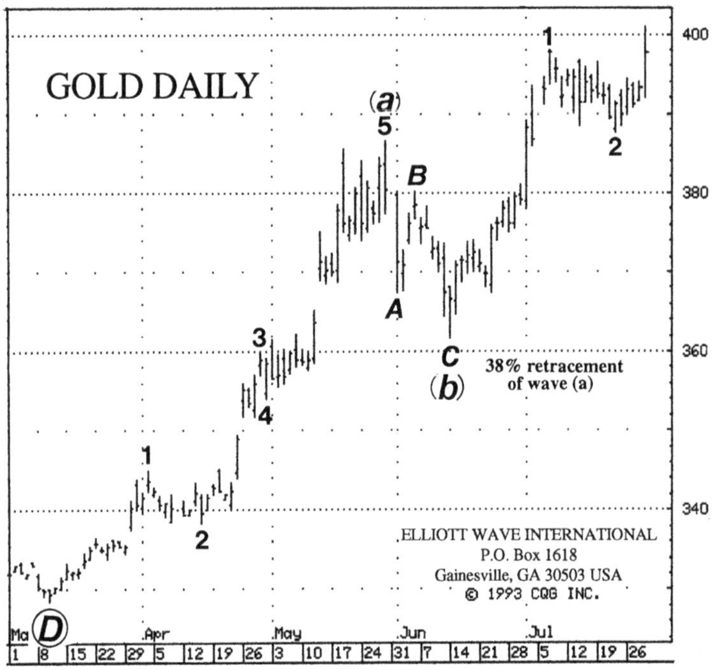

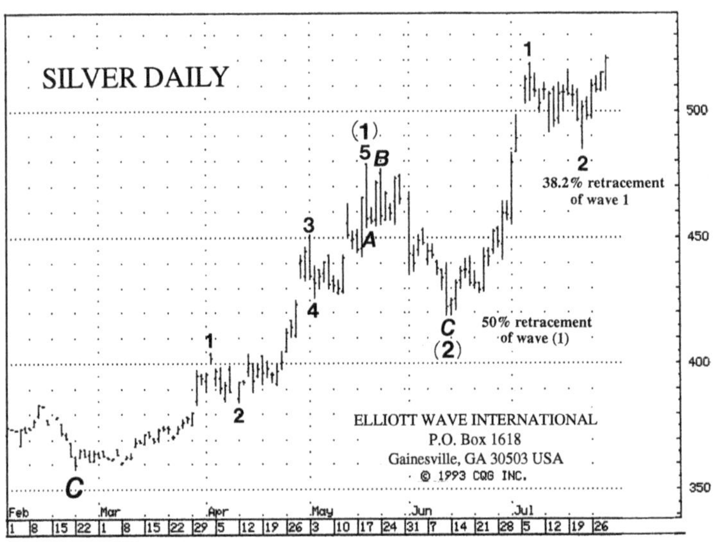

That description proved accurate, as silver soared a full dollar, from $4.19 to $5.19, in just four weeks, matching a gain that in wave (1) took three months. On a percentage basis, that's like the Dow going from 3500 to 4336 in a month! Gold reached a new high as well, at just under $400.

As expected, silver is still outperforming gold dramatically. Cyclic pressure remains up into the fourth quarter, and the potential for silver remains "greater than a triple" from the low of wave (2). As you can see from these articles, newspapers are still reporting *caution and warnings* from analysts (who now say it's "obvious" why gold *has* risen!), so the sentiment area continues to support our outlook.

"Higher volatility," by the way, is precisely the reason you want to be invested in silver in a bull market. Neither is "silver following gold," for three reasons: 1) Silver started up first, and gold followed; 2) silver is moving at twice the pace of gold; 3) silver is in a new bull market and gold is in a bear market rally. So if any such statement is valid, then gold is following silver. Finally, there are always some fundamentals that analysts miss. Here's one from last May, which also spoke to the historic cheapness of silver at the time:

Silver Rally Outshines Gold, but Analysts Warn Against the White Metal's Volatile Track Record

NEW YORK – Looking to ride the rally in silver?

Proceed with extreme caution, analysts say.

Silver broke through the $5 an ounce level last week, an impressive accomplishment after years of languishing at lower prices. But analysts warn that any sign of weakness could send the long-tarnished white metal once again into a major skid.

"Silver at $5 is a distinctly overbought position," says

Silver's blazing pace notwithstanding, dealers and analysts generally agree that silver has merely been riding gold's coattails. The danger, they say, is that the silver futures market is much less liquid—and therefore far more volatile – than is the market for gold.

"Silver started to rally because it typically moves in tandem with gold," says Mr. [redacted]. But he said speculative bets on silver as a tag-along to gold can't sustain further rises in the white metal if industrial demand does not pick up soon in Europe or Japan.

"Silver has been trading in a void, in a vacuum," says

Adding to silver's potential woes, analysts stress, is ample above-ground stocks. There are about one billion ounces of investment and speculative stocks of silver

Whatever the estimate of silver stocks, dealers expect "stale bulls" who bought silver at much higher prices to sell if the price rallies further.

once holders of silver start selling in earnest, the market will be amazed how sharply the price will fall," says

THE WALL STREET JOURNAL
JULY 12, 1993

DON'T LET THE GOLD BUGS GIVE YOU INFLATION NIGHTMARES

BUSINESS WEEK/JULY 19, 1993

Does the rising price of gold signal a new inflationary cycle?

It doesn't. There are plenty of reasons, on both the supply and demand fronts, why prices have risen.

The reason is simple: Economic fundamentals around the globe spell disinflation, not inflation.

$400 an ounce? Maybe.
$800? Forget it

FINANCIAL TIMES MAY 6 1993

MEXICO'S SILVER industry is facing crisis. "Everything you see out there is due to silver" says Mr Raul Rodriguez Marquez, planning minister in the once fabulously rich Mexican state of Zacatecas. "Now, what's certain, and it's no secret, mines are going to close."

Mexico is the world's largest silver producer, accounting for about one seventh of total output. But the silver industry, once the backbone of the country's economy, with production sustaining both New and Old Spain for more than two centuries, is in now trouble.

Hundreds of smaller mines have already been closed or restructured, forcing thousands out of work. Mr Jaime Lomelin of the Peñoles group, the largest silver producer in the world, reckons that no more than 20 low-cost Mexican mines will survive the current shake-out. Given current prices, his group has stopped exploring for more silver.

Earlier this month, the governor of the state of Zacatecas announced closure of the mine at Real de Angeles – the largest open pit silver mine in the world, with annual production of about 250 tonnes. With it would go some 400 to 500 jobs directly and another 800 indirectly.

Mr Rodriguez Marquez, the head of planning, mines and tourism in the state of Zacatecas, says in his state alone about 80 to 90 out of some 270 small mines have closed in recent years.

As you can see on the daily chart of silver, the consolidation that started in early July retraced a Fibonacci 38.2% of wave 1. This correction is labeled wave 2 of (3) (it's wave 2 of (c) in gold), so the "third of the third" (see text, p.68) wave, the strongest part of the advance, will be next. This point in a five wave structure usually sports a gap or two, very heavy volume, and a buying panic. It is also typically accompanied by a change in majority investor opinion from skeptical to bullish. These events should occur over the next couple of weeks. Gold is still on target to peak ideally near $461 but *not above $503* if it is indeed in a bear market rally. Any move above that level would negate the long term triangle shown in the May issue.

Question from a subscriber: "When it comes time to sell silver, should I consider selling the junk coins we bought near $3.50/oz. and try to buy them back lower?" Answer: EWT suggested purchasing bags of junk silver coins last November and February so that you could obtain at the lowest possible price some protection against a future shutdown of the banking system or currency crisis. (Ask the Russians today if they wish they'd stored some silver coins away. It appears prudent to hold tight to them for that very purpose.)

Inflation?

The May-June correction in gold and silver (which EWT called "a last chance to enter at reasonably low prices"), along with the new high in bonds, brought forward some bearish commentary on the precious metals.

Well, either the "inflation scare" returned immediately thereafter, *or* the reason for the metals rally has nothing to do with inflation. An opinion on inflation is *not* a necessary component of any argument in favor of rising gold and silver prices. Indeed, at major trend changes, *insistence upon fundamental support for one's market opinion usually increases the probability that you will miss the turn.*

JUNE 22, 1993

T-bond yield signals end of inflation scare

Long-term interest rates nudged toward a 16-year low Monday.

"The inflation scare has bit the dust," says

USA TODAY

Inflation is a concept different from that of *rising prices*. Inflation is an increase in the money supply. Rising prices are rising prices. Sometimes prices fall during inflation, and sometimes they rise during disinflation or deflation. In the first quarter of 1993, the Wave Principle forecasted a *price rise* in silver without reference to inflation. The debate raging among analysts today, however, is not whether precious metals prices are likely to continue rising, but whether inflation will return to *make* them rise. This, of course, is a fundamentalist question and one that will likely not be answered at any time that is opportune for buying precious metals.

The problem with this line of inquiry is that price rises are not necessarily a commentary on underlying inflation. Some prices can rise for awhile during a period of disinflation. Why? Because if prices have fallen substantially already (as is the case with the precious metals, for instance), they are welcome to a countertrend move – because if supply is restricted (by war, flood or drought), prices can rise — because if government slaps on import controls on a product (such as steel), domestic producers are free to raise that product's prices — because new government regulations work their way into companies' costs, which the customer ultimately must pay through higher prices — because if companies are suffering, some will decide that raising prices is their only hope for survival (although this course of action cannot succeed in the long run) — and so on.

The wave structure in gold indicates that the current rally, projected to $461, will be its last before a substantial decline in price. Inflation (an increase in the money supply) may or may not accompany the uptrend. If it does, news of it will certainly help market psychology reach fever pitch, probably right near the top. However, any increase in inflation is likely to be a temporary phenomenon. The "reflationary" period that followed the 1980-1982 deflation is drawing to a close. The current rally in the precious metals, along with the final high in the stock and bond markets, will end it. When it's over, a monolithic deflation will carry both the stock market and gold prices a long way down.

JULY 30, 1993 — BONUS PAGE

You Are Here

As you can see by the daily chart of silver, prices are in wave 3 of (3). Our "You Are Here" chart, taken from page 27 of *Elliott Wave Principle*, shows the position of silver within the overall progression of Primary wave ①. To quote from page 68 of the book:

> Third waves are strong and broad, and usually generate the greatest volume and price movement. It follows, therefore, that the third wave of a third wave, and so on, will be the most volatile point of strength in any wave sequence. Such points invariably produce breakouts, "continuation" gaps, volume expansions and large gains in the market.

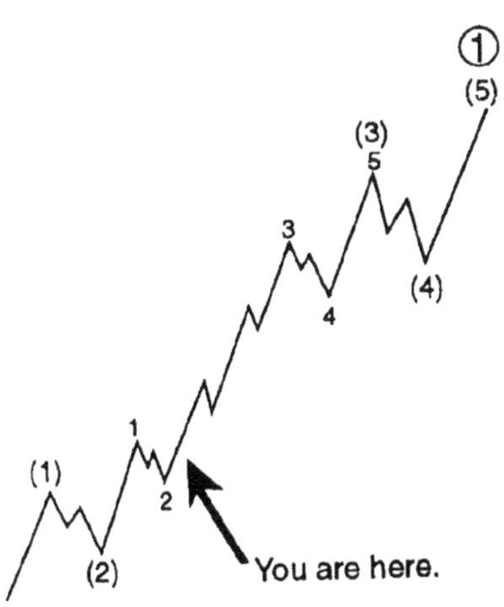

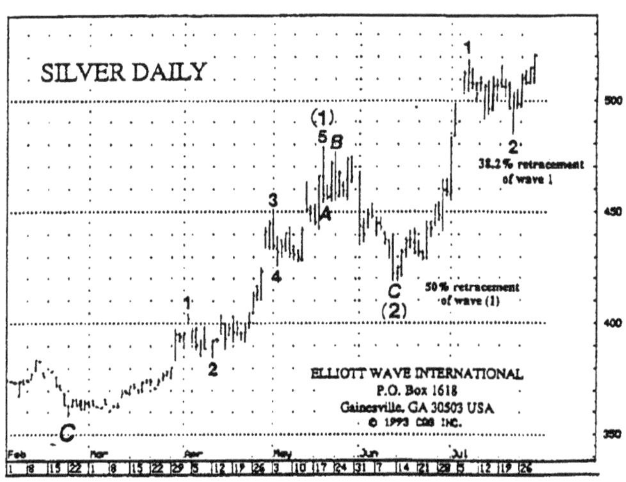

This type of action lies immediately ahead. (There is a remote possibility that silver is completing only wave (1), in which case wave (3) will be delayed a couple of months, but this count is a distant alternate.) Once silver completes waves 3, 4 and 5 of (3), it will trace out waves (4) and (5), per the diagram. Our goal is to recognize the end of wave (5) so that we can exit the market with maximum gain. At that point, wave ① will be over, and wave ②, a substantial correction lasting at least several months, will ensue. Given the clarity of this bull market so far, the odds are quite good that we will be able to identify the upcoming peak.

AUGUST 6, 1993 – INTERIM REPORT

Silver

Our last discussion of silver commented, "There is a remote possibility that silver is completing only wave (1), in which case wave (3) will be delayed a couple of months...." The sharp drop in silver today confirms this count in no uncertain terms. Nevertheless, our earlier conclusion about which wave count was the *better* one was absolutely proper given the evidence and guidelines. The occasional result of dealing in probabilities, however, is that sometimes the lesser probability occurs.

Because the Wave Principle got us into this bull market early, the current correction is simply providing an opportunity to add to long positions if we wish. In fact, we are going to use it to the advantage of new subscribers, and everyone else who would like to add to positions. Here are the guidelines we have to work with:

1) By far, most second waves hold above the low of the preceding second wave of one lesser degree. Thus, the current drop should hold above the June low (where we last added to positions).

2) Most second waves retrace no more than ⅔ of the preceding advance.

3) The June low is $4.16, and a ⅔ retracement is precisely the same, $4.16. This level, then, defines our extreme limit for a normal bull market correction. (These figures are basis the nearby futures contract.)

4) A 38.2% retracement, the minimum expectation, has already occurred, at today's low of $4.73.

5) The most likely outcome is a 50% retracement to $4.49, which would mirror the 50% retracement for wave 2 that occurred in May-June. Corrections following wedge shaped "fives" (see converging lines on chart) are usually more than 38%.

We now have guidelines for adding to positions and for a stop. Those who are 100% invested from our earlier purchases should place a stop on our entire position at $4.10, which is above the $4.08 average entry level for our current holdings. This is the most conservative

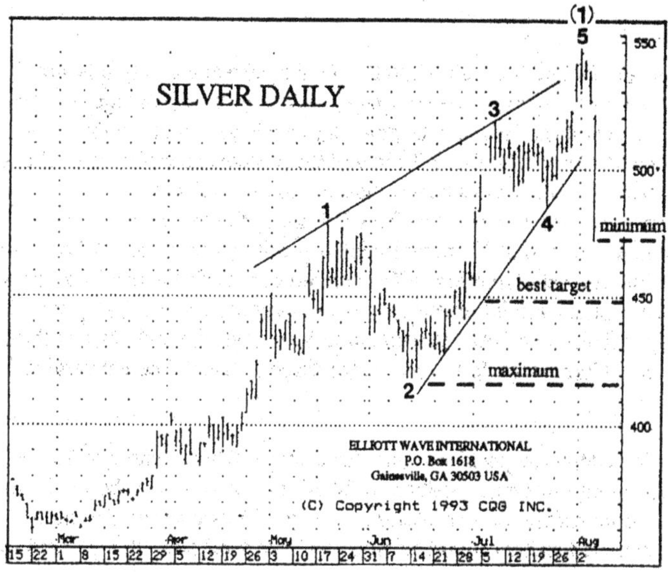

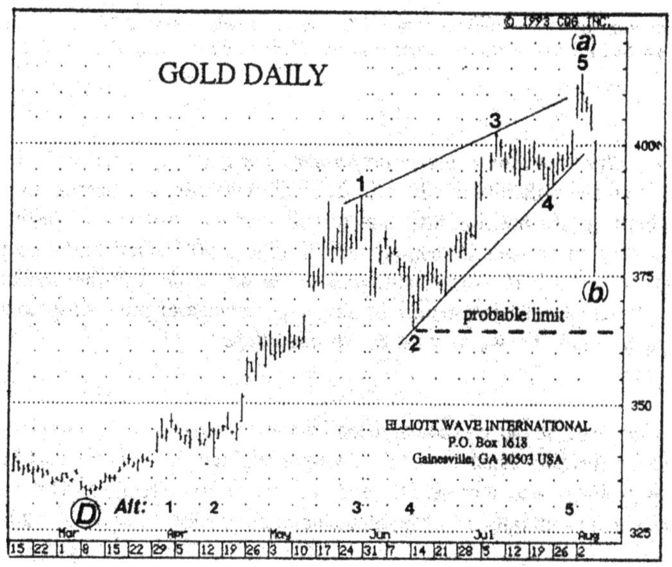

posture. If any futures contract for silver (or the cash price) reaches $4.51, latecomers will be presented an opportunity to enter with the same stop (though with more risk).

Relative Performance

Even after today's reaction, silver remains a better performer than gold, up a net 35% from the February low, as opposed to gold's 14%. The greater volatility of silver (in terms of movement as a percent of its price), far from being a negative, has put us in a better profit position than that of gold owners. In terms of percentage retracement of the rally, moreover, gold is proving more volatile than silver, falling to a 50% retracement so far as opposed to silver's 38.2%! The fact that gold on this basis is more volatile only on the downside is further evidence that silver is the more bullish metal in the current technical environment. Its larger percentage-of-price drop today, if anything, has now provided us with another opportunity that we may use to our advantage.

Gold

Gold is already deep into the area of the preceding second wave of wave (a). If today's low is as far as gold will correct, then a rally for wave (c) would equal wave (a), a normal relationship, at $459, just $2 from our working target of $461. Therefore, gold is probably also at or near the end of its wave (b) correction. The downside limit for a normal correction in gold is $364, which is not only a 61.8% retracement but the low of wave 2 in June.

AUGUST 27, 1993

Gold and silver ended their brief, sharp corrections right at EWT's targets and should now be resuming their intermediate term uptrends.

Gold & Silver

Silver is the only brand new bull market on the investment scene. EWT readers bought bags of silver coins within pennies of the low at $3.51 and accumulated silver mining company stocks from a list of ten last February, the month silver bottomed. Those stocks have doubled since then.

The brief precious metals panic of early August allowed anyone not yet invested a chance to buy at lower prices. *The Elliott Wave Theorist* wrote an Interim Report the day of the drop and made these observations:

> The current correction is providing an opportunity.... We are going to use it to the advantage of new subscribers and everyone else who would like to add to positions. The most likely outcome for silver is a 50% retracement to $4.49.... The downside limit for a normal correction in gold is $364, which is not only a 61.8% retracement but the low of wave 2 in June.... If any futures contract (or the cash price) reaches $4.51, latecomers will be presented an opportunity to enter. [P]lace a stop on our entire position at $4.10, which is above the $4.08 average entry level for our current holdings.

These updated charts are reprinted from that report, showing the downside targets for both gold and silver. As you can see, silver bottomed a week later at $4.48. Gold has slipped to $367 basis December. These precious metals have clearly respected their Elliott wave support levels so far. The ideal development would be for silver to hold above its August 12 low despite the slightly lower low in gold, creating a bullish non-confirmation like the one that occurred in February-March.

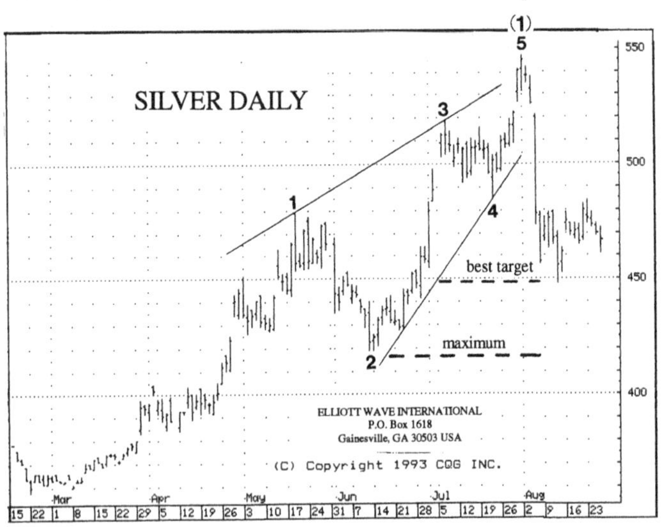

From their lows in the first quarter of the year, gold and silver have traced out five waves up and three waves down, the classic picture of a larger uptrend in progress. The Gold and Silver Stock Index (XAU) also corrected in three waves in a very mild selloff into the upper end

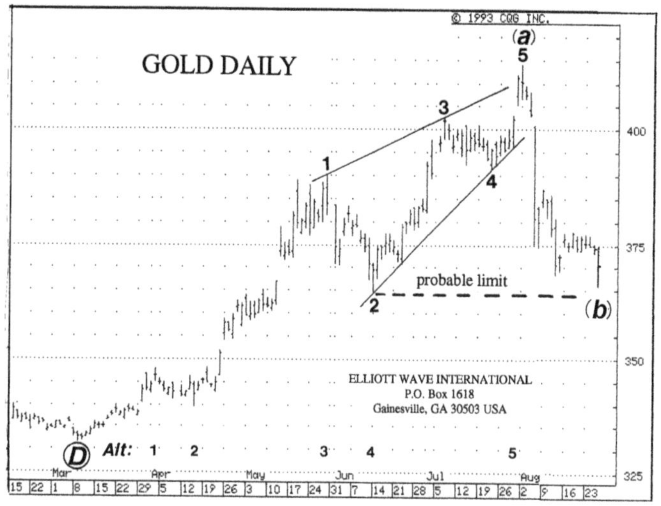

of the range of the preceding fourth wave, a normal zone of support (see text, p.57). The XAU could correct further, to its downside limit of 98 (see dashed line on the chart), but it isn't necessary.

The August panic in the precious metals was accompanied by the breathless announcement that the most famous gold buyer of a number of months ago whom Business Week calls "The Man Who Moves Markets" (a timely curse with which I have some acquaintance, having been headlined with exactly those words in the USA Today of October 9, 1987, at the guru image peak) had sold his holdings, so those who might have been disposed to sell out probably did so.

There are no guarantees in life, which is why our positions have stops. However, the situation in silver this year has led to, as the August Q&A Special Report put it, "extremely specific and highly reliable" conclusions, and those are the ones that when incorporated into investment planning lead to superior results. If EWT's outlook for silver remains on track, silver stocks should double again from this correction low, and silver bullion should rise further than current observers imagine. While there is no way to calculate a specific target this early in the trend, to provide some perspective, EWT has projected a minimum of a triple in silver from the low and more likely a triple from the low of wave (2). There is every reason to maintain this expectation.

The original estimate for the rally peak in gold was $461. If wave (b) ends approximately here, and if wave (c) travels the same length as wave (a), a typical relationship, then gold would peak at $450. The internal structure of the advance, then, is pointing to the same vicinity as a target. If EWT's long term interpretation is correct, gold will *not* rise above the 1987 peak at $502.75. With that in mind, it is interesting to note that if wave (c) is a Fibonacci 1.618 times the length of wave (a), it would peak at $500. Therefore, we now have a minimum and probable target ($450-$461), and a maximum target ($500).

The Gold/Silver Ratio

For years, until near the end of the bear market in precious metals, EWT maintained that despite the historically high gold/silver price ratio and widespread preference for silver, silver was *not* a better buy than gold. Indeed, at the end of its bear market, it had fallen 93%, far outpacing gold's drop of 61.6% (Fibonacci) in the same period. The accompanying chart was the reason for that successful forecast. *Five waves up in the gold/silver ratio was required to mark the end of silver's weaker performance.* As you can see by the chart, for a Fibonacci 13 years the ratio followed Elliott's guidelines perfectly throughout the entire pattern, except for one small wave, 4 of (5), near the top. (It did create a brief hesitation in the line, however.)

When the bear market in silver ended, EWT made the case that silver was now poised to outperform gold, and outperform it has. The gold/silver ratio is now in a downtrend, and based upon the dramatic difference in the Elliott wave outlooks for gold and silver (see discussion, May issue), that downtrend should be lengthy and persistent.

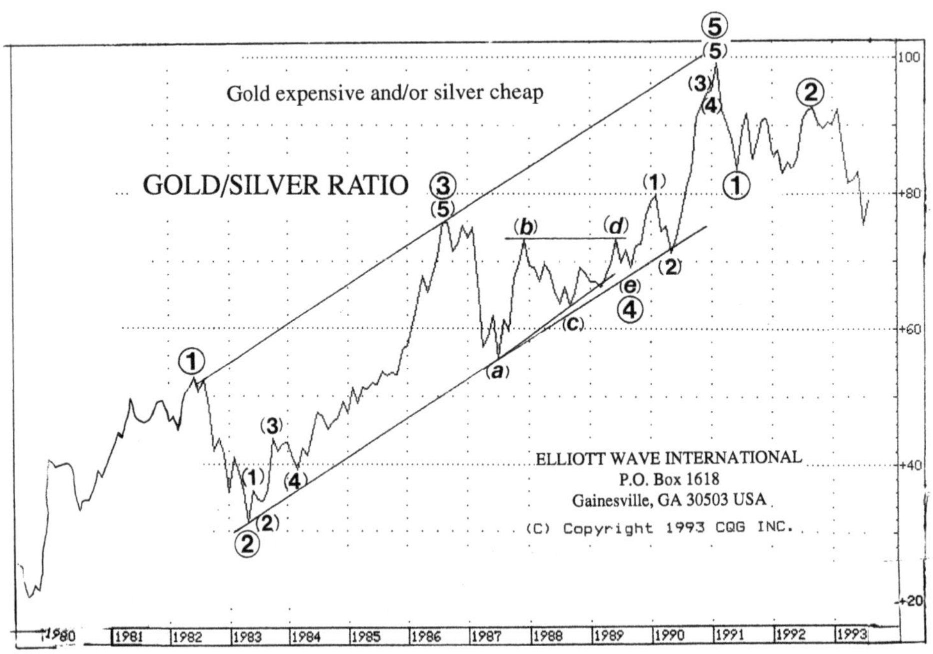

Investment Information

An alert subscriber has brought to our attention the Lexington Strategic Silver Fund (symbol STSLX), one of the Lexington Management family of funds out of Saddlebrook, NJ. The fund is fully invested in 15 silver stocks and is up over 50% on the year. Its total value was only $8m. at year-end 1992, and while that figure has probably doubled by now, it's still a small fund. Some see that as dangerous. It is more likely a sign of an out-of-favor group of stocks that has low prices and few interested investors. You can buy this fund through Charles Schwab brokerage for no load, or pay a load otherwise. Call 800-526-0056 for info.

SEPTEMBER 16, 1993 – INTERIM REPORT

Wave (2) in silver brought prices down 50¢ more than expected and 23¢ more than our "probable maximum." However, this fact does not change the best interpretation of the long term pattern, i.e., that a bull market began last February. Second waves are occasionally deep, exceeding usual retracement percentages but violating no rules. So far, the decline is a clear *three* waves, with waves a and c of equal length, a typical relationship, so it is counted just fine as wave (2).

The gold/silver stock index (XAU) held below support at 98 for only three days and has risen quickly back above it. Our purchases of junk silver near $3.60 and the major investment in silver stocks last February remain in good shape. Those who added to positions at $4.51 took more risk, but right now that risk appears justified. If, contrary to current expectations, the decline from the August high turns into a "five," we will use the rally thereafter to sell. Currently, however, it appears that silver should begin our long awaited wave (3) to the upside.

OCTOBER 1, 1993

Silver has completed the wave (2) pullback within its bull market and is beginning wave (3) to the upside. Gold is still in a bear market but nevertheless should complete its countertrend rally to the mid-400s before resuming the downtrend.

Gold & Silver

The deep reaction in silver prices prompted an Interim Report in mid-September. To summarize, the wave (2) correction is probably over. The analytical difficulty with the silver rally of 1993 is that it can be counted as a "five" or a "three," so the larger picture does not yet allow a high degree of certainty. Producing some comfort is the clear five-wave rally in the Gold and Silver Stock Index (XAU), a bullish sign for the metals complex (see chart). Like silver, that index corrected in three waves and should be starting wave (3) to the upside. There is far less upside potential for gold on a long term basis, since that metal is still in a major bear market. Nevertheless, as long as $325 holds, gold will probably rally with silver and reach the mid to upper 400s.

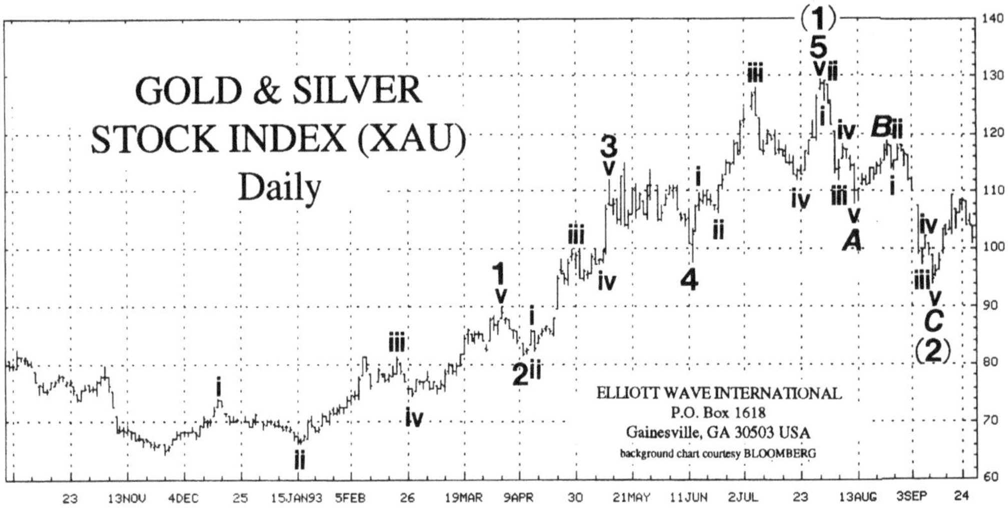

The 5- and 10-year cycles in silver prices were due to bottom in 1992-1993, and they apparently did so. This is a long term bullish development arguing that one way or another, silver is basing for a substantial advance. Of intermediate term concern is the 9-month cycle, which bottomed in June and is not due to bottom again until February.

One compelling analogy mitigates concern about the 9-month cycle. Everyone remembers the precious metals peak of January 1980, but few discuss the secondary peak (or "test") that occurred on September 23, when gold stocks actually made higher highs. This double top in inflation hedge investments was a major distribution pattern in that great year of fear, 1980. It appears that this year is developing along similar lines, but in reverse. A double bottom in inflation hedge investments may be a major accumulation pattern in a great year of complacency, 1993. In 1980, the peaks occurred in January and September, a Fibonacci 8 months apart. In 1993, silver bottomed in February, and a test may have occurred once again in September. A repeat of the eight-month time span would indicate an October low for silver and a November low for gold, since its bottom was in March. The chart shows the picture.

OCTOBER 29, 1993

Silver and gold mining stocks, big winners this year, still have further to go. Silver has begun Intermediate wave (3) to the upside and should soon start rising even faster. Gold is still heading for the mid-400s in its bear market rally.

Gold & Silver

Take a look at the chart of the Gold & Silver Stock Index (XAU) to see how far these stocks have advanced since the wave (2) low just weeks ago. Another few points will put the XAU at a new high for the year. Our preference for silver over gold, both in terms of the commodity and stocks of mining companies, has paid off. Silver continues to outperform gold, and silver stocks continue to outperform gold stocks. Check the March and July issues for lists of our recommended silver mining issues. South African gold mining stocks also ap-

pear attractive. The U.S. has just removed sanctions against that country, and the stocks are even cheaper than usual against North American mining issues. Here's a list, courtesy of Gold Newsletter (2400 Jefferson Hwy, Ste.600, Jefferson, LA 70121). The stock-price leverage increases going down the list, so choose your preferred level of risk accordingly.

GOLD MINE RANKING

Exchange rate for costs: US $1.0=R3.36
Real gold price for dividends: R1 300/oz

TOTAL WORKING COST (US $/OZ)

MINE	COST
Doornfontein	93
Bracken	169
Beatrix	219
Stillfontein	237
Hartebeestfontein	242
Kinross	246
Driefontein	253
Southvaal	254
Elandstrand	264
Randfontein	271
ET Cons	284
Freegold	288
Unisel	294
Western Deeps	299
Western Areas	299
Buffelsfontein	303
St Helena	304
Kloof	305
Loraine	307
Winkelhaak	307
Joel	309
Ergo	313
Afrikander	315
Vaal Reefs	318
Village	319
Harmony	321
Blyvoor	334
Durban Deep	346
Deelkraal	355
ERPM	393

EWT's September 16 Interim Report reiterated our long term bullish outlook for silver, which had just finished wave (2), as you can see on the chart. The October 1 issue said, "Silver is beginning wave (3) to the upside." Wave 1 of (3) is in progress, and within it, subwave ii should end soon. Wave iii, a powerful rally, is due next. Gold continues to trace out non-impulsive structures, further validating EWT's case that while silver has begun a new bull market, gold is merely in a bear market rally and will ultimately fall below its 1993 low. Nevertheless, it should still reach the mid-400s prior to the next downturn.

James Turk, editor of the Freemarket Gold & Money Report (Box 4634, Greenwich, CT 06830), has developed an interesting indicator of investors' confidence in the national currency. Turk's "Fear Index" is obtained by dividing the total value of the nation's gold reserve by the quantity of money as represented by M3, the total of bank deposits and Federal Reserve Notes outstanding. As the next chart shows, the current valuation of the nation's gold reserves is a mere 2.38% of the value of M3, up from a recent low near 2.1%. The only point of greater investor complacency according to this indicator was 1972, from which year gold soared over 1800% and stocks plummeted 45% to 74% in the Dow and Value Line respectively. 1976 was a close second, from which year interest rates skyrocketed from a low near 4% to over 16% in just five years, as gold gained 700%. Turk notes that "buy" signals for gold are signaled by rises in the Fear Index to above its *rising* 21-month moving average. Guess what. A signal was given at the end of May 1993 for the first time since 1986.

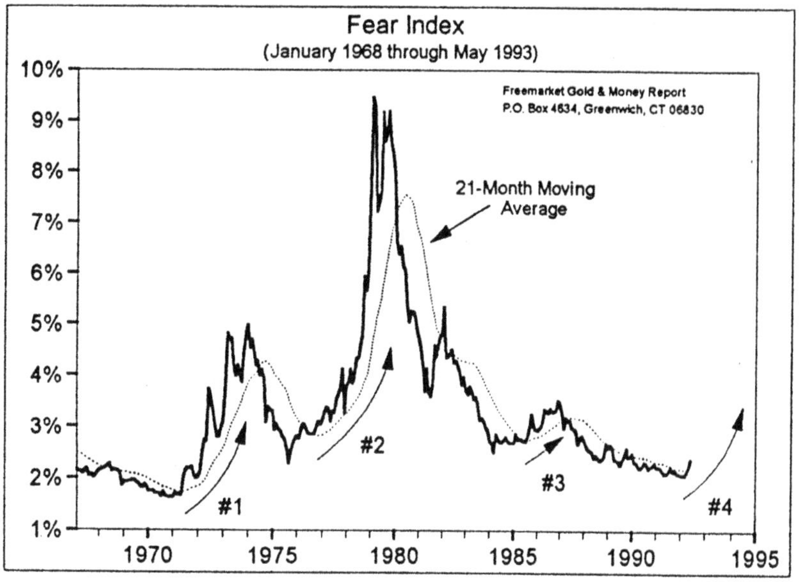

Further supporting the case for a period of renewed investor interest in the precious metals is this chart of the Centennial Precious Metals' Index of Thirty Coins. CPM President Michael Kosares constructed the index using data from Coin Dealer Newsletter for prices of 30 proof and mint state 65 coins suitable for a typical investment portfolio. (For information on CPM's newsletter and coin prices, call 800-869-5115 or 303-393-0322.) Mr. Kosares writes that some time after constructing the index, he came across a description of the Wave Principle and casually decided to see if it would apply. As you can see, the patterns are excellent "Elliott" down to the last subdivision.

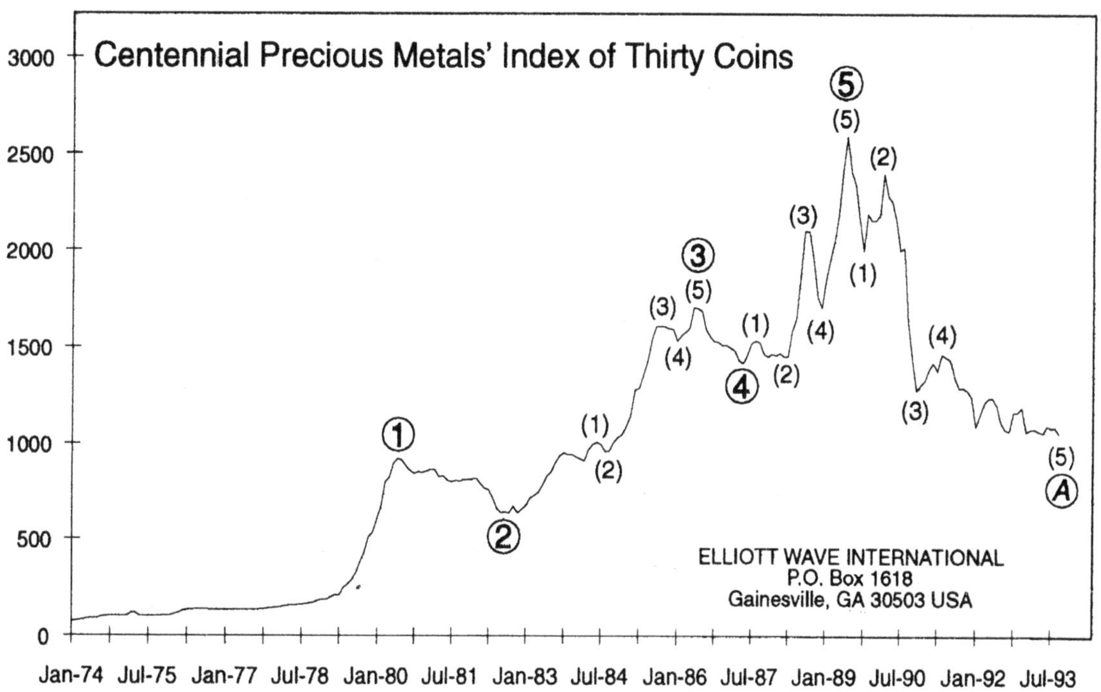

NOVEMBER 24, 1993

Silver and gold mining stocks, big winners this year, still have further to go. Silver is in Intermediate wave (3) to the upside and should soon begin rising faster. Gold is still heading for the mid-400s in its bear market rally.

Gold & Silver

A chart in the October issue described a basing pattern that EWT perceived was under way, as follows:

> In 1980, the peaks [in gold and gold stocks] occurred in January and September, a Fibonacci 8 months apart. This year is developing along similar lines, but in reverse. In 1993, silver bottomed in February, and a test may have occurred once again in September. A repeat of the eight-month time span would indicate an October low for silver, and a November low for gold, since its bottom was in March.

To date, the September test low has held, and a second reaction bottomed on November 2, right in the time zone that should have completed the mopping up of bearish investor psychology toward the precious metals. The news was particularly accommodating. On November 1, it was widely reported that Xerox had developed a specialized type of photography for graphic arts that did not require the use of silver. Headlines trumpeted the news everywhere, inducing fear among investors that by the following week, all photography would be silverless. If there were any "weak hands" remaining on the long side, that news should have shaken them out. Silver registered a short term bottom the next day, and two days later was gapping on the upside.

The price patterns anticipated all of this action. As *The Elliott Wave Theorist* put it succinctly last month, "Wave 1 of (3) is in progress, and within it, wave ii should end soon. Wave iii, a powerful rally, is due next." One glance at the updated chart and you can see that wave ii ended two trading days later at almost exactly a Fibonacci .618 retracement of wave i, and the upside gaps certainly qualify as the start of a "powerful rally" for wave iii. Proof that the wave ii reaction was required regardless of the news is that gold and other precious metals fell concurrently, and they're not used in photography. If the news were the sole reason for the silver drop, gold should have risen as precious metals investors switched favorites.

It is interesting to note that waves i and ii reflect almost precisely the construction of waves (1) and (2). Both sport wedge-shaped rallies followed by sharp a-b-c declines. The look of wave iii might give us a clue as to the look of wave (3).

The pattern of prices in the Gold and Silver Stock Index (XAU) is similarly bullish. As you can see, the XAU traced out a beautiful five waves up from the September low, reaching a new bull market high in November. A wave 2 correction could take the index back to the 117-119 area, which encompasses the previous fourth wave low and the 38.2% retracement level. Like silver, the XAU is best interpreted as being on the verge of a "third of a third" wave to the upside, the most powerful part of any advance.

The pattern of the rally in gold bullion (not shown) from the September low is less certain but appears to be a series of bullish first and second waves. The forecast from months ago that gold should reach the mid-$400s on this intermediate-term recovery remains on track. Basis the nearby futures contract, the best specific target is still $461, at which point the entire rally, wave Ⓔ, will be .618 times the length of wave Ⓒ in the long term triangle (see May issue for a chart). The structure of the rally from March supports this target, in that wave (c) will have traveled .618 times the length of wave (a) past wave (a) (see text, p.107) at $456.50 basis the London fix and $460 basis the nearby futures contract. Other relationships suggest potential targets at $424 and $476 basis nearby futures. The internal wave structure should help indicate which is the most likely termination point as it is approached.

Silver vs. Other Investments

Highly valued stock and real estate markets and lowly valued precious metals reflect a lack of fear about the future among investors. How cheap is silver compared to these investments, which have risen for most of the last 13 years? The next two charts show silver's value against houses and the S&P. As you can see, the ratios this year were different by 21 times (at least; the available data for house prices is annual averages) and 39 times their 1980 levels, respectively. In terms of these two investments, silver is at a *record low price* going back at least *100 years*. The recent drop on the S&P/silver chart is the largest in 25 years of chart history, a momentum change that probably signals a major reversal. [Note: Thanks to the stock mania that took off a year later, the ratio eventually tripled again from there! – Ed.]

EWT's position this year has been long silver and silver stocks, short S&P [traders only] and out of all investment real estate, exactly what it should be according to the implications of these charts. This position has already paid off, particularly in the silver stocks, which are *up 128%* in the nine months since EWT recommended them in

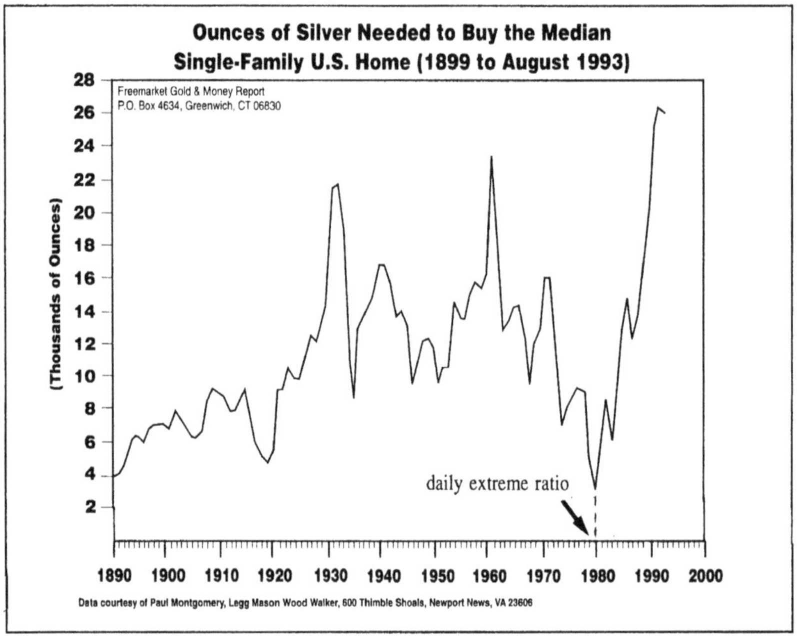

the February 26 issue. The S&P hasn't even advanced that amount from its 1987 crash low *six years ago.* If silver bullion does get going on the upside, these stocks will probably more than double again.

DECEMBER 31, 1993

Gold is still heading for its target in the 400s. Silver has weathered several bearish news announcements and is steadily tracing out a bullish pattern. Making our year were *silver mining company stocks.* This completely sold-out group presented a compelling profit making opportunity in the form of a major bear market bottom. Gold and silver stocks, the best performing group of 1993 (to zero news coverage), are set to accelerate on the upside in wave 3 of (3).

Silver stocks, our "stealth" group (not once in the news) have risen a dramatic 120% in the ten months since *The Elliott Wave Theorist* recommended accumulating them last February. Standard & Poor's does not have a silver stock index, but it does have a gold stock index, and at a 64% gain through November, it was the single best performing S&P group in 1993 among the 87 tracked. The similar XAU index was up over 75%. (Advance notice for January newspaper readers: Most newsletter "rating services" rate only U.S. stock *index* timing, ignoring any non-index recommendations. Their tallies do not reflect our switch.

As indicated then, this portfolio alignment is expected to be temporary relative to our previous long term commitments. When gold and silver reach their upside targets, probably in 1994, we will return to the safety of Treasury bills unless a similar opportunity is presented (which is possible if stock indexes drop precipitously). Currently, there remains far more upside potential ahead in silver than has been realized to date from its $3.50 low. Silver bullion is up 40%, and it hasn't even passed the third of the third wave yet.

Gold & Silver

The December issue showed a chart of the Gold and Silver Stock Index (XAU), labeled with Minor wave 1 of Intermediate (3) having just ended. The near term forecast predicted December's action accurately:

> The XAU traced out a beautiful five waves up from the September low. A wave 2 correction could take the index back to the 117-119 area, which encompasses the previous fourth wave low and the 38.2% retracement level.

The XAU corrected right on schedule, and the pullback low was 117.31, right in the target area. Since then, it's back above 130. Now it's time for wave iii of 3 of (3), a near-vertical rise more powerful than any in the bull market to date. Even though silver stocks are up over 200% from their 1992 lows and gold stocks over 100%, the best is yet to come, as suggested by the accompanying "You Are Here" idealized diagram. Wave (3) in silver bullion has had an orderly beginning as well. Two counts are shown on the chart. The power of the next rise will determine which is correct. For now, it doesn't matter, as both are bullish.

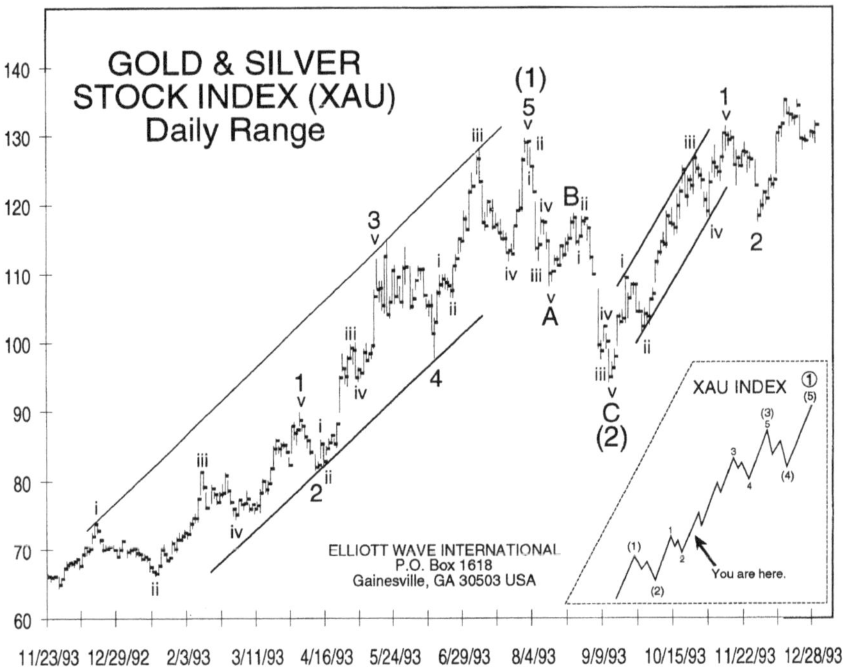

Bad news, real or phony, is typical at price lows. Silver saw two major announcements that served to engender bearish sentiment among investors right at the pullback lows of late October and late November. The first was Xerox's announcement that it had developed a silver-free graphic arts photography; the second was Polaroid's announcement that it had developed a silver-free X-ray process. These announcements provided excellent buying opportunities for those wishing to add to positions (including, perhaps, the people who fed the stories to the media?). Count on it: At the upcoming price peak, news will express *bullish* fundamentals.

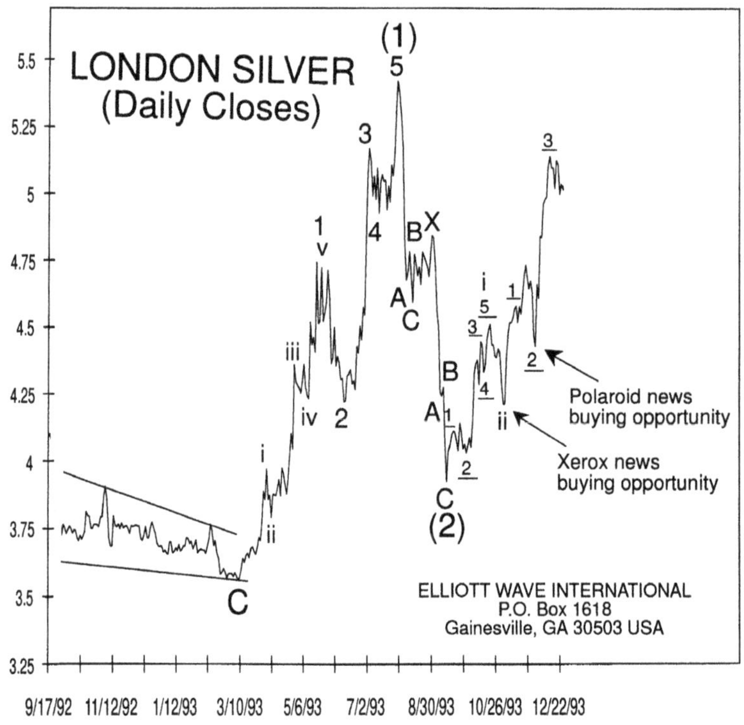

Gold is still on its way to the mid-400s in a bear market rally. The best specific target is still $461 (see previous issues), but anywhere in the $420-$500 range would satisfy the larger Elliott wave pattern. Silver and gold should top out at about the same time in 1994, but the subsequent reaction should be far more damaging to gold, which has yet to complete its long term bear market, and which is still, unlike silver, historically overpriced relative to a basket of commodities.

As published in *Gold Newsletter*, January 13, 1994

Very few technical analysts have earned the widespread respect accorded to Bob Prechter. Numerous financial publications (as well as his peers) have acknowledged Mr. Prechter's extraordinary professional accomplishments. Although he applies Elliott wave analysis in his own publications and has written several books, he only rarely writes for other publications. It is a special honor for Gold Newsletter to present the following article by Mr. Prechter.

ELLIOTT WAVE SURPRISES FOR GOLD AND SILVER

by Robert R. Prechter, Jr.

Despite owning a highly successful gold coin business and a publication called Gold Newsletter, Jim Blanchard was the first conference host to invite me to speak, in June 1980. He knew full well that in a December 1979 article [published January 1980 in *Commodities* magazine] I had taken a stand that the inflationary era was coming to an end, and had become a staunch long term bear on precious metals and a bull on common stocks.

Nevertheless, Jim felt that a contrary opinion at his seminars would be a healthy thing. He even provided space in Gold Newsletter several times during the 1980s for me to reiterate the bearish Elliott wave case, even when gold appeared to be on its way upward again in one of its several major rallies. Each time, the wave patterns indicated that the long term bear market in precious metals wasn't over yet, and Gold Newsletter remained dedicated to giving subscribers both sides of the story. Jim's allowing a dissident voice to address the committed flock attests to his integrity and explains why he's prospered while most other "gold bugs" have long since disappeared from the scene.

One thing I kept promising Jim was that one day, the Elliott wave outlook would change, and he would be the first to know it. That change occurred in early 1993, particularly for silver, thirteen years after the all time peak in 1980 at $50/oz. and after a 93% decline in value.

Understand first that a market forecast is different from a philosophy. As previous articles I wrote for Gold Newsletter explained, I am an unwavering advocate of precious metals as money—not as backing for state controlled money but as money itself, which is its essence in reality. At its best, paper is nothing but IOUs for money (gold or silver), no matter who issues it. At its worst, paper is "IOU–Nothings," as Colonel E.C. Harwood of the American Institute for Economic Research put it long ago when describing the "Federal Reserve Notes" that supplanted silver certificates in 1965. An honest and flexible system would entail notes being marked in grams of metal, without any obfuscating term or intervening, restricting term such as "dollar," "franc" or "yen" getting in the way. The system would also exclude legal tender laws that force consumers to accept certain notes for use as money, which allows theft of value through the degradation of currency by the issuer. In a free system, good money would drive out bad. Who would want to trust his savings or transactions to a suspect currency? Regardless, however, of my firm belief in the desirability of unregulated free market money, it is a simple fact that gold and silver go through bull and bear markets.* Anticipating, recognizing and analyzing market trends is necessary both for financial survival and success. These tasks are the province of technical analysis, which is my field.

A Major Change in Trend

At the price peak in January 1980, precious metals had completed a sequence of "waves," or price movements, that were typical of bull markets that had exploited all of the potential psychological change available in the marketplace. The bull market began in 1967 and lasted thirteen years. At the time, I had no idea how long the bear market would last but became quite certain that silver would ultimately fall over 90% in value and gold over 75%.

As the years went by, price patterns continued to communicate that gold and silver were in bear markets. Gold was often difficult to "read," but silver was a model of clarity throughout its decline. Three benchmarks were very helpful in providing a continuing long term perspective. The first one related to price. The wave structure indicated long term support in the $3.50-$6.50 range, which was the support area typically provided by the "fourth wave" of the preceding bull market, which in this case was the 1974-1978 consolidation. The second and third benchmarks related to time. As shown on a chart in a February 1989 study by The Elliott Wave Theorist, the 5- and 10-year time cycles indicated a probable price low in 1992. Fibonacci time spans, a tool of the Wave Principle, indicated a probable low in 1993. Therefore, the general expectation was for a low in the $3.50-$6.50 range in 1992-1993. While not pinpoint-specific, this outlook kept Elliott Wave Theorist subscribers away from the precious metals markets through all its false starts and set up a useful framework from which to anticipate the low.

Another Major Change in Trend

The story of how The Elliott Wave Theorist handled the approach to the final bottom at $3.51 on February 22, 1993 is told in detail in Jim Blanchard's excellent new book with Franklin Sanders, "Silver Bonanza," so there is no need to reiterate it here. Suffice it to say that following silver's low of $3.505/oz. in February 1991 the pattern of prices suggested one more rise and decline. By June 1991 silver was falling again, and the wave structure was confirming, not only in dollar terms but in Swiss franc terms as well, that the final descent was in progress. The February 1993 low was registered at $3.51, missing the perfect target by just one cent but clearly completing the required pattern. That slightly higher low was another technically bullish portent amidst the most apathetic sentiment toward any market in the world at the time. Silver mining stocks (along with gold mining stocks) had already bottomed the previous November, in 1992. The long term silver target of $3.50-$6.50 in 1992-1993 had been fulfilled, right at the bottom of

*More accurately, it is paper notes that go through bull and bear markets. The valuation of gold and silver in terms of dollars is an inversion of the actual situation. The stabler assets are gold and silver, and a proper designation would be the valuation of the dollar in terms of the metals. Gold did not "rise" to $850/oz. during the 1970s. The value of the dollar had fallen that far in the preceding decades, and the retraction of government price controls in 1971 merely allowed the gold price of the dollar to reflect that fact.

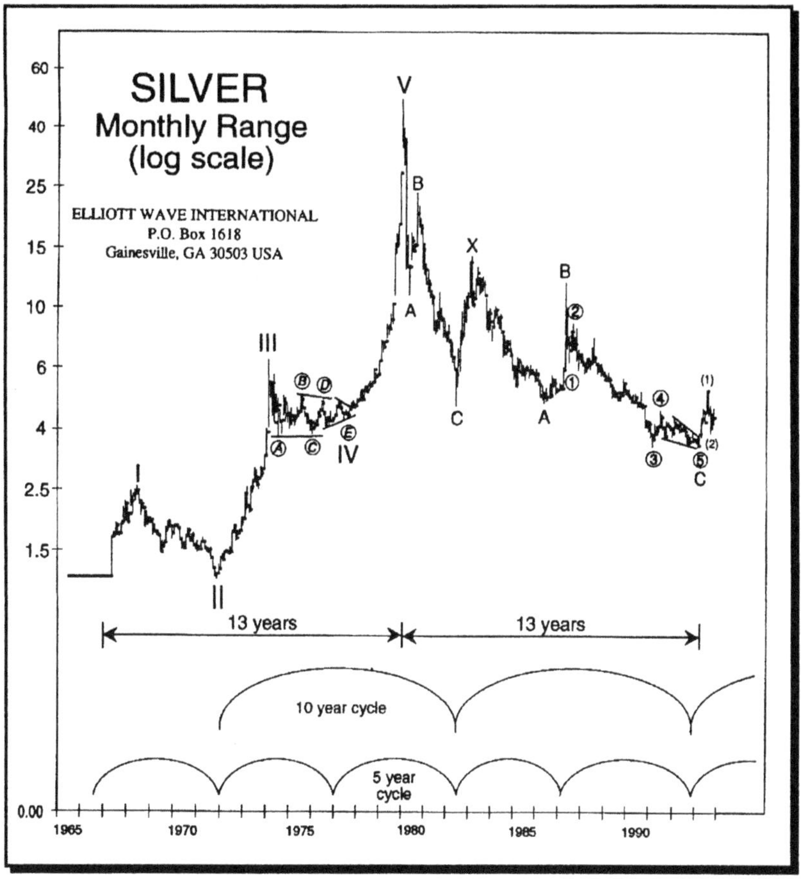

Figure 1

the forecasted range. Figure 1 shows the completed wave count, as well as the idealized 5- and 10-year cycles.

The general aversion to investing in silver has persisted despite the slight recovery off the low so far. Most money managers consider the recent rise to $5 at most a mild curiosity, as if buckwheat prices were bouncing in Bolivia. The recent rise, however, is probably not just a bounce in a bear market but almost certainly the start of something very substantial on the upside. It is possible that silver is in fact starting on a long road back to its centuries-long role as money in Western civilization. Let's get down to specifics.

Price Outlook for Silver

The Wave Principle reveals that in bull markets, advancing waves will trace out a "five wave" pattern—i.e., up, down, up, down, up—according to certain rules of market behavior. As you can see by the labeling of the recent rise in Figure 2, the best interpretation of the pattern is that only waves (1) and (2) are complete. That leaves waves (3) up, (4) down, and (5) up to go. The history of silver reveals that usually the fifth wave (but occasionally the third wave) is the strongest in a bull market sequence. The first wave is

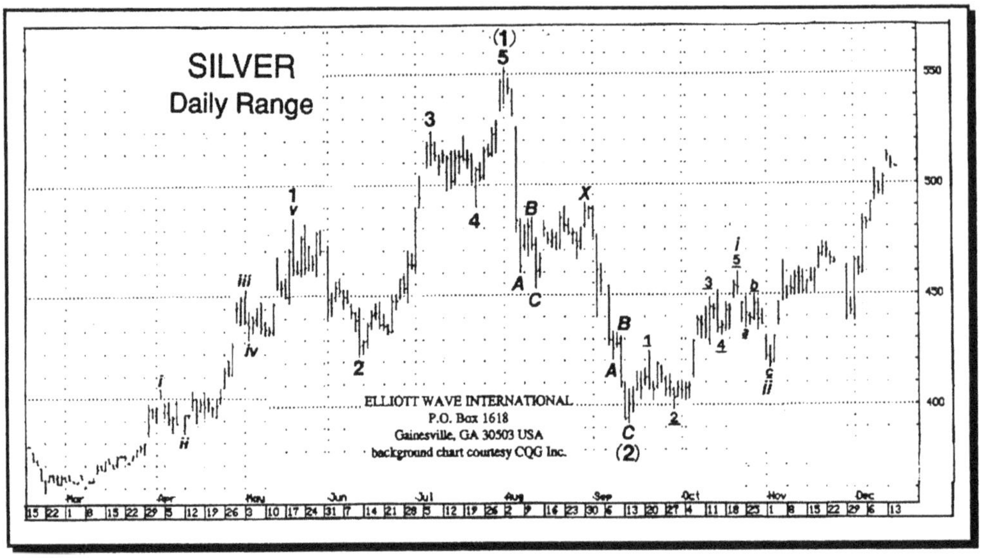

Figure 2

almost always the weakest. Wave (1) saw a rise in silver prices of 57%. Waves (3) and (5) should each be much more than that. From this simple guideline alone, double digit silver appears to be a near certainty in coming months.

Time Outlook for Silver

As you can see in Figure 1, the 5- and 10-year cycles turned upward together a year ago. The combined force of these two cycles should propel silver higher for two years or more. Compared to gold, silver tends to rush upward and reverse more violently, so it lends itself less to the forecasting of tops through cyclic analysis. The wave structure will be the most valuable evidence for calling the next important peak, just as it was for calling the bear market bottom.

The Gold and Silver Stock Index

The gold and silver mining stock index (ticker symbol XAU) has been the best performing stock group of 1993. In early 1993, *The Elliott Wave Theorist* contacted fellow silver bull James Dines (Box 22, Belvedere, CA 94920) to obtain a list of ten silver mining stocks for recommendation in our February 26, 1993 issue. As explained on the front page last April, the shift to owning silver related investments was a major investment policy shift, only the third major portfolio alignment in the history of the publication. In the past ten months, these stocks are up 150%, more than the S&P 500 stock index has risen in the past six years.

You now know enough about the Wave Principle from the "Price Outlook" paragraph above to understand exactly how I view the remaining potential in precious metals mining stocks. The pattern in that group is exactly the same as that for silver bullion, and indicates that wave (3) is in progress. As you can see by the scale, these stocks have already doubled from a year ago. Can the rest of the bull market really cause these stocks to double again, and perhaps yet again? Such an expectation is no less outrageous than the expectation that silver would fall as low as $3.50 from its peak at $50. Keep in mind also that mining stocks represent a drop in the ocean of investment money, most of which is fully invested in bonds and common stocks. A 1% commitment to precious metals by all funds would cause an upward explosion in price for these issues. Don't underestimate the potential.

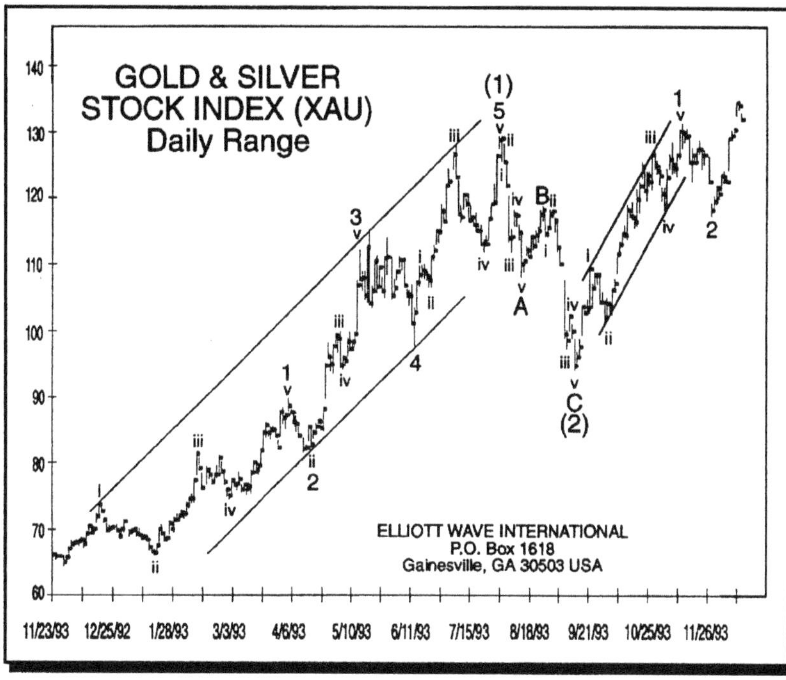

Figure 3

Silver: The Metal of Preference

The Elliott Wave Theorist stated earlier this year in no uncertain terms that the far greater profit potential lay in silver, not gold, and that is still my position. The key is an analysis of the gold/silver price ratio, which in early 1993 had reached not only a historic extreme of nearly 100:1, indicating an untenable undervaluation for silver, but which had also traced out a perfect Elliott wave pattern from its 1980 low, as you can see in Figure 4. It was this developing pattern that forced a bearish posture on the relative attractiveness of silver all during the bear market. While most metals investors saw the 20:1, 40:1. 60:1 and 80:1 ratios as signs that silver

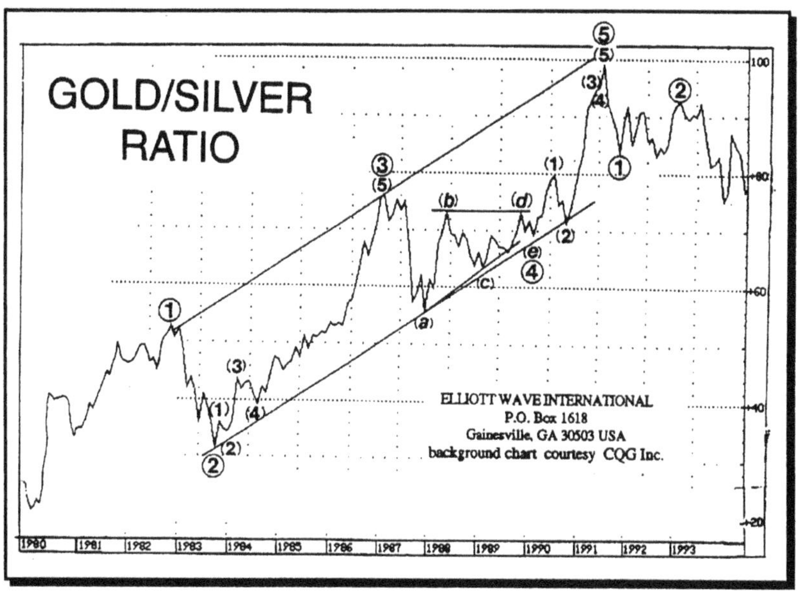

Figure 4

should be owned in favor of gold, the wave pattern clearly indicated that silver would remain weaker until a five-wave pattern in their relative valuation was complete. In early 1991, that indicator reversed in favor of silver, and by early 1993 (at the top of wave ②), it was clear that the new trend was poised to begin accelerating.

The preference for silver at the precious metals' 1993 low has already paid off. While gold stocks have risen 100% or more from their lows, silver stocks have risen an amazing 200%. And they are still undervalued, having advanced from basement level prices that reflected bankruptcy conditions, exactly the kind of conditions that make an attractive long term investment. While in the ideal Elliott wave scenario gold could ultimately rally as much as 40-50% from its 1993 low, silver has the potential to quintuple, providing over eight times the gain.

What About Gold?

While gold will probably rise concurrently with silver, there are three reasons to favor silver. First is the gold/silver ratio, as discussed above. Second is the fact that gold never did reach its ideal downside target under the Wave Principle, as explained below. Third is the long term wave structure. While silver clearly completed a long term bear market pattern, gold better fits an interpretation that indicates still lower prices to come after the current rally is complete.

How in the world could gold at some date in the future fall to substantial new lows while silver holds at a higher level? The first point to make is that it hardly matters; if you are timing the silver market properly and gold moves with it just as strongly, you haven't lost anything by favoring silver. The second point to make is that a "non-confirmation" of this type is not merely theoretically possible. From June 1985, with gold sitting at $284 an ounce and silver at $6 an ounce, you would have been correctly informed if you had heard, "Gold is about to begin a major rise. It will not make new lows on any correction. At the same time, silver is going to be cut in value almost in half." From that point, gold rose to $503 and then corrected to $326, never reaching a new low in those eight years, and then started up again. Silver eroded to substantial new lows at $3.50 and then started up. As you can see, a non-confirmation is not only possible; it's recently happened.

As for the probability of another one occurring in the future, the points that EWT has made in numerous issues over the past year are these:

1) Silver dropped 93% in its bear market, which is a major devaluation. To realize how much that is, consider that gold would have to have fallen to $59/oz. to match it. By contrast, at current prices, gold remains historically overvalued relative to a basket of agricultural commodities. In fact, at the recent gold peak of $400/oz., the ratio is twice the 200-year historical norm and four times the low of that period.

2) The Elliott wave pattern in gold allows for a bull market to be in progress, but the current rise is far better interpreted as part of a countertrend (i.e., bear market rally) pattern dating from the 1982 low. When the current advance is over, gold will have the potential to fall in a major A-B-C pattern, at least to below $200 and ideally

to about $105, the low of the fourth wave in its preceding bull market. Silver would be expected to fall in a similar pattern at the same time, differing only in the extent of the fall, holding above the $3.50 level. (If it doesn't, though, it won't make any-difference, as we would presumably be out of the market to avoid the correction anyway.)

Conclusion

Regardless of gold's ultimate performance, silver has begun a new bull market and is likely to continue outperforming gold. The picture in silver, furthermore, is far clearer, and its pattern should provide for a timely exit when the time comes. Despite nearly universal opinion to the contrary among professionals, silver today provides less risk than gold and far more profit potential. Gold mining stocks are still attractive investments, of course, particularly the South African gold mining issues, which are deeply undervalued and provide a clear second-best choice for investing in today's financial climate. The first choice, though, in my opinion, remains silver and silver mining stocks. Needless to say, both categories of investments provide infinitely less risk than the major stock market averages and most bonds, which have reached a point of multi-century overvaluation and supply.

Silver is often called "the poor man's gold." For this bull market, gold is likely to be the poor man's silver, and silver is likely to be the rich man's preferred store of value. In fact, we may not again see a value or opportunity like $3.50 silver for many years to come.

The Elliott Wave Theorist, 1994

JANUARY 21, 1994 – INTERIM REPORT

The gold and silver stock index (XAU) appears to have just completed five waves up from the September low, contrary to earlier expectations. Support is near 128 and 118. A bearish non-confirmation is in place as well, in that these stocks have risen above their August peak, while the metals themselves have not, implying possibly larger implications to the latest five-wave pattern. The prudent course of action is to *take profits now on all gold and silver stocks, as well as gold and silver.* If this week's highs in the XAU (146.32) and silver ($5.41 basis nearby futures) and the recent high in gold ($397.80 basis nearby futures) are all exceeded, the picture will improve. Use that event, if it occurs, to trigger a return to a 50% long position in those markets. Long term (multi-year) investors in silver, who do not mind the risk of lower prices for awhile, are welcome to hold positions.

JANUARY 28, 1994

After rising for over a year, gold and silver stocks topped out in the third week of January, as per our special bulletin of January 21. Silver and gold prices should decline for some months.

Gold & Silver

It was a surprise on January 20 to see indications of an intermediate-term top in the precious metals complex, which a month ago appeared to be preparing for an upside acceleration. Nevertheless, after four months of persistent price advance, wave structure and rate-of-change behavior were signaling a completed pattern, so an Interim Report was mailed the next day saying so. It is more important to be out of a falling market than to miss a rising one, so for your protection, EWT always takes sell signals seriously. Let's examine in some detail what the indicators were saying at that time.

Wave Structure

On January 18, the Gold and Silver Stock Index (XAU) stalled at a trendline instead of breaking through it as a "third of a third wave" would have done. That stall left behind a choppy pattern typical of fifth waves that lasted seven weeks (a Fibonacci 38.2% of the time for the entire advance from September). The chart shows how that fifth wave fit into the larger pattern from the September low.

Momentum Divergence

At the same time, the rate of price rise for the XAU was *slowing* rather than accelerating as would have been required in a third-of-third situation. As you can see at the bottom of the chart, the 10-week rate of change indicator was stalling at a lower level than it reached in the February-August rally. This "divergence" against the new price high was a technical sell signal.

Price Non-Confirmation

Markets in mid-trend usually display broad and supportive participation by components. Markets that are terminating trends usually fray, with some components continuing in the old trend and some establishing the new one. The technical term for various components falling behind is "non-confirmation." Take a look at the charts of gold and silver bullion prices and notice that neither metal accompanied the XAU to its post-August new high. Remember when silver fell further than expected last September? That event created a deeply oversold condition that helped set up this intermediate term non-confirmation. Notice that there was a smaller non-confirmation at the January 18/19 peaks in the XAU and silver, as gold was holding below its peak of January 5.

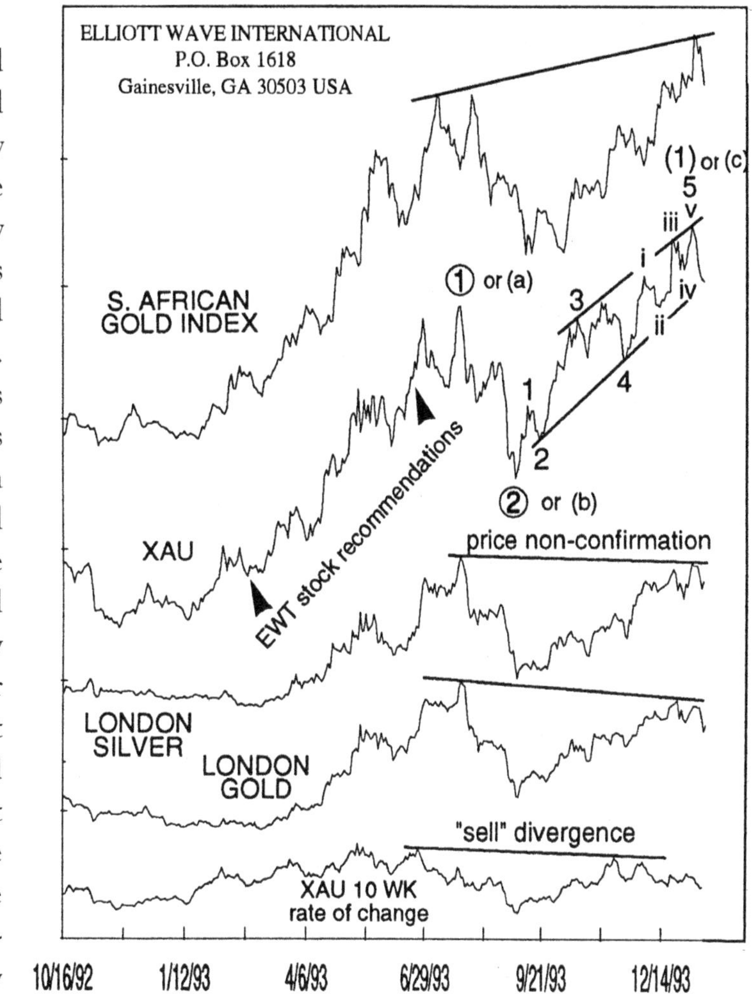

Outlook

The XAU chart shows two labelings for the larger uptrend from November 1992. The rise can be labeled as waves ①, ② and (1) of ③, with (2) now in progress (the bullish count), or waves (a), (b) and (c), completing a countertrend rally (the bearish count).

If the bullish count is correct, the XAU should hold support at 126-128 or 114-118. The first zone marks a .382 retracement of wave (1) and the low of wave ii of 5; the second marks a .618 retracement of wave (1) and the low of wave 4 (see text, pp.28, 57, 115). If one of those support levels is reached at a time when momentum indicators are oversold and a corrective pattern ends, it may be time to reconsider a bullish posture on the precious metals. Also keep in mind this note from the Interim Report: "If this week's highs in the XAU (146.32) and silver ($5.41 basis nearby futures) and the recent high in gold ($397.80 basis nearby futures) are all exceeded, the picture will improve," and we will return to a bullish opinion.

The bearish count is supported by the size of the non-confirmations discussed above. Of course, a bearish outlook here is little problem with respect to *gold*. EWT has maintained staunchly that gold was in a countertrend rise in a larger bear market, albeit with an ideal target 15% higher than it reached. Its long term cycles are still due to bottom late this year. As reiterated numerous times, its long term bear market target, in force for over a decade, is still a long way down, to "below $200/oz., and ideally $105/oz." We'll show the long term picture in gold again soon, depending upon market action.

EWT foreshadowed the current mixed outlook for the two metals back in 1991:

> Gold will have to fall rapidly to achieve the expected 50%-70% further loss in value over the next three years. During that time, silver might build a long base, perhaps involving a first and second wave to the upside, without great upside progress.

That scenario has been developing since silver first reached $3.50 that same year. Since its long term cycles still point up, silver could indeed simply undergo a long "wave 2" correction, holding above $3.50, while gold falls to a new low. However, silver did not rise nearly to the target of double-digit prices that were expected last year. What's more, the long term wave structure in silver *allows* for a break of $3.50, which is why it is prudent to stand aside while the rates of change correct. For the time being, therefore, it is best to maintain a negative intermediate-term opinion on silver and return to a bullish posture if the action and patterns warrant. As stated in the January Interim Report, long term (multi-year) investments in silver, such as the bags of junk silver coins we bought near the low, are a "hold." If gold reaches its downside target, silver will be a buy again, whatever its price.

Review

Both silver mining stocks and South African gold stocks, the two groups specifically recommended in EWT last year, *tripled* from their late 1992 lows. That's a substantial bull market, which puts the recent signs of a top in perspective. For 1993, the four top performing major mutual funds, and 12 out of the top 14, were gold funds. The Lexington Strategic Investments Fund, one of the precious metals funds suggested in EWT, soared a history-making 270% in 1993, and we caught a good portion of the move. A repeat of that performance now appears unlikely from that sector. That's why we said "Thanks for the ride" and stepped aside.

FEBRUARY 25, 1994

Gold and silver stocks are likely to fall in sympathy with stock indexes in general. Gold and silver bullion should decline into March or April.

Gold & Silver

There is little to add to the detailed analysis of recent weeks. Price and momentum non-confirmations signaled at least an interim peak on January 18. Rates of change are moving toward oversold territory, but appear to need more time to form bullish patterns. Silver, our preferred metal long term, moved above its January high and its August high for a brief two days, but was unaccompanied by mining stocks or gold. Recall that our reversion to a bullish stance requires joint new highs by all three components of the precious metals picture. All that the new high in silver accomplished was to leave behind yet another upside non-confirmation, both on the five-month and one-year trends.

The 9-month cycle suggests a low in or near April, which coincides with the intermediate term cyclic outlook for the stock market. Mining stocks suffered substantially in the 1987 crash, so coincident bearish outlooks for the stock market and metals for the next month or so is additional reason to stay on the sidelines for now. From its peak at 146.32, the Gold & Silver Stock Index (XAU) has fallen a bit below first support at 126-128. Next support at 114-118 must hold if the bigger picture is to remain bullish. By a month or two from now, it should be possible to form a more definitive opinion with respect to the mining stocks. Silver should reach an intermediate term low at that time, although the longer-term cycles in gold are still not due to bottom until year-end, when the next 9-month cycle low is due.

MARCH 31, 1994

The precious metals are at a critical juncture. For now, bearish non-confirmations remain in place, but a joint new high in gold and the XAU will signal a renewed uptrend.

Gold & Silver

In January, *The Elliott Wave Theorist* called for an intermediate term correction in the precious metals, particularly the Gold and Silver Stock Index (XAU) and gold. EWT identified support for the XAU (which had peaked at 146.32) at *114-118*, which, as the February 25 issue stated, must hold if the bigger picture is to remain bullish. That issue also called for the low in gold and silver to occur in March or April. The low on March 8 was *117.19*, right in the target zone, a perfect price retracement that also lasted exactly 2/5 of the time of the rise from last September, a common time relationship. What's more, the wave structure of the decline is an excellent A-B-C pattern, which, being corrective in nature, appears to confirm that the XAU is in a long term uptrend. Gold bullion completed a similar correction on March 2. What's more, the latest new high in silver not accompanied by gold is precisely in concert with the differing intermediate term opinions on the two metals that we have held for a year, i.e., that the bear market for silver is probably over, but the bear market in gold is definitely not over.

More Correction?

Despite this seemingly perfect picture, numerous technical problems remain in the precious metals picture, at least at the moment. This A-B-C correction in the XAU could be only part of a more complex corrective pattern that will ultimately be labeled A-B-C-X-A-B-C or

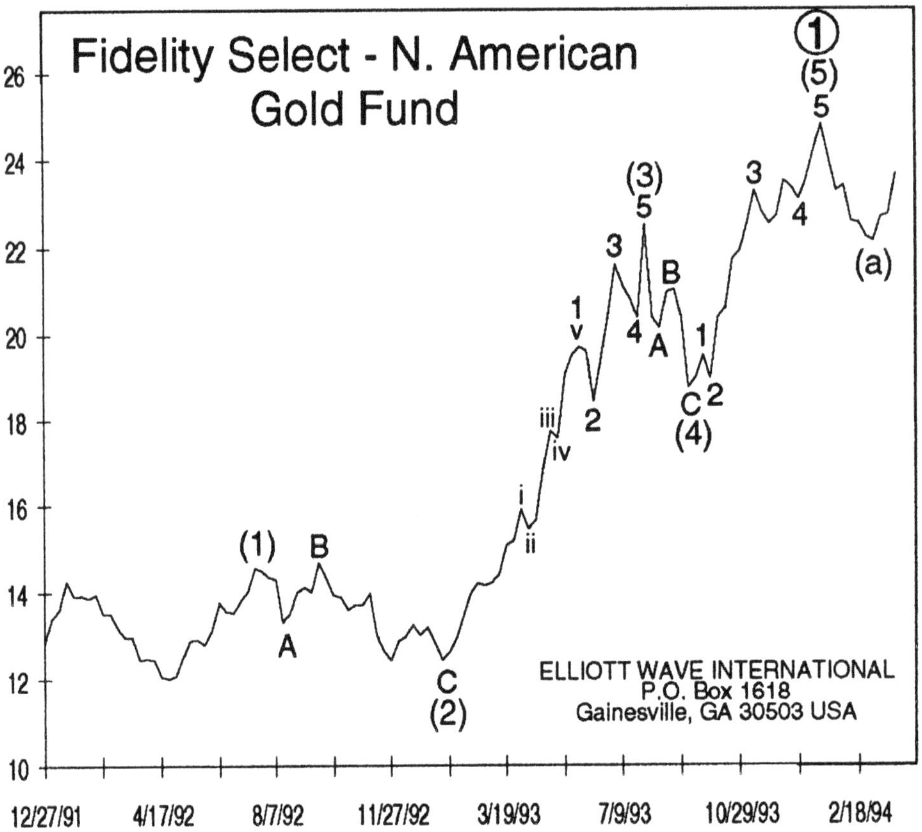
Fidelity Select - N. American Gold Fund
ELLIOTT WAVE INTERNATIONAL
P.O. Box 1618
Gainesville, GA 30503 USA
12/27/91
4/17/92
8/7/92
11/27/92
3/19/93
7/9/93
10/29/93
2/18/94

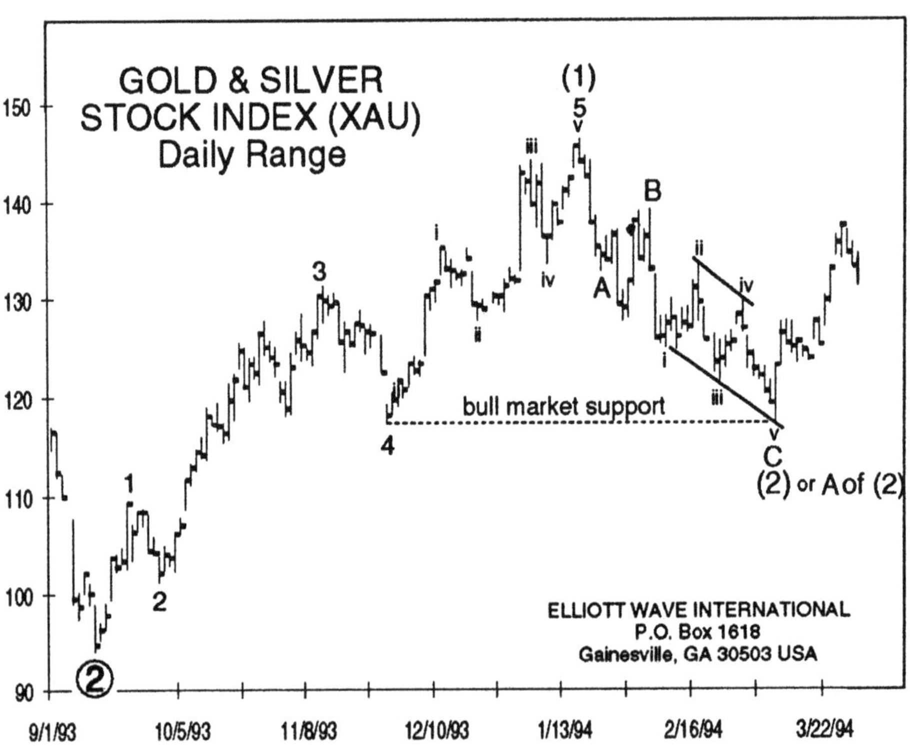
GOLD & SILVER STOCK INDEX (XAU)
Daily Range
bull market support
(2) or A of (2)
ELLIOTT WAVE INTERNATIONAL
P.O. Box 1618
Gainesville, GA 30503 USA
9/1/93
10/5/93
11/8/93
12/10/93
1/13/94
2/16/94
3/22/94

simply a larger A-B-C. There are several reasons to take this potential outcome into account. First, the bearish non-confirmation among the three markets remains intact, as the XAU and gold have not matched silver's new high. Second, the best wave count for silver shows a nearly completed five waves up from last September. As you can see from the daily chart, the February-March period may have contained a triangle, and triangles occur in the position of wave four. Thus, silver could be completing wave five from the low last September. Next, take a look at the chart of Fidelity North American Gold Fund, which holds a mix of stocks slightly different from that of the XAU. This fund depicts a five wave bull market from 1992 *and a correction that still needs wave (c) down.*

A More Important Top In Silver?

Finally, and most important, silver's rally from last year's low has developed in such as way as to undermine EWT's case made back near $3.50 that a major bull market was beginning. In other words, the ride, fun while it lasted, may be ending. Remember last summer when silver fell further than it should have in a normal second wave? The depth of that fall was very characteristic of a B wave. Now, silver has rallied to the point that its advance from September equals that of February-August last year. In A-B-C patterns, the most common price relationship is C=A, and if the internal wave count showing five waves up from last September is correct, silver is about to peak at exactly that relationship. If a Fibonacci 13-month A-B-C pattern is ending in silver, then it is a countertrend rally in a bear market.

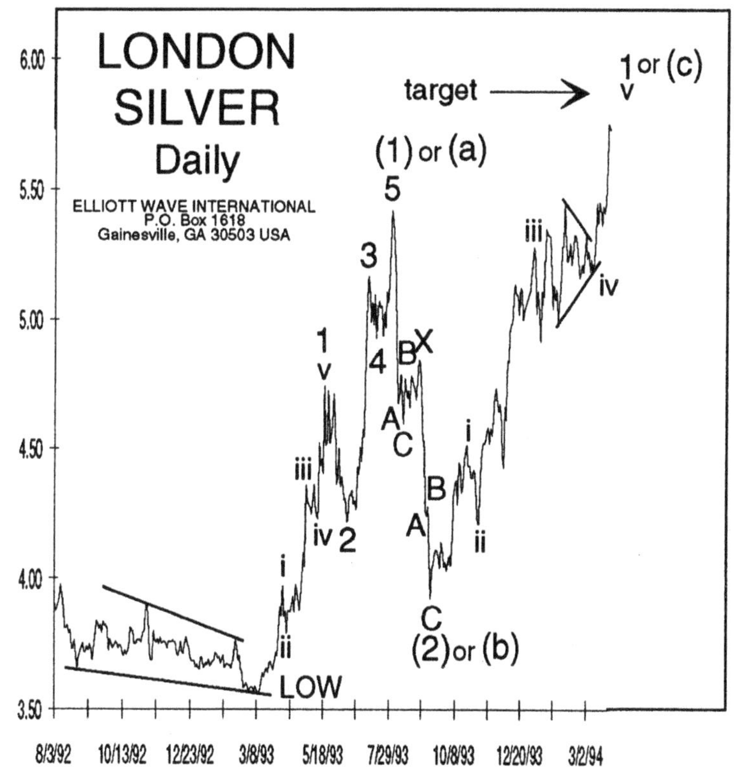

Two targeting methods point to the same level for a near term peak in silver. Basis London fix, v = i by the guideline of equality (see text, p.59) at $5.77, and, if the entire rise from a year ago is a bear market rally, (c) = (a) at $5.78, virtually the same price. The high so far is $5.75. (The equivalent nearby futures contract target is $5.86 + or - $2, and it just hit $5.81.) If silver turns down from this level, it should pull back to the previous fourth wave (see text, p.57) in the $5 - $5.50 range even if it remains in a bull market. All these concerns for the moment are quite real but could be erased rapidly if silver continues to push higher. For now, we will stick with the fail-safe designed in January, that *joint* new highs for the year by silver, gold and the XAU would signal a return to a bullish posture. So far, as noted above, only silver has made a new high, leaving intact the bearish non-confirmations noted back in January.

Gold

These charts show our preferred and second best scenarios for gold bullion. The upper chart depicts the more likely outcome. The bottom chart depicts a double three (see text, p.44), subdividing A-B-C-X-triangle, just like the DJIA formed from 1966 to 1982. The lower chart shows that gold *could* finish its bear market from 1980 without falling to a new low, a scenario that would be far more probable if silver has begun a new bull market. To summarize the outlook for gold, it *may* rally to the mid-400s first, it *should* ultimately fall to its long forecasted downside target of below $200/oz. (and ideally to near $105), but it *may* end its bear market at a much higher level if it meanders sideways for the rest of the year in a triangle pattern. As always, *wave form* should give us the answer in good time, as it did for silver near $3.50/oz. last year. Regardless of the *specific* outcome, *gold remains in a bear market*, and that's all we need to know for now.

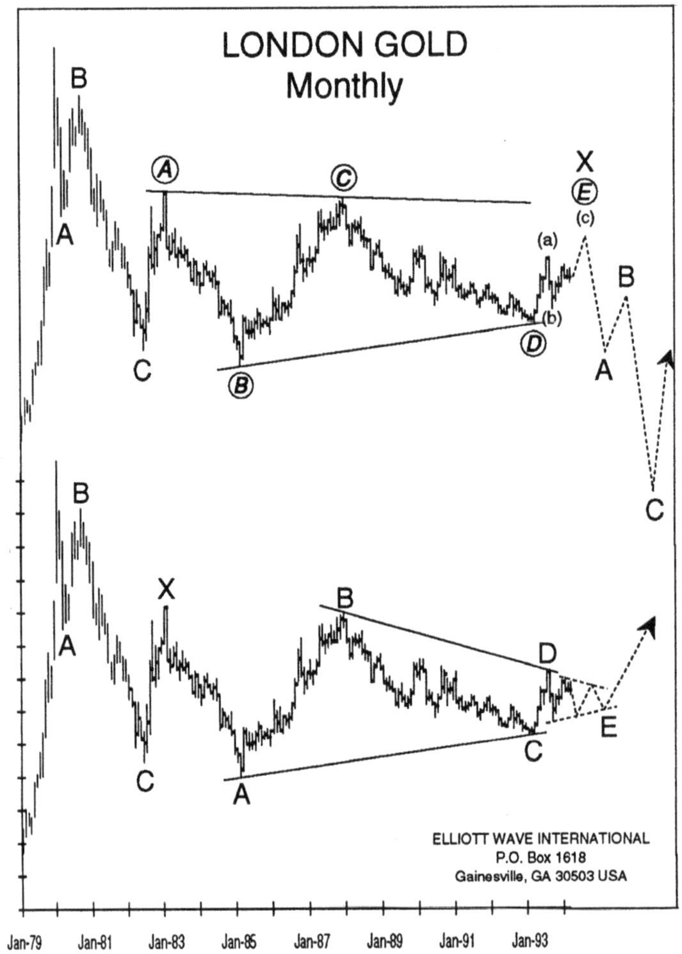

APRIL 29, 1994

Gold & Silver

Our bearish stance on the precious metals and mining stocks since January has been rewarded, as selling in April brought prices to even lower levels. All three markets require at least one more wave of decline. Under the most bullish scenario, both gold and the Gold &

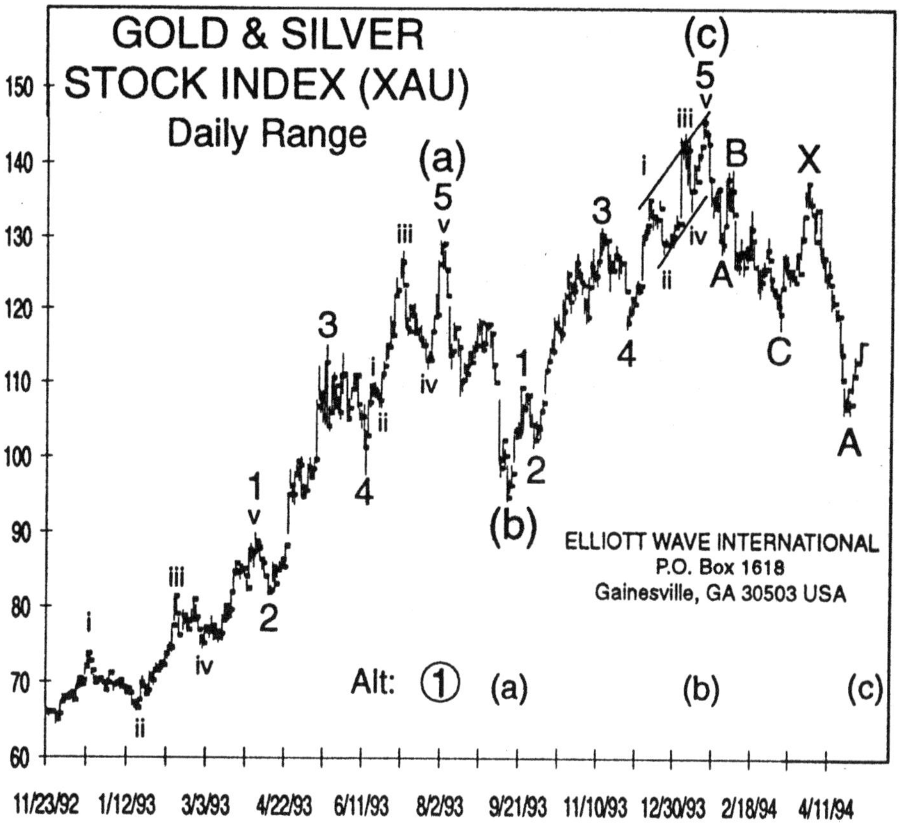

Silver Stock Index (XAU) are in the process of tracing out a double or triple zigzag (see text, p.35) decline, to be labeled A-B-C-X-A-B-C(-X-A-B-C). As you can see by the chart of the XAU, the second wave B is in progress, and the second wave C lies ahead. Silver has completed wave a of an a-b-c correction and is also in wave b, similarly requiring wave c down to finish its pattern. The chart of the Fidelity Select North American Gold Fund shown last month labeled the February low as wave (a), with a rally for (b) in progress. The bearish implication of that labeling was correct, as new lows have since been registered. That fund has support in the 18-20 range.

Momentum indicators confirm prospects for a new low. The 10-day, 24-day and 50-day rates of change on the XAU recently reached their deepest oversold readings of the year. More often than not, a price low will coincide with a divergence, or lesser oversold reading, than was generated in a previous decline within the correction, and to date no such divergence has occurred. If another wave C unfolds as expected, it should produce a divergence buy signal in at least one of these rates of change.

Sentiment into March followed the typical profile of a completed advance. Remember a year ago when newspapers interviewed money managers who derided the idea of buying silver? A month ago, we suddenly heard about which upside target was most reasonable, which hedge fund genius is long and how speculators are betting on further rise. This psychological change supports the case that the price decline is not over yet.

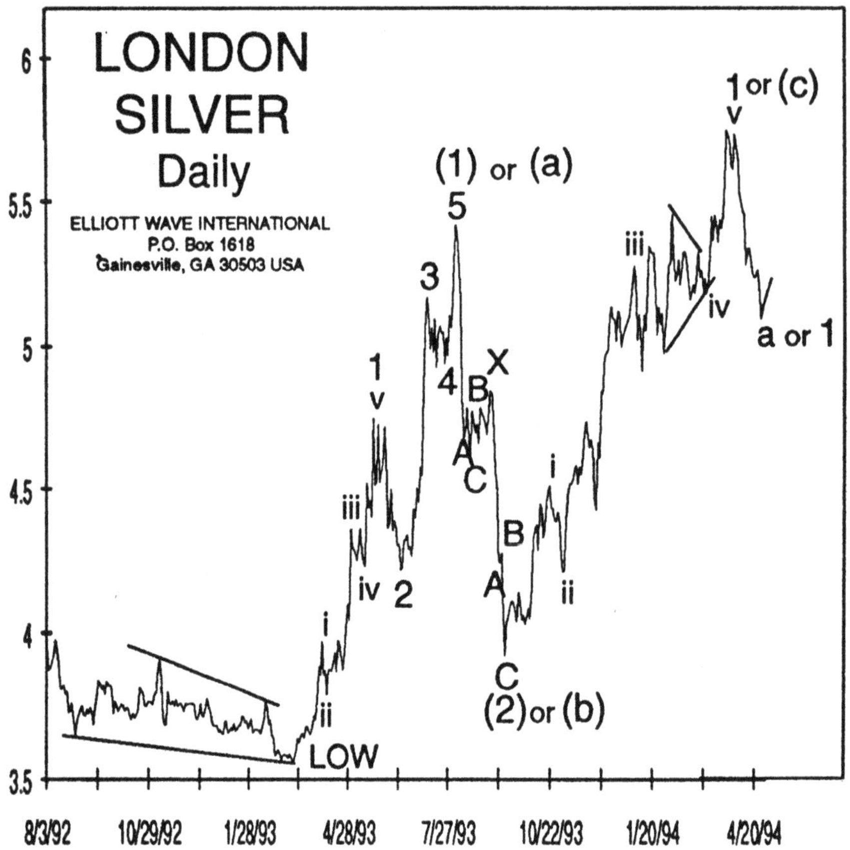
LONDON
SILVER
Daily
ELLIOTT WAVE INTERNATIONAL
P.O. Box 1618
Gainesville, GA 30503 USA
(1) or (a)
1 or (c)
a or 1
(2) or (b)
LOW
8/3/92
10/29/92
1/28/93
4/28/93
7/27/93
10/22/93
1/20/94
4/20/94

SILVER HOURLY
1 or (C)
ELLIOTT WAVE INTERNATIONAL
P.O. Box 1618
Gainesville, GA 30503 USA
background chart courtesy CQG Inc.
3/28
4/ 4
4/11
4/18
4/25

Bear Market?

The above analysis continues to be the most bullish that the wave structure supports. As discussed in detail last month, the entire advances from last year could be bear market rallies. In fact, since the September-January rally in the XAU has been so deeply retraced and since the decline is probably not over, this index joins those of gold and silver in having possibly completed an (a)-(b)-(c) pattern from the 1993 low, as labeled on the chart.

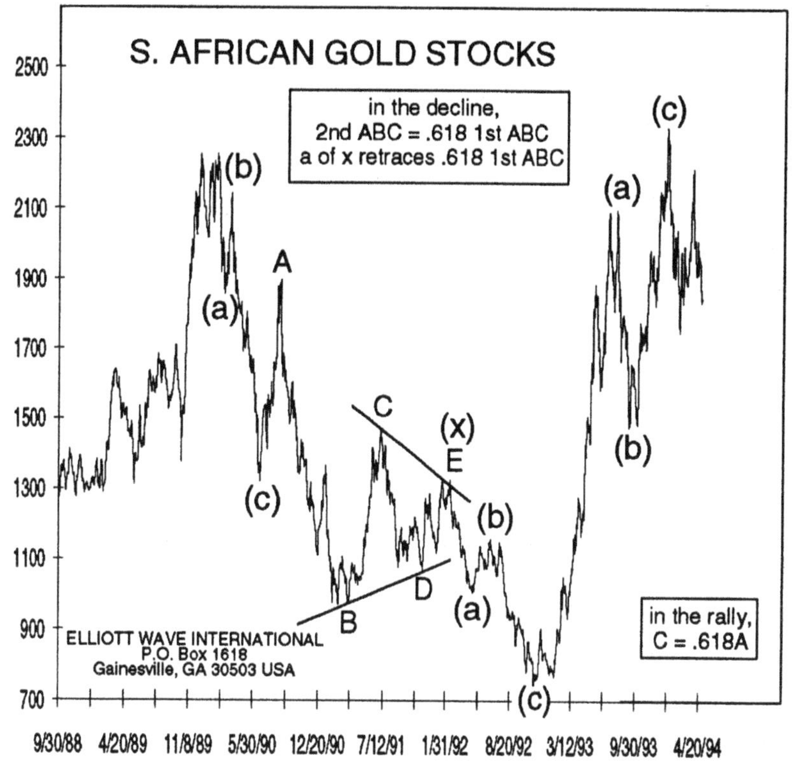

Another chart supporting this case is that of the South African gold mining issues. From late 1992, South African gold shares tripled. As you can see, the pattern was clearly an (a)-(b)-(c) (with a nearly perfect Fibonacci relationship), not a five, implying that gold shares across the board are still mired in a multi-year corrective process made up of repeating (a)-(b)-(c) advances and declines. The long term bearish potential implied by this chart adds weight to the concerns expressed last month, thus provid-

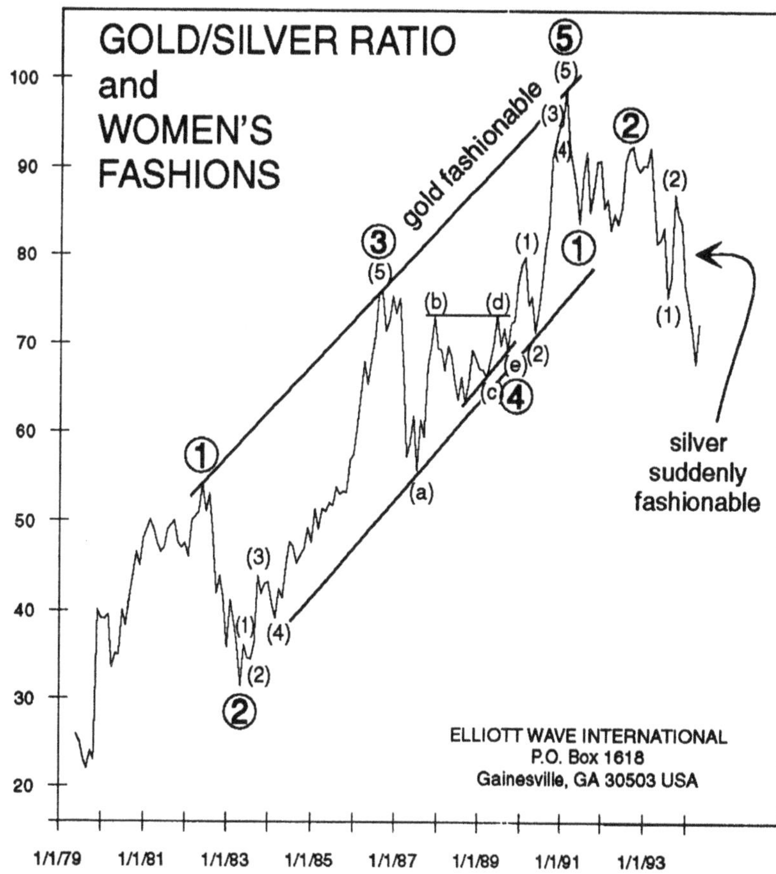

ing an additional reason to remain cautious on the precious metals complex, at least for the time being.

After several years of popularity in women's fashions, gold clothing is suddenly being replaced by silver clothing. This change is the popular cultural manifestation of a mental change that in the financial markets was revealed by a change of direction for the gold/silver ratio. The ratio had been rising since 1980, favoring gold, and held near its high until February 1993. The rise into 1991 traced out a perfect Elliott wave pattern, as *The Elliott Wave Theorist* has shown several times. Either women's fashions lagged the markets in expressing the dominant social mood change or women after a time sensed the change in what men want and began dressing accordingly. You can decide, depending upon your level of political correctness, which one it is.

MAY 26, 1994

Gold & Silver

Gold and silver remain in corrective patterns from their January and April peaks respectively. The clearest picture among the various precious metals related charts is provided by the Gold & Silver Stock Index (XAU). The May issue of *The Elliott Wave Theorist* showed a developing double zigzag count (to be labeled A-B-C-X-A-B-C) that at the time had just completed the second wave A. At this juncture, it appears that the second wave B has just ended, as shown on the updated daily chart.

That the rally from May 20 has been wave B is confirmed by the a-b-c-x-a-b-c structure and the appearance of a *triangle* for subwave x, as shown in the hourly chart. In the double zigzag, the second a-b-c is about equal in length to the first, a normal relationship. The triangle is a beautiful specimen, with clear three-wave subdivisions as well as perfect Fibonacci retracements of .618 at the low of wave a and .382 at the low of wave e.

The peak at 124.08 provides an excellent target for the final low (see dashed lines on the first chart). Within a fairly narrow range, the following relationships will be satisfied on the next decline:

–2nd ABC = 1.618 x 1st ABC at 90.33;

–In 2nd ABC, C = A at 92.42;

–Decline from January = 1.618 of August-September decline at 88.95.

–Support from September low is 94.10.

–The gap at the 88.14 - 89.79 area coincides with the .618 subdivision of the five-wave advance from February to August, 1993. A low at that point would therefore complete a complex pattern retracing .618 of that rise.

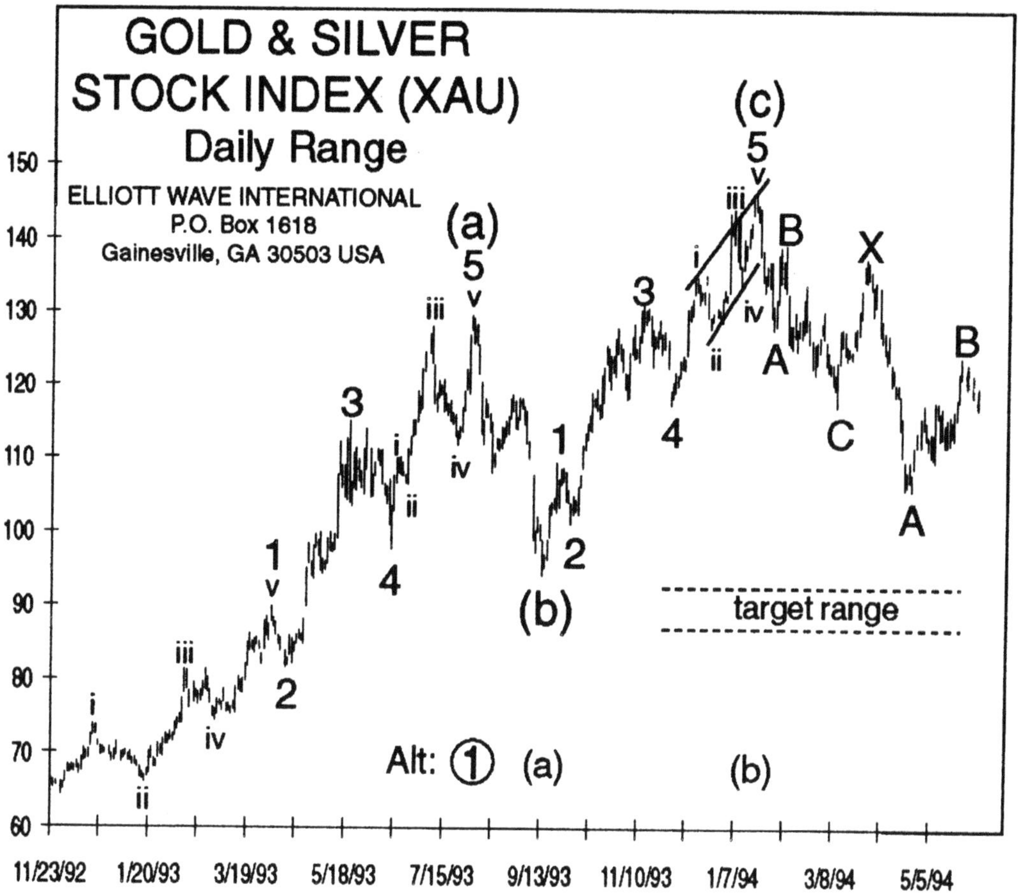
GOLD & SILVER
STOCK INDEX (XAU)
Daily Range
ELLIOTT WAVE INTERNATIONAL
P.O. Box 1618
Gainesville, GA 30503 USA
target range
Alt: ① (a) (b)
11/23/92 1/20/93 3/19/93 5/18/93 7/15/93 9/13/93 11/10/93 1/7/94 3/8/94 5/5/94

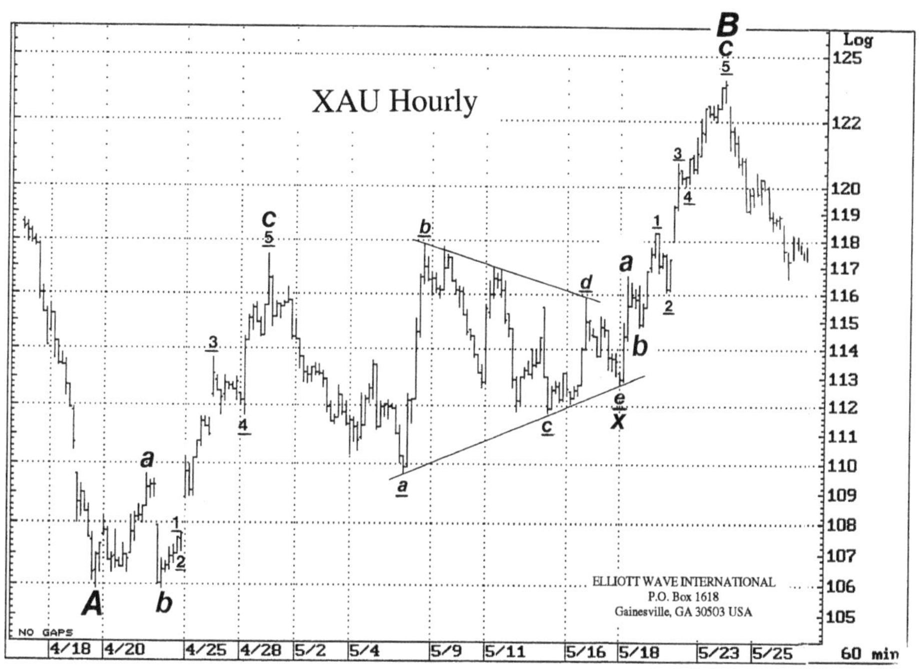
XAU Hourly
ELLIOTT WAVE INTERNATIONAL
P.O. Box 1618
Gainesville, GA 30503 USA
NO GAPS
4/18 4/20 4/25 4/28 5/2 5/4 5/9 5/11 5/16 5/18 5/23 5/25
60 min
Log

Recall that in the first A-B-C decline, C = 1.618 x A, so the wave count in the XAU appears to satisfy all normal relationships. To conclude, the XAU has a downside target zone of 88-94, with 90-92.50 the most strongly indicated range. A drop to that area will complete the correction that began in March, and it should complete the correction that began in January.

JUNE 30, 1994

Gold & Silver

After staying invested for ten months, EWT concluded in January 1994 that the rise in precious metals investments had ended and a correction was due. That correction unfolded on schedule, taking a sideways trend in the metals and a downward trend in mining stocks.

Pattern clarity has waned a bit, which is normal for corrections. Ideally, the correction will continue until the Gold & Silver Stock Index (XAU) reaches its ideal target of 88-94, with 90-92.50 the most strongly indicated zone. However, the level of certainty is low, as the metals *could* be completing triangles. Triangles portend a final rally, so if we miss it, it won't be that critical. The nearby chart shows the best count for the XAU.

JULY 28, 1994

Gold, silver and mining stocks remain in corrective patterns.

Gold & Silver

Judging from letters we receive, many subscribers are extremely interested in gold and silver, and many want to hear a firm opinion. We are extremely interested in gold and silver also, but firm opinions can be issued only when they are warranted. Our long term bullish stance toward silver in early 1993 was as strong as our previous bearish stance, and it paid off well in the mining stocks, which rose 100%. We turned intermediate term bearish in January and have remained that way since, as gold and silver have undergone a correction while the mining stocks have fallen 28%.

One of the characteristics of corrective patterns is their lack of clarity at various times, and this is one of them. The uncertainty in the technical picture that emerged last month was a proper interpretation, evidenced by the fact that these markets have done nothing but drift sideways since then. The put/call ratio on silver futures options jumped in July to its highest level since the price low in April, which is short term bullish. Our most reliable intermediate-term guide is that two important time cycles are due to bottom very late in 1994. So the most reasonable outlook now is for a rally to take place within the corrective pattern, but this is little more than a good guess. Until a corrective pattern clearly ends, it is best to maintain a stand-aside posture toward this group of investments.

Possibly supporting the potential for further price weakness in mining stocks is this chart of copper producer Phelps Dodge, which has risen nearly ten times in value since 1984 and sports a wedge from 1989 to the present. Since prices are near the top of the wedge now, it would be prudent to adopt a bearish outlook until such time as the wedge is penetrated significantly, say by a rise past 70.

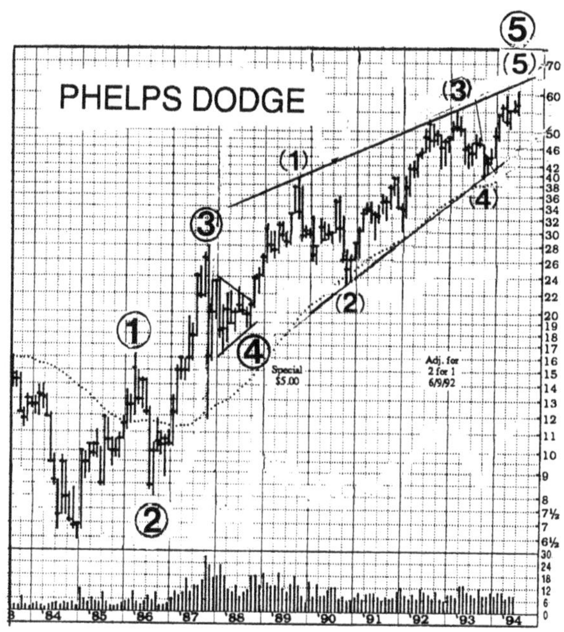

One question we receive often is, Does the price of gold in other currencies support your outlook for gold in terms of dollars? An opinion already justified can be supported by such analysis, such as when EWT showed that the outlook for silver in terms of both the dollar and Swiss francs was bullish early last year. However, when the outlook is uncertain, other ratios are of little value because there is no way to know whether the pattern is indicating a change mostly in the currency or in the metal. A bullish outlook for gold in terms of Swiss francs, Deutsche marks and yen might mean simply that the dollar is about to have a big rally, against which gold could fall. The only thing that matters to most U.S. investors is the price of gold in dollars, since that is the valuation basis of their assets. Other relationships can still be assessed, however, by anyone who wishes to apply the currency analysis in our 100-page monthly, *Global Market Perspective.*

AUGUST 18, 1994 – INTERIM REPORT

Last January, *The Elliott Wave Theorist* recognized an intermediate term peak in gold, silver and mining stocks, ending a ten-month bullish stance. Mining stocks and gold did peak then, and after seven months of correction, a buying opportunity once again appears near.

More compelling, however, is the picture in silver, which continued rallying until April and since then has undergone a clear A-B-C correction lasting just under a Fibonacci 5 months. Now back to just above $5 an ounce, silver appears likely to begin another impulse wave to the upside.

Silver bullion is the most underpriced commodity, indeed perhaps the most underpriced financial asset, in the world. EWT argued strongly in 1993 that, based upon wave pattern analysis, silver was registering a major bottom. It rose from $3.50 an ounce to $5.90, a 69% gain, while silver mining (and gold mining) stocks rose over 100%. Now, just as in February 1993, silver appears to be ending a corrective process, although of smaller degree than last year since the major bottom has already passed. We'll update the visual picture in the next regular issue, due out next week.

If silver is bottoming again, silver mining stocks, which are an underowned stock group to say the least, also have excellent prospects. Promising companies, as recommended by mining stock expert James Dines, include Hecla (HL, NYSE), Coeur d'Alene (CDE, NYSE), Industrias Penoles (Mexico exchange) and Minefinders (MFL, Vancouver exchange).

AUGUST 25, 1994

Gold, silver and mining stocks have completed their multi-month corrective patterns and are poised to climb to new highs in the advance that began early last year.

Gold

The charts of gold and silver shown in this section illustrate why *The Elliott Wave Theorist* has again become bullish on these metals for the intermediate term, as per the Interim Report of August 18. Let's refresh our ongoing long term outlook for gold, which is crystal clear, and relate that to what has just happened.

The 13-Year Triangle

The May 1993 issue of EWT presented a chart (reprinted here) showing that gold had just finished a five-year decline for wave Ⓓ of a contracting triangle (see text, p.41) that dated back to the 1982 low. At the time, EWT projected wave Ⓔ up to $461. The April 1994 issue then labeled wave (a) of Ⓔ as a Fibonacci 5-month rise and wave (b) as a 2-month decline into September 1993.

(Reprinted from the May 1993 ELLIOTT WAVE THEORIST)

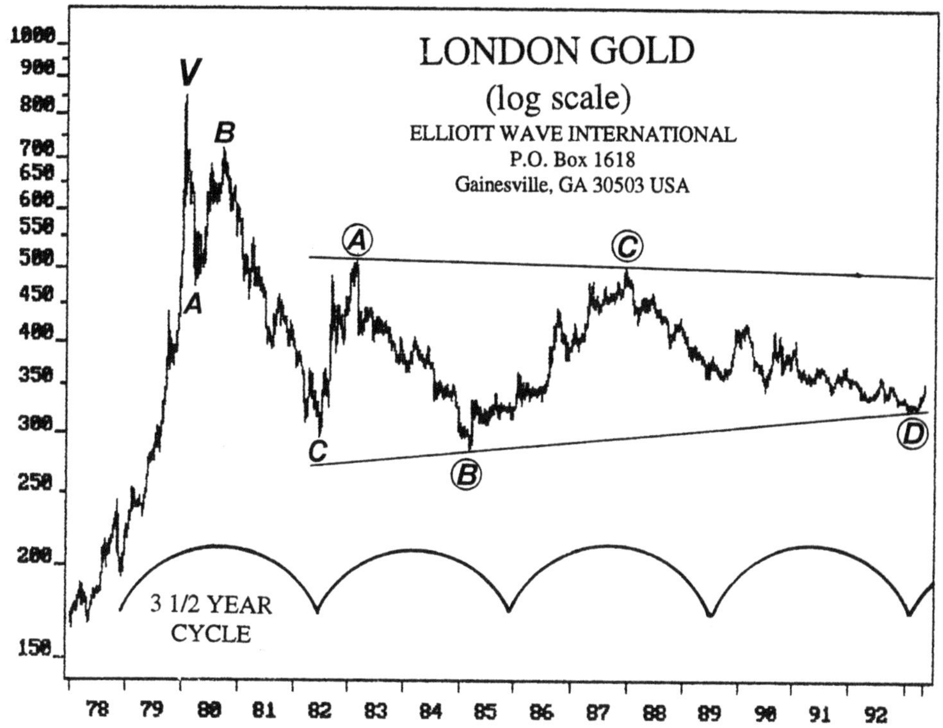

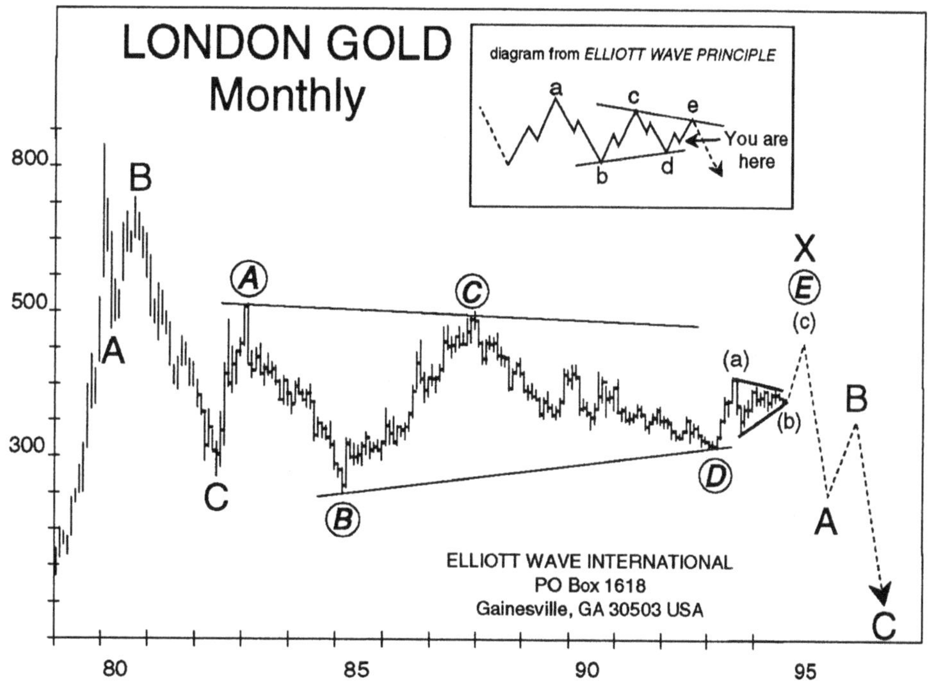

A 13-Month Triangle

Well, that low has indeed held ever since, but wave (b) of Ⓔ has apparently developed into a Fibonacci 13-month contracting triangle, as shown in the updated chart. 369.10 basis the nearby futures contract must hold for this triangle to remain intact. A contracting triangle is a pattern that temporarily interrupts the one larger trend. In this case, the trend from the March 1993 low was up. Triangles also precede the final move in the larger trend, which in this case precisely fits our long term interpretation and confirms that the rise from 1993 is a bear market rally, not a new bull market.

Wave (b) is now over, so wave (c) is ready to launch. Gold should now advance for 3, 5 or 8 months. Since the movement following a triangle tends to be swift and short, we should be alert for the advance to take place in a brief period, i.e., 3 or 5 months. The inset on the updated monthly chart shows exactly where the gold market is within its 13-year triangle.

Upside Target

The original target of $461 basis London fix ($462.40 basis futures) for wave Ⓔ was derived from the observation that alternate waves in a triangle are often related by .618. A peak at that level would make wave Ⓔ .618 as long as wave Ⓒ. Now wave Ⓔ's internal structure is supporting that target. Within Ⓔ, if wave (c) equals wave (a), a typical relationship, it will peak at $456.90 basis London fix ($458.60 basis futures), virtually the same target. This analysis adds confirmation to our conclusion that gold is about to climb to $460 (+ or - $5).

As you can see by the long term chart, the gold market is getting ever closer to the most exciting juncture since it reached $850/oz. in January 1980. The long meandering wave Ⓓ wasted over five years, and wave Ⓔ has taken its time as well. All this time has been spent, however, for a reason. Gold fell in its first A-B-C pattern over a Fibonacci 2 years, and it has been tracing out a triangle that is certain now to end in a Fibonacci 13 years, from 1982 to 1995 (+ or - 1 month). What's more, as you can see on the first chart, the 3½-year cycle's ideal top is year-end 1994. A peak within a few months of that time would be perfectly timed for cyclic pressure to begin exerting itself on the downside. The next 3½-year cycle low is due in the fourth quarter of 1996. That timing is particularly interesting because the first A-B-C decline in gold's major bear market took a bit over two years, in 1980-1982. The second A-B-C, then, could also unfold in a quick two years and bottom with the 3½-year cycle low due in late 1996. If all continues to unfold along expected lines, *The Elliott Wave Theorist* will update the multi-decade picture in gold, as well as the analysis behind our long-standing bear market target, when the rally appears to have run its course.

Important Benchmarks

Near term, if gold slips below $369.10 basis nearby futures, it will have negated the idea that it has just ended wave Ⓔ of a triangle. This benchmark conveniently provides an extremely tight boundary for our bullish opinion. Consider also that if the overall analysis identifying the advance in gold from last year as a bear market rally is correct, then gold must remain below the presumed peak of wave Ⓒ at $502.75/oz. We thus have a 10% range of uncertainty between $460, which it should reach, and $502.75, which it should not exceed. If gold does exceed that level, it will signal a rise to new all time highs and force a return to a long term bullish posture.

Silver

The picture in silver is similarly bullish on the intermediate-term outlook. As you can see by the weekly chart, silver has traced out an A-B-C flat correction with a diagonal triangle (see text, p.31) for wave C, a very reliable sign of completion. Silver, then, is due to make a new high in its advance dating from early 1993. Right on schedule, this advance should allow the metal to rally into the ideal peak in its 5-year cycle (last shown in the January 1993 issue), which bottomed in late 1992. Its next low is due in 1997, shortly after gold's.

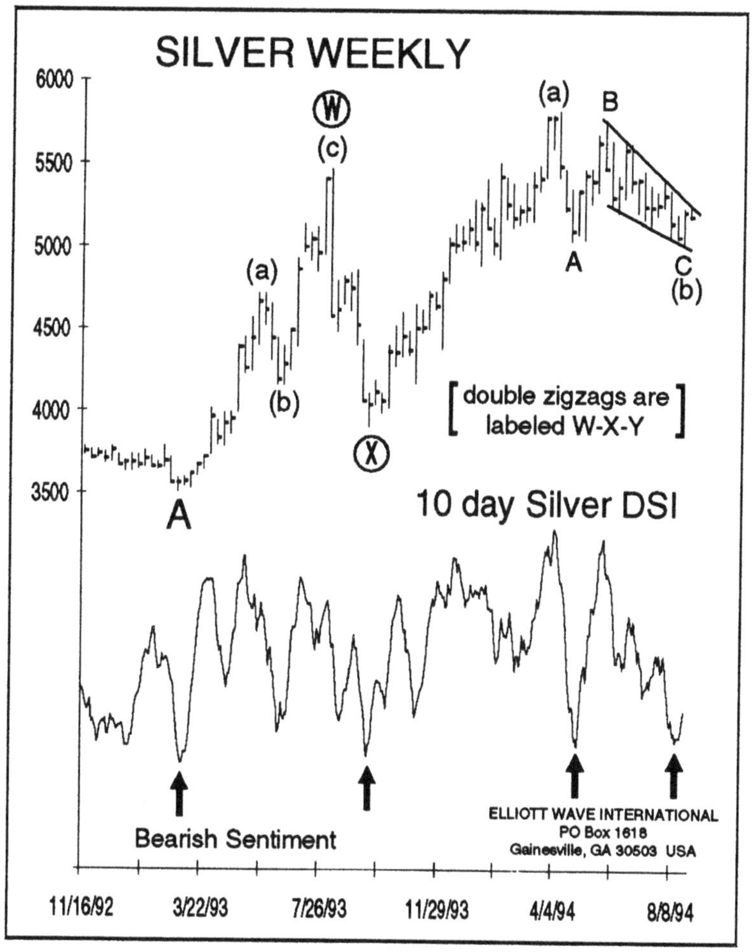

Estimating price peaks in silver is difficult, as silver tends to be extremely volatile at the very end of a precious metals move. However, the wave structure since the 1993 low does provide some basis for conjecture. If the entire advance is subdividing (a)- (b)-(c)-(x)-(a)-(b)-(c), only the final wave (c) is left to go. An examination of the price movements reveals that the second (a)-(b)-(c) is developing so as to be a Fibonacci 1.618 times the size of the first. The second wave (a) is 1.618 times as long as the first, and the second wave (b) would be 1.618 times as deep as the first at $4.90 basis nearby futures. So far, the low is $5.025.

If the second wave (c) now travels 1.618 times as long as the first, it will peak near $7.10. This target implies a 40% gain, twice that expected of gold. Given silver's history of volatility, this target should be considered both the best target and a minimum target, allowing for a spike top bursting briefly but sharply above that level.

This interpretation of silver's pattern, you may notice, puts it in gear with gold on the long term picture, implying that both metals are in bear market rallies. *The Elliott Wave Theorist* will update the very long term picture for both metals in an upcoming issue, presuming the rally takes place as expected.

Sentiment

Market psychology is primed for a rally in the precious metals. As the chart shows, the Daily Sentiment Index (DSI) from MBH Commodities (Northbrook, IL) just reached its lowest level of bulls since the April low of wave a, nearly matching the levels reached at the February and September 1993 lows. At the same time, the put/call ratio on silver futures just registered its highest reading since the wave a low.

Gold & Silver Stocks

EWT has been counting the Gold and Silver Stock Index (XAU) as a double zigzag, with the last wave C expected to fall to the 88-94 area, for a .618 retracement. Suddenly last week, however, wave C appeared to have completed a diagonal triangle, ending at a higher level than expected. If the correction is over, it has nevertheless bottomed quite nicely at a 38.2% retracement of the rise into August 1993 and simultaneously a 50% retracement of the rise into January 1994. Truncations of C waves in zigzags are exceedingly rare, so this conclusion

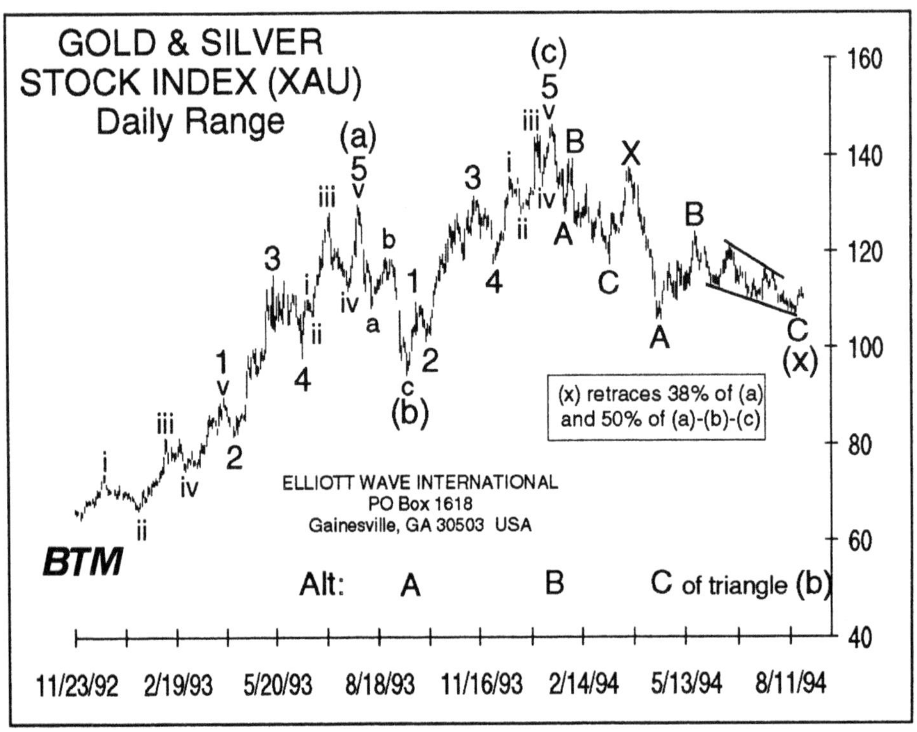

is hardly certain. Nevertheless, a bullish stance here is virtually riskless, since last week's low must hold for this interpretation to remain valid, and that low is very close to the current price. If a turn is indeed at hand, the upside target range is 145-190. Wave form, as well as the upside targets for gold and silver, will help us identify the next peak more precisely.

Those interested in silver stocks should check these names with their brokers: Hecla (HL), Coeur d'Alene (CDE), Minefinders on the Vancouver exchange and Industrias Penoles, traded in Mexico. James Dines (Box 22, Belvedere, CA 94920) prefers HL convertible preferred stock and the CDE convertible debentures to the common. One money manager contacted us to mention the availability of Freeport McMoran Copper and Gold preferred (FXC.D), which is a silver-denominated preferred stock paying 4% interest. (It appears to be the company's way of borrowing money cheaply, with their silver reserves as collateral.) The stock is redeemable at 4 oz. of silver per share in a few years and presumably would change price along with the price of silver. Gold stock investors may use this list, which should do very well if gold rises: Agnico-Eagle (AEAGF), Anglo-American Gold (AAGIY), Avino (AVO, Canada), American Barrick (ABX), Placer Dome (PDG) and Sunshine Mining (SSC). South African gold shares appear ready to go up strongly across the board. All these stocks are considered highly speculative and typically sport wide swings in both directions, so proceed accordingly.

SEPTEMBER 16, 1994 – INTERIM REPORT

Yesterday silver completed its wave 2 pullback at precisely a .382 retracement of its mid-August/early-September rally. Wave 3 is next, so don't be surprised if silver jumps sharply in coming days. Gold and silver stocks have been leaping, and have more to go.

SEPTEMBER 29, 1994

Gold, silver and mining stocks have made substantial progress since EWT's August 18 report calling the end of the seven-month correction. EWT's silver stock recommendations have provided more profit in just 19 months than investing in the S&P, including dividends, has in the past 6 years.

Gold & Silver

The August 18 Interim Report called for an end to the seven-month correction in the precious metals complex. Gold, silver and mining stocks have all risen strongly since then and have nearly fulfilled the forecast that they would climb to new highs in the advance that began early last year. Also as expected, mining stocks and silver bullion have substantially outperformed gold since the August low. Here are the figures from the August low to the September high to date: gold up 4.2%, silver up 9.2%, Gold & Silver Stock Index (XAU) up 21%.

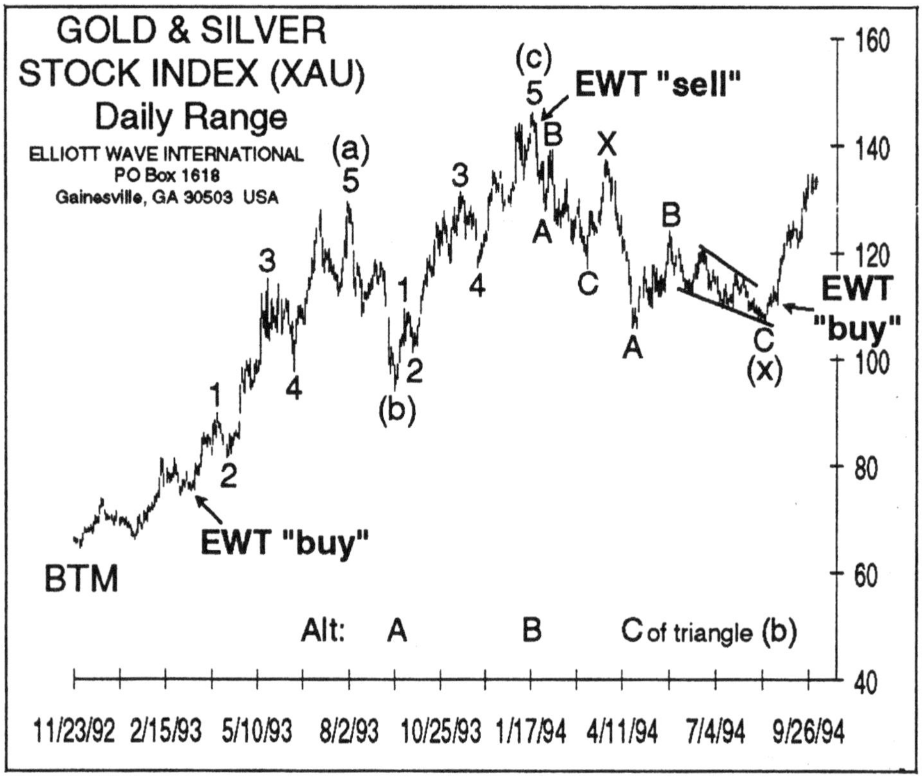

EWT's buy and sell recommendations on silver mining stocks are shown in the chart of the XAU, which in terms of price movement is an excellent proxy for our basket of silver stocks. This strategy has provided more profit in 19 months than holding the S&P during its bull market (including dividends) has in six years. To restate our current list of stocks:

– In the lots of silver category: Avino (AVO), Coeur d'Alene (CDE), Hecla (HL), Industrias Penoles (Mex.Ex.), Minefinders (MFL), and Sunshine (SSC).

– In the mostly gold category: Agnico-Eagle (AEAGF), Anglo-American Gold (AAGIY), American Barrick (ABX), Placer Dome (PDG) and South African gold mining stocks in general.

As mentioned in the September 1993 issue, Lexington Strategic Silver Fund is a reasonably good substitute for those who do not wish to buy individual issues.

The wave structure of the rally has been quite clear. The September 16 Interim Report noted, "Yesterday, silver completed its wave 2 pullback at precisely a .382 retracement of its mid-August-early September rally. Wave 3 is next, so don't be surprised if silver jumps sharply in coming days." September 15 was indeed a short term low, as you can see on the daily chart. The most bearish possibility is that silver has just completed five waves up now. If so, it should

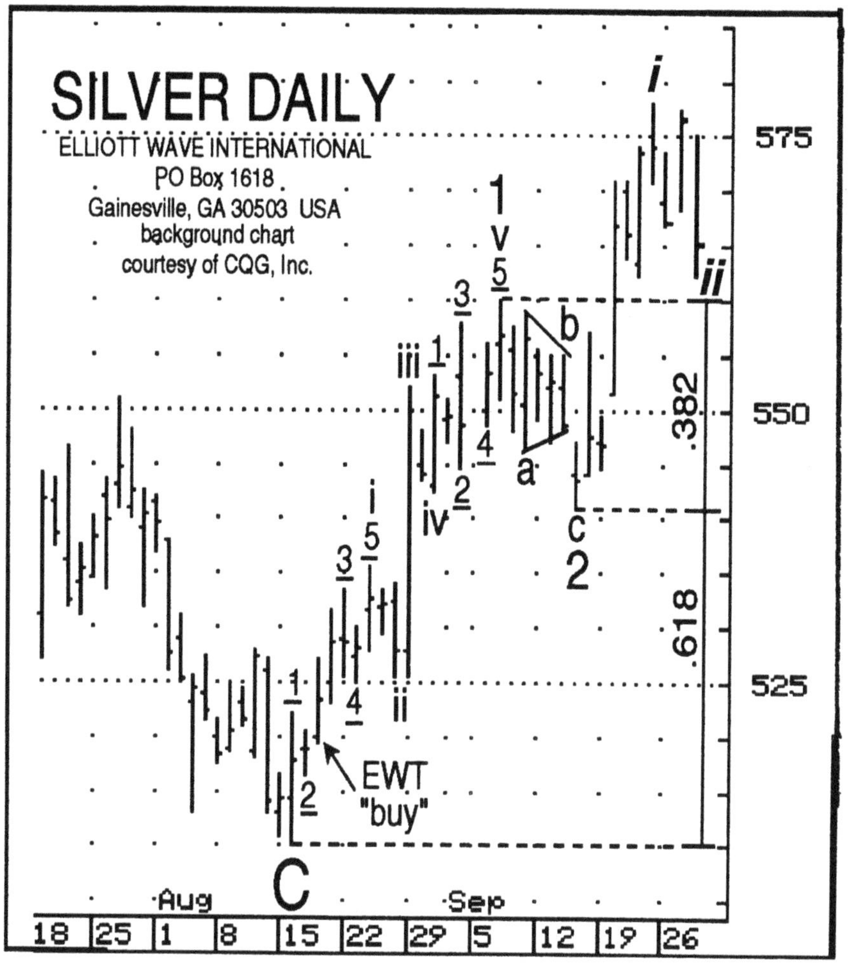

undergo, at most, a .382 retracement to the gap at $5.52 basis December futures, providing a final entry for latecomers.

It is the long term picture that matters most, however, as gold is approaching the long-awaited end to wave X, the upward consolidation dating from the 1982 low. The August 26 issue of EWT detailed that outlook in 2½ pages, so please review that issue if you need an update. Needless to say, EWT will present another major discussion if gold gets close to its rally target of $461 (+ or - $20). In the meantime, expect to see increased commentary on the return of inflation, which will be a necessary rationalization for the rally. Excitement should be substantial at the upcoming peak, since it will mark the culmination of an upward triangle lasting over twelve years.

Favorite photo caption: September 23, in USA Today: "Analyst Sees Gold Going Above $400 An Ounce." Gold had already passed $397.

OCTOBER 28, 1994

Gold, silver and mining stocks are bottoming in a second wave and preparing to rise to new highs for the year.

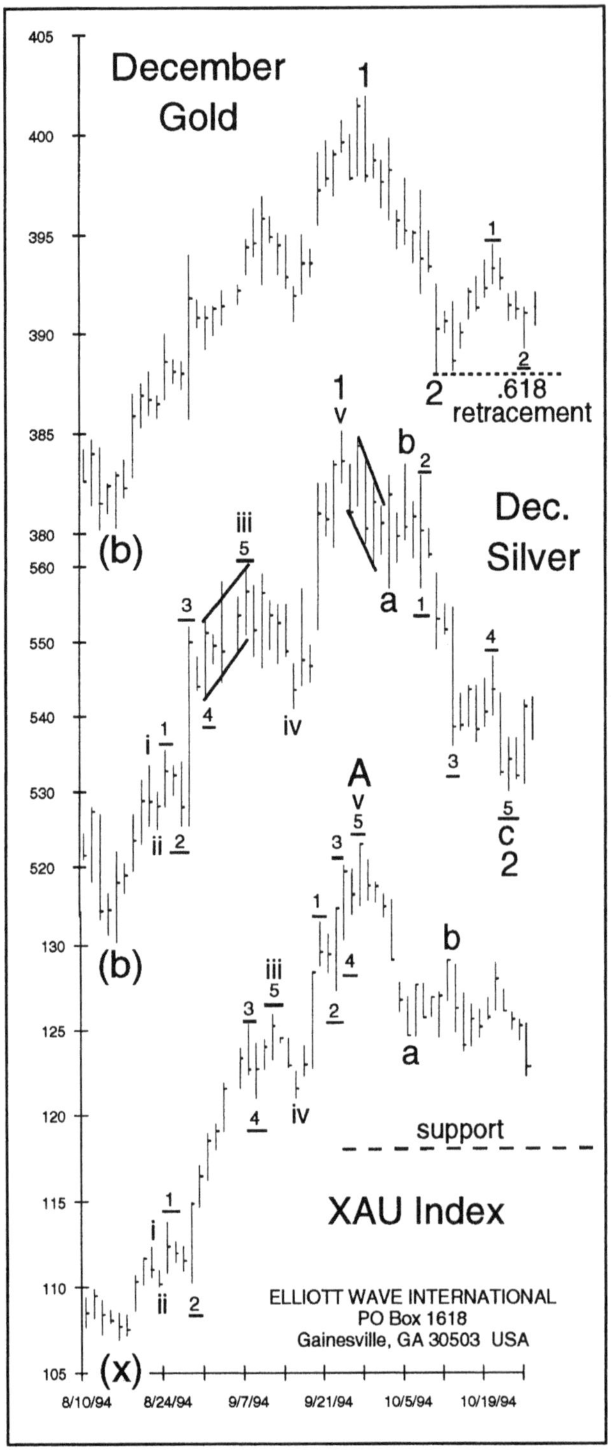

Gold & Silver

The precious metals picture is very exciting. Wave 2 in gold and silver has almost certainly bottomed. Gold retraced exactly .618 of its August-September advance. The biggest surprise was that silver dropped through the .382 retracement level at $5.52, which was the most pullback EWT expected last month. The extra 20 cents down to a 2/3 retracement was briefly unnerving, but the A-B-C structure is so well formed that the preferred count is clear. As EWT said last month, this drop was to provide a final entry for latecomers. The charts tell the story.

The XAU's pattern suggests an end to its correction just below 118, which is not only a .618 retracement but also the point at which waves c and a will be equal, a typical relationship. Any further drop should be unconfirmed by the metals, within which wave 3 of (c) upward is now ready to launch.

When wave (c) finally peaks, gold should be near its target of $461, silver near $7.00, and the XAU over 170. To realize this outcome, gold should stay above $388, silver above $5.30, and the XAU above 115. A break of all three of those levels would upset the bullish picture.

DECEMBER 1, 1994

Gold is days from a low and should advance to $461 by spring of 1995.

Gold & Silver

The November issue of EWT erroneously reported, "Wave 2 in gold and silver has almost certainly bottomed." Instead of bottoming, the metals, particularly silver and most mining stocks, fell sharply throughout the month. For protection, EWT stated that gold, silver and the Gold & Silver Stock Index (XAU) had to hold above $388, $5.30 and 115 respectively to maintain the short term bullish outlook. These stop levels were all triggered, resulting in losses averaging 2% from original entries. Since then, the XAU and silver have fallen 10%.

The persistence of the recent decline in the metals reflects the bottoming of the 9-month cycle. The March 1994 issue of EWT made a forecast that has worked out better than that suggested by the wave patterns of recent months:

> The 9-month cycle suggests a low in or near April, which coincides with the intermediate term cyclic outlook for the stock market. The longer term cycles in gold are still not due to bottom until year-end, when the next 9-month cycle low is due.

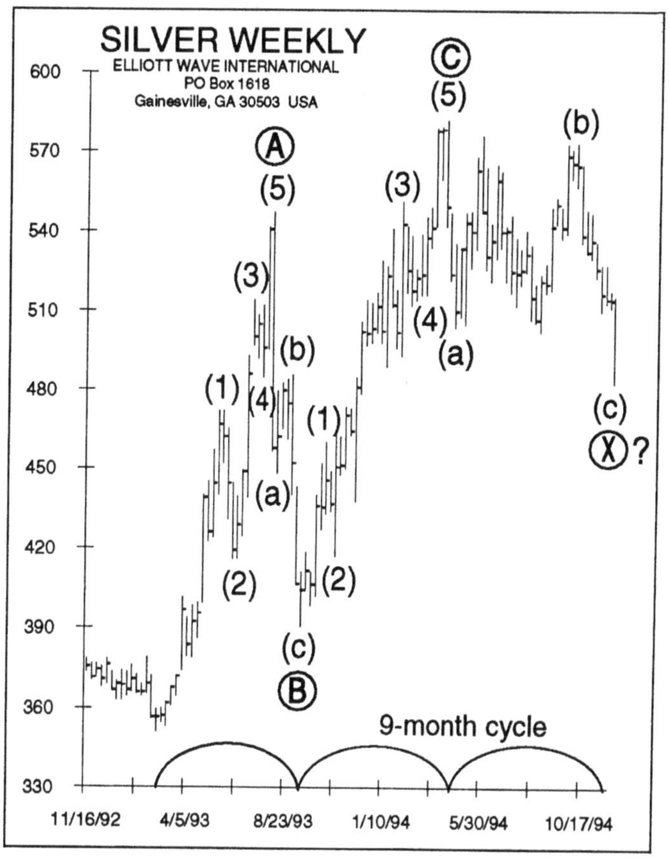

Year-end has now arrived. The current oversold condition suggests that a 9-month cycle, as depicted on the chart of silver, is indeed bottoming. On this basis, the precious metals should reach a low within days and then achieve their upside targets in the spring of 1995.

Elliott Wave Analysis

Silver's deep fall forces a change of wave count. The 1993-1994 advance is now best labeled a simple Ⓐ-Ⓑ-Ⓒ zigzag. The question now is whether the correction since April is an (a)-(b)-(c) for wave Ⓧ of a double zigzag (see text, p.35) or a renewal of the long term bear market. The former conclusion will remain more attractive as long as the nearby contract holds above $4.30, in which case silver will stay on track to advance to the $7 level.

The wave count in gold, which hardly budged last month, still indicates that wave 2 of (c) is bottoming. If gold were to complete a larger flat correction as indicated by the inset on the chart, it would fall to approximately $360. However, time is running out for such a drop. Indeed, gold's relative strength is producing a bullish non-confirmation against the new low in silver. As long as gold holds above $350 basis nearby futures, it should still be on its way to approximately $461.

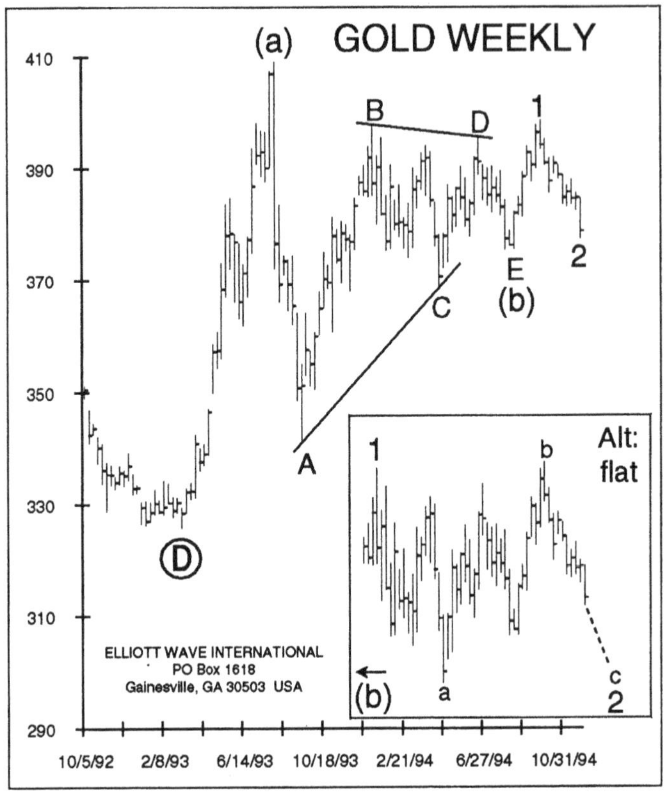

The wild card is the XAU. It outperformed gold on the way up

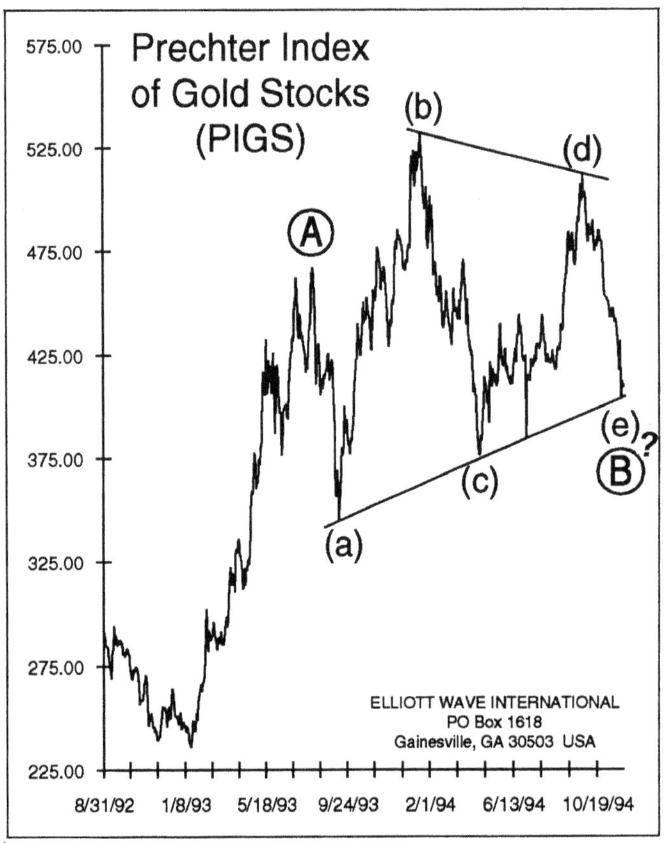

and has fallen further on the way down. The pattern does not indicate a completed correction from the 146.32 high last January. Nevertheless, it is hard to imagine gold and silver reaching their upside targets without mining issues rising in concert. Our own gold stock index can be counted as a completed correction taking the shape of a contracting triangle, as shown here in the chart. Perhaps the XAU will complete its pattern a bit later than gold and silver, then play catch-up on the upside.

The Elliott Wave Theorist, 1995

JANUARY 6, 1995

Silver and the Gold & Silver Stock Index (XAU) bottomed in December in accordance with the 8-month cycle. Gold is bottoming now and should advance to $460 (+ or $5) by April-June. Silver and the XAU should outperform gold by a substantial margin.

Gold & Silver

After triggering our stop level in November, precious metals sold off sharply. Cycles then suggested on December 2, as EWT said, that "Gold is days from a low." The cyclic outlook proved its value by producing a bottom in the metals and the XAU over the next four days. The cycle that EWT used to forecast that low was labeled as 9 months long in keeping with its long-standing rhythm, but in recent years it has actually been running a Fibonacci 8 months, + or - 1/2 month. As you can see on the next chart, it has coincided with the lows for waves A, C, and now E of the triangle.

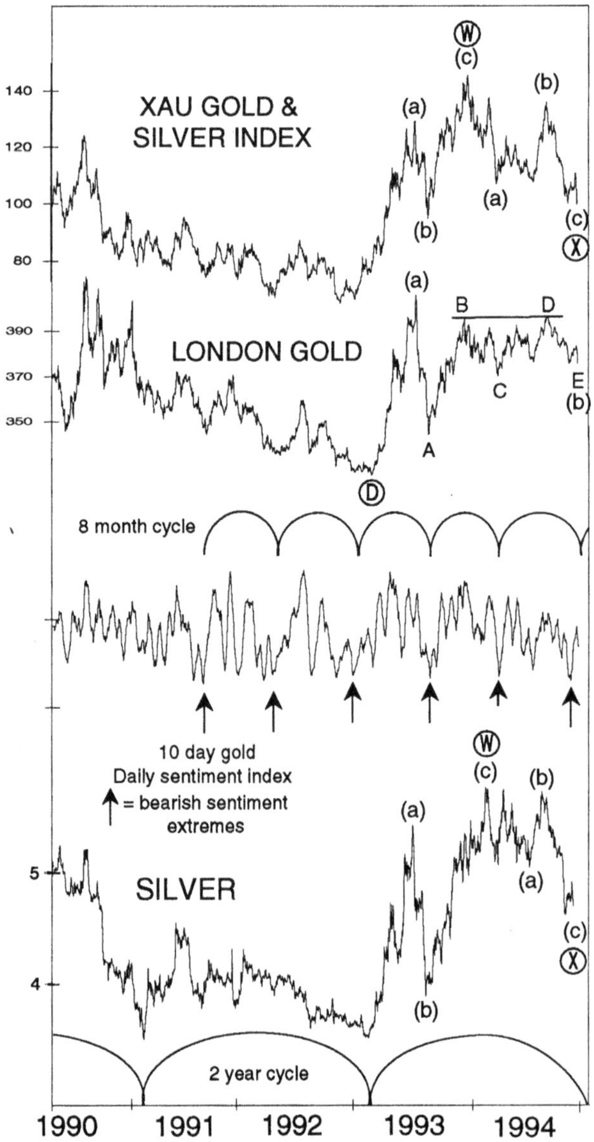

Though the sharp selloff this week is striking fear into the hearts of investors and has driven gold below its December low, as of today (1/5), both silver and the XAU are holding above their December lows by a slim margin in what is probably a bullish non-confirmation typical of a late cycle bottom. Although the XAU could fall as low as 96, the 8-month cycle is now stretched to its limit. From April 22, 1994, the December 5 low was 7½ months later, and January 4 is 8½ months later. Thus, the 8-month cycle should turn up immediately. What's more, there is a case to be made, as shown at the bottom of the chart, that silver is under the influence of a 2-year cycle, which encompasses three 8-month cycles. This cycle is due to bottom and turn up in the first quarter of 1995. The size of this cycle suggests that silver should have a particularly spirited rally this year, once again outperforming gold.

Elliott Wave Analysis

The long-standing conclusion that gold was tracing out a triangle for wave (b) remains the best interpretation of its pattern from mid-1993. Instead of ending in August, however, wave (b) is ending here in January. It is an ascending triangle, i.e., one with a flat top and rising bottoms. Using nearby futures contract prices (including the low-volume January contract), wave B peaked at $399 and wave D at $398.60. This week's low is only $5.40 from the low of wave C, so the decline must stop here to keep the triangle intact. The next best interpretation is that the correction from the January 1994 high is a flat. A break of $350 would negate all bullish interpretations.

Silver was shown last month as finishing wave Ⓧ of a double zigzag upward (to be labeled Ⓦ-Ⓧ-Ⓨ), a count that remains intact. This interpretation now applies to the Gold & Silver Stock Index (XAU) as well, as shown on chart.

Market Psychology

Market sentiment supports the case that a significant bottom is being reached. On December 8, the ten-day average of the Daily Sentiment Index (courtesy MBH Commodities, Northbrook, IL) reflected only 15% bulls, its lowest level in over three years. Though less reliable, the ten-day average of the put/call ratio on gold futures reached 1.18 on December 13, its highest level in over two years. The December 26 issue of Business Week featured a special focus on gold to report, "Precious Little to Cheer About... Experts believe that gold prices will linger or drift down." The sentiment, then, is well reflective of the end of a corrective pattern of Intermediate degree or larger.

Targeting

Gold should now fulfill EWT's forecast to "advance to $461 by spring of 1995." This upside target for gold was derived from the fact that alternate waves within triangles often have a Fibonacci relationship (see text, p.115). The long term triangle dating from June 1982, which appears destined to last a Fibonacci 13 years, will sport this relationship between waves Ⓔ and Ⓒ if Ⓔ peaks at $462.44 basis nearby futures. This target is strengthened by the developing wave Ⓔ, since within it, waves (c) and (a) will now be equal if wave (c) peaks at $457.70. Thus, these two typical wave relationships will be satisfied within a tight $5 range.

As gold undergoes wave (c), silver and the XAU should trace out the rest of their double zigzags. Ideal targets are $6.84 for silver and 180.72 for the XAU, at which levels wave Ⓨ will be equal to wave Ⓦ. These calculations confirm EWT's outlook for the metals' upside potential. A .618 relationship, less likely, would produce peaks at $5.96 and 149.42 respectively.

If wave (c) in gold takes as long as the Fibonacci 5 months of wave (a), it will peak in June. If it lasts .618 times as long as (a), i.e., 3 months, it will peak in April. Half the length of the ideal 8-month cycle, i.e., four months, added to the December-January lows projects an idealized high in April-May. Thus, the combined approaches indicate an April peak, possibly extending to no later than June, with the next cyclic low due in August-September.

JANUARY 26, 1995

The precious metals bottomed in December-January in accordance with the 8-month cycle. Gold should advance to $460 (+ or -$5) by April-June. Silver and the XAU should outperform gold by a substantial margin. A break of the January lows will negate the bullish outlook for the precious metals.

Gold & Silver

The January issue presented another extensive analysis of the precious metals and stood firm on its conclusion, as follows: "Silver and the Gold & Silver Stock Index (XAU) bottomed in December in accordance with the 8-week cycle. Gold is bottoming now."

Gold reached a low that day. Both gold and silver have traced out *five*-wave rallies, which are consistent with a bullish outlook. As you can see by the hourly chart of silver futures, the rally and partial retracement from January 4 to date have apparently completed waves 1 and 2 of a new uptrend. Wave 3 should begin soon and cause an upside acceleration.

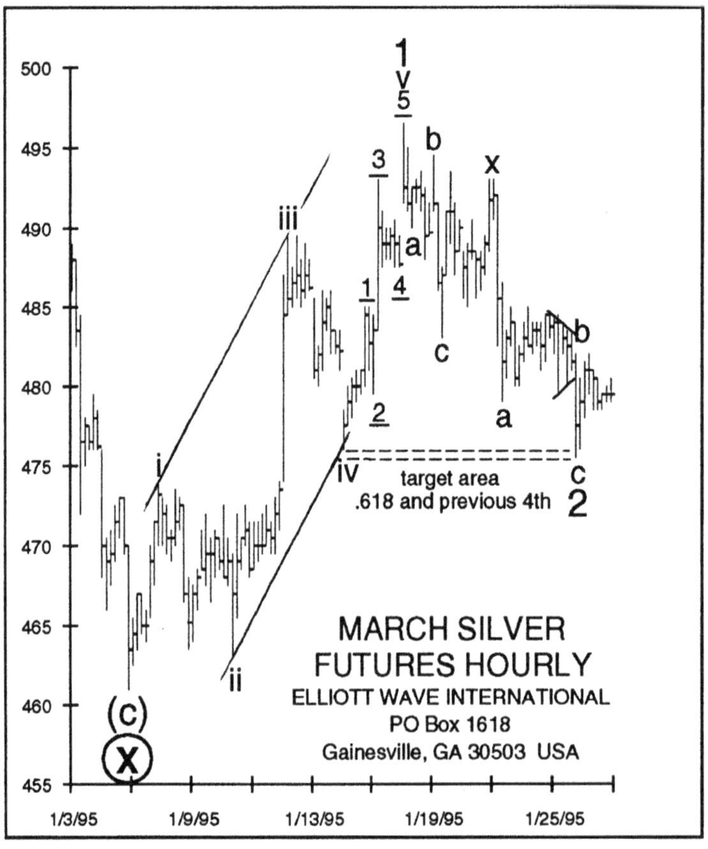

Important: The passage of the 8-week cycle low now allows us to identify the January lows in the precious metals complex as critical to a continued bullish outlook and these targets. A break of those levels ($372 in nearby gold, $4.60 in nearby silver and 98.77 in the XAU) will negate the bullish picture and indicate that the recovery from early December was just a flat correction within an overall downtrend.

Price and Time Targets

To reiterate our forecasts, gold should reach its long standing target of $460 + or - $5 in the second quarter of 1995. The XAU will climb to at least 149.42 and probably 180.72. Silver is more difficult to forecast. Its minimum target is $5.96, its best target based upon internal relationships is $6.84, but given its penchant for dramatic finishes, it could streak to two or three times that level in the final week or two of the advance (see discussion below).

As for timing, the January issue concluded, "The combined approaches indicate an April peak, possibly extending to no later than June, with the next cyclic low due in August-September." It is therefore of interest that silver's Fibonacci 13-year bear market of 1980-1993 and recovery to date mirror precisely its 13-year bear market of 1919-1932 and recovery of 1932-1935. The second chart, courtesy of Past Present Futures (1043 17th Street, Santa Monica, CA 90403), shows that the bear markets (using the centerpoint of a double top as the start time of the first bear market) each lasted 13 years, 1 month and 1 day. If the current recovery carries as long as that of 1932-1935, it will end in June 1995, the last month currently suggested by Fibonacci time sequences. An exact coincidence would cause a peak on June 26. As for the aftermath that EWT has been predicting for years, see the dashed lines in the final chart.

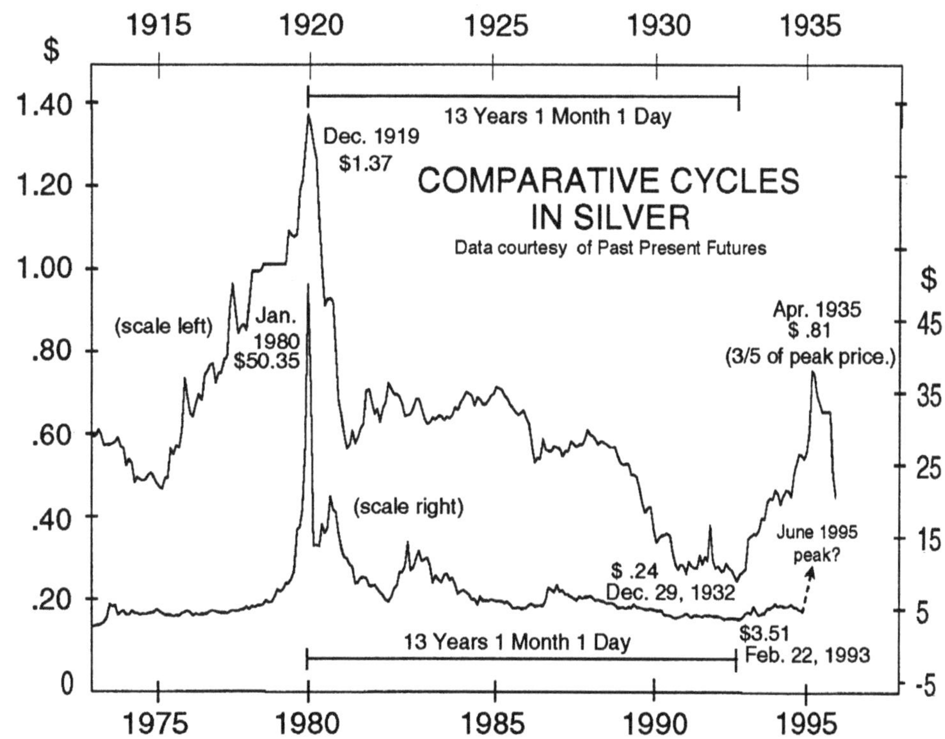

Targeting an Overrun

Since silver often runs up sharply at the end of a gold rally (just as it did in 1935, as shown on the chart), the chances of a repeat performance appear strong. Where might an overrun carry? Cross-time Elliott wave analysis may be helpful in answering this question.

The 1935 peak brought silver back to one cent below a Fibonacci 3/5 of its 1919 peak price. If that were to happen in 1995, it would peak at $29, which given the relatively weak recovery of today's market, appears impossible. A 2/5 ratio would project $19, which is also 5.41 times the $3.51 low of 1992 and therefore exactly a Fibonacci 1.618 times the 3.34 multiple of the 1932-1935 rise. Thus, if silver reaches $19, it will have risen a *multiple* equal to 1.618 times the multiple it gained from 1932 to 1935 and accomplished a *retracement* of the previous bull market equal to .618 of the retracement it made from 1932 to 1935. While there is no corroborating evidence to predict such a price for the second quarter of 1995, it is possible to say that *if* $19 is attained, it will mark the peak.

Gold and Climate

Subscriber C. G. Larson noticed a correlation between the ups and downs of the annual percentage change in the Earth's surface temperature with those of the price of gold. While we lack sufficient evidence to conclude that collective human emotion is linked to physical phenomena, we present the next chart as a point of interest. If our gold forecast is right, we'll have a chilly year or two some time in 1997-2000! [Or whenever gold undergoes its final wave of decline. – Ed.]

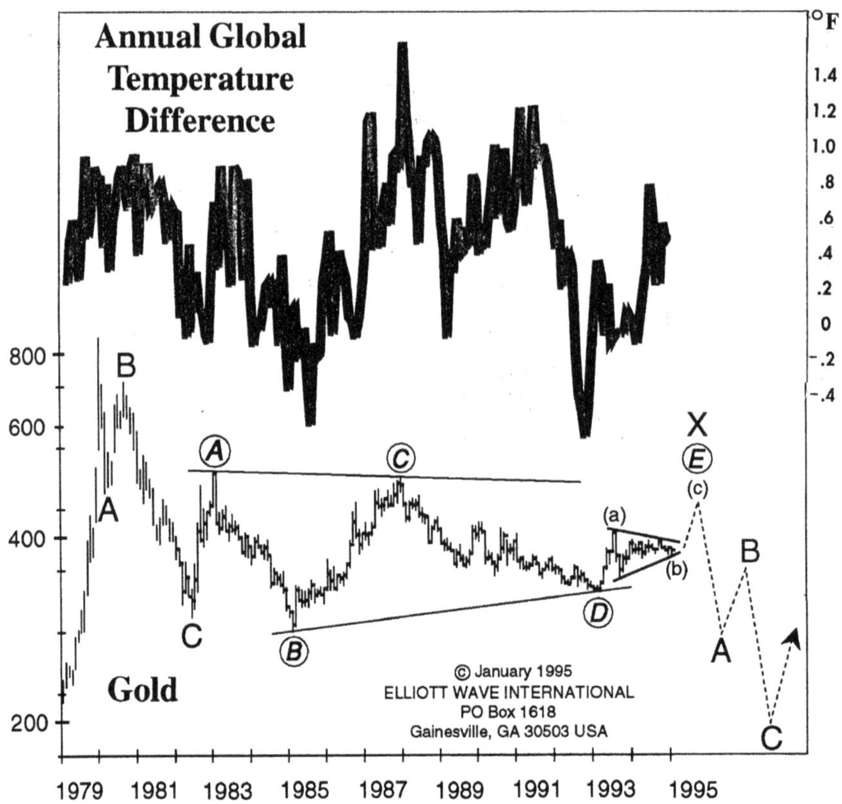

FEBRUARY 23, 1995

Dull though they have been, the precious metals should spring to life now that the 2-year cycle is lifting. Gold should advance to $460 (+ or -$5), probably by June. Silver and the XAU should rise into year-end 1995 and outperform gold by a substantial margin.

Gold & Silver

On January 31, the Gold & Silver Stock Index (XAU) edged to a new low by just two points and has rallied back sharply. Silver slid to a big new low, contrary to expectations. At the same time, gold *held above* its low of two months ago, thereby keeping intact the bullish picture on the entire precious metals complex as presented in the February issue. Evidence continues to accumulate to indicate a very important low in the making.

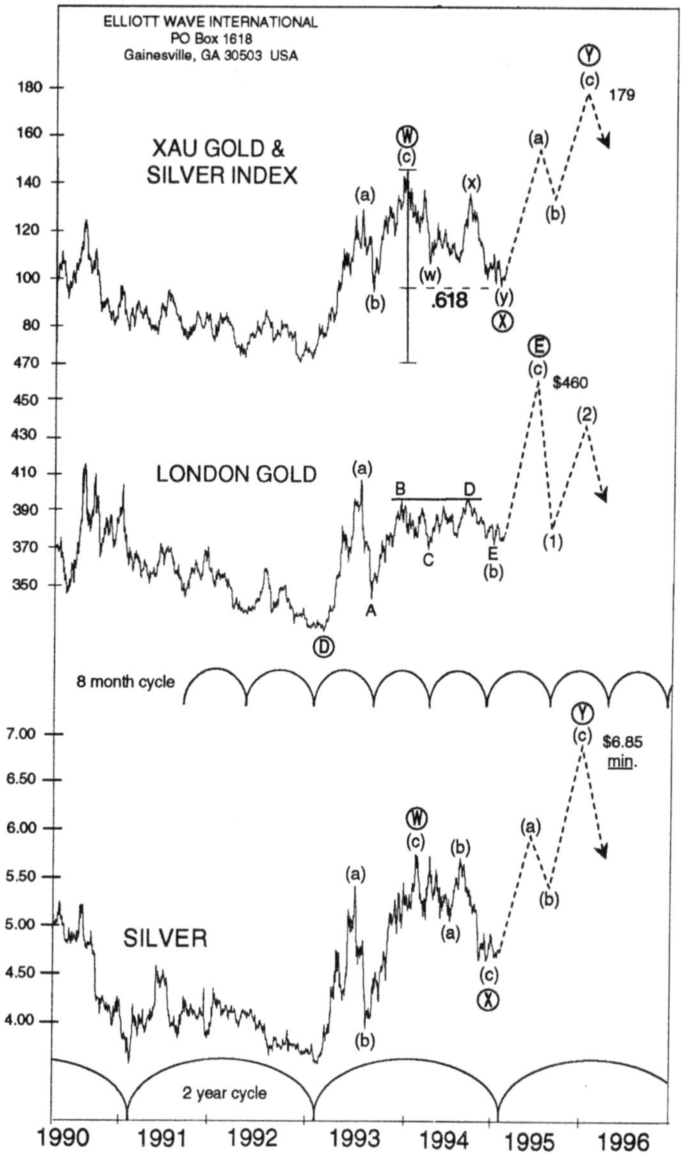

Elliott Wave and Cycle Analysis

The key to the recent behavior of precious metals is the 2-year cycle, which was displayed in the January issue. Its last two bottoms were particularly prominent in silver, which has been relatively weak at this low as well. As explained in the January issue, "This cycle is due to bottom and turn up in the first quarter of 1995." The last two cycle lows occurred in the month of February (with gold in 1993 slipping ever so slightly to a new low in the second week of March), and led to soaring prices. With the 2-year cycle lately struggling to push lower against a rising 8-month cycle, the metals should begin leaping out of first quarter lows as soon as the 2-year cycle exhausts its downward pressure. Based on past bottoms, this event should take place any day now, and certainly before the end of March.

As you can see, all three indexes still sport a bullish outlook, with silver relabeled to match the XAU. Though a new low in March for those two indexes cannot be ruled out, the XAU has already come within one point of an ideal target. The decline of the past 13 months retraces a Fibonacci .618 of the preceding 13-month rise at 95.68, and within the decline, the two subwaves are of equal length at 95.42. Either one of these relationships is worth betting on, so the two together are a powerful indication of support. The low so far is 96.66, just one point away, which is close enough. The same retracement percentage in silver, at which level waves 1 and 5 of (c) would also be equal, indicates strong support at $4.43 + or - .03. If the one-year bullish outlook is to remain intact, these levels should not be seriously penetrated.

Forecasting Details of the Next Advance

(This is a complex section, so take your time.) When the Elliott wave and cyclic outlooks for a market are the same, the probability of success for a forecast increases. Observe from the chart that the wave structures in silver and the XAU call for a *three*-wave advance, to be labeled Y. This advance would be expected to match fairly closely the rally labeled W that took place over the eleven months from February 1993 to January 1994.

The cyclic outlook is perfectly compatible with this Elliott wave outlook. The rising phase of the 2-year cycle calls for about one year of advance. It should be punctuated by a pullback generated by the declining phase of the 8-month cycle. The 8-month cycle bottomed most recently between early December and early January. Eight months later is August-September.

Combining these outlooks, wave (a) in the XAU and silver should take place into about June, wave (b) should unfold as a summer selloff into the 8-month cycle bottom in August-September, and then wave (c) should carry to a new high near year-end.

Now notice that when the XAU and silver last made new highs in wave (c) in early January 1994, gold did *not* make a new high. A repeat of that occurrence is indicated by the wave structure, as all gold needs to complete its bear market rally from 1993 is wave (c). While the patterns in the XAU and silver require a three-wave rally, that in gold requires only *one* rally, a post-triangle thrust (see text, p.42). Thus, gold should once again peak earlier than silver and the XAU, probably in or near June.

As discussed most recently in the September 1994 issue, the high for gold is expected to be very near $460/oz. The subsequent high in the XAU should be 179, where Y will equal W. Silver's minimum target is just under $7, for the same reason. Because dramatic endings are typical in silver, however, it could exceed that level substantially. An ideal scenario for all three metals is shown by the dashed lines on the chart, taking into account all this analysis.

MARCH 10, 1995 – INTERIM REPORT

Gold held its low as necessary, silver reached its downside target, and the XAU has suddenly become active. All these are good signs that the 2-year cycle in the precious metals has bottomed, so our bullish outlook remains intact.

MARCH 24, 1995 – INTERIM REPORT

Gold, silver, the XAU and bonds all remain on track.

MARCH 30, 1995

Silver exploded on the upside today, proving that the 2-year cycle turned up in early March, right on schedule. Gold is still expected to carry to $455. Silver and the XAU have already outperformed gold by a substantial margin (up 20% since the lows) and should continue to do so.

Gold & Silver

The March issue forecast an imminent bottom in the metals complex and sketched out a schematic of the expected rallies through 1995. The conclusion was emphatic: "The metals should begin leaping out of first quarter lows as soon as the 2-year cycle exhausts its downside pressure." As you can see in the charts, the rises in gold and silver from early to mid-March took a five-wave shape, which is a bullish sign for the larger trend. The pullback was composed of three-wave structures. Waves i and ii are over, and today wave iii began, producing a clas-

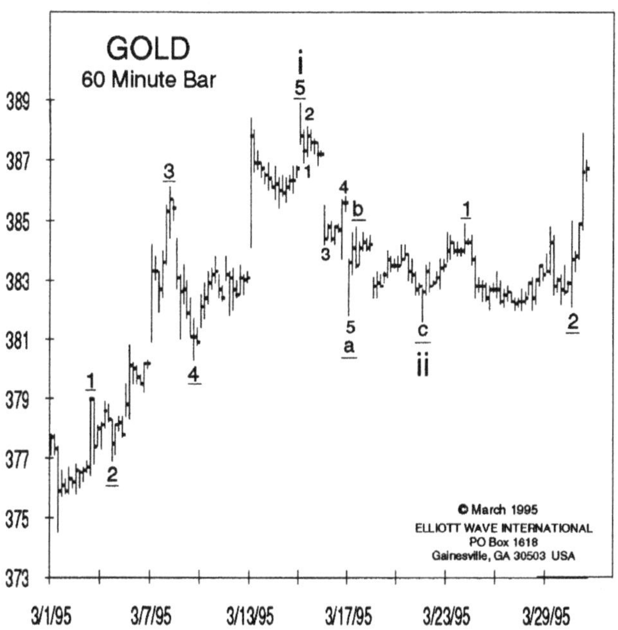

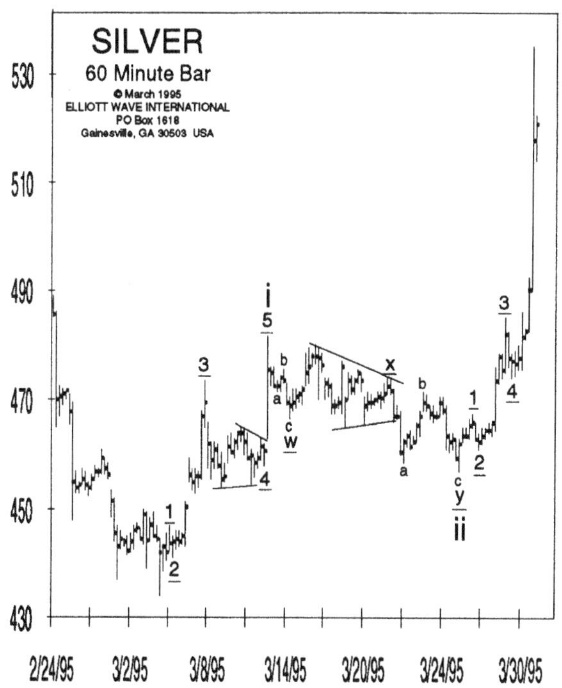

sic upside acceleration. Gold is still expected to rise to $455. EWT has continually forecast that silver and the Gold & Silver Stock Index (XAU) would move faster than gold during the advance. Such has certainly been the case so far, as silver and the XAU are both up 20% since the bottom.

APRIL 27, 1995

Silver has had little trouble following our forecast that it would "outperform gold by a substantial margin," as it exploded to a new 6-year high above $6/oz. Short term, gold, silver and the XAU completed five-wave advances for wave one and are correcting in wave two. Gold is still expected to carry to $455, so upside potential in the precious metals complex remains substantial.

Gold & Silver

The February 24 issue called for the precious metals to turn up sharply from first quarter lows. "This event could take place any day now," said EWT, "and certainly before the end of March." The XAU had already bottomed on January 31. Gold futures then bottomed on March 1, London gold ended its triangle on March 2, and silver bottomed on March 3. The more valuable information was the continuing indication that "silver and the XAU should outperform gold by a substantial margin." No kidding! Silver has already soared 39% to a new six-year high (see chart), and the XAU is up 31%. Gold hasn't even gotten above $400 yet. The better news is that gold still has an upside target near $455. If it keeps moving this slowly getting there, silver and the XAU will have lots of time to continue their powerful performances.

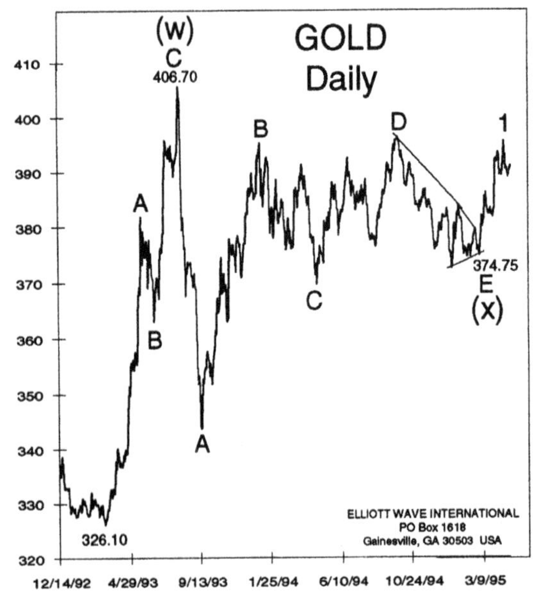

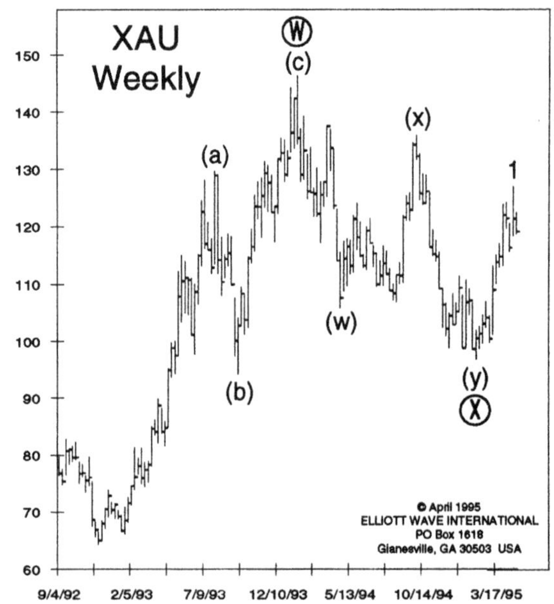

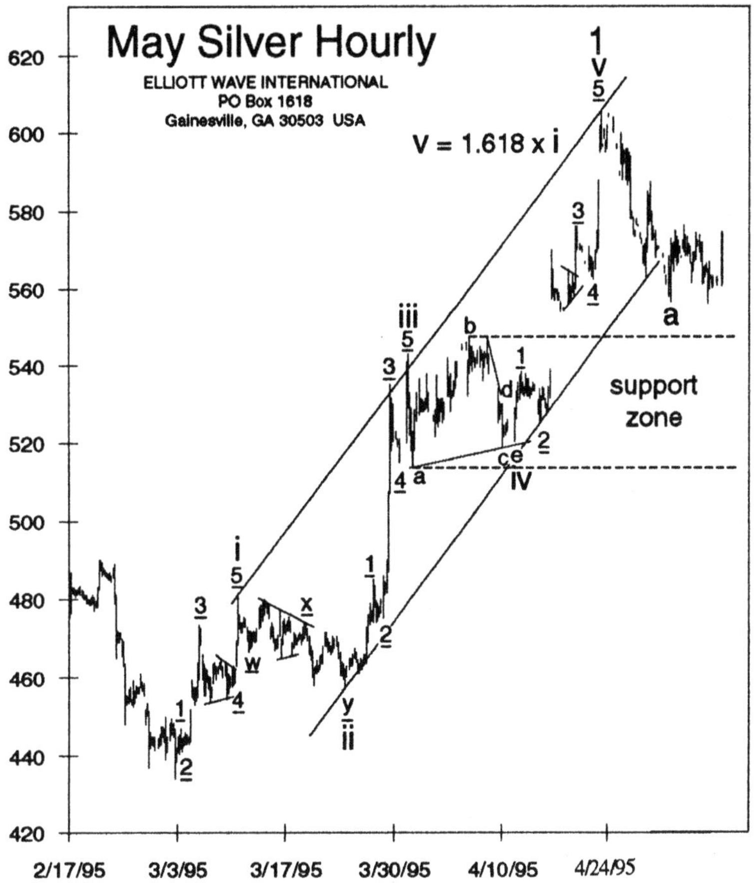

Elliott Wave Analysis

EWT has been labeling the corrective process in gold from the August 1993 high as a triangle wave (b) or (x) correction within an (a)-(b)-(c) or (w)-(x)-(y) advance. As you can see on the daily chart, wave E of the triangle was itself a triangle, the purpose of which was to mark time into the 2-year cycle low.

On a short term basis, the advance in the metals created impeccable five-wave structures for Minor wave 1 of "A", as you can see on the hourly chart of May silver. This impulse wave indicates that the larger trend is up. The current pullback on all three charts is wave 2, which in silver should find support in the area of wave iv between $5.18 and $5.53 basis July futures. The strongest point of support is $5.41, which is a .382 retracement. Wave 3 will be an even stronger advance.

The upside target for gold is still $455-$461 basis London fix. Recall that $461 is the level at which the entire advance from the 1993 low, wave Ⓔ, will be .618 times as long as the preceding advance, wave Ⓒ, which is a typical relationship in triangles. (For a chart of the big picture, see the March issue.) Another common relationship is for "w" and "y" waves to be of equal length. Wave (w) in 1993 rose $80.60. If wave (y) rises the same amount, it will top at $455.35, thus generating our high reliability target range. The XAU's target on the same basis is 179. Silver's target on the same basis is $6.85, but as EWT has expressed before, that is a minimum expectation, as silver often enjoys a near-vertical rise in the final week or so of an advance of this degree. For now, the ultimate target is irrelevant. It was hard work maneuvering for the low in silver and in the XAU as well; all we need do now is ride the wave.

Gold Stocks

Since 1993, gold, and perhaps silver, have been in rallies within long term bear markets, which is why their advances are three-wave structures called double zigzags. What about gold

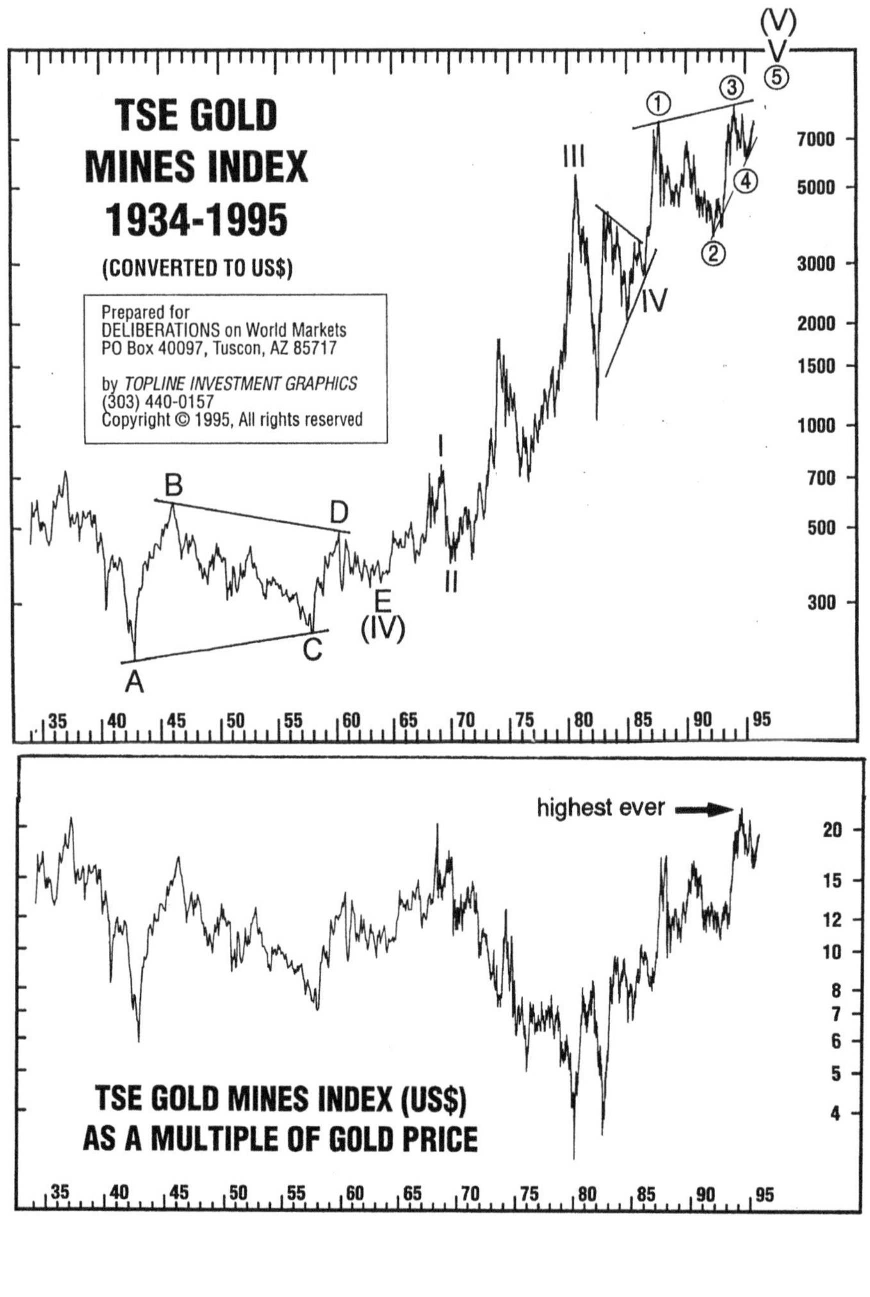

stocks? The long term chart of the Toronto Stock Exchange Gold and Silver Stock Index (many thanks to Ian McAvity of Deliberations for publishing the data) presents a stunning picture of a bull market dating from the 1960s. As you can see by our labeling, the index is in its final wave of advance. Wave V has been tracing out a diagonal triangle (see text, p.31) since 1986. A diagonal triangle is a wedge whose subwaves all comprise three-wave moves, which is why its advance from 1993 is perfectly in tune with those in gold and silver.

The current rise should take this index to a new all-time high and cap the entire three-decade-long bull market. Once that bull market is over, this index will fall 90% or more, right along with all other common stocks. If you were wondering whether gold stocks will be a refuge in the coming deflationary collapse, the answer is no. In fact, gold stocks recently reached their most overvalued level ever in terms of the price of gold bullion, as you can see on the bottom chart. What's more, as EWT has shown numerous times, gold itself is expensive relative to commodities! With the XAU, then, we do not own value; we own overpriced stocks that are simply still in a bull market that is likely to outperform the S&P. The gold stock mania is just another aspect of the Great Paper Asset Mania of the past thirteen years.

Perspective on Performance

We rode the wave in gold and silver in 1993 and we were bearish for the record-breaking bond decline in 1994, earning *The Elliott Wave Theorist* three #1 or #2 rankings in the Commodity Traders Consumer Report rating service. In 1995, we are once again making money in silver. Fine, a few critics say, but being bearish on the S&P for all this time means we missed out on big stock market profits, right? Wrong. From when EWT exited the stock market on October 5, 1987, we earned roughly 24% in T-bill interest during six years and have made 140% with timely investing in gold and silver stocks. The total of 164% is double the S&P's gain of 80%, including dividends, during the same time. In other words, *The Elliott Wave Theorist* not only outperformed the S&P when we were bullish in the 1980s, but our sector timing has outperformed the S&P during the entire time we have been "wrong" on it. Even our traders who sell short have made more trading bonds and metals than they have lost in the stock market in the past two years. So if you hear a critic focus only on whichever market or subsector *The Elliott Wave Theorist* is wrong about, you know he is just that, a critic, not someone who cares about a fair assessment.

To put even our stock market situation in perspective, had wave E fallen another 3% in December, our strategy would have had us 100% long stocks for much of the current rally. Putting up with low probability outcomes from time to time is the cost of making money in markets. For instance, our 7.5% loss in silver on the way down was an unavoidable component of an overall successful strategy that got us 200% invested [for rating services] at an average price of $4.56. The current stock market valuation is such a low probability as to be unprecedented in U.S. history. We can handle even that, because we know that when the stock market finally turns down, we will have our most profitable three years since 1984-1987 and probably ever.

Those who have their money in stocks at that time will ultimately find themselves in the position of Japanese investors today, as shown in the news photo.

REUTER PHOTO

Tokyo businessmen stand behind Shinto priest and pray for the market to rebound.

MAY 30, 1995

Gold, silver and the XAU all pulled back in wave 2 as required and should now be ready for wave 3 on the upside. Gold is still expected to carry to $455, silver to $6.85 and the XAU to 179. The first quarter lows in the precious metals complex are now very important and must hold if the bullish outlook is to remain intact.

Gold & Silver

Gold, silver and the Gold & Silver Stock Index (XAU) have followed our outlook closely. *The Elliott Wave Theorist* forecasted last month that these markets had "completed five-wave advances for wave one and are correcting in wave two." July silver futures were expected to retreat to the $5.18-$5.53 area, which was exceeded slightly in a slip to $5.12 that lasted a matter of minutes and left a spike reversal on the chart. The XAU completed a classic 60% retracement, and gold (not shown) fell back in an a-b-c. The setup is exactly the way we want it.

The precious metals now stand at a crucial crossroads. To remain true to the bullish outlook, they must very soon accelerate their uptrends in wave 3. Anything less than an upside acceleration will throw the outlook in doubt. Like a highly reliable weather pattern, a formation like this one communicates a high degree of *potential* but not certainty. Our risk, however, is well-defined, as the first quarter lows in all four charts must hold for the outlook to maintain its validity. If the patterns resolve as expected, gold should reach its long-standing upside target of $455-461, silver a minimum of $6.85 and the XAU 179.

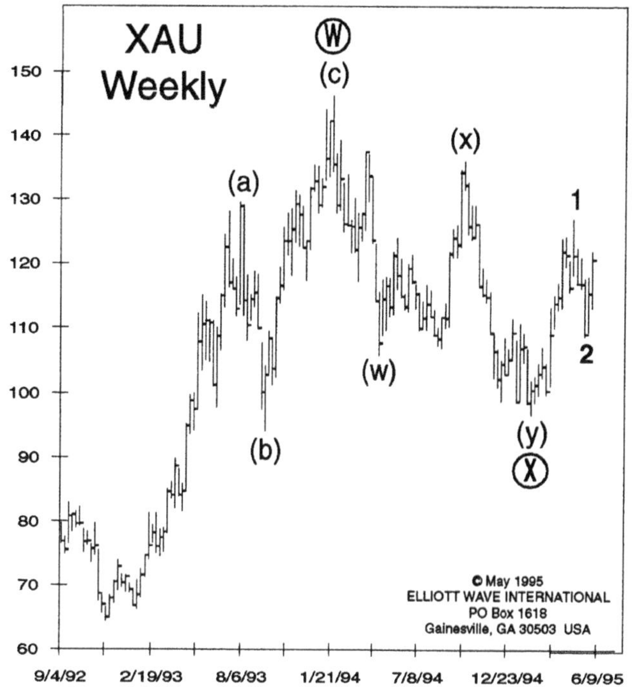

As you can see by the chart, the latest pullback in the metals may have brought our long-maintained Prechter Index of Gold Stocks (PIGS) to the termination point of a 16-month long triangle. This index is a different mix and weighting from the XAU. Its slightly weaker performance in March-May is merely making up for its slightly stronger performance going into the first quarter low. The two indexes are now in exactly the same position with respect to the April 1994 low; they have simply attained it via different patterns.

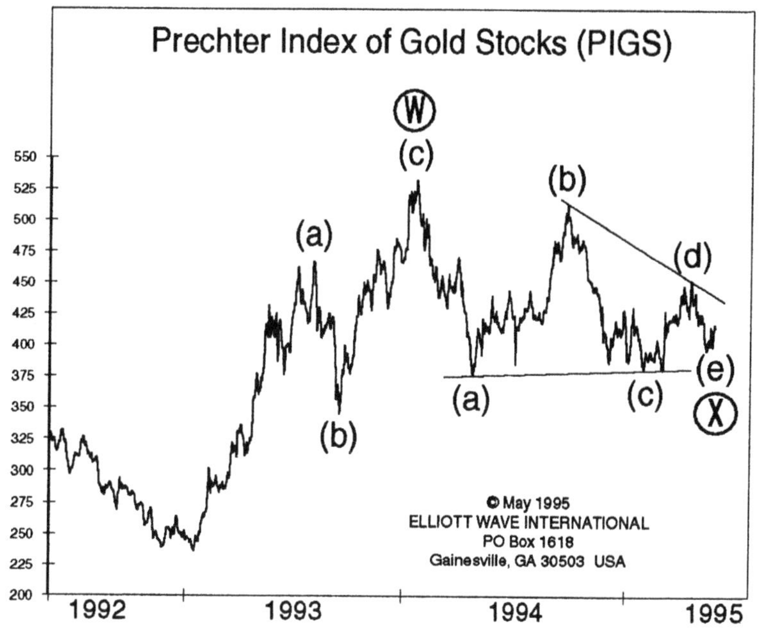

The Latest From A.J.

I called A.J. Frost this evening, and he had some terse words about the markets. "I am very, very bearish on the stock market," says the Grand Pontificator. "We are due for a tumble." Where to invest? "The only place to be is gold and gold stocks," he says," or maybe silver if you can handle the volatility. Regards to all!"

JUNE 30, 1995

The XAU has begun a correction, while gold and silver remain in corrections that began in April. A near term selloff should serve to resolve all three patterns. The intermediate term outlook remains bullish, as gold is still expected to carry to $455, silver to $6.85 and the XAU to 179.

Gold & Silver

The a-b-c rally in gold and the developing triangle in silver over the past six weeks (not shown) have the look of an upward correction that will lead to another selloff. The new 1995 high in the XAU in June was unconfirmed by gold or silver, a short-term bearish event for the precious metals complex. For these reasons, we must allow for a drop in silver to below $5 and in gold to the $370s to finish their multi-month corrective patterns. The 3-month cycle in silver shown in the Interim Report is two weeks late and may prove to be a non-event. The correction in the XAU that began last week might be shallow but could take the index as low as 105 if it is finishing off a larger triangle from July 1993. The essential message from all these developments is that you should consider the intermediate term uptrend to be intact but be positioned to survive a short term drop.

Gold is still expected to climb to $455 and silver to $6.85 later this year, so the intermediate-term outlook for the entire complex remains bullish despite the prospects of a short term selloff. Though the S&P is getting all the press in rising 24% from its December low, it is worth pointing out that the Gold & Silver Stock Index (XAU) rose 30% over the same period and 33.5% from its January 31 low.

At the Crest of the Tidal Wave

(excerpt only; see book for full text)

JULY 1995

Collector Coins

[Note: See previous analyses dated May 28, 1990 and August 1, 1990. – Ed.]

Collector coin prices had registered their secondary peak on April 3, 1990. Beginning on September 11, 1990, they crashed, driving the Numismatic News Coin Index down 30% in six months, signaling that the powerful bull market of decades' duration had ended. By 1993, the brokerage firms' coin funds had collapsed 70% in value. In the fall of that year, one large firm liquidated its entire portfolio at a no-minimum-bids auction.

At this point, EWT's forecast of "a 50% drop in the top end and as much as 95% in the lower tiers" has been substantially fulfilled. This article from September 1992 summarized the result well.

Philadelphia Inquirer — Saturday, September 5, 1992

Prices of rare coins soared after the 1987 stock market crash, as investors sought safe money havens with high rates of return. Rumors throughout the industry that Wall Street planned to create multimillion-dollar, rare-coin investment funds, and sell individual coins through brokers, created a veritable frenzy, with prices of many coins reaching record levels in 1989.

With the onslaught of the recession, a credit crunch among small businesses, and prices that had soared beyond reason, the values of virtually all coins, rare and common, began to tumble in late 1990. Almost overnight, few people wanted to buy them.

Today, many coins carry the same price they had 20 years ago—on average about a 40 percent drop since 1989, dealers say. In some cases, prices have plummeted significantly more. Common date Morgan silver dollars in mint condition, which fetched more than $800 each in 1987, now retail for $125 or less.

Wall Street, which launched a handful of rare-coin funds in 1989 and 1990, has cooled to the idea. A spokesman for Merrill Lynch & Co., which set up three rare-coin limited partnerships, said he did not even know if his company was still involved. An official with the funds later said they were closed to new investors. He declined to say how much value the funds had lost.

The *Numismatic News* Coin Price Index is a broadly based sample of coin grades and is thus representative of typical large coin portfolios. As you can see in Figure 19-3, this index has been in a relentless downtrend since the 1990 peak, having fallen 57.3% to date. The *Coin World* High-Grade Index, which made a higher high in 1990 as shown in [the chart in the August 1, 1990 article], has actually been weaker than the Low-Grade Index since then. Apparently the market has been suffering from an oversupply of the high grade issues that the brokerage firms bought in such quantity back in 1989-1990. Because *Coin World's* index of low grade coins (not shown) has yet to fall below its 1991 low, there is a bullish non-confirmation in place that could lead to another rally phase over the near term. A rally would reflect a heady optimism toward the economy that should accompany some excitement over the prospects for gold at the peak of its wave Ⓔ.

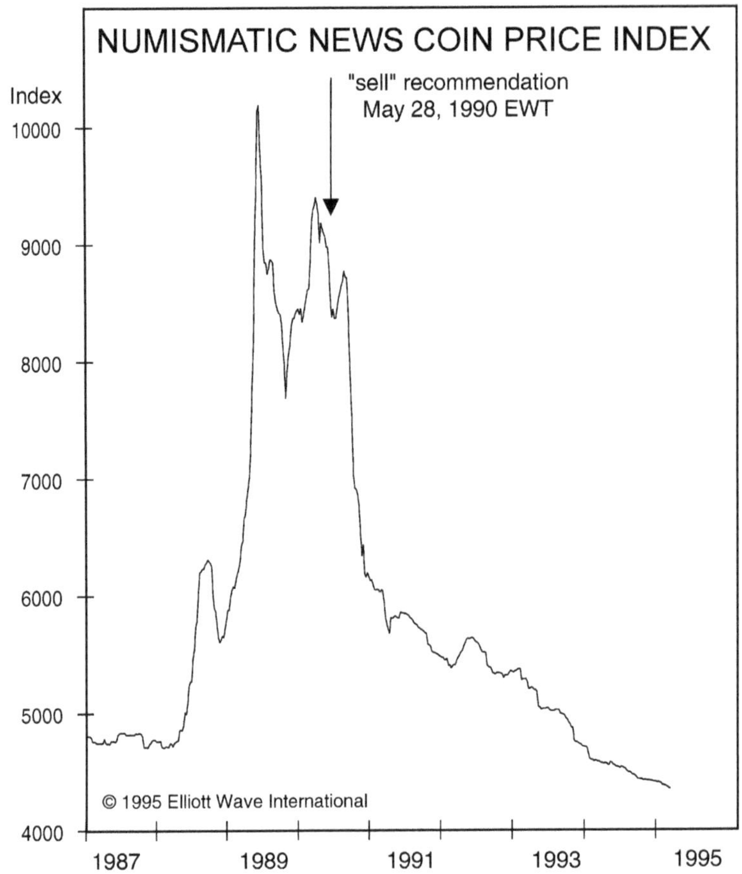

Figure 19-3

Has this selling, and the attendant bearish psychology, signaled the *end* of a short but violent bear market? No, because the long term picture remains bearish. Although coin prices have fallen a lot, premiums over bullion are not yet low. In fact, coin premiums remain higher today than they were when gold was cresting in a panic at $850/oz. in 1980! Consequently, there is still plenty of room for prices to fall even if bullion were to remain stable. If the analysis in Chapter 17 is correct that the upside potential for gold bullion is limited to $500/oz. while the downside potential is as low as $110/oz., the metallic value of collector coins, such as it is, is likely to fall a lot further, making it difficult for coins to close that premium gap. Thus, over the long term, the financial forces indicated for coming years imply that a long term bear market in collectible coins remains in force.

Thus, the balance of evidence indicates that, intermediate term rallies notwithstanding, the average coin is mired in its trend toward a 95% loss in value from the 1989 high. When collector coin prices ultimately hit bottom, the prices of 1989-1990 will be widely acknowledged as having been the product of delusion. After the [next] depression has run its course, coins will present a great buying opportunity for long term investment, and the forces that propel their prices upward will [have a chance to] return.

Analysis for Gold

By definition, the five waves of a triangle each subdivide into three waves. Examine the updated chart in Figure 17-5, and you will see that within wave X, waves Ⓐ, Ⓑ, Ⓒ and Ⓓ have each subdivided into (a)-(b)-(c) or (w)-(x)-(y). Wave Ⓔ should be no exception. Let's see how it is developing. Wave (a) of Ⓔ peaked in July 1993. Wave (b) of Ⓔ has been tracing out a contracting triangle, which is due to end soon. This is a thrilling development because a triangle precedes

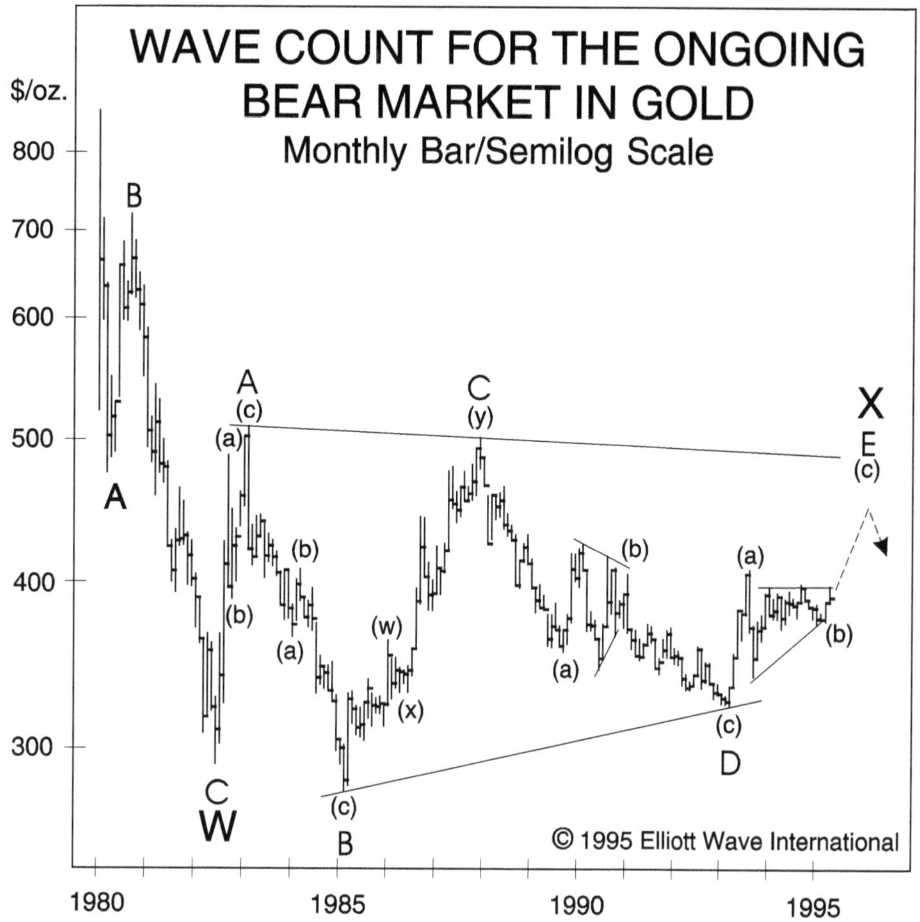

Figure 17-5

the final move in the next larger trend. Since only one rally from the 1993 low has occurred, the fact that only one remains guarantees that the advance will be three waves, thus precisely fitting the requirement for wave Ⓔ. This small event conforms to the entire Elliott wave analysis covering the past fifteen years.

That the rise from 1993 is part of a bear market rally rather than the start of a new bull market will be invaluable knowledge to have when wave Ⓔ tops in coming months. Because wave Ⓔ will cap a recovery pattern of Cycle degree, the bullish psychology attending its peak should be correspondingly intense. Mining issues should reach new all-time highs (see discussion below) and the price of silver should reach a new multi-year high, fueling bullish psychology. "Ⓔ" waves are often accompanied by supporting news, so look for a widely publicized "reason" to own gold at the top of wave Ⓔ.

A Price and Time Projection for the End of Wave X

It has now become apparent why waves Ⓒ, Ⓓ and Ⓔ have taken their time developing. Wave W lasted a Fibonacci **2** years, from 1980 to 1982. Wave X has been tracing out a triangle from 1982 that is fairly certain to last a Fibonacci **13** years, ending in 1995.

As the quotation from February 1992 shows, *The Elliott Wave Theorist* projected wave Ⓔ to carry to the **$420-$500** area before it even began. The specific target of $461 issued two years ago was derived from the observation that alternate waves in a triangle are often related by .618, and a peak at that level would make wave Ⓔ .618 as long as wave Ⓒ. Wave Ⓔ's internal structure now supports that target, because if wave (c) is to equal wave (a), a typical relationship, it would peak in the $450s basis London fix. This cluster makes the **$450-461** area an ideal target.

The entire pattern will remain intact as long as wave Ⓔ tops at or below the peak of wave Ⓒ, which gives it a 10% leeway beyond the ideal target. Wave (c) could stretch to just shy of 1.618 times the length of wave (a) and top at wave E's maximum potential near $500. In fact, given that waves Ⓐ and Ⓒ topped at $511.50 and $502.75 respectively, a rise in wave Ⓔ to near $500 would fit the shape of an "ascending triangle," which is a contracting triangle with a flat top.

To conclude, a rise to the upper half of the $400s is all that remains in gold's 13-year triangle pattern. From that high, and given that the low $500s are not exceeded, the Supercycle bear market will resume with a final Ⓐ-Ⓑ-Ⓒ decline for wave Y of the W-X-Y double zigzag pattern that began in January 1980.

Targeting the Final Low In Gold

The Elliott Wave Theorist's estimate for the ultimate low in gold has been firmly in place since 1982, when the parallel channel for the long term bull market (see Figure 17-1) was penetrated on the downside. Analysis from a few previous issues is excerpted below, demonstrating the long term consistency of this outlook.

> **$103.05** is the level of the bottom of the previous fourth wave of lesser degree if a five-wave sequence occurred from 1967 to 1980. **$111.63** is the point at which wave C from $720 will be 1.618 times as long as wave A from $850 to $474. These two points are generated by two of the most powerful calculations under Elliott, and the fact that they are very close together reinforces their validity.
>
> – February 8, 1982

> **$105** is a center for two Fibonacci multiples. $105 divided by 3 gives the fixed-price low of $35, while $105 multiplied by 8 gives $840, just $10 off the all-time high.
>
> – May 10, 1982

> The previous fourth wave of one lesser degree had a peak price at **$197.50**, an orthodox peak at **$179.50**, and a low at **$103.05**. [This] defines the most likely range for the end of the current bear market, [with] $105 (+ or - $5) as a sensible expectation.
>
> – March 7, 1983 and November 7, 1984

> Wave IV in bullion began at the orthodox top of wave III in March 1974 at $179.50 and ended in August 1976 at $103.05. Until the wave structure indicates otherwise, those prices still mark reasonable minimum and maximum expectations for the ultimate bear market low. For this reason, I have continually reiterated that ultimately gold should fall **below $200**/oz.
>
> – March 5, 1987

> The Wave Principle indicates that gold will fall at minimum to **below $200**/oz., the highest price within wave IV. Using the London fix as a basis, the peak was $197.50 and the low was $103.05. Fibonacci relationships within the bear market strongly support this area as a downside target.
>
> – February 1989

> According to our long standing target, gold still ultimately needs to fall to **below $200/oz.**, probably close to $100, in order to complete the Supercycle bear market that began in 1980.
>
> — October 26, 1990

> Elliott wave price projections still call for an ultimate low **under $200/oz.**, with an ideal target near **$105.**
>
> — January 29, 1993

The target range of $103.05 to $197.50 was provided by the wave structure, as that range encompasses the action of the previous fourth wave, wave IV, as shown by the dashed lines in Figure 17-10. Now that wave X is near its end, does our downside target have any additional support?

As illustrated in Figure 17-10, the main turning point prices in gold's bear market have been related by Fibonacci fractions. $511.50 is ⅔ of $850, $296.75 is ⅗ of $474 and ⅜ of $850, and $284.25 is ⅔ of $720.50.

With these relationships in mind, observe that the prices at the first two lows of the bear market are precisely related by Fibonacci ratios to the ideal downside target calculated by waves

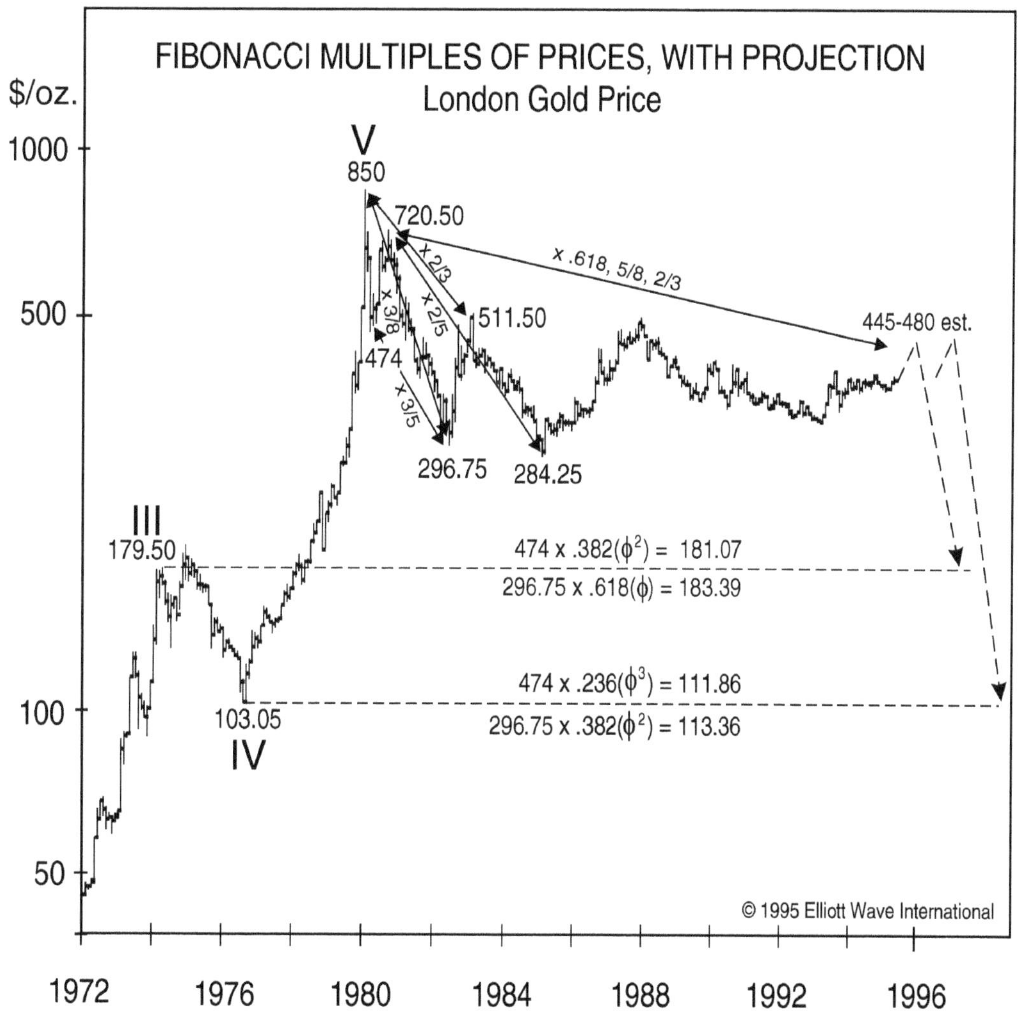

Figure 17-10

lengths. Here are the calculations: $474 x .236 = **$111.86**, and $296.75 x .382 = **$113.36**. How much closer to $112-113 could they be? (Using applicable fractions provides a few dollars' leeway, as $296.75 x ⅖ and ⅓ are $118.70 and $98.92.)

Raising the Fibonacci ratios by one level produces the following prices: $474 x .382 = **$181.07**, and $296.75 x .618 = **$183.39**. (Using applicable fractions provides a few dollars' leeway, as $474 x 2/5 and ⅓ are $189.60 and $158, while $296.75 x ⅗ and ⅔ are $178.05 and $197.83.)

Notice that while the first set of figures is very close to the $103.05 level that marked the end of wave IV in 1976, the second set is very close to the $179.50 level that marked the start of wave IV in 1974. These, of course, are the long-standing (as revealed by the quotes at the start of this section) boundaries of the downside target zone based upon the pattern of the 1967-1980 bull market.

An Academic Exercise

Given all the specific and extreme forecasts in this book, perhaps it would be humorous to say that I am going out on a limb here, but would it not make a mathematically beautiful pattern if within wave Y, wave Ⓐ were to bottom near $182 and wave Ⓒ near $112? In that way, all the Cycle degree lows of the bear market would be intimately related by Fibonacci ratios. An intervening rally for wave Ⓑ might carry to .382 of the value of wave Ⓑ in 1980 at $275 (or up to $20 higher, as suggested by the relationship of the $720.50 level to other turning point values). A rally to that area would also meet tremendous resistance at the 1982 and 1985 lows of $284.25 - $296.75. This scenario is depicted on the left side of Figure 17-11.

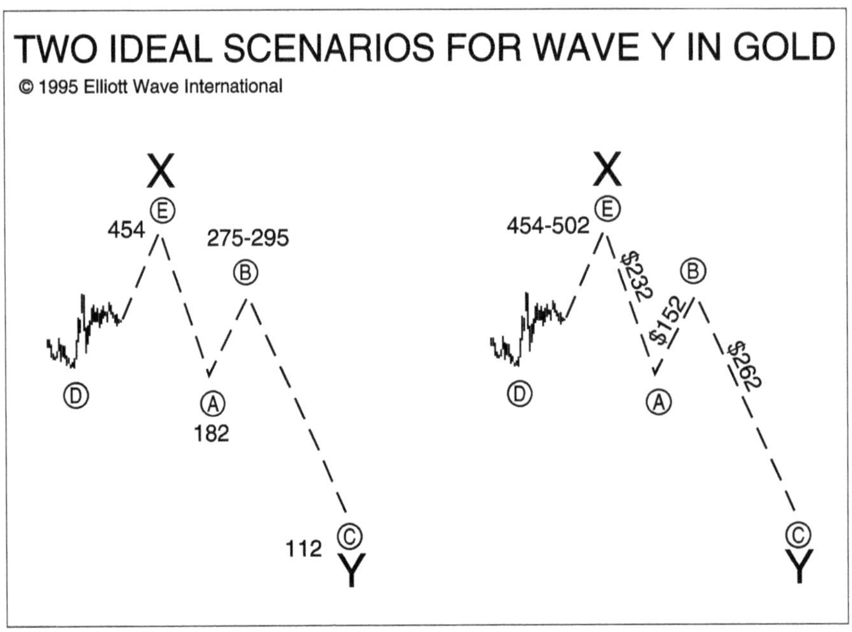

Figure 17-11

As an alternative possibility, the components of wave Y might travel .618 of the corresponding components of wave W, creating a duplicate of the entire structure multiplied by .618. The second most likely possibility, then, is that waves Ⓐ, Ⓑ and Ⓒ of Y will cover distances of $232, $152 and $262. These lengths will have to be projected (downward, upward and downward) from the high of wave Ⓔ when it occurs. If $112 is a reliable forecast for the ultimate low, then waves Ⓔ, Ⓐ, Ⓑ and Ⓒ under this scenario would end at $454, $222, $374 and $112. These levels will have to be adjusted by the amount that wave Ⓔ ends differently from $454. This scenario for wave Y is depicted on the right side of Figure 17-11.

To conclude, until the peak of wave Ⓔ is in, allowing a final adjustment, $112 remains the most attractive target for the final low. $182 is the next most attractive target, which, if it does not mark the final low, has an excellent probability of marking a Primary degree low on the way down. All targets listed herein should be given a few dollars' leeway. Also, they are based upon the London fix prices, which would be exceeded somewhat by intraday futures prices.

Time Considerations

As you can see in Figure 17-12, Fibonacci durations have been evident throughout the period of free market trading in gold. The 13-year advance from 1967 to 1980 subdivides into two periods of 8 and 5 years at the December 31, 1974 peak, which preceded the largest correction of the bull market. Since the bear market began, every major wave has terminated a Fibonacci number of years from the all-time high. From 1980, 2 years later was the low of wave W, 3 years later was the high of wave Ⓐ, 5 years later was the low of wave Ⓑ, 8 years later was the high of wave Ⓒ, and 13 years later was the low of wave Ⓓ. Wave X has taken its time so that it can last 13 years from the 1982 low.

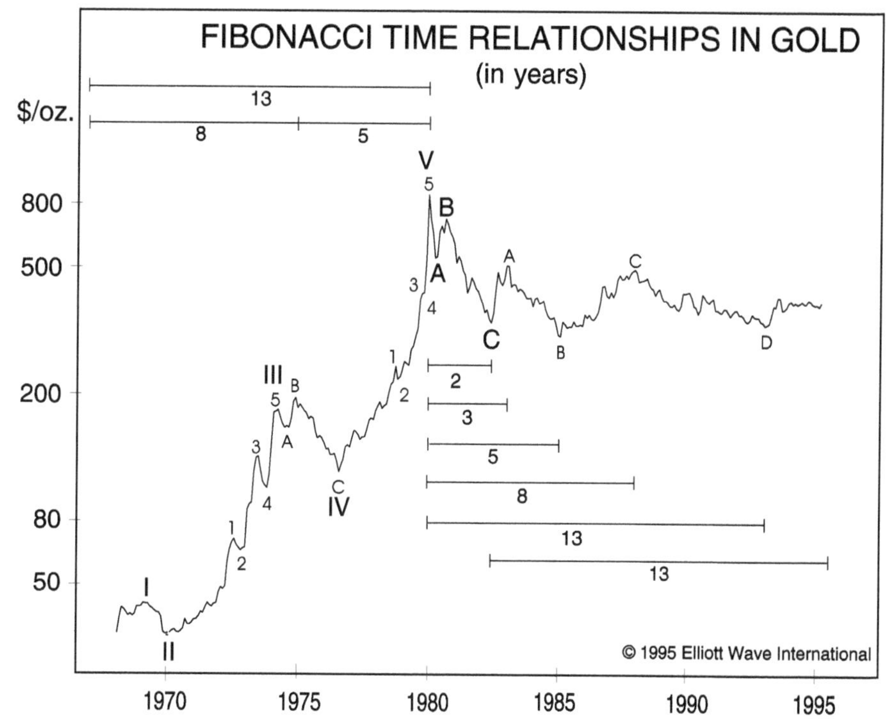

Figure 17-12

While wave X is far enough along to suggest that it will terminate in 1995, there is no way to forecast the length of wave Y. It could be as brief as 2 years, matching wave W; it could last 3 years, bottoming with several investment market cycles in 1998. One attractive termination date for wave Y would be *New Year's Day of 2001 (± a month)*. That way, it will have lasted a fat 5 years from 1995, a lean 21 years from the 1980 peak, and 34 years from the 1967 bottom. Two of gold's biggest turns, in 1974/5 and 1980, came at the cusp of the year, so there is precedent for a turn at that time. [Note: Gold registered a low at $253.50 on February 16, 2001. – Ed.]

These are simply ruminations, as time forecasts at this juncture must be considered unreliable and should be given zero weight relative to pattern and price relationships. If those factors fall in place at a Fibonacci time interval, then the time factor will add some weight to the picture.

Important Caveat

The gold pattern is analytically complex, adding a measure of uncertainty in the outlook. The successful application of every market forecasting approach requires an immediate response to probability-altering developments. At least the Wave Principle provides a knowledge that actually allows one to recognize such developments, mitigating the consequences of any inaccurate conclusion.

If in coming months gold exceeds the 1987 high by as little as $20, it will negate this entire analysis, as neatly packaged as it may appear at the moment. Nor is that level far away, being only 15% above where gold is expected to climb. If the forecasted low prices do not come to pass because the bear market is already over, this section will at least serve the purpose of pointing out the Fibonacci price relationships in gold's bear market as they relate to the previous turning points of $103.05 and $179.50, which began and ended wave IV.

Negation of an analysis does not automatically mean a complete reversal of the resulting stance. For instance, the upper interpretation shown in Figure 17-13 would imply a move

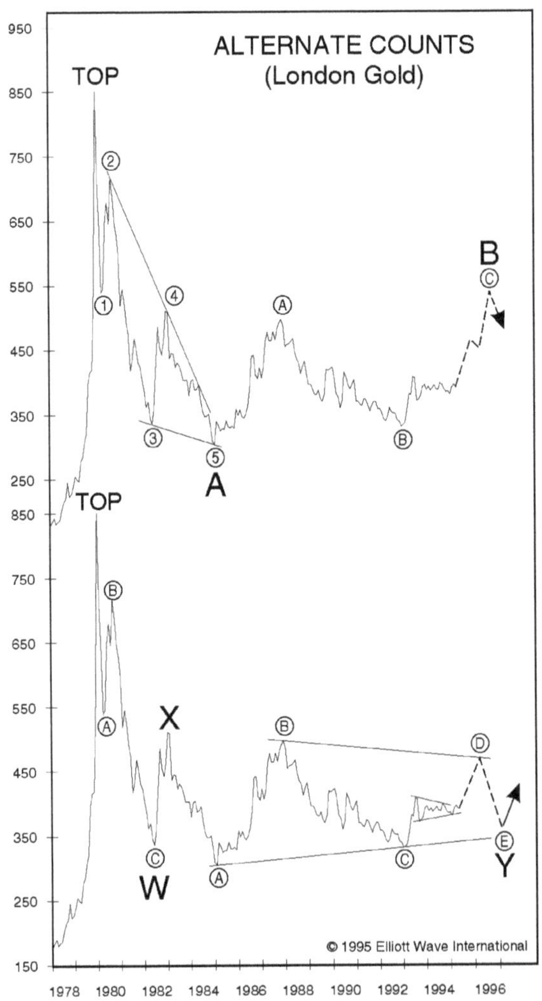

Figure 17-13

somewhat beyond $500, but only by $50-$150, in which case the long term bearish outlook would be delayed but not contraindicated. As shown in the lower half of Figure 17-13, it is also acceptable to count a "double three" nearly completed, where Y is a triangle that is currently in wave Ⓓ. So gold could finish its bear market from 1980 without falling to a new low, and soar thereafter. With silver having fallen 93%, this possibility must be entertained. The market is precise, but it is also a living thing, not a machine. As such, it always has options open, even within the formal structure of the Wave Principle.

A Long Term Analysis of Gold Stocks

Perhaps you have heard the idea that gold mining stocks are not only an inflation hedge, but also a deflation hedge. (Translation: gold stocks will never go down.) This thesis is based upon the observation that shares of gold mining companies soared during the 1930s. This fact is misleading absent the knowledge of two pertinent details. First is the fact, as market analyst Ian McAvity has pointed out, that gold stocks barely budged during the 1929-1932 bear market. Homestake's high for 1929 of 11½ and low for 1932 of 13⅞ reveal little net gain, while Dome Mines was unchanged for the period. It was during the subsequent bull market that gold stocks soared. Second, it is imperative to know that the Federal government in those years maintained a fixed price for its currency (i.e., its IOUs) at $20.67 per ounce of gold. While the deflation caused all other commodities to collapse in dollar value from 1929 to 1933, the relative value of gold remained flat because its "price" in dollars was fixed. Thus, there was no reason for gold mining stocks to participate in the crash. In January 1934, the government devalued the dollar against gold to $35 per ounce (approximately a 1.618 multiple), and mining companies benefited from the windfall dollar profits despite an environment of extremely low inflation. Even with that benefit, the average gold stock from 1932 to 1936/38 rose no more than the five times in value that the DJIA did! Today, the government does not fix the price of its currency to gold and is unlikely to do so any time soon. Without artificial constraints, gold should fall nearly as much in dollar terms as any other commodity during the coming deflation, and gold stocks are likely to fall even more. An analysis of the long term wave pattern for gold shares confirms this conclusion.

Figure 17-14 shows the sixty-year Elliott wave history of the Toronto Stock Exchange Gold Mines Index. This is a thrilling chart. Look at the beautifully formed contracting triangle that took place from January 1936 to November 29, 1963. This can be none other than a fourth wave according to the rules of the Wave Principle. By its size, it is unquestionably of Supercycle degree, so is labeled wave (IV). From the triangle's termination in 1963 commenced an excellent five-wave impulse, labeled I-II-III-IV-V. Each advance in turn sports a five-wave subdivision.

Wave IV was either a contracting triangle or a zigzag. Either way, wave V is tracing out a diagonal triangle, which is an overlapping five-wave structure that takes a wedge shape. Within this pattern, wave ④ is probably complete. The last thing remaining is one rise to a new all-time high. Such a rise will complete waves ⑤, V and (V). Diagonal triangles portend major, violent reversals.

Notice how perfectly this pattern and outlook fit those for gold. Both charts show a low in 1982 followed by a recovery. While gold has gone sideways in a triangle, gold stocks have achieved new highs on each upward thrust. The current outlook for gold calls for one last rally to the $450-$500 area, then a deep decline of over 75%. The current outlook for the TSE Gold Mines Index calls for one last rally to a new all-time high, then the biggest collapse in

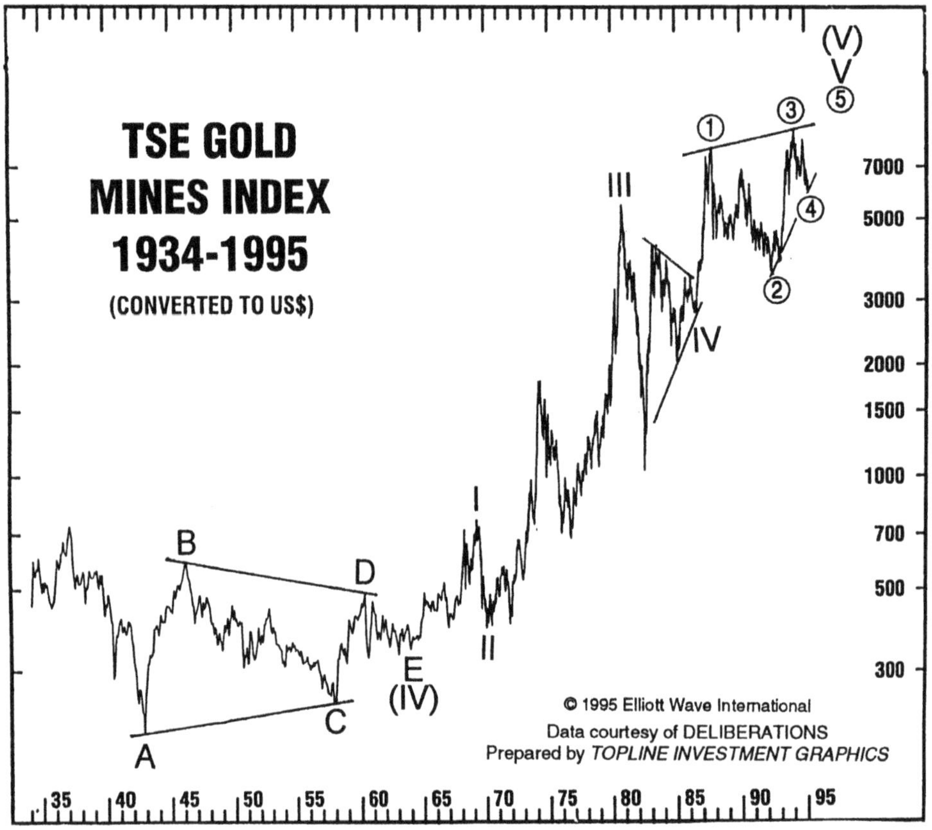

Figure 17-14

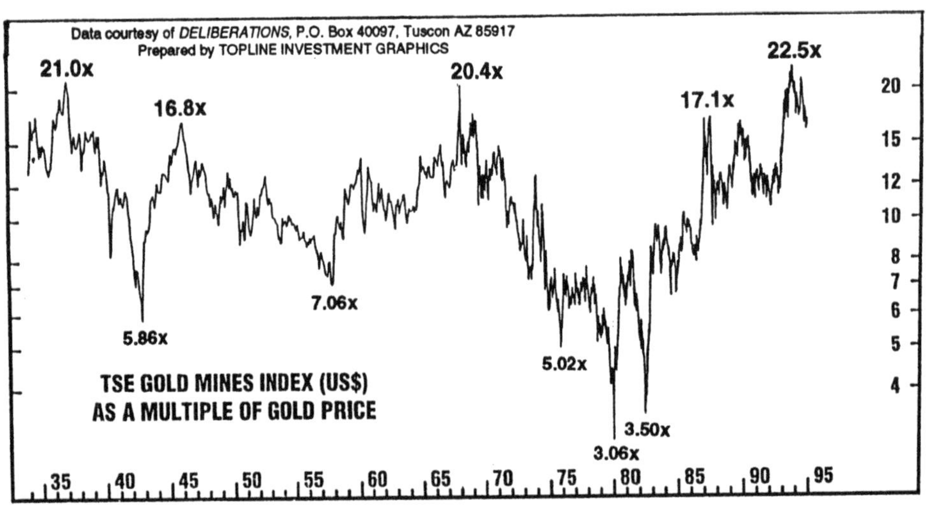

Figure 17-15

its history. If gold's triangle ends in 1995, it will have been a Fibonacci 13 years long. If the stock index were to peak in 1997, its wave (V) will have been a Fibonacci 34 years long. The ideal scenario, then, is for a peak in gold in 1995 ±1 year followed by a peak in mining stocks in 1997 ±1 year. (1996 is likely.)

How low will the TSE Gold Mines Index fall? Support, as with so many markets discussed in this book, is the span of the preceding fourth wave of one lesser degree, which in this case is wave (IV). Wave (IV) covered a range from 205 to 735. This target range portends a decline of at least 90% and possibly as much as 98% for the TSE Gold Mines Index. Favored for a target is the low for wave E of the triangle, which occurred at 344.60, although whenever the index gets below 735, it should be scrutinized closely for signs of a bottom.

This analysis answers the question, "Can we find refuge from the coming deflation by investing in gold stocks?" The answer is no. These equities should experience the same kind of intense deflation that occurred from 1980 to 1982. Look what the TSE gold stocks did in those two short years: They fell 81%. Is a drop of 90%-plus over a longer period of time so unrealistic?

The Valuation of Gold Stocks Relative to Gold

Take a look at Figure 17-15, which depicts the value of Canadian (and by extension, North American) gold stocks relative to gold bullion. First, notice that gold stocks recently registered their highest relative valuation of the entire century, in January 1994. As previously shown, gold itself is expensive relative to commodities and silver, so if gold stocks are at a record valuation relative to gold, then how expensive are gold stocks? The answer is: very.

Now observe that the high and low relative valuations of the TSE Gold Mines Index have always occurred within a few months of major tops and bottoms in the stock market. Gold stock valuation peaked in January 1937; the DJIA peaked in March 1937. Gold stock valuation peaked in January 1946; the DJIA peaked in May 1946. Gold stock valuation peaked in March 1968; the DJIA+Value Line peaked in December 1968. Important stock market lows have corresponded with lows in gold stock valuation as well. The DJIA bottomed in April 1942; gold stock valuation bottomed in October 1942. Gold stock valuation bottomed in June 1982; the DJIA bottomed in August 1982 (in inflation-adjusted terms). This confluence of trends indicates that gold stocks are not purchased solely in a reflection of the relative attractiveness of gold. They are traditionally added to portfolios during common stock bull markets, to the point that they become highly overvalued relative to the price of bullion.

From the 1982 low, gold stock valuation has continued to move in tandem with the DJIA. It soared to a peak in 1987 and crashed, then recovered and pulled back into 1990, all just as the Dow did. It has since followed the continuing rise of wave ⑤ in the DJIA. If the DJIA peaks in 1995 as Chapter 4 suggests, then the relative valuation of gold stocks should reach a final high in 1995, plus or minus a year. The all-time high valuation of January 1994 may stand, though it is more likely to be exceeded as part of the psychological peaking process in gold's 13-year triangle. Either way, the ultimate high in gold stock prices will undoubtedly, and to "disaster-hedged" investors ironically, occur within months of the final high in the Dow Jones Industrial Average.

If an inflationary period were looming, as in the late 1960s, the current high ratio would be irrelevant. A soaring precious metals market would overpower the drop in gold stocks' relative valuation so that gold stocks would still rise, as they did from 1968 to 1980. However, with so many charts pointing to deflation and to a fall in the price of gold, this scenario appears unlikely. A drop in the value of gold stocks relative to gold should prove to have a devastating effect on the prices of those stocks.

Gold Is Still Money

Have you ever traveled abroad and taken a look at the local currency and wondered how the citizens of that country could take seriously what looks like "Monopoly money?" I've got news for you: You're using the same stuff. Monopoly money is the money over which some government has a monopoly. It is the currency of the realm only because the state makes it illegal to use any other type.

Promissory notes issued by a state and declared the only legal tender are always doomed to depreciate to worthlessness because of the natural incentives and forces associated with governments. A state cannot resist a method of confiscating assets, particularly one that is hidden from the view of most voters and subjects. By extension, it is unreasonable to advocate a standard for such notes, which is simply a state's promise that its currency will always be redeemable in a specific amount of something valuable, such as gold. A gold *standard* of this type is only as good as the political promises behind it, reducing its value to no more than that of paper. It could be argued, in fact, that a state-sponsored gold standard is far more dangerous than none at all, as it imbues citizens with a false sense of security. Their long range plans are thus built upon an unreliable promise that the monetary measuring unit will remain stable. Later, when the government's "IOU-something specific" becomes, as Colonel E.C. Harwood put it, "IOU nothing in particular," reliability disappears and the arbitrary reigns. Although the populace tends to retain its confidence in the currency for awhile thereafter, the ultimate result is chaos.

The only sound monetary system is a voluntary one. The free market always chooses the best possible form, or forms, of money. To date, the market's choice throughout the centuries, wherever a free market for money has existed, has been and remains precious metal and currency redeemable in precious metal. This preference will undoubtedly remain until a better form of money is discovered and chosen. Until then, prices for goods and services should be denominated not in state fictions such as dollars or yen or francs, but in specific weights of today's preferred monetary metal, i.e., in grams of gold. Anyone might issue promissory notes as currency, but the acceptance of such paper certificates would then be an individual decision, and risks of loss through imprudence or dishonesty would be borne by only a few individuals by their own conscious choice after considering the risks. Critical to the understanding of the wisdom of such a system is the knowledge that private issuers of paper against gold have every long run incentive to provide a sound product, just as do producers of any product. As a result, risks would be minimal, as the market would provide its own policing. Thievery and imprudence will not disappear among men, but at least such tendencies in a free market for money would not have the potential to be institutionalized, as they are when a state controls the currency. From a macroeconomic viewpoint, occasional losses resulting from dishonesty or imprudence would be extremely limited in scope, as opposed to the nationwide disasters that state controlled paper money has facilitated throughout history, which have in turn had global repercussions. As *Elliott Wave Principle* put it, "That paper is no substitute for gold as a store of value is probably another of nature's laws."

That being said, it is also true, and crucial to wise investing, that markets come in both "bull" and "bear" types. Being a "gold bug" at the wrong time can be very costly in currency terms. For fifteen years, gold and silver's dollar price trends have confounded the precious metals enthusiasts, who for the entire period have argued that $1000 gold and $100 silver were "just around the corner" and that inflation was (and is) due to take off again "any time now." It hasn't happened. With deflation due to gain the upper hand in the investment markets, it is not likely to do so soon, either, short term rallies notwithstanding.

In contrast to the one-note approach, which has had an immense opportunity cost over the past decade and a half, competent market analysis can make your financial decisions timely and profitable. When the end of the deflation arrives, a swift shift to gold will be essential. Its low will present the buy of a lifetime, your last chance to put wealth into the form of real money at an advantageous price.

JULY 28, 1995

The correction in the precious metals complex is near an end. Sentiment measures indicate explosive upside potential. Upside targets remain $455 for gold, $6.85 minimum for silver (with a blowoff to much higher levels probable) and 179 for the XAU.

Gold & Silver

The July issue summed up the outlook for precious metals this way:

> The a-b-c rally in gold and the developing triangle in silver over the past six weeks have the look of an upward correction that will lead to another selloff. We must allow for a drop in silver to below $5 and in gold to the $370s to finish their multi-month corrective patterns. You should consider the intermediate term uptrend to be intact but be positioned to survive a short term drop.

The "short term drop" materialized immediately, with silver slipping to $4.98/oz. and gold to $383/oz. so far basis front-month futures. While each of those lows might be taken out by slight margins in the next few days, intermediate term corrective forces are reaching termination. Indeed, despite all the talk that gold has a "ceiling" at $400 and the deep skepticism about the potential for silver, the precious metals show unmistakable signs of being poised for a dramatic upside run. Let's examine the evidence.

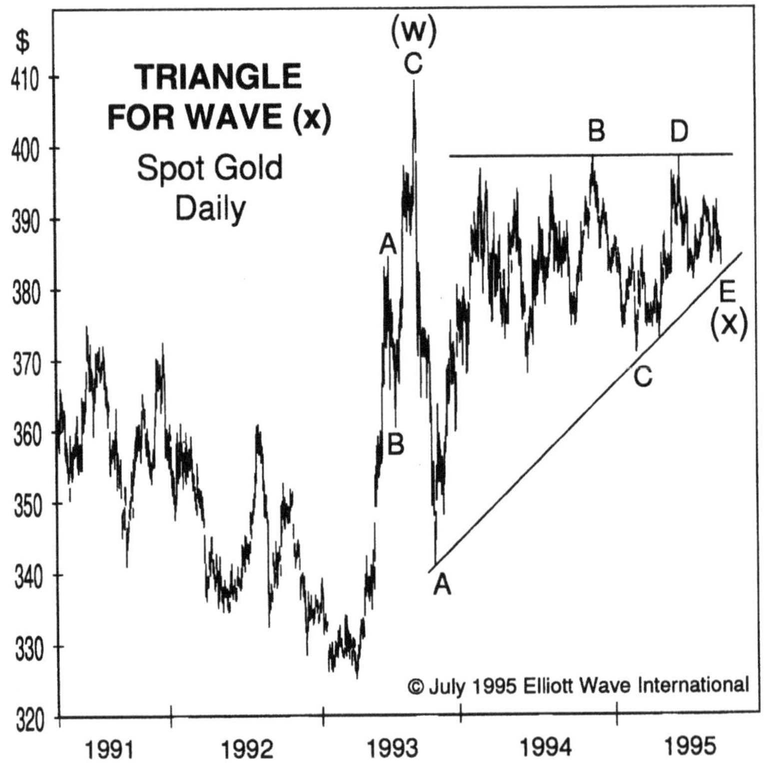

The chart of spot gold reveals a two-year triangle that is days from completion. Long triangles appear in the precious metals during periods of monetary complacency. The stock market over past two years has reflected optimism toward economic matters, and the gold market has done the same. That complacency is about to change rapidly to concern. Triangles portend thrust, so the coming advance in gold should be swift, taking place in a matter of a few months.

Indicators of investor sentiment unequivocally support a bullish outlook. The Commodity Futures Trading Commission tracks the positions of three groups of speculators: small traders, large speculators, and commercials (i.e., businesses involved in precious metals production, distribution and sale). As our daily on-line metals specialist Peter Rehmer points out, all three categories of market participants are telegraphing a bullish message. Small traders have their lowest level of long positions in gold since before the March rally, while their net long position in silver, following eight months of persistent selling, is the lowest in over seven years. Large speculators (not shown), who at minor lows often get the direction right, have become so disillusioned after two years of sideways action that they hold a very low level of longs. Indeed, their silver position is a mere one-tenth of what it was just ten months ago! The dearth of longs is balanced by the group that typically holds substantial short positions to hedge their inventory: the commercials. This group is most often correct on its bets and today holds its smallest net short position in the metals in over three years, as shown in the chart. In an extraordinary short-term development, commercials did *not* take advantage of the July rally to increase their silver hedges, which means that they have reason to believe that their stocks

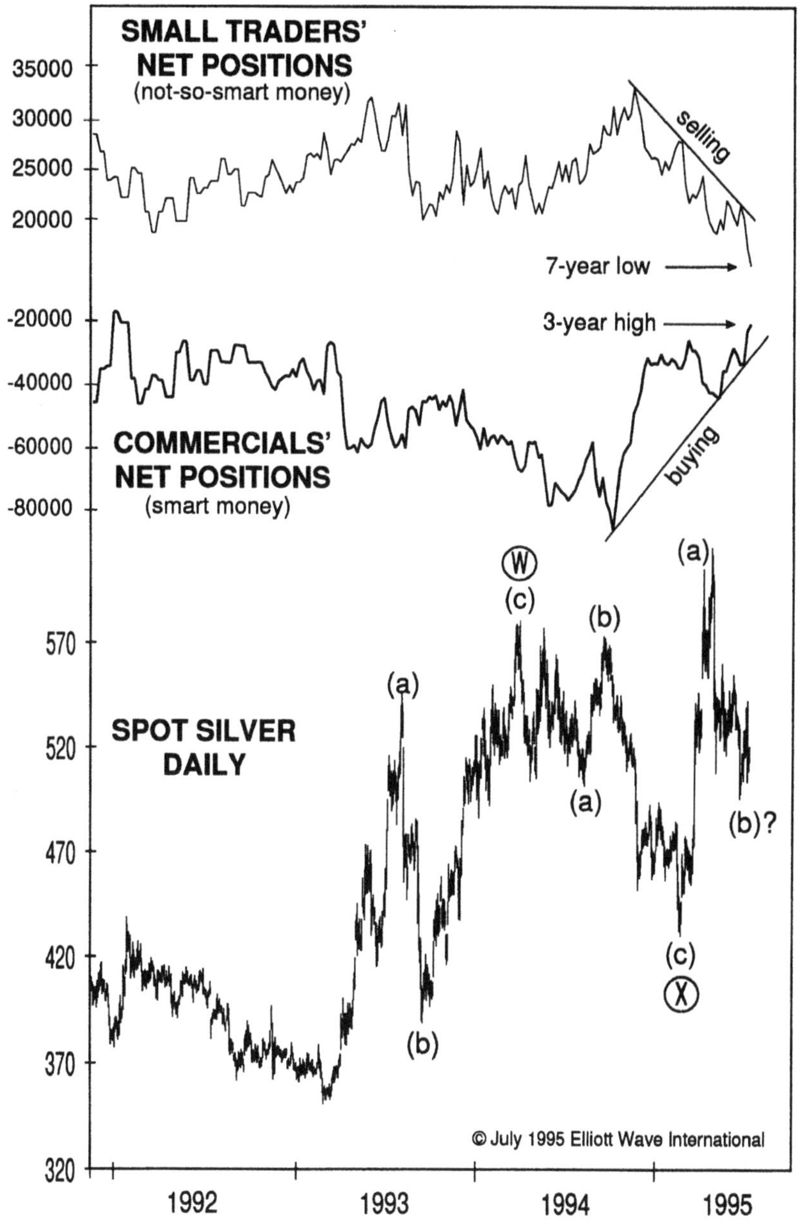

of silver are valued very cheaply and will rise in value in the not-too-distant future.

Other sentiment indicators reflect the same lack of enthusiasm for the metals among traders. In July, the ten-day averages of the Daily Sentiment Index (from Jake Bernstein) for both gold and silver reached their lowest levels since February-March at the last market bottom. Dave Allman observes (see next chart) that in the May-June rally in the XAU, more precious metals mutual fund owners *sold* the rally than bought it! (At the 1993 high, they were "in for the long haul," don't you know?) This behavior is in direct contrast to the trend-following behavior of the preceding two years and indicative of the kind of sentiment shift that usually accompanies major bottoms. In addition, premiums on gold futures options have fallen to extraordinarily low levels as traders conclude that gold will go sideways forever. As Business Week sums up the consensus, "Any rallies will serve as an excuse for producers to sell, driving prices back down...mining stocks will probably trail the broad market...don't look for any payoff soon from buying gold or gold funds...mining stocks should be viewed with caution...barring some huge surprise such as war, financial panic or surging inflation, gold will probably *stay within a narrow range just below* $400, analysts say." As always, this "prediction" is simply a description of the past. The net psychology

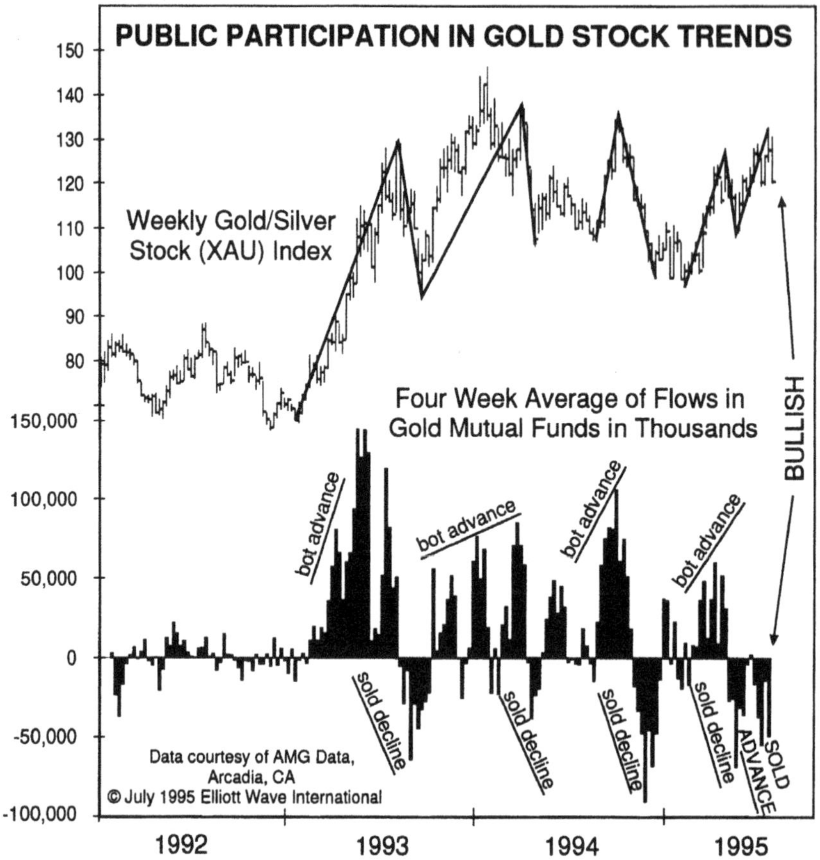

regarding the future of precious metals prices is a subtle but heady mixture that indicates a change directly ahead. That change is in perfect coincidence with our Elliott wave analysis.

Short term, the only risk is that these markets will correct a bit further before taking off, and even this risk is low. The big picture is what matters now, and EWT's outlook remains steadfast: Gold is expected to rise to at least $450/oz., and possibly as high as $500. Silver should reach a minimum of $6.85, at which level waves Y and W will be equal. However, given the tendency of silver to soar during final rallies in gold, combined with the explosive sentiment picture, it is highly likely that silver will rise until it is moving nearly vertically in a "blowoff" to much higher levels. North American gold and silver mining issues are poised to reach new all-time highs in an orgy of buying to cap their three-decade climb. In the process, the XAU should reach at least 179.

SEPTEMBER 1, 1995

Upside targets are still $455 for gold, $6.85 minimum for silver (with a blowoff to much higher levels probable) and 179 for the XAU.

Gold & Silver

Both gold and silver have done the same thing since their early 1994 highs, i.e., corrected slightly, but each has done it in its own way. Silver has staged a roller coaster ride, while gold has played dead. The chart of silver shows three possible resolutions to the corrective process, only one of which requires a drop below the June 30 low. Sentiment toward silver continues to support a very bullish multi-month outlook. The August issue demonstrated that the least informed

speculators have been betting against an advance. Only the commercials have been positioned for a rise. We think that is the way to bet, too, interim motion sickness notwithstanding.

Gold *appears* to be a most boring chart, yet it is technically one of the most exciting. The past two years' range is the narrowest since its fixed-price days at $35/oz., both resulting from and causing widespread disinterest. The latest figures show that the commercials increased their holdings by 44,000 futures contracts in the two weeks ending August 4. Also, as EWI's metals analyst Peter Rehmer points out, volatility has its own ebb and flow, and a long period of quiet is inevitably followed by a "surprising" return to trending behavior. The two-year triangle in gold has reached a point of virtual standstill, while the Daily Sentiment Index dropped this week to only 8% bulls, its lowest reading in six months. This figure reveals a consensus ripe for upset. As you can see by the closeup look on the daily chart, wave E of the triangle is ending its a-b-c pattern as this issue goes to press. The triangle's resolution will lead to an upward "thrust" (see text, p.52), with a minimum target of $450 and a maximum potential of $502.

Cycles On Track

The March issue of *The Elliott Wave Theorist* addressed the timing within the 1995 gold and silver rally this way: "One year of advance...should be punctuated by...the declining phase of the 8-month cycle, [next due to] bottom in August-September." The corrective process this summer in the metals has been perfectly compatible with this outlook. The 8-month cycle is due to turn up *any day* and should carry upward for at least four months, which is why the March issue originally projected *a final high "near year-end."* Because silver has made some upside progress (despite wild volatility) as the 8-month cycle has based, that metal's potential from here is truly explosive and remains the preferred investment.

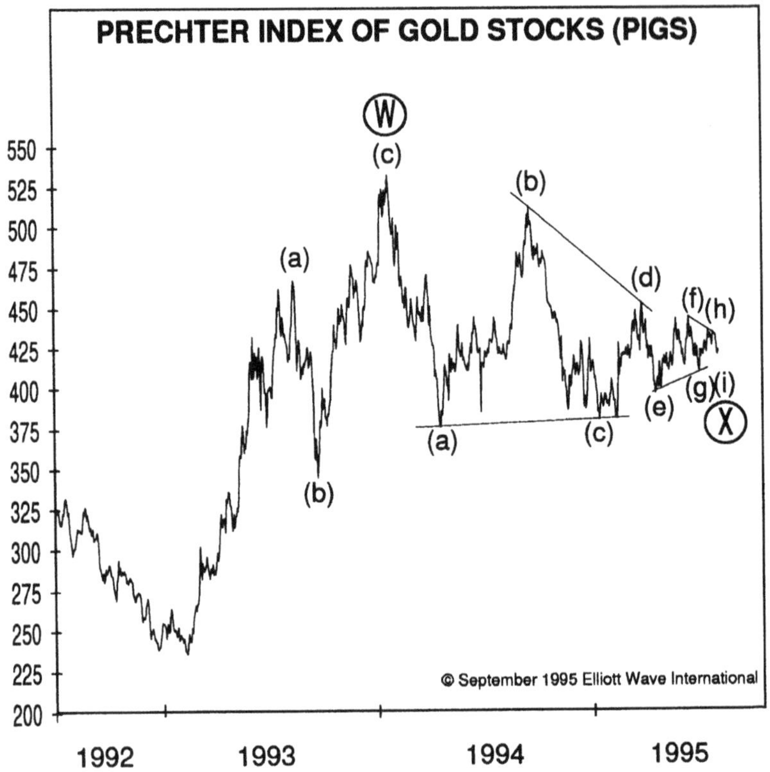

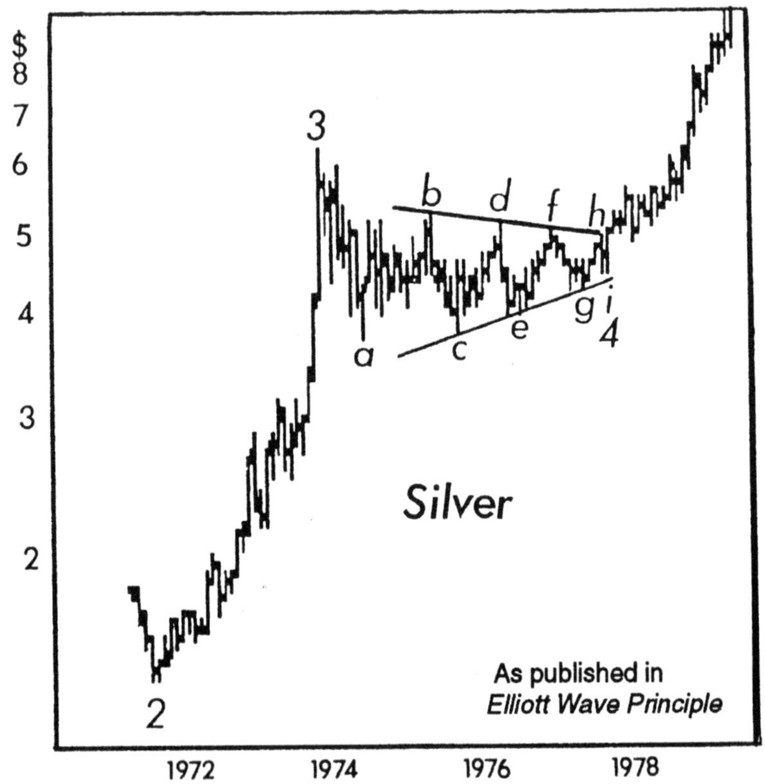

Gold and Silver Mining Stocks

The Prechter Index of Gold Stocks (PIGS) shows a slightly different construction from the Gold & Silver Stock Index (XAU), but it is of no less interest. As you can see in the chart, PIGS has traced out a nine-wave contracting triangle. While this formation is hardly common, the most famous example occurred in another metal-related price, that of silver from 1974 to 1979, as reproduced here from Figure 1-44 of *Elliott Wave Principle*. That triangle lasted a Fibonacci 5 years; this triangle in PIGS has lasted a Fibonacci 21 months. Now is a perfect time for this pattern to resolve with a surge to new all-time highs. Toronto's TSE Gold Mines Index (not shown) shows a developing pattern of first and second waves since March, which echoes the early stages of the impeccable five-wave advance it made in 1993-1994. Thus, gold, silver, the XAU, PIGS and the TSE gold index *all* show patterns compatible with the immediate beginning of an advance in the precious metals complex.

As in 1993, gold and silver mining issues are expected to perform powerfully over the next four to six months. Here is a list of stocks that have potential for a 100% gain or greater. Remember, potential is just that, potential. All speculations have risk, and these are no exception. If you would like more specific coverage of gold and silver mining stocks, I recommend *The Dines Letter* (Box 22, Belvedere, CA 94920) and Doug Casey's *Crisis Investing* (824 E. Baltimore St., Baltimore, MD 21202). The following list is compiled selectively from those two sources: Agnico-Eagle (AEAGF), Anglo-American Gold (AAGIY), Asarco (AR), Avino (AVO), American Barrick (ABX), Cambior (CBJ), Equity Silver (EST/A), Hecla (HL), Industrias Penoles (Mexican; no symbol), Minorco (MNRCY), Royal Oak Mines (RYO), Sunshine Mining (SSC), TVX Gold (TVX) and United Keno Hill (UKH). Some of these are on the NYSE, some on the ASE, some are Canadian. Make sure that you review these with your broker and choose those that are suitable to your financial situation. For those interested in less volatility (and potential), here is a list of fund families that offer precious metals funds: Benham (800-472-3389), Bull & Bear (800-847-4200), Fidelity (800-544-8888), Invesco (800-525-8085), Lexington (800-526-0056), Rushmore (800-343-3355), Scudder (800-225-2470), and U.S. (800-873-8637). It is striking that these funds are only a few percent below their peak prices of 1994, so they appear to have outperformed the averages. Note: In the last move, Lexington Investments outperformed the others. For those interested in more risk and volatility, ask Doug Casey for a copy of his June 1995 issue, which lists four dozen "junior gold" stocks.

SEPTEMBER 29, 1995

Gold and silver have bottomed and are building bases for powerful rallies into December-January.

Gold & Silver

The three market patterns shown last month have developed right along expected lines. The diagonal triangle (see daily chart, September issue) in gold finished subwave $\underline{5}$ down on September 1. The Prechter Index of Gold Stocks (PIGS) is ending wave (i) of a 9-wave triangle. Silver (see last month's chart) has followed the path of a contracting triangle and has finished either wave C or E. The Gold & Silver Stock Index (XAU) has risen 20% from

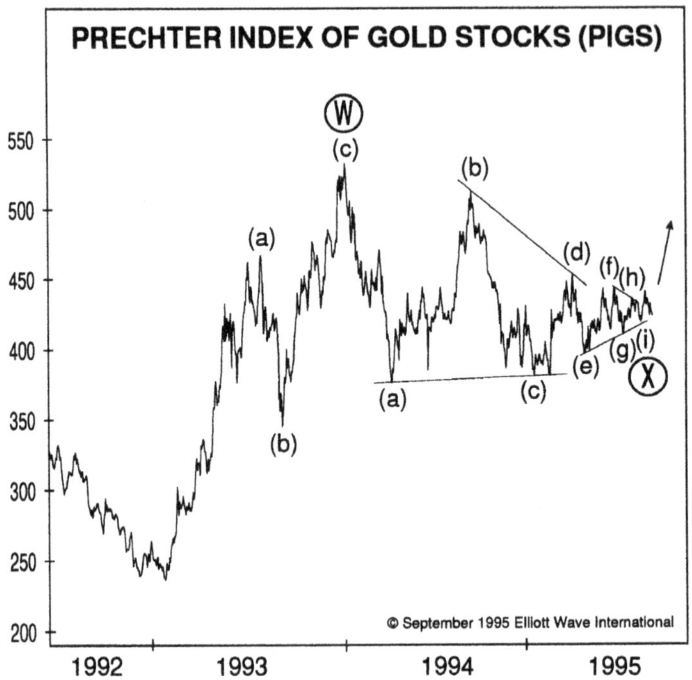

January, so is well above the low we identified at the start of the year. All of these patterns indicate that the price lows for gold, silver and mining stocks have passed. The intermediate term picture in two of these markets is updated here.

The 8-month precious metals cycle bottomed in September and points strongly up into *December-January*. The sentiment picture continues to confirm a very bullish outlook. The smart money continues to accumulate, while small traders in gold futures were actually net short in early September, a very bullish event. The Daily Sentiment Index for gold recently reached a new six-month low. All these indicators are behaving exactly as they did at the start of the 1993 rally. To review a chart of the sentiment picture in silver, see the August issue.

Additional stock ideas: Famed metals specialist Jim Blanchard wrote to make an excellent case for Silver Standard (SSO.V) and Pan American Silver (PAA.T), both Canadian. These are highly leveraged plays on the price of silver and should be added to our list of stocks with potential as high as 100%. Notes on last month's list: Avino is now International Avino Mines, and American Barrick is Barrick Gold Corp. Notes on management: The manager who piloted Lexington Gold Fund to big gains in 1993 is now running the Gabelli Gold Fund (800-422-3554). Lexington Strategic Silver Fund (800-526-0056) is near its 1995 high, so it continues to be managed very well.

Gold's upside target remains $450 minimum, $502 maximum. The XAU should reach 179. Silver is still expected to outperform gold by a substantial margin, reaching at least $6.85, while a blowoff to much higher levels is probable. A drop in gold to below $360 would upset the bullish picture in both metals. The XAU should stay above 96 for the bullish outlook to remain intact.

EDITOR'S NOTE

At this point, Prechter retired from monthly precious metals analysis. As you can see from the preceding commentary, his outlook for the precious metals complex at this point was clear and firm:

1. Gold was still in a long term bear market.
2. It was in a countertrend rally, which was not over. It needed a thrust to the upside to complete wave E.
3. Wave E would end in "December-January," 1995-1996.
4. Wave E had an upside target range of $420-500, with an ideal target of $455. Gold would then resume its bear market.
5. Silver should rally to at least $6.85, with higher potential in a spike.
6. The TSE Gold Mines Index needed one more advance to an all-time high.
7. The target in the Gold and Silver Stock Index (XAU) was 172.
8. Gold stocks would peak in 1996-1998.
9. Then gold stocks would enter the biggest bear market of the past century.
10. The final bottom would occur on "New Year's Day of 2001 (± a month)."
11. Gold's final bottom would occur "below $200/oz."

This essential vision came to pass, with a few exceptions in the specifics:

1. Gold was still in a long-term bear market.
2. It rallied immediately, thrusting from its triangle as expected.
3. It ended wave E in February 1996, almost exactly at the forecasted time.
4. It topped at $415.50, shy of the projected area.
5. Silver went sideways and then lower until mid-1997, when it took off, reaching $7.45 in New York and $7.90 in London in February 1998.
6. The TSE Gold Mines Index rose to a new all-time high, completing the diagonal triangle form (see chart, next page).
7. The Gold and Silver Stock Index (XAU) topped at 155, shy of the target. Still, its gain of 40% in the three months from November to January was greater than the rise in the S&P over the preceding two years.
8. Gold stocks topped in February 1996, within the broadly forecasted time.
9. Gold stocks resumed their bear market, ultimately falling to a new bear-market low in their largest decline in a century (see chart, next page).
10. Gold made a bottom at $251.70 on August 26, 1999 and another one at $253.50 on February 16, 2001, just days past the time forecasted six years earlier in *At the Crest*.
11. Down from $850, gold came within $52 of the target range.

As published in *At the Crest of the Tidal Wave* (1995)

Forecast:

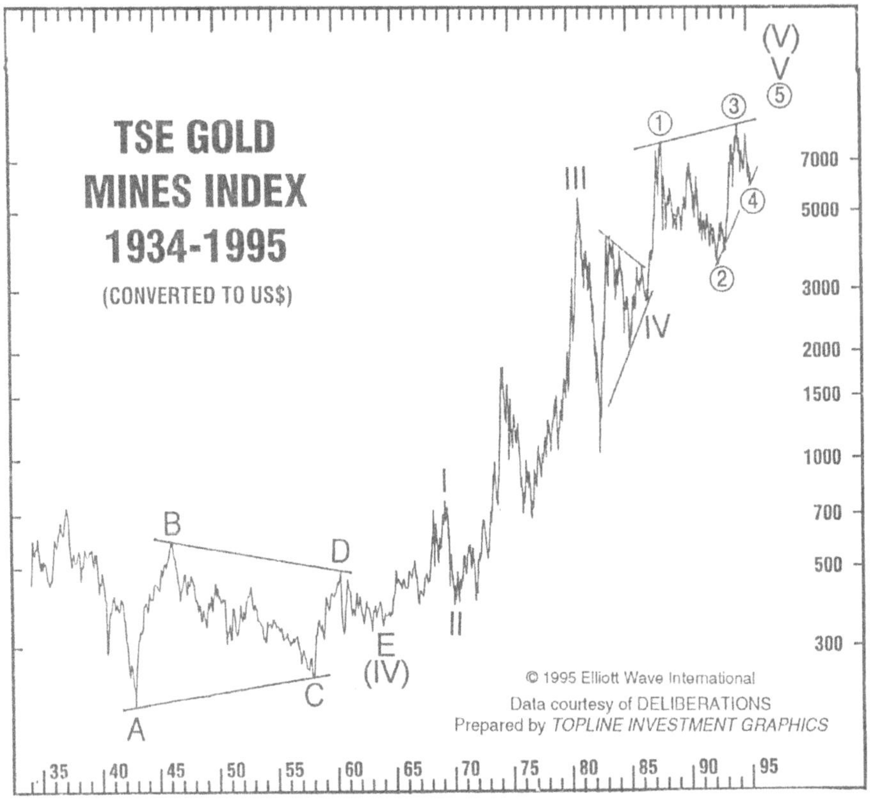

Outcome so far:

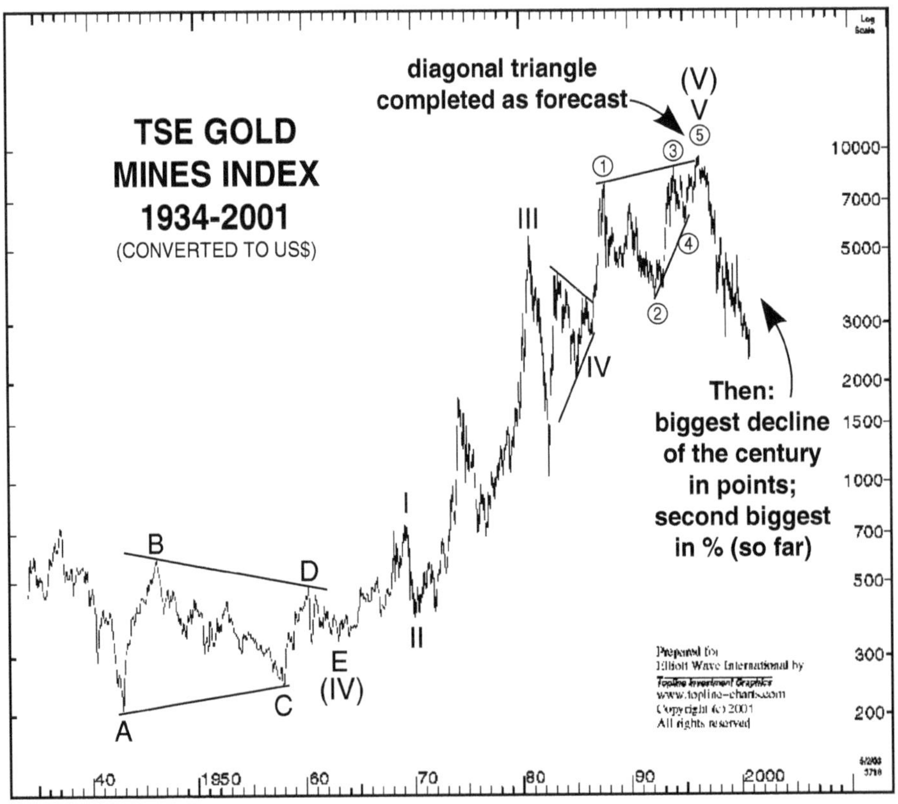

Prechter hereby ceased regular precious metals commentary, but he did address the metals whenever he had something important to say. We close with two Special Reports and a Q&A, the only comments that Prechter wrote on the precious metals from October 1995 through 2001 when gold made its final low for this period. The February 16, 2001 Special Report was published on the exact day of that year's low for spot gold at $253.50. Though hardly a perfect forecast, it was a uniquely bullish voice at that juncture and a major change in tone for a bear of 21 years.

The Elliott Wave Theorist, 1999

JULY 9, 1999 – SPECIAL REPORT
GOLD IS APPROACHING EWT'S LONG TERM TARGET

[spot gold price $257.40]

Introduction

Gold has reached its lowest level in 20 years. Almost no one cares. Why? Because today's investors are caught up in the *current* mania, the one involving the stock market. Casualties from the *precious metals* mania of 1970-1980 are swelling daily. Investors should pay attention, because the experience that gold bulls have been going through is a preview of what the stock market bulls will be going through when the bear market in equities takes hold.

Retrospective

Over the past two decades, *The Elliott Wave Theorist* has held high the bear flag with respect to the price of gold. At the manic peak, the January 1980 issue of *Commodities* (now *Futures*) magazine reported EWT's position that "Elliott counts suggest important tops in silver, gold, the major commodity market indexes and short-term interest rates." Two years later, gold had collapsed from $850 to $297. EWT called for several rallies along the way since then, most of which materialized, but the long term wave count continued to insure that the bear market was not over.

Idealized Triangle

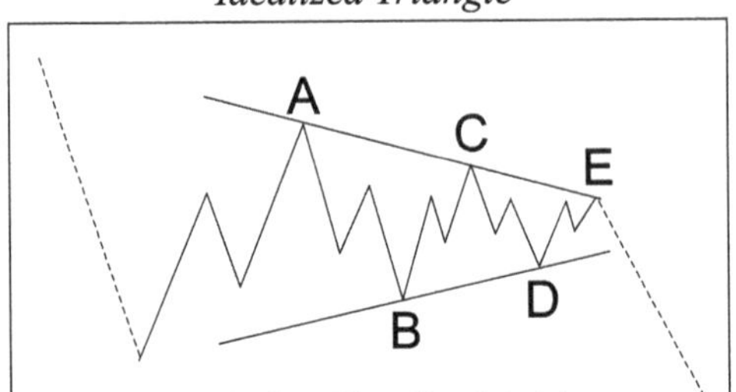

Illustration from *Elliott Wave Principle*

Chapter 17 of *At the Crest of the Tidal Wave* gives an abbreviated review of some of EWT's gold analysis. EWT's main focus over the bulk of these years was tracking the development of a contracting triangle (see text, p.48). While most observers presumed it was a base, wave analysis recognized it as a temporary respite within the major downtrend. The triangle began in 1982 and was finally coming to an end as *At the Crest* came out. Here is the analysis from mid-1995, as quoted in that book (see illustration):

> By definition, the five waves of a triangle each subdivide into three waves. Examine the updated chart, and you will see that within wave X, waves Ⓐ, Ⓑ, Ⓒ and Ⓓ have each subdivided into (a)-(b)-(c) or (w)-(x)-(y). Wave Ⓔ should be no exception. Let's see how it is developing. Wave (a) of Ⓔ peaked in July 1993. Wave (b) of Ⓔ has been tracing out a contracting triangle, which is due to end soon. This is a thrilling development because a triangle precedes the final move in the next larger trend. Since only one rally from the 1993 low has occurred, the fact that only one remains guarantees that the advance will be three waves, thus precisely fitting the requirement for wave Ⓔ. This small event conforms to the entire Elliott wave analysis covering the past fifteen years.

Figure 17-5 from At the Crest (1995)

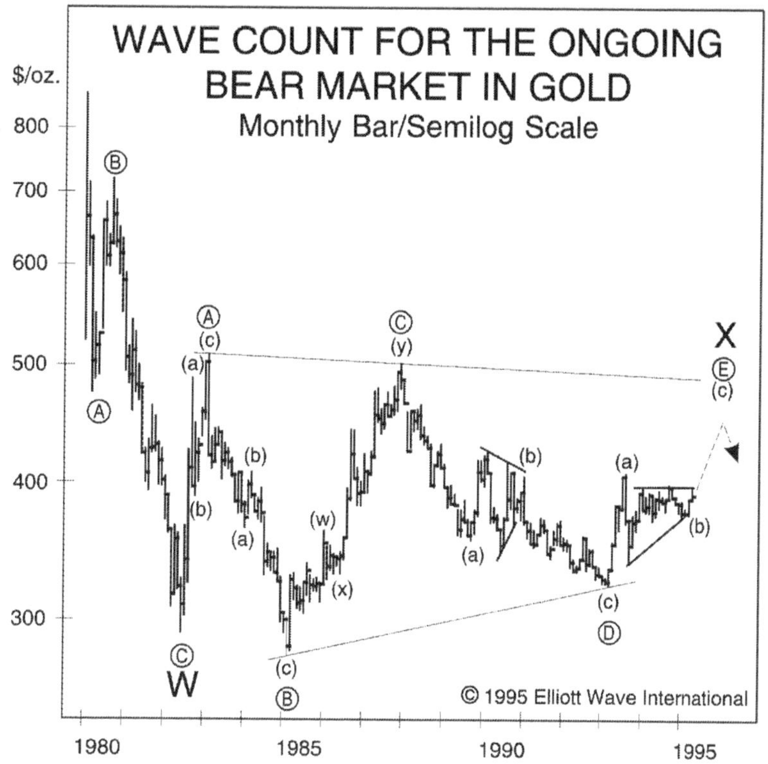

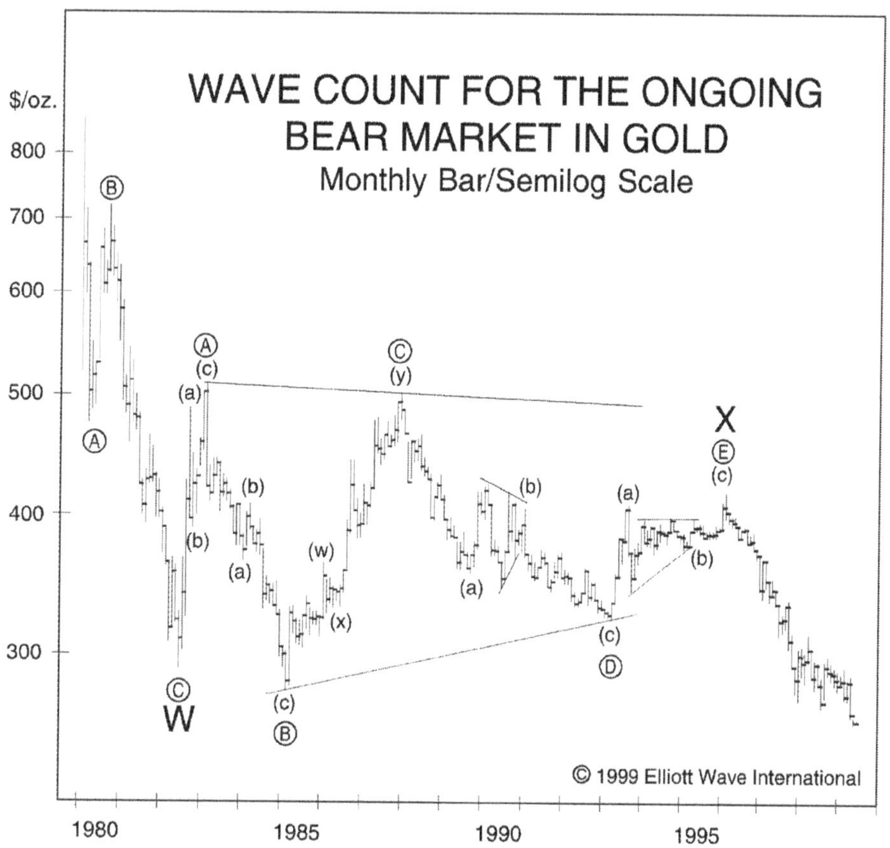

That the rise from 1993 is part of a bear market rally rather than the start of a new bull market will be invaluable knowledge to have when wave Ⓔ tops in coming months. Because wave Ⓔ will cap a recovery pattern of Cycle degree, the bullish psychology attending its peak should be correspondingly intense. Mining issues should reach new all-time highs, and the price of silver should reach a new multi-year high, fueling bullish psychology. "E" waves are often accompanied by supporting news, so look for a widely publicized "reason" to own gold at the top of wave Ⓔ.

It has now become apparent why waves Ⓒ, Ⓓ and Ⓔ have taken their time developing. Wave W lasted a Fibonacci **2** years, from 1980 to 1982. Wave X has been tracing out a triangle from 1982 that is fairly certain to last a Fibonacci **13** years, ending in **1995**.

As the quotation from February 1992 shows, *The Elliott Wave Theorist* projected wave Ⓔ to carry to the **$420-$500** area before it even began. The specific target of $461 issued two years ago was derived from the observation that alternate waves in a triangle are often related by .618, and a peak at that level would make wave Ⓔ .618 as long as wave Ⓒ. Wave Ⓔ's internal structure now supports that target, because if wave (c) is to equal wave (a), a typical relationship, it would peak in the $450s basis London fix. This cluster makes the **$450-461** area an ideal target.

Targeting the Low

Throughout the years, EWT has maintained that gold would ultimately fall "below $200/oz." The best initial targets based on pattern were $179.50 and $103.50, the start and end of wave IV, a normal stopping area (see text, p.64). To most people, these levels appeared ludicrous when first indicated and still do. However, with gold now at $260, these levels no longer look so far away.

At the Crest took eight pages to detail a price and time projection for the end of wave Y and therefore the end of the bear market. I will not repeat all the analysis here since Figure 17-10 from the book, reproduced on the next page, summarizes the Fibonacci relationships that relate wave Y to wave X. As you can see, it illustrates two downside projections, one near $182 and the other near $112. These projections are just a few dollars from the ideal targets based upon pattern (see dashed lines), so they strengthen my conviction about them.

There is one aspect of the analysis that has suddenly become especially interesting. Figure 17-11 presented my attempt to forecast even the *details* of wave Y. Here is the commentary that went with it:

> Given all the specific and extreme forecasts in this book, perhaps it would be humorous to say that I am going out on a limb here, but would it not make a mathematically beautiful pattern if, within wave Y, wave Ⓐ were to bottom near $182 and wave Ⓒ near $112? In that way, all the Cycle degree lows of the bear market would be intimately related by Fibonacci ratios. An intervening rally for wave Ⓑ might carry to .382 of the value of wave Ⓑ in 1980 at $275 (or up to $20 higher, as suggested by the relationship

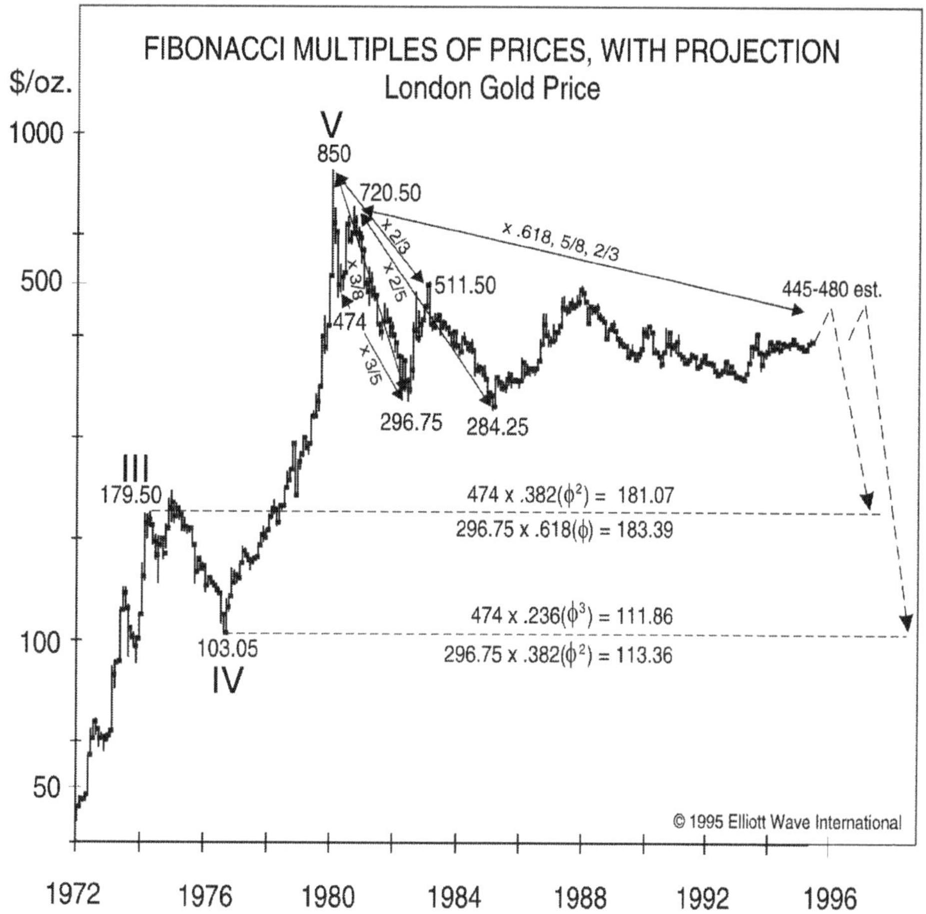

Figure 17-10 from At the Crest *(1995)*

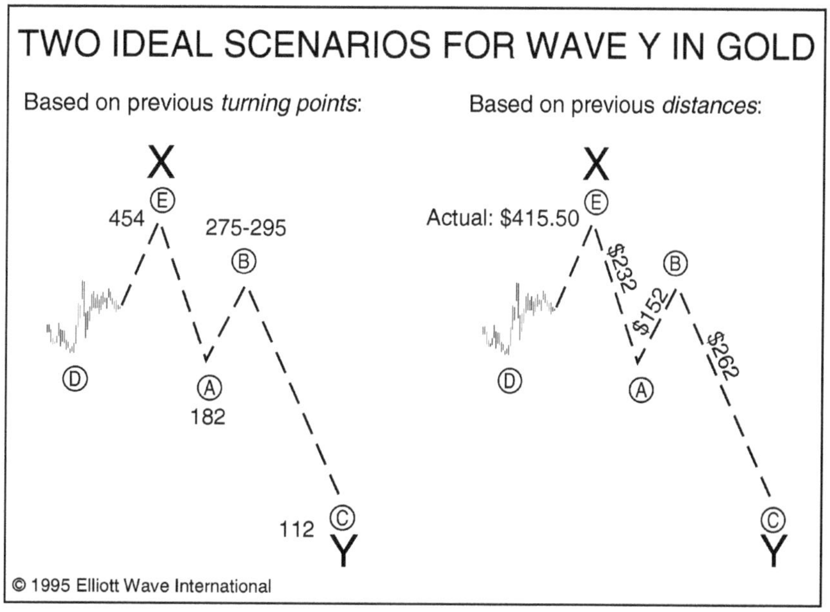

Figure 17-11 from At the Crest *(1995), with added notes*

of the $720.50 level to other turning point values). A rally to that area would also meet tremendous resistance at the 1982 and 1985 lows of $284.25 - $296.75. This scenario is depicted on the left side of Figure 17-11.

As an alternative possibility, the components of wave Y might travel .618 of the corresponding components of wave W, creating a duplicate of the entire structure multiplied by .618. The second most likely possibility, then, is that waves Ⓐ, Ⓑ and Ⓒ of Y will cover distances of $232, $152 and $262. These lengths will have to be projected (downward, upward and downward) from the high of wave Ⓔ when it occurs. If $112 is a reliable forecast for the ultimate low, then waves Ⓔ, Ⓐ, Ⓑ and Ⓒ under this scenario would end at $454, $222, $374 and $112. These levels will have to be adjusted by the amount that wave Ⓔ ends differently from $454. This scenario for wave Y is depicted on the right side of Figure 17-11.

To conclude, until the peak of wave Ⓔ is in, allowing a final adjustment, **$112** remains the most attractive target for the final low. **$182** is the next most attractive target, which, if it does not mark the final low, has an excellent probability of marking a Primary degree low on the way down. All targets listed herein should be given a few dollars' leeway. Also, they are based upon the London fix prices, which would be exceeded somewhat by intraday futures prices.

Initially disappointed that wave Ⓔ topped below what I thought was an ideal projection, I now notice that the actual peak level has served to turn my *two* ideal scenarios into *one*, at least with respect to wave Ⓐ of Y and possibly for the whole bear market. The first scenario called for a *low near $182* regardless of its starting level, while the second scenario called for a *drop of $232* regardless of its starting level. Given that wave Y started at $415.50, a *drop of $232* projects a target of $183.50, a near match to $182! In other words, we now have one scenario for the current drop, and it satisfies all the relevant Fibonacci relationships. ($182 is an average of two projections. Notice from Figure 17-10 that one of those projections was $183.39, essentially the same as $183.50.)

Conclusion

Regardless of any near-term rallies or how long it eventually takes, gold should reach an important bottom near **$183**. This level *could* mark the end of the entire bear market from 1980. I would give that event a 40% probability, leaving open a 60% probability that a low at that level will mark only the end of wave A. Either way, a substantial advance should ensue. If we are to see a final wave Ⓒ thereafter, it should meet the lower target less than three years from today (see time projection on page 355 of *At the Crest*). All these projections rely on gold's not exceeding $415.50.

Gold bugs have counseled accumulating gold for years at what looked like low prices but were actually high prices. The current decline will force many holders to despair and sell. We should take advantage of what may turn out to be a historic opportunity and take a position in gold when it drops below $200/oz. We will watch the rally thereafter to re-examine the outlook for waves Ⓑ and Ⓒ and to make further decisions.

THE ELLIOTT WAVE THEORIST, 2001

FEBRUARY 16, 2001 – SPECIAL REPORT
BEGIN CHANGING YOUR THINKING TOWARDS GOLD AND SILVER

[the day of that year's low in spot gold at $253.50]

I have been long term bearish on gold and silver for 21 years. *The Elliott Wave Theorist* called most of the rallies in the 1980s and 1990s as well, making the metals our most successful market since our publication began. Figure 1 shows the wave count since 1968. EWT identified most of these complex wave labels during the bear market in real time.

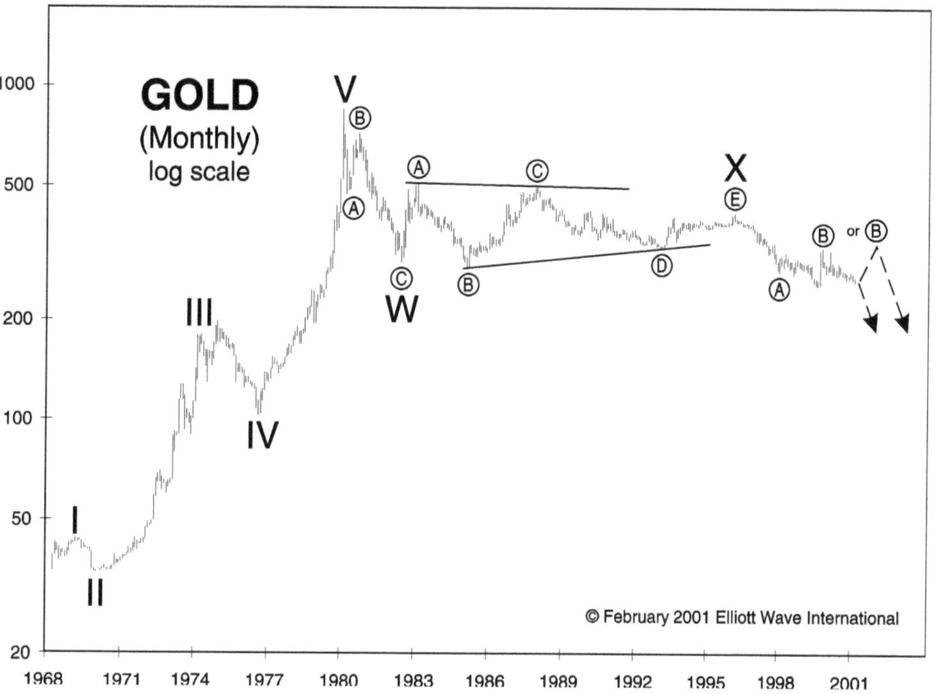

Figure 1

It is time to begin thinking differently about the precious metals. For those 21 years, we saw each intermediate-term rally in gold and silver as a short selling opportunity. Now it is time to begin thinking about how and when to buy.

My two best long-term targets for gold are still below $200/oz., so the intent of this report is not to issue a "buy signal." It's to get you mentally on the side of what has finally become a distinct minority. Figure 2 shows a close-up of wave Y. As I see it, this wave is incomplete and requires wave Ⓒ down. The only question is whether wave Ⓑ of Y is over. If it is over, then gold is already in its final washout. If it is not over, then gold will soon embark on a $100 rally to about $360 before wave Ⓒ begins. The dashed lines on Figure 2 show these two scenarios.

If I don't think the bear market is over, why bring up the subject? The answer is that market psychology toward gold and silver reflects so much complacent pessimism, even aggressive pessimism, that anyone who knows markets cannot ignore it. It alone justifies beginning to pay attention to, if not accumulate, gold and silver. Remember in the late 1990s when stock mania enthusiasts shouted, "Cash is trash"? It would have been a good time to cash in their "hot stocks." Today, if there is a consensus anywhere, it is that gold and silver are trash. This means we are getting close to the final bottom.

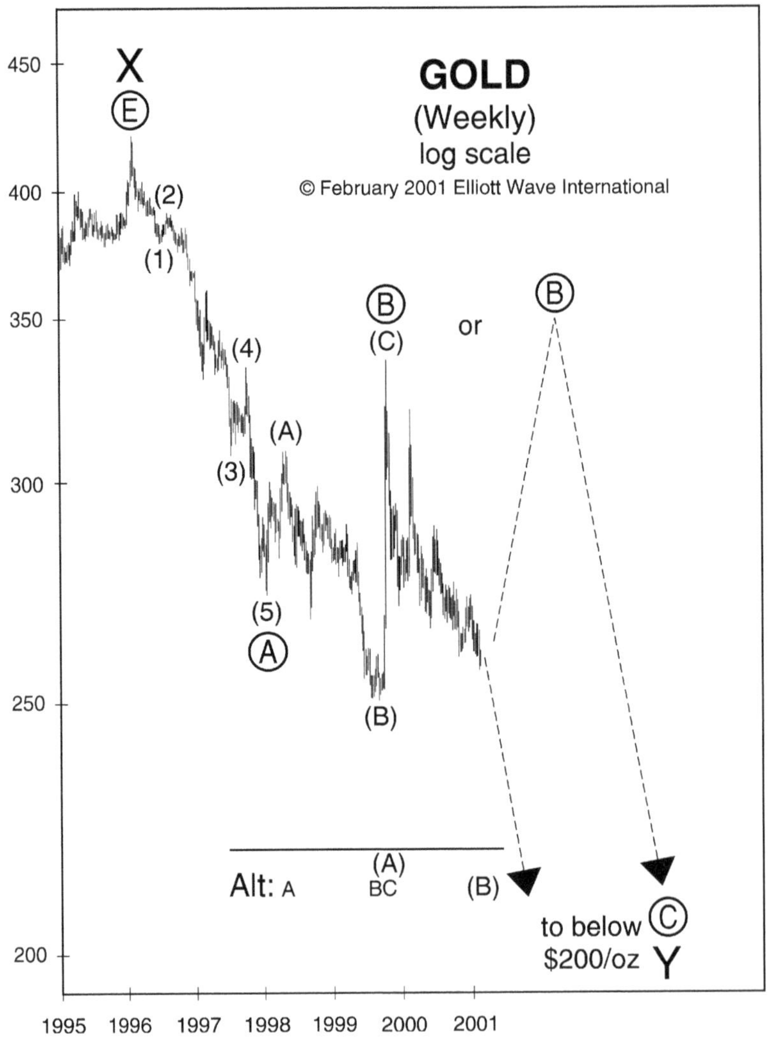

Figure 2

Throughout the 1980s and 1990s, "gold bugs" welcomed every rally as the start of the great move to quadruple digits. Now there are no high-visibility gold bugs. Gold bug publications, out of necessity, have switched to touting anything but gold. Famous long-term bears on the U.S. economy have thrown in the towel after sometimes as much as twenty years of pessimism and embraced the idea of a new era of prosperity in which gold plays no part. An article that has just appeared in Barron's shows what most market participants think. I was going to quote excerpts from it, but it is so packed with fodder for contrary opinion that I'm simply going to reproduce the whole thing on the next page. Read every bit of it to get a feel for how the majority is thinking and acting right now.

Certainly, this psychology befits the final stages of a bear market of over two decades' duration. It is no guarantee of an imminent low, however. We need simply recall the ridiculously bullish psychology attending the stock mania in 1996 to understand that even historic extremes can become more extreme. In the case of stocks, it continued for another four years. If wave Ⓒ in gold lies ahead, as I believe it does, then the psychology toward gold and silver

BARRON'S • MARKET WEEK February 12, 2001

Cheryl Strauss Einhorn

Tarnished!

Nobody expects gold prices to turn up soon

IT'S DIFFICULT TO FIND ANY POSITIVE news in the depressed gold market. At around $260 an ounce, the metal continues to trade near its cost of production, and almost no one believes it will rally soon.

Just last week, for instance, when **Harmony Gold**, the world's sixth-largest producer, announced its intention to buy two mines from the world's largest miner, **Anglogold**, Harmony's banks asked the company to put a hedging program in place – something Harmony had never done before. "Financing is tough to come by these days" in the unpopular gold-mining sector, says Ferdi Dippenaar, Harmony's director of marketing. "We've always been unhedged," he says. "But our banks wouldn't lend us the money any other way."

The market took the news badly, falling almost $2 an ounce Tuesday, in part because forward sales are considered bearish–they add supply and suggest that producers expect prices to fall before the loan is repaid.

Dippenaar says he understands why the banks required the company to hedge their price risk: "There doesn't seem to be anything on the horizon that will make gold prices go up."

As a result, Harmony agreed to purchase a put option, giving it the right, but not the obligation, to sell one million ounces of gold – about 40% of the company's annual production – at about $260 apiece.

And as if that weren't enough bad news for one week, on the same day, Tuesday, Anglogold announced that it would continue to hedge half of all of its production for the next five years. The company expects to mine just over seven million ounces of gold this year.

"We are an industry incapable of realizing good returns for our shareholders," says Dippenaar.

He blames hedging in part, for allowing companies to "stay in business longer than perhaps they should be" and for making supplies seem larger than they are. "There is a perception of a continuous flow of gold from a very fragmented industry," he says.

Brokerage houses seem to agree. In another sign of the times, ABN Amro gold analyst Todd Hinrichs threw in the towel and stopped covering the industry a few weeks ago. "I've capitulated and moved on," he says. He is now covering manufacturing. "The gold industry is essentially a very difficult place to make a dollar," he observes. "There is nothing positive. It's as bad as it gets."

Another problem: As the stock-market value of gold companies has shrunk, along with their profits, mutual-fund managers no longer want to own them. In fact, the industry's market value now is about $20 billion, which is just larger than **Caterpillar**'s alone. Put another way, **Barrick Gold**, considered to be one of the best-positioned producers because of its hedges, has a market value of about $5 billion; **General Electric**'s market value is 100 times as large.

Of course, while prices have slid, good money has been made on the short side, by those betting they will continue to retreat. Right now, Commodity Futures Trading Commission statistics show that bearish bets are at their highest level in years.

Because prices for future delivery of gold trade at a premium to those for metal to be delivered today – a phenomenon known as contango – traders can make money off the spread by selling futures. "The shorts have a good thing going," says Hinrichs.

Even the ever-bullish World Gold Council, an industry group sponsored by the gold companies themselves, is finding it tough to come up with a new catalyst to boost prices. "U.S. inflation can't keep falling," says George Milling Stanley, the Gold Council's New York analyst. "The U.S. dollar can't keep strengthening and the depressing impact of central-bank sales shouldn't continue, given the Washington Accord," he says, referring to the pact that 15 European central banks put together to limit official sales of gold. Still, he admits, "all these things continue to weigh on prices."

Why? Demand. It just isn't there. "Unfortunately there is nothing positive on the horizon," says Dippenaar.

will get even blacker before the metals reach bottom. The developing deflation should help pull gold down to one of my downside targets. For an update on those, read *At the Crest* or just be patient. *The Elliott Wave Financial Forecast* has been right on top of gold and silver over the past year. If gold breaches $200/oz., EWFF and the Update will be zeroing in on a great buying opportunity. (If you are an active institution, be sure to check out our on-line Metals Specialty Service, with full coverage around the clock, at www.elliottwave.com/specialtyservices.)

To me, the ideal outcome would be a sharp rally now, completing a more complex wave Ⓑ up, and then the start of wave Ⓒ down. Wave Ⓑ in 1980 retraced 61.8% of wave Ⓐ; the recent wave Ⓑ has retraced 50%, leaving a bit of room for gold to take out its October 1999 high. Such a rally would force the now-confident shorts out of the market just before the final collapse. However, market trends in their final throes are sometimes relentless. We can bet that if wave Ⓒ continues directly down from here and some short sellers make money, they will be doubly short at the final bottom, convinced that gold is going all the way back to $35.

I can think of a number of strategies that would make sense here. Review your own situation and decide how you wish to proceed. The main thing is, it's at least time to put gold and silver on your long-term radar screen as pending buys. Sometimes people need to be psychologically prepared to act. We have been staunchly oriented one way all these years, and it's time to begin anticipating a change.

AUGUST 24, 2001
A Q&A WITH ROBERT PRECHTER

[metals comments excerpted; spot gold price $273]

Q: How will gold and silver respond?

A: I'm very excited about them. I've been bearish on them for 21 years. I wrote something in February where I said, "Look, you need to start thinking about getting your mechanisms in place to buy gold and silver, because we're coming into a major long term buying opportunity." I'm not sure that I'm going to be able to pinpoint it. I said from the beginning that gold should go under $200 an ounce before the bear market is over. The last drop could be in tandem with a last rally in the Dow, or it could be the first part of the bear market deflation when people sell every asset, even their best ones, in order to cover debts and try to stay alive. I'm not sure quite how this will play out, but I do know that we are probably between three weeks and two years of the greatest buying opportunity for gold – maybe ever.

Q: Do you still see gold dropping to the $200 level?

A: Yes, but I'm also trailing a buy stop. If it goes high enough, I'm going to say, that was it, I missed it; get in. I'm also not against people beginning to buy it already. Silver is just above $4 now. I think it could go as low as $3, but don't forget, it once was $50, so $4 is cheap.

Q: I know, I rode it all the way down, earning a lot of brutal experience.

A: Compared to where it's going, I don't care if it does go down to $3. You should own physical, begin to accumulate physical, and every time the central banks and the scared people and the people in debt sell gold and silver, buy some.

Q: You said $3.00 on silver. That's very interesting, because we've got two bottoms in 1991 and 1993 at $3.50. So if it broke through $3.50....

A: That would crystallize psychology on the bearish side, which is your opportunity to buy.

Q: What about silver relative to gold? If you had a chart 45 feet long where each foot represented a century, only in the last 15 inches would the ratio ever rise above 16:1. I think that has something to do with the physical ratio, and for the rest I just have to call it mysterious. Do you think that silver will outperform gold?

A: I have no idea. I think you should own some of both. There is some industrial use for silver, and some people say that's going down because of digital photography, but who knows what'll be invented tomorrow? For many years and in many cultures, silver was more prized than gold. That could return, but I can't predict that. What I can predict is the dollar's collapse, so you need to buy something real that will hold its value while that happens.

POSTSCRIPT

Well, we all know what happened to the dollar in the three years immediately following. As for gold and silver, they could be off on a new adventure if gold ended wave ⓒ of y in 2001. Or they may simply be in a flashy bear market rally.

Whatever is in store for the metals, the analysts at Elliott Wave International are assessing their prospects every day, week and month. For general coverage of markets (including Prechter's occasional Special Reports), please investigate our Financial Forecast Service at www.elliottwave.com/store. For intense coverage of the metals, please see our Metals Pro Service at www.elliottwave.com/Trader-Analysis/Pro-Services.

It was quite a task to collect all this material, but we hope you agree that the journey was worth it. We trust that your future dealings with the precious metals will be pleasant and profitable.

Elliott Wave International is the world's largest financial market forecasting firm. It publishes forecasts and analyses of every major market in the world on every time frame.

If you would like to avail yourself of EWI's precious metals forecasting, please investigate the following services:

The Financial Forecast Service
Moderate metals coverage, along with stocks and bonds
Learn more at www.elliottwave.com/wave/goldffs

The Metals Pro Service
Intensive metals coverage
Learn more at www.elliottwave.com/wave/goldps

Elliott Wave International

www.ingramcontent.com/pod-product-compliance
Ingram Content Group UK Ltd.
Pitfield, Milton Keynes, MK11 3LW, UK
UKHW051241300926
15471UKWH00015B/1601

9 781616 041267